PRENTICE-HALL HISTORY SERIES
CARL WITTKE, PH.D., EDITOR

A History
of the
Modern and Contemporary
Far East

MEMORIAL TO DR. SUN YAT-SEN AT NANKING.

To stimulate political action, Sun's followers have deified him in the memory of China's masses.

A HISTORY OF THE MODERN AND CONTEMPORARY FAR EAST

*A Survey of Western Contacts with Eastern Asia
During the Nineteenth and Twentieth Centuries*

by

PAUL HIBBERT CLYDE

Department of History, Duke University

New York

PRENTICE-HALL, INC.

1937

TO MY FRIEND
H. S.

Preface

THE following pages do not attempt to present a complete history of the Far East in modern and contemporary times. That story, told even within the briefest compass, would fill several volumes. The narrative here set forth is concerned primarily with, first, the impact of western imperialism upon the Far East in the nineteenth century and, second, the challenge to western imperialism brought about by the rise of Japan to the position of a so-called great power in the twentieth century. The scene is essentially China, which in a very true sense has been "The Middle Kingdom"—the center of the Orient.

Although this history is concerned in the main with the contacts between the West and the Far East, the author has attempted to provide enough background in the institutional life of China and Japan to make possible an understanding of the conflicts that arose.

The author is all too conscious of the limitations that are inseparable from a brief survey of this kind. For one who seeks a definitive interpretation, each chapter might well be expanded into a volume. Generalizations, of which such generous use must be made by the writer of a broad survey, frequently fail to convey the intended qualifications in meaning. This is particularly true of the years since the Washington Conference (1921-1922). The most important materials necessary for a study of this period are not yet available to the historian. The narrative therefore must be accepted as tentative.

Some of the interpretations here presented are at variance with traditional American attitudes toward the Far East in recent years. Future evidence may tend to substantiate or to destroy them. In any event, it is the author's hope that they may prompt more American students to further investigation.

The spelling of geographical and personal names always presents a difficult problem. The author has not followed any conventional system but has attempted to give the form with which western readers are apt to be familiar.

The writer is indebted to a host of historians and investigators whose works he has used freely in compiling these pages. Where the conclusions stated are not his own, due credit is given in the footnote citations. He is also indebted to a number of publishers who have graciously granted permission to quote from copyrighted material. These permissions are acknowledged in the first footnote citations. To that modest but invaluable friend, Ippei Fukuda, Associate Editor of *Contemporary Japan,* the author extends his thanks for many of the portraits of Japan's statesmen and soldiers. He wishes also to mention the encouragement that has been constantly extended to him by the editor, Dr. Carl Wittke, and staff members of Prentice-Hall, Inc. He is likewise indebted to President Frank L. McVey of the University of Kentucky, where the following pages were written.

As always, he remains in obligation to the three men who first awakened in him an interest in the Far East—his instructors at Stanford University: Dr. Payson J. Treat, Dr. Yamato Ichihashi, and the late Dr. Frank A. Golder. Such merits as this volume may possess are due largely to the background of their guidance. Its demerits must be attributed to the author alone.

P. H. C.

Contents

ix

Maps and Illustrations

CHAPTER I

The Politico-Geographic Setting

THE modern international history of the Far East, as western students are prone to view it, is to a significant degree a product of European and American expansion. Following closely upon the first voyages of discovery in the late fifteenth and early sixteenth centuries, Europe's sea-going pioneers of empire carried the colonial movement to the Pacific slope of Asia. From these beginnings, which today are only four centuries old, have developed complex territorial, commercial, and cultural relations between what are commonly referred to as the West and the Far East. First contacts between the western world and the extreme Orient are not of this recent origin. On the contrary, they may be traced to very ancient times—to the first twelve centuries of the Christian Era, when Europe's life was affected profoundly by the civilization of Asia. In contrast, the period of modern contacts, dating from the sixteenth century, has been marked by the impress of western civilization upon Asia. At first the process was slow, and in general it may be said that the modern, twentieth-century Far East is a product of western influence covering no more than the past one hundred years. To be sure, formal relations between China and eastern Europe date back to the Russo-Chinese Treaty of Nertchinsk (1689); yet it was not until the close of the so-called Opium War, when China and Great Britain signed the Treaty of Nanking (1842), that the wall of Chinese exclusiveness was broken by the impact of forces which were distinctly western. Japan did not emerge from more than two centuries of official seclusion,

I

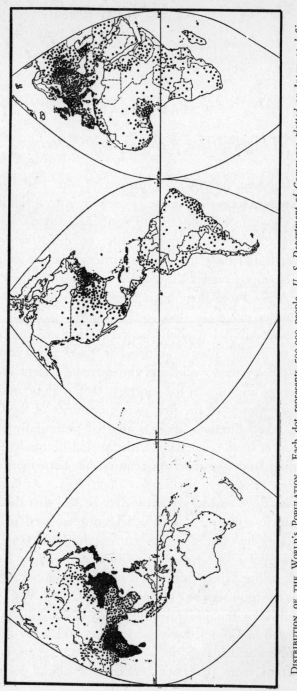
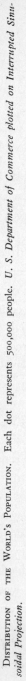

Distribution of the World's Population. Each dot represents 500,000 people. U. S. Department of Commerce plotted on Interrupted Sinusoidal Projection.

dictated by the Tokugawas, until a decade later (1854), when Commodore Perry's black ships sailed triumphantly, with a treaty of amity, from the waters of Yedo Bay. To these modern beginnings is to be traced the Far East of contemporary times.

The geographical setting for the movements to be related in succeeding pages cannot be given in a brief and simple statement. Furthermore, terms which are frequently employed (such as "the Far East," "Eastern Asia," "the extreme Orient," and so forth) fail always to suggest fixed and known geographical areas or definitive political boundaries. In general, however, they possess a common if not a precise meaning and will be used to designate those regions comprising: (1) the vast and ill-defined area called China, (2) Siberia, from Lake Baikal to the Pacific, (3) the Empire of Japan, including Korea, or Chosen, (4) the Philippines and other islands of the northwestern Pacific, and (5) the southeastern peninsula of Asia, known generally as Indo-China.

These areas include the far-eastern portions of the world's largest continent. Asia, probably the original home of the human race, covers almost one third of the land surface of the globe, is larger than the combined areas of North and South America, is half as large again as Africa, and is more than four times the size of Europe. Within its borders and shores, containing some seventeen million square miles of land, live, according to some estimates, 950 millions of people, almost one half of the world's population. In Asia, too, the geographer finds the highest of mountains, where Everest towers to more than 29,000 feet; many of the greatest river systems—the Yangtze in China is 3,100 miles from its source to the sea; and finally, the gigantic Asian plateau, extending almost the entire length of the continent.

The physical picture of Asia is dramatic and compelling, yet for many this natural grandeur is surpassed by the achievements of its peoples. It appears that western Asia was the first home of human culture, from which two of the world's greatest civilizations took their birth: the Indian, in the valleys of the Indus and the Ganges, and the Chinese, along the banks of the Yellow and the Yangtze Rivers. Asia, too, contributed perhaps more than is known to the civilization of Europe, a circumstance of more than passing significance, for in the nineteenth and twentieth centuries the impact of European civilization upon Asia has seemed to challenge the entire fabric of its ancient culture. All of the great religions had their origin in Asia, from the Hinduism of India, the Confucianism of China, the cults of Judaism, Taoism, and Shintoism, to the more recent systems of Christianity and Mohammedanism. In fact, no other continent provides the student with such diversity of life, be it in physical environment, in race, in color, in language, in religion, or in methods of livelihood.

Until the dawn of modern times the civilization of China, the dominant culture of eastern Asia, was all but unknown to western lands. Mountains and seas were almost impassable barriers. Western man judged the values of life usually in terms of his own environment and his own customs. Not infrequently he attributed the latter to divine inspiration. The ways of other peoples, beyond the mountains or across the seas, were different; therefore they were inferior. Even in modern times, when physical barriers no longer impede contacts, provincialism is often treated as a virtue. Likewise, the Europeans and the Americans who knocked at the doors of China in the middle nineteenth century were to the Chinese mere "barbarians." The Westerner in turn was inclined to regard the average Oriental as something less than human. Fixed attitudes of this type still prevail, fostered by both ignorance and parochialism. Centuries of isolation have created profound contrasts in the lives of eastern and of western peoples. When, therefore, a century ago Europe's impact was first felt in the extreme East, the conflict, though fought with bayonets and battleships, was in reality a conflict of differing human ways, standards, and values.

China

Just as Asia is the greatest of the continents, so China is the largest political and cultural unit of Asia. Before the days of what is now the Chinese Republic, China was the "Middle Kingdom"—the center of civilization. At least, so said the Chinese. With its more than four million square miles of land,

POLITICAL AND PHYSICAL MAP OF ASIA. *Base map according to J. Paul Goode, plotted according to Alber's Equal Area Projection.*

no modern empires save those of Great Britain and Soviet Russia have exceeded it in area. With its dense mass of human life, estimated (for no one really knows) as perhaps in excess of 450 million, no state, no nation, no empire has surpassed it in population. Yet this physical and human magnitude has been overshadowed by the complexity of China's physical environment and the diversity in the life of her peoples. "What is China?" asked one of the delegates at the Washington Conference in 1921. That question still awaits an answer. Politically, the western world has thought of China as comprising five great areas: (1) China proper, (2) Manchuria (now Manchoukuo), (3) Mongolia, (4) Sinkiang, and (5) Tibet.

China Proper

In the days of the Manchus (1644-1912), China proper consisted of eighteen provinces,[1] reaching from Kwangtung, on the shores of the south China seas, to Chihli in the north, where the Great Wall (built during the third century B.C.) wandered inland from the sea; and from Shanghai, on the eastern coast, to the western mountains of Szechwan. This was the China of the Chinese, as distinct from the greater Chinese Empire, in which lived alien, tributary, and subject races. These latter, though occupying great areas, were numerically weak. The bulk of China's population in modern times has always been within the eighteen provinces. In 1926, the population, exclusive of Mongolia, Sinkiang and Tibet, was estimated as high as 485,000,000; of this total all save 24,000,000 (allotted to Manchuria) lived within the eighteen provinces. The area of China proper is about 1,530,000 square miles, or approximately half the size of continental United States. The largest of the provinces include: (1) Szechwan, in the west, 155,800 square miles, popu-

---

[1] The names of these provinces were: Chihli (now Hopei), Shantung, Kiangsu, Chekiang, Fukien, Kwangtung, Kwangsi, Kweichow, Hunan, Kiangsi, Anhwei, Hupeh, Honan, Szechwan, Shansi, Shensi, Kansu and Yunnan.

lation in excess of 50,000,000 (the area of Germany is 186,000 square miles); (2) Yunnan, in the southwest, 153,000 square miles, population in excess of 11,000,000; (3) Kansu, in the northwest, 147,000 square miles, population in excess of 7,000,-000; (4) Kwangtung, on the southern coast, 86,000 square miles, population in excess of 36,000,000 (about the area of England, Scotland, and Wales); (5) Kwangsi, also in the south, 84,000 square miles, population in excess of 12,000,000. The smallest of the eighteen provinces is Chekiang, on the central eastern coast, 39,000 square miles, population in excess of 24,000,000 (the area of the State of Tennessee is 42,000 square miles). It will be noted that some of the larger provinces have a relatively small population, such, for example, as Kansu and Yunnan. Many of the smaller provinces, in contrast, are densely populated: Hopei, 38,000,000; Honan, 35,000,000; Hunan, 40,000,000; Kiangsu, 34,000,000; and Shantung, 34,000,000.

Geographically, China proper may be described in terms of three great river basins: the Hwang Ho, or the Yellow River, in the north; the Yangtze Kiang basin, in central China; and the Si Kiang, or West River, in the south. The basin of the Yellow River, covering some 600,000 square miles, contains in the neighborhood of 100,000,000 people. Probably the first Chinese settlements were made in the valley of the Wei Ho, in the Yellow River basin, about 3,000 B.C. From there the Chinese spread to the east and south. Their early movements were favored by such geographic conditions as a temperate zone, diverse resources, and, as they moved onward, an extended coast line. Difficulties of travel either by land or by sea gave the early Chinese the protection of relative isolation. The only gateways by land were in the north, and these were closed before the dawn of the Christian Era by a man-made barrier, the Great Wall.

The valleys of the Yellow River constitute what is commonly called North China. It includes six of the eighteen

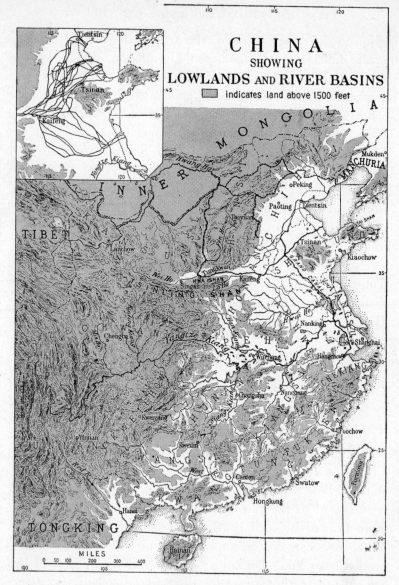

CHINA
SHOWING
LOWLANDS AND RIVER BASINS

indicates land above 1500 feet

The essentially mountainous character of western and southern China is illustrated.
The Tsingling Range, a part of the Hwang Ho-Yangtze divide, forms the natural
boundary between northern and southern China. Scale 1:20,000,000. The inset
shows changes in the lower course of the Hwang Ho and the seaward extension of the
shoreline. *Courtesy of the "Geographical Review," published by the American Geographical Society of New York.*

provinces: Kansu, Shensi, Shansi, Hopei, Honan, and Shantung. The climate here is more severe than in the south, the people are larger and sturdier, and millet and wheat instead of rice form the staple diet. In its lower reaches the Yellow River has followed two courses to the sea. For nearly a hundred years it has flowed north, to empty into the Gulf of Chihli. In previous centuries it made its way southward and emptied into the ocean south of Shantung province. Changes in the course of the Hwang Ho have wrought untold havoc, giving it the unhappy name of "China's Sorrow." There are indications also that in the twentieth century the Yellow River will again change its course.

The Yangtze basin, in central China, is by far the largest and richest of China's natural divisions. This great stream, with its tributaries, is the essential factor in China's communications. The basin which it forms absorbs sixty per cent of China's foreign trade. Here the climate is temperate. It is the region where rich crops of tea, rice, silk, and cotton are grown. China's manufacturing industries are located in the Yangtze basin, which supports a population of at least 180,000,000. Although the Yangtze is not the longest river in the world (its length of 3,100 miles is exceeded by that of the Yenesei, the Mississippi, the Nile, and the Amazon), its basin covers 750,000 square miles. Naturally many of China's great cities are in the Yangtze Valley, including ports at which much of her commerce is conducted: Shanghai, Chinkiang, Wuhu, Hankow, Changsha, and Chungkiang. To the Chinese the Yangtze is known as "kiang"—*the* river." Directly or indirectly it is the most significant single geographic factor in the lives of approximately half of China's millions.

China's third natural division, the basin of the Si Kiang or West River, is smaller than the basin drained by the Hwang Ho or the Yangtze, but it lies wholly within China proper, while the Yangtze includes part of Tibet, and the Hwang Ho, the outer northwest territory. The basin includes the greater

part of four southern provinces, which have an area of less
than 400,000 square miles and a population of some 60,000,000.
This southern area is marked off distinctly from central and
northern China by mountains, broken by two famous passes,
the Cheling and the Meiling. These mountains, known as
the Nan Shan, reach from the highlands of Yunnan to the
shores of the Pacific near Amoy, a distance of some 900 miles.
Of the four provinces drained by the West River, only Kwangtung is on the coast. The others (Kwangsi, Kweichow, and
Yunnan) all depend for their outlet on the Si Kiang. These
southern regions are quite distinct from the rest of China.
The climate is tropical or semitropical. The people are not of
pure Chinese blood. Their mountainous isolation has given
these southern Chinese a spirit of political independence not
shared by their northern brothers. It is in the south that

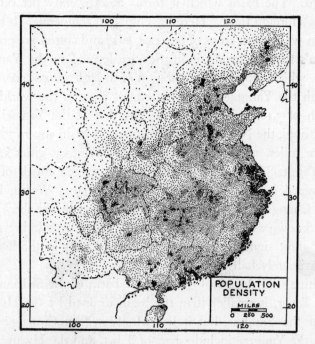

POPULATION DENSITY IN CHINA. Each dot represents 25,000 people. *From Daniel
R. Bergsmark, "Economic Geography of Asia."*

most of China's great revolutions have had their origin. The
inhabitants of Kwangtung, too, have had a longer history of
contacts with western peoples. In or near the delta of the West
River are located those historic spots that have played so striking a part in the record of China's contacts with the western
world: Canton, Macao, and Hong Kong.

Along these three great rivers the life of China has had its
greatest development. Even in the twentieth century they are
still the principal means of communication. Millions of Chinese know no other home than the river junks in which they
are born, are married, survive for a time, and finally die. The
physical isolation of one region from another has been an important element in shaping a society in which the family, the
village, and the local community provided almost all there was
of government, the central administration remaining largely
decorative.

Manchuria (Manchoukuo)

Northeast of China proper lies Manchuria (now Manchou-
kuo), known in the days of the Manchu Dynasty as the Three
Eastern Provinces. The area of the three provinces (Fengtien,
Kirin, and Heilungkiang) was 363,700 square miles, approximately the area of the Canadian province of British Columbia.
Of all the lands bordering on China proper its soil is the most
fertile. Between its mountain ranges, the Khingan, on the
northwest, and the Changpai, on the southeast, is the extensive
Manchurian plain, watered by the Sungari and the Nonni
Rivers. To the west grazing lands extend into Mongolia. In
recent times the southern valley of the Liao River and the
plains to the north of it have attracted millions of Chinese
farmer-immigrants from the crowded and ill-governed areas of
Shantung, in China proper. The present population of Manchuria, numbering more than 33 millions, is, as a result of this
recent migration, predominantly Chinese. Prior to the twentieth century, while the Manchu Dynasty still ruled in Peking,

Manchuria was not open to immigration. It was the private domain of the conquering Manchu race. Only in this sense was it a part of China. Its modern development dates only from the advent of Russia and Japan as exploiters of its great natural and strategic wealth. Its agricultural crops consist principally of soya beans, kaoliang, millet, and wheat. Of these the first is the most important. The forest lands of Manchuria, covering nearly 90 million acres, abound in larch, birch, oak,

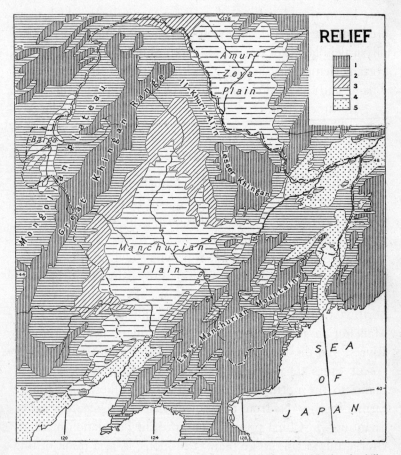

MANCHURIA. The numbers refer to: 1, mountains; 2, uplands and higher foothills; 3, lower foothills; 4, plains; and 5, lowlands. *Courtesy of the "Geographical Review," published by the American Geographical Society of New York.*

spruce, and Korean pine. Among its minerals are coal, iron, and gold. Coal reserves have been estimated as in excess of three billion metric tons. Iron is plentiful but of low grade. Of all the areas which in 1911 constituted the Manchu Empire, Manchuria occupied first place in transportation, since it was there that Russia and Japan had pioneered in railway building. Manchuria's strategic position has combined with its natural wealth to create one of Asia's principal battlegrounds.[2]

Mongolia

West of Manchuria and north of China proper lies Mongolia, an immense area of table and grazing land, desert, and mountains, reaching far into the heart of Asia. With its area of 1,367,000 square miles it is almost as large as China proper. Politically, Mongolia consists of two great regions: Outer Mongolia, bordering in the north on Siberia, with a population of probably 1,000,000; and Inner Mongolia, whose population may be 2,000,000 or 2,500,000. Outer Mongolia, which today is an "independent" state closely affiliated with Soviet Russia, has never considered itself a part of China. In fact, there has never been a period when the Chinese either conquered or controlled all of Mongolia. Mongolia's relationship as a dependency of China arose because of two circumstances: Manchu overlordship in Mongolia, and the Manchu conquest of China. As long as the Manchus ruled in Peking, the Mongols recognized the suzerainty of China. In contrast, since the establishment of the Chinese Republic in 1912, the Mongols of Outer Mon-

[2] Southwest of Manchuria is the Province of Jehol. It is largely mountainous, and divides the valleys of the Liao and the Lwan Rivers. The northeast portions belong geographically to Manchuria. Politically and administratively Jehol was for long a special district controlled from Peking, but in 1928 it was made a fourth province of Manchuria. This action followed the victory of the Nationalist armies in north China. At the same time Peking (the northern capital) became Peiping (northern peace), and the former metropolitan province of Chihli (direct rule) was renamed Hopei (north of the river). After the Manchurian incident of 1931 Jehol was incorporated as a part of Manchoukuo.

golia have remained virtually independent of any Chinese control. Inner Mongolia, by reason of its geographical position and as a result of Chinese immigration, has been more susceptible to control from Peking. This region is known by various subdivisions, such as southern Inner Mongolia and eastern Inner Mongolia. Today it is better known under the names of provincial administrative areas created by the Chinese as late as 1929 in an effort to extend their control over the Mongols. These are the provinces of Ninghsia, Suiyuan, Chahar, and Jehol, of which the last was, as already mentioned, incorporated with Manchoukuo in 1932. In general it was the policy of the Manchus, and this policy has also been followed by the Chinese Republic, so to influence the political organization of the Mongols as to prevent any unification among them which might weaken the control of Peking. This was effected in Inner Mongolia by subjecting the inhabitants directly to the several frontier provinces of China. Since the creation of Manchoukuo, in which there is a considerable Mongol population, the new state has sought to extend its control further into eastern Inner Mongolia beyond the borders of Jehol.

Sinkiang (The New Dominion)

West of Mongolia is another of China's so-called dependencies—Chinese Turkestan, or Sinkiang. Originally conquered by the Mongols in the thirteenth century, it was subjected in later times to almost constant civil wars and to foreign invasion from the north and the west. Since 1881 it has been subject to Chinese rule. The area of the New Dominion is about 400,000 square miles, with a population of 2,000,000. The majority of the people are Turkomans, the Chinese forming but a small proportion. Much of the country is desert, fringed by mountains along the frontiers. The climate is continental, with hot summers and severe winters. Valuable minerals are found particularly in the south: jade, gold, copper, oil, and coal. China's policy has sought to prevent exploitation of these resources. The weaving of coarse, hand-made cotton cloth is the most widely developed industry. The surplus is exported to Russia, to which there is now easy access over the Turkestan-Siberian Railway, a part of the Soviet railway system completed in 1930.

Tibet

Due south of Chinese Turkestan and west of China proper is Tibet, the last of the great "dependencies," frequently called the "Roof of the World." It is a vast watershed of lofty mountains and deep valleys where rise the great river systems of both China and India. The Yellow, the Yangtze, and the Mekong Rivers all flow from Tibet. This huge territory of nearly one million square miles includes the Lama Kingdom, the semi-independent native states under Chinese protection, and the territory of Kokonor, controlled by the Chinese Amban in Kansu province. The inhabitants are Mongol, numbering slightly in excess of three million. Commercially and industrially Tibet has been of little consequence in world affairs; but politically she has been subject to the rivalries of powerful neighbors. Tibet's close association with China dates from the early years of the Manchu Empire, but by the close of the nineteenth century China's practical control had been lost, though her suzerain rights there were recognized by Great Britain and Russia as late as 1907. In 1912, contrary to treaty obligations, Yuan Shih-kai declared Tibet an integral part of China, but, his armies being defeated, the country has since remained virtually independent of·Chinese control.

French Indo-China

South of China proper lies the peninsula of Indo-China, the eastern slope of which was for long under the nominal suzerainty of China but in modern times has been absorbed as colo-

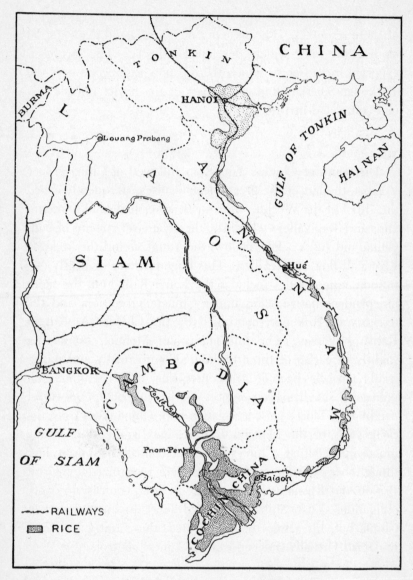

MAP OF FRENCH INDO-CHINA, SHOWING POLITICAL DIVISIONS, RAILWAYS, AND CHIEF
RICE-PRODUCING REGIONS. *From Daniel R. Bergsmark, "Economic Geography of Asia."*

nies or protectorates of France. The states of French Indo-China include: (1) Tonkin, in the north, on the borders of China proper (protectorate), (2) Annam, stretching in a long belt along the eastern coastline (protectorate), (3) Laos, in the interior bordering Siam (virtually a colony), (4) Cochin China, in the extreme south (a French colony), and (5) Cambodia (a protectorate). The area of these states is 277,000 square miles, considerably larger than the homeland of France and slightly larger than the State of Texas. Population is in excess of 21,000,000. Agriculture is the chief industry and rice the prevailing crop, with approximately ten per cent of the total land area in cultivation. Cambodia is one of the richest areas. Its plains, which extend south into Cochin China, have been formed by the Mekong River and provide a rich soil for crops. Cochin China itself is really the delta of the Mekong; here the land is but a few feet above sea level and is extremely rich. Annam, with its long coastline, has a highly developed fishing industry. The principal land crops are rice and tea. The agricultural life of Tonkin, in the north, is built largely around the delta of the Red River, where rice is widely cultivated. Mountains predominate in the western sections. Of all these states Laos is the most mountainous, the least developed, and the least accessible. Its forest lands are its richest endowment, but lack of transportation facilities has prevented effective exploitation.

Eastern Siberia

Another region which has played a vital part in the history of the modern Far East is eastern Siberia, in particular the territory east of Lake Baikal and north of Manchuria and eastern Mongolia. The area of Siberia as a whole is about 5,000,000 square miles, with a population in the neighborhood of 15,-000,000. This population is composed largely of immigrants from European Russia, with a sprinkling of native races. Since the time of Peter the Great, Siberia has been the great Russian frontier. Its earliest settlers from Europe were fur-traders, convicted criminal and political offenders, and fugitives from the law. Across Siberia in modern times the Russians moved to the shores of the Pacific, where, in 1860, they founded Vladivostok (dominator of the East). From eastern Siberia, too, they penetrated Mongolia and Manchuria as far south as the borders of China proper. From this far eastern empire Russia hoped, in the days of the last Tsars, to control China, to absorb Manchuria and Korea, and to emerge as a great power on the Pacific. Until very recent times Siberia was thought of by most western peoples (when thought of at all) as a species of no man's land, a fit habitation for wild beasts and fugitives from the law. Today Siberia must be described in different terms, for its development both in agriculture and in industry is one of the significant movements since the World War. The completion of the Trans-Siberian Railway, linking European Russia with the Pacific at the opening of the twentieth century, made colonization on a large scale possible for the first time.

In Tsarist Russia, Siberia was considered mainly as an avenue to political and economic influence in the Far East. The Soviet authorities, while not abandoning this objective, have made it their first object to develop the resources of Siberia itself. Raw materials are being exploited and heavy industries such as iron and steel introduced. The character of development varies from place to place. In northern Siberia are the marshy tundra plains, where the climate is so cold as to prevent the growth of trees. Agriculture is impossible, and there is little mineral wealth. South of the tundra is the northern coniferous forest belt, an area in which future colonization is quite possible. Southwestern Siberia, the black earth belt, contains the richest land and is the most thickly settled. In the extreme south and in the east, highlands, containing the bulk of the mineral wealth, predominate.

On the extreme Pacific slope Russian settlement is sparse,

due primarily to the rugged and mountainous nature of the land. Vladivostok, at the southern tip of the Maritime Province, is the only large city. The northern half of the island of Sakhalin, which lies off the mouth of the Amur River, belongs to Russia and contains considerable mineral wealth. Finally, northern territorial waters of Siberia are a lucrative fishing ground, a circumstance that has led to much controversy between Japan and Russia.

The Japanese Empire

Japan is predominantly an island empire. With the exception of Chosen (Korea) and the Kwantung leasehold in south Manchuria, all Japanese territory is insular.[3] In addition to its insularity, the Japanese Empire is exceedingly small: 263,000 square miles, less than the area of the single state of Texas, yet its total population is close to 100,000,000. The islands, contrasting sharply with the massive land areas of the Asiatic continent, extend as a chain for nearly 3,000 miles along its coast. Far to the north and reaching almost to the shores of Kamchatka are the Kurile, or Chichima (Thousand Isles). To the west, and close to the Maritime Province of Siberia, is Sakhalin (Karafuto), the southern half of which is Japanese territory. Then come the four main islands of Japan proper: Yezo or Hokkaido (30,000 square miles); Hondo or Honshiu, the main island (87,000 square miles), approximately the size of the State of Minnesota; Kyushu (14,000 square miles); and Shikoku (7,000 square miles). Off the coasts of these main islands are hundreds of small ones. Reaching southward again, the Loochoo (Ryukyu) chain extends almost to Taiwan, or Formosa (14,000 square miles), and Hokoto (the Pescadores). Further to the east in the Pacific, approximately south of Hon-

---

[3] Manchoukuo is not to be considered among these exceptions for though it is controlled in varying degree by Japanese policy, it is neither legally nor actually an integral part of the Japanese state.

shiu, lie the tiny Bonin Islands. Again far to the south and stretching over a vast expanse of ocean, though still in the northern latitude, are the mandated islands (the Marianas, the Carolines, and the Marshalls, 830 square miles).

Japan Proper

Japan proper, consisting of the four main islands and smaller ones off their coasts, has an area of 148,000 square miles and a population in 1937 of 70,200,000. It is some 10,000 square miles smaller than the State of California. Population density per square mile is approximately 450, exceeded only by that of Belgium, Holland, and England. In reality practical density is even greater than in these, for Japan proper is a mountainous country in which scarcely more than fifteen per cent of the land is arable. When Japan feeds her peoples from the crops of her own soil, 3,000 persons must be supported from the produce of each square mile of arable land. In Japan problems of food and population cannot be described as academic. They are distinctly modern, since Japan's population has doubled within the past 75 years.

Prior to the World War Japan was predominantly a land of agriculture. Since then she has undergone a profound industrial change, bringing by 1935 something of an equilibrium between agriculture and industry. Although the development of the factory system in Japan dates only from the Chino-Japanese War (1894-1895), the nation had become by 1934 a serious rival to western industrial states in world markets. Rice still remains the staple product of Japanese agriculture, exceeded in volume only by the rice crops of India and China and in quality by none. The domestic crop is in some years sufficient for home consumption, but more frequently foreign rice is imported. Sericulture was until very recent years second in importance to rice in Japan's economic structure. Today it is relatively less important in view of the rise of the great textile industries: cotton, woolens, and rayon. The fishing industry is the most highly developed in the world. Fish and rice are the staple foods of every Japanese meal.

Geography, in some respects, has produced more striking effects upon the Japanese than upon any other oriental people. Their land is beautiful in a unique sense: a satisfying picture of mountains, pine forests, valleys richly green in paddy fields,

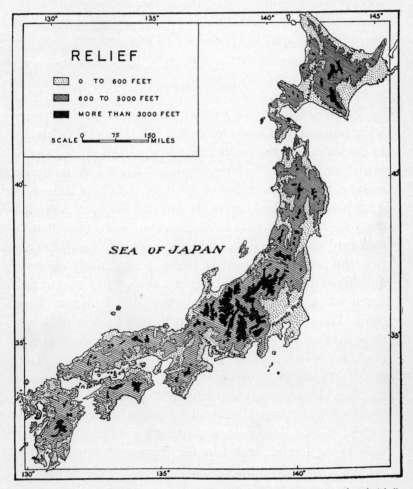

RELIEF OF JAPAN PROPER. *From Daniel R. Bergsmark, "Economic Geography of Asia."*

islands, and ocean bays. Probably no people are so attached to their homeland as are the Japanese. As an insular race the Japanese take naturally to life upon the sea. Their national expansion in modern times has always involved the development of sea power and the control of maritime routes. In a modern world of industrial wealth, the poverty of their own islands in industrial resources has been a pronounced stimulus to national ambitions. Only 83 years have elapsed since Japan was opened to world intercourse by the black ships of Commodore Matthew C. Perry. Today she is one of the great powers. Geography has played a vital part in that transformation.

Chosen (Korea)

Separated from Japan proper by the narrow Korean Straits is the peninsula of Chosen, or Korea, as it is commonly known in the West. On the north and west it adjoins the borders of Manchuria and the Maritime Province. Its area, 85,000 square miles, is approximately that of the State of Idaho. Since 1910 it has been an integral part of the Japanese Empire. Although enjoying an early cultural development, Korea has been a backward state in modern times. A weak state lying between powerful neighbors, she recognized at various times the overlordship of both China and Japan. Such wealth as she possessed was squandered by a corrupt and unintelligent ruling class. The spirit of the people was thereby broken, rendering them a fit subject of conquest at the hands of more vigorous neighbors. Today, under Japanese rule, Korea enjoys an ordered and efficient government and an increasing national wealth. The country is scenically most attractive. Mountains, of which Kongo-san (Diamond Mountain) is world-famous, abound in every landscape, their denuded slopes now covered with young forests planted by the Japanese conqueror. It is essentially an agricultural country. More than eighty per cent of its 20,000,000 people are engaged in farming. Rice is the

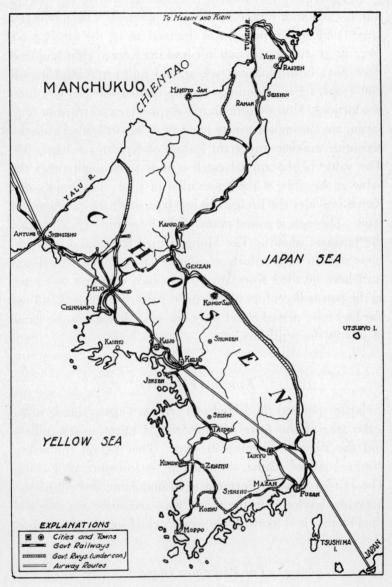

CHOSEN (KOREA) IN 1935.

staple crop, and, although the area of arable lowland is not large (perhaps ten per cent of the total area), the soil is good. In contrast with Japan, two thirds of the Korean crop is upland rice. Soya beans, tobacco, wheat, and millet are other important crops, some beginnings having been made also in cotton production. Korea's agricultural surplus is exported mostly to Japan, accounting for ninety per cent of export trade. Fisheries constitute another important feature of Korean economic life. The value of the annual catch is now some eight times the value at the time of the annexation in 1910. Geographically, Korea provides the bridge linking Japan and the mainland of Asia. Through it passed many of the migrations which settled the Japanese islands. The Mongols used Korea as a stepping-stone in their futile efforts to conquer Japan, and Hideyoshi in turn later invaded Korea in his proposed conquest of China. In the past half century all the great powers of Europe and the Far East have played either the game of diplomacy or the game of war in the peninsula.

Taiwan (Formosa)

Japan acquired the Island of Formosa (14,000 square miles —the area of the State of Maryland is 12,300 square miles) and the Pescadores group in 1895. They lie off the south-eastern coast of China, dominating the province of Fukien. The eastern slope of Formosa is mountainous, but cultivation is highly developed in the west. Rice and sugar are the principal crops. It is likewise the world's chief source of camphor.

The Philippine Islands

South of Formosa and southeast of China proper are the Philippines, which the United States received from Spain at the close of the Spanish-American War. There are some 7,000 islands in the Philippine group, with an area of 114,000 square

miles (slightly larger than the State of Nevada). Population
is in excess of 14,000,000. The largest islands are Luzon, in the
north (40,000 square miles), and Mindanao, in the south
(36,000 square miles). Others in the group include: Cebu,
Mindoro, Negros, Samar, and Palawan. The Philippines are
tropical. High mountains, rich plains, abundant forests, and
perpetual summer provide the principal endowments of the
land. Although probably more than fifty per cent of the total
area is arable land, not more than twelve per cent was under
cultivation in 1930. The principal crops are rice, abaca, sugar,
tobacco, and cocoanuts. Industry is not developed, but commerce between the islands and the United States has been of
some importance. Politically, in very recent years the Philippine Islands have been a disturbing factor in Far Eastern
affairs. In 1898 their acquisition made the United States an
Asiatic power. More recently their aspirations for political
independence have led to conflicts of policy within themselves
and within the United States. Their value to the United States
commercially and strategically has been both affirmed and
challenged. Their ability to maintain their independence has
been questioned by American imperialists. Japan has been
accused in the American press of coveting their rich resources.

These are the principal areas, briefly sketched, with which
the following pages are in large part concerned.

SELECTED BIBLIOGRAPHY

For the geography of Asia in general the most useful single volume is Lionel W. Lyde, *The Continent of Asia* (London: 1933),
especially chs. 29-38. A less detailed treatment is given by Daniel
R. Bergsmark, *Economic Geography of Asia* (New York: 1935), in
which Pts. 4-6, dealing with eastern Asia, contain bibliographical
references of value. Herbert E. Gregory surveys "The Geography of
the Pacific" in *Problems of the Pacific,* J. B. Condliffe, ed. (Chicago:
1928). H. Foster Bain, *Ores and Industry in the Far East,* rev. ed.,
(New York: 1933) gives the most satisfactory concise treatment of

industrial geography. Of importance, too, is L. D. Stamp, *Asia: An Economic and Regional Geography* (London: 1929). Political implications of geography are discussed ably in such works as: L. H. D. Buxton, *The Peoples of Asia* (London: 1925); G. M. Dutcher, *Political Awakening of the East* (New York: 1925); F. R. Eldridge, *Trading with Asia* (New York: 1923); V. C. Finch and O. E. Baker, *Geography of the World's Agriculture* (Washington, D. C.: 1917); C. C. Huntington and F. A. Carlson, *Environmental Basis of Social Geography* (New York: 1929); C. K. Leith, *World Minerals and World Politics* (New York: 1931); J. R. Smith, *The World's Food Resources* (New York: 1919); R. H. Whitbeck and O. J. Thomas, *The Geographic Factor, Its Role in Life and Civilization* (New York: 1932); and E. W. Zimmermann, *World Resources and Industries* (New York: 1933).

Atlases

Many atlases serving as aids in the study of far eastern history are available, among which may be mentioned: *The Times Survey Atlas of the World* (London: 1922); *Putnam's Historical Atlas* (New York: 1927); and J. G. Bartholomew, *A Literary and Historical Atlas of Asia* (New York: n. d.).

China

Among the most valuable works on China is Julean Arnold, *China: A Commercial and Industrial Handbook* (Washington, D. C.: 1926). C. W. Bishop has two informative articles: "The Geographic Factor in the Development of Chinese Civilization" in *The Geographical Review,* XII (1922), and "The Rise of Civilization in China with Reference to its Geographical Aspects" in *ibid.,* XXII (1932). *The China Year Book,* H. G. W. Woodhead, ed., (Shanghai), always contains illuminating material on Chinese geography. The best single volume by an American scholar on Chinese geography is G. B. Cressey, *China's Geographic Foundations* (New York: 1934). Instructive articles by the same author are: "The New Map of China" in *The Geographical Review,* Oct. 1930; and "The Geographic Regions of China" in *The Annals of the American Academy of Political and Social Science,* Nov. 1930. Among important studies on Chinese agriculture may be mentioned: J. L. Buck, *Chinese Farm Economy* (Chicago: 1930), and by the same author, "Chinese Rural Economy" in *Journal of Farm Economics,* XII (1930); F. H. King, *Farmers of Forty Centuries* (New York: 1926); W. H. Mallory, "China—Land of Famine," American Geographical Society Pub. No. 6, 1926. For general collateral reading the following are suggestive: F. J. Goodnow, *China, An Analysis* (Baltimore: 1926), ch. 1; K. S. Latourette, *The Chinese, Their History and Culture,* 2nd ed. rev., (New York: 1934) I, ch. 1, "Geography and its influence on the Chinese"; by the same author, *The Development of China,* 3rd ed. (Boston: 1924) ch. 1; W. A. P. Martin, *The Awakening of China* (New York: 1907) Pt. 1; Paul Monroe, *China: A Nation in Evolution* (New York: 1928) ch. 2, the people and the physical background; *An Official Guide to Eastern Asia,* 5 vols. (Tokyo: 1913-17) vol. 4, "China"; E. H. Parker, *China* (London: 1917) ch. 1; L. Richard, *Comprehensive Geography of the Chinese Empire,* trans., rev., and enlarged by M. Kennelly (Shanghai: 1908); E. T. Williams, *China Yesterday and Today* (New York: 1923) ch. 1; and S. Wells Williams, *The Middle Kingdom,* rev. ed., 2 vols. (New York: 1907) chs. 1-5. On population see P. M. Roxby, "The Distribution of the Population in China" in *The Geographical Review,* XV (1925).

Manchuria (Manchoukuo)

The most reliable information on geography, agriculture, and industry is contained in the five reports entitled *Report on Progress in Manchuria* (Dairen: The South Manchuria Railway Co., 1929-36); at first edited by Dr. Seiji Hishida, they are now being compiled by Roy H. Akagi; both are Japanese scholars of repute and are assisted in the work by the staff of the research office of the railroad. The reports cover all phases of Manchurian development. They are now supplemented by *The Manchoukuo Year Book* (Tokyo: 1933-); see in particular issue for 1934, ch. 1. *An Official Guide to Eastern Asia* (Tokyo), I, "Manchuria and Chosen" is useful. Other worthwhile references include: "Agriculture in Manchuria and Mongolia" in *Chinese Economic Journal,* I (1927); Chu Hsiao, "Manchuria—A Statistical Survey of its Resources, Industries, Trade, Railways, and Immigration" in *Problems of the Pacific* (Chicago: 1930); *North Manchuria and the Chinese Eastern Railway* (Harbin: 1924); Owen Lattimore, *Manchuria, Cradle of Conflict* (New York: 1932); P. Kropotkin, "Russian Exploration in Manchuria" in *The Geographical Journal,*

II (1898); J. R. Stewart, "The Resources of Manchuria" in *The Journal of Geography*, XXXI (1932); B. P. Torgasheff, "The Mineral Wealth of North and South Manchuria" in *Chinese Economic Journal*, IV (1929).

Mongolia, Sinkiang, and Tibet

See references above on China. Other studies include: R. C. Andrews, "Explorations in the Gobi Desert" in *National Geographic Magazine*, LXIII (1933); Charles Bell, *The People of Tibet* (London: 1928); E. Bradshaw, "Sino-Russian Relations in Sinkiang" in *The Journal of Geography*, XXXI (1932); Owen Lattimore, "Caravan Routes of Inner Asia" in *Geographical Journal*, LXXII (1928); H. D. Robinson, "Mongolia, Its Trade Routes and Trends" in *Commerce Reports* (Washington, D. C.: Jan. 6, 1930); J. F. Rock, "The Land of the Yellow Lama" in *National Geographic Magazine*, XLVII (1925); R. C. F. Schomberg, "The Habitability of Chinese Turkestan" in *Geographical Journal*, LXXX (1932); A. L. Shelton, "Life Among the People of Eastern Tibet" in *National Geographic Magazine*, XL (1921); Sir M. A. Stein, "Innermost Asia, Its Geography as a Factor in History" in *Geographical Journal*, LXV (1925); and P. H. Stevenson, "Notes on the Human Geography of the Chinese-Tibetan Borderland" in *Geographical Review*, XXII (1932).

French Indo-China

Outstanding in the literature on this section is Sir Henry Bell, *Foreign Colonial Administration in the Far East* (London: 1928), and H. Cordier, *Histoire des relations de la Chine avec les puissances occidentales, 1860-1900*, 3 vols. (Paris: 1901-02), chs. 12-25. Other works to be consulted are: R. K. Douglas, *Europe and the Far East, 1506-1912*, rev. ed. (Cambridge: 1913), ch. 18; N. D. Harris, *Europe and the East* (Boston: 1926), ch. 11; H. Lorin, *La France puissance coloniale* (Paris: 1906); C. B. Norman, *Colonial France* (London: 1886); and H. A. Franck, *East of Siam* (New York: 1926).

Eastern Siberia

Literature on eastern Siberia in English is somewhat fragmentary. Among the best brief accounts is Boris Baievsky, "Siberia—Its Resources and Possibilities" in *Trade Promotion Series*, No. 36 (Washington, D. C.: 1936). See also P. P. Goudkoff, "Economic

Geography of the Coal Resources of Asiatic Russia" in *The Geographical Review*, XIII (1923). A brief but useful account is given by H. K. Norton, *The Far Eastern Republic of Siberia* (New York: 1923), ch. 1, "The Land of Siberia." S. Novakovsky has an interesting article "Climatic Provinces of the Russian Far East in Relation to Human Activities" in *The Geographical Review*, XII (1922). For a picture of Siberia in the middle nineteenth century the reader should consult E. G. Ravenstein, *The Russians on the Amur* (London: 1861). Additional references containing geographical materials are: E. K. Reynolds, "The Economic Resources of the Russian Empire" in *The Geographical Review*, I (1916); G. F. Wright, *Asiatic Russia*, 2 vols. (New York: 1902); R. L. Wright and B. Digby, *Through Siberia* (New York: 1913).

The Japanese Empire

1. Japan proper

Detailed information is given in *An Official Guide to Japan* (Tokyo: 1933), ch. 2. Political features of geography are stressed in G. A. Ballard, *Influence of the Sea on the Political History of Japan* (New York: 1921). C. W. Bishop gives a valuable treatment of "The Historical Geography of Early Japan" in *The Geographical Review*, XIII (1923). For the island of Hokkaido see D. H. Davis, "Present Status of Settlement in Hokkaido" in *The Geographical Review*, XXIV (1934). H. H. Gowen, *An Outline History of Japan* (New York: 1930) gives, in chs. 1-2 a brief but clear summary on geography, race, and language. The geographical factor is noted by Seiji Hishida, *International Position of Japan as a Great Power* (New York: 1905). Helpful suggestions are found in E. Huntington, "Geographical Environment and Japanese Character" in *Japan and Japanese-American Relations*, G. H. Blakeslee, ed. (New York: 1912). Annual issues of *The Japan Year Book* are invaluable. For the Japan of Tokugawa times no student can afford to neglect Engelbert Kaempfer, *The History of Japan*, 3 vols. (Glasgow: 1906), vol. 1, Bk. 1 of which is devoted to a general description of the Empire. K. K. Kawakami, *Japan in World Politics* (New York: 1917) treats, in ch. 1, the Japanese instinct of self-preservation. Brief sketches on the relation of geography to Japanese history are given in K. S. Latourette, *The Development of Japan*, 2nd ed. (New York: 1926) and J. H. Longford, *Japan* (Boston: 1923). A very worth-while introduction to the subject has been given by Sobei Mogi and H. Vere Redman, *The Problem of the Far East* (London: 1935). Chapters on geography are contained too in David Murray, *Japan,* 6th ed. (London: 1919) and in Inazo Nitobe, *The Japanese Nation* (New York: 1912). On numerous phases of Japan's economic problems in their relation to geography one should consult J. E. Orchard's contributions, among which may be mentioned: "Can Japan Develop Industrially?" in *The Geographical Review,* XIX (1929); "The Pressure of Population in Japan" in *ibid.,* XVIII (1928), and *Japan's Economic Position* (New York: 1930). Perhaps the best single volume on Japanese rural life is J. W. R. Scott, *The Foundations of Japan* (London: 1922). For special agricultural activities see G. T. Trewartha, "The Tea Crop" in *Journal of Geography,* XXVIII (1929); and by the same author: "The Suwa Basin—A Specialized Sericulture District in the Japanese Alps" in *The Geographical Review,* XX (1930), and "Notes on the Physiographic Diagram of Japan" in *The Geographical Review,* XXIV (1934).

2. *Chosen (Korea)*

Considerable material on geography is contained in the *Annual Report on Administration of Chosen* (Keijo). A chapter is devoted to geography in each of the following: Henry Chung, *The Case of Korea* (New York: 1921); Alleyne Ireland, *The New Korea* (New York: 1926); and W. F. Sands, *Undiplomatic Memories* (New York: 1930). *An Official Guide to Eastern Asia* (Tokyo), vol. 1, contains accurate descriptive and statistical data.

3. *Taiwan (Formosa)*

In addition to many of the references given on Japan, there is much geographical material on Formosa in many of the earlier reference works on China.

4. *The Japanese Mandate (Nanyo)*

The best official source is Japan, *Annual Report to the League of Nations on the Administration of the South Seas Islands.* For accounts by travelers see, Willard Price, *Pacific Adventure* (New York: 1936), and Paul H. Clyde, *Japan's Pacific Mandate* (New York: 1935).

CHAPTER II

China: An Historical Background

THE China to which western imperialists sought access in the middle of the nineteenth century was, in contrast with their own youthful states, a product of antiquity. Centuries before the beginning of the Christian Era, its peoples, its manners, customs and modes of thought, and its institutions—social, economic, and political—had reached the fullness of their development and then had become stereotyped. Had Confucius revisited his native land in the year 1800, he would have found with few exceptions the same China from which he passed in 479 B.C. Centuries before the coming of the Westerners Chinese life had become a fixed "way." Time had consecrated China's philosophy, had endowed it with a maturity and a finality which rendered it immune from questioning. This fixed, conventional Chinese mind may be explained only by reference to an historical development reaching back through many centuries.

Chinese History

The traditional beginnings of Chinese history are not without their interest. There was first, it is said, a period when Nothing existed, though more ambitious chronologers have laid claim to an era antecedent even to this. In the course of ages Nothing became Unity (a point at the center of a circle), a convenient if not convincing First Cause. Again countless ages appear to have passed before our First Cause emerged as

31

two entities or principles: the one active, positive—the male; the other passive, negative—the female.

The interaction of these Two Principles resulted in the production of all things, as we see them in the universe around us, 2,269,381 years ago. Such is the cosmogony of the Chinese in a nutshell.[1]

The more modest of Chinese historians, however, think it well enough to begin things with an emperor who ruled only 2,800 years before the Christian Era. The beginning of agriculture, the invention of wheeled vehicles, and numerous other achievements are sometimes attributed to this era. This is, nevertheless, so patently a period of myth and legend, about which virtually nothing is known, that modern historians pass over it to the eighth century B.C. as the starting-point of authentic Chinese history.

As early as the twenty-first century B.C. the Chinese appear

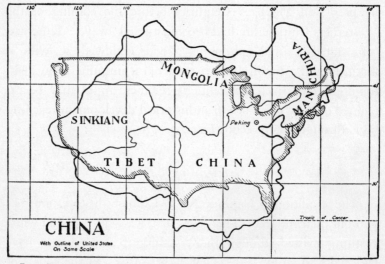

From Paul Monroe, "China: A Nation in Evolution." The Macmillan Company, New York, 1928.

CHINA, WITH OUTLINE OF CHINA ON SAME SCALE

[1] H. A. Giles, *A History of Chinese Literature.* D. Appleton-Century Company, New York, 1927. p. 3.

to have been settled in the upper valley of the Yellow River in what are now the provinces of Shansi, Shensi, Kansu, and Honan. Although numerous legendary figures had occupied the throne in previous centuries, the appearance of the Hsia Dynasty (2205-1766 B.C.) marks the beginning of a semihistorical period. The Hsia were followed by the Shang (1766-1122 B.C.) and they in turn by the Chow Dynasty (1122-249 B.C.).

During the Chow period "the government was not yet in name an Empire; but the overlord governed through a feudal nobility of graduated rank (duke, marquis, count, etc.), the members of which were in command each of an assigned district, as was the case in the Holy Roman Empire in Europe; and, as in that Empire in its latter centuries, these feudal nobles by degrees asserted their semi-independence, giving only a nominal allegiance to their sovereign." [2]

The greatest exponents of Chinese thought lived during these years: Laotze (Old Philosopher, born 604 B.C.), from whose teachings Taoism has evolved; K'ung Fu-tze (Confucius, 551-479 B.C.), who formulated China's great ethical codes; and his greatest disciple, Mencius (372-289 B.C.).

Internal anarchy and feudal strife, against which Confucius had protested, destroyed the power of the Chow, and China was ruled (249-206 B.C.) by the Tsin Dynasty, the fame of which rests upon the name of the First Heavenly Emperor (Tsin Shih Huang-ti). It was he who first consolidated the Empire by abolishing feudalism, built the Great Wall, and attempted to unify political theory and practice by the burning of the classics, hoping thereby that the nation would look to the future and not to the past.

The Han Dynasty (206 B.C.-220 A.D.) is still venerated by the Chinese as a golden age. It was an era of economic prosperity and cultural development. Communication was made

---

[2] Dr. H. B. Morse, *The Trade and Administration of China*, 3rd rev. ed. Longmans, Green & Company, London, 1920. pp. 2-3.

easier by the building of roads, bridges, and canals. Literature revived with the introduction of Buddhist books from India; China's own classics were restored and engraved on stone. The system of official examinations, which survived until the beginning of the twentieth century, dates from this period. The boundaries of the Empire were extended on all sides to include the provinces of Fukien, Kwangtung, Yunnan, Szechwan, and Liaotung.

Again internal strife was responsible for the collapse of a dynasty, and on the passing of Han the Empire was for a time divided into three kingdoms. Tartar invasions from the north having become more serious, the capital was moved south to Nanking. After several centuries of almost constant civil strife, a semblance of political stability was restored with the advent of the Tang rulers (618-907 A.D.). Boundaries were again extended, particularly in the west, while Chinese officials controlled also the political life of Korea. Nestorian missionaries reached China at this time, receiving some official favor.

A number of minor dynasties preceded the Sung (960-1280). In the northeast China was now open to the advance of the Tartars, who, by establishing their capital at Peking, forced the Sung south of the Yangtze. In this extremity China appealed to the Mongols, who, after defeating the Tartars in 1234, turned upon the Chinese and, under the leadership of Kublai Khan, founded the Yuan or Mongol Dynasty (1280-1368). It was during the reign of Kublai Khan that Marco Polo was received at the court of Peking. The Mongol power, however, lasted less than a century, being displaced by the last native Chinese dynasty, the Ming (1368-1644). Although conflict with the Tartars continued on the northern frontier, internally China enjoyed an orderly and stable government, and, during the early years of the dynasty, a measure of prosperity. The power of the Empire was felt in all the border vassal states, while at home the arts flourished, scholarship was encouraged, and trade increased. The period saw, too, the coming of European merchants: the Portuguese at Canton (1515-1517), the Spaniards from their new colony in the Philippines (1575), the Dutch (1604), and finally the English (1637).

Yet all was not well. Ambitious Chinese generals rebelled against the waning power of the Mings, and in the north the threat of invasion remained, this time from the Manchus, a Tartar tribe occupying what is now Kirin province in Manchuria. These Tartars, in 1618, invaded Liaotung, setting up their capital at Mukden. The capture of Peking by Chinese rebels, in 1644, and the suicide of the last Ming emperor, together with the appeals of loyal Ming generals for their assistance, afforded the Manchus their opportunity to enter Peking and found the Tsing (Manchu) Dynasty (1644-1912). Like their Mongol predecessors, the Manchus were foreigners who, by military power, imposed their rule upon China. Their capacity to control is amply attested by the duration of their sway; but like no other dynasty before them the Manchus faced a problem for which both they and their Chinese subjects were equally unprepared: the impact on eastern Asia of the imperialistic West. For more than a century Manchu and Chinese alike sought to halt the western advance. By failure the dynasty, like others before it, forfeited the mandate of "Heaven," and in the stormy days of 1911-1912 abdicated in favor of the Republic.

No less striking than its antiquity is the uniform character of China's history. Century after century dynasties might rise and fall, civil strife be rampant, or feudal anarchy prevail at the expense of the central government, yet the foundations of China's civilization proved to be singularly stable.

She had mastered . . . fundamental arts of life at a time when the West was still ignorant of them. Like her peasants, who ploughed with iron when Europe used wood, and continued to plough with it when Europe used steel, she had carried one type of economic system and social organisation to a high level of achievement, and was not conscious of the need to improve or supersede it.[3]

This stability, this uniformity, which centuries before the dawn of the Christian Era had been engraved on the Chinese pattern, may be explained in large part by a profound loyalty to generations that had passed. As far into the past as history bears record, ancestor worship has controlled the social, political, and economic activities of the Sons of Han. The cult of the ancestor was perhaps common to all ancient societies, but in China its sway has remained even to the twentieth century. It is still *the* basic religion, the way of life, to China's millions. Through ages its sway was unchallenged, until with the impact of modern western thought the old order was shaken, and the oldest of existing social structures began to give ground to the new. How has this cult of the dead served China so well and so long?

Religion in China

In contrast with western Christian notions of human depravity, the Chinese have regarded human nature as essentially good; and to this path of goodness man is held by human rather than divine means: by education, by proper forms of conduct or ethics, and by government. If proper rules are constructed and observed, rules that govern every situation in life, then life itself will be stable, the good in man will be preserved, the structure of society will be firm, and government in the political sense will be largely unnecessary. Such is the philosophy upon which Chinese life was built.

Heaven, the power of deity, had endowed man with the five virtues: benevolence, justice, reverence, wisdom, and sincerity. These, the bases of life, were conserved and developed by education. So it came about that the Chinese were not so concerned with the origin of evil and its eradication as with

---

[3] R. H. Tawney, *Land and Labour in China.* George Allen & Unwin, Ltd., London, 1932. p. 11.

the origin of good and its preservation. The idea of the *Tao,* "the way or path," became all-important, and, since ways might differ, it followed that all religions might contain some truth. To the Chinese, who could find aid and comfort in each of China's religions, whether it be Confucianism, Buddhism, or Taoism, the exclusiveness preached by Catholic Christianity seemed absurd and unintelligent. He was tolerant of all that might assist him in finding the "Way." This broad, all-inclusive attitude of the Chinese was obviously repellent to the Christian missionary. His object was to destroy the edifice of Chinese religious thought in order that it might be replaced with an exclusive Christian doctrine. To him, China's very tolerance was a vice, and irrefutable evidence that the Chinese were not a religious people. In this conclusion there was grave error, for on the subject of ancestor worship China would tolerate no tampering with established custom and belief.

The Family: the Unit of Society

Among the Chinese, the family was, and to a large extent still is, the most important constituent of society. The individual and society as a whole were merely manifestations of this unit. Family, too, had a far wider significance than in the West. It included all those who had died, all the members still living, and future generations of the group yet unborn. The welfare of the deceased depended wholly upon the care of their needs and upon their worship by the living. Perpetuation of the family became imperative. The individual was of value only as a link in this continuous family chain, a link between generations of the dead and those yet to be born. Since the happiness of those who had gone depended upon right conduct on the part of the living, perpetuation of the family was an urgent responsibility. As long as the system worked, responsibility remained within the family, thus minimizing the necessity for the external controls of government.

The purely religious aspects of ancestor worship were no less striking:

Here is a religion without priesthood, without church or temples, without monks or monasteries, without processions, without a sacred book, with no Deity, without revelation, without any supernatural element save that of the immortality of the soul—and yet it penetrates into every daily act of life of practically every individual of the largest unified aggregation of human beings living together in the most enduring of social structures.[4]

The orthodox Westerner who regards his Christian creeds as divine revelation stamps ancestor worship with the stigma of superstition; yet both are but manifestations of an identical concept: the immortality of the soul. And so in every Chinese household there is a shrine or temple before which reverence it paid daily to the ancestral spirits. At least twice a year more elaborate ceremonies are performed at the family graves; and when a member of the family dies, the intricate ritual of the funeral procession and the long period of mourning are but added evidence that those who remain have left nothing undone to speed the soul on a happy journey.

Since the establishment of the Republic in 1911 the grip of ancestor worship upon China's intellectuals has noticeably weakened. With the masses its power remains unbroken. Nor is this surprising. Even in the western world there are not lacking people who still cling to outmoded and irrational forms of religious thought.

Taoism

Since ancestor worship is the foundation and the frame of the Chinese religious structure, it expresses itself in the completed edifice in various ways. The religion of Taoism is, if

---

[4] Paul Monroe, *China: A Nation in Evolution.* The Macmillan Company, New York, 1928. pp. 88-89.

one take account of the founder, the oldest in China. Laotze is said to have been born in 604 B.C. Undoubtedly one of China's greatest teachers, his life and work have been beclouded by legend. Early chroniclers, for example, affirmed that he was born of a virgin. What, if anything, Laotze actually wrote is not known; but he is credited with some notable observations on life. These, preserved by ancient scholars, were published with much padding, probably in the second century B.C., in a work called *Tao Te Ching*. Whatever the circumstances of Laotze's life may have been, it is beyond question that he was a man of profound thought. Six centuries before the birth of Christ he had expounded the essence of Christian ethics: "Recompense injury with kindness." It is probable, however, that Laotze did not regard himself as primarily a religious teacher, and certainly not as the founder of a religion. His philosophy was that of the *Tao,* the Way of Life, as set forth by earlier writers. Patience, humility, calmness, and deliberation were extolled; while luxury, vulgar show, boastfulness, and military glory were condemned.

Out of this simple "Way" succeeding generations built Taoism, a thing so immaterial and miraculous as to suggest speculative Hindu philosophy rather than doctrines of the old Chinese sage. Naturally in practice among the unthinking and the illiterate, Taoism became "the most elaborate and complicated system of magic, myths, spells, charms, incantations, demonology, and all similar forms of superstitious practice that any society has developed." [5]

Its control of the spirit world gave it an immediate place in the scheme of ancestor worship. Man's every act was affected by spirits either friendly or hostile. Here lay the power of the Taoist priest to decide the proper time for the building of a house, the solemnization of a wedding, or the burial of a corpse.

---

[5] *Ibid.* p. 102.

Confucianism

If influence upon one's fellow man be accepted as an adequate standard, K'ung Fu-tze (Confucius, 551-479 B.C.) remains the greatest character that China has produced. He was born in the state of Lu (the modern province of Shantung) of a titled but impecunious family. In his early life there was nothing to indicate the power he was destined for two thousand years to wield over his race. At the age of fifteen he was a student; at nineteen, he married, and for three years he filled minor public offices. At twenty-two, gathering about him a group of students intent on mastering the classics, he began his fruitful career as a teacher. Thirty years later his fame as a scholar brought recognition in the form of an official appointment as magistrate of an important city and minister of justice in his native state. His fame as an administrator was soon widespread. Government, however, was little more than a feudal anarchy against which one man could not prevail, and Confucius, wearied by the dissipations of his own and the intrigues of rival princes, resigned his office and sought voluntary exile. For thirteen years he wandered from state to state engaged in teaching and literary pursuits before returning finally to the home of his ancestors to die.

Of the Four Books and the Five Canons, conventionally known as the Confucian classics, Confucius was in part editor rather than author. Their character may be summarized as follows:

The Four Books include: (1) *The Analects,* or dialogues of Confucius with his disciples; (2) the *Book of Mencius,* containing the sayings of this sage; (3) the *Great Learning,* an outline of Confucian ethics; and (4) the *Doctrine of the Mean.* The Five Canons contain: (1) the *Book of Changes,* an elaborate and philosophical interpretation of the Sixty-four Hexagrams; (2) the *Book of History,* a fragmentary history covering the period 2400-619 B.C; (3) the *Book of Poetry,* a collection of more than three hundred poems of the Chou period; (4) the *Book of Rites,* dealing with ceremonial procedure; and (5) *The Spring and Autumn Annals,* a history of the state of Lu.[6]

In these volumes is found the substance of the Confucian philosophy, a philosophy whose influence on the moral, social, and political life of the Chinese it is perhaps impossible to overrate. It was essentially a code of conduct by which man might be governed in his relations with his fellow man. These relations included that of prince to minister, parent to child, husband to wife, brother to brother, and friend to friend. The five constant virtues of benevolence, righteousness, propriety, wisdom, and fidelity were stressed, and, in following these, man looked for wisdom to the sages of the past. Whether Confucianism is to be regarded as a religion is a subject on which scholars differ. Confucius himself was seemingly opposed to reliance on the supernatural, and, when asked concerning the gods, replied that he knew little about them. If man could not understand life, it was unreasonable to suppose that he could understand death. Certainly Confucianism as practiced by the masses lacks the external paraphernalia of religion in the conventional sense: a priesthood, sacraments, and the dogma of supernatural revelation. As suggestive of Confucian thought the following may be cited:

Learning without thought is labor lost. Thought without learning is intellectual death.

The study of the supernatural is injurious indeed.

In mourning it is better to be sincere than to be punctilious.

A plausible tongue and a fascinating expression are seldom associated with true virtue.

Return good for good; for evil, justice.

---

[6] See E. D. Thomas, *Chinese Political Thought.* Prentice-Hall, Inc., New York, 1927. pp. 28-29.

The commander-in-chief of an army may be carried captive, but the convictions even of the meanest man cannot be taken from him.

And so Confucianism, without the mysteries, the rewards, or the terrors of religion, with no heavenly pledges and no hell, directed man in his duty both to his family and to society rather than in the worship of an unknown spirit world.

Buddhism

Buddhism, which was introduced into China probably in the first century of the Christian Era, is today, as practiced by the Chinese masses, as far removed from the pure doctrines of the founder as is Taoism from the philosophy of Laotze. The term "Buddha" is not a proper name but a title meaning "The Enlightened One." Gotama, the founder, was born in northern India on the borders of Nepal about 563 B.C. He was the son of a wealthy and powerful prince. After marriage and the birth of a son he became dissatisfied with the transient character of worldly things, renounced the world, and began to wander in search of truth. After a revelation, which appears to have come to him suddenly, he spent the remainder of his life in spreading his doctrine. He was primarily a moral teacher concerned with *right* living and the spiritual training necessary to this end. In contrast with Confucius, who was a humanist, Gotama was the founder of a religion. Essentially a "protestant," he held that nothing was to be taken on authority; to all doctrines was to be applied the test of personal experience and reason. He stressed inwardness of life and the suppression of desire as a means of winning spiritual freedom. Wisdom and love were regarded as the greatest of virtues. Self-discipline was the first aim of all. He urged the usual virtues common to conventional morality in civilized lands.

China was in many ways an unpromising field for Buddhism. The emphasis of Buddhism on introspection and the inner life was not in harmony with the practical bent of the Chinese mind. Its exhortation to the celibate life could have little appeal in a land of ancestor worship. Its corporate organization was an object of suspicion. Yet Buddhism was accepted widely. Its dogmas were elastic and adaptable to new needs. Monasticism, if not popular, could at least be made useful to the Chinese family. Filial piety became inseparable from the Buddhist creed in China, while its masses for the dead filled a needed gap in the Confucian system. This latter had little to say of the dead, but Buddhism offered ready information and a profound faith. The Buddhist monk became an essential agent in the worship of ancestors.

Buddhism, however, brought more than religion from India. Indian science and art came too. Chinese astronomy was enriched; the written language, by the adoption of foreign terms, became less rigid; Chinese sculpture, and later painting, took on new and finer forms; and block printing was used in the making of books. By the time of the Tang Dynasty (618-907 B.C.) Buddhism had reached the height of its influence. But against its conception of individualism and progress, the Confucian code of conformity and conservatism triumphed at the close of the Sung Dynasty, a triumph which has persisted into modern times. From this and other causes the grip that Buddhism once had upon the Chinese people seems steadily to have waned, while its intellectual interest and spiritual power lost in a measure their vitality.

Government in China

Historically speaking, and in the sense in which western peoples use the term, the Chinese have not been politically minded. Centuries ago an anonymous Chinese poet noted this attitude in *The Husbandman's Song:*

Work, work,—from the rising sun
Till sunset comes and the day is done
I plough the sod
And harrow the clod,
And meat and drink both come to me
So what care I for the powers that be? [7]

Furthermore, any consideration of government as it existed in China during the Manchu Dynasty, when foreigners made their first major contacts with the Empire, must take account of two widely differing political theories. In Europe and the Americas the individual was the unit of society; in China the family was the unit. Thus society did not consist of a mass of individuals controlled directly by the laws of a central and perhaps remote government, but rather by laws of groups of individuals (the family), each member being responsible to his fellow members and controlled in his daily conduct not to any great degree by laws either central or local but by custom and tradition as fixed by the Confucian system. Therefore, the central administration, as will presently appear, though clothed in theory with the unlimited powers of autocracy, was in fact of less practical consequence than the magistrate of a single village. In the early years of the Manchu Dynasty, as in previous centuries, the system worked well enough, but the coming of the foreigner with his demand for contact with a responsible administration forced gradually the assumption of greater control by central authorities.

Since the middle of the thirteenth century China has been twice conquered by the foreigner: the Mongols in 1260 and the Manchus in 1644. But by neither of these conquests was the political life of the people appreciably affected. Domestic customs and institutions were not disturbed. The Manchus maintained garrisons at strategic points and reserved for their nobles certain important positions in the metropolitan ad-

---

[7] H. A. Giles, *Gems of Chinese Literature* (Verse), 2nd rev. ed., Shanghai, 1923. p. 12.

ministration; yet even here Chinese influence carried perhaps equal weight with that of the Manchu, while in the provincial and local administrations it was of even greater importance. By thus associating the Chinese official class with themselves in the government of the Empire, the Manchus gave a stability and a permanence to their regime which otherwise it could never have possessed.

China's government as it existed under the Manchus may then be considered under the following four divisions:

1. The Emperor, the court, and the Manchu nobles.
2. The central or metropolitan administration.
3. The provincial administration.
4. The township and village.[8]

At the head of the state was an Emperor possessed of theocratic, patriarchal, and autocratic powers. He was a sovereign by divine right—the "Son of Heaven." His was the accountability (a consequence of his sins) if famine, flood, or pestilence befell the people. He, too, was the father of the nation, clothed in theory with autocratic powers; yet these powers were not to be exercised according to arbitrary will but in conformity with practice established through the ages. Succession passed in the male line to the Emperor's ablest rather than his oldest son, not excluding the offspring of concubines. When there was no direct heir, succession passed to a lateral branch of the family in the younger generation. The new Emperor could thus by adoption perform the ancestral rites to the departed sovereign.

This Manchu Emperor ruled over a territory which included the eighteen provinces (China proper) and the four great dependencies: Mongolia, Manchuria, which enjoyed privileged status because it was the homeland of the dynasty,

---

[8] For this summary of government the writer is indebted in large part to Dr. H. B. Morse, *The Trade and Administration of China,* 3rd rev. ed. Longmans, Green & Company, London, 1921. Chapter 2.

Tibet, after 1700, and Sinkiang, after 1789. Beyond these "dependencies" lay the vassal states, varying in number from time to time and recognizing in a somewhat informal manner the overlordship of the Middle Kingdom. Payment of tribute was the tangible evidence of this vassalage, and its bearers have come in the course of China's history from as far as Arabia, Malabar, Ceylon, eastern India, the East Indies, Indo-China, Loochoo, Sulu, and Korea. China, however, while at various times asserting her suzerainty over all or several of these states, did not assume the natural responsibility of controlling their foreign relations, a circumstance which was to be the cause later of grave diplomatic disputes. Furthermore China's practice of regarding her neighbors as vassals, led her, in the nineteenth century, to regard the Westerner in similar fashion. He too would be received only as the bearer of tribute.

Since the Emperor was an absolute sovereign, his edicts were the law of the land. In practice, however, he was in no sense free from certain powerful controls. He was bound by:

. . . the unwritten constitution of the Empire, the customs which . . . [had] come down from time immemorial, through generations of both rulers and ruled, and further by established precedent as defined in the edicts of his predecessors, even those of previous dynasties.[9]

He was likewise bound by the opinions of his ministers, and if not bound, at least influenced by his more personal attendants within the palace. The Emperor was also the source of honors and patronage. He selected the future Empress from a group of daughters of Manchu nobles designated by his ministers. He might also choose secondary consorts from the same group, and finally an unlimited number of concubines from the families of Manchu nobles and freemen. The Emperor's nobility consisted of the imperial clansmen, tracing their descent directly to the founder of the dynasty; the hereditary

---

[9] Dr. H. B. Morse, *op. cit.,* p. 37.

nobility, direct descendants of the eight princes who co-operated in the conquest of China; and certain Chinese families, such as the Duke of Yen, a descendant of Confucius.

The function of the Emperor's metropolitan administration was negative rather than positive: to check rather than to direct the actions of provincial officials. This was true at least until the middle of the nineteenth century, when contacts with western nations forced the central government, though reluctantly, to assume greater responsibility in the nation's affairs. The administrative divisions of this government may be set forth briefly as follows:

1. The Inner Cabinet or Grand Secretariat, though of great importance under the Mings, had with the Manchus become merely a court of archives. Membership, which was limited to six, conferred the highest honor to which Chinese officials could aspire.

2. The Grand Council, the Emperor's chief advisory body. Its membership usually did not exceed five.

3. The Tsungli Yamen (1861-1901) was first organized as a ministry of foreign affairs, but tended in time to function as a cabinet, taking over in large part the work of the Grand Council.

Under these policy-forming bodies actual administration was carried on by a number of boards, at first six, and later nine in number:

1. The Board of Civil Office, controlling appointment to all official posts: the patronage.

2. The Board of Revenue, controlling such finances as were paid to the Imperial treasury.

3. The Board of Ceremonies.

4. The Board of War, controlling the provincial (Chinese), not the Manchu military.

5. The Board of Punishments, a department of criminal justice dealing primarily with wayward officials.

6. The Board of Works, caring for official residences throughout the Empire.

To these boards were added:

7. The Board of Foreign Affairs (Wai-wu Pu), in 1901 succeeding the Tsungli Yamen.
8. The Board of Commerce, in 1903.
9. The Board of Education, also in 1903.

There were also other departments of interest. The Court of Censors, through its unlimited power to criticize, was a constant check, at least in theory, upon the activities of government. The College of Literature (Han-lin Yuan) controlled until 1903 the educational system.

Provincial Administration

Under this impressive but somewhat inactive metropolitan administration the provinces of China enjoyed a large measure of autonomy. As long as the general policy of the central government was followed and its revenues were received, the province was left free to administer local affairs as it saw fit. However, all provincial officials, from the highest to the lowest, were appointed, transferred, and dismissed by Peking. Appointments were normally for a three-year term, and no official could assume office in the province of his birth. By this means the personnel was constantly shifting, and every official ruled among strangers. Care was also taken to select officials residing at a given post from various political parties or factions in order that each might act as a check on his fellows. By this general policy the central government maintained a kind of imperfect control: imperfect, since there was a complete lack of reciprocal responsibility among the provinces themselves. If an uprising occurred in the province of Kiangsi, the rebels would most probably be driven across the border into Fukien. It was then the duty of that province to deal with the matter.

The principal official of the provincial administration was a viceroy or governor. With him might be associated a Tartar general in command of the Manchu troops. There was also a treasurer, who transmitted revenues to Peking; a judge, who passed on appeals from the prefectural and district courts; a salt commissioner, who controlled both the manufacture and sale of this article; a grain commissioner (in some provinces); and the literary chancellor, who supervised the civil service examinations.

Local Government

Again, for purposes of administrative supervision, the province was divided into a number of units. The smallest and most important of these was the district. A number of districts (from two to six) formed a prefecture, while two or more prefectures were grouped in a circuit under a supervising official known as the *taotai*. The district (hsien) was composed of a walled city (in larger cities only half or third of the city) and the adjacent country with its towns and villages. Here the magistrate was the chief official, responsible for all affairs. His functions were many and varied. He was judge in first instance in cases both civil and criminal. He collected all the local revenues excepting special tributes, the salt tax, and likin.[10] All local units of government functioned under his care. He combined, too, in his person the functions of registrar of land, and famine commissioner, not to mention moth and locust commissioner. He was the local representative of the provincial treasurer in caring for official buildings. In general it was his business to maintain order and to care for both the physical and the moral welfare of his people. The towns and villages were governed by their own officials, nominated by the village elders and confirmed by the magistrate.

Measured by the standards of modern political practice, the

---

[10] Taxes levied on the inland trade crossing provincial boundaries, and so forth.

central administration of the Chinese Empire would hardly be regarded as government at all. Superficial observation would lead to the belief that in its passive and negative attitudes there was little that could serve to maintain the state or the nation. In a measure this was true; yet factors were present which, in their time and place, did preserve social solidarity and thereby rendered binding political mechanisms in large part unnecessary. The system by which the civil service was recruited may be cited as illustrative.

In China, education by means of formal schools was not regarded as a function or a duty of the government. The wealthy employed private tutors for their children and might in some cases establish a free school as an act of benevolence. But the average Chinese boy enjoyed no formal school education. At the close of the nineteenth century not more than three per cent of the people were literate. From this small group, however, came the most influential men of the state—the scholars, for it was only through scholarship that a man might rise to official position and thus gain honor. The studies by which this goal might be reached were, if modern standards be applied, exceedingly dreary. Mastery of the characters of the language was in itself a heavy task. After the more elementary books had been completed, there remained not only the Confucian classics but in addition nearly two hundred other books which the prospective civil servant was required to know. Much of the work was pure memorization in what today would be termed philosophy, ethics, poetry, and some so-called history. There was virtually no science and no encouragement of independent and critical thought.

Such unity as this system of education possessed resulted directly from the system of civil service examinations prescribed and conducted by the government. Only by passing one or more of these examinations might the candidate enter public office and thus gain distinction. There were four series of examinations, the first being held in the district and prefectural cities twice every three years. In the district only about two per cent of the candidates were passed. These were admitted a few weeks later to the prefectural examinations, where somewhat more than fifty per cent were likely to be successful. They were then eligible for minor posts and could qualify to enter the provincial examinations. The provincial examinations were held every three years in the capital cities. Great examination halls were erected, sometimes capable of accommodating 14,000 candidates, who ate, wrote, and slept in their "cells." The examination lasted nine days, divided into periods of three days each, between which the candidates were permitted to go home for one night. Policing the halls was a difficult task. Frequently candidates, and on occasion even the chief examiner, might go insane, a fact not surprising in minds taxed for years with memorization of the classics. Then came the metropolitan examination at Peking, where rarely more than six per cent could pass, and finally the palace examination where, in the presence of the Emperor, those candidates who had survived struggled for the highest honors. If China lacked a political machinery which the West could understand, she nevertheless possessed virile substitutes. Her social solidarity was imbedded in the Confucian system, while her official hierarchy was fashioned to a common mold: the mold of the Confucian classics, standardized even before the dawn of the Christian Era.

SELECTED BIBLIOGRAPHY

For bibliographies on China the student should consult two great works of H. Cordier: *Bibliotheca sinica: dictionnaire bibliographique des ouvrages relatifs à l'empire chinois,* 2nd ed., 5 vols. (Paris: 1904-24), and *Bibliotheca indosinica: dictionnaire bibliographique des ouvrages relatifs à la peninsule indochinoise,* 4 vols. (Paris: 1912-13).

General works on the history of China are numerous and are of unequal value. The following merit consideration: Captain F. Brinkley, *China: Its History, Arts and Literature,* 4 vols. (Boston:

1902); D. C. Boulger, *The History of China,* rev. ed., 2 vols. (London: 1898); D. C. Boulger, *A Short History of China,* 2nd ed. (London: 1900); H. Cordier, *Histoire générale de la Chine,* 4 vols. (Paris: 1920-21); Li Chi, *The Formation of the Chinese People . . .* (Cambridge: 1928); R. Grousset, *Histoire de l'Extrême-Orient,* 2 vols. (Paris: 1929); H. A. Giles, *China and the Chinese* (New York: 1902); H. A. Giles, *The Civilization of China* (London: 1911); H. H. Gowen and J. W. Hall, *An Outline History of China* (New York: 1926), of which pts. I and II by Dr. Gowen are recommended; Marcel Granet, *Chinese Civilization* (New York: 1930); L. A. Lyall, *China* (New York: 1934), in particular chs. 1-5 on religion, education, and government; K. S. Latourette, *The Chinese, Their History and Culture,* 2nd ed. rev., 2 vols. in one (New York: 1934) is recommended highly; by the same author is a brief account, *The Development of China,* 3rd ed. (Boston: 1924); A. F. Legendre, *Modern Chinese Civilization* (London: 1929); Paul Monroe, *China: A Nation in Evolution* (New York: 1928) is very readable; Mary A. Nourse, *The Four Hundred Million* (Indianapolis: 1935) is brief but suggestive; E. H. Parker, *China: Her History, Diplomacy, and Commerce . . .,* 2nd ed. (London: 1917); F. L. H. Pott, *A Sketch of Chinese History* (Shanghai: 1923); Anna L. Strong, *China's Millions* (New York: 1935); Leang-li T'ang, *The Foundations of Modern China* (London: 1928); S. Wells Williams, *The Middle Kingdom,* rev. ed., 2 vols. (New York: 1907) is a standard work; E. T. Williams, *China Yesterday and Today* (New York: 1923), in particular, chs. 2-17; by the same author a work of less value, *A Short History of China* (New York: 1928); E. T. C. Werner, *China of the Chinese* (New York: 1920); and Richard Wilhelm, *A Short History of Chinese Civilization* (New York: 1929).

Many of the above references contain material on Chinese government. Further references on this subject include: Sih-Gung Cheng, *Modern China* (Oxford: 1919), ch. 1, the historical conception of Chinese government; P. C. Hsieh, *The Government of China 1644-1911* (Baltimore: 1925); W. F. Mayers, *The Chinese Government,* 2nd ed. (Shanghai: 1886); H. B. Morse, *The International Relations of the Chinese Empire,* 3 vols. (London: 1910-18), I, ch. 1, "The Government of China," and ch. 2, "Taxation in China"; also the excellent account by the same author, *The Trade and Administration of China,* rev. ed. (London: 1920); T. Z. Woo, "The Rule of Succession to the Throne in China" in *The Chinese Social and Political Science Review* (Oct. 1925).

The reader who is interested in the religious life of China will wish to consult: Samuel Beal, *Buddhism in China* (London: 1884); M. Broomhall, *Islam in China* (London: 1910); Paul Carus, *Chinese Philosophy* (Chicago: 1902); W. J. Clennel, *The Historical Development of Religion in China* (London: 1926); M. M. Dawson, *The Ethics of Confucius* (New York: 1915); R. T. Douglas, *Confucianism and Taoism* (London: 1889); J. Edkins, *Chinese Buddhism* (London: 1890); H. A. Giles, *Musings of a Chinese Mystic* (London: 1920); H. A. Giles, *The Travels of Fa-hsien* (London: 1923); L. Hodous, *Buddhism and Buddhists in China* (New York: 1924); K. S. Latourette, *A History of Christian Missions in China* (New York: 1929), the standard work, sympathetic in tone; W. E. Soothill, *The Three Religions of China* (London: 1913).

The most convenient works on Chinese literature are by H. A. Giles: *A History of Chinese Literature* (New York: 1927); *Gems of Chinese Literature,* 2 vols. (Shanghai: 1923).

E. F. Fenollosa, *Epochs of Chinese and Japanese Art* (New York: 1913) is a most valuable work. For the contribution of Chinese art see Adolph Reichwein, *China and Europe* (New York: 1925). A convenient reference volume, though brief, is H. A. Strong, *A Sketch of Chinese Arts and Crafts,* 2nd ed. (Peiping: 1933). T. F. Carter, *The Invention of Printing in China and Its Spread Westward* (New York: 1924) should also be noted.

A small but invaluable volume is H. B. Morse, *The Guilds of China* (London: 1909). A. H. Smith treats *Village Life in China* (New York: 1899), and Sing Ging Su develops the subject of *The Chinese Family System* (New York: 1922). J. D. Ball, *Things Chinese* (London: 1904) is a useful reference work. For further reference the student should consult two articles in *The American Historical Review* by K. S. Latourette, "Chinese Historical Studies During the Past Seven Years," XXVI (1921), and "Chinese Historical Studies During the Past Nine Years," in *ibid.,* XXXV (1930).

CHAPTER III

Early and Feudal Japan

THE Empire of Japan, measured in terms of Chinese history, is comparatively a youthful state. When Confucius in the sixth and fifth centuries B.C. was indoctrinating his countrymen with an ethical system of human relationships, Japan was a battleground for roving warring tribes whose exploits are recorded but dimly in myth and legend. Even today the origins of the Japanese remain a matter of dispute beyond the mere generalization that the "race is a compound of elements drawn in prehistoric times from different parts of the Asiatic mainland, and perhaps from Indonesian islands such as Borneo, Java, the Celebes and the Philippines." [1] In this compound the Mongolian strain is strong if not predominant.

Of the contacts which may have been made in prehistoric times between the Asiatic mainland and Japan, it is impossible to speak; but there is some certainty that by the first century A.D. the Han influence of China had penetrated the islands. Fragments of history in this early period have been recorded by Chinese historians, while in Japan itself the principal written sources are two official records: the *Kojiki* (Record of Ancient Things) and the *Nihon-shoki* (Chronicles of Japan), in which myth, legend, and history are mixed with little discrimination.

The real beginnings of the Japanese state appear to date from about the beginning of the Christian Era. At this time clans of the southern island of Kyushu moved eastward along

---

[1] G. B. Sansom, *Japan: A Short Cultural History.* D. Appleton-Century Company, New York, 1931. p. 3. The writer is indebted to this excellent work for much in the following summary of Japan's early history.

the southern shores of Honshiu to the province of Yamato, where something in the nature of a central state was established. By the seventh century this state exercised a limited control over western and central Japan as far east as the modern city of Sendai. The supremacy of these Yamato sovereigns, however, was not unchallenged. The two official records, the *Kojiki* and *Nihon-shoki,* were compiled with a view to strengthening their dynastic claims.

For this purpose, then, were fabricated those involved though interesting myths which reveal the divine origins of the Japanese state. According to the chronicles, the grandchild of the great Sun Goddess was sent to rule the islands of Japan. From Heaven, he alighted on the island of Kyushu, carrying as tokens of his divine mission a mirror, a sword, and a jewel: a pledge that the dynasty should rule forever. This was the first Emperor, known to history as Jimmu, who, with his hosts, moved eastward to Yamato and celebrated his victories with services to the Sun Goddess (again according to the chronicles) on February 11, 660 B.C. This is the date which is now regarded officially as that of the founding of the Empire, though in reality the expedition to Yamato occurred more probably at the beginning of the Christian Era.

Introduction of Foreign Culture

During succeeding centuries the Japanese established political relations with various kingdoms in Korea, from whence came skilled workmen and scholars able to read the Chinese classics. Among the more notable of these was one Wani, who came as tutor to the heir apparent, and at this time (405 A.D.) the Chinese written language was adopted for official purposes. Here was an event of more than passing importance. The power of government could be extended by written order, and the way was now paved for the introduction of things Chinese.

The material culture of this early Japan was crude indeed, yet its social and religious life was of a comparatively high order. The indigenous cult, known today as Shinto, was a pantheism, a nature worship, not highly developed, and yet based on "appreciation rather than fear." It follows naturally that "much that is kindly and gracious in the life of the Japanese today can be traced to those sentiments which caused their remote ancestors to ascribe divinity not only to the powerful and awe-inspiring, such as the sun and the moon and the tempest, or to the useful, such as the well and the cooking pot, but also to the lovely and pleasant, such as the rocks and streams, the trees and flowers." [2]

The Sun Goddess occupied a position of paramount importance, for she was not only the central divinity in this early worship but also the ancestress of the imperial house. Purity was the essence of religion. Uncleanliness, even the material uncleanliness of the person, was to be avoided at all cost. Thus, preparation for all religious observance consisted of washing the body and putting on clean garments. And here, deep-rooted in time and tradition, lies the origin of a modern characteristic of the race: its desire to be scrupulously clean.

Such in barest outline is the early religion of the Japanese. In essence it was a nature worship, but in time, as fostered by the ruling classes, it became an organized cult closely linked with the political system. Nor is it correct to describe Shinto simply as ancestor worship.

Ancestor worship, as practised in Japan, is a cult imported from China. The objects of worship of the early Japanese were nature deities, and not their own deified ancestors. It is true that the noble families claimed descent from the gods whom they worshipped, but making your god into an ancestor and making your ancestor into a god are not the same thing. [3]

As already indicated, Japan's cultural life in these early centuries was enriched by contacts with Korea, through which

[2] Ibid. p. 45.   [3] Ibid. p. 53.

came Chinese learning. The process was gradual. It is probable that Chinese civilization had been impressing itself upon the life of the islands since the third century, but it was not until about the middle of the sixth century (552-621 A.D.) that there "occurred the greatest event of Japanese history, the conversion of the nation to Buddhism," [4] for with the Buddhist priest came virtually the entire institutional life of China. The influence of the new learning was fostered by Prince Shotoku Taishi, who ruled Japan as regent during the reign of the Empress Suiko. He patronized not merely the outward forms of Buddhism (temples, pagodas, vestments, and ceremonies) by which the masses might be attracted, but also, and more important, its moral and intellectual gifts. To him early Japan was likewise indebted for the so-called constitution of 604 A.D., a code of moral injunctions designed to check oppression and to create a new ideal in government.

The Great Reform

Shotoku Taishi died in 621, but already he had laid the foundations for a new political and economic life patterned on the Chinese model. To these changes, inaugurated in the years 645-650, has been given the name of *Taikwa,* or Great Reform. This reform contemplated a new system of taxation and of local government, and, in its economic aspects, of land tenure, involving, in theory, a greater centralization of power. But in practice, powerful families who could not expediently be deprived of their lands had their titles confirmed on the theory that they were now held as grants from the Throne. In addition they were given official posts or court rank. The government also undertook to appoint governors in the provinces; but here too the practice was to confirm the existing authority of the most powerful local chief, who now, in theory again, de-

[4] B. H. Chamberlain, *Things Japanese,* reprint of 5th rev. ed. J. L. Thompson & Co., Kobe, 1927. p. 231.

rived his powers from the Imperial administration. In fact, the emphasis in the edicts of 645 was on the economic rather than on the political organization of the state. The forces which controlled the court were not concerned primarily with the extension to remote regions of their direct political control. Their immediate concern was a more effective means of collecting wealth from the provinces.

Later by the Code of Taiho (Great Treasure, 701-704), the administrative machinery of a reformed central government was devised. Unhappily this code tended to preserve the interests of the court aristocracy of birth at the expense of the people. Here Japan followed merely the forms of the Chinese system, neglecting the vital principle that in China the official aristocracy was not one of birth but of learning. Yet, while allowing for these and other limitations, the reforms of this era were not without value. The gradual strengthening of the central power by depriving the territorial nobility of their autonomy was an essential step in the march toward statehood. In 645 China was already an old and highly developed nation; Japan was not. Her capital shifted from one imperial manor to another with the beginning of each new reign. She was yet to develop towns and cities that might compare with those of China.

The First Permanent Capital

And now for the first time in their history the Japanese built a permanent capital—the city of Nara, which remained the seat of the Imperial Court until 784. This Nara period is one of the great epochs of Japan's history. The study of Chinese language and literature became the chief intellectual pursuit of the court aristocracy; but it was a learning designed to ornament the lives of the privileged and not to enrich society as a whole. Although there was much in the minutely organized structure of Chinese society which appealed to the

Japanese, the conservatism of the Confucian system was in no sense fitted to their needs.

Buddhism, too, flourished, and before the close of the Nara period six distinct sects of the religion had appeared. The wealthy lavished gifts upon the church, which soon became the possessor of large and valuable tax-free lands. Economically it came to be without a rival, while its potential power in politics attracted to the priesthood men whose sole purpose was material gain. Nara was not a great period in Japanese literature; but to it must be ascribed those remarkable examples of early architecture: the Golden Hall, pagoda, and gate of the monastery of Horyuji, perhaps the oldest wooden structures in the world and as notable for their beauty as for their age. In contrast, however, to the cultural and artistic advance Nara was a barren period in politico-economics. A large and ever-growing privileged and leisured class bore more and more heavily on a farming population already crippled by heavy taxation.

Political Life in Kyoto

In 784 the capital was moved from Nara. The motives for this expensive undertaking may have been varied, but principal among them was the desire to remove the court from the growing dominance of Buddhism. A new city called Heian-kyo (the modern Kyoto) was built, and there in 794 the new capital was established. This was the work of the Emperor Kammu (782-805), an able and enlightened ruler. His successors, however, during the greater part of the Heian period (794-1192), were dominated by the powerful Fujiwara family. This clan monopolized civil office and maintained control of the court by a kind of "supervising statesmanship." Originally men of great capacity, the monopoly of power held by the Fujiwaras led them eventually into corrupt and effeminate ways. They no longer produced able men, and this at a time (1073-1128) when a monarch of great energy, Shirakawa, occupied the throne. It was he who enlisted support from two great military clans, the Taira and the Minamoto. By means of their aid he overawed and precipitated the downfall of the Fujiwara, protected the court from turbulent soldier-priests who had become virtually a law unto themselves, and subdued rebel tribes in the more distant provinces.

The Rise of Military Clans

With the death of Shirakawa confusion again prevailed at court. In the factional strife among retired emperors who sought to regain their power, the Taira and Minamoto warriors supported rival claimants. Kyoto was the scene of almost constant strife until the appearance of Taira Kiyomori. For seventeen years (1166-1183) his Taira followers occupied all important offices of government and controlled the most lucrative domains in the Empire. His greatest rival, Yoritomo, of the Minamoto clan, was banished; but in 1181 the Minamoto, on the death of Kiyomori, rose in revolt, drove the Taira from Kyoto, and in 1185 exterminated the last of their forces in the battle of Dannoura (near Shimonoseki). Such in outline was the political story of the Heian period. It has been aptly summarized in the following words:.

... during the first half of the Heian period the monarchy became a dyarchy; bureaucratic control gave way to hereditary privilege; land ownership evolved from individual small-holding to feudal tenure; the revenue system utterly collapsed; and the administration of justice depended no longer upon codes but upon summary rules and precedents. Half-way through the 11th century the imperial government had lost most of its power and much of its prestige; the whole country was ravaged by family feuds and civil war; and such law as prevailed was the house law of the clans. Daylight robbery was rife in the capital and bandits flourished on the main highways by land and by sea. It is not a pretty picture; but it is redeemed by the rise of a vigorous, self-reliant class of rural magnates, and by the growth of an independent national culture, freed to some extent—

though not entirely, for that would be impossible—from the almost overwhelming influence of Chinese models.[5]

Heian Civilization

Culturally, the Heian epoch was notable in many ways, chief among which was the growth of a native literature. Japan had now developed her own native script, the *kana* syllabary. Chinese still remained the medium of the pompous, learned scholar, but since Heian life was essentially frivolous, the native language proved a more suitable medium for the literature of such a society. The scholars continued to write in Chinese their dull expositions on Chinese thought, while Japanese court ladies composed those triumphs which still remain the prized treasures of Japanese literature. Among the great works of the period were the *Kokinshu,* an anthology containing more than eleven hundred short poems; the *Genji Monogatari,* a romance written by Lady Murasaki; and the *Makura no Soshi,* or *Pillow Sketches,* of Lady Sei Shonagon.

Establishment of Dual Government

The victory of the Minamoto clan at Dannoura in 1185 marked in some respects a turning point in the history of Japan. For many centuries the nation was to be ruled by military men. Yoritomo established himself at Kamakura, three hundred miles from the Imperial Court at Kyoto. There on the seacoast he set up a military and feudal government known as the Baku-fu, or military camp. It does not appear that he sought to replace the ruling dynasty, though in effect the latter was soon deprived of all practical power, retaining merely the name of sovereignty. Yoritomo, at Kamakura, was situated strategically to control his vassals; and on this control, rather than on the replacing of the dynasty, his power depended. He

---

[5] G. B. Sansom, *op. cit.* p. 216.

sought in fact to increase the prestige of the Imperial Court, sought its sanction for his policies, accepted court rank, and finally was appointed Seii-Tai-Shogun (Barbarian-Subduing Great General). The court thus retained a degree of prestige and a certain negative authority, though real power rested in the hands of the Minamoto leader. The title of Shogun was not new, but it held now an entirely new significance; for, instead of temporary power for a single and specific commission, it now conferred general powers, permitting the holder to assume the initiative in controlling the military feudal clans. In a word the administrative machinery of the state passed into the hands of the Shogun, where, almost without interruption, it was to remain until the restoration of 1868.

There were now two capitals [in Japan], Kiōto and Kamakura, and two centres of authority: one, the lawful but overawed emperor and the imperial court; the other, the military vassal [Yoritomo of the Minamoto], and a government based on the power of arms.[6]

The Hojo Regency

With the death of Yoritomo (1199) control of the Baku-fu[7] passed to the powerful Hojo family. Tokimasa, head of this clan, was both a vassal of the Minamoto and the father-in-law of Yoritomo. By intrigue he deposed the first of Yoritomo's sons, on whose behalf he had acted as regent. A second son was assassinated, and though by this act the Minamoto line became extinct, the Hojo regency persisted until 1333. Here was a triple façade of government in which the Hojo ruled as regents for a succession of infant Shoguns who were replaced as soon as they grew old enough to be troublesome; while in turn these infants ruled for an emperor who retained only imperial prestige and the title of sovereign. Many of the Hojo

---

[6] W. E. Griffis, *The Mikado's Empire,* 11th ed. Harper & Brothers, New York, 1906. Vol. I, p. 146.

[7] Military camp—that is, the government of the Shogunate.

regents were men of great ability, and their "rule was marked by economy, justice and moderation." Unhappily the later regents were not of this caliber. Loyalist leaders clamored for the return of Emperor Godaigo, whom the Hojo had banished. Armies dispatched to quell the uprising supported the royalist cause, and under the leadership of Ashikaga Takauji the Hojo themselves were overthrown. Ashikaga became Shogun, his family holding the office from 1334 to 1573. These were troubled years, the period often being called the Ashikaga anarchy.

Feudal fights; border brawls; the seizure of lands; the rise of great clans; the building, the siege, and the destruction of castles, were the staple events. Every monastery was now a stronghold, an arsenal, or a camp. . . . Villages, cities, temples, monasteries, and libraries were burned. . . . War was the only lucrative trade, except that of the armorers or sword-makers. . . . It was the Golden Age of crime and anarchy.[8]

And yet, though an age of turmoil, it was not an age of decay, for new institutions were emerging toward a more highly developed feudal society.

In the midst of this ferment the arts flourished as never before. Artists and men of letters found refuge in the Buddhist church or attached themselves to some wealthy baron-patron. A love of pomp and luxury promoted lavish expenditure. The Shoguns built their summer palaces in Kyoto, the Kinkakuji (Golden Pavilion) and Ginkakuji (Silver Pavilion). The ancient classical dance, the *No,* and the art of the ceremonial tea were further developed, while in painting, the beauty of a Japanese landscape was re-created by the immortal Sesshu.

The Rule of Oda Nobunaga

The closing years of the Ashikaga rule were chaotic in the extreme. The authority of the central government was all but

---

[8] W. E. Griffis, *op. cit.* pp. 194-195.

destroyed. The prime need was for a leader to restore it. The task fell to Oda Nobunaga, who prepared the way for unification of the dismembered empire. Taking the imperial house as his rallying point, Nobunaga drove the last of the Ashikagas from power in 1573 and made himself master of the provinces about Kyoto. Nobunaga himself was assassinated in 1582, but his work was carried forward by Hideyoshi (1536-1598), sometimes known as the Napoleon of Japan. By military force he subjected the barons to a centralized control such as Japan has never before experienced. He then assumed the title of kwampaku (regent) and later of taiko (commander-in-chief). Not content with his supremacy as war lord of the Empire, he sought the conquest of Korea, from which he hoped to descend upon China. For six years (1592-1598) his armies occupied the Korean peninsula, only to be withdrawn after his death. From the military point of view these campaigns were as vainglorious and futile as Napoleon's later march to Moscow; yet indirectly they were not without profit, for with the returning armies came skilled Korean potters to whose instruction is attributed in part at least the exquisite beauty of the old Satsuma ware.

Hideyoshi had conquered the barons of Japan; it remained for his successors to build a political structure that could consolidate this conquest. The infant son of the taiko had been left to the protection of five trusted generals, of whom the foremost was Iyeyasu, of the Tokugawa family. In the struggle for power which followed the taiko's death, Iyeyasu was victorious. The taiko's son was set aside and probably slain, Iyeyasu becoming Shogun in 1603.

The Rise of the Tokugawas

Japan now entered upon a period of government more stable than anything which she had heretofore enjoyed, for, under the first Tokugawa Shoguns, the system of feudalism

reached maturity. Iyeyasu broke with the past by building
and residing in the new city of Yedo (later known as Tokyo).
Here, free from the enervating influences of the imperial court
at Kyoto, he ruled Japan. Furthermore he was not content to
see Yedo merely a second Kamakura; it was to be the commercial and cultural center of the Empire as well. The Emperor
and the Imperial Court were shorn of all save their ancient
dignity and limited ceremonial functions such as appointment
of the Shogun. Iyeyasu granted the Imperial family adequate
income, yet neither the sovereign nor the court nobles could
own land or engage in the administration of public affairs.
Officials of the Shogun resided at Kyoto both to direct and to
command the sovereign.

Of much greater significance to the Tokugawa was the
problem of controlling the daimyo, or feudal barons. Here
distinctions were made on the basis of past loyalty to the Tokugawa house. Those barons who had always supported the clan
were known as fudai, or hereditary vassals; those who had only
submitted after Tokugawa's rise to power were known as
tozama, or outside lords. These latter included many of the
more wealthy and powerful clans; and, since they constituted
the greatest potential threat to the Shogunate, they were compelled to contribute heavily to public undertakings, to reside for
several months of each year at Yedo, and to leave their wives
and families as hostages during their absence. Feudal holdings
were redistributed so as to place the fudai daimyo at strategic
points to crush any attempt by the tozama against the Shogunate. The building of feudal castles was strictly limited,
if not proscribed. Large commercial centers such as Osaka
were brought under the direct control of the Yedo government, which, in addition, checked carefully the movement of
travelers from one province to another. In essence the system
was a military dictatorship of the Tokugawas over their vassals, and in the case of each vassal, a dictatorship of the military caste over all other groups in society.

Development of Tokugawa Feudalism

The system, however, was pre-eminently feudal. Within each fief the daimyo retained full administrative powers, levying taxes and collecting revenue according to the laws of the fief. No contribution was made to the Shogunate; its income was derived from the vast Tokugawa estates added by conquest and confiscation during the rise of Iyeyasu. The armies, too, were feudal. The Tokugawa forces were composed of the direct retainers of the clan, but in time of emergency the feudal barons might be called upon to furnish contingents of their fighting men. The very existence of these semi-independent feudal armies was, obviously, an ever-present threat to the Shogun's authority, this being particularly true in western Japan where resided some of the more powerful tozama. In the main, the Tokugawa policy was moderate. Nevertheless the successors of Iyeyasu did not hesitate to use severe punitive measures where occasion arose. Where surplus funds might encourage a daimyo to revolt, he was "honored" with the Shogun's command to execute public works. As late as 1753 the daimyo of Satsuma was ordered to repair at great cost the levees of the Kiso River, 750 miles from his fief. By such measures, rather than by direct military attack, the Tokugawas suppressed any threat to their power.

The Social Structure of Feudalism

This decidedly stable politico-feudal society naturally produced a conventionalized social order. When, in former times, civil strife was more or less constant, men of ambition might rise from lowly origin to positions of privilege. Now stability led to a crystallized social order in which movement from class to class all but disappeared. At the peak of the social edifice was the civilian court nobility, the kuge. In matters of honor they were unrivaled, but since they were without property and depended on income granted by the Shogun, their political influence was small. Next to the kuge in this grouping of privileged society stood the daimyo, rated according to revenue and precedence at the Shogun's court. Below the daimyo stood the hatamoto, the lesser vassals of the Tokugawa, and the gokenin, who filled minor administrative posts in the Shogunate. Below these again, but still members of the privileged caste, were the samurai, the hereditary fighting men. They were vassals either of the Shogun or of the barons, and they alone enjoyed the privilege of wearing the two swords. Their income was paid by the lord and was small, as befitted men trained to live a frugal and austere life and to find happiness in the honor of their calling. During the Tokugawa period there were some two million of these samurai representing about 400,000 households.

Among the plebeian population social distinctions were not less severe. The farmer was the aristocrat of the plebs, for did he not provide the rice on which the nation must live? Furthermore he carried much of the tax burden, and thus for very practical reasons could not be denied some honor. On occasion he might be elevated to the samurai class. As in the case of the Satsuma clan, not a few of the samurai were also farmers. Next in the social scale of the commoners came the artisan. This was natural and logical in a state where honor centered in the career of the military man. The artisan fashioned the sword, and this in turn was the soul of the samurai. Below the artisan again was the merchant who merited the conventional contempt of society as a whole. He produced nothing himself, and yet he waxed rich by disposing of what others had produced. Finally there were the social outcasts, the eta, or hinin, scarcely to be counted as members of human society. These were the groups whose hereditary occupations involved some form of religious pollution, or whose calling was beyond the pale of respectability: professional entertainers, executioners, beggars, and those who handled dead bodies.

Seclusion and Peace

The Tokugawa Shoguns gave Japan more than two centuries of seclusion and peace, though by no means a peace without problems. They essayed a task of the greatest difficulty: perpetuation of a politico-military organization when there were no wars to be fought. The privileged military class was largely unproductive; its requirements in arms and raiment were elaborate and costly; and it proceeded on the notion that farmer and merchant should continue to produce what their betters would consume. Society was an ill-balanced structure which could not indefinitely endure. Daimyo and samurai lived beyond their means, and in their attempts to shift the burden of debt to the farmer precipitated the collapse of rural economy and its replacement by mercantile interests. A new money economy initiated a gradual but none the less complete undermining of the whole feudal structure. By 1700 "the samurai still had their dignity, the consciousness of high social standing; but the commoners [meaning the people of the towns] had most of the money and most of the fun." [9]

The Appearance of Urban Economy

Obviously, the Shogunate and the daimyo looked askance on this newer and growing town populace. The money economy on which it was based gave it a new power which was openly flaunted in costly apparel, extravagant living, and luxurious entertainments. The townsman wanted entertainment, and he possessed the money to pay for it. These tendencies were particularly strong in the period of Genroku (1688-1703). Against them the ruling classes might protest and issue edicts. Their own lives frequently failed to exemplify the simplicity they preached, and the very wealth expended by the daimyo paid eventually for the pleasure of the new mon-

[9] G. B. Sansom, *op. cit.* p. 463.

eyed aristocracy of the cities. New schools of the arts depicted the life of the wealthy commoner in the cafés, the theaters, and gay houses of ill fame. Popular novels (ukiyo-soshi) and pictures (ukiyo-e) revealed the ways of the worldly city dweller. All this was repugnant to the ruling classes, the daimyo and samurai. In it they saw or pretended to see a flaunting of the stern code of the warrior, and still more (though this could not be mentioned), the rise of a new moneyed class threatening the entire fabric of feudal aristocracy both socially and politically.

The Philosophy of Bushido

To meet this threat recourse was had to Confucian doctrine. The past, or at least such portions of it as were proper, should form the pattern for the present. With this end in view it was by no means difficult for the ruling intelligentsia to formulate codes of conduct based on stern virtues such as simplicity. The evolution of the philosophy of Bushido was the result.

The term *Bushido* (The Way of the Warrior) is of comparatively recent origin. The cult, or set of ideas for which it is the label, is on the contrary of ancient origin. These ideas varied from time to time and were not highly conventionalized until well into the Tokugawa period, and then, as already indicated, to serve specific ends of the ruling military caste. The philosophy of Bushido was founded on early conceptions of the soldier's duty. In periods of feud and strife there was need for some standards of loyalty among the fighting men. Thus "rectitude, courage, benevolence, politeness, sincerity, honor, disdain of money, and self-control" constituted a set of ideals pointing the way for the samurai class. But, since virtue is only as strong as those who profess its practice, the conduct of the samurai rarely attained the ideal. In the early days of feudalism the warrior code was largely a mere sentiment between lord and vassal based on direct personal service as occasioned in battle; but in the Tokugawa period it took on much of the appearance of a tangible and systematized code which the ruling class regarded as necessary in controlling in times of peace the unruly qualities of the turbulent samurai. By these steps Bushido became a practical code associated primarily, because of its origin, with the warrior class, and yet developing a broader significance as an ethical guide to commoner as well as soldier.

The Revival of Philosophy

The intellectual interests of the early and the middle Tokugawa period were centered largely, as already suggested, in Confucian philosophy. The Shogunate, though it was never a champion of what might be termed free intellectual inquiry, gave its official support to this learning. However, the enthusiasm for Chinese thought did not go unchallenged. Among the Tokugawa philosophers were those who reacted in favor of the ancient native literature of Japan itself. To them must be ascribed the revival of Shinto, with its emphasis upon the divine origin of the imperial line. This new emphasis hastened, if it did not actually cause, political consequences of the greatest importance. Ever since the rise of the Minamoto clan, at the close of the twelfth century, Japan had been ruled by successive Shoguns. Furthermore, after 1600 the Tokugawas had strengthened the political edifice of the Shogunate until it appeared as a permanent machinery of the feudal state. But the renaissance of early Japanese studies now revealed the Shogun as a usurper of imperial authority, or at best as a mere delegate of the Throne. In the light of this revelation loyalty to the throne became an ideal destructive of loyalty both to the feudal lord and to the Shogun. By the opening of the nineteenth century the Shogunate was already threatened by many and by powerful enemies. It had long since outlived its usefulness, its ability to meet the needs of the time. Its doom had already been written in the rise of an urban, mercantile class. And now these enemies possessed a political weapon, the revived ideal of loyalty to the throne, by which the Shogunate itself was soon to be destroyed.

SELECTED BIBLIOGRAPHY

There are two major bibliographies on Japan with which the student should be familiar: Fr. von Wenckstern, *A Bibliography of the Japanese Empire,* vol. 1, (Leiden: 1895), vol. 2, (Tokyo: 1907), and O. Nachod, *Bibliography of Japan,* 2 vols., 1928.

There are two works of great importance by K. Asakawa, *The Early Institutional Life of Japan* (Tokyo: 1903) and *Documents of Iriki* (New Haven: 1929), the author being one of the foremost Japanese scholars in the United States. There are two comprehensive studies by Captain F. Brinkley, *Japan, Its History, Arts and Literature,* 8 vols. (Boston: 1901), and *A History of the Japanese People* . . . (New York: 1915). A sketchy but interesting account is J. I. Bryan, *History of Japan* (London: 1927). In *The Cambridge Modern History,* vol. 2 (Cambridge: 1909), see ch. 28 by Sir E. M. Satow, "Japan" [under the Tokugawas and during the early Restoration]. E. W. Clement, *A Short History of Japan* (Chicago: 1915), in chs. 1-11 covers the period to the close of the Tokugawa period. W. E. Griffis, *The Mikado's Empire,* 2 vols., 12th ed. (New York: 1913) still remains a study of importance. H. H. Gowen, *An Outline History of Japan* (New York: 1927) is suggestive but rather superficial. K. Hara presents a nice attempt to provide *An Introduction to the History of Japan* (New York: 1920). Emile Hovelaque, *Le Japon* (Paris: 1921) summarizes the Tokugawa period in bk. 2, ch. 10. More detailed studies will be found in R. Hildreth, *Japan as It Was and Is,* E. W. Clement, ed., 2 vols. (London: 1907). Perhaps the most valuable source on early Japan is Engelbert Kaempfer, *The History of Japan,* 3 vols. (Glasgow: 1906), in particular, vol. 1, bk. 2, the early history of Japan; vol. 2, bk. 3, the religion of Japan; vol. 2, bk. 5, the author's travels to the capital. J. H. Longford has written two volumes of value to the general reader: *The Story of Old Japan* (London: 1910), and *Japan,* in the series *The Nations of To-Day,* John Buchan, ed. (Boston: 1923). In his *Development of Japan* (New York: 1926) K. S. Latourette gives (chs. 2-5) a readable though superficial survey to 1853. Among the monumental works on Japanese history is J. Murdoch, *A History of Japan,* 3 vols. (Kobe, Tokyo, New York: 1903-26). Another is A. R. La Mazelière, *Le Japon, histoire et civilisation,* 8 vols. (Paris: 1907-23), in particular vol. 3, "Le Japon des Tokugawa." J. W. Robertson-Scott, *The Foundations of Japan* (London: 1922) is a fine study. Best of all single-volume works on early Japanese history is G. B. Sansom, *Japan: A Short Cultural History* (London: 1932). This work closes with the end of the Tokugawa period; it is an excellent study. For wealth of material no study compares with Y. Takekoshi, *The Economic Aspects of the History of the Civilization of Japan,* 3 vols. (London: 1930), a condensation of a much larger work in Japanese.

Some of the religious aspects of Japanese history may be studied in: W. G. Aston, *Shinto: the Way of the Gods* (London: 1905), which may be used with the same author's *A History of Japanese Literature* (New York: 1899). M. Anesaki has written the story of *Nichiren, the Buddhist Prophet* (Cambridge: 1916), and a *History of Japanese Religion* (London: 1930), both of the highest scholarship. Lesser but worth-while studies are: C. N. E. Eliot, *Japanese Buddhism* (Oxford: 1935); A. Harada, *The Faith of Japan* (New York: 1914); A. Lloyd, *The Creed of Half Japan* . . . (New York: 1912); I. Nitobe, *Bushido, the Soul of Japan,* 10th ed. (New York: 1906); K. Nukariya, *The Religion of the Samurai, a Study of Zen Philosophy* (London: 1912); L. Pagés, *Histoire de la religion chrétienne au Japon depuis 1598 jusqu'à 1651,* 2 vols. (Paris: 1869-70); M. Steichen, *The Christian Daimyos* (Tokyo: 1903).

There are two excellent studies by J. H. Gubbins touching the late feudal period: *The Progress of Japan, 1853-1871* (Oxford: 1911), and *The Making of Modern Japan* (London: 1922). Yamato Ichihashi gives a fine summary of the "Economic Life of Japan, 1600-1868" in the *Journal of Economic and Business History,* vol. IV, no. 1, Nov. 1931. W. Dening has written *The Life of Toyotomi Hideyoshi,* 3rd ed. (Kobe: 1930). G. A. Ballard, *The Influence of the Sea on the Political History of Japan* (New York: 1921) devotes ch. 3 to the Tokugawa period.

On literature and art the reader is recommended to consult: E. F. Fenollosa, *Epochs of Chinese and Japanese Art,* 2 vols. (London:

1912); A. Waley, *The No Plays of Japan* (New York: 1922); A. Waley (translator), *The Tale of Genji,* by Lady Murasaki (Boston: 1925-34); A. Waley (translator), *The Pillow Book of Sei Shonagon* (Boston: 1929); A. S. Omori and K. Doi (translators), *Diaries of Court Ladies of Old Japan* (Boston: 1920); "Yone Noguchi" in Ippei Fukuda, *New Sketches of Men and Life* (Tokyo: 1934).

CHAPTER IV

Early Western Crusaders

WESTERN contacts with China and Japan, although they did not assume major importance until well into the nineteenth century, have an ancient and fascinating history. The influence of the Hellenistic kingdoms in western Asia penetrated China. The wares of the western and the eastern worlds were exchanged in cities of central Asia by merchants from China, India, Asia Minor, Greece, and Rome. At the beginning of the Christian Era there was already an extensive commerce between the Mediterranean world and India, but few, if any, western traders had gone beyond Ceylon. The Greeks and Romans had some vague notions concerning China as the land of silk, an article highly prized in Europe and at times exchanged for its weight in gold. This commerce, such as it may have been, whether by the overland routes through central Asia or by sea to India, was necessarily limited to articles of small weight and great value and was subject to the hazards of wars, tributes, and robberies.

The Nestorian Christians

By the time of the Tang Dynasty (618-907), however, there is more tangible evidence that man was conquering, by slow degrees, to be sure, the physical barriers between the East and the West. Nestorian Christianity seems to have entered China at this time. By an active missionary policy it had spread widely from Mesopotamia through India and central Asia, from these outposts finally reaching China. The record of this

Nestorian effort had been preserved on a monument erected at Hsianfu in 781 but not discovered until the seventeenth century. From this and other sources the belief is now held that the Nestorians reached China in 635, were honorably received by the Tang Emperor, and were instructed to prepare translations of their sacred books and to preach their gospel. Churches were built in several cities, and though at times the faith was persecuted, it persisted in China proper for at least two centuries. Both for its leadership and for its converts Nestorian Christianity seems to have depended on foreign residents of the Tang Empire rather than on the Chinese themselves.

The Arab Trade

The period of The Five Dynasties (907-960) and of the Sung Dynasty (960-1280), though one of political weakness, was also one of cultural brilliance. The invasions and wars in the north encouraged the southward movement of the Chinese, thus increasing the relative importance of the Yangtze Valley and the southern coast. Here foreign trade, conducted at such marts as Ch'uanchow in Fukien and at Canton, received a great impetus. This trade was rigidly controlled by the Sungs, who derived a considerable revenue from it. An imperial embassy was sent abroad to encourage trade. Foreign merchants, most of whom at this time were Moslem Arabs, were well treated. For the most part they were permitted to settle disputes among themselves according to their own laws. Many of them married Chinese women, and some at least appear to have occupied high office in the state. Among the foreigners, too, was a colony of Jews. The Chinese had thus developed an important commerce with southern and western Asia long before Europe gave evidence of a tangible desire to reach the Far East, and when this desire did appear, the principal motive prompting it was fear.

The First Catholic Contacts

The early decades of the thirteenth century witnessed the westward advance of the Mongols and their two invasions of eastern Europe. The news of their conquests spread terror to the thrones of Europe, and embassies were dispatched to learn of the new conquerors and perchance to enlist their aid against the Mohammedan foes of Christianity. Pope Innocent IV sent a mission, headed by Friar John de Plano Carpini, to protest against the Mongol invasion of Christian lands and to determine the extent of Mongol power. Carpini reached the capital of the Grand Khan, whom he invited to become a Christian, in 1246. In the following year the embassy returned to Europe bearing a letter from the Khan in which the Pope was counseled to proceed to the East and there pay homage to the Mongol Power.[1] A few years later (1253-1255) Friar William of Rubruck, acting as the envoy of Louis IX of France, reached the court of Mangu Khan, the elder brother of the great Kublai. Here, for he did not go beyond Mongolia, Friar William gathered strange reports of "Cathay [China, which] touches the ocean," and even of stranger lands beyond. Back in Europe he reported that a bishop rather than a preaching friar would be a fitter person to establish relations with the Mongol Empire. Thus by the arduous labors of these early travelers was Europe adding slowly to its knowledge of the Far East.

The Polos in China

By far the greatest of these early contributions was *The Book of Marco Polo.* Shortly after the Mongols had established their sway in China (1260), two Venetian merchants, the brothers Nicolo and Maffeo Polo, reached the court of Kublai Khan, not far to the north of Peking, where they were

---

[1] In his journey to the East, Carpini was preceded by Rabbi Benjamin of Tudela, who set forth from Spain about 1160 and probably reached the frontiers of China.

well received. Through them Kublai requested the Papacy to dispatch to his court a mission of one hundred Christians, "men of intelligence, acquainted with the seven arts, and qualified to prove that idols were of the devil and that the law of Christ was better than the law he and his people knew." Whatever the reasons may have been (perhaps a decline in the crusading-missionary spirit), the Church of Rome did not respond to the Khan's invitation. Instead, the Polo brothers, accompanied this time by Marco, Nicolo's son, returned to China, arriving in 1275. There they remained for seventeen years, and Marco enjoyed the special favors of Kublai, being appointed on numerous occasions to important missions to distant parts of the Empire, and even to the governorship of cities. In 1292 the return journey to Europe was made by sea to the Persian Gulf and thence overland to Europe. *The Book of Marco Polo* was dictated a few years later, and long remained the chief source of medieval knowledge on the Orient.

Early Development of Catholic Missions

For some years after the return of the Polos the overland route to China appears to have remained open, and considerable intercourse seems to have developed. This security depended largely upon the friendship of the Mongol Empire, and was to disappear with its decline. In the meantime further contact with China was developing by sea. Friar John of Montecorvino, a Franciscan, reached China by way of India in 1292. For perhaps thirty-five years he preached in the Chinese capital (Peking) and established two churches with a membership of several thousand. Later, in 1307, he was created archbishop of Peking, and other missionaries were dispatched to aid in his work. These religious efforts appear to have prospered, for at the death of Archbishop John (1328) the mission claimed the conversion of "more than 30,000 infidels." But with the passing of the Mongol power went also the prosperity of the missionaries. In China the early Ming Emperors, while not proscribing completely contacts with Europe, did not encourage the coming of foreigners. The early Christian communities, both Nestorian and Catholic, disappeared.[2]

The Portuguese Reach China

In the early years of the Ming Dynasty (1368-1644), while China was yet recovering from the chaos which accompanied the collapse of the Mongols, Portuguese navigators were penetrating the southern Atlantic to the Cape of Good Hope, which was rounded in 1488. Ten years later Vasco da Gama, by this same route, arrived on the coast of India, while his successors in 1511 reached Malacca, in the Malay Peninsula. From these advanced trading posts, which now could be reached by the ocean route, the Portuguese were soon in contact with Java, Siam, Indo-China, and the southern coast of China proper.

Rafael Perestrello was probably the first of these Portuguese navigators to reach China. This was in 1516. Other traders followed. In 1517 Fernando Perez de Andrade arrived with eight ships at St. John's Island, some 75 miles southwest of Macao. With two of these ships he reached Canton, there receiving the viceroy's permission to trade; while others of his countrymen extended the trade past Amoy to Foochow and Ningpo. Unfortunately such distinction as there may have been between these early European navigators and pirates was decidedly ephemeral. Reports reaching China of their brutal treatment of the Mohammedans were amply substantiated by their high-handed treatment of many Chinese. It is not surprising therefore that a Portuguese envoy from the viceroy of India, who had succeeded in reaching Peking, was hustled

---

[2] A contemporary of Friar John in the Far East was Friar Odoric, another Franciscan, who reached China about 1321. He appears to have visited Foochow, Hangchow, and Peking, and in his journal speaks of the Yellow River "which runs through the midst of Cathay, and does great harm in the country when it overflows the banks, or breaks the channel."

back to Canton and thrown into prison. The Canton trading post was attacked and destroyed in 1522, though another, which survived for many years, was soon established nearby at Lampa. Later, and it would seem with good cause, the Portuguese were driven from Ningpo and Amoy. Thus for a period the Portuguese retained only a precarious position on islands south of Canton.

For this ill fortune the Portuguese had chiefly themselves to thank. Truculent and lawless, regarding all Eastern peoples as legitimate prey, they [although professing Christianity] were little if any better than the contemporary Japanese pirates who pillaged the Chinese coasts. The Ming [emperors of China] can scarcely be censured for treating them as freebooters.[3]

In time, probably in 1537, the Portuguese traders established themselves at Macao, a small peninsula joined by a narrow neck of land to the Island of Heang-shan, which lies in the delta to the south of Canton. The first occupation of this desolate spot appears to have been somewhat informal; but, as a result of bribery, and later the payment of an annual rent, the foreign invaders were permitted to remain. Across the narrow isthmus the Chinese constructed a wall with but one gate, in order that the movements of the foreigner might be the better controlled. The settlement grew rapidly, yet for several centuries the fundamental question of sovereignty within its borders remained a matter of dispute. Usually a Chinese official resided at Macao, governing the city, theoretically at least, in the name of the Emperor, and deciding cases in which Chinese alone were involved. In addition it would seem that the Chinese continued to exercise fiscal jurisdiction—a point of some consequence, for to Macao came all ships destined for the China coast. Nevertheless the Portuguese claimed in Macao the right of exclusive jurisdiction, though it was not until 1887 that this claim was conceded and full sovereign rights were

---

[3] K. S. Latourette, *The Chinese: Their History and Culture,* 2nd rev. ed., 2 vols. in one. The Macmillan Company, New York, 1934. Vol. I, p. 313.

granted by the Chinese. From its establishment until the cession of Hong Kong to the British in 1842, Macao remained the center of western contacts with China, whether commercial or religious. After this date its importance steadily declined. Its harbor being unsuitable for the merchantmen of modern times, it could not compete successfully with either Hong Kong or Canton; it became little more than a picturesque point of historical interest whose chief claim to present fame consists in its large revenues from gambling and the sale of opium.

Growth of Portuguese Missions

The advent in south China of the Portuguese traders prepared the way for renewed missionary efforts by the Roman Catholic Church. Francis Xavier, who had already founded his church in Japan, died off the coast of Kwangtung (1552), thwarted in his ambition to carry Catholic Christianity to the Chinese. His successor was Matteo Ricci, an Italian, who had joined the Society of Jesus in 1571. Ricci arrived at Canton in 1582. During succeeding years he prosecuted his work in both Kwangtung and Kwangsi provinces. His early preaching in Nanking and Peking met with little response; nevertheless he succeeded later (in 1599 and 1601, respectively) in founding missions in Nanking and Peking. In the latter city he remained until his death (1610).

The religious propaganda of Ricci and his successors met with notable success. By 1617 the number of converts is said to have been 13,000; by 1650, 150,000; and by 1700, 300,000, among whom were numerous princes of the blood, mandarins of the first rank, and other courtiers. Doubtless this rapid growth was attributable to many causes, among which should be noted in particular the scholarly attainments of the Jesuits. In their missionary work they employed every intellectual and mechanical device which the Europe of their day could suggest: clocks, horological instruments, gauges, glass prisms, mathe-

matical and astronomical instruments, and geographical, architectural, literary, and religious works. Without this equipment
it may be questioned whether they would have won the official
recognition which was soon accorded them. Ricci himself
prepared for the Chinese a map of the world. Some of his
successors corrected the Chinese calendar, while others were
appointed by the emperor to the post of state astronomer. In
1692 the Emperor Kang Hsi issued a decree granting freedom
of worship and extending protection to the Roman churches
throughout the Empire.

Even these official favors did not exempt the Jesuits from
persecution. In 1616, at the instigation of an official of the
Board of Rites, a number of missionaries were expelled, in
cages, to Macao. Again in 1664 other Jesuits were forced to
leave Peking for Canton. But apart from several instances
such as these, they were permitted to pursue their work un-
molested.

A far greater obstacle to the work of the church than persecution by the Chinese was the attitude of the missionaries
themselves. For nearly fifty years after the arrival of Ricci the
Jesuits had been the only missionaries in China; but in the
seventeenth century they were followed by the Dominicans
(1631), the Franciscans (1633), the Augustinians (1680), and
the Paris Foreign Missions (1683). With the arrival of these
competing orders many of the missionaries devoted themselves to the pursuit of puerile and petty jealousies rather than
to the winning of converts to the church. These decidedly
un-Christian rivalries resulted in what may best be termed the
rites controversy. The essential points in this essentially child-
ish dispute may be summarized as follows. The Jesuits, as the
first missionaries in the China field, permitted their converts to
perform the Chinese ancestral rites as ceremonies of a civil and
commemorative character. They also employed the Chinese
character *Tien* (Heaven) in referring to the Christian God.
As against these Jesuit practices, members of the religious orders

that entered China in later years asserted that *Tien Chu* (Lord of Heaven) was the correct Chinese character for God, and that the ancestral rites were heathen customs that should be forsaken by the Chinese convert. The dispute, which raged on among the missionaries for the better part of a century, was carried to both the Emperor in Peking and the Pope in Rome. In 1700 the Manchu Emperor Kang-hi ruled in favor of the Jesuits, but in Rome the Papacy supported their critics. A somewhat humorous situation resulted. No missionary could go to China as a representative of the Roman Church unless he accepted the Papacy as the highest authority on the translation of Chinese religious terms; and such as accepted this authority the Manchu Emperor would not receive. The net result of this extraordinary episode was that in 1724 all missionaries, save a few who were retained for scientific work, were expelled. Nevertheless, the church fared far better than it deserved, for many of its converts retained their faith, and courageous missionaries, at the risk of their lives, entered China secretly to minister to their needs.

The Spaniards in the Philippines

It was only a matter of some five years after the first Portuguese navigators had landed in south China that Spaniards reached the East by crossing the Atlantic, rounding Cape Horn, and penetrating the Pacific. In March, 1521, Ferdinand Magellan, a Portuguese by birth but sailing under the flag of Spain, discovered the Mariana or Ladrone Islands, and later in the same month reached Samar in the Philippines. At Cebu Magellan found a native population already familiar with China. Junks from Siam were trading in Philippine waters, while in the markets of Cebu brass gongs and other articles gave evidence of an extensive trade with the Chinese. The Spaniards, however, were seeking not the Philippines but the Spice Islands, which lay to the south. As it happened, these islands, according to the line of demarcation of 1494, lay, as did also the Philippines, in the Portuguese half of the world. The Philippines were, in fact, a secondary consideration, and it was not until the passage of some years that Spain undertook seriously their conquest and exploration. Manila was founded in 1571. By this time Chinese trade with the islands had grown to considerable proportions. Chinese junks brought their wares to exchange for native products; and, since in the Philippines the Spaniards failed to find the coveted wealth of the Spice Islands, the China trade presented a possible alternative. But Spain could not enter the China trade directly, as the land of the Mings was recognized as lying in the Portuguese half of the world. Thus it developed that Chinese junks in increasing numbers made the voyage to Manila, while the Chinese population of the Philippines grew at a pace so alarming to early Spanish colonizers that numerous massacres resulted. Some of the early adventurers, projecting the conquest of China, petitioned the home government to dispatch the necessary forces, naïvely estimated at about sixty soldiers. The first Spanish friars, reaching China from the Philippines in 1575, entered into their bitter rivalry with the Jesuits, as already related. Spain's influence in China, however, did not extend beyond these missionary and indirect trading contacts. In fact, Spain offered no serious challenge to the claims of Portugal in the Far East.

The Dutch in the Far East

By the beginning of the seventeenth century developments had taken place in Europe which were soon to have their repercussions even in eastern Asia. The Dutch had already emerged as the leading maritime merchants of Europe, while the English (1588) had dealt a staggering blow to the sea power of Spain. The chief agencies of these two rising powers both in trade and in colonization were the United Dutch East India

Company and the English East India Company. Both commenced their activities in the first decade of the century, seeking to destroy the colonial and mercantile monopoly which Spain and Portugal, supported by the Papal blessing, enjoyed.

As early as 1604, and again in 1607, the Dutch reached Canton and attempted to open trade; but on both occasions permission was denied at the instigation of the Portuguese at Macao. Thus baffled in their efforts, the Dutch sought in 1622 to capture Macao, and for two years continued these attempts, using the Pescadores Islands, southwest of Taiwan (Formosa), as their base. In turn the Chinese now exerted themselves to expel by force the invaders from the Pescadores; but, failing in this, induced them by negotiations to exchange the islands for Formosa, over which China exercised at best only the most tenuous suzerainty. Here the Dutch maintained themselves for a number of years. After expelling the Spaniards, who had constructed a fort on the island in 1626, they met with a similar fate at the hands of the Chinese in 1661. Nevertheless, they continued an intermittent trade along the southern coast of China for many years, seeking the while to form direct contacts with the government in Peking. Missions were dispatched to the capital (1655, 1665, and 1795), where the Chinese insisted upon, and the envoys performed, the humiliating kowtow (nine prostrations). Yet this subservience brought little gain to the Dutch. The western trader was in no sense welcome, and the new Manchu rulers of China, having by the close of the seventeenth century established themselves firmly in power, were disposed to admit him only on such terms as they saw fit. Not until 1762 was a Dutch factory [4] built at Canton. The coming of the Dutch gave the Chinese their first contact with Europeans of the Protestant faith, and, though the Dutch sent no missionaries, their traders, who had tasted the bitterness of religious persecution, did not fail to warn the Chinese against the political dangers inherent

---

[4] A factory was a trading post.

in the Roman Catholic system whereby the spiritual allegiance of Chinese converts was transferred from Peking to Rome.

The English Reach China

Although the English had preceded the Dutch in their efforts to open trade with China, their first ship, with its envoys, was lost at sea in 1596. The first English vessel to reach China was dispatched in 1635 by the English East India Company, under license from the Governor of the Portuguese colony of Goa, to Macao. This was followed by a squadron of English vessels commanded by Captain John Weddell and sent by the Courten's Association, which at the time enjoyed the favors of King Charles I. Weddell arrived at Macao in 1638 and proceeded to Canton, where the Chinese, after attempting to repel his ships, finally consented to trade. The English East India Company did not enter China actively until 1664. In the south commerce was hampered by the ancient hostility of the Portuguese. Farther north the trade was conducted both at Amoy and in Formosa until in 1715 the English company was allowed to erect a factory at Canton.

Other European nations played but an inconspicuous role in this China trade. The first French ship to reach Canton arrived in 1699. During the eighteenth century Sweden (1731), Prussia (1753), and Denmark (1782) sent their first merchant ships to Canton, but no sizeable trade resulted from these efforts. The first American ship, *The Empress of China,* sailed in 1784.

First Russian Contacts with China

While these sixteenth and seventeenth century contacts of western Europeans were being made with China by the ocean route, the Russians, too, had been moving to the east by way of Siberia. Explorers, fur traders, and fugitives from the law penetrated as far as the Pacific, which, in time, gave rise to such settlements as Tobolsk, Tomsk, Yakutsk, Nerchinsk, and many others. In Far Eastern Siberia there was a natural tendency for the Russians to move southward toward the valleys of the Amur River; but here they came into conflict with tribes that, theoretically at least, recognized the suzerainty of China. Albazin was founded by the Russians on the upper Amur; frequent conflicts occurred between the Cossacks and Chinese forces sent to repel them, and it was not until 1689 that a boundary settlement was finally reached in the Treaty of Nerchinsk, the first that China signed with a western power. By it China retained the Amur valley. In succeeding decades Russia sent a number of embassies to Peking, resulting in the development of some overland trade, and permission to establish a Russian church in Peking. A settlement of the western boundary was made in 1727, two permanent trading stations were established on the frontier, and the Chinese dispatched to St. Petersburg their only embassy to a foreign court.

The Westerners Reach Japan

When Portuguese navigators cast anchor off Canton in the early years of the sixteenth century, China was not the only far eastern land of which Europe had at least some knowledge. Many years earlier those Europeans who had been privileged to read the pages of Marco Polo had seen these strange words:

Chipangu is an Island towards the east [from China] in the high seas, . . . and a very great Island it is. The people are white, civilized, and well-favoured. They are Idolaters, and are dependent on nobody. And I can tell you the quantity of gold they have is endless. . . . You must know that he [the king of this island] hath a great Palace which is entirely roofed with fine gold, just as our

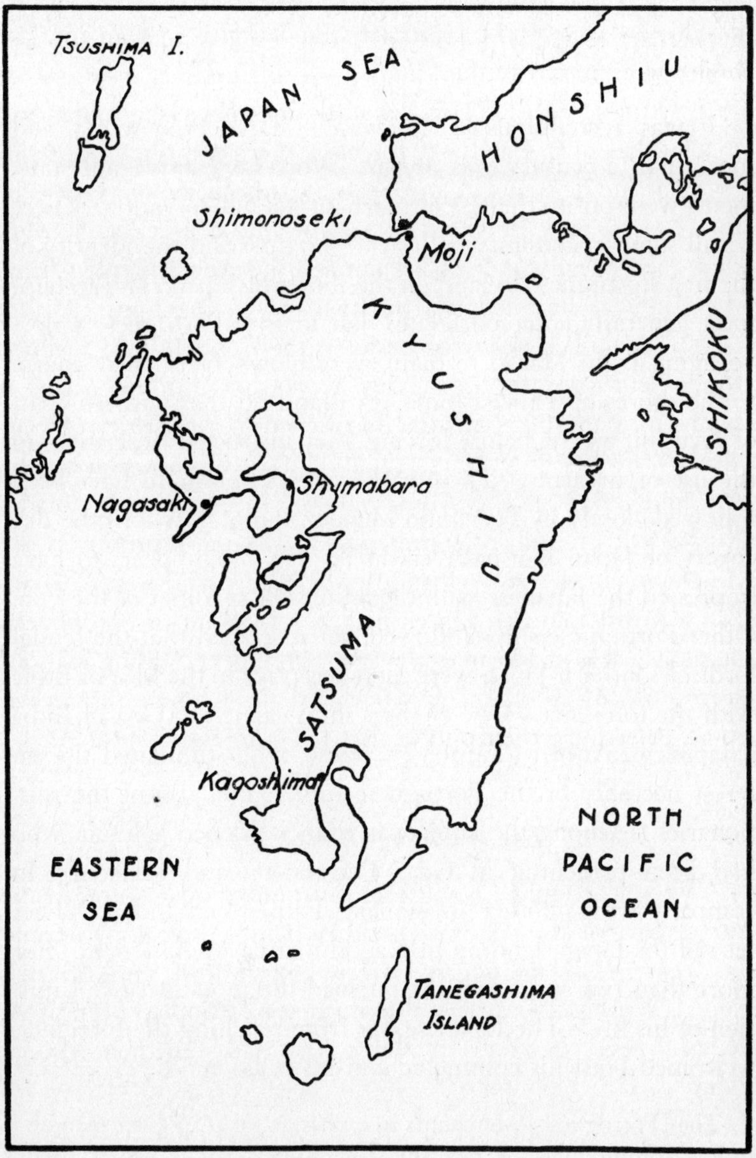
TSUSHIMA I.
JAPAN SEA
HONSHIU
Shimonoseki
Moji
KYUSHIU
SHIKOKU
Shimabara
Nagasaki
SATSUMA
Kagoshima
NORTH
PACIFIC
OCEAN
EASTERN
SEA
TANEGASHIMA
ISLAND

SOUTHWESTERN JAPAN, WHERE THE PORTUGUESE FIRST LANDED AND WHERE THE DUTCH AND CHINESE TRADE WAS CONDUCTED DURING THE TOKUGAWA PERIOD.

churches are roofed with lead, insomuch that it would scarcely be possible to estimate its value.[5]

It was a credulous age in which Marco Polo wrote, and more than a century was to pass before his extravagant statements were put to the test of more intimate observation. There is still some uncertainty both as to the time and the identity of the first Portuguese to land on the shores of Japan. The account most generally accepted relates that in 1542 Portuguese sailors voyaging from Macao to Siam were blown from their course to the shores of Tanegashima, an island off the southern coast of Kyushu, where, before leaving, they instructed the natives in the use of firearms. These early visitors appear to have been followed closely by Fernando Mendez Pinto, to whom the discovery of Japan is usually credited. He, too, appears to have impressed the Japanese with the admirable qualities of the gun. Other Portuguese ships followed, for it seemed that the feudal lords of southern Japan were most receptive to the idea of trade with the foreigner. One of their ships carried to Goa in India a Japanese, Anjiro (Yajiro) by name, who stimulated the interest not only of the Portuguese traders but also of the missionaries. Among the latter was Francis Xavier, a Jesuit, who had been preaching in Goa, Travancore, and Malacca. In company with another missionary, Father Fernandez, Xavier set sail for Japan, landing in Kagoshima in August, 1549. For more than two years he now pursued the most successful mission of his life. The Japanese, far from repelling the foreigner, welcomed both his commerce and his religion.

The [Portuguese] Merchants in exchange for their European and Indian commodities, as raw silk, fine stuffs, druggs, wines, medicines, and a great variety of other both natural and artificial curiosities, became possess'd of immense treasures, and the golden marrow of the country. The fathers of the Society [of Jesus] on their side

---

[5] Sir Henry Yule, editor, *The Book of Ser Marco Polo*, 3rd rev. ed. Charles Scribner's Sons, New York, 1926. Vol. II, pp. 253-254.

gain'd the hearts of the people, always greedy of novelties, by the meek and comfortable doctrine of the Gospel. . . .[6]

Catholic Missions in Japan

Xavier remained in Japan only a little more than two years. From Kagoshima in Satsuma he moved to Hirado and later visited Kyoto, seeking vainly an audience with the Emperor. In November, 1551, he left Japan, dying the following year off the coast of south China. Other Jesuits, however, followed him to Japan, where their work testified to the highly tolerant spirit of the Japanese. They were heard respectfully by all classes of the people, including Buddhist priests. It is of course doubtful whether the first Japanese converts possessed any adequate understanding of the new religion, for, as one authority has observed, "Japanese is a difficult language and Christianity is hard to explain." There was, to be sure, a certain resemblance between Catholic ritual and that of Buddhism, and one official document of the time described the Jesuits as teaching the Law of Buddha.

Other causes, too, contributed to the early success of Christianity. The feudal barons desired the profits of the foreign trade. They observed the deference paid by the Portuguese traders to the missionaries, and they concluded naturally that where the missionary was, there too would be the trader. This tendency was marked in particular among the barons of Kyushu, who on occasion ordered the mass conversion of their subjects to Christianity and even instigated persecution of the Buddhists; but if no foreign ship arrived, the populace was as often commanded to revert to its native faith.

Although the Japanese were attracted by the learning and dignity of the Jesuits, they were at a loss to understand their intolerance.

---

[6] Engelbert Kaempfer, *The History of Japan.* The Macmillan Company, New York, 1906. Vol. II, p. 154.

. . . Jesuits did not study the feelings of others, and their zeal easily took the form of an aggressive bigotry, though it must be granted that they displayed a splendid courage which undoubtedly gained them the respect of the military class. Xavier . . . made the bad mistake of insisting that all the dead who had not been Christians during their lifetime would burn for ever. To a people who had never believed seriously in the flames of hell, and who paid to the memory of their ancestors a most reverent devotion, this was a revolting doctrine; . . .[7]

Thus, while gaining converts, the missionaries also aroused bitter opposition. The great majority of their adherents were people of lowly station, many of whom had enjoyed such medical care as the missionaries could offer. Later in the century, however, a number of barons in the western country were converted, which meant also the forcible conversion of their retainers. There was some success too in Kyoto, where a small group of Jesuits were received by the Shogun, and later by Nobunaga (1568), who befriended them in his desire to curb the political power of Buddhism. Yet as late as 1582 the Jesuits numbered their converts at not more than 150,000, most of whom resided in Kyushu and had been forced to adopt the foreign faith by their feudal rulers. In fact, as time was to show, formal Christianity as introduced by the Jesuits had little influence on the national life or thought of Japan.

Arrival of the Spaniards

Until 1592 the Portuguese had been the only Europeans to reach Japan. In 1581, when Philip II of Spain ascended the throne of Portugal, he confirmed his Portuguese subjects in their exclusive right to the Japan trade, and four years later the Papacy conferred upon the Jesuits the sole right to enter Japan as missionaries. When Hideyoshi (1591) was planning the conquest of China, he sent an embassy to Manila demanding

[7] G. B. Sansom, *Japan: A Short Cultural History*. D. Appleton-Century Company, New York, 1931. p. 408.

that the Spaniards there recognize him as their suzerain. The result was two Spanish missions to Japan from the governor of the Philippines, carrying among their number four Franciscan friars, who, in the guise of ambassadors, entered Japan in violation of the papal order. Other priests' soon followed and were permitted to remain on the understanding that they should not preach Christianity. Having accepted this prohibition, they proceeded immediately to violate it by conducting service in Nagasaki, Kyoto, and Osaka. Though at first favorably disposed toward the foreign priests, Hideyoshi had become suspicious of political implications in the Jesuit policy. In confirmation of his fears, he now observed the Spanish priests openly defying his authority and promoting (as in China) sectarian warfare with their Jesuit colleagues. Finally the idle boasting of a Spanish pilot that the missionary was but preparing the way for political conquest led Hideyoshi to act. In February, 1597, six Franciscans, three Japanese Jesuits, and seventeen Japanese laymen were crucified at Nagasaki. It must be conceded, however, that the Spanish and Portuguese priests brought this punishment upon themselves. As early as 1587 Hideyoshi, after subjecting the daimyo of Satsuma, where most of the Christians lived, issued an edict ordering the foreign missionaries to leave Japan within twenty days. This edict was directed only against the priests, not against their religion. The Japanese still desired the visits of the Portuguese traders, and, to encourage them, the edict was modified to permit priests to accompany the ships so long as they did not remain in Japan. For several reasons the law was not enforced. The priests defied the law; many of them were protected by friendly barons in Kyushu; and Hideyoshi was already engaged in war both at home and abroad. It is thus obvious that when in 1597 the first crucifixions took place at Nagasaki, the foreign priesthood was fully aware that it had defied the nation's law. Curiously (it is probable that he feared stoppage of the trade) Hideyoshi did not interfere with the Jesuits, though they too had defied his laws. The six unfortunate Spanish priests were, of course, regarded by the Church as martyrs, and despite the fact that they had entered Japan by fraud and had defied its laws, they were canonized by Rome in 1627.

Iyeyasu's Foreign Policy

With the passing of Hideyoshi (1598) control of government in Japan passed to the able founder of the Tokugawa Shogunate, Iyeyasu, whose views on foreign relations and trade were probably more enlightened and liberal than any which prevailed in Europe at the time. During his rule the Spaniards, the Dutch, and the English were all welcomed in Japanese ports. The exclusion edict against the foreign priests was not revoked, yet Iyeyasu for a time tolerated their presence. Friars of the Spanish orders at Manila again entered Japan, and in 1608 the Papacy revoked the restriction which had granted the field solely to the Jesuits. In 1600 the first Dutch ship arrived. It was one of a fleet of five vessels which had sailed by way of the Straits of Magellan, and, blown from its course, sought shelter in the harbor of Bungo. The pilot of the vessel was an English sailor, Will Adams, who was employed by Iyeyasu as adviser in matters of commerce and navigation. Other Dutch ships came in 1609, and a factory was set up at Hirado. News of the Dutch success stimulated the English, one of whose ships reached Hirado in 1613. Iyeyasu, following his liberal policy, extended to these first Englishmen on his shores a charter for free trade and urged them to construct a factory at his capital, Yedo (the modern Tokyo). Captain Saris, however, preferred Hirado, where the Dutch were already established, and there the English factory was located. Because of incompetent management it was abandoned in 1623, a time when the Dutch were still plying a most lucrative trade with Japan. In the meantime Iyeyasu's views on Catholic Christianity had experienced a gradual and withal a profound change.

As already noted, Iyeyasu had at first adhered to a most tolerant attitude toward the priests, his motives being closely linked to commercial policy. He communicated with the Spaniards in the Philippines, offered to open the ports of eastern Japan to Spanish ships, and let it be understood that the edicts against the missionaries would not be enforced. With him the promotion of commerce was a primary objective, and at the time he had no thought of excluding the foreigner. But it was soon apparent that, while the Spaniards were eager to send missionaries, they had but a secondary interest in the Japan trade. Iyeyasu grew suspicious of their motives, a change of view which was reinforced by the arguments of the English and Dutch Protestants, who pointed out that foreign priests were in no sense essential to foreign trade. It was patent to this able Japanese ruler that the foreign priests—Portuguese Jesuits and Spanish Dominicans—who claimed to speak for the same god were, none the less, bitter in their attitude to each other and probably antagonistic to his un-Christian government. In 1612, therefore, he took the first step to curb their pretensions by proscribing the Christian faith. All the Franciscan churches and many of those of the Jesuits were destroyed. The following year a number of Japanese Christians were executed in Yedo, the capital, and in 1614 suppression of the foreign faith was ordered throughout the Empire. Naturally this order did not fall with equal effect on all parts of the country. The foreign missionaries were not harmed, and some of the feudal barons refused to act against native Christians in their domains.

Upon the death of Iyeyasu, in 1616, affairs of state passed into the hands of Hidetada, who determined to enforce the laws against Christians. Although, during the following years, a few Spanish priests were beheaded, the laws were not even yet fully enforced. The government directed its efforts toward having the native converts peaceably abandon the foreign faith and to encouraging the priests to leave the country voluntarily.

For the most part these efforts failed. The priests were defiant, and many converts followed their example.

Accurate figures will probably never be available, but an estimate that 280,000 Japanese and a few foreigners suffered punishment of some kind between 1614 and 1635, principally imprisonment or exile, with some executions by beheading, crucifixion, burning, and the *fosse* (ditch), even if exaggerated, testifies to the stanchness of the loyalty of these early Japanese Christians.[8]

In view of the fact that Hidetada believed that the work of the Spanish missionary and trader was but the prelude to political invasion, it is surprising that his policy was not enforced sooner and with still greater vigor.

The Policy of Exclusion

Gradually more vigorous measures were adopted, and these were soon to result in an almost total exclusion of the foreigner from Japan. The Spaniards, who were the first to suffer, were ordered (1624) to leave the country. All direct relations between Japan and the Philippines were thus severed. For some years the laws respecting Christianity and the foreigners underwent no further change. Meanwhile Hidetada had been succeeded by his son Iyemitsu, who ranks as one of the greatest of the Tokugawa administrators. To the general policy of his predecessors he adhered with even greater vigor. By a single executive act (1636) Japan's trade on the high seas was proscribed. No Japanese vessel might proceed abroad. No Japanese subject might leave his country; anyone doing so and attempting to return would suffer death. For this revolutionary policy, Christianity was a primary cause, for Japanese converts had been going abroad and receiving instruction either at Macao or in the Philippines, from whence they returned to propagate the faith in their native land. More stringent regu-

[8] Payson J. Treat, *The Far East,* rev. ed. Harper & Brothers, New York, 1935. p. 179.

lations were at the same time placed upon all foreigners, including the Dutch at Hirado, while the Portuguese traders had to confine their activities to a small island, known as Deshima, in the harbor of Nagasaki in Kyushu.

The next year (1637) witnessed the Shimabara revolt, in which numbers of native converts were implicated. The causes of this rising were probably two. It arose as a protest against both feudal oppression and the persecution of Christians. After severe fighting the rebels were defeated, most of them being put to death. But this was not all. Portuguese missionaries were believed to have incited their converts to revolt, and, as a result, all subjects of the Spanish king (the thrones of Spain and Portugal were at the time united) were forbidden to set foot on the shores of Japan. Furthermore, it was decreed that if any Portuguese ships came to Japan, both ship and cargo would be burned, and those on board would suffer death. In defiance of this order Portugal dispatched an embassy of seventy-three persons in an effort to prove its innocence of the Shimabara revolt. The fate which awaited these emissaries in Japan was indeed conclusive evidence of the nation's new policy. All were sentenced " . . . to be beheaded, excepting twelve men of the lowest rank, who were to be sent back to Macao, to bring their countrymen the news of this unhappy success, along with a most proud and threatening message from the Emperor, containing in substance, that should the King of Portugal himself, nay the very God of the Christians, presume to enter his dominions, he would serve them in the very same manner." [9] A second embassy sent to Japan after Portugal had regained her independence from Spain failed also.

Japan in Seclusion

In this manner Japan entered upon a long period of exclusion and seclusion that was not to be broken until the middle

[9] Engelbert Kaempfer, *op. cit.* pp. 166-167.

of the nineteenth century. Nevertheless, her contacts with the oriental and western worlds were not severed completely. The Dutch were permitted to carry on a limited trade at the so-called island of Deshima, in Nagasaki harbor. There, confined to what was virtually a prison, they were permitted, under rather humiliating limitations, to conduct their trade. The Chinese, too, were allowed to send a small number of trading junks annually to this port.

With the establishment of this policy of exclusion, Japan embarked on a course far different from that originally contemplated by Iyeyasu. For its adoption the political implications of Catholic Christianity must be held largely responsible. Instead of a liberal policy which encouraged foreign trade and foreign contacts, the nation now turned exclusively to itself. What might have happened had Japan continued to develop foreign intercourse lies solely in the field of speculation. It is at least notable that it was during the period of Japanese exclusion and seclusion (1638-1854) that western powers built and consolidated major portions of their colonial empires. Had Japan been in more intimate touch with world affairs, perhaps she too would have played a leading role in those struggles.

Selected Bibliography

China

One of the most satisfactory accounts is given by H. Cordier, *Histoire Générale de la Chine,* 4 vols. (Paris: 1920-21), and by the same author, *Le Consulat de France à Canton au XVIIIe siècle* (Leiden: 1908). R. K. Douglas gives a good account in his *Europe and the Far East,* rev. ed. (Cambridge: 1913), ch. 1. J. B. Eames in his *The English in China* . . . (London: 1909) covers the subject from 1600 to 1843. J. W. Foster, *American Diplomacy in the Orient* (Boston: 1904) treats of the first American contacts in ch. 1. Dealing specially with Macao are C. A. Montalto de Jesus, *Historic Macao* (Hong Kong: 1902), and George W. Keeton, "The International Status of Macao before 1887," in *The Chinese Social and*

Political Science Review (July, 1927). H. B. Morse, *The International Relations of the Chinese Empire* (London: 1910) vol. 1, ch. 3, "Early Foreign Relations" is indispensable. Less usable but of value is E. H. Parker, *China, Her History, Diplomacy, and Commerce . . .* 2nd ed. (New York: 1917). More detailed material will be found in E. H. Pritchard, *Anglo-Chinese Relations During the Seventeenth and Eighteenth Centuries* (London: 1930). The Russian phase is presented in George Timkowski, *Travels of the Russian Mission through Mongolia to China . . .* 2 vols. (London: 1827) and deals with the years of 1820-21. P. J. Treat gives a concise, clear summary in *The Far East* (New York: 1928). S. Wells Williams, *The Middle Kingdom,* rev. ed., 2 vols. (New York: 1907) is rich in material.

Japan

R. H. Akagi, *Japan's Foreign Relations* (Tokyo: 1936) devotes ch. 1 to Japan's pre-treaty foreign relations. Capt. F. Brinkley, *A History of the Japanese People* (New York: 1915), chs. 32, 37. C. R. Boxer, *A Portuguese Embassy to Japan, 1644-1647* (London: 1928). Dr. Seiji G. Hishida in *The International Position of Japan as a Great Power* (New York: 1905) gives a scholarly account in ch. 4. For a detailed account of Christian influence there is P. F. X. de Charlevoix, *Histoire de l'établissement, des progrès et de la décadence du christianisme dans le Japon,* 3 vols. (Rouen: 1715). H. Davis, *Japan, from the Age of the Gods to the Fall of Tsingtau* (New York: 1916). W. E. Griffis, *The Mikado's Empire,* 12th ed., 2 vols. (New York: 1913), vol. 1, ch. 25. J. H. Gubbins, *The Making of Modern Japan* (London: 1922), ch. 2. R. Hildreth, *Japan as It Was and Is,* 2 vols. (London: 1907), vol. 1. Engelbert Kaempfer, *The History of Japan,* 3 vols. (Glasgow: 1906) gives the best account of Nagasaki and the early foreign trade, in vol. 2, Bk. 4. J. H. Longford, *The Story of Old Japan* (London: 1910), chs. 13-15, and by the same author, *Japan* (Boston: 1923). J. Murdoch (in collaboration with I. Yamagata), *A History of Japan* (Kobe, Tokyo, New York: 1903-26), see vol. 2. M. Steichen, *The Christian Daimyos* (Tokyo: 1903). The most scholarly observations, though brief, on early foreign contacts with Japan are made by G. B. Sansom, *Japan, A Short Cultural History* (London: 1931).

CHAPTER V

The Canton Trade

THE earlier contacts of Europeans with China, which have
been surveyed briefly in the preceding chapter, had, by
the close of the seventeenth century, laid the foundations for
a considerable trade. Half a century earlier European trade
with Japan had been closed (save for the limited privileges
retained by the Dutch and the Chinese), with the result that
the China market alone remained. From 1638 until the middle
of the nineteenth century the far eastern trade was primarily
a China trade. The peculiar circumstances in which this
trade was conducted, the politico-economic policies of the trading nations, and the character of the international merchants
themselves—these, and other factors, created the confused and
irritating state of affairs which in 1840 resulted in what is
usually called the "Opium War" and the placing of China's
foreign commerce on a regular and a treaty basis (1842-1844).
Furthermore, since these treaties contained certain principles
which, for nearly a century now, have determined the real
character of China's foreign relations, it would seem obvious
that the causes giving rise to them are worthy of some consideration.

British Primacy in the China Trade

China's foreign maritime trade in the eighteenth and the
early years of the nineteenth century was shared by many
western states. With the beginnings of the Portuguese, the
Spanish, the Dutch, the English, and the Russian (overland)
trade, the reader is already familiar. The French too sent

occasional ships to Canton after 1660, to be followed by the Americans more than a century later. Other flags also were represented at rare intervals: those of Sweden, Prussia, Hamburg, Bremen, Austria (by Belgians), and some of the Italian states. Peruvians, Mexicans, and Chilians as well appeared in Chinese waters; but the trade of all these lesser states was of minor consequence. By the beginning of the nineteenth century the British predominated in the China trade, while the Americans, whose trade had begun only as late as 1784, soon occupied second place.

At an early date (1685) the right to erect a factory (trading post) at Canton was secured by the English East India Company, but it was not until many years later (1715) that a decision was reached to dispatch ships to Canton at regular intervals and to maintain a permanent staff there. By the close of the century, a sizeable commerce having developed, the British government determined in 1792 to dispatch an embassy to the court of Peking in the hope of removing "restraints and exactions" on the Canton trade, and of securing the liberty of trading at other ports. Lord Macartney, who headed the embassy, was permitted to proceed in 1793 to the Chinese capital, where his reception was marked by great splendor and dignity, though the conveyances in which he traveled were decorated with banners bearing an inscription in Chinese characters, "Ambassador bearing tribute from the country of England." Lord Macartney was even permitted an audience with the Emperor without performance of the objectionable kowtow, to which the Dutch on their earlier embassies had always submitted. If the British grew optimistic at this apparent leniency of the Chinese court, their hopes were in vain, for the embassy resulted in not a single advantage to the existing trade of the East India Company at Canton. Even this dismal failure, however, was not without its amusing side. Early on the morning of his audience with the Em-

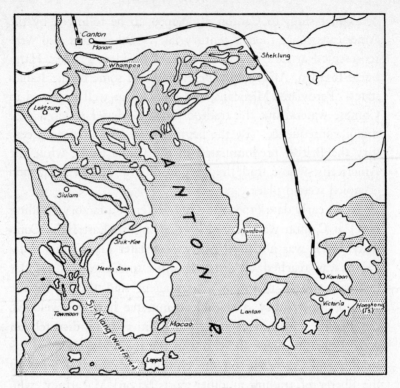

THE DELTA OF THE SI KIANG OR WEST RIVER AT CANTON.

peror, Lord Macartney proceeded to the Palace accompanied by a most impressive suite.

From the darkness of the morning, a considerable confusion arose in the intended order of the cavalcade; but as parade is useless when no one can see it, the failure was of little consequence.[1]

The Macartney embassy was soon followed by the mission of Lord Amherst. In 1814 a British ship of war made a number of American captures in Chinese waters near Canton. Chinese officials instructed the agents of the East India Company to order the naval vessel to leave Chinese waters; and when the agents pleaded lack of jurisdiction over a public ship,

---

[1] Lord Macartney, *Embassy to China*, abridged. London, 1797. p. 81.

the Chinese threatened to stop British trade. The incident itself was soon amicably settled, but it led to the decision by the British government to dispatch a second, the Amherst, embassy, the object of which was "a removal of the grievances which had been experienced, and an exemption from them and others of the like nature for the time to come, with the establishment of the Company's trade upon a secure, solid, equitable footing, free from the capricious, arbitrary aggressions of the local [Chinese] authorities, and under the protection of the Emperor, and the sanction of regulations to be appointed by himself." [2]

Lord Amherst experienced at the hands of the Chinese none of the courtesy which had been accorded his predecessor. He was hurried from Taku to Peking as a "tribute bearer," under a constant barrage of arguments to induce him to perform the kowtow. His refusal at Peking to be pushed into an immediate audience without court dress or credentials resulted in the demand that he leave the capital instantly, and with this demand he had no alternative save to comply. The embassy was an even more impressive failure than that of Lord Macartney, who at least had received hospitable treatment. Amherst, on the contrary, and what was more, his government, had been subjected to gross insult, while the Chinese enjoyed a full diplomatic victory. Perhaps foreign governments would now realize that they must approach Peking as humble vassals, the bearers of tribute. Perhaps the foreign traders, and in particular the agents of the English East India Company, would now realize that the Canton trade must be conducted on such terms as the Chinese saw fit to dictate. These implications of Lord Amhert's failure were not without their effect at Canton. Opinion among the foreign traders already was crystallizing. There were but three alternatives: (1) the Canton trade could be abandoned; (2) it could be continued under what the for-

---

[2] Dr. H. B. Morse, *The International Relations of the Chinese Empire.* Longmans, Green & Company, London, 1910. Vol. I, p. 56.

eigner regarded as the unreasonable and arbitrary Chinese regulations; or (3) force might be employed to compel China to adopt a more liberal and regular commercial policy.

The "Exactions" of the Canton Trade

What then were the "restraints and exactions" on the Canton trade of which the British (and other foreign nationals at Canton) complained?

In 1757 the Chinese government proclaimed Canton the sole port at which foreign trade might be conducted. On the actual course of trade this decree had, in itself, little effect, since for a matter of some fifty years commerce had tended to desert the northern ports where the exactions of local officials were more than the traffic would bear. Its real importance may be attributed to the fact that after 1757 Canton enjoyed a monopoly in which the Chinese arbitrarily dictated the terms on which the foreigner might have access to his markets for silk and tea. For the most part the advantage was all with the Chinese. In the first instance there was a natural advantage. The western trader wanted China silk and China tea and was ready to pay well for it, while China wanted few, if any, products which a western market could offer in return. On this circumstance the Chinese merchant could capitalize, while his government drew revenue from a multitude of commercial taxes, and while his officials at Canton waxed rich on "squeeze," a euphonious synonym for bribery. Furthermore, neither taxes nor "squeeze" were standardized. They could be and were raised or lowered with unpredictable irregularity, and against them the foreigner had but one weapon. He might refuse to trade; but this neither he nor the Chinese desired.

There was always the danger, however, that the Chinese government might prohibit foreign trade. China had not sought this trade; it had been imposed upon her by the western world. Regarding herself as the Middle Kingdom, completely satisfied with her supposed pre-eminent position, she had looked upon all other states as her vassals. Her neighbors, in the act of presenting tribute, conceded their inferior status; as a reward they might be permitted to trade with China, but only upon such terms as the Emperor, the Son of Heaven, might prescribe. There was no place in the Chinese scheme of things for commercial or political treaties between equal and independent states. It was but natural that when the Westerners reached the Far East, China should apply this same code to them. As long as the foreigner was willing to trade peaceably, as long as he accepted the regulations that China imposed, and as long as he did not attempt to destroy Chinese procedure by the imposition of his western notions, the commerce would continue. For many years, in fact for more than three centuries, the foreign trader bowed to the Chinese view. At Macao and Canton he traded when and how China, the suzerain, permitted. But as time passed, as regulation became more irksome and more arbitrary, as the value and the potentialities of the foreign trade grew, as the vitality of the Manchu regime declined, and as the foreigners became more conscious of an ability to impose their will upon China, the trader became less inclined to accept the Chinese code. The arbitrary regulations appeared more and more burdensome as he pictured the larger profits that would flow from a trade founded upon liberal commercial treaties. Such thoughts, of course, never occurred to the Chinese, as their methods of regulating the trade clearly show.

A Gentleman of Consequence

At Canton the most important of the Chinese officials who controlled the foreign trade was known as the Hoppo. His power to regulate import and export duties at his own discretion made him a person of great consequence. What these charges would amount to on a given cargo was a matter wholly beyond prediction. The Hoppo, too, exercised some control over those "unofficial" duties which lined the pockets of officials, great and small, and were paid by the Chinese and the foreign merchants alike. Until these demands were met, the grasping official could and did involve the trader in a circle of official red tape. But the most effective organization or instrument through which the Hoppo and other officials controlled the trade, and waxed rich upon it, was the Co-Hong. This was a group of twelve or thirteen Chinese, known as the "security merchants," who, after 1755, enjoyed a monopoly of all trade with the foreigners. For this privilege they paid dearly—at times as much as a quarter of a million dollars. The position was worth the price. They fixed the price of the silk and tea which the traders sought. They determined the market value of the imports that came to Canton in the western ships. Their task in most cases was lucrative, but it was also trying. While seeking to accumulate a fortune, they were obligated to meet every demand of an avaricious officialdom. Theirs was the nice and delicate problem of taxing the trade for all it would bear. Here their responsibility did not end. In return for their envied monopoly, the Hong merchants were responsible to the Hoppo for the behavior of the foreign traders at Canton or in Chinese waters. For any breach of law or custom it was only necessary for the Hoppo to threaten the Co-Hong. If it failed to win redress from the offenders, further "taxes," or perhaps the entire stoppage of the trade, were threatened.

Despite these facts, the relations between the foreigners and members of the Co-Hong were surprisingly agreeable. Each had a common objective—the amassing of profits. Each realized that the other was essential to this end. The foreigner might grumble at the irregular burdens which his ships and his goods had to bear; yet he knew that his security merchant was the best friend he had on Chinese soil. The personal relationship between them was in many cases most intimate and friendly. The largest transactions were carried on without written bond, a circumstance to which no special significance need be attached. It was merely a recognition by both parties that integrity was the best guarantee of continued profits.

Social Restraints on the Foreigner

There were many other ways, too, in which the trade and the daily activities of the foreigners were controlled. The factories at Canton were situated on the river bank just outside the walled city, and to this latter the foreigner was denied access. His ships were forced to lie at anchor below the city, thus adding to the cost of handling cargo. When at Canton his movements were confined to the narrow limits of the factory grounds. He was denied the use of sedan chairs—the most honorable conveyance for travel. He could not row on the river, and only on rare occasions was he permitted to visit the flower gardens on the opposite bank. The markets of the walled city, with their variety of wares, were as far from his view as though they had been on the opposite side of the world. No foreign women could be brought to the Canton factories; and, when the trading season was over, the foreigners must return to Macao, there to await a new season and new fleets of ships. It was all part of a system, an historical heritage, by which China impressed the foreigner with his inferior and ignoble status.

If the traders became restive, if they agitated for a commercial treaty to regularize duties and other impositions, the fact is not surprising. The Macartney and the Amherst embassies, which have already been mentioned, were evidence that the British government was moving in this direction. And yet, the trader was timid as well as restive. Despite all the impositions the Canton trade was profitable, and the trader was inclined to bear exasperating burdens rather than to risk by diplomatic pressure an entire stoppage of the trade. Both the commerce and the methods under which it was conducted might therefore have continued indefinitely had it not been for three factors of the utmost consequence. The first was the development of the opium traffic; the second the question of jurisdiction; the third the abolition by the British government of the monopoly in the China trade so long enjoyed by the East India Company.

The Opium Problem

The precise time at which opium was first used by the Chinese is not known. Though the opium-producing poppy is mentioned in Chinese literature as early as the Tang Dynasty (618), its early use in China, as elsewhere, appears to have been for medicinal purposes. In India opium was eaten, but it was the Chinese who popularized its use for smoking. This practice evidently was derived from the smoking of tobacco, which was introduced into China by Spaniards from the Philippines early in the seventeenth century. The Dutch, who controlled Formosa after 1624, mixed opium with tobacco as a preventive against malaria; from there this habit spread to China, where gradually it became the practice to smoke opium alone. As early as 1729 the Chinese government prohibited the sale of opium, without, however, imposing any penalties upon the smoker. The importation of foreign opium, which was started by the Portuguese, increased rapidly during the middle years of the eighteenth century. By 1800 its effects upon the people had become so apparent that the Emperor prohibited not only importation of the drug, but also cultivation of the poppy in China. This was a serious blow, for, until this time, opium had been carried to China like any other article of commerce, and in fact was welcomed since it reduced considerably the unfavorable balance in the Westerner's trade.

Although Chinese officials at Peking may have desired sincerely to stop the opium traffic, the local officials at Canton and Macao had not the slightest intention of doing so. For twenty years the edict was virtually unheeded. The Co-Hong ceased to deal in opium at Canton, and the British East India Company prohibited its transportation in company ships, but none the less the drug continued to enter China at Macao, or from the Whampoa anchorage below Canton, and after 1821 from receiving ships that could move from one anchorage to another as safety required. Occasionally some overzealous official might seem to apply the law; but not until 1836 was there "any real attempt to stop, or even to check, the trade."

The emperor might prohibit the trade, and might renew the prohibition by repeated edicts; the viceroy might issue his proclamation in strict accordance with the Imperial orders, and both viceroy and Hoppo might enjoin on the Hong merchants to obey the law; but viceroy, Hoppo, governor, admiral, magistrate, and down to the smallest person with the slightest connexion with a government office, all connived at the continuous breach of the law, provided only that they found therein their personal profit.[3]

The foreign traders were only too anxious to see the traffic increase. The moral objections that later generations have raised against the smoking of opium were rarely voiced by traders in the early years of the nineteenth century. The point of view was that if the Chinese wanted opium and were willing to nullify their own laws to get it, that was not the concern of the trader. All were willing to participate in the shipment of a product for which the Chinese (because the trade was illegal) paid in cash. The best-quality opium came from the British provinces of Bengal and Behar in India, where its manufacture was a monopoly of the East India Company. Parsees were the first carriers of this product. Later the Company participated directly in the carrying trade; but after 1800 its ships carried no opium, and this privilege was granted on

[3] *Ibid.* p. 183.

license to individual British and Indian shippers. American vessels, too, carried opium both from India and from Turkey.

Forces whose power it is difficult to estimate thus contrived to nourish the growth of an illegal and morally destructive traffic. The foreigner supplied the opium because the Chinese would buy it, and because, together with raw cotton, it was almost sufficient to pay for the exports of silk and tea. Its sale was the one means by which the trade could be balanced. To destroy it would bring serious consequences to the legitimate trade. On the other hand Chinese officialdom was woefully corrupt. In 1800 it was still within its power to enforce the law. Forty years later the traffic had grown to such proportions, had become so involved with legitimate trade, that any attempt to stop it would lead inevitably to the most serious consequences.

The Question of Jurisdiction

The second problem contributing to the coming crisis in relations between China and the western nations was the question of jurisdiction. It was inevitable that disputes should arise when rough and ready sailors from foreign ships came ashore at Chinese ports. Woundings and homicides could easily result, and the settlement of these matters, as will appear, was in no sense a simple affair. To the crews of ships that had made the long and arduous voyage to Macao and Canton, shore leave was a well-merited reward. The sailor availed himself of whatever temptations a foreign and novel city had to offer. Brawling and drinking were constant companions, and not unnaturally killings sometimes resulted. The surprising thing is that homicides were so few. Their consequences, however, were none the less troublesome. It would appear that the Chinese had no desire to shield their own nationals from punishment, but they insisted that justice should take its course according to Chinese ideas and methods, which the foreigner looked upon as decidedly barbarous. When the Chinese insisted that they must apply the same law and procedure in the case of crimes committed by foreigners, trouble was bound to result. Until 1844 the American traders adopted the view that they must abide by Chinese law. At times, too, the English showed some tendency in this direction; but an opinion gained steadily in weight that whatever the merits or demerits of Chinese law might be in theory, its practice was such as no self-respecting Westerner could accept. The Chinese viewpoint is easily understood. Prior to the coming of the Westerners, China had had relations only with vassal states that always had acknowledged their inferiority. The advent of the Westerner had served merely to reinforce China's conception of her own superiority. The Portuguese traders were little better than pirates; the Spaniards were bloodthirsty; the Dutch were lawless; while the English, with little provocation, had, in the earliest days, used their cannon against Canton. It was little wonder then that the Chinese believed that the outer barbarians should be ruled as beasts rather than by the precepts of law and reason. It was less to be wondered that the barbarian disagreed with this view.

Another objection that the foreigner entertained arose from the acknowledged corruption of the Chinese courts. In decisions affecting foreigners money was more effective than evidence, and the average judge was disposed to give more credence to testimony of a civilized Chinese than to that of a foreign barbarian. Furthermore, torture was inevitably applied to a victim of the courts. This device, of course, was by no means unknown in Europe, but it appeared in more sinister guise when practiced by Orientals against members of the "white" races. But even more objectionable than these features of Chinese justice was the legal theory of responsibility.

The Yellow River bursts its banks; the governor of Honan begs the emperor to deprive him of his titles, since he is responsible. A son commits an offence; the father is held responsible. A bankrupt absconds; his family are held responsible in body and estate. A shopman strikes a blow and goes into hiding; his employer is held responsible for his appearance. A province is overrun by rebels; its governor is held responsible . . . The result is that nothing which occurs goes unpunished; if the guilty person cannot be found, convicted and punished, then the responsible person must accept the consequences—father, family, employer, village, magistrate, or viceroy.[4]

How such a theory worked at Canton may be readily surmised. If a Chinese killed a foreigner, he was apprehended and strangled. The man who paid the penalty might not be the one who committed the crime; but at least someone was strangled, and the law of responsibility was satisfied. If a foreigner killed a Chinese, there was no reason, in the Chinese view of things, why the same principle should not apply. If the culprit could not be found, then some other foreigner would do, and if no foreigner was surrendered, the entire trade might be threatened. This theory the English could not accept. They demanded, too, a fair trial for the accused.

One of the most infamous cases illustrative of this sort of thing was the Terranova affair. Terranova was an Italian seaman serving on the American ship *Emily* of Baltimore. In 1821 he was accused by the Chinese of having caused the death of a Chinese woman. Although the Americans were convinced of Terranova's innocence, and thoroughly aware that the Chinese would not give him a fair trial, they nevertheless yielded to Chinese demands. Terranova was tried on the *Emily* by Chinese authorities and found guilty. His surrender was demanded by the Chinese. The Americans hesitated. The Chinese stopped the trade and arrested the ship's Hong merchant, who owed considerable sums to Americans. This decided the matter: the trade was worth more than the life of a single seaman, so Terranova was surrendered and

---

[4] *Ibid.* p. 115.

later strangled. The financial credit of the American merchants had been saved.

A New Status for British Trade

The third factor contributing to the approaching crisis in Anglo-Chinese affairs had its inception in 1833 when by an act of Parliament the English East India Company lost the monopoly of British trade at Canton. Vital changes were to result. As long as the Company was established at Canton, it had controlled all British subjects there, had enjoyed a limited privilege to trade, and had, in large part, accepted to this end the regulations, irregular and arbitrary, imposed by the Chinese. In other words the British had acquiesced, until 1833, unwillingly but in the interest of trade, in China's assumptions of superiority. After 1833 all this was changed. Instead of British interests at Canton being represented by an agent of the Company, they were now in the hands of a direct representative of the British Crown. Lord William Napier, with two associates, was selected as chief superintendent of trade and was instructed to seek by all practical means to develop a "good and friendly understanding" with the Chinese. However, it was obvious from the first that Lord Napier, as representative of the Crown, would not accept the inferior status which the Chinese had accorded agents of the Company. He would demand recognition of equality; and this the Chinese with equal stubbornness would refuse.

The issue was soon drawn. Lord Napier proceeded to Canton from Macao without securing the consent of the Co-Hong. There he attempted to deal directly by "letter" with the Chinese officials. Naturally he failed, and for two reasons. From the Chinese view his communication should have been labeled a "petition" (the form used by vassal states), and furthermore it should have been transmitted through the Hong merchants. Being ordered to return to Macao, he at first refused. The Chinese thereupon ordered the English trade stopped. After an attempted show of force, which proved to be inadequate, Napier had no alternative save to comply; returning to Macao, he died there on October 11, 1834. His mission had failed completely. The Chinese had refused any concession toward equality and were more convinced than ever that in stoppage of the trade they possessed a weapon before which the British and other foreigners would always yield.

SELECTED BIBLIOGRAPHY

An Account of Lord Macartney's Embassy to China (London: 1797). Peter Auber, *China, an Outline of Its Government, Laws and Policy* . . . (London: 1834). Sir John Barrow, *Travels in China* (London: 1804). D. C. Boulger, *The History of China,* new and rev. ed., 2 vols. (London: 1898). *The Cambridge Modern History,* vol. II (New York: 1909) ch. 28, Sir E. M. Satow, "China and Her Intercourse with Western Powers, 1815-1871." J. M. Callahan, *American Relations in the Pacific and the Far East, 1784-1900* (Baltimore: 1901). Henri Cordier, "Américans et Français à Canton au XVIIIᵉ Siècle" in *Journal de la Société des Américanistes de Paris,* 1898. Henri Cordier, *Histoire Générale de la Chine,* 4 vols. (Paris: 1920-21). J. F. Davis, *Sketches of China,* 2 vols. (London: 1841). J. F. Davis, *The Chinese,* 2 vols. (London: 1836). Tyler Dennett, *Americans in Eastern Asia* (New York: 1922), chs. 1-4, present an excellent summary of American interests. F. R. Dulles, *The Old China Trade* (Boston: 1930) is a very readable account. E. J. Eitel, *Europe and China: the History of Hongkong to 1882* (London and Hongkong: 1895). W. H. Ellison, "American Beginnings in the Pacific and the Far East" in the *Proceedings* of the Pacific Coast Branch of the Am. Hist. Ass'n, 1927. J. B. Eames, *The English in China* . . . (London: 1909). R. B. Forbes, *Remarks on China and the China Trade* (Boston: 1844). J. W. Foster, *American Diplomacy in the Orient* (Boston: 1904), ch. 2. Rodney Gilbert, *The Unequal Treaties* (London: 1929), ch. 3, "The Foreigner's struggle for equality in China," 1800-1842. Rev. Charles Gutzlaff, *A Sketch of Chinese History,* 2 vols. (London: 1834), and by the same author, *Journal of Three*

Voyages Along the Coast of China (London: 1840). K. S. Latourette, "The History of Early Relations between the United States and China, 1784-1844," in *Transactions of the Connecticut Academy of Arts and Sciences,* vol. 22 (New Haven: 1917), a very scholarly account. By the same author, "Voyages of American Ships to China, 1784-1844," in *ibid.,* vol. 28 (New Haven: 1927). By the same author, *The Development of China,* 4th ed. rev. (Boston: 1929). Two works by R. M. Martin, *British Relations with the Chinese Empire* (London: 1832) and *China: Political, Commercial and Social,* 2 vols. (London: 1847). The two standard works by H. B. Morse, *The International Relations of the Chinese Empire* (London: 1910), vol. 1, ch. 4, "The Canton Factories and the Co-Hong," and *The Trade and Administration of China* (London: 1920) ch. 1, "Sketch of Chinese History," and ch. 9, "Foreign Trade." The most extensive of all the scholarly studies by H. B. Morse is his great 4-volume work, *The Chronicles of the East India Company Trading to China* (Cambridge: 1926). Mary A. Nourse, *The Four Hundred Million* (Indianapolis: 1935) ch. 15. D. E. Owen, *British Opium Policy in China and Japan* (New Haven: 1934). E. H. Parker, *China, Her History, Diplomacy, and Commerce* . . . 2nd ed. (New York: 1917), ch. 5. C. O. Paullin, *Diplomatic Negotiations of American Naval Officers, 1778-1883* (Baltimore: 1912) and by the same author, "Early Voyages of American Naval Vessels to the Orient" in *Proceedings of the United States Naval Institute,* vol. 36 (Annapolis: 1910). Josiah Quincy, *The Journals of Major Samuel Shaw, the First American Consul at Canton* . . . (Boston: 1847). Edmund Roberts, *Embassy to the Eastern Courts* (New York: 1837). A. J. Sargent, *Anglo-Chinese Commerce and Diplomacy* (London: 1907). William Speer, *China and the United States* (Cincinnati: 1870) ch. 11. Sir G. L. Staunton, *An Authentic Account of an Embassy from the King of Great Britain to the Emperor of China,* 2 vols. (London: 1797). A. W. Ward and G. P. Gooch, eds., *The Cambridge History of British Foreign Policy,* 3 vols. (Cambridge: 1922-23), vol. 2, ch. 5, "India and the Far East" (1833-49) by G. P. Moriarty. W. W. Willoughby, *Foreign Rights and Interests in China,* rev. ed., 2 vols. (Baltimore: 1927), vol. 2, ch. 43, opium in China. S. Wells Williams, *The Middle Kingdom,* rev. ed., 2 vols. (New York: 1907), ch. 21. S. Wells Williams, "Recollections of China Prior to 1840" in the *Journal of the North-China Branch of the Royal Asiatic Society,* new ser. no. 8 (Shanghai: 1874).

CHAPTER VI

The Opium War and the Settlement

THE British government was not prepared in 1834 to pursue an aggressive policy in China. Lord Napier's instructions from Lord Palmerston, Foreign Secretary in the ministry of Lord Grey, had emphasized the need of caution. Napier, however, had never interpreted this to imply submission on his part to diplomatic rebuffs or insults at the hands of the Chinese. Appealing vainly to the use of force when confronted with their refusal to deal with him as an equal, both he and his country suffered a diplomatic defeat. Napier's embarrassing position at Canton does not appear to have been thoroughly understood by his government. Shortly before his death he protested to London that the government had not given him the support necessary to preserve its dignity in the Far East. As a statement of fact this was undoubtedly true; but it fell on the unsympathetic ears of the Duke of Wellington (Foreign Secretary in the short ministry of Peel, 1834-1835), whose new instructions accused Napier of undue aggressiveness and affirmed the necessity of a policy of conciliation. Whatever the misunderstandings may have been between the home government and its representative in China, it was now clear that existing trade was not, for the moment at least, to be jeopardized by further demands for diplomatic equality. Results appeared to justify the method. For two years (1834-1836) the British bowed to Chinese assumptions of superiority, while the merchants continued to enjoy the profits of the trade.

This quiescent policy was not to be of long duration. With the assumption of office in 1835 by the Whig ministry of Lord

Melbourne, Palmerston again occupied the post of Foreign Secretary. Sir George Robinson, then Chief Superintendent of British trade at Canton, was replaced the following year by Captain Charles Elliot. Elliot's request to visit Canton, made upon his arrival at Macao *through the medium of the Hong merchants,* was granted. It seemed that he, too, was going to follow the quiescent policy; but such was not the case. Palmerston had determined upon a more aggressive attitude; he instructed Elliot to seek direct communication with Chinese officials upon terms of equality. The Chinese, of course, were equally determined to resist these advances. Palmerston, resorting to a demonstration of force, dispatched to the scene a small British squadron, which arrived off the China coast in July, 1838; the Chinese, however, declined to be impressed.

The Chinese Government and Opium

Coincident with these events there appeared among Chinese officialdom a surprising interest and activity relative to the opium traffic. It will be recalled that the Imperial ban on the importation of opium had, with the connivance of central and local officials, remained a dead letter for nearly forty years, while the merchants, both Chinese and foreign, waxed rich on the contraband trade. There was some discussion of legalizing the traffic in order that it might be controlled and made to yield a revenue; but instead the Peking government decided on its suppression. Responsibility for this decision must go almost exclusively to the Emperor Taokwang, for in 1838:

. . . only a few individuals high in the official world honestly desired to abolish the trade in opium; but among them was the emperor, who . . . in 1820, succeeded to a licentious and rotten court, a disorganized and corrupt government, and an empire honeycombed by rebellion and disorder.[1]

---

[1] Dr. H. B. Morse, *The International Relations of the Chinese Empire.* Longmans, Green & Company, London, 1910. Vol. I, p. 213.

Having enjoyed some success in reforming the metropolitan administration, he now sought to rid China of the illicit opium traffic. To this end he appointed in December, 1838, Lin Tse-su, viceroy of Hupeh and Hunan, as Imperial High Commissioner, with orders to proceed to Canton and to wipe out the opium trade. Lin reached his post in March, 1839, and within eight days had ordered the foreigners to surrender all opium in their possession, and to give bond, on penalty of death, that they would import no more. Chinese troops and war-junks surrounded the foreigners in their factories, and all trade was stopped.

The foreign merchants were now faced with a situation having no precedent. They were at last confronted by a Chinese official who was determined to enforce the law regardless of consequences. Convinced that this was the case, Captain Elliot ordered the surrender of all British-owned opium, amounting to more than 20,000 chests. To the astonishment of all, the surrendered opium, valued at about $10,000,000, was now mixed with lime and salt and poured into the river. The next question was the giving of bond that no further opium would be brought in the foreign ships. The Americans and other merchants agreed to this demand, but the British refused, and on Captain Elliot's orders (May 22, 1839) all British subjects left Canton for Macao. In July a Chinese was killed at Kowloon as a result of rioting between Chinese and British and American sailors. Fines and imprisonment were imposed on the sailors by Captain Elliot, but the Chinese were not satisfied, and Commissioner Lin demanded the surrender of the accused on the charge of murder. When this was refused, food supplies were cut off at Macao; the British were ordered to leave, and accordingly in August took refuge on the Chinese island of Hong Kong. The Chinese now attempted to seize the accused seamen, and in November a fleet of war-junks approached the two British naval ships at Hong Kong. The resulting engagement destroyed four of the Chinese vessels. Lin was more determined than ever. Since the British would neither give bond nor surrender the seamen, their entire trade would be stopped. A decree to this effect was issued by the commissioner on November 26, and two months later it was confirmed by Peking.

These developments finally forced the British government to adopt a specific and positive policy. The policy of "submission," which had been followed by the East India Company during its period of monopoly control, had give place, in the absence of positive instructions from London, to a so-called "quiescent" policy, which was really an absence of any definite line of action. Such was the state of affairs from 1834 to 1839, when the Chinese made an issue on the opium traffic. This forced the British to take up the larger question of diplomatic equality in official relations with Peking. The new British policy was formulated on February 20, 1840, in instructions from Lord Palmerston to Admiral George Elliot and Captain Charles Elliot, who were to act as British plenipotentiaries. A letter from Lord Palmerston to the "Minister of the Emperor of China" reviewed the difficulties which had arisen since 1833, and observed that "the Queen of Great Britain has sent a Naval and Military Force to the Coast of China, to demand from the Emperor satisfaction and redress for injuries inflicted by Chinese Authorities upon British subjects resident in China, and for insults offered by those same Authorities to the British Crown."

In brief, Lord Palmerston's argument was that Chinese action had been unjust and precipitate. She had permitted the law against the importation of opium "to sleep as a dead letter" for many years, so that "both Natives and Foreigners should be taught to consider it as of no effect." Then suddenly, "and without sufficient warning," it was enforced with the "utmost vigor and severity."

. . . it is notorious [said Palmerston] that for many years past, that importation has been connived at and permitted by the Chinese

Authorities at Canton; nay, more, that those Authorities, from the Governor downwards, have made an annual and considerable profit by taking money from Foreigners for the permission to import Opium; and of late the Chinese Authorities have gone so far in setting this Law at defiance, that Mandarin Boats were employed to bring opium to Canton from the Foreign Ships lying at Lintin.

Had China, Palmerston continued, "after giving due notice," seized the opium instead of seizing "peaceable British Merchants," the British government "would not have complained." But "the injuries" inflicted on British subjects and the "insults" offered to the British Crown could no longer be ignored. They would be met by demands:

First—The British government regarded the surrendered opium as a ransom exacted by the Chinese as the price of the lives of the superintendent and the imprisoned British merchants at Canton. For this surrendered property China would be required to pay at full value.

Second—Since successive British superintendents of trade at Canton had been subjected to indignities, China would be required to treat all British officials accredited to her "in a manner consistent with the usages of civilized Nations, and with the respect due to the Dignity of the British Crown." In a word, China was to bow to equality with the foreign barbarian.

Third—To insure the future security of British trade, and to protect British merchants from "the arbitrary caprice either of the Government at Peking, or its local Authorities at the Sea-Ports," China would be required to cede permanently an island off her coast, though this demand might be waived if an otherwise satisfactory treaty were granted.

War Becomes Inevitable

Naturally, the China that for so long had prescribed the terms on which western traders might visit her shores was in no sense prepared to accept Lord Palmerston's demands. War was now inevitable. Palmerston's letter was delivered to Chinese officials at the Pei-ho River in the north during August, 1840, but without result. A British squadron blockaded Canton, demanding payment for the opium; this not being forthcoming, it bombarded the city (January, 1841). This brought concessions from the local officials, and a draft treaty was signed, only to be disavowed later by both governments. Toward the close of winter hostilities were renewed, while Canton, which lay at the mercy of the British fleet, was ransomed for $6,000,000. At the same time Commissioner Lin, who alone among Chinese officialdom had attempted to enforce the Emperor's law, was rewarded with removal from office and exile to the distant lands of Ili. Meanwhile Sir Henry Pottinger had arrived in China as Britain's chief plenipotentiary. With more adequate forces he moved northward, meeting with no effective resistance. By October, 1841, the Chinese cities of Amoy, Tinghai, Chinhai, and Ningpo had all surrendered to British arms. In the following spring, when operations were renewed, other cities were taken: Chapu, Woosung, Shanghai, and Chinkiang. Early in August, 1842, Nanking, the southern capital, was at the mercy of the British fleet and the war was over.

The military defeat of China was decisive. A small but effective British force (never more than 7,000) had destroyed whatever remained of the Manchu military prestige. Yet it was merely the beginning of a century of defeat administered by western arms. In 1842 China was humbled; she was reduced to helplessness. Accordingly three imperial commissioners, officers of the highest rank, signed on the deck of a British battleship the treaty which legally at least ended the days of China's diplomatic superiority among the nations of the world.

The Treaty of Nanking

The Treaty of Nanking is one of the most important commitments ever signed by representatives of a Chinese government. Although its terms were broad, and required more explicit definition in later agreements, it was this treaty which set forth in the main the principles that were to govern China's relations with foreign states for the succeeding century. Most important of its provisions was that affirming the principle of diplomatic equality between China and Great Britain. The properly accredited officials of both states would henceforth conduct their business as equals, according to the standards of western diplomacy. The days when an envoy of the British Crown could be accorded the same treatment extended to a tribute-bearing vassal from Korea were gone. Likewise were gone the days when China might confine her foreign trade to Canton under the cramping monopoly of the Co-Hong. Instead, five ports were opened to British merchants: Canton, Amoy, Foochow, Ningpo, and Shanghai; and at these ports the British might trade in an open market with such Chinese as they chose. Furthermore these new ports would be open for residence to the foreign traders. Commerce would now be conducted under a fair and regular tariff of export and import duties: a conventional tariff, fixed by treaty, and thus subject to revision only upon the consent of Great Britain. By this one provision China signed away a large measure of fiscal independence, a not unimportant limitation upon her sovereignty. In addition, Great Britain received the Island of Hong Kong, which her merchants were soon to use as a base for their rapidly expanding commerce along the entire China coast. Finally China paid for the war with an indemnity totaling $21,000,000. Of this sum $12,000,000 was for the cost of the military and naval expedition; $3,000,000 was to cover debts due British merchants by members of the Co-Hong; while the remaining $6,000,000 was to pay for the surrendered opium, the "ransom" exacted by China for the lives of British traders who had been confined in the Canton factories in March, 1839. With the writer's interpretation of the war the Chinese have been loath to agree. To them opium has always appeared as the cause; hence the derogatory name—the Opium War— by which it is generally known. But to the critical student, whether western or Chinese, opium was no more than the immediate cause, the pretext. The real elements of conflict, intensified year after year in the decade which preceded the war, cannot be dismissed as a mere squabble of traders at Canton; rather must they be viewed as the impact, infinitely complex, of conflicting and antagonistic civilizations. For centuries China had regarded her own as the only respectable civilization. But when her high commissioners affixed their seals to the Treaty of Nanking, this view was no longer tenable. A scrap of paper, symbolic of the might of British arms and in the larger sense of the vitality of the western world, had destroyed it. It is not too much to say that here in 1842 are to be found the real origins of the Chinese revolution which in 1911 ushered in the so-called Republic, a revolution pre-eminently the product of the penetration of western ideas.

Since the Treaty of Nanking dealt in principles rather than details, its provisions were supplemented by further Chino-British negotiations completed during the succeeding year (1843) and embodied in the Treaty of the Bogue. Among the matters dealt with were trade regulations. A tariff schedule, promulgated at Nanking on July 22, also was incorporated. Quite as significant, too, was the inclusion of a somewhat incomplete provision for extraterritorial jurisdiction. In explanation of this, it is necessary to recall that for many years the foreign traders at Canton and Macao had been unanimous in condemning Chinese notions both of the theory and the practice of justice. At Macao the Portuguese had sought to retain exclusive jurisdiction over their nationals, and in 1833 an order-in-council legalized the establishment of a British court of criminal and admiralty jurisdiction at Canton under the control of the chief superintendent of British trade there. It was not surprising then that in 1843 the British demanded that British criminals be tried and punished according to British law administered by a British consular court. Here was a second major instance in which China signed away an essential element of sovereignty. Only in later years was she to know the dangers of harboring in her seaports a foreign population over which her courts had no power. Lastly, the negotiations of 1843 resulted in a treaty provision for most-favored-nation treatment. If China granted to other foreign states "additional privileges or immunities," they would be enjoyed likewise by British subjects. Since this clause was soon inserted in treaties subsequently negotiated by other powers, it will be seen that the rights of any one power consisted of all the privileges granted in all the treaties. Following the precedent of the British, other powers secured similar concessions in treaties negotiated between 1844 and 1847.

The United States acted first (July 3, 1844); then France (October 24, 1844); and finally Norway and Sweden (March 20, 1847). Belgium tried, but failed (1845). Of these various treaties, the most important was that secured by Caleb Cushing, representing the United States. Its real value can be best seen through a brief summary of developing American interests in China in the decades immediately preceding the so-called Opium War.

American Interests in China

The beginnings of American interest in Asia date from the close of the Revolutionary War. John Ledyard, an American who accompanied Captain Cook to the Pacific (1776-1781), was among the first to tell his countrymen how furs from the northwest coast of America might be sold in Canton at enormous profit. The result was the voyage of the *Empress of*

China, the first American ship to sail direct for Canton (1784). Other ships soon followed, and the trade prospered, for the American-China traders enjoyed numerous special favors from their government. Like the European traders of the same period, the Americans went to China to buy silk and tea; and they were confronted with the same problem of finding an outward cargo. At first there were miscellaneous cargoes which might be changed several times before the ship reached Canton. Later, furs, ginseng, and opium were prominent commodities; but the heavy balance which still remained could only be met by shipments of silver. There was no single route by which this early American trade with Asia was conducted. Ships which crossed the Atlantic might call at Mauritius. In India American vessels were received on a most-favored-nation basis. After 1800 they carried a conspicuous share of the trade along the coasts of Arabia and Persia, and there was some trade with Batavia. Those traders who carried furs to Canton made the voyage of course by way of the Horn and across the Pacific.

Between 1784 and 1811 Americans were the most serious rivals of the British in the export of tea from Canton. Their ships were neither so large nor so numerous as those of the East India Company, yet in the season of 1805-1806 they carried from Canton eleven million pounds of tea in thirty-seven ships, as against British exports of twenty-two million pounds in forty-nine ships. At Canton the position of the Americans contrasted somewhat with that of their British cousins. Though they traded with greater individual freedom, they possessed neither the credit nor the powerful backing of the English East India Company, nor did they enjoy any protection from their home government. The first official representative of the United States in China was Major Samuel Shaw, who, after making a number of voyages to the Far East, was named consul at Canton by the Continental Congress acting on the recommendation of John Jay. Since no salary was attached to the post, it may be assumed that the Congress regarded its position in the Orient as a matter of honor rather than of interest. And many more years were to pass before the American consulate in China could boast of an American interpreter. It would seem that the early American trader felt little need of official backing as long as he was permitted to trade on terms as favorable as those enjoyed (or at least tolerated) by his British rivals.

At Canton in the decade preceding the Anglo-Chinese war (1830-1840) American merchants observed with some anxiety the growing tension between the Chinese and the British. In the main the Americans could not but desire the same trading concessions sought by the English. Yet like many a British trader they feared that a policy of force, if unsuccessful, would destroy the existing trade. In May, 1839, when Commissioner Lin had forced the surrender of the foreign-owned opium, a group of American merchants at Canton memorialized their government for a commercial agent to negotiate a treaty and a naval force to protect their persons and property. Although expressing no sympathy with the opium traffic, they could find no excuse for the "robbery" committed on the British. They foresaw that England would use armed force, and "it is our belief that this is necessary." They recommended that the government of the United States take joint action with such powers as England, France, and Holland to secure: (1) resident ministers at Peking; (2) a fixed tariff on exports and imports; (3) the liberty of trading at ports other than Canton; and (4) Chinese assent to the principle that, until their laws are made known and recognized, punishment for offenses committed by foreigners against Chinese or others shall not be greater than is applicable to a like offense by the laws of the United States or England. It was the belief of these American traders that the appearance of an American, British, and French fleet in Chinese waters would effect the necessary revision in the system of trade "without bloodshed." Britain, they believed, would use armed force, and this they regarded as necessary or "there will be no dealing with the Chinese."[2]

In the meantime Americans at Canton had turned over their Indian opium to Captain Elliot for surrender to the Chinese; but when the English withdrew to Macao and later to Hong Kong, the Americans remained at Canton (against the protests of Captain Elliot), doing a most lucrative business in carrying from Hong Kong cargo after cargo of British goods which could not enter the river in British ships.

The events of 1839 and 1840 served, for the first time, effectively to focus American public attention upon the China trade. Merchants of the Atlantic seaboard became apprehensive lest their interests be adversely affected by British policy. Reports of American missionaries lent color to the popular notion that England sought only to force opium on an innocent and helpless China. In fact the whole Anglo-Chinese struggle was soon seized upon as a convenient medium through which Americans might express their traditional anti-British prejudices.

Thus began the myth in the United States, at a time when the Americans at Canton were riding rough-shod over Commissioner Lin's embargo on English trade, and smuggling the English cargoes for the season, both in and out of the port, that the American in China was an angel of light. This complacency is entirely comparable with the contemporaneous misrepresentations in England of Chinese ethics and foreign policy.[3]

The Mission of Caleb Cushing

Happily there were some few well-informed Americans, of whom John Quincy Adams was one, who would not permit prejudice to run riot with the facts. But such was the popular hatred of England, and the desire to assume the moral role, that when Adams, in December, 1841, delivered an address in

[2] U. S., H. doc. 40, 26-1. Memorial dated Canton, May 25, 1839.

[3] Tyler Dennett, *Americans in Eastern Asia*. The Macmillan Company, New York, 1922. p. 105.

which he pointed to China's refusal to recognize the principle of equality among states as the real cause of the war, he could find no public support, and the pious editor of the *North American Review* refused to print the address. Later the entire question was placed before Congress on December 30, 1842, in a special message by President Tyler, calling for appointment of a resident commissioner in China to care for the commercial and diplomatic affairs of the United States. This post was conferred upon Caleb Cushing, of Massachusetts, a brilliant lawyer, a member of the Committee on Foreign Affairs, and an intimate friend of President Tyler.

The instructions which Cushing received from Webster, then Secretary of State, were the first major and official statements of United States policy toward China. The principal objective, the very core of American policy, has not changed from that day to the present time. Cushing was to secure the entry of American ships and cargoes, on terms as favorable as those enjoyed by the English, into the ports opened to British trade by the Treaty of Nanking. In securing this objective he was to employ the utmost tact, and to impress the Chinese with the peaceful character of his mission. If possible, he was to reach the Emperor at Peking, but in no case was he to perform the kowtow. The instructions concluded with these words:

Finally, you will signify, in decided terms and a positive manner, that the Government of the United States would find it impossible to remain on terms of friendship and regard with the Emperor, if greater privileges or commercial facilities should be allowed to the subjects of any other Government than should be granted to the citizens of the United States.

Cushing reached Macao on February 24, 1844, where he established himself with some pomp and ceremony. His arrival and the splendor of his mission created considerable amusement among the British, who wondered what Mr. Cushing might do that had not already been done. And indeed there was some point to this question. The British had fought the war; they had won the Treaty of Nanking and the supplementary Treaty of the Bogue; and the Chinese had already opened the trade at the new treaty ports to all foreigners. The American merchants themselves entertained some fears as to Cushing's intentions, and one of them wrote from Canton:

> As Americans we are now on the very best terms possible with the Chinese; and as the only connection we want with China is a commercial one, I cannot see what Mr. Cushing expects to do.

Neither was Cushing's arrival agreeable to the Chinese. Since the Americans were interested only in commerce, the Chinese could see no need for a treaty. But Cushing's threat to proceed to Peking brought the speedy appointment and the arrival of an Imperial commissioner at Macao, where a treaty was soon signed. In principle (save for the indemnity and the cession of territory), the American treaty followed the policy already laid down in the two British treaties. In some respects it was decidedly superior, for the Americans enjoyed the advantage of the British experience. Perhaps the most important contribution of Cushing's treaty was its clear statement on extraterritoriality and the extension of the principle to civil cases. It was a decided improvement over the statement which had appeared in the British trade regulations of 1843. This, together with the emphatic statement of most-favored-nation treatment, was to form the permanent basis of American policy in China.

Thus by 1844 an American diplomat had given the finishing touches to the commercial policy of the West. In the pursuit of this policy England had fought the Chinese. For this, in America, she had reaped the odious charge of aggression, and the stigma of attempting to force opium on the Oriental. The average American conceived his own country to be quite free of such iniquities. Yet curiously he found no inconsistency in the eagerness of his government to win for Americans every commercial and diplomatic advantage extracted from China by

British imperialists. His complacent piety blinded him to the fact that "it became ingloriously, yet very profitably, the rôle of the United States pacifically to follow England to China in the wake of war, and to profit greatly by the victories of British arms." [4]

SELECTED BIBLIOGRAPHY

The American Secretaries of State and Their Diplomacy, S. F. Bemis, ed., 10 vols. (New York: 1927-29). J. O. P. Bland, and E. Backhouse, *Annals and Memoirs of the Court of Peking* (London: 1914). Sih-Gung Cheng, *Modern China* (Oxford: 1919), ch. 6 on extraterritoriality. Chinese Maritime Customs, *Treaties, Conventions, etc. between China and Foreign States,* 2 vols. (Shanghai: 1917). J. F. Davis, *China During the War and Since the Peace* (London: 1852). Tyler Dennett, *Americans in Eastern Asia* (New York: 1922), chs. 5-8, gives an excellent summary of the relations of the Americans to the Anglo-Chinese War, the American share in the opium trade, the preparations for the Cushing mission, and the policy of Cushing. John W. Foster, *American Diplomacy in the Orient* (Boston: 1903), ch. 3, the first Chinese treaties. C. M. Fuess, *The Life of Caleb Cushing,* 2 vols. (New York: 1923). Rodney Gilbert, *The Unequal Treaties* (London: 1929), ch. 4, the first "unequal treaties." Philip Joseph, *Foreign Diplomacy in China, 1894-1900* (London: 1928) devotes ch. 1 to the early treaties with foreign powers—an excellent study. G. W. Keeton, *The Development of Extraterritoriality in China,* 2 vols. (London: 1928). P. C. Kuo, *A Critical Study of the First Anglo-Chinese War* (Shanghai: 1935), one of the best recent studies. L. A. Lyall, *China* (New York: 1934), ch. 7, the "First War between England and China." For the treaties see Hunter Miller, ed., *Treaties and other International Acts of the United States of America* (Washington: 1931———) vol. 4, 1835-46. It is still difficult to improve on H. B. Morse, *The International Relations of the Chinese Empire,* vol. 1 (London: 1910), chs. 10-11, "War and Negotiations" and "The First Treaty Settlement." V. S. Phen, "The Most-Favored-Nation Clause in China's Treaties" in *The Chinese Social and Political Science Review,* Oct. 1924. A. J. Sargent, *Anglo-Chinese Commerce and Diplomacy* (London: 1907). George N. Steiger, *China and the Occident* (New Haven:

---

[4] *Ibid.* p. 159.

1927), chs. 1-2, the opening of China. Wei Yuan, *Chinese Account of the Opium War,* E. H. Parker trans. (Shanghai: 1888). E. T. Williams, *China Yesterday and To-Day* (New York: 1929), chs. 18-19, early foreign intercourse and the first foreign wars. W. W. Willoughby, *Foreign Rights and Interests in China,* 2 vols., rev. ed. (Baltimore: 1927) vol. 1, ch. 2, most-favored-nation clauses in the China treaties. S. W. Williams, *The Middle Kingdom,* rev. ed., 2 vols. (New York: 1907), chs. 22-23.

CHAPTER VII

The Treaties on Trial

WHEN the struggle commonly called the Opium War was ended, when the British had tucked away their two treaties (Nanking, 1842, and the Bogue, 1843), and when Mr. Cushing had sailed away with his treaty (1844), relations between China and the West had been placed, as far as treaties and legalities were concerned, on an entirely new basis. Between 1839 and 1843 the British, and in the larger sense the western world, had taught the Chinese what was considered to be a well-deserved lesson. A handful of British troops and a few ships had revealed how worthless was the Manchu bannerman as a soldier, had destroyed the monopoly of the Co-Hong, had opened new ports to foreign trade, had secured extraterritorial rights for the foreigner, and finally, and most significantly, had forced the proud and exclusive Chinese (Manchu) Court to deal diplomatically, as an equal, with the detested barbarian. To the foreigner all this seemed clear and decisive; to the Chinese it was quite otherwise, and naturally so. Excepting a few Chinese merchants, officials, and bannermen in a few coast towns, the British war had not touched China. A small group in her official hierarchy recognized what it considered as a temporary inability of China to resist British arms, and the Emperor accepted this verdict. Accordingly, China signed the treaties, not because she was converted to the system for which those treaties stood, but purely from necessity. In a still broader sense, the great bulk of the Chinese people had, as yet, no knowledge of and no contact with the foreigner. These people were dominated by the small but all-powerful literati who monopolized government office, and whose minds had been sealed, by the dead hand of the Confucian system and training, against all that was new or irregular.

These things being so, it was but natural that China should seek by every available means to nullify a treaty settlement that she regarded as destructive of every principle on which her assumptions of national superiority were based. To Westerners, this attitude in itself was justification for a second war. But there were other reasons for friction. The first treaties were experimental. As the years passed, their weaknesses and their deficiencies became more obvious; and, in the movement to revise and supplement what had already been won, the British again assumed leadership. By 1856 the issue was clearly drawn. The Chinese were not yet convinced that the new order in international affairs must be accepted, while the British, now joined by the French, were determined not only to enforce existing treaties, but also to supplement and expand their terms. In fact, the second European, or the *Arrow* War (1857-1858), as it is frequently called, was a direct product of these clashing attitudes toward existing treaties. In order then to see more clearly how this struggle developed, it will be necessary to review in some detail specific issues arising between the Chinese and the foreigners between the years 1844 and 1856.

The Treaty of Nanking, as the reader is already aware, effected revolutionary changes in the commercial relations of China and the West. Of these changes, the most conspicuous was the opening to foreign trade of the four new treaty ports: Shanghai, Ningpo, Foochow, and Amoy. Since it was at these ports that the foreigner was to have access to the markets of China, and since it was here that he would experience his most intimate contacts with the Chinese, some analysis of conditions at the ports is desirable. For this purpose the two ports of Shanghai and Canton offer significant contrasts.

The Unique Position of Shanghai

Shanghai, the most northerly of the five ports, was opened to foreign trade as a treaty port on November 17, 1843. Situated on the Woosung River about twelve miles from where it joins the Yangtze, and with a population of some 270,000, it was already an important center of China's inland and coasting trade, and gave prophetic promise of becoming the principal port in China's exports of silk and tea. The origin and character of the first foreign "settlement" at Shanghai, which has developed since into the greatest of Chinese seaports, is thus a matter of uncommon interest.

In Canton, and in some of the chief Treaty Ports opened for foreign trade under later treaties, the British Sovereign and other Foreign Powers obtained from the Chinese Emperor areas of land, known as "Concessions," as sites for the trading establishments and residences of their subjects. These concession areas were leased by the Chinese Government to the Foreign Power concerned, which then proceeded to lay out the land leased in suitable lots, and granted leases of these lots for long terms to its own subjects, and also in some cases to other foreigners. Thus at Canton there are the British and French Concessions on Shameen; at Tientsin there were at one time no less than eight separate foreign Concessions; and at Hankow five. In these ports the foreign community of each Concession set up, under the authority of the Foreign Power holding the Concession, its own municipal government, presided over by its own Consul, and thus there came into existence, in contiguous Concession areas, a number of separate municipal governments, each exercising independent authority.

But this was not the system adopted at Shanghai. Some attempt appears to have been made by the [British] Consul, Captain Balfour, to obtain from the Chinese Government a grant or lease of a defined area, in which Crown leases could subsequently be issued to British subjects, but, in view of the Taotai's objections to this proposal, the British authorities were content to enter into an agreement with the Chinese authorities as to the setting apart of an area in which British subjects might acquire land from Chinese owners. It was arranged that a British purchaser of land, as soon as he had entered into an agreement with a Chinese owner, should report his agreement to the British Consul, who, in turn, reported it to the Taotai, and that the Taotai should issue to the British subject concerned, through his Consul, a title in the form of a perpetual lease, under which a small annual rent was reserved for payment to the Chinese authorities, the theory being that, as all the land in China belonged to the Emperor, there could be no out-and-out sale of Chinese land to a foreigner, and that foreigners, instead of becoming owners, must be content to be lessees.[1]

In the case of Shanghai, the settlement was at first exclusively British, and foreigners of other nationalities, in order to acquire land, secured consent of the British Consul. This procedure proved objectionable, in particular to the Americans, and the right of all foreigners to lease land within the settlement and to register such land at their own consulates was soon recognized. In this manner there grew up a system whereby each foreign consul exercised jurisdiction over his own nationals, and at the same time participated in general supervision of settlement affairs. For a brief period separate American and French settlements existed at Shanghai, but in 1863 the American and the British were united to form an international settlement with a single municipal government. The French area continued to remain separate.

When the Shanghai settlement was first established, it was supposed that the area would be inhabited exclusively by foreigners. For some eight years such was the case. In 1853 there were only five hundred Chinese residents, most of whom were servants or shopkeepers supplying the needs of the two-hundred-odd foreign residents. In this year, however, Chinese authority in areas adjacent to the settlement having broken down completely as a result of rebellions and civil war, the foreign area was soon swarming with homeless and often desti-

---

[1] *Report of the Hon. Mr. Justice Feetham, C.M.G. to the Shanghai Municipal Council,* 4 vols. Shanghai, 1931-1932. Vol. I, p. 27. The taotai, an official of the Chinese central government, was the administrative official of a district known as a "circuit," and in this case was also superintendent of customs of the province in which Shanghai was situated.

tute Chinese refugees. By 1854 the Chinese population of the settlement exceeded 20,000. In this manner the whole character of the settlement was changed: a small group of foreign merchants (renters of settlement land) governed through their municipal organization a population predominantly Chinese. The origin of this foreign municipal control is not without interest.

In 1853 the Chinese authorities were unable to afford protection to the Settlement against the dangers resulting from rebellion and civil war, and the Foreign Powers concerned had to come to the rescue of the Settlement community, which had also taken such measures as its limited resources permitted for the purpose of its own protection. This emergency, and the sudden influx of Chinese refugees, had revealed to the inhabitants of the Settlement their weakness so long as they remained an unorganised community consisting of groups of foreigners belonging to different nations, each living under their own laws and subject to the jurisdiction of their own Consuls. They found themselves in need both of organised provision for protection against dangers from without, and of improved machinery for purposes of internal administration, but before these needs could be effectively met it was necessary for the community to acquire some degree of unity under a constitution which would be accepted as binding on all its members.[2]

Accordingly in 1854 the foreign settlement community provided itself with an elected representative government, a common police force, and adequate powers of taxation.

The development of this new international municipality beyond the walls of the old Chinese city of Shanghai was exclusively a product of the foreigners' trade. Within a year after the opening of the port, eleven foreign firms, English and American, were represented at Shanghai by a foreign population of twenty-six persons. Ten years later this population exceeded two hundred. Here traders were no longer hampered by such monopolistic agencies as the Co-Hong. There was business and opportunity for all. In 1844, forty-four foreign

<hr/>

[2] *Ibid.* Vol. I, pp. 35-36.

ships of a total tonnage of more than 8,000 entered Shanghai. Eight years later the number of ships was 182, with a tonnage of 78,000, while in 1855, 437 ships entered, their tonnage totaling 157,000. The value of exports from Shanghai, which in 1846 was $7,000,000, had increased by 1853 to $23,000,000. In fact, such was the prosperity of the port that between 1846 and 1852, its share in China's total export trade rose from one seventh to considerably more than one half. A number of factors contributed to this end, of which two may be mentioned. Shanghai lay on the border of the largest and finest silk-producing area in China, and soon predominated over all other ports in the export of silk. Furthermore, at Shanghai the initial relationship between the foreign traders and the Chinese was devoid of the unhappy memories so closely associated with the earlier trade at Canton.

During 1843 and 1844 Foochow, Ningpo, and Amoy, the remaining new ports designated by the Treaty of Nanking, were also opened to foreign commerce. Contrary to general expectations, their trade grew but slowly, and thus their position in China's newly developing relations with the West was not one of great importance. At Canton, however, the situation was quite otherwise.

Chinese Resistance at Canton

Canton, it will be recalled, had, until 1842, enjoyed a monopoly of the foreign trade. Here the foreign traders and the Chinese had accumulated fortunes; but here, too, had also arisen the grievances, real or imaginary, and the hatreds which had finally produced war. At Canton the foreigner had been subjected to "insults" by high-handed Chinese officials. At Canton these same officials had been forced to bow to the power of British guns. Now that the war was over, it was but human for the British and other foreigners to assert their newly won equality; and perhaps no less human for the Chinese to seek evasion. The issue was soon drawn. No sooner had the city been opened in its new status as a treaty port (1843) than the intensity of its antiforeign attitude became apparent. The foreigners wished to escape from the cramped and unhealthy quarters of the old factory grounds outside the walled city, but of this the Chinese would not hear. Their hostility increased. As proof of their national equality, the British demanded the right of entry to the walled town. This resulted only in inflaming the populace further. The local authorities asserting that they could neither control public sentiment nor protect foreigners in the crowded streets of the city, it was agreed, in 1846, to postpone indefinitely the "opening" of the city. Numerous attacks on foreigners in the neighborhood of Canton had already occurred, and when in 1847 a group including several Englishmen and an American was stoned at a nearby village a British fleet attacked the Bogue Forts, commanding the approach to Canton, while the city itself lay at the mercy of British guns. In these circumstances the Viceroy agreed to "open" the walled city in April, 1849, but his decision was not approved by the Emperor despite the warnings of Lord Palmerston. For a time at least, victory was with the Chinese; but a first cause had thereby been created for another European war.

The Obligations of Extraterritoriality

For this unhappy situation thus developed at Canton, both foreigners and Chinese were responsible. The latter had no legal basis for their unrestrained hostility to the foreigners; neither had the former any treaty basis for claiming entry into the walled city. In other respects, too, the official attitude of many of the foreign powers left much to be desired. In extraterritoriality the foreign states had won a right of the greatest consequence; yet for many years after 1843 they were guilty of a shameful disregard of their responsibilities. To this statement the British offer the only exception. Under grants of extraterritorial jurisdiction, China surrendered the right to punish foreigners guilty of crimes upon her soil. Such culprits were subject only to the laws of their own nation as administered in a consular court. It was therefore the duty of the treaty powers not only to establish courts at the open ports, but also to provide jails. In the years prior to the second European war (1857) Great Britain alone took adequate steps to meet this need. A British criminal court, provided for in 1833, functioned at Canton after 1839. An act of the British Parliament in 1843 authorized British legal jurisdiction on foreign soil, and under this act machinery was set up for the adminstration of extraterritoriality in China, including provision for jails. Not until 1848 did the United States by Congressional act provide for American consular courts, and even then no provision was made for the maintenance of jails. Habitual American criminals in the China ports could be confined only on a national ship, or, as frequently happened, by courtesy in a British jail. As late as 1858 American criminals were released from the British jail in Shanghai because the American consul had no funds to meet jail expenses. Two years later the United States passed its first appropriation for consular jails in China.

Quite as objectionable, from the standpoint of justice, was the fact that, with the exception of Great Britain, most of the early foreign consuls were resident merchants whose consular duties were secondary to their private business interests. To vest such persons with judicial authority was at best a questionable procedure. The Chinese soon learned that it was virtually impossible to secure the conviction of a foreigner who had harmed one of their countrymen. It is little wonder that they were slow to grasp the "superior" virtues of western codes and procedures.

If there was little justice in the early consular courts, there was less among the foreigners themselves. There were three groups in the foreign population that seeped into the treaty ports after 1842: merchants, missionaries, and seamen. The name "seaman" covered a multitude of sins, for the crews of early China ships carried a motley assortment of adventurers, soldiers of fortune, and criminals. There on Chinese soil, yet beyond the reach of her laws, and subject only to the inadequate control of merchant consuls, these brigands served as advance agents of a type of western culture which no decent Chinese could respect.

The Coolie Trade

It was likewise in these middle years of the century that the coolie trade was matured and refined in a species of frightfulness unsurpassed in the most prosperous years of slave traffic. The gradual liberation of black slaves in the western world turned the attention of planters, particularly in Cuba and Peru, to alternative sources of cheap, steady, and effective labor. As early as 1839 there was some emigration of British East Indians to British Guiana; but flagrant iniquities associated with this trade soon brought its stoppage by the British government. Nevertheless the value of coolie labor had been proved, and a new source was found in China. Just when the first shipments of Chinese coolies occurred is uncertain; but it is clear that by 1847 the trade was developing rapidly. Nominally, the coolies migrated as voluntary contract laborers committed to work for a term of years under specified conditions contained in the contract. In reality the migration was only partly voluntary, for thousands of coolies were kidnaped by Chinese and by foreigners alike. Furthermore, once they were confined on board the coolie ships, their contracts were valueless. With few, if any, exceptions the ships themselves were floating hells in which the wretched victims festered and often died before reaching American shores.

In a sense the coolie traffic was more inhumane than the slave trade. The slave, having no prospect of freedom, entertained little hope of a better life. The coolies, on the contrary, were beguiled with the promise of gainful labor and eventual return to their native land with the profits of their toil. When, however, word of the shameful violation of contracts reached China, the recruiting of coolies became more and more difficult, while the means employed by recruiting agents grew even more unscrupulous.

The first task of the coolie was to survive the long trans-pacific voyage. Cramped within the narrow and sweltering inner decks of the coolie ship, with inadequate ventilation, unwholesome food and water, and rarely allowed exercise, he fell an easy victim to disease. To save food and water, and to protect those who were still sound, these victims were often thrown overboard while still alive. The ships that sailed from Hong Kong were probably under stricter supervision than those from any other port, yet of the 23,928 coolies shipped from this port between 1847 and 1857, bound for Cuba, more than 3,000 died on the voyage.

Those who survived had little to anticipate in their new home. Both in Cuba and Peru the coolies, with their contracts, were sold at auction. Some found decent owners, but the majority were worked under conditions which made death a welcome reward. So loathsome indeed had the traffic become that no government retaining a vestige of honor could afford to remain indifferent. The initiative in curbing the trade came from the British and the Americans. The English Passenger Act (1855), which restrained some of the worst abuses, served only to concentrate the coolie business at the Portuguese town of Macao. In the same year the Chinese Emperor by imperial edict forbade emigration of contract laborers. Concurrently, representatives of the United States in China sought legislation to prohibit American participation. In 1856 Dr. Peter Parker (Commissioner of the United States in China) warned Americans that they would forfeit the protection of their government in any difficulties arising from the coolie trade. In 1860 a report laid before the American Congress showed that foreigners were chartering American vessels and that the coolie trade was thus being thrown to an alarming degree into American hands. Early in 1862 the Congress, despite its preoccupation with civil war, passed an act which effectively barred its citizens and ships from the traffic.

Unfortunately most of the powers remained indifferent. In 1866 France blocked the adoption of rules which would have controlled the trade effectively. Meanwhile the United States continued its efforts toward complete suppression, Secretary of State Seward instructing Mr. Burlingame (American Minister in China, 1867) "to make use of all authority, power and influence at your command, toward preventing and discouraging the carrying on of the traffic." Finally in 1874, after the United States and Great Britain jointly had condemned Portugal for harboring and perpetuating the evil at Macao, the trade was prohibited there.

It is quite true that in the years following the Nanking settlement foreigners might claim justly that China had failed in observance of the treaties; but these shortcomings appear as trifles when compared with the profits in human blood extracted by western planters, shipowners, and captains through the lucrative coolie trade.

Another feature of Chino-foreign relations was known as convoying. The southern coasts of China were infested with native pirates who preyed mercilessly on the coasting trade of their fellow countrymen. In this situation, the foreigners, and in particular the Portuguese, discovered a new road to profits. With well-armed foreign ships they offered (for a generous monetary consideration) their services as convoys. At first the charges were reasonable, and the Chinese junk owners willingly accepted the protection. Later, their greed excited, the Portuguese raised their charges to excessive heights and *forced* the junk owners to engage their services. Those who refused lost their ships and frequently suffered the most revolting deaths at the hands of these Portuguese freebooters.

So desperate was the plight of the Chinese traders that by 1857 they had appealed to their own pirates for protection. In the conflicts that ensued between Chinese pirates and the Portuguese brigand-convoys the latter were defeated, but the evils of the convoy system lingered for many years.

A further blot on the record of Westerners in these years was the opium trade, which continued to grow and to prosper. Although the opium question was the occasion if not the cause of the first Chino-British war, the treaties had scrupulously avoided the subject. Thus, while by the law of China opium importation was still prohibited, foreigners and Chinese conspired to flood the ever-growing market with this contraband and destructive drug. Between 1840 and 1858 it is estimated that the annual importation had increased almost three hundred per cent, and, as previously, most of the opium came from India. Its effects on the Chinese were devastating; but as long as their government could not or would not enforce its laws, there was little hope that the foreigners would forego a trade so profitable.

Demands for Treaty Revision

In summary it may be said that by 1854 the foreigner's abuse of extraterritoriality, his traffic in coolies, his crimes committed in the name of convoying, his profits in opium, and his use of the gunboat policy at Canton had served to reinforce the traditional view of the Chinese that the foreign barbarian was an uncouth and troublesome creature with whom he should have as few dealings as possible. Unhappily for China, the view entertained by the troublesome foreigner himself was just the reverse, for he was now intent on making more intimate and inclusive the treaty relations established in 1842. In the American and French treaties of 1844 provision had been made for revision after twelve years, and the British claimed this same privilege on the basis of most-favored-nation treatment.

This made the Treaty of Nanking revisable in 1854. The British and other foreigners alike were no longer content with existing treaty rights (even had China observed them); in addition to these, they now sought further privileges. The full scope of Britain's policy to revise her China treaties was set forth in instructions from Lord Clarendon to Sir John Bowring (February 13, 1854). Bowring, while insisting on China's recognition of the *right* of immediate revision, was nevertheless allowed discretion, in view of China's domestic chaos resulting from the Taiping Rebellion, to delay the actual work of revision. Meanwhile he was to seek co-operation with the Americans and the French, whose treaties would become revisable in 1856. Specifically, he was to seek "access generally to the whole interior of the Chinese Empire as well as to the cities on the coast: or failing this, . . . free navigation of the Yangtze Kiang and access to the cities on its banks up to Nanking. . . ." He was to effect legalization of the opium trade; to seek abolition of internal transit duties on goods imported from foreign countries or purchased for exportation to foreign countries; to secure effectual suppression of piracy on the China coast; and to obtain regulation of the emigration of Chinese laborers. In addition, the British government desired "the permanent and honourable residence at the Court of Peking of a Representative of the British Crown" or provision for direct and unobstructed correspondence with that government; while in the provinces there was to be no obstacle to "ready personal intercourse" between the British representative and the high local authorities. Lastly, in any difficulties of interpretation connected with the revised treaty, the English text alone would be regarded as official.

In part at least, the explanation of this extensive British program of treaty revision may be traced to China's official attitude since 1844 toward the representatives of the foreign governments. In this period, as formerly, it was the Chinese desire to keep the foreigner as far removed from Peking as possible. To accomplish this end, the Canton viceroy was entrusted with the office of high commissioner for Foreign Affairs, and with him alone foreigners were expected to deal. In 1848 John W. Davis, the American commissioner, after great difficulty, secured an interview with the high commissioner for the purpose of presenting his credentials. He was treated "with extreme rudeness" both by the viceroy and also by the governor. Four years later this same governor (Yeh Ming-chin) became high commissioner, and from this time "the practice of ignoring the foreign representatives became a part of the settled policy of the Chinese government." [3]

A French representative remained at Macao fifteen months awaiting vainly a personal interview. Of the various successors to follow Mr. Davis as American representative in the period to 1855, none succeeded in securing an interview. The high commissioner was always "too busy," and in any event would have to await the arrival of "an auspicious day," which never came. Two American commissioners (Humphrey Marshall and Robert McLane) proceeded to Nanking in the hope of making direct contact with officials, only to be referred back to Canton. The British considered themselves subject to an even greater grievance in China's persistent refusal to permit foreigners within the walled city of Canton. Nevertheless, the English government had adopted in the main a relatively mild policy after 1843. It had failed to gain the right of admittance to Canton, this failure being hailed with delight by the anti-foreign Canton populace. The foreigners could also observe that Kiying, who had negotiated the American treaty with Cushing (1844), and who alone of all high Chinese officials had made a serious effort to carry out the treaties, had been degraded by the Chinese throne; while Commissioner Yeh, who played to the popular sentiments of the Canton mob, was applauded alike by the populace and by the Emperor.

---

[3] Dr. H. B. Morse, *The International Relations of the Chinese Empire.* Longmans, Green & Company, London, 1910. Vol. I, p. 411.

The Gunboat Philosophy

Thus in 1854 when Clarendon disclosed British policy to Bowring, the foreigner in China was of a mind not only to extend his commercial rights but also to convert China, forcibly if necessary, to western codes of diplomacy. Nevertheless, the British government was not as yet committed to a policy of war. There was to be no precipitate action. England hoped for a co-operative policy in which France and the United States would join. In China, Great Britain had already made friendly gestures toward the United States. She had let it be known that she sought no exclusive privileges for herself, and, in particular, that she had conceded every claim of Americans to equal rights in the new foreign settlement in Shanghai.

Direct overtures for a three-power alliance (France, Great Britain, and the United States) to effect revision of the treaties were made by the British Ambassador, Lord Napier, to Secretary of State Cass in March, 1857. By this time both England and France had concluded that the further opening of China to foreign trade could be effected only by war; but to this course neither Buchanan nor Cass would agree, despite the fact that American grievances against China were of a most serious character. As one historian has said:

The President could have laid before Congress the facts that China had failed to observe the stipulations of the Treaty of Wanghia (1844). He could have pointed out that the Government of China had failed to protect the lives and property of American citizens in China and that failing in that, China had evaded payment of claims for reparation. Diplomatic correspondence had been impeded, interviews with the Imperial Commissioner at Canton, and with the Governor General at Foochow had been repelled, and a letter of President Pierce to the Emperor of China had been treated with indignity, having been returned to the commissioner without answer, and with broken seals. On the basis of these facts President Buchanan might have asked Congress to authorize a military and naval expedition to China to demand reparations. Had Congress yielded to this request he might have sought its further approval for the joint expedition with Great Britain and France. Two American commissioners in China had recommended such a course. Lord Napier urged it. The American residents in China, for the most part, would have approved. But to neither of these propositions was it even remotely possible that Congress would have given its assent. Public opinion would have seen in them only a trick by which England was seeking the aid of the United States in her efforts to secure the legalization of the opium trade.[4]

With these facts before it, the American administration declined the British proposal. Considerations of policy dictated that there should be no alliance with England. Nevertheless, the importance of the matter required that the United States should be represented ably in China if and when Great Britain again resorted to a policy of force. The administration made haste, then, to appoint William B. Reed as envoy extraordinary and minister plenipotentiary to China.

It will be recalled that whereas in 1854 the instructions received by Sir John Bowring had required him to pursue a cautious policy, in 1857 both England and France had determined on a policy of force. Fortunately for these European imperialists, incidents were not lacking which could be used to justify warlike measures.

France Finds a Pretext

The reader is already aware of the disregard by some members of the Catholic priesthood of the laws of the heathen lands which they entered. Already in earlier times this intractable attitude had been responsible for their expulsion from both Japan and China. Although the first treaty settlement (1842-1844) stipulated that foreigners should remain close to the treaty ports, a French priest, Father Auguste Chapdelaine, in 1853 entered Kwangsi Province. His work was not interfered

---

[4] Tyler Dennett, *Americans in Eastern Asia.* The Macmillan Company, New York, 1922. pp. 303-304.

with until February, 1856, when he and some of his converts were arrested by a Chinese magistrate on a charge that they were rebels. This charge was a natural one, for Kwangsi had witnessed the beginnings of the Taiping Rebellion, which in its origins had a strong Christian flavor. Since the priest had violated both the express stipulations of the treaty and the law of China that forbade persons from entering the country to propagate religion, and in view of the Christian character of the Taipings, whose movements were now widespread in the south, it is not surprising that he and two of his Chinese converts, after being tortured, were put to death. But, unhappily for the Chinese, the execution of the priests violated the extra-territorial rights of France. News of this so-called "judicial murder" reached Canton in July, 1856. Demands for punishment of the magistrate were formulated immediately by the French representative, while in Paris news of the event was not unwelcome. The death of a priest was a small price for the political opportunities which were thereby opened. France was now in a position not only to assist Great Britain in forcing a revision of the treaties, but also to come vigorously to the aid of the Catholic Church in China. In October France and England were able to agree on a common policy of force.

The Affair of the Lorcha "Arrow"

The British were equally fortunate in finding a pretext for a policy of war. Hong Kong, it will be recalled, had become a British port in 1842. Its authorities had adopted the questionable practice, under a local ordinance, of granting British registry and the right to fly the British flag to Chinese coasting vessels. The result was most stimulating to Hong Kong's trade, but destructive of the reputation of the flag, for by this means it was used to cover the coolie trade, convoying, piracy, and opium smuggling.

A Chinese lorcha, named the *Arrow*, owned by a Chinese,

captained by an Irishman, and manned by a Chinese crew, was lying in the river off Canton on October 8, 1856 when she was boarded by Chinese officers who, it was claimed, tore down the British flag and carried away the crew. Harry S. Parkes, the British consul, immediately addressed Commissioner Yeh, demanding that this public insult be publicly atoned, that the crew be returned to the vessel, and that if there were any charge against them, it be prosecuted through the proper extra-territorial channels. Commissioner Yeh replied that the subject of the arrests was a notorious pirate and his gang; that the British flag had not been flying and thus could not have been hauled down; that the lorcha was owned by a Chinese and not entitled to British registry. As it happened, and this Yeh did not know, the British registry of the *Arrow* had expired eleven days previously, though Consul Parkes claimed that she was still entitled to British protection since she had not yet been able to reach Hong Kong to renew the certificate. That the flag was flying and was hauled down there is little doubt, and less doubt that the *Arrow* was legally entitled to British pro-tection.

The most serious offence committed was the arrest of the crew without a warrant from the consul. A British ship in Chinese waters is British soil, and all on board, persons or property, are under British protection.[5]

To the second demand of Consul Parkes, Yeh offered to return nine men, retaining three for further examination. He still refused to admit the right of British protection. In the meantime the developments had been reported to London, where Lord Clarendon supported fully the actions of Sir John Bowring at Hong Kong and Consul Parkes at Canton. The policy was debated vigorously in Parliament, and when the government failed on a vote of censure in the Commons, Lord Palmerston dissolved Parliament and was returned to office

---

[5] Dr. H. B. Morse, *op. cit.* Vol. I, p. 425.

with a substantial majority. Under the increasing British pressure Commissioner Yeh finally surrendered the twelve captives, but tendered no apology. The matter was now placed in the hands of British naval authorities. The Barrier Forts below Canton were soon taken, and fire was then directed to the viceroy's yamen (official residence) within the city. That unhappy official replied by a proclamation ordering extermination of the English barbarians. War was now inevitable. For the second time China would be confronted with foreign gunboats.

In summary, it must appear that the causes behind the Second European or the *Arrow* War were highly complex. Fundamentally, however, its origins were not different from those which had brought on the first war in 1840. China still regarded herself as the Middle Kingdom. She was still convinced of her superiority. She had neither the desire nor as yet the ability to change. Her mental ways were fixed. The foreigner was equally determined that she should change. He was determined that she should accept his treaties and observe them. Between these two extremes there was no compromise. If the Chinese would not learn willingly, then they must be forced to learn. The process may have been cruel, but it was old and hallowed by the march of history. In ages long gone by, China had used the same weapon against border states, had made them her vassals, and had imposed her civilization upon them. Now it was the turn of the West, by the same process, to impose its ways on China.

SELECTED BIBLIOGRAPHY

M. J. Bau, *The Foreign Relations of China* (New York: 1921), ch. 1 gives a Chinese interpretation of the opening of China. *The Cambridge History of British Foreign Policy,* 3 vols. (Cambridge: 1922-23), vol. 2, ch. 9 has a clear summary by F. W. Buckler, "India and the Far East, 1848-58." A. H. Clark, *The Clipper Ship Era* (New York: 1910). J. F. Davis, *China During the War and Since the Peace,* 2 vols. (London: 1852). Robert Fortune, *A Journey to the Tea Districts of China* (London: 1852). Tyler Dennett, *Americans in Eastern Asia* (New York: 1922), chs. 9-12, 14-16 cover the more important American activities during the period, including the work of such American commissioners as Humphrey Marshall, Robert McLane, and Dr. Peter Parker. J. W. Foster, *American Diplomacy in the Orient* (Boston: 1904) ch. 7. Richard Feetham, *Report to the Shanghai Municipal Council,* 4 vols. (Shanghai: 1931-32) is rich in material. W. J. Hail, *Tseng Kuo-fan and the Taiping Rebellion* (New Haven: 1927). F. L. H. Pott, *A Short History of Shanghai* (Shanghai: 1928). S. Lane-Poole and F. V. Dickins, *The Life of Sir Harry Parkes,* 2 vols. (London: 1894), vol. 1, *Consul in China.* C. S. Leavenworth, *The Arrow War with China* (London: 1901). K. S. Latourette, *The Chinese: Their History and Culture* (New York: 1934). C. A. Montalto de Jesus, *Historic Shanghai* (Shanghai: 1909). T. T. Meadows, *The Chinese and Their Rebellions* (London: 1856). The most satisfactory collateral reading is H. B. Morse, *The International Relations of the Chinese Empire* (London: 1910) vol. 1, chs. 12-16. These chapters discuss such subjects as international readjustment from 1843 to 1850, the treaty ports, Chinese antiforeignism at Canton, piracy and convoying, and the affair of the *Arrow.* Mary A. Nourse, *The Four Hundred Million* (Indianapolis: 1935), ch. 16, the "Taiping Rebellion." Laurence Oliphant, *Narrative of the Earl of Elgin's Mission to China and Japan* (New York: 1860), chs. 1-20. Sir G. T. Staunton, *Miscellaneous Notices Relating to China* (London: 1850). A. J. Sargent, *Anglo-Chinese Commerce and Diplomacy* (London: 1907). C. A. M. Smith, *The British in China and Far Eastern Trade* (London: 1920). S. W. Williams, *The Middle Kingdom,* rev. ed., 2 vols. (New York: 1907).

CHAPTER VIII

The Treaties of Tientsin and Peking

THE plight of China in 1857 was indeed a sorry one. Her relations with the hated foreigner were about to precipitate a second and more disastrous war. To many of the foreigners the stubborn and superior attitude of Commissioner Yeh at Canton was both the immediate and the fundamental cause of the conflict. In reality that unhappy gentleman was merely a fair sample of China's dominating official class: a class which politically at least was living wholly in the past. It was convenient for this class to lay all China's ills at the door of the foreign barbarian. His commerce, his piracy, his opium, and his presumptuous treaties were the root of all of China's ailments. Such was the view which officials at Canton had spread among the populace. It was the argument which the politician, ancient and modern, has invariably used to cover his own sins. In the China of 1857 those sins were legion.

The Manchu Dynasty had ruled at Peking since 1644. Though an alien house imposing its will upon the Chinese by force, it had, by able leadership, consolidated its power in a system of government whereby it ruled with, rather than over, the conquered Chinese. As long as this government was benevolent, and prosperity prevailed, the conquered race was content to believe that the mandate of heaven belonged to the Manchus.

. . . during the heyday of the dynasty China attained a fresh level of material prosperity, probably higher than ever before. In the latter part of the seventeenth and through most of the eighteenth century, indeed, it was the most populous and possibly the most prosperous realm on the planet. . . . From the standpoint of order and justice it was probably as far advanced as any state of the time, for that was before the humanitarian movement had ameliorated the laws, the courts, and the prisons of the West. In total wealth, too, it very possibly surpassed every other nation of the period.[1]

These were the years when China could boast of great rulers. K'ang Hsi (1662-1723), a contemporary of Louis XIV of France, William of Orange in England, and Peter the Great in Russia, was undoubtedly their equal. Ch'ien Lung (1736-1796) was both a conqueror and a statesman. In the days of his prime, affairs of state were controlled with the utmost vigor; but, in his later years, there appeared the first symptoms of the Manchu decline. Secret societies, the germ organisms of revolt, again appeared, and to combat this danger the Manchus had no effective weapon. The Chinese mind had long since ceased to be original. Intellectual life was sterile. The goal of all learning was to know what the ancients had done and to be guided accordingly. Thus in the heat of the first foreign impact (1840-1842) it never occurred to the official Chinese mind that new methods might be necessary to meet new problems. Ch'ien Lung was succeeded by incompetent rulers, and the new Emperor, Hsien Feng, who ascended the throne in 1850, inherited "a legacy of corruption, misgovernment, discontent, and rebellion." [2]

In the two decades which preceded the first British war widespread revolts had occurred with alarming frequency in such areas as Kwangsi, Shansi, Kweichow, Kiangsi, Hainan, Hupeh, and Formosa, all indicative of growing political discontent. In most cases these revolts were of purely domestic origin; in part, however, their inspiration arose from foreign contacts, and in particular from the teachings of foreign missionaries. This was the case with the Taipings.

---

[1] K. S. Latourette, *The Chinese: Their History and Culture,* 2nd rev. ed. The Macmillan Company, New York, 1934. Vol. I, pp. 327-328.

[2] Dr. H. B. Morse, *The International Relations of the Chinese Empire.* Longmans, Green & Company, London, 1910. Vol. I, p. 411.

The Taiping Rebellion

A Chinese student, a native of Kwangtung province, who attempted unsuccessfully to pass the civil service examinations at Canton, acquired some pamphlets summarizing the teachings of Protestant missionaries. Hung Hsiu-ch'uan (for this was his name) was later the victim of a severe illness during which he is reputed to have enjoyed some astonishing visions, which subsequently he interpreted as of divine origin. This experience, coupled with his reading of Christian tracts, convinced Hung that he had been ordained to restore the worship of the true God. The movement which he thereupon undertook was at first purely religious, and, externally at least, not unlike Protestant Christianity. With this, however, were mixed indiscriminately native Chinese beliefs. In the course of time this new religious sect acquired a character decidedly political, in this way becoming associated with discontented groups. Its object now became the overthrow of the Manchu regime and the establishment of the Taiping (Great Peace) Dynasty, with Hung as the new sovereign. The first uprisings occurred in Kwangsi as early as 1848, and by 1852 the Taipings were moving northward into Hunan Province. In the following year they had reached the Yangtze River, and moving now eastward, captured first Wuchang and later Nanking, where they set up their capital. From here they attempted vainly to penetrate the north and to drive the Manchus from Peking. After laying waste the countryside and wreaking incalculable damage, they were finally overthrown more than a decade later (1865). It is difficult to put one's finger on the real nature of the Taiping movement. In the main it was a protest against Manchu incompetence. It was also an attempt of non-propertied groups to dispossess the wealthy classes. Western thought in the form of Christian religious fanaticism was another of its elements. When one recalls the intense poverty of the Chinese masses, their tendency to seek relief through secret rebel societies, and the flagrant abuses which were sapping the vitality of Peking, it is not to be wondered that the Taipings enjoyed even a temporary success. Their failure was due to three things: Hung lacked genius; wealthy Chinese rallied to the support of the Manchus; and finally the foreign powers threw their support against the rebels.

With this background in mind it will now be possible to trace the relation of the Taipings to the foreign powers, and the effects of their movement on China's foreign relations in the decade preceding and also during the *Arrow* War.

While the Taipings were enjoying their first major success and were already well established in their new capital at Nanking, and the Manchus had demonstrated their total inability to cope either with them or other rebellious movements, the foreign traders and their consuls were already of the mind that the treaties should be revised, and this by force. In September, 1853, Shanghai itself was captured by revolting bands, who expelled the imperial officials. All these forces working together raised the question as to whether the foreign powers should not recognize the Taipings and thus hasten the downfall of the Manchus. In return for this aid the Taipings would be required to guarantee all the commercial and diplomatic privileges which the foreigners desired. For such a course the western powers would have full support from the Protestant missions but vigorous opposition from the Roman Catholics. At the time the United States was represented in China by a commissioner, Humphrey Marshall, who, like most of the foreigners, believed the eventual success of the Taipings to be assured. It was his belief that:

. . . the highest interests of the United States are involved in sustaining China—maintaining order here, and gradually engrafting on this worn-out stock the healthy principles which give life and health to governments. . . .

How this was to be done Marshall did not specify, but he set about to thwart any steps by Great Britain or Russia to take advantage of China's domestic turmoil.

Shanghai and the Rebellion

An occasion for full discussion among the foreign powers on the subject of policy toward both the Chinese government and the Taipings soon arose. When in 1853 Shanghai fell to rebel bands more or less associated with the Taipings, the Chinese officials deserted their customs house located in the foreign settlement. This raised the question whether Shanghai had thus become a free port, since the Chinese government was no longer capable of collecting the duties. British and American consular authorities immediately notified their nationals that the consuls themselves would collect the duties during the absence of Chinese officials. The British consul required his merchants merely to deposit promissory notes, which in fact were never paid, while the Americans were at the disadvantage of having to pay in specie. Nationals of powers that had no consul at Shanghai paid nothing. In their dominating capacity, too, the British stipulated that the Shanghai foreign settlement must remain neutral in the conflict between the imperial forces and the rebels; but in reality the settlement merchants were constantly giving aid to the rebels in the form of supplies. Ships entered and cleared the port without paying duties. Early in 1854 Commissioner Marshall ordered that American vessels be cleared without payment of duties, and now the British merchants, who were still required to deposit promissory notes, were at a disadvantage. Meanwhile it was becoming increasingly clear that the foreigners could gain little by recognition of the Taipings, even though the imperial forces had as yet failed to retake Shanghai, and the government was urgently in need of the customs revenue. To meet this situation Robert M. McLane, who had succeeded Marshall early in 1854, sought co-operative action with his British and French colleagues. The plan proposed to the Chinese called for a Chinese customs house at Shanghai controlled by a board of foreign inspectors. To this proposal both the local viceroy and the taotai agreed. In detail it called for the appointment of foreign inspectors of customs, and subordinates, both Chinese and foreign, all acting under the authority of the taotai. The expense of the new system was to be met from customs revenue, and records were to be kept in both the English and the Chinese language. In this way began the Imperial Maritime Customs service, a Chinese service staffed, however, largely by foreigners, which in later years was to be extended to other ports of the Empire.

By 1855, the initiative of the Taipings being already spent, it was clear that the foreign powers would continue to deal with the government at Peking. Policies in the two succeeding years, as the reader is already aware, had developed rapidly. England and France had both agreed to force, if necessary, a revision of the treaties. The *Arrow* affair and the execution of Father Chapdelaine had provided the pretexts for war. The United States had refused to co-operate with the European allies in a policy of force, but at the same time, in order not to lose any advantages this policy might win, had appointed William B. Reed as Minister Plenipotentiary to China, where he arrived in November, 1857. Reed's instructions indicate that the policy of the United States (excepting, of course, the use of force) was not in principle unlike that of the Europeans. Their objects, in fact, were described by Secretary of State Cass, as "just and expedient." Reed was to make clear that the United States sought "enlargement of opportunities for trade"; that it did not desire legalization of the opium traffic; and that it would insist on the enforcement of existing treaty rights. Russia also was seeking to profit by whatever victories the British and French might win, and to this end was now represented in China by Count Putiatin.

The Foreigners Rebuffed at Canton

At Canton in the closing months of 1857 Commissioner Yeh persisted in his habitual attitude of contempt for the foreign envoys. The special missions from England and France to revise the treaties, headed by Lord Elgin and Baron Gros, respectively, had already arrived in south China. The reply of these dignitaries to Commissioner Yeh was the bombardment of Canton (December 28, 1857), and, with the occupation of the city, the unfortunate Yeh was captured and sent to India, where later he died. British and French troops continued to hold Canton, while their envoys and also those of the United States and Russia proceeded north to Shanghai.

The Foreigners Invade North China

The four envoys had co-operated, while still at Canton, in drafting simultaneous notes to the Chinese government making it clear that as far as treaty revision was concerned, the powers had a common policy. These notes were sent to Shanghai for delivery to Peking, but the Chinese made it known that negotiations must be confined to Canton. Thereupon the envoys determined to proceed beyond Shanghai to the Pei-ho, where their very presence would be disturbing to Chinese officialdom. Here negotiations were opened by the Chihli viceroy. The British and French regarded his powers as inadequate and refused his overtures, and, though Mr. Reed held some discussions with him, these too were soon broken off. Again the European allies assumed the initiative, demanding the surrender of the Taku Forts at the mouth of the river in order that they might advance safely to Tientsin. When this was refused, the forts were assaulted and taken. And now, with the approach to the nation's capital in enemy hands, the Chinese appointed two high commissioners to negotiate a settlement and a revision of the treaties. The work, completed during June, resulted in the four famous Treaties of Tientsin.   The negotiations were separate but simultaneous.   The Russian treaty was signed on June 13; the American on June 18; the English on June 26; and the French on the following day.

The Treaties of Tientsin

Because of the co-operative policy that had been followed by the powers, the Tientsin Treaties formed in reality a single settlement.   England and France exacted indemnities to cover their military and naval expeditions.   With this exception, the settlement was a common settlement.   The Russians and the Americans had not used force, and their treaties contained little of importance; but since they insisted on the most-favored-nation clause, they fell heir immediately to the enlarged concessions won by British and French arms.   These concessions were to prove of the utmost import in China's future foreign relations. As summarized from the British treaty, they included the following:

1. China would receive a British ambassador or other diplomatic agent who might reside at Peking permanently or visit the capital occasionally at the option of the British government. This ambassador should "not be called upon to perform any ceremony derogatory to him as representing the sovereign of an independent nation on a footing of equality with that of China."   The ambassador was to be given the full protection of the Chinese government and "his letters and effects shall be held sacred and inviolable."   China agreed to nominate one of the highest ranking officials with whom the ambassador should conduct his official business either personally or in writing "on a footing of perfect equality."

2. Article VIII of the treaty provided that: "The Christian religion, as professed by Protestants or Roman Catholics, inculcates the practice of virtue, and teaches man to do as he would

be done by. Persons teaching it or professing it, therefore, shall alike be entitled to the protection of the Chinese authorities; nor shall any such, peaceably pursing their calling, and not offending against the laws, be persecuted or interfered with."

3. Article IX provided: "British subjects are hereby authorized to travel, for their pleasure or for purposes of trade, to all parts of the interior, under passports which will be issued by their consuls, and countersigned by the local authorities. . . . If he [the British subject] be without a passport, or if he commit any offense against the law, he shall be handed over to the nearest consul for punishment. . . ."

4. Articles X and XI provided that British merchant ships might trade on the Yangtze River, and that additional treaty ports should be opened, including: Chefoo, in Shantung province; Chinkiang, in Kiangsu; Hankow, in Hupeh; Kuikiang, in Kiangsi; Kiungchow in Hainan; Newchwang, in Manchuria; Swatow in Kwangtung; Wenchow, in Chekiang; and Nanking, in Kiangsu (by the French treaty).

5. Article XVI dealt with extraterritorial rights in criminal cases: "Chinese subjects who may be guilty of any criminal act toward British subjects shall be arrested and punished by the Chinese authorities, according to the laws of China. British subjects who may commit any crime in China shall be tried and punished by the consul, or other public functionary authorized thereto, according to the laws of Great Britain. Justice shall be equitably and impartially administered on both sides."

6. Finally, the treaty contained the most-favored-nation clause. Provision was also made for revision of the tariff.

Such was the importance of the Tientsin settlement that some comment on its terms seems to be justified. While the foregoing summary is taken from the British treaty, it must be emphasized that it represented the policies of all four powers: England, France, Russia, and the United States. To be sure, the United States and Russia had refused to employ force, but they were insistent that they enjoy all privileges which a policy of force had won for England and France.

The most striking gain won by the foreigners in the Tientsin Treaties was the right of their governments to maintain ambassadors or ministers at Peking. On the assumption that China was now to be opened to full diplomatic intercourse with the West, this was a reasonable demand. The foreigners had long since discovered that even their most temperate requests could be and were easily sidetracked as long as they were obliged to deal with local officials at the open ports of the south. The delay and evasion which China had constantly practiced in dealing with foreigners would now be more difficult. But, in the larger sense, the penetration of foreign diplomats to Peking, the Forbidden City, seemed like a crushing blow to China's old official exclusiveness. The western diplomat was now at the very door of the Imperial Palace.

The grant of toleration to Christians, to missionaries, and to their converts has been a subject of much controversy. To toleration in principle there could be no objection; but in 1858 toleration was won as a result of war and became a legal treaty concession. The missionaries, particularly the Catholics, were already well aware that many elements in Christian doctrine had proved disruptive of China's cultural heritage; yet, since their very object was to destroy this heritage, it was but natural that they should accept the new status for themselves and for their religion. After 1858 the Chinese were quite justified in regarding Christianity in China as a political as well as a religious weapon of the western world.

The right of foreigners to travel in the interior was another concession on which opinions have differed. The traders of 1858 had chafed at the restrictions which confined them to the treaty ports. They were businessmen intent on profits, and these same profits, they felt, would depend in turn on freedom of access to the entire country. Against this point of view the Chinese could argue that the people were not yet ready to receive foreigners beyond the port towns, and that because the foreigner enjoyed extraterritoriality, and when in the interior would be far removed from his nearest consul, China could exercise over him only an ineffective control.

Assuming again that enlarged trade with the foreigners was now an accepted policy, there could be little valid objection to the opening of the ten new treaty ports (nine in China and one in Formosa), though in fact it did give rise to new difficulties, and some of the ports were not opened until many years later (Nanking, for instance, was not opened until 1899). The admission of foreign vessels to the Yangtze trade could not be defended easily. It was a most valuable concession to the foreigner, for the Yangtze Valley was the richest area of all China. Large quantities of produce would now be carried in foreign instead of Chinese vessels. It is to be noted, too, that in demanding access to China's coasting and inland trade the West was departing radically from custom as established among European and American states. But the powers were not dealing with the West; they were dealing with that curious thing called China. And this is more evident when it is recalled that the Tientsin settlement gave to foreign warships the right not only to visit ports on the coast but also to enter the Yangtze and other rivers.

The Opium Trade Legalized

The British treaty also contained the following provision:

Whereas the tariff fixed by Article X of the Treaty of Nanking, and which was estimated so as to impose on imports and exports a duty at about the rate of five per cent *ad valorem,* has been found, by reason of the fall in value of various articles . . . to impose a duty upon these considerably in excess of the rate originally assumed as above to be a fair rate, it is agreed that the said tariff shall be revised. . . .

Accordingly negotiations which resulted in a new schedule were commenced at Shanghai. Its most notable feature was the inclusion of opium, importation of which was thereby legalized at a duty of about $45 on 133 pounds. This new legal status of opium was a result of British policy, which, since 1842, had been entirely consistent. The argument was this. Since the first British war the importation of opium (a contraband trade) had increased steadily. Although most of the opium was produced in India, other sources of supply were available, and therefore prohibition by the British authorities was not likely to prove effective in stopping the trade. It was the business of China to enforce her laws against an illicit traffic; and, although England would not give protection to subjects violating those laws, neither would she undertake to enforce the laws for China. The Chinese had already proved themselves incapable or unwilling to enforce their law, and this could leave but one alternative. The prohibition should be removed, and opium importation legalized at a fixed duty and under strict regulation. This was the policy, then, which was translated into fact in the supplementary negotiations of 1858. China had failed to free herself of the opium evil because she had failed to enforce her own laws. As will appear later, this same weakness was to react again and again to her disadvantage in subsequent years.

The attitude of the United States at this time to the opium question is also of interest. Mr. Reed had been instructed by his government that:

The United States does not seek for their citizens the legal establishment of the opium trade, nor will it uphold them in any attempt to violate the laws of China by the introduction of that article into the country.

The treaty which Mr. Reed signed at Tientsin made no mention of opium. Nevertheless, the American envoy had come to the conclusion that, of the evils associated with opium, legalization of the traffic was the least objectionable. He assured Lord Elgin of his support to this end, and by so doing appears to have violated the spirit of his instructions. His action aroused no undue criticism in the United States.

One aspect of the Tientsin settlement remains for comment. In the first British war (1840-1842) the English had demanded "equality." By this they meant of course not the abstract principle, but rather "diplomatic equality." The same was demanded in the Treaties of Tientsin, under which British and other foreign ministers at Peking were to be received "on a footing of equality." Because of the emphasis upon this principle of diplomatic equality, it is worth while to note that the actual treaties of 1858 in no sense (save the diplomatic) established a status of equality. The earlier treaties (1842-1844) had already deprived China of control over foreigners and over her tariff. In 1858 these limitations were made more definite, while in addition foreign ships were admitted to her river trade, and an alien religion was given the legal protection of the treaties. China, the Middle Kingdom, was no longer entitled to the name. The western powers had shattered her superior position, and, far from granting her a status of equality, had denied to her essential attributes of real sovereignty.

The Renewal of Hostilities

The Treaties of Tientsin were approved by the Chinese government in 1858, before the British and French forces left Tientsin. They were not to become effective, however, until ratified copies had been exchanged at Peking. The Russian treaty was the first to be exchanged. The new Russian minister proceeded to Peking by the overland route and met with no difficulties. The British, the French, and the American representatives, accompanied by ships of war, arrived at the mouth of the Pei-ho in June, 1859. The British envoy had received special instructions from his government to proceed to Peking by way of Tientsin. At Taku it was discovered that the Chinese had strengthened the forts and had blocked the mouth of the river. The British were informed by the local Chinese officials that they would be received at Pehtang, farther north on the coast, but that China would repel any attempt to enter the river at Taku. The British and the French now demanded that they be permitted to proceed by Taku to Tientsin, and, on again being refused, attempted to storm the forts and break the barrier. In this they failed and were forced to retire to Shanghai. During the engagement the commander of the American naval forces, who occupied a neutral position, had, none the less, come to the assistance of his British cousins, explaining his action with the statement that "blood is thicker than water," all of which was very scientific but had little to do with the commander's official instructions.

In the meantime John E. Ward, the American envoy, who was restricted neither as to place nor as to the route to be followed in the exchange of his country's treaty, proceeded to Pehtang, where the Chinese had provided carts which carried him and his mission to Peking. This was unfortunate. Mr. Ward, who came from Georgia, was a southern gentleman of some distinction, but, being sadly ignorant on the finer points of far eastern diplomacy, he permitted the Chinese to take full advantage of his inexperience. Mr. Ward should have demanded sedan chairs, the mode of conveyance used by the highest Chinese officials. The cart in which he actually rode was the type of vehicle used to carry Koreans and other tribute-bearers to the Chinese capital, and over it floated banners describing the occupant as a tribute-bearer from the United States. This was obvious proof that the Chinese government was holding tenaciously to the empty pretense of its superior position. In Peking the Chinese demanded that Mr. Ward perform the kowtow, which, of course, he refused; and, with what must have been a splendid southern dignity, replied that "although he was willing to 'bend the body and slightly crook the right knee,' he was accustomed to kneel only to God and woman." [3] Thoroughly disgusted, Mr. Ward returned to Pehtang, where the American ratified treaty was now exchanged.

While these events were transpiring, England and France had again determined to use coercion. Additional forces were sent to Shanghai, and with these the allied envoys returned to Taku. The Chinese repeated their offer to receive the ambassadors at Pehtang; but the allies stormed the Taku forts (August 21, 1860) while their military forces advanced on Tientsin and Peking. The Chinese retired in hopeless confusion, and when the foreigners reached and entered the city, the Emperor and his court had fled north to the mountains of Jehol. During the march on Peking the Chinese had captured thirty-nine foreigners, including the private secretary of Lord Elgin, who were presumably protected by a flag of truce. It was the Chinese belief that by holding these hostages they could force the British to accept more moderate terms. These prisoners were subjected to such cruelty that, when finally rescued, eighteen had already died. Lord Elgin thereupon determined that the Chinese government must pay for this treachery, and accordingly he ordered the burning of the Summer Palace, which French troops had already occupied and looted. These buildings had been erected at great cost and included structures of European style designed by the early Jesuits. In many respects they were architectural monuments embodying both occidental and oriental style. Whether or not their destruction was the proper price for the lives of eighteen Europeans seized treacherously is a matter of personal interpretation. For the Chinese, their ruins stood as a constant reminder of the vigor and perhaps the ethics of the western "barbarian" world.

---

[3] Tyler Dennett, *Americans in Eastern Asia.* The Macmillan Company, New York, 1922. p. 342.

The Peking Conventions

With the Chinese capital now at their mercy the allied envoys could proceed to exact another treaty settlement and to exchange the ratified treaties of 1858. This work was finished with the signing of the British convention of Peking on October 24, and the French convention the following day. For the most part these conventions were identical. The Chinese Emperor expressed his "deep regret" for the action of his soldiers in opposing the allies at Taku in 1859. The British and the French (and therefore other treaty powers) would maintain permanent legations in Peking. Additional indemnities were provided, and Tientsin was added to the ports now open to foreign trade and residence. Great Britain received Kowloon, on the Chinese mainland directly across from the island of Hong Kong, as protection against attack on the British harbor. France secured the restoration to the Roman Catholic Church of all property which had been confiscated since 1724. This provision would obviously work great injustice on innocent Chinese who had long since acquired the property; but this fact does not appear to have troubled the conscience of either the French government or the Church: both could assert that an imperial edict of 1846 had promised restoration to Roman Catholics of religious establishments. The Chinese text of the French convention (which was not the authoritative one) also contained a troublesome provision allowing French missionaries to rent and purchase land and to erect buildings in all provinces. Finally, the conventions legalized, under regulation, the coolie trade.

The most curious phase of events in China during 1860 remains to be told. The Taiping Rebellion, which had spread north to the Yangtze and Nanking in 1853, had spent most of its force. For various reasons it had by 1860 regained some of its early vigor, and some of its rebel bands were threatening to advance upon the wealthy and populous city of Shanghai, with its foreign settlement. In this extremity Chinese authorities appealed for protection to the English and French, who agreed to defend the Chinese city and the foreign settlement against any attack. On August 21, 1860, British troops, assisted by some French, repelled the Taipings from the walls of Shanghai. This was the very day on which in the north British and French troops were storming the Taku forts and beginning their march on Peking.

So ended the struggle to determine on what, terms China should do business with the western world. The period of conflict was by no means over; but for the time being China was thoroughly beaten. Her incapable and corrupt government was still harried by the threats and ravages of internal rebellion. On her seacoasts she had watched with dismay the steady advance of the hated foreigner, who by his relentless policy of force had broken every barrier raised against him. These were the foreigners (Englishmen, Frenchmen, Russians, and Americans) who had not scrupled to turn China's domestic turmoil to their own advantage. Less than a century later they in turn (with pious phrases) would censure others who reapplied the policy they had devised. In part at least by 1860 China had learned the more obvious lessons that western guns and bayonets could offer. For several decades her foreign relations would run, if not happily, at least more smoothly than in the years since Commissioner Lin had ruled at Canton.

SELECTED BIBLIOGRAPHY

D. C. Boulger, *The History of China,* new and rev. ed., 2 vols. (London: 1898), vol. 2, chs. 14-15. H. Cordier, *L'Expédition de Chine du 1857-58* (Paris: 1905); by the same author, *L'Expédition de Chine de 1860* (Paris: 1906). Algernon Cecil, *British Foreign Secretaries 1807-1916* (London: 1927). Baron de Chassiron, *Notes sur le Japon, la Chine, et l'Inde, 1858-1859-1860* (Paris: 1861). G. W.

Cooke, *China; Being the "Times" Special Correspondence from China in the Years 1857-58* (London: 1858). Tyler Dennett, *Americans in Eastern Asia* (New York: 1922), chs. 16-18. R. K. Douglas, *Europe and the Far East,* rev. ed. (Cambridge: 1913). J. W. Foster, *American Diplomacy in the Orient* (Boston: 1904), ch. 7. Rodney Gilbert, *The Unequal Treaties* (London: 1929), ch. 5, the elaboration of the treaties, 1858-1860. W. J. Hail, *Tseng Kuo-fan and the Taiping Rebellion* (New Haven: 1927). Philip Joseph, *Foreign Diplomacy in China 1894-1900* (London: 1928), ch. 2, "The Commercial Privileges of the Foreigners in the Nineteenth Century." S. Lane-Poole and F. V. Dickins, *The Life of Sir Harry Parkes,* 2 vols. (London: 1894). C. S. Leavenworth, *The Arrow War with China* (London: 1901). W. F. Mayers and others, *The Treaty Ports of China and Japan* (London: 1867). C. B. Maybon and Jean Fredet, *Histoire de la Concession Française de Shanghai* (Paris: 1929). Marquis de Moges, *Souvenirs d'une ambassade en Chine et au Japon en 1857 et 1858* (Paris: 1860). H. B. Morse, *The International Relations of the Chinese Empire,* vols. 1 and 2 (London: 1910 and 1918), vol. 1, chs. 17-18, and 21-26 covering such topics as: the rise of the Taiping Rebellion; the relation of Shanghai to the Rebellion; the work of Elgin and Gros at Canton; the treaty negotiations of 1858; opium, 1842-58; the treaty settlement of 1858; the hostilities at Taku, 1859; and the final settlement, 1860; in vol. 2, see chs. 4-5, on the Taiping Rebellion; and chs. 1-2, on the development of the customs service. Laurence Oliphant, *Narrative of The Earl of Elgin's Mission to China and Japan* (New York: 1860), chs. 33-34. D. E. Owen, *British Opium Policy in China and India* (New Haven: 1934). R. S. Rantoul, *Frederick Townsend Ward* (Salem: 1908). A. J. Sargent, *Anglo-Chinese Commerce and Diplomacy* (London: 1907). W. E. Soothill, *China and the West* (London: 1925), ch. 10. G. E. Taylor, "The Taiping Rebellion: Its Economic Background and Social Theory," in *The Chinese Social and Political Science Review,* Jan. 1933. S. W. Williams, *The Middle Kingdom,* rev. ed., 2 vols. (New York: 1907).

CHAPTER IX

Russia on the Pacific

ONE of the longest and, at the same time, least-known land
frontiers in the history of political geography is that
which in the later nineteenth and early twentieth century
marked the boundary between China and Asiatic Russia. From
the northern tip of Korea, not far from Vladivostok, it extended northward along the Ussuri River to its junction with
the Amur, and then up the course of that river to lose itself in
the uncharted wastes of mountain and desert that divide in
uncertain fashion Mongolia from Siberia. From this westward
course it veered far to the south into the very heart of central
Asia, running between Sin-kiang (the most western of China's
dependencies) and Russian Turkestan (Kirghiz). Rarely has
this frontier been free from wars or their rumors. Even in
these middle years of the twentieth century it remains a constant threat to peace: a sort of geographical mystery winding
its way through a remote continent. Since the emergence of
the new state of Manchoukuo the far eastern sections of the
frontier have become more familiar to western readers; but to
the west, where China, Russia, and British India merge, the
mystery still remains. Today this frontier has become an international boundary across which Russian communism seeks to
march to the conversion of China. It was not always so. Only
five centuries ago Siberia was uninhabited save for small and
scattered bands of wandering tribesmen, while the Mongolian
frontier was nothing more tangible than a broad expanse on
the outer edge of which Chinese political control, such as it
was, ceased to function.

Early Russian Expansion

Russian expansion eastward across the Urals into Siberia began in the time of John the Dread (1533-1582). In 1581 a Cossack under sentence of death for rebellion led a band of brigands against western Siberian chieftains and occupied the valley of the Obi River. These conquests were handed to the Tsar in return for full pardon. The movement thus begun soon gained momentum. The misgovernment that prevailed in European Russia drove many peasants toward the frontiers, and some of them entered Siberia. Before 1638 these Russian pioneers had pushed eastward as far as the Lena River, where Yakutsk was founded. Behind them settlements had already been established at Tobolsk (1587) and Omsk, on the Irtish. In general the advance was not difficult. The country was populated but sparsely, and although all the rivers flowed generally to the north, most of the portages between their upper tributaries were neither long nor difficult to cross. Even had the obstacles been greater, it is unlikely that they would have impeded for long the bold advance of the adventuresome Cossacks. In 1638 a group of these Cossack brigands crossed from the upper waters of the Lena to the shore of the Pacific, where the town of Okhotsk now stands.

The Character of Russian Settlement

In this new and vast dominion of Siberia the Russians employed themselves in two ways. In the western plains and valleys near the Urals the peasant could settle in the quiet pursuits of agriculture. To the east, mountain barriers had pushed the Russian advance further to the north in the upper valleys of the Lena. Here the climate was severe and the country more difficult of access. It was, nevertheless, rich in fur-bearing animals and soon attracted hunters, trappers, and fur traders. Thus far it would appear that the Russians had no knowledge of the Amur Valley, which lay south and across the mountains from the Lena. The watershed between these great rivers was inhabited by bands of Tartars, from whom the Cossacks learned of the rich and more hospitable lands of Manchuria. Crossing the mountains, their first explorers reached the Amur in 1643 not far from where Blagoveschensk is now situated. Five years later other Cossacks had discovered the Shilka, a tributary of the upper Amur, lying directly east of Lake Baikal. A southern movement by the Cossacks was now prosecuted with great vigor. Between 1649 and 1651 a Cossack, Khabarov by name, advanced down the Amur from the Shilka, driving the native tribes from their homes or slaughtering the men where resistance was encountered (native women were made captive). Villages were plundered and burned, crops seized, and as the march proceeded, the natives were forced to pay tribute. At Albazin, on the upper Amur, Khabarov found a site suitable for a frontier fort. In 1651 he wintered at the junction of the Ussuri and the Amur—the present site of the town of Khabarovsk. Here the first conflict with the Chinese occurred. The Amur tribes had appealed to Peking, but the Chinese force, a thousand strong, sent to their assistance were soon dispersed by the small but well-organized Cossack band.

A few years later (1654-1655) Russia dispatched a diplomatic mission to Peking in the hope that regular relations might be established. It failed. The Chinese insisted upon the kowtow, and were none too anxious to have any dealings with a country that claimed as subjects such brigands as the Cossacks of the Amur. While the mission was in Peking, the Cossacks continued their marauding, invading even the valley of the Sungari. In 1658 the Chinese succeeded in all but destroying these bands, but their fellows still occupied the upper Amur. Here the Cossacks were entrenched at Albazin and Nertchinsk. The former was destroyed by the Chinese (1685) but rebuilt almost immediately by the Russians. Again the Chinese laid

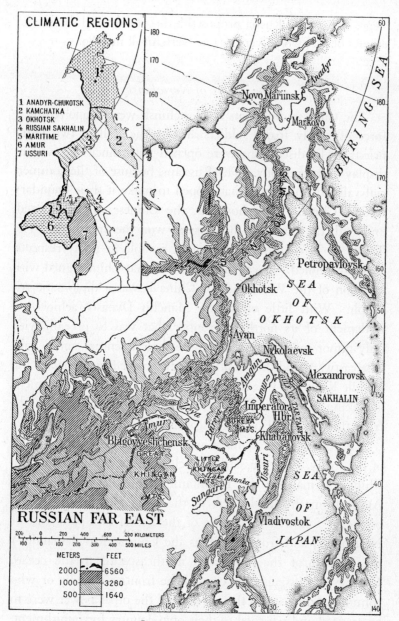

CLIMATIC REGIONS

1 ANADYR-CHUKOTSK
2 KAMCHATKA
3 OKHOTSK
4 RUSSIAN SAKHALIN
5 MARITIME
6 AMUR
7 USSURI

RUSSIAN FAR EAST

METERS — FEET
2000 — 6560
1000 — 3280
500 — 1640

Courtesy of the "Geographical Review," published by the American Geographical Society of New York.

171

siege. This time Russia proposed a diplomatic settlement, and envoys of the two powers met at Nertchinsk in 1689.

The Treaty of Nertchinsk

The Chinese diplomats at Nertchinsk were supported by a force of nearly 10,000 soldiers and by the skill of two Jesuit priests. The discussions were opened with much extravagant display and ceremony. The Russians, because of the commercial value of the Amur, had hoped to make it their boundary against China. This, however, the Chinese stoutly resisted, and with the threat of their troops won the argument. The Treaty of Nertchinsk, a document notable in many respects, was soon signed. It was the first treaty that China signed with a nation of the West, and for China it was a diplomatic triumph. With little effort the Manchu Dynasty achieved a settlement of its northern frontier that was to prevail, with only minor modification, for more than a century and a half. The eastward and then southerly advance of Russia toward the Middle Kingdom was checked effectively, and the government at Peking was able to attack internal problems of empire free from the threat of Cossack brigands on the Amur.

The boundary settlement was the most important feature of the treaty. The Russians had claimed the Amur, while the Chinese demanded the mountain divide that separates the Amur from the headwaters of the Lena. In the treaty the boundary followed the course of the Shilka to a point east of Nertchinsk, and from there (as the Chinese had demanded) the summit of the mountains northeastward to the ocean. Chinese or Russians who crossed the frontier illegally or who committed offenses on the territory of the other power were to be arrested and returned to their own country for punishment. Trade across the Russo-Chinese border was now legal, with Nertchinsk as the principal point of exchange, but in later years Kiakhta dominated the caravan route across Mongolia to Peking.

Russo-Chinese Commerce

Russia was eager to take advantage of commercial opportunities opened by the Treaty of Nertchinsk and to this end sent embassies to Peking in 1692 and again in 1719. To a certain degree the Chinese reciprocated in the dispatch of a mission to the Tartar groups of southern Russia on the Don and Volga Rivers. In time the trade between Russia and China assumed considerable proportions. It centered at the Russian town of Kiakhta, south of Lake Baikal. The frontier at this point had been fixed by a treaty in 1727, and the trade which developed was strictly a trade by barter under strict official control. The Chinese brought silk and cotton fabrics and tea, which they exchanged for Russian broadcloth, skins, and furs. As would be expected, the natural difficulties of such a long caravan route across Siberia from European Russia and then through Outer and Inner Mongolia to Peking placed definite limitations on the growth of the trade.

Apart from their commerce, the Russians enjoyed another contact with Peking. The Chinese capital harbored a small Russian colony made up of prisoners of war and deserters from Russian forces in the Amur country. The men of this colony served in the Manchu army and were permitted to erect their own church at Peking. Early in the eighteenth century Russian priests were permitted to join this colony, and later by treaty provision a regular ecclesiastical mission consisting of priests and students of the Chinese language was established.

While these commercial and religious contacts were developing, the Russians were advancing their frontier along the northeastern Pacific slope of Siberia. Their knowledge of Kamchatka, Sakhalin, and the Kurile Islands was soon extensive, and eventually their settlements had crossed the northern Pacific to the coasts of America. They also made numerous but fruitless efforts to open commercial relations with Japan, which was still sealed from foreign contacts by the Tokugawa policy of exclusion and seclusion. It was this Russian interest in the islands of the western Pacific which led in 1805 to a request for permission to navigate the Amur. This request, which was disturbing to the Chinese, was promptly refused. There was evidence, in fact, that the settlement of Nertchinsk, which for more than a century had blessed the Amur region with comparative peace, was becoming irksome to advancing Russia. The boundary, as defined in the Nertchinsk treaty, remained on paper only, and as Russian settlement increased, border disputes and violations became more frequent. This was inevitable in a region where Russian pioneers were moving toward an area where China exercised at best a most informal control. The situation was ripe for colonial expansion. All that was needed was official sanction and support.

The Era of Mouraviev

In 1846 Tsar Nicholas I ordered a thorough investigation and a report on the entire question of the Amur in its bearing on Russia's eastward expansion. In the following year Nikolas Mouraviev, a man of capacity and of action, was appointed governor general of eastern Siberia. One of Mouraviev's first official acts was to provide for exploration of the Amur River and the seacoast near its mouth. It does not appear that the governor general was at all disturbed by the fact that the Amur lay completely within the territory of a foreign and friendly power. Border disputes had occurred, to be sure, but in themselves they were of little consequence. Economically Russia was certainly not starved for land, and only on the basis of political prestige could she at the time justify the attempt to gain a more solid footing on the shores of the Pacific. There was, in fact, no real need for the policy which Mouraviev adopted in

1847. Its general character is now not difficult to analyze. By the Treaty of Nertchinsk, Russian colonization in Pacific Asia had been confined to inhospitable frozen lands north of the Stanavoi Mountains. To the south of these mountains lay the fertile Amur Valley, commanding what seemed like an admirable approach to the Pacific. Furthermore, since China had failed effectively to garrison the Amur frontier, its occupation would entail small cost. A better example of a pure policy of political expansion than that on which Mouraviev embarked in 1847 would be difficult to find.

The work of exploration was undertaken by Captain Nevelskoi. In 1851 Nikolaievsk was founded at the mouth of the Amur. This and other nearby posts were to serve the trading interests of the Russian-American Company. Protection of the Amur, too, would require that Russia hold the Island of Sakhalin, and its occupation was authorized by the Tsar in 1853, despite claims which Japan could assert. The following spring witnessed the outbreak of the Crimean War, and the full implications of Mouraviev's policy now became more obvious. The two great commercial pioneers in the northern Pacific, the Hudson's Bay Company and the Russian-American Company, had agreed to remain neutral in the war between their respective governments, but this did not deter the British and French from attacking Russia's Pacific base at Petropavlovsk. The real value of the Amur for transporting supplies to the Pacific was now evident. In May, 1854, Mouraviev led his first expedition down the river. It included troops and munitions of war. Other expeditions followed, and with them came not only soldiers but colonists with livestock and provisions for permanent settlement. At the Congress of Paris (1856) Russia could afford to accept defeat in Europe, for in the Far East the fortunes of war had already placed her in practical possession of what was legally Manchu land. With peace now restored in Europe, Mouraviev sat firm in the valley of the Amur. His colonists, coming down the river in increasing numbers, settled on its banks. There had been no war between China and Russia, no troubled background of serious disputes, yet the Manchus had already lost their northern frontier. It now remained for Russia by diplomatic action to give the stamp of legality to her newly won conquest. The methods she employed were highly instructive.

When the Crimean War was ended, England and France were free, as the reader will recall, to adopt a policy of force to compel China to revise the first treaty settlement. That policy, applied from 1857 to 1858, resulted in the Treaties of Tientsin, which have already been discussed. The United States and Russia joined in this policy to the extent of sending ambassadors to China, not to use force, but to demand that their countries enjoy whatever advantages were won by British and French arms. Accordingly, when peace was declared in Europe, Russia lost no time in sending Count Putiatin to the Far East. His object was to negotiate a commercial treaty which would admit Russian vessels to such China ports as were open to other powers. Until this time Russian trade had been confined to the overland route. Putiatin attempted to enter China at Kiakhta and, when refused, proceeded down the Amur, which was already controlled by Mouraviev, to the Pacific. Arriving at the mouth of the Pei-ho in August, 1857, he delivered his instructions to Chinese officials. Since the Chinese were unwilling to conduct further business at this place, it was finally agreed that the Emperor's reply should be delivered to Putiatin at Canton. This explains the appearance of Putiatin in south China. Here, joining the British, French, and American envoys, he proceeded to Tientsin, where the treaties bearing the name of that place were signed in June, 1858. The Russian Treaty of Tientsin, like the American, was of secondary importance, but by the most-favored-nation clause it conferred on Russia all the new privileges won by England and France.

Russia Occupies the Amur Country

However, while Russia played only a minor role at Tientsin, her concurrent actions on the Amur were of a different character. Here Mouraviev had been instructed by his government to deal directly with local Manchu officials. In 1857 he had received additional reinforcements, enabling him to hold securely the entire territory northward from the left bank of the river. Late in the year (October) Russia incorporated officially this new dominion under the name of the Maritime Province of Eastern Siberia. Opening negotiations with the Tartar general commanding China's forces, Mouraviev secured a treaty which was signed at the river town of Aigun on May 28, 1858. As a result the Amur now became the legal as well as the actual boundary between Manchuria and eastern Siberia. In addition Russia was admitted to joint occupation with China of the territory on the Pacific coast lying east of the Ussuri, pending a final decision on this frontier. Both the Ussuri and the Sungari, the latter flowing through the heart of Manchuria, were to be open to Russian merchants and travelers.

Thus did Russia, at the expense of the Manchus, increase immeasurably her Asiatic domain. Rarely, if ever, has a province been added to the empires of Europe at less cost. The Manchus were in no position to offer resistance. In China proper their power was still threatened by the Taiping rebels. On the seacoast they were confronted with the military and naval forces of England and France, who at the very moment were forcing signature to the Treaties of Tientsin. In the face of these trials it was but natural that Peking could give little consideration to the Amur. Mouraviev was never scrupulous as to the means to be used. He followed the method that imperialists have so often found convenient; he occupied the territory first and did his talking later.

Annexation of the Maritime Province

Despite the gains won in the Treaty of Aigun, Russia was not yet satisfied. China too refused to ratify the treaty. Count Putiatin, meanwhile having retired from China, was replaced there by General Ignatiev, whose first task was to exchange the ratified copies of the Russian Treaty of Tientsin. This was accomplished without difficulty in April, 1859. The question of the Amur still remained. The Russians, not content with joint occupation of the Pacific coast east of the Ussuri, also wanted a delimitation of the Mongolian-Siberian frontier far to the west and better agreements there for trade. The solution of these problems came from an unexpected quarter. When in 1859 the English and French again attacked the Taku forts to break their way through to Peking, Chinese resistance was due in part to assistance rendered by Russia. Although the extent of their co-operation is not known, there is reason to believe that the Russians had planned the new defenses of the river and that some of them fought with the Chinese. When Chinese resistance was finally broken, and the allies reached Peking in 1860, General Ignatiev was presented with a situation dear to the diplomatic heart. Having been in close touch with the allies during their advance, he soon convinced Prince Kung (heading the Peking administration) that it was his efforts which saved the city from such destruction as befell the Summer Palace. Here, then, was positive proof of Russian friendship and concern for China's welfare. When Ignatiev asked for a new treaty to replace the one made at Aigun, therefore, China could not well refuse. The Convention of Peking was signed on November 14. Its most striking feature was the full cession to Russia of the Manchurian seacoast from the Amur to the Korean border. It also provided for a settlement of the far western frontier. Russian traders might proceed to Peking from Kiakhta, and other trading posts would be established to the west.

By the close of 1860, Russian policy in China enjoyed a success unparalleled by that of any other foreign state. Without engaging in war she was to reap all the advantages, commercial and diplomatic, won by England and France in the Treaties of Tientsin. In the north, by a policy both logical and unscrupulous, she had opened the Mongolian frontier to her traders and had fixed her boundary along the course of the Amur and far south along the Pacific coast to the very borders of Korea. By conquest and colonization, yet without war, she had deprived the Manchus of 350,000 square miles of territory. Manchuria was now completely cut off from the sea, while Russia possessed a new road to the ocean. Even before Ignatiev signed the Peking Convention, annexing the seacoast or Maritime Province, Russia's objective had been made clear. At the southern extremity of the new territory Mouraviev had selected the harbor and site of Russia's future fortress on the Pacific, Vladivostok, "dominator of the East." As a slogan suggestive of Russia's needlessly aggressive policy no better name could have been chosen.

As later and more complicated phases of Manchurian history are discussed in subsequent chapters, events of 1858 and 1860 should not be forgotten. It was in these years that the real character of Russian far eastern policy was revealed. On that policy must rest in considerable measure responsibility for catastrophes which were to follow.

SELECTED BIBLIOGRAPHY

G. Cahen, *Histoire des relations de la Russie avec la Chine sous Pierre le Grand (1869-1730)* (Paris: 1912). P. H. Clyde, *International Rivalries in Manchuria,* rev. ed. (Columbus: 1928), chs. 1-2. Henri Cordier, *Histoire des relations de la Chine avec les puissances occidentales, 1860-1900,* 3 vols. (Paris: 1901-02), vol. 1, ch. 6. F. A. Golder, *Russian Expansion on the Pacific 1641-1850* (Cleveland: 1914), chs. 1-2; this is the standard work on the subject. S. Hsu, *China and Her Political Entity* (New York: 1926) deals with

China's relations with Korea, Manchuria, and Mongolia; see ch. 2. Alexis Krausse, *Russia in Asia* (London: 1899) covers the period 1558-1899. T. C. Lin, "The Amur Frontier Question between China and Russia, 1850-1860," in *The Pacific Historical Review*, Mar. 1934. A. Lobanov-Rostovsky, *Russia and Asia* (New York: 1933), ch. 1, the Russian occupation of Siberia, and ch. 6, the annexation of the Amur region, 1858-1860. H. B. Morse, *The International Relations of the Chinese Empire* (London: 1910), vol. 1, ch. 19, the Treaty of Aigun. H. K. Norton, *The Far Eastern Republic of Siberia* (London: 1923), ch. 2, Russian colonization of Siberia. Leo Pasvolsky, *Russia in the Far East* (New York: 1922), ch. 2, the colonization of Siberia. E. G. Ravenstein, *The Russians on the Amur* (London: 1861), chs. 1-11. "Vladimir" (Z. Volpicelli), *Russia on the Pacific and the Siberian Railway* (London: 1899). The best concise summary is P. J. Treat, *The Far East* (New York: 1928), ch. 11.

CHAPTER X

Revolution in Nineteenth-Century Japan

IN resuming the story of western contacts with Japan, it will be recalled that early in the seventeenth century the first Tokugawa Shoguns, fearful of the political implications of Catholic Christianity, expelled the troublesome priests and closed the country to all foreign intercourse save for the annual visit of a Dutch ship and a few Chinese junks at Nagasaki. There followed a period of more than two centuries (1638-1854) in which Japan adhered to this policy of exclusion and seclusion. These were years of peace in which feudal society was developed and conventionalized on lines exclusively Japanese and free from foreign influence. The reader has already observed (chapter 3) some of the difficulties which beset the Tokugawa rulers. The feudal structure had already outlived its usefulness, but it continued to survive, supported by the weight of tradition. The maintenance in idleness of the noble and the fighting (samurai) classes placed an unbearable burden upon the farmer, while concurrently there was appearing a new commercial and urban populace possessed of wealth and eager for power. A revolution in the political, social, and economic structure of the Japanese state was in preparation many years before Perry's ships entered Uraga Bay.

While Japan was living behind closed doors, western states were developing a new society, new theories of government, and new conceptions of national wealth. It is only necessary to recall that between 1638 and 1854 Europe witnessed the Glorious Revolution in England, the perfection of the absolute monarchy in France, the Anglo-French wars for control of colonial empires in America and India, the successful revolt of thirteen English colonies, the French Revolution and the wars of Napoleon, and the major beginnings of the industrial revolution with its emphasis on economic doctrines of *laissez faire*. By the first half of the nineteenth century popular middle-class nationalism had triumphed over the crumbling edifice erected by Metternich. Both Europe and the United States (the latter had by that time reached the Pacific Ocean) were prepared for a new era of industrial and commercial expansion. Western commerce was to invade every corner of the globe. By 1840 the first war by a western power was being fought in China.

Japan's knowledge of this changing, threatening western world was obviously imperfect. The policy of exclusion and seclusion had worked all too well. Yet, while this was so, the Tokugawa Shogunate was not in complete ignorance of external affairs. Much information had entered Japan with the annual Dutch ship at Nagasaki. Disquieting as these reports often proved to be, councilors of the Shogun could still argue that the national policy was secured by the very remoteness of the country's position.

Early Nineteenth-Century Contacts with Japan

This alleged security was of short duration. As related in the preceding chapter, the Russians had crossed Siberia and reached the Pacific in 1638, the very year in which the Portuguese were expelled from Japan. Their subsequent explorations brought them inevitably in contact with the Japanese Islands. Attempts were made by the Russians in 1792 and again in 1804 to open relations, but without success. Later British and French explorers appeared in Japanese waters. The Dutch trade at Nagasaki was carried under the American flag during the Napoleonic Wars, and the Russian-American Company chartered an American vessel and attempted to open commerce at the same port. A British ship of war visited Nagasaki in 1808, and while the British held Java (1811-1816), British vessels replaced the annual Dutch ship. The *Morrison,* an American ship, attempted in 1837 to return some Japanese sailors who had been blown from their native shores. In China the so-called Opium War soon followed, and with the opening of five Chinese ports by the Treaty of Nanking, interest in the trade of Japan was renewed. In the decade that followed the outbreak of war in China a number of foreign ships visited Japanese ports. These included British surveying vessels and French and American ships of war. All this activity seemed to foreshadow the breakdown of Japan's seclusion policy. This change, whatever it might be, was of particular interest to two western powers: Russia and the United States.

Russia's eastward expansion through Siberia had not been arrested permanently when her explorers reached the shores of the Pacific. They acquired some knowledge of the Island of Sakhalin early in the seventeenth century. By 1700 they had completed exploration of the Kamchatka peninsula and soon learned of the Kurile Islands, which stretch in a long chain southward toward Japan. In the course of the next twenty-five years two Russian expeditions explored these islands. Early in the nineteenth century the Russians penetrated to the southern Kuriles, which, however, had now been occupied by Japan. Consequently, as early as 1800 the Tokugawa rulers were aware that their policy of seclusion was threatened from the north, and when in 1847 Russia under Mouraviev's leadership became active on the Amur, there could no longer be any doubt that the exclusion policy was doomed.

American Interests in Japan

The interests of the United States in Japan in the middle nineteenth century were primarily commercial. In 1846 Great Britain and the United States settled the Oregon question, and before the end of the decade California, too, was American territory. The way was now open for new developments in transpacific commerce, in particular the direct trade between San Francisco and China. Japan lay in the course of this trade, and, with the appearance of steamships, coaling stations would be essential. For many years, too, American whalers had operated in the north Pacific. They required ports of call for supplies and repairs. Likewise it was desired that American shipwrecked seamen be accorded hospitable treatment when cast on Japanese shores.

Diplomatic efforts to meet some of these problems were made by the United States as early as 1832. Edmund Roberts, American Minister to Siam, carried letters of credence, but did not reach Japan. In 1846 Commodore Biddle visited Japan with a letter of credence which had been entrusted to Alexander H. Everett, then American commissioner to China. A more ambitious effort was made in 1851 when Commodore Aulick was directed to visit Japan and to secure a treaty of amity and commerce. This proposed treaty was to include the right to buy coal, the opening of one or more ports to trade, and adequate protection for shipwrecked seamen and property. Aulick was recalled before his mission could be undertaken, and the task was entrusted to Commodore Matthew C. Perry, a brother of Oliver H. Perry of Lake Erie fame.

Commodore Perry's Instructions

The instructions which Perry carried to Japan were evolved from this growing interest of the United States in the Pacific and far eastern trade. They set forth that his object was: (1) to guarantee protection for shipwrecked American seamen and property, (2) to gain permission to secure supplies, especially coal, and (3) to open one or more ports to American trade. Perry was to seek these objectives by argument and persuasion. Should he fail, he was to inform the Japanese that the United States would not tolerate any but humane treatment of shipwrecked seamen. Perry was also cautioned that his mission was "necessarily of a pacific character, and [that he was not to] . . . resort to force unless in self defence in the protection of the vessels and crews under his command, or to resent an act of personal violence offered to himself, or one of his crews."

He was to be "courteous and conciliatory, but at the same time firm and decided." These instructions were followed by Perry with marked success. He sailed from Norfolk, Virginia, on November 24, 1852, and assembled his squadron of six vessels at Shanghai. He visited both the Loochoo and the Bonin Islands, and with four ships of war, anchored in Uraga, a part of Yedo (now Tokyo) Bay on July 8, 1853.

The arrival of Perry did not take the Japanese by surprise. They had been warned of his coming by the Dutch, who probably stressed the naval and military character of his expedition and sought also to replace their limited trade at Nagasaki by a broader commercial convention. Thus, although not surprised, the Japanese were relieved when Perry on this first visit remained only ten days. In that short time he accomplished a great deal.

He succeeded in impressing the Japanese with the strength of his squadron, containing the largest naval force and the first steamers ever seen in Japanese waters, and with his own good will. He refused to go to Nagasaki or to deal through the Dutch; he refused to accept presents unless some were received by the Japanese in exchange; and he insisted upon treatment suitable to his position as the representative of a great Power. His mixture of "firmness, dignity, and fearlessness" made a deep impression on the Japanese. He succeeded, therefore, in having the President's letter received, "in opposition to the Japanese law," by two of the high officials of the Shogun's court . . .; and he sailed away, promising to return in the spring for an answer.[1]

---

[1] Payson J. Treat, *Diplomatic Relations between the United States and Japan.* Stanford University Press, 1932. Vol. I, p. 11.

The Shogun's Dilemma

Perry's visit confronted the government of the Shogun with the most serious problem the Tokugawas had been called upon to face. Furthermore, as the reader is aware, the vitality of the administration had been weakened by domestic movements, political, economic, and social. Thus the Shogun, instead of assuming full responsibility for whatever decision was reached, took the unprecedented step of referring President Fillmore's letter to the Mikado and the daimyo (feudal barons). The preponderant opinion favored expelling the foreigners when they returned, but fortunately there were a few leaders who realized the futility of armed opposition to Perry's force. The latter was now hastening his return, spurred on by rumors that French and Russian squadrons planned to visit Japan, and on February 13, 1854, with seven vessels, he again entered Yedo Bay. Negotiations were conducted at the village of Yokohama, later to become one of Japan's first seaports, and on March 31 a treaty was signed. The discussions were conducted in a most friendly spirit, and gifts were exchanged, those from the United States including a miniature railway, telegraph instruments, books, weapons, and alcoholic beverages of various kinds. Entertainment, which was lavish on both sides, included a dinner given by Perry on board his flagship. While the Commodore and his senior officers feasted the chief Japanese commissioners at the commander's table, the following scene was enacted among American and Japanese officers of lesser rank:

The Japanese party upon deck, who were entertained by a large body of officers from the various ships, became quite uproarious under the influence of overflowing supplies of champagne, Madeira, and punch, which they seemed greatly to relish. The Japanese took the lead in proposing healths and toasts, and were by no means the most backward in drinking them. They kept shouting at the top of their voices, and were heard far above the music of the bands that enlivened the entertainment by a succession of brisk and cheerful tunes. It was, in short, a scene of noisy conviviality, and of very evident enjoyment on the part of the guests. The eating was no less palatable to them than the drinking, and the rapid disappearance of the large quantity and variety of the viands profusely heaped upon the table was quite a marvel, even to the heartiest feeders among the Americans. In the eagerness of the Japanese appetite, there was but little discrimination in the choice of dishes and in the order of courses, and the most startling heterodoxy was exhibited in the confused commingling of fish, flesh, and fowl, soups and syrups, fruits and fricassees, roast and boiled, pickles and preserves.[2]

It was significant that at the very moment when the Japanese government was making one of the most momentous decisions in its history, its representatives could, nevertheless, enter wholeheartedly into this interchange of hospitality.

The Perry Treaty

The treaty of twelve articles which Perry secured was not important because of its content, and, as will be seen, it was soon replaced by other conventions. Its importance lay in signalizing Japan's break with more than two centuries of exclusion and seclusion. Specifically it provided for permanent peace between the two nations. Two ports were to be opened for supplies: Shimoda immediately, and Hakodate a year later. Other articles assured good treatment for shipwrecked Americans and their freedom from such restrictions as were applied to the Dutch and the Chinese at Nagasaki. Provision was made for discussion of unforeseen problems, should they arise. A limited trade would be permitted under temporary

---

[2] Francis L. Hawks (compiler), *Narrative of the Expedition of an American Squadron to the China Seas and Japan, Performed in the Years 1852, 1853, and 1854, under the Command of Commodore M. C. Perry, United States Navy.* Published by order of Congress by A. O. P. Nicholson, Washington, 1856. Vol. I, p. 375.

Japanese regulations. American ships were to secure supplies through the agency of Japanese officers, and they were to call only at the open ports, except in cases of distress. Finally, the treaty contained the most-favored-nation clause.

Although this treaty did not open Japan to full commercial intercourse, it was, in the light of two centuries of exclusion, a remarkable achievement. Perry's success was due to many factors. His own "firmness, sagacity, tact, dignity, patience, and determination" must be given full value. It is also to be observed that though Perry's mission was peaceful, the Japanese were fully impressed with the strength of his naval force and were perhaps not uninfluenced by his threat that more ships might be sent if the wishes of the United States were not met. Perry also profited by what the British had already done in China. Through the Dutch at Nagasaki the Japanese knew of the first European war, the defeat of China, and the imposition of the first treaties. Many of them realized that in the face of these events exclusion could not be prolonged indefinitely. This view was also supported by the advance of the Russians from the north and the arrival at Nagasaki on August 22, 1853, of Putiatin with four ships. The frequent appearance of Russian vessels in Japanese waters had in fact been more alarming to the government of the Shogun than any other single factor. All of these contributed to Perry's success, but they fail to provide a complete explanation. To them must be added internal factors of the utmost consequence. A full discussion of these cannot of course be given; some suggestions, however, have already been made (chapter 3). Many Japanese had, through the Dutch, informed themselves rather adequately on European life and culture. They were already partially conscious of the imminent collapse of their worn-out feudal structure. Perhaps some few realized that the development of cities, commerce, and an urban population based on a moneyed and a non-feudal economy would soon destroy the exclusion policy even should Perry fail.

Treaties with Other Powers

Perry's treaty was soon followed by others of similar character. England and France had carried the Crimean War against Russia into the northern Pacific, thus making access to Japanese ports even more desirable. Accordingly, when Admiral Sir James Stirling with four vessels reached Nagasaki on September 7, 1854, he had no difficulty in securing a treaty for Great Britain, including a limited form of extraterritoriality. A few months later Admiral Putiatin obtained a treaty at Shimoda (February 7, 1855). It fixed the Russo-Japanese boundary in the Kurile Islands and provided for fuller extraterritorial rights. Finally, the Dutch were freed from the restrictions which confined their trade at Nagasaki. Their new treaty was signed January 30, 1856. Because of the most-favored-nation clause the rights of any one power consisted of the sum total of concessions granted in all the treaties. In 1856 these included: (1) permission to secure supplies at Shimoda, Hakodate, and Nagasaki; (2) permission to trade through Japanese officials and under their regulations at these ports; (3) the right of male residence at Nagasaki; (4) permission to appoint consuls at Shimoda and Hakodate; and (5) the right of extraterritorial jurisdiction.

Three of these treaties (the American, the British, and the Russian) were approved by the Mikado in February, 1855. At the time, the importance of this step was not realized by the foreigners. The treaties had been negotiated by the government of the Shogun and were signed under the title of "tycoon" (great lord). By the foreigners it was assumed that the Shogun was the proper authority to control diplomatic affairs. In a sense this was so. What the foreigner did not know was the extent to which the authority of the Shogun had already been weakened. The result was that when Perry first arrived, the Shogunate was unwilling to accept full responsibility for granting a treaty and so had referred the matter for approval to the Emperor at Kyoto. Since the influence of the Shogun with the Imperial Court was still strong, approval was soon given, and with this support the Shogun could for the time being silence opposition to the new policy. The Imperial approval insured general acceptance of the treaties, but the fact that this approval was sought at all revealed a fatal weakness in the Shogunate's power. It had not been the practice of the Tokugawas or their predecessors to consider the will of the Throne. They did so now largely because what remained of their feudal supremacy was little more than a political fiction. So great a change, too, in the national policy led obviously to bitter disagreement among political groups, and even among those who had favored signing the treaties the feeling was strong that no further concessions should be made. No general trade would be permitted and foreign contacts would be held to a minimum.

The Arrival of Townsend Harris

This was the view held by the more liberal Japanese leaders in 1856 when the United States was appointing its first consul to reside at Shimoda. The choice fell upon Townsend Harris, a merchant of New York, who had been engaged in the China trade and had been named (though he did not serve) as consul at Ningpo. Harris proceeded to the East by way of Siam, where he negotiated a treaty granting extraterritoriality and a conventional tariff. He reached Shimoda on August 21, 1856. The town was a small and inaccessible place at the southern extremity of the Izu peninsula about sixty miles from Yedo. Its harbor was small and had been rendered almost useless by a tidal wave that had visited the place the previous year. Cut off from the hinterland by mountains, no products which could serve in any future export trade were accessible. If it were true that the Japanese hoped to isolate the first American consul-general in a perfectly useless spot, they could hardly have chosen a better place. Harris was not welcome. The Japanese insisted that according to their text of the Perry treaty, a consul was to be appointed only if both powers desired it. Nevertheless Harris landed, took up his residence in a temple, erected a flagstaff, and watched the *San Jacinto* sail away. With his interpreter, C. J. Heusken, he was to wait fourteen months before he was again visited by an American naval vessel, and eighteen months for further instructions from the Department of State.

The main object of the Harris mission was to secure a full treaty of commerce, but Harris himself realized that this could not be accomplished at once. The Japanese were suspicious of him and spied upon his every movement. He therefore set about first to gain their good will and confidence and then to secure a convention which would grant formally to the United States all that was contained in the British, Russian, and Dutch treaties. His patience, his honesty, and his tact were soon rewarded, and in June, 1857, the first of several conventions was signed. It granted the right of residence at Shimoda and Hakodate to Americans, permission to obtain supplies at Nagasaki, and criminal extraterritoriality. At the same time the Dutch and the Russians were able to revise and improve upon their earlier treaties.

But the most important part of the work entrusted to Harris still remained. He must gain consent to visit Yedo, to be received by the Shogun, to present a letter from the American President, and to negotiate a full commercial treaty. While at Shimoda, Harris had discussed these subjects at length with the officials. At times the prospects appeared hopeless. It was more than two centuries since a foreign representative had been received in audience by the Shogun. Nevertheless enlightened counsel prevailed, and Harris was notified that his request would be granted. Only once did the Japanese mention a prostration similar to the kowtow, and when Harris replied that its mere mention was repugnant, the matter was

dropped. His journey to Yedo was accompanied by all the
dignity due a great feudal lord. He was assigned an official
residence near the Shogun's castle, and on December 7, 1857,
he received an audience with the great tycoon. Harris, unsupported by gunboats or marines, had won a diplomatic victory
of the greatest magnitude. It was also a victory for the more
liberal and intelligent members of the Shogun's court. In
marked contrast with China, these men were prepared to cast
tradition aside and to accept the full responsibilities of a new
international order.

While still in Yedo, Harris presented his case for a commercial treaty. These conversations were conducted principally
with Lord Hotta, a liberal daimyo whose post amounted to
that of minister for foreign affairs. The arguments presented
by Harris are not without interest. He sought to convince the
Japanese that the limited intercourse established by the first
treaties was no longer adequate. He stressed the new commerce growing in the Pacific, the threatening advance of England and France in China, and the encroachments of Russia
in the north. In a manner that was not entirely disinterested
or free from prejudice and half-truths he pictured the policy
of the United States as entirely peaceful and free from aggressive tendencies. Japan's advantage, he said, lay in negotiating
an honorable commercial treaty with the United States—a
treaty that would remove any excuse for aggression by European states. These arguments falling upon receptive ears,
Harris was notified on January 16, 1858, that the Shogunate
had agreed to the principal terms of a treaty. General trade
and a resident American Minister at Yedo were thereby agreed
to, and negotiations were continued to complete the details of
the pact. These provided a long and at times difficult task for
Harris, who presumed to act not only as a representative of
the United States but also as an instructor to the Japanese in
the new art of western diplomacy and international law. Today it is fitting that, in recognition of this effective service, his

name should be held in high respect by the Japanese. Harris was a teacher as well as a diplomat; a somewhat rare patriot who believed that the honor of his own country was proportional to its consideration for other states.

Domestic Politics and Foreign Affairs

The negotiations were all but completed during January and February, 1858, and the treaty was to be signed in April. But now a new difficulty arose. The reader is aware that at the time of Perry's mission there was already powerful opposition among the daimyo toward the new foreign policy. The Shogun had carried the day by securing the Emperor's approval of the new treaties. The opposition was silenced, but only temporarily. In 1858 it flared up anew, led, be it noted, by the Prince of Mito, leader of one of the branches of the Tokugawa family. The Shogun was thus constrained to secure again the Emperor's approval before the new American treaty should be signed. A representative was accordingly sent to Kyoto in January, but the court nobility (kuge), never on favorable terms with the Shogunate, and now assured of the support of many of the feudal lords, withheld the Imperial sanction. In March, Lord Hotta proceeded to Kyoto but was no more successful than his predecessor. Meanwhile Harris had appeared again at Yedo to sign the treaty, only to learn that nothing could be done until the return of Hotta. Postponement was the only alternative. Harris waited impatiently. Late in July an American warship reached Shimoda, bringing first news of the Tientsin Treaties, which had been forced upon China after the second European war. In these reports Harris saw both a danger and an opportunity. If the Europeans now turned their guns against Japan, his own policy would be in jeopardy. Could the threat of English and French warships be used to secure signature of the American treaty? Harris thought it could. He argued with the Shogun's officials that their best interests depended on signature of the American treaty before the European squadrons arrived. There was bitter division in the Shogun's government, for Imperial approval was still withheld. Finally, it was decided that the treaty should be signed. Harris had triumphed. In a peculiar way it was a personal victory. Unsupported by naval or military forces of his country, this American diplomat had won the full confidence of his Japanese colleagues. In the moment of crisis this confidence was probably decisive in winning the American treaty.

The terms of this important document (signed July 29, 1858), which governed relations between Japan and the United States until 1894, must be briefly summarized. Diplomatic representatives might reside at the capitals of both powers, and consular agents at the open ports. New treaty ports were to be opened for general commerce.[3] Extraterritorial jurisdiction was granted in civil and criminal cases. The importation of opium was prohibited, in contrast to procedures which had been and were even then being followed in China. Americans might practice their religion freely. There was to be most-favored-nation treatment and right of revision of the treaty after July 4, 1872, on one year's notice by either party. Finally, Harris secured a conventional tariff providing for a general duty on exports of five per cent and on imports of five per cent on raw materials, twenty per cent on manufactures, and thirty-five per cent on liquors.

One can only speculate as to what policy England and France would have pursued in Japan had Harris failed. As it was, when their representatives arrived fresh from war and diplomatic victories in China, there was nothing to do but to conclude treaties almost identical with that signed by the American envoy. This was soon accomplished: the Dutch

---

[3] Kanagawa was to be substituted for Shimoda. Nagasaki and Hakodate would be opened in July, 1859; Niigata, in January, 1860; Yedo, for residence only in January, 1862; Hiogo and Osaka (but not for shipping) in January, 1863.

treaty was signed August 18, the Russian August 19, the British August 26, and the French October 7.

Owing in considerable measure, though by no means exclusively, to the work of Perry and Harris, Japan had now taken her place in the family of nations. Her policy of exclusion had been set aside peaceably. Full commercial treaties had been concluded with leading western states. These changes appear simple enough on paper. In reality, they were fraught with dangers of the utmost consequence, and to these some attention must now be given.

Selected Bibliography

R. H. Akagi, *Japan's Foreign Relations* (Tokyo: 1936) devotes ch. 2 to "Japan Reopened" and ch. 3 to "Restoration and Consolidation." R. Alcock, *The Capital of the Tycoon* . . . 2 vols. (London: 1863). Capt. F. Brinkley, *A History of the Japanese People* (New York: 1915). J. M. Callahan, *American Relations in the Pacific and the Far East, 1784-1900* (Baltimore: 1901). M. E. Cosenza, ed., *The Complete Journal of Townsend Harris* (Garden City: 1930). W. G. Dickson, *Gleanings from Japan* (Edinburgh: 1889), a volume of later nineteenth-century descriptions. J. W. Foster, *American Diplomacy in the Orient* (Boston: 1904), ch. 5, the opening of Japan. W. E. Griffis, *The Mikado's Empire,* 2 vols. (New York: 1906), vol. 1, Bk. 1, which surveys Japanese history to 1872. W. E. Griffis, *The Japanese Nation in Evolution* (New York: 1907). W. E. Griffis, *Townsend Harris, The First American Envoy to Japan* (Boston: 1895). H. H. Gowen, *An Outline History of Japan* (New York: 1927), ch. 24 on Perry's mission. The two excellent works by J. H. Gubbins: *The Progress of Japan, 1853-1871* (Oxford: 1911) and *The Making of Modern Japan* (London: 1922). S. L. Gulick, *Evolution of the Japanese* (New York: 1903). Katsuro Hara, *An Introduction to the History of Japan* (New York: 1920), for cultural influences. F. L. Hawks, *Narrative of the Expedition of an American Squadron to the China Seas and Japan, Performed in the Years 1852, 1853, and 1854, Under the Command of Commodore M. C. Perry,* 3 vols. (Washington: 1856). Richard Hildreth, *Japan* (Boston: 1855), chs. 44-45, the opening of Japan, 1840-1854. Charles E. Hill,

Leading American Treaties (New York: 1922), ch. 11, the Perry and Harris treaties with Japan.

Seiji G. Hishida, *The International Position of Japan as a Great Power* (New York: 1905), ch. 5, the Perry mission. Sobei Mogi and H. Vere Redman, *The Problem of the Far East* (London: 1935), ch. 1. A. H. Mounsey, *The Satsuma Rebellion: an Episode of Modern Japanese History* (London: 1879). David Murray, *Japan*, 6th ed. (London: 1919), ch. 13, Commodore Perry. J. B. Moore, *Digest of International Law* . . . 8 vols. (Washington: 1906). Laurence Oliphant, *Narrative of the Earl of Elgin's Mission to China and Japan* (New York: 1860), chs. 21-32. J. J. Rein, *The Industries of Japan* (New York: 1889). R. R. Rosen, *Forty Years of Diplomacy*, 2 vols. (New York: 1922), vol. 1, ch. 3, the revolution of 1868 in Japan. Frank E. Ross, "The American Naval Attack on Shimonoseki in 1863," in *The Chinese Social and Political Science Review*, Apr. 1934. H. Satoh, *Lord Hotta, the Pioneer Diplomat of Japan*, 2nd ed. (Tokyo: 1908). Sir E. M. Satow, *A Diplomat in Japan* (London: 1921). M. Takizawa, *The Penetration of Money Economy in Japan* (New York: 1927). Four works by P. J. Treat, all of which are worthy of close study: *The Far East* (New York: 1928); *Japan and the United States 1853-1921*, rev. ed. (Stanford University: 1928), chs. 2-4; *The Early Diplomatic Relations between the United States and Japan 1853-1865* (Baltimore: 1917); *Diplomatic Relations Between the United States and Japan 1853-1895*, 2 vols. (Stanford University: 1932).

Additional references include: C. O. Paullin, *Diplomatic Negotiations of American Naval Officers, 1778-1883* (Baltimore: 1912). S. W. Williams, *A Journal of the Perry Expedition to Japan 1853-1854* (Tokyo: 1910). I. Nitobe, *The Intercourse between the United States and Japan, an Historical Sketch* (Baltimore: 1891). Tyler Dennett, *Americans in Eastern Asia* (New York: 1922), ch. 21. J. H. Longford, *The Story of Old Japan* (London: 1910). Count S. Okuma, compiler, *Fifty Years of New Japan*, 2 vols. (London: 1909).

CHAPTER XI

Revolution in Nineteenth-Century Japan (Continued)

JAPAN now entered upon a period of bitter internal strife, the real nature of which it was difficult for the foreign states to comprehend. By signing, without the Emperor's approval, commercial treaties which in a very real sense opened the country to foreign intercourse, the Tokugawa Shogunate incurred the wrath of powerful feudal groups. Among these were elements that were determined stubbornly to maintain the historical policy of seclusion. Though misguided and ignorant of external affairs, they were none the less sincere. Other forces of the opposition were drawn from ambitious leaders of the feudal nobility who hoped to profit by the embarrassments of the Tokugawa government. Their tireless search for arguments through which the Tokugawas might be attacked had now been rewarded, for had not the Shogunate concluded treaties reversing the whole national policy *without the consent of the Mikado?* Two centuries earlier this argument would have been worthless, for the Mikado was then treated as little more than a decorative puppet. Now the situation had changed. Historical studies had revealed the Shogun as a usurper of the Imperial prerogatives and had pointed the way to a restoration of the Emperor as a *de facto* ruler. Here was the golden opportunity. By opposing the new foreign policy of the Tokugawas the rival feudal lords could appear as champions of the Throne.

Rise of the Western Clans

The chief opponents of the Shogunate were the great feudal clans of western Japan, in particular the Satsuma and the Choshu. These western daimyo had felt the heavy hand of the Shogunate in the days when the Tokugawas were consolidating their feudal dynasty. Being envious of the high estate of the Tokugawas, they were in no sense free from sentiments of revenge. They enjoyed, too, a certain strategic advantage in their geographic position in western Japan, where they were far removed from any immediate control by the Shogun's officials in Yedo.

Complicating the situation still further were dissensions within the Tokugawa house and among its principal allies, the fudai daimyo. Many branches of the Tokugawa family had been virile in their opposition to the new foreign policy. They were also divided on the question of the ruling Shogun's successor. All this made it quite clear that the family could not control its own councils and would have little prospect of leading the nation. And yet at this very moment Japan, having concluded treaties with principal foreign states, could ill afford to indulge in a weak or vacillating policy. Accordingly, after signing the Harris treaty, the Shogun's advisers again sought the Emperor's approval. His reply did sanction the treaties, but only as a temporary expedient to be abandoned as soon as the barbarians could be expelled and the old policy of seclusion restored. In this way the Imperial Court accepted leadership in an antiforeign policy. In this it was supported by the western daimyo, by some of the Tokugawa allies, and even by a few members of the Tokugawa house. But it must not be forgotten that this antiforeignism was in part at least only incidental to a movement by these same groups to profit by breaking the power of the Tokugawa Shogunate and by restoring the Emperor to the position of *de facto* as well as *de jure* ruler of the state. A mixture of motives prompted this policy. There were those among the privileged feudal society who desired sincerely the restoration of the Emperor to actual power. Others were interested merely in gaining power for themselves by destroying the Tokugawa regime. With this domestic turmoil Japan's new foreign obligations under the treaties were soon deeply involved.

July, 1859, was a critical month in Japanese affairs. The new commercial treaties were to become operative at the ports of Kanagawa, Hakodate, and Nagasaki. So great was the danger of attacks upon foreigners that the Shogunate refused to open Kanagawa, which lay on the Tokaido (Great Highway) leading to Yedo, but encouraged them to settle at Yokohama, soon to become one of Japan's greatest seaports. The immediate danger was twofold. Ultra patriots among the samurai would not hesitate to embarrass the Shogunate by attacking foreigners. Conversely, many of the first foreigners to reside in Japan came directly from China. In general they regarded Orientals as inferiors to be treated with little respect. There was danger that they would assume the same attitude in Japan. This being so, it is surprising to note that in the years 1859 to 1865, when foreigners were denounced by every supporter of the Throne, only twelve Westerners were killed. One of the more notable cases was the murder of Heusken, interpreter at the American Legation, in January, 1861. On this occasion the foreign representatives, with the exception of Harris, withdrew from Yedo to Yokohama in protest against the Shogun's failure to give the legations adequate protection. Harris took the broader view that the administration was doing everything in its power and that foreigners should not expose themselves unnecessarily to attack. He therefore remained in Yedo, and for a time was the only diplomatic representative in the city. He understood far better than his colleagues the difficulties of the Yedo government and was opposed to any policy of united pressure such as had been applied so effectively in China.

The Murder of Richardson

In September, 1862, C. L. Richardson, a Britisher visiting from Hong Kong, was killed on the highway near Yokohama while riding with three compatriots, two men and a woman. The assassins were samurai in the feudal procession of the father of the Lord of Satsuma, a leader of the anti-Shogun and antiforeign party supporting the Throne. This influential personage had just served upon the Shogun a summons ordering him to appear in Kyoto to explain his conduct before the Throne. There are various accounts as to what happened. There is no evidence that Richardson intended to be offensive. Nevertheless, he and his companions failed to dismount while the feudal procession passed by. For this he sacrificed his life, while his companions were wounded. Although foreigners in Yokohama demanded immediate military action, saner counsel prevailed. The case was reported to London and instructions were awaited. Arriving early in the following year (1863), they included the following demands: (1) payment of an indemnity by the Shogun of 100,000 pounds; (2) an indemnity of 25,000 pounds to be paid by Satsuma, and (3) trial and execution of the assassins in the presence of a British naval officer.

These demands came at a most unhappy moment in the Shogun's career. He had already been summoned to Kyoto to explain his conduct, which could mean only that those opposed to his government and his policy were now virtually in control of the Throne. This proved to be true, for on June 5 the Emperor ordered that all ports be closed to foreign commerce on June 25 and that the daimyo drive foreigners away. Meanwhile, the negotiations on the British demands continued at Yokohama, where the British and the French now offered to use their naval forces on behalf of the Shogun against the antiforeign lords. This offer the Shogun declined. On June 24 the British indemnity was paid and the powers notified of the Emperor's exclusion decree. Their reply declared that the treaties must be enforced, which, of course, the Shogun fully realized. For the moment his policy would be one of delay, while he rested on the hope that some change could be effected in the unreasonable attitude of his opponents.

Choshu Attacks the Foreigners

According to the Imperial decree, the expulsion of the foreigners and the discarding of the treaties were to be carried out by the Shogun's government. No authority was given to the daimyo to act independently. But when June 25 passed without action on the part of the Shogunate, the Lord of Choshu, a tozama daimyo, whose lands controlled the western entrance to the inland sea, fired on an American ship lying off Shimonoseki. Later, French and Dutch vessels were also fired upon, while one American and several French war vessels hastened to attack Choshu forts. It was now evident that the Shogun was unable to control the western barons, and the British had already determined to take action against Satsuma to enforce compliance with the demands arising out of the Richardson affair. Accordingly, a British squadron appeared at Kagoshima in August, 1863. The negotiations broke down, and the resulting bombardment, assisted by a typhoon and fire, resulted in the destruction of more than half the town. Without securing acceptance of their demands, the British sailed away. Three months later envoys from Satsuma called upon the British *chargé*, agreeing to pay the indemnity and to continue the search for the guilty. They also requested assistance in securing in England a naval vessel for their clan. The significance of the incident is obvious. Satsuma had never been genuinely antiforeign, and from this time on the clan followed a liberal foreign policy. Antiforeignism was merely the cloak hiding a determination to destroy the Shogunate.

And now events took an unusual turn at Kyoto, where the

antiforeign and anti-Shogunate forces were in control. Dissension appeared in their councils, and Choshu leaders were accused of attempting to seize the person of the Emperor. Their troops were therefore ordered to leave the capital, and when they attempted a *coup d'état,* the Shogun was ordered by the Emperor to deal with the rebellious clan. At this juncture, Sir Rutherford Alcock, the British Minister, returned to Japan determined to unite the foreign powers in a joint expedition against Choshu. The purpose of this was to give support to the Shogunate in the hour of its need and to demonstrate to the hot-headed clans that it was no longer safe to tamper with the treaty rights of foreigners. Alcock's plan was supported by his diplomatic colleagues, and so, contrary to his instructions from London, he set about to organize a joint naval expedition, consisting of British, Dutch, and French ships and one small American vessel, which sailed from Yokohoma in August, 1864. No negotiations preceded the engagement off the Choshu coast. The fleet went straight to the task of silencing the batteries, a feat that was accomplished by September 8. On Choshu the lesson was as effective as the previous affair at Kagoshima. Clan leaders agreed to open the straits, not to repair the forts or to build new ones, and to pay an indemnity covering the cost of the expedition. This clan, too, now turned to the West for armaments and advice that would create an effective military machine. Since the Shogun could not permit the foreign powers to negotiate with a single clan, a convention was soon concluded whereby the indemnities were assumed by the Shogunate. Payment of large sums, however, proved most embarrassing to the government, and since the powers were more interested in new treaty ports and new concessions, the opportunity was favorable for a second naval demonstration.

Under the leadership of the new British Minister, Sir Harry Parkes, it was planned to assemble the naval forces of the powers at Osaka, close to Kyoto, where pressure could be most effectively brought to bear on the antiforeign forces surrounding the Throne. This time no American vessel participated, for none was available. The demands stated that two thirds of the Shimonoseki indemnity would be remitted if Hiogo and Osaka were opened immediately, if the Emperor gave his approval to the treaties, and if the tariff were reduced to a general five per cent. A vigorous debate ensued among the factions now surrounding the Throne, the Shogun pointing out that refusal to meet the demands would inevitably mean war, a war in which Japan could expect nothing but defeat. The reply was delivered on the final day permitted by the Allies' demands. The Emperor, and this was most important of all, had agreed to ratify the treaties; the tariff would be reduced; and the full indemnity would be paid, for Japan was not prepared to open Hiogo and Osaka until 1868. Thus the most serious problem, the opposition of the imperialists to the treaties, was disposed of. The western daimyo were no longer aligned against the foreigners. But their determination to overthrow the Shogunate and restore the Emperor still remained.

The End of the Shogunate

In February, 1867, the Emperor Komei, leader of the antiforeign forces, died and was succeeded by his fourteen-year-old son, Mutsuhito. And now the daimyo of Tosa counseled the Shogun to relinquish his administrative powers in order that a united government might be established, enabling Japan to take her place as an equal among the nations. The Shogun himself favored the proposal, which was supported also by a conference of some forty daimyo. Accordingly, in November the Emperor accepted the surrender of the Shogun's administrative powers but entrusted him with the conduct of foreign affairs and the defense of the realm until a further conference of the daimyo could be held. This meant that though the Tokugawas were deprived of much of their power, they still retained a pre-eminent position among the feudal nobility. This being more than their rivals could tolerate, a palace revolution took place on January 3, 1868, and the clans of Satsuma, Tosa, Echizen, and Owari gained control of the young Emperor. An Imperial decree now abolished the Shogunate and initiated a complete reorganization of the government according to the wishes of the rebellious clans. The Shogun himself had no desire to oppose these Imperial commands, even in the matter of surrendering his lands and revenues. He now withdrew from Kyoto to Osaka, where he was soon surrounded by loyal Tokugawa troops who, however, were of no mind to accept this summary treatment accorded their lord. Their influence precipitated civil war in which Tokugawa forces sought to free the Emperor from his new advisers. In this they failed completely. Even before their final defeat all hope of restoring the Shogunate was lost. Dual government, which had existed in Japan since the days of Minamoto Yoritomo, was now destroyed, and the Emperor again took his position as direct ruler of the state, though controlled, of course, by the clans that had effected his restoration. At first it was supposed by some that one of the western clans would replace the Tokugawas in some office similar to, if not identical with, that of Shogun, but it was soon realized that this would merely perpetuate the dual system in a revised form. There was likewise a growing consciousness that neither the dual system of government nor the feudal structure of society was compatible with Japan's new foreign obligations.

The Emperor Receives Foreign Envoys

How great a change had already been effected in the imperialists' point of view may be seen in the memorial of western daimyo of February, 1868, advocating a general housecleaning in court procedure and the reception of foreign envoys by the Emperor. The invitation which followed was promptly accepted by the representatives of Great Britain, the United States, France, the Netherlands, Prussia, and Italy. Preparations for this signal reception were marred by the assassination of eleven French sailors by soldiers of the Tosa clan, but the government showed its good faith by accepting in full the French demands and again repeated its invitation to the Imperial audience. Later, when Sir Harry Parkes was on his way to the Imperial Palace in Kyoto under escort of British and Japanese soldiers, attempts were made on his life by two fanatical samurai who regarded his approach to the Emperor as an insult to the Imperial House. Despite these unhappy occurrences, the government of the Mikado, by granting the audience, had now given full proof of its resolve to meet the foreign powers according to the custom of western states. This decision, it should be recalled, was made promptly and with energy the moment the Emperor had been restored. It contrasted most favorably with the contemporaneous and stubborn attitude maintained by the Chinese, as will appear in the following chapter.

The Emperor's Charter Oath

The new advisers of the young Emperor had by their voluntary grant of the Imperial audience given evidence of the enlightened policy they proposed to follow. This was confirmed in April, 1868, by the Emperor's oath, which was expressive of principles on which the restored government was to be based. The bearing of this document on Japan's development since the days of the Restoration can hardly be overemphasized.

1. A deliberative assembly shall be formed, and all measures decided by public opinion.
2. The principles of social and political economics should be diligently studied by both the superior and the inferior classes of our people.
3. Everyone in the community shall be assisted to persevere in carrying out his will for all good purposes.

4. All the absurd usages of former times will be disregarded, and the impartiality and justice displayed in the working of nature be adopted as the basis of action.

5. Wisdom and ability will be sought after in all quarters of the world in order to firmly establish the foundations of the Empire.

Whatever may have been the mixed motives prompting this Imperial decree, the fact remains that the Emperor's oath was later to serve as the real foundation and justification for Japan's progressive and liberal growth. To demonstrate further the break with the past, the capital was moved from Kyoto to Yedo, which was renamed "Tokyo," or "Eastern Capital."

The Abolition of Feudalism

But a new Japan that could take its place among the nations as an equal had not yet been created. It is true that the dual system had gone and that the Emperor now headed a so-called central government. In fact it was not a unified government, for Japan was still organized as a feudal state subject to all the decentralizing influences of that system.

As long as the feudal system existed there could be no adequate national revenues, no effective military and naval services, no uniform laws. The revenues of the new government [formed in 1868] came principally from the lands confiscated from the Tokugawas and their rebellious vassals—all the rest passed into the treasuries of the feudal lords. The imperial armies which had defeated the rebels had been furnished by the loyal daimyos and maintained by them. Feudalism broke up that unity and centralization which was necessary if Japan were to hold her own with the thoroughly organized states of the West. The supporters of the emperor realized this perfectly, but how was feudalism to be brought to an end? [1]

In Europe at a much earlier period feudalism had fallen gradually before the assault of kings supported by the middle

---

[1] Payson J. Treat, *The Far East,* rev. ed. Harper & Brothers, New York, 1935. pp. 231-232.

class. In Japan the legal and many of the tangible aspects of feudalism were surrendered by the voluntary act of prominent feudal leaders. Early in 1869 the daimyos of Satsuma, Choshu, Tosa, and Hizen, the leaders of the Restoration, submitted a memorial in which they requested the Throne to accept their lands, their possessions, and their men in order that there might be a central government in fact as well as in name. This revolutionary proposal revealed not only the profound patriotism of the clan leaders but also their intelligent appraisal of Japan's new position in international affairs. Within an amazingly short time, 241 of the 276 feudal lords, following the lead of the great clans, had likewise offered their estates to the Emperor. It has been argued that self-interest, the hope of enjoying greater power in the new central government, prompted the daimyo to this action. Self-interest was undoubtedly a factor in cases of some of the more ambitious samurai, but it is neither a complete nor a major explanation of the end of feudalism. Loyalty to the Throne played a part, though perhaps not the greatest. The intelligent and informed leaders knew that feudalism had outlived its usefulness in a state which now proposed to join the family of nations of the world.

The process by which the change was effected may be briefly related. The first step was the appointment of the feudal lords as governors of their respective estates, where they retained one tenth of their former revenues. Local administration was paid for out of local revenues, the balance being turned over to the central government. In August, 1871, feudalism was ended officially by an Imperial decree. The fiefs were now reorganized into prefectures. Old titles, such as daimyo and kuge, were abolished. The temporary governors were removed from their posts and new appointees named by the Emperor. The former daimyo still retained a tenth of their incomes, while the central government assumed the pensions of the former samurai.

The Feudal Heritage

The problems that resulted from this sudden and complete reorganization of Japanese society were complex and at times baffling. It was simple enough to create the new central government on paper. It was more difficult to create the actual government out of a society whose whole tradition and experience were feudal. Of consequence was the fact that the new government was itself composed of able samurai who as privileged members of the old society did not now underestimate the task before them. To be sure, some of the feudal lords profited by the change. The samurai, on the contrary, suffered both in honor and in income. They were forced to adjust themselves to a society for which their traditions and training were ill suited. They were no longer the only men entitled to bear arms, for the soldiers of new Japan would be called from all ranks of society. Accordingly, they were encouraged to enter peaceful occupations, which many did. Others found the adjustment too great. They lived on unhappily in, but not as a part of, the new era. Their memories were of a Japan that was gone, where the greatest honor was their privilege of carrying the two swords. To the rising middle class of the towns and ports the abolition of feudalism brought immediate and permanent economic rewards. Under the new treaties, trade prospered and wealth increased. The farmers, freed from feudal exactions, paid a uniform tax. But their apparent new freedom was short-lived. In the course of a few decades they were to find themselves bound as effectively by the money power of the cities as they had been previously by obligations to the feudal lord. Finally, the feudal tradition of loyalty to the clan could not be wiped out by the mere declaration. Yet despite all these problems a great and an essential step had been taken. Feudal ideas were to persist long after the events of 1871. They rested, however, no longer on any legal basis. That basis the makers of new Japan had wisely destroyed.

The Era of Enlightened Government

The new era on which Japan now entered is known as "Meiji" ("Enlightened Government"). It was a period of re- markable change. In contrast with the more than two cen- turies of almost complete seclusion, the nation now turned to accept all that the West could offer. The ideas and products of a western industrial world entered Japan with amazing rapidity. Modernization made feverish haste as though to atone for those lost centuries of exclusion. The bitter opposi- tion to foreign contacts which marked the years 1853 to 1865 gave place to an often indiscriminate enthusiasm for anything new and western. This was not an unnatural reaction. Japan was a small and compact land. Her peoples were homogeneous and the language uniform. As a race they were industrious, ambitious, and eager to learn. Furthermore, they had been disciplined by the feudal order and were ready to accept the guidance of the new national government which spoke for a restored and venerated Emperor.

Even before the official abolition of feudalism, railways, tele- graphs, a merchant marine, and a postal system had been intro- duced. The first railroads, though built by foreign engineers and with foreign capital, were owned by the Japanese—a strik- ing contrast to procedures which were to develop later in China. The construction of the first western-style vessels was of particular interest because of the policy followed during Tokugawa days. After the seclusion edict of 1636, junks could not be built in excess of seventy-five tons. They had no keels and could be used only in the coasting trade. Two years before the Restoration, the seclusion edict was repealed (1866), and Japan purchased, and commenced the construction of, commer- cial sailing and steam vessels. This was the beginning of her remarkable development on the sea. The domestic postal service, begun in 1871, was soon expanded to all parts of the Empire, the nation being admitted in 1876 to the International Postal Union. Another mark of western progress was the adoption in 1873 of the Gregorian calendar. Previously, Japan had reckoned time by the lunar month, as had China. Today the change appears as a small matter, yet it was not effected without causing concern to the more conservative.

Post-Restoration days also witnessed a remarkable growth of the press and periodical literature. Although attempts were made to found newspapers as early as 1861, the first daily paper did not make its appearance until ten years later. Others followed rapidly, until today the Japanese press is an institution as highly developed as that of the United States. Magazines and periodicals of various types made their appearance in increasing numbers, while books on both scientific and literary subjects were translated from western languages.

More striking than this was the development of Japan's new educational system. The reader will recall that the Emperor's oath of 1868 had declared that knowledge should be sought throughout the world. A department of education was formed in the year that feudalism was abolished, and the first educational law set forth that "all people, high or low, and of both sexes, should receive education, so that there should not be found one family in the whole empire, nor one member of a family, ignorant and illiterate."

This was a radical departure from previous policy. In feudal Japan, education had not been confined to the classics, but it had been restricted to men of the upper classes. Women in general did not receive instruction. Thus, promulgation of the new educational policy meant not only that Japan was breaking with the past but also that she was taking a step far in advance of many western states at the time.

Elementary schools were rapidly organized, under the guidance of David Murray, an eminent American educator. By 1874 the school enrollment reached 1,590,115, or one-third of the children of school age. Higher schools were added, and universities, where German influence was strong, were developed. As a result of this educational policy the people of Japan to-day are among the most literate in the world, and this fact must always be reckoned with when Japanese affairs are under consideration.[2]

Toward Christianity the Restoration government adopted a liberal policy. The practice of Christianity had been forbidden in Japan since the beginning of the Tokugawa Shogunate, but in spite of this, some Catholic communities had survived secretly in western districts. When the new treaties were concluded following Perry's mission, foreigners were permitted to practice their religion (Christianity), but its propagation was still under ban. Townsend Harris, following the unfortunate precedent which had been established two years previously in China, in 1860 asked for a treaty guaranteeing toleration of Christianity. The Japanese wisely refused. They realized that Christianity was again becoming a problem, for in 1859, Catholic missionaries, in violation of the treaties, had visited the Christian communities in western Japan and renewed their propaganda. Arrests and confinement of some of the native believers followed, and the old edicts were renewed. Later about 3,000 native Catholics were arrested and placed in control of various daimyos who were under orders to destroy the faith. When foreign envoys protested that an intolerant policy would not win respect, the government permitted these unfortunate Christians to return to their homes. The responsibility of the Catholic Church for the intolerable actions of its priests appears to have passed unchallenged. The problem was indeed grave. Happily for the nation, the makers of new Japan were more tolerant than the foreign priests. In 1873 the anti-Christian policy was abandoned voluntarily. The decision was one of enlightened and liberal statesmanship, though, as will later appear, it opened the way for future problems of conflict between the state and the Catholic Church.

---

[2] *Ibid.* p. 241.

Another striking feature of post-Restoration Japan was the appearance of an army and a navy modeled after fighting forces of the West. Some beginning in introducing western military tactics had been made by a few daimyo even before the arrival of Perry. The character of his fighting forces and the naval units that visited Japan in succeeding years were sufficient to convince even the most antiforeign groups that the old tactics of the samurai were now useless. Some of the Tokugawa troops were accordingly trained under French military advisers, and in 1871 the principle of conscription was adopted. For a time, French instructors were retained in the new Imperial army, but with the rise of German military prestige, these were replaced by German advisers. In naval matters the Japanese turned to England, where advisers were engaged in 1873. Naval cadets were sent to study in both England and America. The clan tradition was particularly strong in the fighting services, the dominant military leaders being drawn from the Choshu, while those of the navy came principally from the Satsuma.

Thus in the space of a few years from the Restoration, through the abolition of feudalism, Japan experienced a revolution quite as significant as those European upheavals of the eighteenth and nineteenth centuries with which western students are more familiar. Japan had embarked on a new and, in 1871, still uncharted course. In main the nation was solidly behind its leaders, prepared for whatever consequences the new policy might bring. Yet it would be a mistake to assume that the revolution of 1854 to 1871 was effected without leaving some bitterness and wide differences of opinion on future policy. That this was so will become more apparent in the next and later chapters.

CHAPTER XII

A Lingering Dynasty

CHINA: 1861-1890

IN 1861 it seemed that the days of the Manchus were numbered. The dynasty that had ruled China since 1644 was practically dead. Its bannermen were no longer a conquering race. Their identity was all but lost in a China which, to be sure, they had subdued, but had not conquered. Socially and culturally they had made no contribution to Chinese life. In the realm of government and politics their contribution was more substantial. Yet even here the Manchus had merely superimposed their control on China's native and ancient system of government. In the early days of the dynasty when wisdom and vigor prevailed, this foreign rule was accepted and even welcomed. But in the nineteenth century the dynasty had been subjected to a series of shocking blows. Internal revolts had culminated in the Taiping Rebellion. With gunboats and bayonets, the western nations had opened China to their trade. Humiliating treaties had reduced the Son of Heaven to a mere equal of western sovereigns. Foreign diplomats resided in the Imperial capital, while in the interior alien missionaries preached under treaty guarantee an alien faith designed to supplant both the religious and the ethical culture of the Chinese people.

Peking's Immediate Problems

Two problems demanded immediate attention. The Emperor and his court had fled from Peking when, in 1860, the

British and the French attacked and entered the city. Now that the panic was passed, the court must return and establish an administration capable of meeting the new treaty obligations which the European allies had imposed. Secondly, this reconstructed government must deal with the Taiping rebels, who still occupied large sections of the Yangtze Valley. Both problems were complex in the extreme.

In the spring of 1861, Frederick Bruce and M. de Bourboulon, the British and French Ministers, respectively, entered Peking, there to establish their permanent residence. Anson Burlingame, the new American Minister, arrived a few months later. A representative of Prussia, with other members of the Zollverein, also appeared, but, though the Chinese granted him the commercial privileges won by the powers in 1858, they refused for the time to permit him a residence in Peking. This refusal was not without its significance. The unhappy events which befell Peking in 1860 were caused in no small measure by the uncompromising attitude of the extreme antiforeign court party. This group, ever since 1842, had counseled armed resistance to the foreigners. In 1861 its influence was still great. Even when the court fled to Jehol, its reactionary leaders, from this safe retreat, continued to demand the impossible—the execution of all foreign prisoners. Fortunately for China, Prince Kung, brother of the Emperor, had been entrusted in September, 1860, with the humiliating task of treating with the foreign armies.

Prince Kung was confronted with the impossible task of creating friendly relations with the foreign powers under the terms of the treaties of 1858 and the conventions of 1860, of securing the Emperor's consent to the conventions, and of reconciling the stubborn court party to its new international obligations. The prospects were not encouraging. The Emperor was a degenerate and a weakling, whose ill health kept him a prisoner at Jehol, where he died in August, 1861. Ambitious members of the court now conspired to control the future sovereign. Two factions emerged, the one headed by Imperial and Manchu princes, the other by Yehonala, the beautiful and gifted but intensely antiforeign concubine of the late Emperor. It was she who in 1856 had borne the sovereign his first and only son. From that moment her influence increased steadily until she dominated every thought of her weakling husband. To her must be credited much of the antiforeign policy in which the court had persisted since 1856. Her enemies had succeeded in excluding her from the Emperor's presence at the time of his death, and had secured an Imperial edict naming a new administration from which both Yehonala and Prince Kung were excluded. It was this conspiracy which forced Prince Kung, still acting in Peking as prime minister, and Yehonala, the former concubine and now the Empress Dowager, to combine forces. Their plans were executed with ruthless energy. The conspirators were overthrown, and Yehonala emerged ruler of the court. In no small measure this victory on behalf of her son was due to Prince Kung, and in accepting this help the former concubine was forced to abandon her pronounced antiforeign views. By the close of 1861 the foreign powers could breathe more easily. They would continue to deal with Prince Kung, the only high minister of the court who had demonstrated his qualities of statesmanship or who realized the fatal results that would follow if the old antiforeign policy were resumed.

Suppression of the Taipings

While this palace revolution was enacted in the north, Taiping rebels still ravaged the lower Yangtze, defying the Manchu power and complicating its relations with the foreigners. Although in the early stages of the rebellion the powers had essayed to remain neutral, they had also in 1860 defended the city of Shanghai against rebel attack at the very moment when British and French troops were likewise fighting Imperial forces in their advance upon Peking. From this time on, foreigners perceived that the interests of their trade lay in supporting the Manchu government, in spite of its short-comings, against the pillage and ruin which everywhere followed the Taipings. The eventual destruction which overtook the Taipings was due in part to the Chinese themselves and in part to aid which they received from the foreigners. Among the Chinese there appeared at this time two men who in ability were unsurpassed by any of their countrymen: Tseng Kwo-fan and Li Hung-chang. The former had rid his own province, Hunan, of rebels as early as 1853 and subsequently regained Hupeh and most of Kiangsi. By 1860 his objective was Nan-king. In these exploits his chief lieutenant was Li Hung-chang. Together these two civilians brought to China's fighting forces abilities and a spirit of leadership such as previously had been completely lacking.

But the imperial soldiery had lost all military feeling, and to restore their confidence more was needed than the quality of their leaders; and this was found in foreign support.[1]

Gradually the prohibition against the enlistment of foreigners in the Imperial forces was removed, and this in turn paved the way for foreign leadership in "shock battalions" of Chinese troops organized to break the last of the Taiping power.

One of the most distinguished foreigners engaged in this service was Frederick Townsend Ward, of Salem, Massachusetts, who, as an officer on an American trading vessel, visited China in 1851. Later he was employed on China coasting steamers, from which he transferred to a Chinese war vessel. Naturally of an adventurous spirit, he proposed to organize a company of foreigners to capture the city of Sungkiang (west and south of Shanghai) from the rebels. The cost was to be met by wealthy Chinese merchants of Shanghai. After some

---

[1] Dr. H. B. Morse, *International Relations of the Chinese Empire.* Longmans, Green & Company, London, 1910. Vol. II, p. 68.

reverses, Ward succeeded so well that the Chinese government
contributed to his cause, and adventurers of all types, mostly
deserting seamen from foreign ships, flocked to his banner.
This was a natural enough pretext for hostility on the part of
foreign authorities. Ward was arrested by the British in 1861
and turned over for trial to the American consul, but by this
time he had secured Chinese citizenship and was accordingly
released. He continued his attacks on the Taipings with forces
composed exclusively of Chinese but officered by foreigners.
This force now became known as "The Ever-Victorious Army,"
and before it the power of the Taipings was dwindling rapidly when Ward unfortunately was killed. Ward's command
fell, successively, to other foreigners: Colonel Edward Forrester
and General Henry Burgevine, Americans; Captain John Yate
Holland, a British officer of marines; and, in March, 1863,
Major Charles Gordon, of the British Royal Engineers.

The Ever-Victorious Army now numbered some 5,000
troops excellently trained by its foreign staff. In assaults on
Taiping strongholds to the hinterland of Shanghai, it was
assisted by a small Franco-Chinese force. The fall of Soochow
soon forced the rebels back upon Nanking, their capital. Gordon, feeling that the remainder of the task could be left to the
Chinese, disbanded his force, and his British officers returned
to their regiments. In July, 1864, Nanking surrendered to
Imperial forces under Tseng Kuo-fan. The rebel leader had
already committed suicide, and thousands of his followers were
put to the sword. With these tragic events, the great rebellion
which for eleven years had ravaged the Yangtze Valley was
ended. By war, famine, and disease it had cost upwards of
20,000,000 lives. Although the followers of the Taiping were
all but exterminated, the rebellion had already proved the
weakness of Manchu power. Without foreign aid it is improbable that the Manchu Dynasty could have triumphed. As it
was, its power was weakened beyond repair. The rumblings
of revolt still remained, for their causes had not been removed.

The suppression of the Taipings, coupled with the fairly intelligent leadership of Prince Kung in the Peking administration, encouraged the hope that China was through with old ways and prepared for new. Many foreign residents entertained a lively admiration for Chinese character and culture. The gunboat policy, it was thought, had surely convinced the Chinese of the futility of resistance. Therefore there was reasonable expectation that the antiforeign policy would gradually disappear, the government would rebuild its decadent machinery on western lines, trade would prosper, and, in short, all would be well. Even some of the foreign merchants at the treaty ports held this view, while among the foreign diplomats at Peking it was particularly strong, as evidenced by the dispatches of Sir Frederick Bruce, the British Minister, and Anson Burlingame, representing the United States. Little could be expected, however, until China herself showed a more positive interest in things western.

Although the treaty powers were all represented in China by ministers and consuls, China had no official representation among western states, her only recorded embassy to the West in modern times being the one dispatched to St. Peterburg in 1733. The assumption had been that, since Chinese civilization was superior to all others, China had nothing to learn from the West and certainly no obligation to be represented there. A few Chinese, including Prince Kung, had in the years of strife between 1842 and 1860 realized the fallacy of this view, and when in 1866 Robert Hart, Inspector-General of the Chinese Customs Service, went to Europe on leave, he was accompanied by Pinchun, a Manchu, who had been commissioned by Peking to investigate and report on what he saw. This gentleman visited most of the courts of northern Europe, where he was accorded the respect due an envoy. Unfortunately, he was endowed with all the bigotry that one mind could well carry. He detested the discomforts of travel and the outlandish customs of western peoples. He reported to his fellow officials in Peking what most of them wished to hear, that China had nothing to learn from a crude and uncivilized Europe.

The Burlingame Mission

It was most surprising then, in November, 1867, that the Chinese Emperor announced the appointment of Mr. Bur- lingame, the retiring American Minister, as China's ambassador extraordinary to all courts of the world. This remarkable move was due in large measure to the advice of Mr. Hart, who since 1861 had urged the Chinese government to move in the direction of what the West termed "progress," and to this end to establish diplomatic representation through which China might convey directly her views and in turn be ac- curately informed on the temper and policies of western gov- ernments. Mr. Hart's counsel was sound, but it was not for these reasons that Peking appointed Mr. Burlingame. The treaties of 1858 and 1860 seemed to the Chinese unduly harsh. Their effects, too, had been widespread. Peking had lost pres- tige; the provinces, revenue. Peking had made the treaties; the provinces, according to the Chinese system, must carry them out. The Chinese had discovered, as Mr. Bruce informed Earl Russell, that, "the conclusion of a treaty is the commence- ment, and not the termination, of difficulties," for the Manchu administration was so feeble that even had it desired, it could not have forced the provinces to observe treaty obligations against their will. The tendency of the provincial authorities to evade the treaties, and of Peking to evade responsibility for acts of the provinces, strengthened the demands of foreign traders for a still more vigorous policy when, in 1868, the British treaty would be subject to revision. Fear of these de- mands and the hope that they might be forestalled were the determining motives on which Peking selected Anson Bur- lingame as its ambassador at large.

To counter the movement for stiffening the treaties; to prevent the disordered state of the country . . . from leading to armed intervention and naval demonstrations: these would provide a sufficient reason for any statesman to make sure that his country's case was properly and clearly represented to the rulers of other nations. The rulers of China had, however, a third reason for the step they now took—a desire to resist the pressure, constantly applied to them, to "develop" their country; to build railways, open mines and erect telegraph lines, not because they wished them, but because others thought that a great and rich country like China ought to have them. They might wish to have them, but they preferred, conservative as they were by tradition, to have them in their own time; and delay is the instinctive aim of every Chinese statesman.[2]

The Mission in the United States

The Burlingame mission sailed from Shanghai in February, 1868. High Manchu and Chinese officials were associated with the chief ambassador, in addition to a large number of Chinese and some European secretaries. From San Francisco to Washington the mission was received with an enthusiasm not unlike that which small boys accord a circus. Burlingame himself was an idealist and above all an orator. He pictured the oldest nation of the world seeking westernization through the medium of the youngest nation. China, he said, was extending its arms toward "the shining banners of Western civilization." How strange these words must have sounded in the conservative ears of Prince Kung and his Manchu associates at Peking! But of this Burlingame had no thought. In Washington his official reception was most favorable. The American government, following the lead of popular sentiment, accorded a Presidential reception, while negotiations for a treaty were opened by Secretary William H. Seward and Burlingame. From these discussions a curious document emerged and was duly signed July 28, 1868. For no apparent good reason it recognized the territorial integrity of China;

[2] *Ibid.* Vol. II, pp. 192-193.

conceded her exclusive control over her inland trade and navigation, except in so far as these were already forfeited by treaty;
provided for the appointment of Chinese consuls in American
ports; guaranteed reciprocal freedom from religious persecution; and granted reciprocal rights for residence and travel and
access for students to the schools of both countries. Finally
the treaty recognized "the inherent and inalienable right of
man to change his home and allegiance, and also the mutual
advantage of the free migration and emigration of their citizens and subjects, respectively, from one country to the other
for the purposes of curiosity, or trade, or as permanent residents."

Likewise, China was to enjoy freedom from American
interference in her future development. As an expression of
pious and ill-considered statements on future American policy,
this treaty, as subsequent pages will show, was a masterpiece.
It was drafted by Secretary Seward. The last provision was
the only one that China desired, while from the American
side cheap oriental labor for the Pacific Coast was the principal
objective.

Policy of the British Government

In London Burlingame's mission was not treated as a spectacle. Nevertheless, the results were far more tangible and
practical. Here Burlingame stated that the mission had two
purposes: (1) to destroy the impression that China had
adopted a retrograde policy, and (2) to prevent western powers
from adopting an aggressive policy such as would make all
progress in China impossible. Lord Clarendon's reply was brief
and without ambiguity. China was assured that the British
government would not apply unfriendly pressure inconsistent
with the independence and safety of China. Secondly, it was
the desire of the British government to deal directly with
China's central authorities and not with provincial officials;
but this policy was stated on the understanding that China

should observe faithfully the obligations of the treaties, and on the reservation that force would be used only to protect foreign life and property immediately exposed. From London the mission went to Paris, Stockholm, Copenhagen, The Hague, Berlin, and St. Petersburg, where in February, 1870, Burlingame died.

The spectacular mission he had headed was a failure. To be sure most Americans accepted Burlingame's oratory at its face value. Unconsciously perhaps, he contributed to the uninformed sentimentality which has been so characteristic of popular American notions on China. His treaty with Seward was a useless expression of principles which in a few years both the American government and the American people were to treat as "a scrap of paper." In Europe, Burlingame's oratory was of no value. Lord Clarendon's statement of policy merely recognized what was already obvious. England would be reasonable *if* China observed the treaties. But that was precisely what China was not likely to do. Peking lacked the power, even if it possessed the will, to enforce the treaties. Contrary to Mr. Burlingame's expressed view, China had as yet shown not the slightest interest in "the shining banners of Western civilization" and would have been heartily glad to be rid of them.

The fantastic nature of the Seward-Burlingame treaty was soon revealed. In the very year it was signed (1868), the British treaty of Tientsin was subject to revision. To neither country had it proved completely satisfactory. The Chinese complained that it granted too much; the British, particularly the merchants in the ports, that it granted too little. Between 1861 and 1867 a number of questions had been settled, temporarily at least, by compromise; but the foreign merchants abhorred compromise. They wanted free commercial intercourse and would be satisfied with nothing less. On the contrary, the Chinese wanted to restrict what had already been granted. As early as 1867 Peking sought the opinions of high provincial officials on a number of rights which it was felt the British would soon demand in their program of treaty revision. These included: (1) the reception of foreign envoys by the Emperor, (2) a Chinese embassy to the West, (3) construction of railroads and telegraphs, (4) exploitation of coal and other mineral resources, (5) the right of foreign merchants to reside and trade in the interior, and (6) increased privileges for foreign missionaries. Many of the replies counseled stubborn resistance to the foreigner and all his ways, but Li Hung-chang advocated a more practical course. Discarding the popular Chinese view that foreigners could not be trusted, he observed that "the outrageous craft and malignity of the Chinese exceeds even that of the foreigners." It was for China to adopt the modern instruments which had given strength to the West. An audience on terms of equality should be granted and legations established abroad. The work of the missionaries should be watched with care, and any attempt to annex Chinese territory should be resisted.

At the same time the foreign merchants at Hong Kong, Shanghai, and other treaty ports were memorializing their governments for a treaty revision that would redress their real or imagined grievances. As against their demands Sir Rutherford Alcock, the British Minister at Peking, advised his government to wait. China, he believed, would go much further if coercion were not applied. This policy, he said, would never satisfy the merchants, but the latter had lost whatever consideration was due them, since they had no appreciation of the obstacles to change created by Chinese law and custom, and were themselves guilty of "fraudulent practices and want of good faith." Accordingly, Lord Clarendon decided to delay the matter of full treaty revision until 1872 and 1873, when the Emperor would attain his majority, and in this view the other treaty powers concurred. An immediate attempt to remedy some obvious evils was made in the British-Chinese convention of October, 1869, but this failed of ratification because of the arrogant opposition of English merchants both in China and at home. Not unlike the Chinese, these gentlemen, too, had their theory of "superiority." Nowhere has their philosophy been given better expression than in these words:

Pressure, indeed, there must always be here [in China] if anything is to be achieved for the advancement of foreign interests and commerce. In one way or another, however we may disguise it, our position in China has been created by force—naked, physical force; and any intelligent policy to improve or maintain that position must still look to force in some form, latent or expressed, for the results.[3]

The Policy of J. Ross Browne

Such was the view of the great majority of foreign commercial residents at the very moment when Burlingame was painting before his American audience an ideal and imaginary China. His successor as American Minister at Peking, J. Ross Browne, revised the picture on more realistic lines, and for this he was recalled. Yet the very government that recalled him had already adopted his views. Browne lacked neither appreciation nor admiration of Chinese character, yet he did not hesitate to label as "without foundation" the impression prevailing in the United States (and encouraged by Burlingame) "that the Government of China is peculiarly friendly to our country, and that great advantages to our commerce are about to accrue from this preference." To the administration in Washington, Browne soon became an unqualified annoyance. His dispatches destroyed with rather cruel logic the entire thesis whereon rested the Burlingame-Seward treaty. Of the China he observed in 1869, he noted that foreign rights had been secured by force and were maintained by force. China, he said, did not possess independence in fact, for she had

---

[3] Alexander Michie, *The Englishman in China*. Charles Scribner's Sons, New York, 1900. Vol. II, p. 321.

already signed it away in the treaties. The diplomatic language of Seward's China treaty had become a mockery.

I question whether it is a good policy to proclaim, in the solemn form of a treaty, that we will not interfere in the internal affairs of the [Chinese] Empire, when [in fact] our very presence is an interference. . . .[4]

To Browne the logic of the American position in China was clear. The treaty rights which foreigners held in China had been extorted by force. So long as China remained antiforeign, these rights could be maintained only by co-operative pressure among the powers, backed if necessary by force.

All I contend is that having forced obligations upon her, we must compel her to observe them, or recede from the position which we have undertaken to maintain.

Mr. Browne's analysis of the position of the foreigners and their governments in China was sound; but in 1869, as on many later occasions, neither the American people nor their government welcomed unpleasant truths.

The Position of the Missionaries

Although the commercial clauses of the treaties were argued by diplomats and merchants, they were by no means the only cause of friction. Christian missionaries had been a permanent source of irritation in China since the very beginnings of western intercourse. Toleration of Christianity had been granted in the Tientsin Treaties of 1858 both to foreigners and to Chinese converts. In this way the treaty powers assumed the legal right to demand that China accord full toleration to her Christian subjects. Likewise, by the Peking Convention of 1860, French diplomacy had forced the restoration to the Roman Catholic Church of property which earlier

---

[4] Paul H. Clyde, "The China Policy of J. Ross Browne. . . ." *The Pacific Historical Review,* September, 1932.

the Chinese had confiscated. By the same treaty, French missionaries could lease or buy land and build houses in any of the provinces. Protestant missionaries claimed the same rights, and so the way was paved for a renewal of Christian proselyting. In the years following 1860, Roman Catholic and Protestant missionaries penetrated every province of the Empire. By the closing decade of the century, converts to Roman Catholicism numbered half a million, and to Protestantism some 55,000. The primary object of the missionary was destruction of whatever religions existed in China and their replacement by Christianity. As by-products, incidental to this religious crusade, the missionaries carried to China some knowledge of western medicine, of democratic politics, and of education. These by-products may or may not have benefited the Chinese. Certain it is, however, that they created much unrest among a populace already none too well disposed toward its government.

The teachings of the orthodox missionary were intolerant of the whole Chinese social, political, and religious structure. His propaganda threatened the Chinese family system and the honors paid to the ancestors. Many Chinese found it difficult to reconcile Christian love and Christian intolerance. Others were impressed by the contrast between Christian doctrine as taught by the missionary and Christian conduct as shown by the foreigners in the treaty ports. Some could hardly forget that the right of the missionaries to reside in China rested on treaties which Christian powers had forced upon China at the cannon's mouth. In fact, it appears that the great majority of intelligent Chinese could see no reason to abandon their own religions for an orthodox Christianity whose superiority was at least debatable.

These reactions, coupled with the great increase in missionary activity, led not unnaturally to pronounced anti-Christian feeling and in some instances to revolting excesses. Wild and fantastic rumors were circulated among the ignorant masses by unscrupulous Chinese. It was commonly believed, for instance, that Christian hospitals and orphanages extracted the eyes of children, and used them to make foreign medicines. All missionaries, irrespective of nationality, suffered with the growth of anti-Christian sentiment. The Protestants were for the most part British and American, and their position became a problem of real concern to their governments. Among the Roman Catholic missionaries the French predominated. Over them France exercised a sort of protectorate which was used most effectively to increase her political influence at Peking.

The Tientsin Massacre

The most notorious outbreak against the missionaries in the period under review occurred at Tientsin in 1870. A mob destroyed the Roman Catholic orphanage and adjoining church. A number of French residents of the city, including the consul, two priests, and ten Sisters of Charity, were killed. Three Russians and between thirty and forty Chinese servants were also slain. Alarm spread among foreigners at all the treaty ports, and British, French, and American warships appeared at Tientsin. France made immediate demands, which resulted in the death or banishment of the chief conspirators. China paid an indemnity of 250,000 taels and dispatched a mission of apology to France. Peking likewise proposed a number of rules to govern the work of missionaries, but as these would have restricted their work, only the American Minister was prepared even to discuss them.

While it cannot be denied that the Chinese mob and many of the officials were guilty in 1870 of an outrageous crime, it is also true that the missionaries, their church, and their governments shared responsibility. At the time of the Tientsin massacre the United States was represented in China by one of its most able Ministers, Frederick F. Low. His dispatches reveal some facts too frequently forgotten.

In my opinion [he said] one of the great underlying causes of the unrest of the Chinese, which exhibits itself in hostility towards foreigners is to be found in the unwise action and illegal assumptions of the Roman Catholic Missionaries; which assumptions have, to a great extent, the countenance and support of the French Government.

Mr. Low referred to the fact that the Catholic missionaries "assumed to occupy a semi-official position" and "claimed the right to protect the native Christians from persecution." An earlier crisis had been averted only by the timely warning of the French Minister who "informed the missionaries that their assumptions were not warranted either by treaty right or good policy." Notwithstanding this, Mr. Low observed that:

It is asserted by the Chinese, with strong probability of its truth, that the missionaries still claim this right, and exercise it wherever local officials are found that can be frightened or coaxed into compliance. This they can do with impunity where there are no Consuls; and even where there are diplomatic or consular officers it is seldom the case that the united power of the clergy fails to silence opposition; and they are left untrammelled to gain all the power possible on the principle that, "the end justifies the means."

Many of the Protestant missionaries, in Mr. Low's opinion, entertained the same view as the Catholics, and he concluded:

An ill-defined suspicion pervades the native [Chinese] mind that some political design lies beneath the honest exterior of the missionaries, and they are constantly watching with a suspicious eye for the hidden mystery which they can neither see nor understand. I regret to be compelled to say that the unwise action of the French missionaries—to say nothing of the French Government—has rather added to than lessened these suspicions.

If the Officials could be undeceived in regard to the real purposes of the missionaries, and if the missions in China could be conducted by really honest and sagacious men I doubt if anything more than a passive resistance would be met with, which would soon be overcome by friendly intercourse and mutual forbearance. But so long as the Roman Catholic missionaries, blinded by religious zeal, and forgetful of the ignorance and prejudices of this people, continue the illegal and unwarrantable assumptions which have characterized their course hitherto, so long may we expect to hear of the hostile attitude of the people towards them, which will occasionally take the form of insurrections, riots and bloodshed, the destruction of missionary establishments and the ill treatment of native Christians —in which Protestants will be likely to suffer also; and [Mr. Low added a most prophetic touch] when these unhappy results occur, the moral sentiment of the civilized world will be shocked at the intelligence of *"religious persecutions,"* perpetrated by the Chinese without cause, provocation or excuse, deserving punishment and dire retribution.[5]

But neither the Church nor the government of France gave heed to the words of Minister Low. In fact, they seemed intent on wounding Chinese pride wherever possible. As evidence of this it is necessary to recall only that the church of Notre Dame des Victoires at Tientsin was built on the site of a Chinese Imperial temple, the cathedral at Canton on what had been the viceroy's yamen, and the Pehtang cathedral at Peking on land from which its towers looked down upon the Imperial Palace.

Selected Bibliography

J. O. P. Bland and E. Backhouse, *China Under the Empress Dowager* (Philadelphia: 1910). J. O. P. Bland, *Li Hung-chang* (New York: 1917). Knight Biggerstaff, "The Official Chinese Attitude toward the Burlingame Mission" in *The American Historical Review,* July, 1936. Frederic Bancroft, *The Life of William H. Seward,* 2 vols. (New York: 1900). M. J. Bau, *The Foreign Relations of China* (New York: 1921), ch. 2, the loss of dependencies, 1860-95, gives the conventional Chinese view. J. Bredon, *Sir Robert Hart* (New York: 1909). D. C. Boulger, *Central Asian Questions: Essays on Afghanistan, China and Central Asia* (London: 1885). P. H. Clyde, "Frederick F. Low and the Tientsin Massacre" in *The Pacific Historical Review,* Mar. 1933. P. H. Clyde, "Attitudes and Policies of George F. Seward, American Minister at Peking 1876-1880: Some Phases of the Co-operative

---

[5] Paul H. Clyde, "Frederick F. Low and the Tientsin Massacre." *The Pacific Historical Review,* March, 1933.

Policy" in *The Pacific Historical Review,* Dec. 1933. *The Cambridge Modern History* (New York: 1910), vol. 12, ch. 17, Sir R. K. Douglas on China 1858-1905. Mary R. Coolidge, *Chinese Immigration* (New York: 1909), the most valuable work on the subject. H. Cordier, *Histoire des relations de la Chine avec les puissances occidentales, 1860-1900* (Paris: 1901-02), and the same author's *Histoire générale de la Chine . . .* 4 vols. (Paris: 1920). W. H. Dawson, "Foreign Encroachments in China" in *The Cambridge History of British Foreign Policy* (Cambridge: 1923), vol. 3. Charles Denby, *China and Her People* (Boston: 1906). Edward B. Drew, "Sir Robert Hart and His Life Work in China" in *Recent Developments in China,* Geo. H. Blakeslee, ed. (New York: 1913).

R. K. Douglas, *Europe and the Far East 1506-1912,* rev. ed. (New York: 1924) remains one of the best brief English surveys, though scanty on American materials. Tyler Dennett, *Americans in Eastern Asia* (New York: 1922). E. J. J. Diguet, *Annam et Indo-Chine française* (Paris: 1908). John W. Foster, *American Diplomacy in the Orient* (Boston: 1903), ch. 8, Chinese immigration and exclusion. H. A. Giles, *The Civilization of China* (New York: 1911). F. E. Hinckley, *American Consular Jurisdiction in the Orient* (Washington: 1906). Tetsu Koizumi, "The Formosan Aborigines" in *Contemporary Japan,* June, 1932. R. S. Gundry, *China and Her Neighbors* (London: 1893). C. Holcombe, *The Real Chinese Question* (New York: 1900). S. Hsu, *China and Her Political Entity* (New York: 1926). K. S. Latourette, *A History of Christian Missions in China* (New York: 1929), the most complete and authoritative account. By the same author, *The Chinese, Their History and Culture,* 2nd ed. rev., 2 vols. in one (New York: 1934). Archibald Little, *Li Hung-chang, His Life and Times* (London: 1903). L. A. Lyall, *China* (New York: 1934), ch. 8, a survey of the years 1842-1894. H. F. MacNair, "Chinese Emigration" in *The Chinese Social and Political Science Review,* Apr. 1923. By the same author, *The Chinese Abroad* (Shanghai: 1924), ch. 1, the relation of China to her nationals abroad, and ch. 2, Chinese emigration. Alexander Michie, *The Englishman in China . . .* 2 vols. (Edinburgh: 1900). H. B. Morse, *The International Relations of the Chinese Empire* (London: 1918), vol. 2, ch. 6, on the co-operative policy, ch. 8, on emigration and the coolie trade, ch. 9, on the Burlingame mission, chs. 10-12, on treaty revision and the Tientsin massacre, chs. 13-14, on the audience question and the Chefoo convention, ch. 18, on Hong Kong and Macao.

C. B. Norman, *Colonial France* (London: 1886), and by the same author, *Tonkin, or France in the Far East* (London: 1884). H. Norman, *The Peoples and Politics of the Far East* (New York: 1895). Mary A. Nourse, *The Four Hundred Million* (Indianapolis: 1935), ch. 17, "The Empress Dowager." G. M. H. Playfair, *The Cities and Towns of China* (Shanghai: 1910). W. W. Rockhill, *Diplomatic Audiences at the Court of China* (London: 1905). G. F. Seward, *Chinese Immigration in its Social and Economic Aspects* (San Francisco: 1881). William Speer, *The Oldest and the Newest Empire* . . . (Hartford: 1870). Payson J. Treat, "Early Sino-Japanese Diplomatic Relations," in *The Pacific Historical Review,* Mar. 1932. By the same author, *The Far East* (New York: 1928), ch. 12, France and Great Britain in Indo-China, and ch. 13, problems of peaceful intercourse. T. F. Tsing, "Sino-Japanese Diplomatic Relations, 1870-1894" in *The Chinese Social and Political Science Review,* Apr. 1933. E. T. Williams, *China Yesterday and To-Day* (New York: 1929), ch. 20 on Ward and the Taiping Rebellion, and ch. 21 on Burlingame and oriental immigration. F. W. Williams, *Anson Burlingame and the First Chinese Mission to Foreign Powers* (New York: 1912). S. W. Williams, *The Middle Kingdom,* rev. ed., 2 vols. (New York: 1907). Francis Younghusband, *Among the Celestials* (London: 1898). R. Wilhelm, *A Short History of Chinese Civilization* (New York: 1929). Wu Ching-ch'ao, "Chinese Immigration in the Pacific Area" in *The Chinese Social and Political Science Review,* Jan. 1929.

CHAPTER XIII

A Lingering Dynasty
(Continued)

CHINA: 1861-1890

IN 1842 China by the Treaty of Nanking had been forced to concede the principles of equality in diplomatic correspondence. In 1858 the Treaties of Tientsin admitted the foreign envoys to residence at Peking, the capital. Nevertheless, opposition to accepting in full the diplomatic practices of the West had not been removed. The government still clung to whatever remnants of alleged superiority still remained. Among these was the question of audience. According to western practice, when an envoy arrived in China, he should be received in audience by the Emperor in order to present his credentials. But to permit an audience would imply that the Son of Heaven was a mere equal of western sovereigns, and so all such requests had been denied. Between 1861 and 1873 the Chinese government used as a convenient excuse or explanation the fact that the Emperor was a minor. Such evasion could not be prolonged indefinitely. The treaty powers had long since determined that the audience must be granted, and to them 1873, the year of the young Emperor's majority, seemed the appropriate time. Many of the foreigners felt that the granting of the audience would remove all the disabilities, real or imaginary, under which they labored in China. While not concurring in this view, the American Minister observed:

... while I am not sanguine that audience of the Emperor will prove such a panacea as some appear to imagine, still my opinion is that a failure on the part of foreign Governments to insist upon it will confirm the high [Chinese] officials in their arrogance and conceit which will be damaging to foreign interests and lead to the interruption of friendly relations at no distant day.[1]

As a result, then, of combined pressure exerted by the powers, the Chinese government conceded the audience in 1873 on the assumption by the Emperor of his majority and full powers. For four months prior to the date of audience the Chinese ministers engaged the foreign envoys in an interminable wrangle, demanding that the envoys kneel before the throne. Three bows were finally accepted as a substitute. The audience was held on June 29, the Japanese Ambassador, outranking the ministers of the other powers, being received first. The audience had been granted. Western envoys had stood in the presence of the Son of Heaven. Western diplomacy, backed by the possible threat of force, had gained its point. Yet the Chinese ministers were not without their victory, too. The audience had been held in the "Pavilion of Purple Light," which in the past China had used in granting audience to tributary and vassal states. The suggestion was as pointed as it was subtle.

The Margary Affair

The audience question had no sooner passed than China's foreign relations were again disturbed by an incident involving primarily the British. Great Britain's annexation of Upper Burma moved the British boundary to the borders of Chinese territory in the province of Yunnan. Several British expeditions had failed to penetrate this region, but one organized in 1874 promised greater success. The British Legation in Peking was asked to provide passports and an interpreter from the consular service. The man selected as interpreter was Augus-

---

[1] United States Department of State (Archive Section), *China Despatches.* Vol. 32, no. 142.

tus Raymond Margary. Accompanied by six Chinese he proceeded up the Yangtze and through Yunnan across the border into Burma, where he joined the expedition. In 1875, when the expedition entered Yunnan, it met with resistance, and Margary, together with a number of his Chinese companions, was treacherously slain. News of this outrage reached Sir Thomas Wade, the British Minister in Peking, in March, and within eight days he had presented demands for redress. These related not only to the murder of Margary but also included extraneous matters, touching upon the audience question, the development of foreign trade, and taxation of foreign goods in China. Traditional diplomacy was again at work. The British Minister was utilizing an incident, the murder of a national, as the convenient pretext for pressing the settlement of outstanding questions.

For a year and a half, stormy negotiations followed between Sir Thomas and the Chinese Foreign Office, terminating in signature of the Chefoo Convention on September 13, 1876. This convention consisted in reality of three settlements:

Section 1. The Margary Case. Proclamations approved by the British Minister were to be issued in all the provinces. Appropriate regulations were to provide for the regulation of the frontier trade between Burma and Yunnan. A second mission might be sent from India and for five years British officers might be stationed in Yunnan. Indemnity was to be paid to the families of the murdered and to meet claims of British merchants. An Imperial letter expressing regret was to be carried by mission to London.

Section 2. Official Intercourse. China was to invite the foreign representatives to consider a code of official etiquette in order that the same regard might be shown foreign representatives in China as in other foreign countries. The powers were likewise to be invited to consider measures for the more effective administration of justice at the open ports.

Section 3. Trade. China was to open four additional treaty ports. She was also to name six places on the Yangtze to be opened not as treaty ports but as ports of call for steamers.

There was much criticism of this settlement both among Chinese and foreigners, and since two thirds of it required the assent of all the treaty powers, much delay was inevitable. It was not ratified by the British government until 1885. Nevertheless, the Margary affair served to open a multitude of questions. In 1876, George F. Seward, then American Minister at Peking, submitted to his diplomatic colleagues a memorandum covering the main issues in dispute. It revealed how wide was the gulf between foreign demands and Chinese concessions. The audience with the Emperor was still regarded as unsatisfactory; letters of credence were not properly received; high Chinese officials still failed to accord the envoys a respect which was their due; there were conflicts in the commercial law, flagrant defects in the Chinese courts, and so on. In fact, the Chefoo agreement settled nothing, for, though the Chinese ratified it, England waited for nearly a decade.

The Chinese in the United States

Turning from these commercial wrangles between China and the British, it is now necessary to review one of the most unhappy phases of China's relations with the United States. Early in 1848 news had reached Hong Kong of the discovery of gold in California. Chinese immigrants were attracted immediately. Several hundred arrived at San Francisco in 1849, and several thousand the following year. At the beginning of 1853 there were probably 25,000 Chinese in California. These immigrants were for the most part free agricultural peasants. They were young, thrifty, and industrious. Contrary to what was often asserted at a later time, they were not paupers, lepers, or criminals. Furthermore, in these early years of the immigration, the Chinese were welcomed and "considered almost indispensable; for in those days race antipathy was subordinated to industrial necessity, and in a heterogeneous community where every Caucasian expected to be a miner or a speculator, the reticent, industrious, adaptable Chinese could find room and something more than toleration. They were highly valued as general laborers, carpenters and cooks; the restaurants established by them in San Francisco and in the mines were well kept and extensively patronized. . . . Whatever the white man scorned to do the Chinaman took up; whatever white men did, the Chinese could learn to do; he was a gap-filler, doing what no one else would do. . . ." [2]

But even in these pleasant years when Californians were referring to the Chinese as brothers and equals and were stuffing their pockets with religious tracts, hatred against them was rising in the mining regions. The cry was soon raised, "California for Americans." As early as 1855 the governor was denouncing the Chinese to satisfy his constituents, anti-Chinese memorials were in circulation, and many anti-Chinese bills were offered in the legislature. It was just at this time that the notorious coolie trade to Cuba and Peru was at its height (see p. 138), and it became common practice for senators and representatives from the Pacific Coast and many of the newspapers to charge that the Chinese in California came under similar servile contracts. This was willful misrepresentation, but no weapon was scorned by those who wished to see the Chinese ousted from the United States. In fact, the Chinese had become a political question. The Civil War prevented an earlier aggravation of the problem, and the transcontinental railroad construction that followed it absorbed all available Chinese labor. The Central Pacific was finished in 1869, at which time the roads were employing nearly 10,000 men, of whom some 9,000 were Chinese. Without their services the

---

[2] Mary Roberts Coolidge, *Chinese Immigration*. Henry Holt & Company, New York, 1909. pp. 21-22.

railroad would not have been completed within the time required by law. As railroad laborers, the Chinese had proved themselves "peaceable, industrious and economical, apt to learn and quite as efficient as white laborers." These facts were of course related directly to the Seward-Burlingame Treaty of 1868, in which the United States had pledged itself to the principle that man posseses an inherent and inalienable right to change his home and allegiance.

Defying all forecasts, the completion of the railways did not usher in an era of prosperity on the Pacific Coast. On the contrary, land values failed to rise; thousands of white and Chinese laborers were thrown upon the market. The California State Democratic platform in 1869 was rabidly anti-Negro, anti-railway and anti-Chinese. The Republicans, too, found it expedient, politically speaking, to be nominally anti-Chinese. It is not surprising, therefore, that California experienced a disgraceful regime of unconstitutional anti-Chinese legislation. The memorial of the California Senate to Congress (1876-1877) was perhaps the most striking example of a partisan document, under the guise of an impartial investigation of the Chinese, designed to inflame race prejudice and to win an election. As one able commentator observed:

It must be inferred that the politicians who produced the Address and the Memorial, counted on the testimony never being read.[3]

Meanwhile, despite the protests of fair-minded Californians, the Chinese had been subject to outrageous abuse. Until 1867 the guilty elements were drawn largely from the adventurous and the criminal. But after this date there was a pronounced relationship between attacks upon the Chinese and political campaigns. In July, 1868, J. Ross Browne (then on his way to Peking as American Minister) informed the State Department from San Francisco that:

---

[3] *Ibid.* pp. 94-95.

[The Chinese] do not seek to interfere in our political struggles; they are peaceful and law-abiding; they are always willing to bear their equal burden of taxes; and all they ask is to be treated with common humanity. It is a noticeable fact that the only strenuous opposition to them is from an alien population, who upon the principle of discrimination urged against the Chinese would themselves be excluded. [Here Mr. Browne had reference to "the lower classes" of Irish.] But the fault is not so much with the laboring classes who pour into our country from Europe, as with the political charlatans who mislead them.[4]

Despite testimony of this type, it was becoming more and more evident that the Chinese were to be sacrificed for political expediency, and, since most of the state legislation against them had been declared unconstitutional, the negotiation of a new treaty and federal legislation were the only recourse. In 1876 a joint special commission of Congress was appointed to investigate Chinese immigration. Unfortunately, even its findings were based on political considerations rather than on the facts. The views of Senator Oliver P. Morton, published after his death, affirmed, in contrast to his less scrupulous colleagues, that prostitution was no greater among the Chinese than among the whites and that they gambled no more than the early white settlers under similar conditions. Nevertheless, by 1880 the Pacific Coast had determined that "the Chinese must go."

The Angell Mission

It is not surprising, therefore, that when in 1879 George F. Seward, American Minister in Peking, was instructed to inform the Chinese government on the trend of sentiment in California and to inquire what measures it might be willing to adopt, he replied that he had first to allay China's justifiable

---

[4] United States Department of State (Archive Section), *China Despatches.* Vol. 25, no. 1.

resentment resulting from the treatment her subjects had received on the Pacific Coast. Not satisfied that the question could be handled by Mr. Seward, the American government appointed in 1880 a commission consisting of James B. Angell, President of the University of Michigan, John F. Swift, of California, and W. H. Trescot, a former Assistant Secretary of State, to negotiate a new treaty with China. On the subject of Chinese immigration, which was the real problem before the commission, it received, curiously, no instructions other than a reference to the platforms of the two major political parties, both of which had sought to win California by playing to popular anti-Chinese prejudice.

On the basis of this background, then, a new immigration treaty between the United States and China was signed on November 17, 1880. In glaring contrast to the principle of "inherent" and "inalienable" free migration to which the United States had pledged itself in 1868, the first clause of the new treaty stated:

> Whenever in the opinion of the Government of the United States, the coming of Chinese laborers to the United States, or their residence therein, affects or threatens to affect the interests of that country . . . the Government of China agrees that the Government of the United States may regulate, limit, or suspend such coming or residence, but may not absolutely prohibit it. The limitation or suspension shall be reasonable and shall apply only to Chinese who may go to the United States as laborers. . . .

Obviously the purpose of the commissioners was to find a practical solution which would not violate the principle established in 1868. They felt that they had found it in the provision that the United States might "suspend" but not "absolutely prohibit" Chinese immigration. However, there was difference of opinion as to what would constitute a "reasonable" suspension, and in 1882 President Arthur vetoed a bill which would have suspended Chinese immigration for twenty years on the ground that it was a practical violation of the treaty. He accepted an amended bill in which the term of suspension was ten years. But regardless of Presidential vetoes and interpretations of the treaty, Chinese exclusion had, by 1882, become a national policy. Since as early as 1849 Chinese had been denied the rights of citizens in California, and now their naturalization was forbidden. More drastic legislation to enforce exclusion was passed in 1888 and again in 1892. Two years later, what was already an accomplished fact was given legal recognition in a new treaty with China by which the United States might prohibit absolutely the immigration of Chinese laborers for ten years. In reality, this was the end of the Chinese "problem," for in 1902 the exclusion legislation of 1888, without treaty sanction, was renewed and applied to American insular possessions, and in 1904 it was made perpetual.

In terminating this brief review of Chinese immigration to the United States, certain conclusions are inescapable. The Chinese were welcomed so long as labor on the Pacific Coast was scarce. When this was no longer true, their competition was resented. Political leaders, taking advantage of this situation and willfully distorting the facts, accused the Chinese of constituting a vicious element destructive of American standards. That these blanket charges were generally unfounded has long been known. To relieve political pressure and also to meet the real needs of limitation, the American government was forced to modify its views on free immigration, but even this did not satisfy popular demands. Exclusion legislation against the Chinese was finally made permanent without modification of treaty obligations. As a former American President has said:

> . . . in the effort to carry out the policy of excluding Chinese laborers, Chinese coolies, grave injustice and wrong have been done by this nation to the people of China, and therefore ultimately to this nation itself.

The French in Indo-China

At the very moment when China was being rebuffed by the methods which Americans chose to adopt in the exclusion of Chinese immigrants, she was affronted with even less scruple by a great European power—France. The origins of this dispute were rooted in the peculiar political conditions prevailing in the great southern peninsula of Indo-China. The states of this region had all at one time or another recognized the suzerainty of China. The eastern part of the peninsula contained Cochin China, Cambodia, Annam, Laos, and in the north, against the borders of China proper, Tongking. It was about these states that French interests and the Franco-Chinese disputes centered. It was here that France hoped to rebuild her shattered colonial empire and maintain her prestige in the Far East. Steps in this direction were taken as early as 1787, when, through the instrumentality of a French Roman Catholic bishop, France concluded a treaty with the fugitive king of Cochin China, as a result of which the sovereign was restored and his territory extended far to the north to include Annam and Tongking. As recompense, French missionaries were permitted to carry on their religious propaganda under royal favor. However, later sovereigns ordered them from the country. Many refusing to go, and as a consequence suffering death, the inevitable followed. Between 1843 and 1856 French naval and military forces appeared on the coasts of Annam with demands for the release of prisoners and grants of religious freedom. The imperialistic technique worked smoothly. Pretexts for further encroachment soon followed, and by 1862 France had forced Annam to accord religious freedom, to pay an indemnity of $4,000,000, and to cede in full sovereignty three of the southern provinces. In the following year Cambodia was made a French protectorate, and in 1867 further provinces of Annam were annexed. With these successful advances to its credit, French policy now turned its attention to the north of the peninsula, where the Red River flows through Yunnan and Tongking to the sea. The opening of this river to French commerce would, it was believed, be a valuable asset. In the treaty signed in 1874, France acknowledged the independence of what was left of Annam and remitted the unpaid portion of the 1862 indemnity, while Annam opened new ports and the Red River to navigation and agreed to the annexation of the provinces France had seized in 1867. The Franco-Prussian War preventing further aggression, it was not until 1882 that France was prepared to carry the policy further. She now demanded a new treaty and, when this was refused, seized Hanoi, the principal town of Tongking. Hue, the capital, was also captured, and two treaties were signed in 1883 and 1884. By these Annam became a French protectorate.

These developments could hardly have failed to involve the Chinese. By the new treaties, France had displaced China, without consulting her, as the suzerain power over Annam; and Chinese troops, at the invitation of Annam, had been sent across the border and engaged the French. The circumstances attending this open challenge to China's overlordship in the Far East, the shifting and unscrupulous character of French diplomacy, the contemporaneous advances of Russia and Japan, and finally, the helplessness of China herself, clearly foreshadowed her fate at the close of the century, which will be related in a subsequent chapter. Her plight as seen by the Viceroy Li Hung-chang in 1883 was expressed in these words:

... China had no friends. Russia was menacing her on the north. Germany had invaded her territory at Swatow. Japan had taken the Loo-Choo Islands. England held Hongkong, and was forcing upon her a traffic in opium that meant the misery and ruin of her people. France was sending an expedition to dismember her empire. [And] the United States had passed an act excluding Chinese from her soil, Chinese, alone, of all the races in the world.

This was indeed a dismal, a disheartening picture; but, as John Russell Young, at the time United States Minister at

Peking, informed the Viceroy, China had largely herself to blame.

She must first show the world [said Minister Young] that she has a Government. There is now no government in Peking.

Ewing Galloway.

LI HUNG-CHANG. The most distinguished of China's 400 millions at the close of the nineteenth century—"great, not because he is so much in advance of his countrymen, but because he is not so far behind as they are. . . ."

China, instead of dealing with foreign powers, was simply "trifling." The most ordinary questions that could be settled in an hour were allowed to linger for months with no result. The Foreign Office at Peking showed not the remotest desire to encourage diplomatic relations. The result was irritation

and friction. In these circumstances Li Hung-chang was called
upon to face the advance of France in Annam. On the one
hand were the demands of France, on the other the demands
of "an unreasonable war party in the Yamen [Chinese Foreign
Office] composed of men who had never heard a gun fired in
their lives, but spent their time in clamoring for war."

In this situation the proper course for China was made even
more uncertain by the irregular policy of France. Early in
1883 it had appeared that France was seeking a settlement
satisfactory to China on the basis of recognition of China's
suzerainty over Annam, in return for which France would be
allowed practical possession and the right of opening the country to trade. But all this was changed when a French officer
was killed in Annam and M. Lacour was appointed to head
the French Foreign Office. The French Minister at Peking
was recalled, and his successor was instructed to deliver an ultimatum declaring that China had no rights in Annam and that
any assertion of them would be regarded as an act of war. A
partial explanation of this policy was given by the retiring
French Minister, M. Bourée.

. . . the whole business [French policy in Annam] is a mining
operation. The [French] Government is at the mercy of speculators. It all means an operation on the Bourse. There are fine mines
in this country, and the influences represented by M. Tricou [the
new French Minister to China] and M. Lacour are entirely speculative. They wish to plunge France into a war to make money.

Views of Minister Young on China

While this assertion was undoubtedly true, a far larger
question was involved in the Franco-Chinese crisis in Annam:
the question of the legal relationship between China and the
border states over which she claimed to be suzerain. This
question had already arisen both in Korea and Formosa. A
conversation between Li Hung-chang and John Russell Young

in 1883 illustrates not only the problem but also the divergence
of views between China and the western powers on the subject
of sovereignty. In discussing China's problem in Annam, Mr.
Young informed Li that China had invited controversy and
aggression by her own uncertain policy.

Why did not the emperor define the actual limits of China and
say to the world that this was his territory, and he would defend it.
The world would respect such a declaration. But China claimed
dependencies, and then declined the responsibility of governing
them. In Formosa when the Japanese asked for reparation because
of the murder of Japanese seamen by Formosan savages China answered that she was not to blame for the acts of savages. Japan sent
an expedition to punish the authors of the outrages, and China at
once came forward and paid an indemnity to Japan to leave the
country. In the West we should call that an ignoble act.

If [Minister Young continued] Formosa were Chinese territory,
why submit to the indignity of a foreign army invading the soil?
The same thing happened in Corea. The crew of an American
ship was murdered by Coreans. My predecessor Mr. Low asked
redress from the Yamen. He was informed that China was not
responsible for Corea. We were compelled to deal with Corea in
our own way. Why does not China define her territory?

The Viceroy [Li Hung-chang] said that the limits of the empire
were well defined. There was China, and there were the tributaries
of China. These tributaries were self governing, except in the fact
that they owed the emperor an allegiance, which was satisfied by
acts of tribute and ceremony. These offices done, the emperor never
interfered in the internal affairs. At the same time their independence concerned China, and he could not be insensible to any attack
upon it.

I [Young] replied that in modern times and under the forms of
civilization which now prevailed, there were no such institutions as
tributary states. A colony was as much a part of the empire as the
capital. . . . China should follow it [this rule], and save herself
embarrassments by consolidating her empire, and having the world
know the exact limits of her territory.

His Excellency [Li] said that he saw no reason why the outside
nations should destroy relations that had existed between China and
these outlying nations for ages. . . . Why should France come in

and disturb them? It was an act of aggression, and only convinced him that China had no friends among the nations.[5]

The above conversation between John Russell Young and Li Hung-chang clarifies a problem that was to plague China in her foreign relations far into the twentieth century. Briefly the facts were these: China's old position as the Middle Kingdom, exercising suzerainty over a surrounding circle of vassal states, was tenable so long as China's supremacy in the Far East passed without challenge. But events of the nineteenth century had changed all this. The coming of the English, the Russians, the French, and the Americans had resulted in treaties which had deprived even China herself of full sovereignty. This being so, there was little chance that these powers would respect China's overlordship in distant border states. In reality China was no longer the Middle Kingdom, yet she clung tenaciously to the theory. Her policy from 1883 to 1885 was, as Minister Young observed, one of "delay."

Time is the Oriental's most trusted ally. To employ this delay, by persistent appeals to public opinion in Europe and the United States, in the hope that the peaceful ways of China . . . her want of enterprise, her desire to live at home, undisturbed and not disturbing, would awaken sympathy.

In many respects this policy was natural, for, said Minister Young:

The internal condition of China is so unique, that in dealing with it, we have a problem which cannot be solved by any recognized law of diplomatic mathematics. You have the most absolute of monarchies; the most democratic of democracies. You have a most conservative and patient people to whom tradition is a religion, and precedent a commandment, and yet who have maintained within the present generation the greatest rebellion of the century. You have the most skeptical of men, who believe in nothing but what they see with their own eyes, or read in the books of Confucius; the most credulous of men, who apprehend the fate of a dynasty in the nebula of a star, or the flushing of the sun at sunset.

---

[5] *Ibid.* Vol. 65, no. 230, Young to Frelinghuysen; Peking, August 8, 1883.

And, he added:

China is permeated with secret societies. Some take moral forms; namely, against tobacco and opium. But no one doubts that, beneath the desire to attain higher excellence in the observance of moral and sanitary laws, political considerations exist. For the Chinaman is a chattering, imaginative, inquisitive politician, living among his fellow shopkeepers, and watching with suspicion every token in the sky, every movement of the foreigner, every act of the high officials.[6]

And so while Li Hung-chang complained of the foreigners and Peking officials clamored for war, neither the dynasty nor the people of China were prepared for what war with a modern European power entailed, and this Li Hung-chang well knew. Consequently, in 1884 the treaties between France and Annam were accepted on the useless understanding that France would respect the fiction that China was still overlord in Annam. However, further clashes occurred in Tongking between French and Chinese forces, in which the former were defeated. France turned to reprisals. A French naval force was sent to Formosa and hundreds of Chinese were slain at Foochow. In desperation China declared war. The disastrous conflict which might have ensued was prevented through the efforts of Sir Robert Hart, and a treaty of peace was signed June 9, 1885. The French position in Annam was recognized, together with the right of French subjects to trade across the Chinese frontier. France waived her demands for an indemnity but "secured a possible advantage through the understanding that should China decide to build any railways she would call upon France, who would give her every facility to secure in France the personnel she might need, but this was not to be considered as an exclusive advantage in favor of France."[7] It was, nevertheless, the beginning on which the later "spheres of influence" were to be built.

---

[6] *Ibid.* Vol. 67, no. 308.

[7] Payson J. Treat, *The Far East,* rev. ed. Harper & Brothers, New York, 1935. p. 131.

Events in Western China

In her far western dependencies during the same years, China enjoyed more success. Since the middle of the century there had been some border trade with Russia across the frontier of Ili. At the time of a Mohammedan rebellion (1871) Russia occupied the area on the pretext of preserving order. Just when it appeared doubtful that China would regain her control, one of her few able military leaders, Tso Tsung-tang, re-established her sovereignty (1878). A treaty negotiated the following year restored two thirds of the province to China, while Russia was to receive 5,000,000 rubles to cover the expenses of her occupation. This treaty was not acceptable to China, but in 1881, after war had been threatened, a second was signed. The entire province was restored to China, the Russian indemnity was increased to 9,000,000 rubles, and her trading privileges across the frontier were defined more explicitly.

As the student looks back to China's relations with the western powers during the years 1861 to 1890, he finds few signs of encouragement. It is true that in the main it was a period of peaceful intercourse, but peaceful only in a relative sense. No major wars such as those of 1840 or 1857 and 1858 marked the period, but there were many years in which the threat of war was present. Among the foreigners in China no element was satisfied. In Peking the diplomats dealt with a government whose daily policy was evasion. The Christian missionaries confronted a populace that regarded them with distrust, if not hatred. The merchants in Shanghai and Canton chafed at treaties that denied them unqualified access to China's markets. On the Chinese side, discontent was quite as pronounced. Throughout the Empire there was restlessness and often open rebellion. Many Chinese believed that the dynasty had outlived its usefulness. For many years its authority had been challenged by the Taipings, and it had failed utterly to stop the advance of the hated western barbarians. In this complex tangle of relationships, this impact of the modern West upon the ancient East, virtually nothing, in the years 1861 to 1890, was settled. For the moment, China's policy of evasion had triumphed. The day of reckoning had been postponed. It had not been forestalled.

For bibliographical references
see the preceding chapter.

CHAPTER XIV

A Political Invalid: Korea

A NEW and a disturbing influence made itself felt in international politics of the Far East as the nineteenth century drew to a close. Since the first English victories in 1840, the great powers of the West had pressed aggressively upon China. They had robbed her of many of the attributes of a sovereign state. They controlled her tariffs, enjoyed extraterritoriality, annexed portions of her territory when it was convenient to do so, and, as has been seen in the preceding chapter, denied her overlordship in the border states of Indo-China. It was a slow process, for China's resistance had been persistent and stubborn. Nevertheless, an eventual victory for western imperialism in one or more of its many forms appeared certain. These advances at the expense of China had not been made without the development of pronounced rivalries: rivalries among the British, the Russians, the French, and the Americans. To a degree these rivalries had been checked on the ground that a common co-operative policy was the best means of preserving and increasing foreign rights and privileges in China. In addition, all the western powers represented civilizations that had much in common. It was assumed, too, that these civilizations were superior to that of China, and that therefore China must submit eventually to western ways of living and western methods of thought. This being so, it was somewhat disturbing, after 1870, to discover that a rival power, one that was neither western nor Christian, was also seeking a share in whatever spoils might be gathered from China. That power was Japan.

New Japan and Her Neighbors

The advent of Japan into the select circle of consequential powers is a phenomenon of very recent date. When Commodore Perry entered Uraga Bay, in 1853, Japan was still a feudal state. She possessed no centralized government, and the policy of exclusion and seclusion was in full force. The Emperor lived in retirement at Kyoto, while the Shogun still exercised what was largely a *de jure* control over the feudal barons. Less than two decades later (1871) this political structure had been destroyed and replaced by one which externally at least was entirely new. The Emperor had been placed at the head of the state. Feudalism had been abolished. A central administration had been established and treaty relations with foreign states adopted as the national policy. Like China, her neighbor, Japan was subject to limitations upon her sovereignty in the form of conventional tariffs and extraterritoriality. Unlike China, Japan was already showing an enthusiasm to learn and to profit by whatever the West had to offer. Her territory was compact, her peoples homogeneous, her culture unified; and as a result, a national consciousness was rapidly growing. For two and a half centuries she had lived within a policy of exclusion. She was now to examine the merits of a policy of expansion.

Japanese Expansion

The territorial extent of Japan at the time of the Restoration (1868) was not great. It consisted of the four main islands: Honshu or Hondo (87,000 square miles), Kyushu (14,000 square miles), Shikoku (7,000 square miles), and Yezo or Hokkaido (some 30,000 square miles). There were also innumerable small islands off the coasts. In all, the area was considerably less than that of the State of Montana. To the north, Japan in 1875 acquired exclusive control of Chishima (the Kurile Islands, which are thirty-one in number, with an area of 6,000 square miles), but in doing so sacrificed claims previously made to the Island of Sakhalin, where Russian influence had steadily increased since the period of Mouraviev's expansion on the Amur between 1847 and 1858. At about the same time, Japan reasserted successfully her much earlier claims to Ogasawara (the Bonin Islands), in which England and the United States had shown some interest. These were the territories that were obviously Japanese and therefore subject to the new central administration. Japan likewise claimed sovereignty over the Loochoo Islands (fifty-five in number, with an area of 6,000 square miles), stretching southward from Kyushu, but this claim was contested by China. Finally, the Japanese were not uninterested in the status and fate of Korea. This peninsula, like Annam, was traditionally a tributary of China, but complicating this relationship was the fact that until 1832 Korea had paid tribute also to Japan. With the growth of western influence in China, the territorial expansion of Russia along the Amur and south to Vladivostok, and the unification of Japan under the Restoration, it was natural that the Japanese should no longer remain indifferent to the future of Korea. Annexation of territory had already become a significant feature of western policy in the Orient. This fact was no secret to the makers of the new Japan, and it formed the basis of their evolving foreign policy. The first step was to consolidate Japan's claim to the Loochoo Islands. The second was the assertion of Japanese interests in Korea. Both cases constituted a challenge to China's claim to overlordship in border vassal states.

The Case of the Loochoo Islands

The case of the Loochoo Islands may be disposed of briefly. In 1871, the year that feudalism was abolished, Japan dispatched an envoy to China to conclude a treaty. The negotiations were conducted at Tientsin with Li Hung-chang. The Chinese treated their diplomatic guests with scant courtesy, and ridiculed the western dress which they wore. Nevertheless, they consented to a treaty, the terms of which were reciprocal and more favorable to China than her treaties with western powers. Japan did not secure most-favored-nation treatment, and thus her commerce was placed at a disadvantage. In contrast to the full extraterritoriality enjoyed by western powers in China, this treaty provided on the subject of criminal jurisdiction that in the treaty ports of each country, jurisdiction over alien criminals would be exercised by national officials and the resident consul, while in the interior, jurisdiction of the national officials would prevail. The fact that these rights were inferior to those enjoyed by Westerners in China aroused opposition to the treaty in Japan, but despite this the two countries proceeded to exchange ratifications in 1873. It was on this occasion that the Japanese Ambassador and the western ministers were received in audience by the Chinese Emperor in the "Pavilion of Purple Light."

One of the questions that the Japanese and Chinese discussed was the subject of their common claim to the Loochoo Islands and the nature of Chinese responsibility in Formosa. The respective claims of the two powers to the Loochoo Islands were historically of long standing. Loochoo was another of the border vassal states. It had paid tribute to China since 1372 and to Japan as early as 1451. In 1609 the islands had been conquered by the feudal Japanese state of Satsuma, in southern Kyushu. Matters remained in this indecisive state until in 1871 more than sixty Loochoo Islanders were wrecked on the coast of Formosa and promptly put to death by the local savages. This was not the first time that this sort of thing had occurred. The shipwrecked nationals of various powers had suffered death at the hands of Formosans. A conspicuous case was that of the American bark *Rover,* which was wrecked in 1867. The crew was murdered. Two American war vessels conducted a punitive expedition, driving the savages into the hills.

The Status of Taiwan (Formosa)

Since China claimed that Formosa was a part of her Empire, the Japanese Ambassador held that China, because of her failure to control the savages, was responsible for the Formosan outrages. China attempted to sidetrack the issue by asserting that she did not interfere with or control the natives of southern Formosa. At this point the Japanese said that China gave verbal consent to a Japanese punitive expedition, and in support of this there is the statement of the American Minister at Peking, Mr. Low:

> Were Japan or any other nation to undertake to chastise the aborigines residing on the island of Formosa, in retaliation for injuries committed by them, China would, I apprehend, offer no objection.[1]

Whatever the facts may have been, a Japanese naval and military force went to Formosa in 1874, exacted vengeance on the southern natives, and occupied a portion of the island while demands were addressed to Peking for a settlement of the diplomatic questions involved. The negotiations were protracted, but finally, through the influence of the British Minister at Peking, a settlement was reached by which China was to pay an indemnity of 100,000 taels for the families of the murdered Loochoo Islanders, and an additional sum of 400,000 taels for the roads the Japanese had constructed in Formosa during the period of their occupation. The incident had served to demonstrate that China's ancient theory of vassal states was no longer tenable or practical. The day when China could claim to be sovereign in a territory and at the same time avoid responsibility for the acts of the inhabitants was fast drawing to a close. This was precisely the position she had tried to assume in Formosa.

Japan had won a technical and also a practical victory on

---

[1] United States Department of State (Archive Section), *China Despatches.* Vol. 33, no. 221, enclosure 1.

two points. She had forced China to pay for her failure to control the Formosans. Secondly, in signing the treaty, China had given technical recognition to Japan's right to protect the Loochoo Islanders. This being so, there could be little argument as to the status of the islands. On this point, though China continued to protest, no one was willing to listen to her. Meanwhile, these islands were incorporated in the Japanese state as a prefecture. Loss of the Loochoo Islands was in itself not a serious blow to China, for actually she had never governed them. It was, however, a most serious threat to her theory of overlordship in all border states, and this fact Li Hung-chang soon recognized.

The Status of Korea

While these events were in progress, Korea, too, had become a center of interest. This peninsula, of 85,000 square miles in area and about 700 miles in length, adjoined Manchuria, the homeland of the Manchus. Throughout its history it had been subject to periodic invasion from China and had developed a civilization essentially Chinese in character, but in the main had remained practically autonomous. In the south, Korea was separated from Japan by a strait some 120 miles in width. It thus formed a natural bridge from the mainland of Asia to the island empire. It was probably through Korea that the early Japanese made their way to Japan. By the same route the Mongols had attempted their invasions, and Hideyoshi in return had hoped to conquer China. In general it may be said that from the time of the Mongol Dynasty in the thirteenth century, Korea had been regarded as a vassal state of China. It was in this early period that a native dynasty adopted, as the name of the country, Chosen (Land of Morning Calm). The Manchus conquered Korea before their invasion of China, but were content to accept its allegiance as a vassal state. While, therefore, Korea enjoyed autonomy at home, she was subject to the suzerainty of China. Korean sovereigns held their position by the grace of the Chinese Emperor, and annually sent embassies to pay tribute at the court in Peking.

The early relations between Japan and various Korean states had been intimate, and it was through Korea in the main that Chinese learning penetrated Japan. In time, these relations were gradually broken, and, at the time of the Mongol invasions of Japan, they had practically ceased. Since the Koreans had assisted in these invasions, their coasts were for many years attacked repeatedly by Japanese pirates. After rather feeble attempts on the part of the Japanese Shoguns to curb piracy, three Korean ports were opened to Japanese trade in 1443, and residence of Japanese merchants was permitted at these ports under rigid restriction. Fusan, in the south, was one of these ports. Hideyoshi's attempts in the last decade of the sixteenth century to use Korea as a means of conquering China resulted only in enormous bloodshed, the destruction of life and property, and, finally, in gaining the bitter ill will of the Koreans. Under the Tokugawas, Japanese relations with Korea were renewed after 1600. Fusan was again opened to Japanese trade, and Korea agreed to dispatch a mission of respect to Yedo whenever a new Shogun was appointed. The cost of these missions, which was paid in part by Japan, proved excessive, and after 1790 they were required to proceed only as far as the Island of Tsushima, in the Korean Strait. The last of these missions was received there in 1811. From this time on, Japan had little time to devote to Korean affairs, the Shogunate being too concerned with threats to the policy of exclusion occasioned by the arrival in Japanese waters of western ships. There followed the mission of Perry and, in 1868, the Restoration, when Korea again became a matter of interest to Tokyo.

Western Influence in Korea

Of western influences, Christianity was the first to reach Korea. It came by way of China. Persecution inevitably followed, the first victims being a Chinese priest and seven Korean converts, who were executed in 1801. A French priest arrived in 1836; others soon followed. Their converts soon numbering over 9,000, persecution was renewed. To French demands for an explanation Korea responded that she was a vassal of China and that the missionaries were in league with rebels (the native Christians). By 1860 Korea had acquired a European neighbor. Russia had taken the Manchurian seacoast (the Maritime Province) and had founded Vladivostok within easy reach of the Korean frontier. Four years later a youth ascended the throne of Korea. He was controlled by his father, the Tai Won Kun, noted alike for his cruelty and his bitter opposition to all foreigners and their ways. The Russians were now pressing for the right to trade at Gensan, and the murder of French priests and their converts in 1866, coupled with the destruction of an American ship, the *General Sherman,* and its crew in Korean waters, focused the attention of both France and the United States on the peninsula. A French naval expedition, resulting in nothing but the destruction of one Korean city, was regarded as a failure. The American Secretary of State, William H. Seward, proposed a joint Franco-American expedition to demand redress from the Korean King. However, France found it inexpedient to act and the matter was dropped. In 1867, American naval vessels visited Korean waters, and George F. Seward, Consul-General of the United States at Shanghai, was commissioned to secure a treaty of amity and commerce. This plan, too, was dropped on receipt of unfavorable news from Korea.

China's Policy of Evasion

Japan's modern interest in Korea had been reawakened in 1861 when the Russians occupied the island of Tsushima, in the Korean Strait, from which they were finally forced to retire by a British squadron. Japanese concern was again aroused in 1866, when French priests and native Korean converts were murdered. It is important to note, in view of later Chinese policy, that at this time "Prince Kung, foreseeing that the assertion of Chinese suzerainty over Korea . . . would lead directly to a demand on China for reparations to be paid to France, adopted the characteristically Chinese policy of evading responsibility for these claims. This act of the Chinese Government, while appearing to be the easiest way out of a difficulty, was a repudiation by China of suzerainty over the peninsula. The French Chargé, Bellonet, [at Peking] had forthwith seized upon this repudiation, and proceeded against Korea as an independent kingdom." [2]

It was thus France and not Japan that took the first step toward breaking whatever ties existed between Korea and the Middle Kingdom, and on this occasion China repudiated claims that she was later to reassert.

Japan, in 1867, had offered to mediate between the United States and Korea over the General Sherman affair. When in the same year the Shogunate was overthrown, an envoy was sent to Seoul to announce the change of government and to invite peaceful relations. These overtures were rejected by the Tai Won Kun in the belief that Japan had adopted the ways of the hated Westerners. Accordingly, Japanese commissioners were sent to investigate conditions in the peninsula. They reported that its independence was threatened both by the political pretensions of China and by the advance of Russia on the northern coast. A second Japanese diplomatic mission was repelled in 1869, and a similar fate befell others in 1871 and 1872. These continued affronts aroused the anger of the more aggressive elements at Tokyo, and for a time there was danger of war. This attitude of the Japanese may be understood when it is recalled that in 1871 the United States was represented in

[2] Tyler Dennett, *Americans in Eastern Asia.* The Macmillan Company, New York, 1922. p. 433.

Korean waters by a fleet of five ships commanded by Admiral John Rogers, who was accompanied by the American Minister at Peking, Frederick F. Low. During the course of this un-welcome visit, a Korean fort fired on an American survey party. No apology was offered, whereupon the Americans destroyed five Korean forts and killed or wounded some 350 natives. The possibilities, if any existed, of negotiating a Korean-American treaty were thus ended, and the expedition sailed away. Commenting on these events, Minister Low ob-served that the Korean Court evidently believed that all the western powers were tributary states of China, and that China by mere mandate could prevent further efforts on the part of the United States to open the country.

The apparent ignorance of the rulers of that country [Korea] in regard to the relations existing between China and Western nations is a formidable barrier in the way of intercourse for any purpose. Until it can be removed all attempts at friendly negotiation must, of necessity, fail; and it is too much to expect that the Chinese Government will, of its own accord, enlighten the [Korean] King, by stating the real facts, when such knowledge would lessen the subserviency and veneration of a vassal to its suzerain. . . . My ex-perience leads me to doubt whether good will, gratitude or inter-national good faith would induce the rulers of this country [China] to take such a step.[3]

To these various developments in Korea, Japan could no longer remain indifferent. She took occasion therefore, when exchanging ratifications of the Chino-Japanese Treaty of 1871, to inquire as to China's responsibility for the acts of Koreans. This, it will be recalled, was at the time of the crisis over For-mosa. The Chinese declined to accept responsibility, main-taining that, though Korea was a vassal state, it nevertheless retained the right to declare war and to make peace with for-eign nations.

[3] United States Department of State (Archive Section), *China Despatches*. Vol. 31, no. 102.

Here, then, was an absurd relationship. China claimed to be suzerain and yet evaded all responsibility when it was convenient so to do. Consequently, Japan resumed her efforts to renew direct relations with the peninsula. These efforts gave promise of success when the Korean government consented to receive a letter and to send an envoy to Japan. However, in 1875, the envoy who carried the letter was denied an audience, and a Japanese gunboat engaged in surveying the mouth of the Han River was fired upon. Following precedent as established by the French and the Americans, the Japanese landed and destroyed some fortifications.

A Leaf From Perry's Notebook

Tokyo now proposed to act in Korea as the United States, more than twenty years earlier, had acted in Japan. The government, as the United States had done in the case of Perry, dispatched a mission advising Korea to open relations with foreign states. China, being informed of these plans, counseled Korea to yield. The Japanese force consisted of only two gunboats and three transports carrying less than eight hundred men. The Koreans were advised in advance of their coming, and, as in the case of Perry in Japan, time was permitted for deliberation. The result was a Korean-Japanese treaty of commerce, signed February 26, 1876. Its first clause was of the utmost importance. Korea was recognized as an independent state enjoying the same sovereign rights as Japan. Intercourse between the two countries was to be on terms of equality. Old restrictions on trade at Fusan would be removed, and two additional ports would be opened to commerce. In addition, Japan was to enjoy extraterritorial privileges. A supplementary treaty including trade regulations and prohibiting the importation of opium into Korea was signed in August. For a time Japan was represented at Seoul by a *chargé* who in 1880 was succeeded by a resident minister.

The First American-Korean Treaty

Encouraged by the success of Japan, other powers sought treaties with Korea. Commodore R. W. Shufeldt, representing the United States, failed to secure a treaty in 1880, largely, it would seem, because he had used the good offices of the Japanese. His efforts were blocked also by Li Hung-chang, who, however, was willing that the United States should approach Korea through China. This willingness did not arise from any desire on the part of China to assist or favor the interests of the United States in Korea. On the contrary, it was based on the fear that Korea was in danger of falling under the influence of Japan or Russia.[4] The theory was, then, that if the United States were in treaty relations with Korea, China would be able to rely on American support there against other powers. So it was that through the assistance of Li Hung-chang, Shufeldt secured a treaty in 1882. He resisted successfully the efforts of Li to insert a clause stating that Korea was a dependent state of China. In place of this, the Korean King pledged "his own sovereign powers" to maintain the treaty. Its content was similar in most respects to the Japanese treaty of 1876. A treaty with Great Britain was negotiated the same year and a supplementary convention in the following year. A treaty with Germany was concluded in 1883, one with Italy in 1884, and one with France, subjecting Korea to missionary propaganda, in 1886. Thus, so far as treaties and their legalities were concerned, Korea had emerged as an independent state. On the basis of these treaties, she was no longer a tributary of China. But this meant nothing to Li Hung-chang and the Chinese Foreign Office. Discussing the Korean question with John Russell Young in 1883 (after the Japanese, the American, and the British treaties had been signed), Li gave full expression to China's policy when he said:

---

[4] *Ibid.* Vol. 59, May 1, 1882, with enclosure.

I am King of Corea whenever I think the interests of China require me to assert that prerogative.[5]

This was the Li Hung-chang through whose efforts Commodore Shufeldt had won a treaty with Korea, yet that naval officer did not hesitate to describe the famous Chinese leader in these terms:

Li Hung-chang . . . sits in his viceregal chair at Tientsin, the gate of the capital of China, regulates the ingress and the egress of foreign diplomats to the Court, and defines the foreign and dictates the domestic policy of the country. Li Hung-chang is, therefore, the absolute and despotic ruler of 400,000,000 of people. Yet such is the system of this Government that he lives upon the mere breath of the Empress, an ignorant, capricious and immoral woman. A word from her and his power would vanish with the morning mist, and his courtiers would shrink from him as a man with the plague.

He is fifty-nine years of age, six feet two inches in stature, has a cold, clear, cruel eye, and an imperious manner. He is a thorough Oriental and an intense Chinaman. This implies contempt for Western nations and hatred for all foreigners. . . . He keeps together an incongruous Empire and an effete dynasty by the repressive force of an indomitable will. He suppresses rebellions by decapitation, and quiets the turbulent with the bamboo. Yet he is great, not because he is so much in advance of his countrymen, but because he is not so far behind as they are. . . .[6]

Domestic Politics in Korea

The opening of Korea to foreign intercourse was accompanied by much domestic unrest. The liberals who favored the new treaty policy became the target of ignorant and conservative fanatics. These latter were encouraged by the Tai Won Kun, who assumed leadership of the antiforeign and pro-Chinese party. The Korean Queen, in contrast, found her main support in the liberal and pro-Japanese factions. Until

[5] *Ibid.* Vol. 65, no. 230.
[6] *Ibid.* Vol. 60, no. 108, enclosure.

1883 the Japanese were the only foreign residents at the open ports, and it was against them that the antiforeign outbreaks were directed. In 1882 the Tai Won Kun lent his support to a conspiracy designed to do away with the Queen. When the lady escaped, the rebels turned their attack on the Japanese in the capital, who were forced to fight their way twenty-six miles to the coast at Chemulpo, where they were rescued by a British ship. The situation being most serious, both China and Japan dispatched troops to Korea, the former still acting on the theory of Chinese suzerainty. The Tai Won Kun was taken to China, while the Japanese, refusing to negotiate through the Chinese, dealt directly with the Koreans. The convention that resulted called for punishment of the guilty, an indemnity of 550,000 yen, a mission of apology, further commercial privileges, and a Japanese garrison in the Korean capital. This last requirement followed the precedent established by the British and the French at Yokohama after the opening of Japan. These terms were readily complied with by the more progressive leaders, who now controlled at Seoul, and the Japanese garrison was soon reduced to a legation guard and the indemnity to 150,000 yen. This happy turn of events was of short duration.

Intrigues at the Korean court soon precipitated a new crisis. The Queen's party now being supreme, with the Tai Won Kun a prisoner in China, it soon reverted to the antiforeign, pro-Chinese attitude. All that remained of the so-called liberal party were a few young Koreans, lacking experience and leaning on the Japanese for support. Since China was at the time involved with France over Annam, the Korean reformers believed their hour to act had come. They attacked the palace at Seoul, murdering some of the reactionary ministers, but again the Queen escaped. The reformers forced the King to call for Japanese protection. Arriving at the palace grounds, Japanese forces sent in response to this request were attacked by Chinese troops, defeated, and forced to retire fighting their way to the sea. More than thirty Japanese were killed, almost all by Chinese troops. There was real danger of a Chino-Japanese war. China, as the reader is aware, was at the moment engaged in conflict with France, which had been attempting for two years to embroil Tokyo and Peking.[7] Fortunately the schemes of France did not bear fruit. The Japanese government adopted a firm but not an unreasonable attitude in the light of what had occurred at Seoul. Two diplomatic missions were promptly dispatched: one to Seoul under Inouye, the other to Tientsin under Count Ito. At Seoul the Japanese demands were soon met. These included punishment of the guilty, an indemnity of 110,000 yen, and a mission of apology.

The Tientsin Convention

Actually these negotiations were little more than incidental to the real discussions which took place at Tientsin. There in 1885 Ito and Li Hung-chang, the outstanding leaders of their respective states, attacked the problem of Korea. It was difficult for China to acknowledge in the form of a treaty that her former vassal was now a free and independent state, though in reality the evidence was clear. Not only Japan, but also the United States, England, Germany, and France, had by treaty acknowledged the sovereignty of Korea. This question, therefore, was not included in the Tientsin Convention, so China again "saved face." The terms agreed to provided that both countries would withdraw their troops from Korea, neither would send instructors to drill the Korean army, and if, as a result of future troubles, either power should send troops to the peninsula, it would notify the other that it was doing so. China also apologized for the attack of Chinese troops on the Japanese Legation in Seoul. In this way a temporary settlement was reached, but, since China still clung to the theory of suzerainty, it would not be regarded by Japan as conclusive.

[7] *Ibid.* Vol. 73, no. 583, enclosure 2.

Yuan Shih-kai in Korea

Far from relaxing China's interest or influence in Korea, Li Hung-chang took steps to increase it. His chief lieutenant in this work was Yuan Shih-kai, who became China's resident-general at Seoul. It was Yuan's business to control all important acts of the Korean government and to block any move which might increase the influence of Japan or Russia. In general, Yuan was eminently successful. Russia had re-entered the Korean scene in 1884 through the efforts of P. G. von Mollendorff, an adviser of the Korean government, who induced the ministry to conclude a convention whereby Russia would lend instructors to the Korean army in return for the use of a Korean naval port. To Japan, this appeared as a direct threat to her own security at home; China saw in it the replacement of her influence in Korea by that of Russia; and Great Britain foresaw a disturbing increase in Russian prestige. The British were the first to act, dispatching a naval force in 1885 to Port Hamilton, an anchorage in a group of islands off the southern coast of Korea from which Russian movements could be watched. Here the British remained for nearly two years, by which time it was apparent that Russia was not prepared to occupy Port Lazareff, which the Koreans had offered her. Encouraged by the British action, Li Hung-chang forced the Korean ministry to repudiate the Russian agreement. The scales had again turned in China's favor, and of this Li and Yuan took full advantage. In violation of an agreement with Japan, Yuan secured the right to connect Peking and Seoul by telegraph. Control over Korea's foreign relations was increased. In 1888, efforts were made to prevent the Koreans from sending a minister to the United States. No nation could deal diplomatically with Seoul free from Yuan's influence, if not his control.

This condition was particularly obnoxious to Japan, whose policy thus far had been remarkable for its restraint. At this point an incident occurred to arouse the Japanese further. A Korean progressive who had taken refuge in Japan was lured to Shanghai and there murdered by a group of his fellow countrymen. The Chinese authorities, acting in a truly remarkable way, sent the murderer and the body of his victim to Korea, where the criminal was rewarded while the dismembered and murdered corpse was displayed publicly. It is hardly surprising that news of these events inflamed Japanese opinion and that there were demands for war. The belief had been widespread—and it still persists—that Japan had long sought some such pretext to intervene and to bring Korea under her control. But if such a desire did exist, "there was nothing in the conduct of the Japanese government to support the contention. To be sure, Japanese publicists, from the early Meiji days, had advocated such a forward policy, but their views were no more influential than those of American expansionists who have advocated time and again the conquest of Mexico and all the countries to the Isthmus of Panama. If the Japanese government had sympathized with these views it had ample cause for action when, in 1873, it firmly refused to adopt the most influentially supported war proposals, and again when, in 1882 and 1884, the Japanese Legation was attacked and the Japanese representatives driven from the country. During these years the official conduct of Japan had been correct in every detail. It had accepted the principle of Korean independence and it had furthered all plans for progress and reform which would have enabled Korea to maintain this independence. It had failed in its endeavors to secure from China a relinquishment of her ancient claims of suzerainty." [8]

In fact, the days when Japan would be patient were fast drawing to a close. As one diplomat in Peking had said, there could be no security in northeastern Asia while Korea "has a government of sand."

---

[8] Payson J. Treat, *The Far East,* rev. ed. Harper & Brothers, New York, 1935. pp. 293-294.

SELECTED BIBLIOGRAPHY

R. H. Akagi, *Japan's Foreign Relations* (Tokyo: 1936), ch. 4, "Japan, Korea and China." K. Asakawa, *The Russo-Japanese Conflict* (Boston: 1904). H. N. Allen, *Things Korean* (New York: 1908). Capt. F. Brinkley, *A History of the Japanese People* (New York: 1915). A. J. Brown, *The Mastery of the Far East* (New York: 1919). Henry Chung, *Korean Treaties* (New York: 1919). Henry Chung, *The Case of Korea* (New York: 1921), ch. 2 on diplomatic relations between Korea and Japan—a one-sided view. Tyler Dennett, *Americans in Eastern Asia* (New York: 1922), chs. 24-25. Chesney Duncan, *Corea and the Powers* (Shanghai: 1889). John W. Foster, *American Diplomacy in the Orient* (Boston: 1904), ch. 9. W. E. Griffis, *A Modern Pioneer in Korea* (New York: 1912). W. E. Griffis, *Corea the Hermit Nation*, 9th ed. (New York: 1911). J. H. Gubbins, *The Making of Modern Japan* (London: 1922). R. S. Gundry, *China and Her Neighbors . . .* (London: 1893). Angus Hamilton, *Korea . . .* (Boston: 1910). Seiji Hishida, *The International Position of Japan as a Great Power* (New York: 1905), ch. 7. S. Hsu, *China and Her Political Entity* (New York: 1926), ch. 3, the Korean problem to 1890. H. B. Hulbert, *History of Korea* (Seoul: 1905). Stephen King-Hall, *Western Civilization and the Far East* (London: 1924), ch. 4. S. A. Korff, *Russia's Foreign Relations during the Last Half Century* (New York: 1922). A. H. S. Landor, *Corea . . .* (London: 1895). J. H. Longford, *The Story of Korea* (London: 1911). H. B. Morse, *The International Relations of the Chinese Empire* (London: 1918), vol. 3, ch. 1, the Korean question. Harold J. Noble, "The United States and Sino-Korean Relations, 1885-1887" in *The Pacific Historical Review*, Sept. 1933. Count S. Okuma, *Fifty Years of New Japan*, 2 vols. (London: 1909). C. O. Paullin, *Diplomatic Negotiations of American Naval Officers 1778-1883* (Baltimore: 1912). R. T. Pollard, "American Relations with Korea, 1882-1895" in *The Chinese Social and Political Science Review*, Oct. 1932. W. W. Rockhill, *China's Intercourse with Korea from the 15th Century to 1895* (London: 1905). John Ross, *History of Korea* (Paisley: 1879). W. F. Sands, *Undiplomatic Memories* (New York: 1930). P. J. Treat, *Japan and the United States* (Stanford University: 1928), ch. 8. By the same author, "China and Korea 1885-1894" in *Political Science Quarterly*, Dec. 1934, a most scholarly treatment of the subject.

CHAPTER XV

Government in Early Modern Japan

1868-1900

MODERN Japan is frequently said to have achieved a political revolution unparalleled in the world's history. Superficial observers are prone to remark that in 1871 Japan was still a feudal state. In 1889, only eighteen years later, she was a united, centralized state, equipped with most of the forms of western constitutional government. No nation, they observe, has ever wrought such a complete transformation in such a brief period of time. From statements of this kind, erroneous, or at least misleading, conclusions have sprung. Some of these are, for example, that what England required centuries to do, Japan achieved in less than two decades, and that the virtue of political change is dependent on the speed with which it is accomplished. There is, to be sure, ample evidence to demonstrate that Japan, in the closing years of the nineteenth century, revolutionized both the form and, in considerable measure, the character of her government. Nevertheless, it is to be noted that the makers of the new Japan and the people whom they ruled were a product of a deeply rooted feudal society. To change the external appearance of this society, in the same manner as Peter the Great changed Russian society by clipping the beards and the coat-tails of the peasants, was relatively a simple task. To alter its habits of thought was more difficult. It is with this thought in mind that one may best approach a survey of Japan's government in the closing decades of the nineteenth century.

Philosophy of the Ruling Classes

The opening of Japan to foreign intercourse in the years from 1853 to 1865 was the occasion rather than the cause of radical reforms in government. True it is that feudalism was unworkable in a society of modern nations and was thus doomed to disappear when Japan opened her doors, but it is also true that feudalism had outlived its usefulness within Japan and was ready to collapse long before Perry disturbed the waters of Uraga Bay in 1853. Some of the causes leading to the decline of feudal efficiency have already been suggested in chapter 3. It is important to recall that Japan had long been suffering from profound unrest. Much of this sprang from economic causes, and in attempting to meet it, the Tokugawa Shoguns, like ruling classes at all times and in all places, appealed to and sought to enforce a higher morality. Virtue in its numerous forms—industry, sobriety, obedience, and piety—was, they said, the answer to these ills. It was this attitude which resulted in the full development of the cult of Bushido, the Way of the Warrior, which by the eighteenth century had become no longer a code exclusively for warriors but rather a system of ethics by which to control a feudal society in times of peace. Bushido was adapted beautifully to feudal conditions, but as feudalism crumbled under economic stress, the principles of its moral code were likewise called in question.

Result of a Changing Economy

The real problem which faced the Tokugawas was economic. During the early Tokugawa Shogunate, Japan had prospered. Agriculture, industry, and distribution had all improved, resulting in a higher standard of living. Then obstacles appeared. An agricultural economy gave place to a mercantile economy. Money was substituted for rice as a medium of exchange, thus reducing the power of the samurai, the privileged fighting order, and curtailing the productive power of the peasants, while that of the merchants was increased. The appalling condition of the farmers, who constituted the mass of society, grew steadily worse. They now needed money instead of rice to buy commodities, whose price in terms of silver was constantly rising. Many fell into debt, a result of high rents and crop failures; others moved to new land or became wandering laborers either in country or town. Some farmers could not support their families, for the daimyo and their vassals demanded higher taxes to meet their obligations to the merchants of the city. To be sure, some of the peasants prospered, and some of the feudal lords (particularly the tozama in western Japan) treated their peasantry well, but major readjustments in economics and government were becoming the demand of the majority.

The Social Collapse of Feudalism

Socially, as well as economically, the feudal system was breaking. In the nineteenth century the rigid class distinctions of earlier times became somewhat confused. Impecunious daimyo adopted the sons of wealthy merchants, or, releasing their retainers, hired servants from the cities. Farmers moved to the towns. Wealthy merchants purchased farms. Commoners from city and farm became samurai either by adoption or purchase, while the latter, deserting the honored status of the fighting class, sought fortune in urban life. Feudalism was no longer a nicely classified order, for social confusion was closely linked to economic distress.

Finally, as already related (chapter 11), the feudalism of the Tokugawas was challenged by the political aspirations of powerful western clans such as Satsuma and Choshu. Chafing under the restraints which Tokugawa had for two and one half centuries imposed upon them, these clans had led the revolution of 1868 to 1871 through which the Shogunate had been destroyed, the Emperor restored to *de facto* power, and feudalism abolished. Although this revolution was carried on largely by men of the samurai class, it was not solely of their making, for every group in Japanese society demanded change.

The country was full of restless spirits, dissatisfied with their condition and thirsting for activity. There were nobles who wanted independence and foreign trade, to develop the resources of their domains; samurai who wanted opportunities to use their talents, whether as soldiers or as officials; merchants who wanted to break the monopolies of the guilds; scholars who wanted to draw knowledge from new springs; humble peasants and townsmen who wanted just a little freedom from tax and tyranny.[1]

Leaders of the New Japan

These were the forces that had brought political upheaval to modern Japan. The formal structure of feudalism was now gone. What sort of political edifice would take its place?

The abolition of the Shogunate in 1867 and the restoration of the Emperor to *de facto* power were attributed directly to the military power of a group of western clans: Satsuma, Choshu, Tosa, and Hizen. In each of these clans was a group of able samurai who had long directed public affairs for their lords in their respective feudal domains. Thus when Tokugawa was defeated, the task of building a new administration about the person of the restored Emperor fell to these men. For capacity and distinction, many of their names are unsurpassed in Japan's history. From Satsuma came Toshimizu Okubo and Takanon Saigo; from Choshu, Koin Kido; from Tosa, Shojiro Goto; and from Hizen, Taneomi Soyeshima. To this distinguished company was added naturally the ancient court nobility, the kuge, who had suffered under the dominance of the Shogunate. Among their ablest men were Tomomi Iwakura and Sanetomi Sanjo. These men, samurai

---

[1] G. B. Sansom, *Japan: A Short Cultural History*. D. Appleton-Century Company, New York, 1931. p. 516.

and kuge, shaped the new government. They were the real power surrounding the Throne, now occupied by the youthful Emperor Mutsuhito. Since both samurai and kuge represented privileged orders in feudal society, their object was to create not a democratic state, but one in which, through the instrumentality of the Emperor, they might secure and insure power for themselves. This personal, class, and selfish motive did not preclude motives of a generous and patriotic character, for in the Restoration and the abolition of feudalism "one is compelled to acknowledge that the noble classes did exchange a valuable reality of individual power and wealth for a combination of a strengthened throne and a speculative personal compensation." [2]

The First Non-Feudal Government

The government which replaced the Shogunate, following the Restoration, was known as the "Sanshoku," or "Three Offices." It consisted of a council divided into two groups: gijo, the higher councilors, and sanyo, the lower. It included some kuge, but most of its members were daimyo and samurai. Various departments were also formed, composed of members of the Council, so that policy was both formed and administered by the same group. It was this government that formulated the Emperor's charter oath (see p. 205), declaring that "an assembly widely convoked shall be established, and thus great stress shall be laid upon public opinion." Whatever the purpose may have been, it was this statement which formed the basis and bulwark of later liberal and democratic movements. In the same year the Council was enlarged, and its name was changed to "Daijokwan." The councilors of the Sanshoku were now united in an upper house. Membership in the larger lower house was still restricted to members of

[2] Harold S. Quigley, *Japanese Government and Politics*. D. Appleton-Century Company, New York, 1932. p. 27.

the privileged classes. Its function was to deliberate on matters submitted to it by the upper house. It met in 1869, representing 276 clans, under the name of "Kogisho" ("Assembly"). Since all its members were drawn from the military orders of the clans, no commoners being included, it was not a truly representative body. Feudalism, it should be recalled, still prevailed. Furthermore, its powers were advisory, not legislative. It was abolished in 1873.

The abolition of feudalism was accompanied by further revisions in the new central government. These proving to be ineffective, in 1875 a major reorganization resulted in a government which distinguished more clearly between the executive, legislative, and judiciary functions. These agencies were known as the "Daijokwan," the "Genro-in," and the "Daishin-in"; or, respectively, the "Privy Council," the "Senate," and the "Supreme Court." Outwardly, this reform indicated a greater degree of separation of powers. In reality, the council remained supreme, the reform being a guarded concession of the conservatives to those who desired a more representative government. But this did not settle the matter. Wide divergence of opinion had already appeared among the Emperor's advisers. Some favored rapid progress, others a more cautious evolution. To the samurai as a class, the abolition of feudalism had brought economic distress. In the leveling process they had lost both honor and wealth, and to most of them readjustment to the new order seemed difficult, if not impossible. These dissatisfied groups, trained in the philosophy of arms, were a restless element; it was they who urged the government to a forward policy in Korea and Formosa (see pp. 258 and 266). Happily, more judicious advisers prevailed, and an aggressive foreign policy, which would have involved Japan in war, was avoided at a time when all energies could properly be devoted to internal reform.

The Rise of Liberalism

Liberal forces, too, were growing in power, led by Taisuke Itagaki, of Tosa, and Shigenobu Okuma, of Hizen. To the influence of these men and their followers may be attributed the Imperial decree in 1881, informing the nation that parliament would be called in 1890 to inaugurate a constitutional regime. In preparation for this change, a number of preliminary steps were taken. Much of the initiative in this work must be credited to Hirobumi Ito, who was chairman of a commission on constitutional investigations. He created a new nobility in 1884 with the familiar western ranking of prince, marquis, count, viscount, and baron. This, a gesture to the wealthy and former noble classes, provided a legal group from which members of a future House of Lords might be selected. Likewise, it guaranteed a conservative leaven for future popular government. In 1885, a cabinet (Naikaku) was formed, headed by a Minister President, with each minister responsible for a department, and three years later the Privy Council was reorganized, designed as an advisory body to the Emperor. The general lines of the executive body and its departments were therefore complete before the promulgation of the constitution or the first meeting of the legislature.

These direct preparations for a constitutional regime were supplemented by others of an earlier and indirect character. An assembly of prefectural governors had been formed as early as 1875. This body was in no sense popular, yet it was a first step toward consulting local opinion. More effective measures were taken in 1878, when provision was made for elected assemblies in the prefectures and the largest cities. Members of these bodies were elected by the male inhabitants who were twenty-five years of age and paid a land tax of five yen or more. Their powers extended to the budget and revenue, and, although their acts might be vetoed by the governor, this veto could be set aside by the home minister. These assemblies were not legislative in the full sense of the word, but they did mark the beginnings in Japan of elective and representative bodies.

The First Political Parties

Concurrent with these developments was the appearance of political parties. Among the leaders of government, such men as Itagaki of Tosa and Okuma of Hizen rebelled against the overwhelming influence of Satsuma and Choshu office holders. The groups which soon formed about these two leaders were composed of diverse elements, but in the main they sought to protest against clan control and to prepare for a more truly representative government. The Jiyuto (Liberal Party) was formed in 1881, the year in which the Emperor gave his promise of constitutional government. Itagaki was president; his first lieutenant was Shojiro Goto. The platform demanded a single-house parliament, manhood suffrage, and a strong foreign policy, this last as a sop to the discontented samurai. A second party, the Kaishinto (Progressive), was organized in 1882 under the leadership of Okuma. Its program, more moderate than that of the Jiyuto, advocated a bicameral legislature of the English type, limited manhood suffrage, internal reform, and a less aggressive foreign policy. A third and decidedly reactionary party, the Rikken Teiseito (Imperialist), was also organized in 1882. Genichiro Fukuchi, an editor, was one of its principal founders; its prime objective was to preserve absolute monarchy as a principle.

The programs of all three parties at their inception were highly theoretical, being concerned principally with the question of what type of government the constitution should provide. The Jiyuto thinkers wanted popular sovereignty, á la Rousseau. The Kaishinto men thought it sufficient to restrain the monarchy within constitutional limitations, emphasizing the importance of a Diet. Both of these groups were strongly opposed to the Prussian type of constitution, which was supported by the Teiseito leaders on historical grounds.[3]

These parties were embarrassing to the government, and it sought to curb them in many ways. The press law of 1875, revised and strengthened in 1883, destroyed freedom of speech and of the press. Laws of 1880 had already brought all public meetings and associations under rigid police supervision. So vigorous in fact was this suppression that the Liberal Party was dissolved in 1884, while the Progressives lost all effective political influence. Parties, as such, thus virtually ceased to exist until the first meeting of the Diet in 1890. However, this did not mean that the government had killed popular political interest. Goto organized the Daido Danketsu (General Agreement Association) in 1887. It was a brief and unsuccessful attempt to unite liberals, progressives, and conservatives against the government. A number of violent incidents occurred, too, all indicative of unrest under the government's repressive policy. The two most effective agencies at the government's command were the peace preservation law of 1887 and the police. The former prohibited all secret societies and secret meetings, provided for confiscation of presses publishing materials regarded as dangerous to peace and order, and imposed severe penalties. This law was enforced with great rigor. Count Aritomo Yamagata, of Choshu, Minister of Home Affairs and the dominating personality in the cabinet, banished from the capital more than five hundred persons, including the most important party men.

Drafting the Constitution

While these events were occupying the political stage in Japan, practical preparations were being made for drafting the constitution. Eleven years before the Imperial decree promised a constitution, Ito had been in Washington to study the Ameri-

---

[3] *Ibid.* p. 202.

can system of government. This experience was of great value
as an introducion to western political procedure, though it
contributed little of a positive character to Japan's new government. The men entrusted with the task of constitution making had two essential objec-
tives. First, they must frame
a government that would give
due consideration to the historical position of the Emperor as the divine head of
what was to be a highly centralized state. Second, they
must take account of a
changed economy in Japan's
domestic society, of the increasing need and demand for
representative institutions, and
of the nation's new contacts
with western powers. To
combine these two objectives
as realities in a single instrument of government was not
an easy task, for it is obvious
that they are antagonistic
rather than harmonious or complementary.

Japan Tourist Bureau.

HIROBUMI ITO. Most distinguished
of Japan's modern statesmen: Prime
Minister, bureaucrat, party leader, author of the Constitution, and Genro.

In 1882 Ito was again selected to study abroad, this time in
Europe, where he met Bismarck and discussed constitutional
problems with the German authority Gneist. It was from these
associations that Ito drew the more positive elements for his
proposed constitution. On his return to Japan in 1884, he was
appointed to draft the instrument. With him were assistants
who had traveled widely: Myoji Ito, Tsuyoshiaki Inouye, and
Kentaro Kaneko. All were members of the former feudal
clans, and they were now constituted as a bureau attached to
the Imperial household, as indicative of the high importance

of their work. When the completed document was laid before the Emperor, a question arose as to how it should be ratified. Some favored Imperial sanction alone, while others like Itagaki and Okuma desired action by a constitutional convention. Ito followed a compromise course by creating (as already mentioned) the Privy Council, whose secret discussions of the draft extended from May, 1888, to January, 1889. On February 11, the official date of the founding of the Empire in 660 B.C., Emperor Mutsuhito presented the constitution to the people. Officially it was to be regarded as a voluntary gift from the Throne. What, then, was the character of this document which was to shape Japan's political future?

Character of the Constitution

Its seven brief chapters, containing in all seventy-six articles dealing with the Emperor, the rights and duties of subjects, the Imperial Diet, the Ministers of State and the Privy Council, the Judicature, and finance and supplementary rules, are "a model of concise statement." In the main it is a statement of principles susceptible of legislative interpretation and thus less likely to require amendment.

"The Empire of Japan," reads Article I, "shall be reigned over and governed by a line of Emperors unbroken for ages eternal." This was bold prophecy, yet it was based on a profound historical tradition—the continuous rule of the divine Yamato Dynasty since the very founding of the state. Here was a principle of unbroken unity—a stablizer in all national affairs. Other articles proclaim that the Emperor is "sacred and inviolable." He is "the head of the Empire, combining in Himself the rights of sovereignty," which he exercises according to the provisions of the constitution. He issues Imperial ordinances covering emergencies when the Diet is not in session, holds supreme command of the army and navy, determines their organization and peace standing, and declares war, makes peace, and concludes treaties with foreign states. However, the Emperor's power over the fighting services is limited by the control of the Diet over appropriation bills. Declarations of war and the conclusion of treaties do not require the Diet's approval, and thus foreign relations are beyond the legal control of the legislature.

Chapter 2 of the Constitution sets forth the rights and duties of Japanese subjects. None of these is unqualified, for all are to be enjoyed subject to law. Nevertheless, the normal guarantees found in western constitutions are included. Among the rights are those of equal appointment to public offices, liberty of abode and of changing the same, freedom from illegal arrest or detention, guarantees of trial by properly appointed judges, freedom of the home from illegal entry and search, the secrecy of private mail, and rights of property. Religious toleration and liberty of speech, writing, publication, and association are also included. The duties of subjects require service in the military or naval forces, the payment of taxes, and the exercise of the above-mentioned rights within the limitations of law.

Chapter 3 deals with the Imperial Diet. This was to be a bicameral legislature including a House of Peers and a House of Representatives. The provision for two houses was natural, for though in Japan all individuals were equal before the law, there was in social relations a powerful aristocracy. The House of Peers could be expected to support the Throne and the privileged society. The framers of the Constitution had an additional purpose in mind.

If the House of Peers fulfills its functions [wrote Ito in his *Commentaries*], it will serve in a remarkable degree to preserve an equilibrium between political powers, to restrain the undue influence of political parties, to check the evil tendencies of irresponsible discussions, to secure the stability of the Constitution, to be an instrument for maintaining harmony between the governing and the governed.[4]

On the other hand members of the House of Representatives were to regard themselves as representing the people of the entire country. In the House they should, said Ito, speak freely according to the dictates of the individual conscience. Membership in the House of Peers was to be limited to the Imperial Family, the orders of nobility, and persons nominated by the Emperor. Representatives in the lower house were to be elected by the people according to the provisions of the election law. Simultaneous membership in both houses was not permitted. It was also stipulated that "every law requires the consent of the Imperial Diet" (Article 37). Provision was made for annual sessions and also extraordinary sessions when necessary. Members of either House may not be held responsible outside the House for opinions or votes given within, and during a session are free from arrest.

Japan Tourist Bureau.

TSUYOSHIAKI INOUYE. Genro and one of the principal draftsmen of the Constitution of 1889.

In its original form the House of Peers consisted of five groups: (1) Imperial princes, (2) princes and marquises, (3) counts, viscounts, and barons, who were entitled to elect one fifth of their total number for terms of seven years, (4) Imperial nominees selected by the Emperor because of meritorious

---

[4] Hirobumi Ito, *Commentaries on the Constitution of the Empire of Japan*, 2nd ed. Tokyo, 1906. pp. 71-72.

services or erudition, and (5) representatives of the highest taxpayers, selected in each prefecture and nominated by the Emperor. In 1925 these rules were modified. The most important changes included raising the eligible age of princes and marquises, placing a definite limitation on the number of counts, viscounts, and barons to sit in the House, and adding four representatives of highest taxpayers. For the first time, too, non-titled members might exceed the titled. Obviously, then, the House of Peers has been more than a collection of hereditary titles. Its membership includes men of property, others who have given distinguished service to the state, and representatives of the nation's highest scholarship. Despite these redeeming features, it has been regarded as essentially a seat of privilege, and it is debatable whether it has fulfilled the larger stabilizing purpose that Ito had in view.

The House of Representatives, though supposedly the mouthpiece of the people, was in fact elected by the propertied classes. The election law of 1889 conferred the suffrage on male subjects twenty-five years of age who paid a direct national tax of fifteen yen annually. This meant that only one per cent of the population voted. The property qualification was reduced to ten yen in 1900, increasing the voting strength to about two and one half per cent. In 1911, a manhood suffrage bill passed the House of Representatives but was defeated by the Peers. However, the suffrage tax was reduced again to three yen in 1919, and manhood suffrage was enacted in 1925, with the age limit still twenty-five years. Elections under this law were held in 1928, when more than eighty per cent of the qualified voters cast their ballots (some twelve and one half million). Members of the House of Representatives, who must be thirty years of age, are elected for four-year terms. The original membership was 300, but this has now been increased to 466.

The functions and powers of the Japanese Diet present an interesting but also a complex subject. Constitutionally, its

Piet

function is to assist the Emperor in the legislative process. It may assist in revision of the Constitution, and it controls (though not in an unqualified manner) finance. So far as powers are concerned, the Houses are on a basis of equality. Amendments to the Constitution must be initiated by the Throne and approved by both Houses of the Diet. The relation of the Diet to finance presents a problem of great difficulty, for the expenditures and the revenues of the state require the consent of this body. Nevertheless, Ito regarded the Japanese budget not as a law but rather as a guide to be observed by the administration. It is therefore executive rather than legislative, only certain of its items requiring the Diet's approval. As an example of items over which the Diet had no direct control may be cited "those already fixed expenditures based by the constitution upon the powers appertaining to the Emperor," such as the ordinary expenditures required to maintain the administration. Normally when such expenditures, and others of like nature, are deducted from the budget, there remains only about one third of the total on which the Diet actually takes action. If, as has happened, the Diet fails to vote the budget, the government carries on with the budget of the preceding year increased perhaps by deficiency appropriations.

The government is not dependent upon the Diet for an annual vote of revenues; on the other hand, new taxation may not be levied without the Diet's consent.[5]

Foreign relations are beyond the scope of the Diet's powers. However, the Foreign Minister addresses the Diet annually on this subject, and the Diet's influence, even if not constitutional, cannot be ignored.

There is no mention in the Japanese Constitution of a cabinet, but Chapter 4 provides for Ministers of State and a Privy Council. Both cabinet and Council had been created and were functioning before the Constitution was promulgated.

[5] Harold S. Quigley, *op. cit.* p. 192.

The respective Ministers of State [reads Article LV] shall give their advice to the Emperor, and be responsible for it.

All Laws, Imperial Ordinances and Imperial Rescripts of whatever kind, that relate to the affairs of the State require the countersignature of a Minister of State.

As a practical consideration, then, the Ministers of State function as a cabinet, and, with some exceptions, have accepted joint responsibility for policies adopted. On the question as to whom the Ministers are responsible, the Constitution is ambiguous, but in practice, cabinets have inclined more toward Imperial responsibility than toward recognition of Diet control. This has been the occasion of a most significant constitutional struggle between those forces that would limit cabinet responsibility to the Throne, and those that believe that the life of a government should depend on popular support in the Diet. In Japan, this latter principle was disregarded entirely until in 1898 Okuma headed a short-lived party cabinet. Other less successful attempts followed, a strong party government not being achieved until the premiership of Hara in 1918. The struggle for responsible party government has gone on from that day to the present, but since 1931 the fortunes of the political parties have been at a low ebb (for reasons which will appear later) and so-called "national" cabinets have become the order of the day.

The Privy Council, as already noted, was created by Ito in 1888. It was to be composed of persons who had rendered great service to the state. This body has been continued by the Constitution and is to give advice when consulted by the Emperor. Among the matters on which its opinion may be asked are interpretations of the Constitution and international treaties and agreements. Its original membership numbered twenty-six. Ministers of the Cabinet are also Councilors. Legally, appointments are made by the Emperor; in practice by the Premier in consultation with members of the Council and elder statesmen.

A factor of the utmost consequence in Japan's constitutional government is the strategic position accorded the military and the naval services. An Imperial notification in 1889 stated that:

With the exception of military or naval affairs of grave importance which, having been reported directly to the Sovereign by the Chief of Staff, may have been submitted by His Majesty for the consideration of the Cabinet, the ministers of state for war and the navy shall report to the minister president.

This notification, combined with those articles of the Constitution that conferred on the Emperor the supreme command of the army and navy, their organization, and their peace standing, established a principle whereby the civilian ministers were precluded from advising the Emperor on "the supreme command." For this purpose the Ministers of War and the Navy and the chiefs of the army and navy general staffs have direct access to the Throne. In this capacity they may advise the sovereign on tactics, strategy, and plans for national defense. It is also to be noted that these officials must be high-ranking officers of the fighting services. The Ministers of War and the Navy thus occupy a dual position: as members of the Cabinet they report on general and military affairs to the Throne through the Minister President, as all members of the Cabinet do; as instruments of the supreme command, they report directly to the Throne independently of the Cabinet. This in itself gives them a highly privileged position, and, since no cabinet can be formed without two high-ranking officers, the exact limits of their potential influence are difficult to determine. In a country which had so recently emerged from feudalism and whose constitution derived its chief inspiration from Prussia, a favored position for the military was to be expected. Yet this historical explanation provided small comfort for Japanese liberals, who looked forward to the day when popular government, as expressed by the House of Representatives and a responsible cabinet, would prevail.

The Genro or Elder Statesmen

These then were the principal agencies, executive and legislative, with which Japan entered upon a constitutional career. Their importance should not be underestimated, and yet even their combined powers were probably less than those of an extraconstitutional group which must now be mentioned—the "Genro," or "Elder Statesmen." This term was applied originally to a group of five distinguished men who dominated Japan's political life after 1880 through the first thirty-five years of constitutional government. They included: Hirobumi Ito, Tsuyoshiaki Inouye, and Aritomo Yamagata, of Choshu; and Iwao Oyama and Masayoshi Matsukata, of Satsuma — a striking evidence of the degree to which these western clans controlled the new Japan. All these men were samurai. Their rise to fame was due to personal ability. To their number was added at a later time Taro Katsura, of Choshu, and Kimmochi Saionji, of the civilian aristocracy. Others of semi-genro status were Shingenobu Okuma, of Hizen, and Admiral Gombei Yamamoto, Admiral Sukenori Kabayama, and Count Keigo Kiyoura, of Satsuma. Although these men as Genro had no constitutional status, it was to them that the Emperor turned for advice on all important matters, just as in the family system of the Orient, the head of a household sought counsel from its oldest and most

Japan Tourist Bureau.

PRINCE ARITOMO YAMAGATA. Military bureaucrat, founder of the modern Japanese army, Genro, and personification of the military tradition.

experienced members. At the turn of the century, the Genro frequently held the highest posts, both civil and military, and at the same time acted extraconstitutionally as the Emperor's highest advisory council. Where the views of Cabinet and Genro were in conflict, the policy of the Elder Statesmen became the policy of the Throne. The Emperor might be advised by Cabinet, Privy Council, and the supreme command; but it was the Genro who gave final expression to the Imperial will. Today, with the exception of the aged Prince Saioji, the Genro have passed from the scene, to the loss not alone of Japan.

The Feudal Tradition Survives

In concluding this brief survey of the background and the instruments of constitutional government in Japan, a few general conclusions may be stated, though all of them are approximations and involve some degree of error. Japan's entire system was dominated by the unique position of the Emperor. He embodied the divine origins of the state; his constitutional powers were comprehensive. The Constitution provided a framework for representative government, but all the organs of the executive (Cabinet, supreme command, and the advisory Privy Council) were responsible to the Throne rather than to the Diet, and above even these stood the Genro, legally responsible to no one. Japan did not acquire parliamentary government in 1890, nor was it Ito's intention that she should do so. In terms of western political forms and theory, the nation lacked experience. Local loyalties and the feudal and clan tradition still persisted, for custom was far more vigorous than law, and a transition to the practice of responsible government would necessarily be slow. This was especially true in Japan, where the masses were accustomed to respect official authority. Nevertheless, public opinion soon learned to express itself. Political parties demanded popular institutions, which to some degree were provided in the Diet. When, however, the House of Representatives sought to increase its power, it was opposed vigorously by executive organs and also by the great body of permanent officeholders, the bureaucrats, who, in Japan as elsewhere, are apt to have little sympathy with the "political" representatives of the people. In the struggle that has ensued between these forces, bureaucracy has been threatened, but it has not been overcome.

SELECTED BIBLIOGRAPHY

N. Asami, *Japanese Colonial Government* (New York: 1924). K. Asakawa, "Some of the Contributions of Feudal Japan to the New Japan" in *Japan and Japanese-American Relations,* Geo. H. Blakeslee, ed. (New York: 1912). *The Cambridge Modern History* (New York: 1910), vol. 12, ch. 18 by J. H. Longford on Japan, 1871-1902. E. W. Clement, *A Short History of Japan* (Chicago: 1915), ch. 14 on constitutional government. A series of scholarly articles by Kenneth Colgrove: "Parliamentary Government in Japan" in *American Political Science Review,* vol. 21; "Labor Parties in Japan" in *ibid.,* vol. 23; "The Japanese Privy Council" in *ibid.,* vol. 25; "The Japanese Emperor" in *ibid.,* Aug. and Oct. 1932; "The Treaty-Making Power in Japan" in *American Journal of International Law,* vol. 25; "Powers and Functions of the Japanese Diet" in *American Political Science Review,* Dec. 1933, and Feb. 1934. W. E. Griffis, "The Development of Political Parties in Japan" in *North American Review,* Nov. 1902. W. E. Griffis, "The Elder Statesmen in Japan" in *North American Review,* Feb. 1906. S. L. Gulick, *The Evolution of the Japanese* (New York: 1903). Kengi Hamada, *Prince Ito . . .* (Tokyo). A. S. Hershey and S. W. Hershey, *Modern Japan* (Indianapolis: 1919), chs. 12-13 on government and politics. Eki Hioki, "A General Survey of the Judicial System of Japan" in *The Chinese Social and Political Science Review,* July, 1926. D. C. Holtom, *The Political Philosophy of Modern Shinto* (Chicago: 1922). Kikujiro Ishii, *Diplomatic Commentaries,* trans. and ed. by W. R. Langdon (Baltimore: 1936), ch. 11, the constitution and foreign policy of the Japanese nation. H. Ito, *Commentaries on the Constitution of the Empire of Japan* (Tokyo: 1889). U. Iwasaki, *Working Forces in Japanese Politics* (New York: 1921). T. Iyenaga, *The Constitutional Development of Japan 1853-1881*

(Baltimore: 1891). William P. Ker, "Treaty Revision in Japan" in *Pacific Affairs,* Nov. 1928. Naokichi Kitazawa, *The Government of Japan* (Princeton: 1929). J. H. Longford, *The Evolution of New Japan* (New York: 1913). J. H. Longford, *Japan* (Boston: 1923), ch. 15, constitutional reform. N. Matsunami, *The Constitution of Japan* (Tokyo: 1930). W. W. McLaren, *A Political History of Japan During the Meiji Era* (New York: 1916), to be used with caution. Of greater value is the same author's *Japanese Government Documents* in the *Transactions of the Asiatic Society of Japan,* vol. 42, pt. 1, (Yokohama: 1914). Masataro Miyake, "The Japanese Judiciary" in the *Trans-Pacific* (Tokyo: June 26, 1930). Sobei Mogi and H. Vere Redman, *The Problem of the Far East* (London: 1935), ch. 2 gives an excellent brief analysis. Tomio Nakano, *The Ordinance Power of the Japanese Emperor* (Baltimore: 1923), see in particular ch. 1, on the fundamental characteristics of the Japanese Constitution, and ch. 15 on European sources of the Constitution. K. Okakura, *The Awakening of Japan* (New York: 1904). S. Okuma, *Fifty Years of New Japan,* 2 vols. (London: 1909). H. S. Quigley, *Japanese Government and Politics* (New York: 1932), the best single volume in English on the subject. Tatsuji Takeuchi, *War and Diplomacy in the Japanese Empire* (Garden City: 1935), Pt. 1, Japan's constitutional organization and Pt. 3, the conduct of Japanese foreign relations. Kenzo Takayanagi, "Occidental Legal Ideas in Japan" in *Pacific Affairs,* Aug. 1930. Yosaburo Takekoshi, *Prince Saionji* (Kyoto: 1933), chs. 40-50, Japanese politics, 1890-1900. G. E. Uyehara, *The Political Development of Japan 1867-1909* (London: 1910). H. E. Wildes, *Social Currents in Japan* (Chicago: 1927), ch. 2 on the press in early modern Japan. See also successive issues of *The Japan Year Book* (Tokyo).

CHAPTER XVI

The Chino-Japanese War

THE year 1894 was a notable one in the history of Japan. Treaty revision became an accomplished fact, and the nation embarked on a war with its great and populous neighbor, China. Both events were to be of immense consequence. They provided the external or surface evidence that Japan had come of age. No longer could she be regarded as a weak and subservient oriental state. Fortunately, revision of the treaties preceded Japan's victory in the China war, from which one may conclude that Japan's right to treaty autonomy came as a result of her remarkable domestic progress in politics and law, and not (as has been frequently said) because of her naval and military victories over the Chinese. Taken together, revision of the treaties and a victorious war indicated both that Japan had put her house in order and that she was now in a position to influence her neighbors.

The Conventional Tariff

In the nineteenth century Japan's relationships with western powers revealed marked similarities to and differences from the experiences of China. Unlike China, Japan had accepted in good grace the coming of the Westerner and thus had avoided such losses as befell China in the wake of the wars of 1840 and 1857. But like China, she was, nevertheless, subjected to treaties which imposed conventional tariffs and rights of extra-territoriality. The extraterritoriality enjoyed by foreigners in Japan dated back to the Russian treaty of 1855, was found also in the Dutch and the American treaties of 1856 and 1857, and was amplified further in the commercial treaties of 1858. The conventional tariff dated from a four-power agreement of 1866 that replaced earlier tariff regulations. In general, this agreement established the rates on exports and imports at five per cent. This precluded any possibility of Japan's charging arbitrary rates had she desired to do so, but, more than this, it prevented the government from drawing any considerable revenue from foreign trade, and this at a time when the new government of the Restoration was urgently in need of funds. Finally, the conventional tariff was an infringement of Japanese sovereignty and thus objectionable to a patriotic and a proud people.

This same objection applied with equal, if not greater, force in the matter of extraterritoriality. The demands of foreign states for this privilege signified that they had no regard either for Japanese law or its administration. As in the case of China, the western powers could argue that Japanese laws lacked uniformity, that torture was employed, and that penalties were revolting or at least too severe. It is true that in Japan abuses of extraterritoriality by the foreigners were less frequent than in China; yet when they did occur, they resulted in justifiable and vigorous public protests difficult for the new government to ignore. A constant cause of friction was the question of whether foreign nationals were subject to Japanese law or only to their own national laws. The United States took the generous view that the former interpretation was correct, but as in China, Great Britain alone made adequate provision for the trial and punishment of her subjects.

Both the Japanese government and the public looked forward to the day when these early treaties might be revised and the stigma of the conventional tariff and extraterritoriality removed. But revision would depend on consent of all the treaty powers, and this was difficult to obtain. The government in Tokyo hoped, as early as 1872, for success, basing its claim for revision primarily on the American treaty, and to this end dispatched a mission headed by Iwakura to the western powers to announce its readiness to revise the treaties as soon as certain reforms had been effected. The mission was a distinguished one including such names as Kido, Okubo, Ito, and Yamaguchi. The United States was already prepared to revise the treaties, but these early negotiations failed because of Japan's desire and America's unwillingness that the questions be dealt with by a general conference in Europe. At all events, the mission was not without tangible results, for Japanese legations were established in Washington, London, Paris, Berlin, Vienna, and St. Petersburg. Perhaps of even greater value was the knowledge of things western gained by these leaders in government. Their attitude contrasted strikingly with the complacent prejudice and self-satisfaction of contemporary statesmen in China.

It was now becoming more evident in Japan that judicial reform must precede the abolition of extraterritoriality, but tariff revision was regarded as suitable for immediate discussion. The first step in this direction was a treaty concluded with the United States on July 25, 1878. Japan's right to control her own tariff was recognized, export duties were to be abolished, and two additional ports were to be opened to trade. This seeming victory was neutralized by the fact that the treaty was not to be effective until similar treaties had been signed by the other powers. In comparison with the United States, British commercial interests in Japan were large, and the British were not yet prepared to surrender valuable tariff advantages.

Meanwhile, the Japanese had been making some progress with judicial reform. A penal code replacing feudal law was promulgated in 1871, but it was based largely on Chinese models. Work was now commenced on new codes under the supervision of M. Boissonade, a French jurist. The results, a penal code and a code of criminal procedure, were promul-

gated in 1880. They were based primarily on French procedure. The Japanese government now believed that the powers
would be prepared to surrender their extraterritorial privileges,
but again it was disappointed. Conferences were held in
Tokyo from 1882 to 1887 with all the foreign representatives.
The United States again supported Japan's proposals. The
European powers were more conservative. Finally a draft
treaty was prepared by which extraterritoriality would be surrendered gradually, during which period (to 1903) foreign
judges would sit in Japanese courts. The tariff, too, was to
be increased. Unsatisfied with this proposal, Japan sought to
negotiate treaties again with individual powers. Such a treaty,
free from objectionable features, and based on terms of equality, was negotiated with Mexico in 1888, and less favorable
treaties were signed with the United States, Germany, and
Russia. Another was being negotiated with Great Britain,
but when the proposed terms were made public, Japanese
opinion was solidly against them, and an attempt was made
on the life of Okuma, who had conducted the negotiations.

By 1890, Japan had completed portions of the new civil
code, and in the same year the first meetings of the Imperial
Diet were held. Although this body had no direct control
over foreign relations, many of its members demanded treaty
revision so vociferously that the subject was impressed on the
public mind. In 1893 the lower house went so far as to
address the Throne, requesting the abolition of extraterritoriality and the conventional tariff. The government determined to attack the problem from a new angle. If Great
Britain, whose interests surpassed those of all other powers in
Japan, could be convinced that the time for revision had
arrived, other powers would follow her example. Working
on this theory, Tokyo initiated negotiations at London. In
July, 1894, revision of the British treaty was completed.
Somewhat tardily to be sure, the English government was at
last ready to concede that Japan was entitled to treatment as

an equal. Many matters were dealt with in the treaty, but its outstanding feature was the provision that extraterritoriality should be abolished in 1899. Full tariff autonomy was not granted at this time, the rates ranging from five to fifteen per cent on the principal imports. Notwithstanding, this victory was a great one for Japanese statesmanship. Other nations adopted in the main the British policy. Treaties with the United States, Germany, and France soon followed. Before the close of the century, a period of less than three decades since the formal abolition of feudalism, consular jurisdiction was merely a memory, and the worst features of the conventional tariff had been removed. The Mikado's government could regard these successes with justifiable pride.

Sixteen days following the signature of the revised Anglo-Japanese treaty in London, Japan declared war upon China. With the background of this conflict, whose object was to establish a Korea independent of Chinese control, the reader is already familiar (chapter 14). To its more immediate causes some consideration may now be given.

Causes of the Chino-Japanese War

The Tientsin Convention of 1885, which has already been discussed, had appeared to offer at least a temporary solution of the troublesome Korean question. This hope was frustrated by many factors, but the principle ones were two in number: (1) the autocratic, incapable, and corrupt Korean government, and (2) a new policy on the part of China. The reader is already well aware that China for centuries had regarded Korea as a vassal state and at the same time had evaded responsibility for events there. This anomalous state of affairs was at the root of the troubles which had already occurred in Indo-China, Formosa, and Korea. It lay in the peculiar interpretation which China had given to the term "vassal state." During the entire period of the Ming Dynasty

(1368-1644), and of the Manchus (after 1644), China expected no more of Korea than the payment of a nominal tribute, the sending of an annual mission, and the right of investiture of each new Korean sovereign. Neither the western powers nor Japan had objected to this empty form of Chinese control, and it was only when China attempted to exercise a more positive influence that objections were raised.

It was, therefore, not the old tributary relations which had existed in the Ming and Manchu days which were to be questioned, but a new policy of direct interference in the foreign and internal affairs of Korea. This policy was inaugurated by Li Hung-chang in 1885, and carried out by his protegé, the Chinese Resident Yuan Shih-kai, between 1885 and 1894. It was this *new* policy which brought on the war between Japan and China, not an attempt on the part of the former to destroy an *old* relationship. And it is the confusion of the *old* vassalage with the Li-Yuan policy which has misled many Western and Chinese commentators.[1]

After 1876, Japan recognized Korea as an independent state. This same policy was followed by the United States in the treaty of 1882. Great Britain, on the other hand, was more inclined to support the Chinese, and China seemingly had learned nothing by her recent experiences in Formosa and Annam. This new Chinese policy was described in 1890 by Augustine Heard, the American Minister in Korea:

It is a curious fact [he said] that it is only since China lost all right to that assumption, if she ever had any, that she claims the vassalage of Corea. Whatever may have been the relations of the two countries in the past, the signing of the treaty with the United States in 1882 made a new starting point, when the position of Corea was defined [as independence], and defined with the consent, if not with the initiative of China. . . .

Up to this time China had practically held aloof, and when summoned to make amends for Corea by France and the United States on well known occasions she absolutely repudiated all responsibility.

---

[1] P. J. Treat, "China and Korea, 1885-1894," *Political Science Quarterly*. Vol. 49, p. 510, December, 1934.

China's New Policy in Korea

China's new and positive policy was foreshadowed in 1882, the very year in which the United States recognized by treaty Korean independence. It was in that year that Li Hung-chang imposed commercial regulations on the peninsula. These regulations recognized Korea's tributary position and extended to the Chinese commercial privileges which were to be enjoyed by no other foreigners. For a time the annexation of Korea was considered seriously in Peking, but a compromise settlement was reached in the appointment of Yuan Shih-kai as Resident. Chinese influence now dominated the Korean administration. A telegraph system built with Chinese money and under Chinese direction connected Chemulpo and Seoul with the Manchurian border, and by 1886 the American *Chargé* at Seoul was reporting that "China now aims at something at least akin to incorporation of Korea into her own Empire." It is unnecessary here to enter into the minute details of Yuan's policy of intrigue. Suffice it to say that by means of his work Korea's treaties with the foreign powers were reduced to a mockery. Hugh O. Dinsmore, who became American Minister at Seoul in 1887, reported that Korean political affairs were approaching a crisis.

China is slowly but surely tightening her grasp upon this government and its king. The spirit of resistance seems almost to have died out of the Koreans and there is an apparent acquiescence on the part of a number of foreign representatives.

The Koreans do not impress me as having any affection or strong attachment for the Chinese. On the contrary there is among the common people a well defined dislike for them, but they fear them and it is under the influence of this fear that they are gradually yielding to Chinese supremacy. . . .

The Chinese representative memorializes, provides, dictates and directs, all under a system of intimidation mixed with an affectation of disinterested kindness.

During these years (1885-1892) Japan had played a passive role in Korea. She had made no noticeable effort to counteract the influence of Yuan. The conduct of her representatives, as reported by various American Ministers in Korea, had been "both correct and moderate." Together with the United States, she had stood for a policy of Korean independence. Her commercial interests in Korea were larger than those of any other country; she looked to the time when more Korean ports would be opened to trade, and to this end had invited the diplomatic assistance of the United States. This policy of moderation gave place in 1893 to one of vigor. The immediate occasion for this change is not clear, but a number of factors may have influenced the policy. During the earlier years of the period, Japan's foreign policy had centered on revision of the treaties, and there was little time for Korean affairs. After 1890, the Imperial Diet made it more difficult for the government to ignore any phase of foreign relations in which there was popular interest. In 1893, Yuan's misgovernment of Korea produced the first provincial rebellions, and warships of various powers were dispatched to Chemulpo. Since 1889, too, a number of specific instances of treaty violation had occurred, and for these, Japan had received no satisfaction. The days of the passive policy were ended.

The Tong-Hak Insurrection

The occasion for dramatic events soon to follow was provided by activities of a Korean religious society, known as the Tong-Haks (Men of the Eastern Religion), who revolted in March, 1893. The uprising, though primarily religious, attracted political malcontents and evinced a pronounced anti-foreign trend. Foreign warships assembled at Chemulpo. A year later in Tokyo three Koreans attempted to assassinate one of their liberal countrymen living there in exile, while at almost the same time Kim Ok Kiun, leader of the Korean liberals, was enticed to Shanghai from Japan and there murdered by a Korean assassin. The dismembered body of Kim was later displayed publicly in Korea, whither it had been carried on a Chinese gunboat. The incident served to inflame Japanese public opinion, though the government remained calm. Scarcely had these events passed than the Tong-Haks were again in rebellion, their efforts this time being directed mainly against the oppressive Korean government. Again foreign warships assembled at Chemulpo. It appears that the Korean administration had no faith in its own troops, and so a Chinese force was requested through Yuan Shih-kai, the Resident. On June 6, 1894, after a second request had been made, fifteen hundred Chinese troops were dispatched from Tientsin and more were promised, while Japan was notified of the action taken, according to the terms of the Tientsin Convention (see p. 264).

Considering the policy which Li and Yuan had followed during the preceding ten years, it was hardly to be wondered that Japan was no longer content for China to act in Korea alone. Japanese troops were soon on their way. They entered Seoul two days after the Chinese had landed at Asan. Here was a situation which the Korean King had not foreseen. He requested the Chinese to withdraw, but this they did not propose to do so long as the Japanese remained. Nor did the Japanese propose to leave, for, unhappily, China, in giving notice to Japan that troops would be sent, had explained that the purpose was "to restore the peace of our tributary state." This statement, coupled with the record of the Li-Yuan policy, created a demand from the Japanese press and public that China's pretensions in Korea be ended. Accordingly, Japan now proposed to China that the two powers send commissioners to Korea to investigate measures of reform. China replied immediately that she could not interfere in Korean domestic affairs, and much less could Japan, who had recognized Korea's independence. The reply was perhaps clever, but the Japanese government, recalling the ten-year record of Li and Yuan, was not impressed by it. It informed China that Japan's interests in Korea arising from geographical and commercial considerations were too far-reaching to be ignored and that the Japanese troops would not be withdrawn until there was some guarantee of future good government in the peninsula.

Japan now acted quickly. She demanded a statement as to whether Korea regarded herself as independent or as a vassal of China. Although the question was embarrassing, for Chinese troops were still in the capital, the government replied that it was independent. There followed extensive proposals for reform, which Korea accepted, at least formally. China, alarmed by these developments, sought vainly for assistance from Great Britain, Russia, and the United States, and, though the ministers of these powers counseled peace at Tokyo, their efforts failed. Meanwhile, Japan informed China that her failure to co-operate in Korean reform could be interpreted only as a desire to complicate matters further. In Seoul, the Korean administration, with Chinese troops on one side and Japanese on the other, was asking the Japanese to withdraw, on the pretext that reforms could not be initiated in the presence of foreign troops. The Japanese retorted that it was the Chinese who must leave and that all agreements between Korea and China that infringed the former's sovereign rights must be abrogated. When nothing came of this suggestion, Japanese troops on July 23, 1894, seized the King and instructed his father to head a new administration. On the following day, Korea's treaty with China was abrogated, and the Japanese were instructed to drive the Chinese troops from the land. If the Chinese resisted, war was inevitable. But it was not, as frequently stated, a war which Japan had forced upon China to avoid domestic revolution in Japan. Mr. Edwin Dun, American Minister in Japan, and at the time the best-informed American diplomat in the Far East, wrote in July:

Japan views with alarm the possibility of the Korean peninsula being absorbed by one of the great western powers and believes that a continuance of existing conditions of corruption and oppression in the administration of Korea must result in the entire disorganization of the government of that country and not only leave Korea helpless prey to any power that may covet her territory, but give a valid excuse for armed occupation by such a power, in the name of law, order and humanity. It is my opinion that Japan has not now ulterior designs of territorial aggrandizement; that her object is, as stated to me by Mr. Mutsu, to bring about such reforms in the Korean administration as may lead, not only in name but in fact, to the autonomy and sovereign independence of that country.

The Japanese Government cannot now draw back. They have committed themselves to a task that the nation insists shall be accomplished.

While China continued to seek foreign intervention and to profess that hers was a policy of peace, Li Hung-chang was sending 8,000 troops from Tientsin to Korea to thwart whatever moves the Japanese might make. This was prior to Japan's seizure of the Korean King. On July 25, Chinese and Japanese warships exchanged shots off the Korean coast, and Captain Togo, commanding a Japanese cruiser, sighted one of Li Hung-chang's transports. It was a British vessel, the *Kowshing,* with a human cargo of twelve hundred Chinese troops bound for Korea. Togo demanded her surrender, and when the Chinese refused to permit the British officers to deliver the ship, she was sunk with the loss of a thousand lives. A few days later (July 29), Japanese troops defeated the Chinese forces in Korea at Asan. China now broke off diplomatic relations (July 31), both countries declaring war on the following day. The issue was Korea: tributary or free. On the day that diplomatic relations were broken, China addressed the American Minister at Peking, asserting that the peninsula had been a tributary of China for many years. In Li's determination to maintain Chinese dominance, it was convenient to forget that Japan in 1876, the United States in

1882, and other European states had all recognized that Korea was independent. China's case in 1894 was lamentably weak, for neither legally nor on the basis of her record in Korea could she lay any just claim to support. Japan, on the contrary, could well assert that she was fighting for independence and reform for Korea.

To most Westerners, even those in the Far East, Japan's military and naval victories came as a surprise. The size and potential wealth of China, coupled with her vast resources in population, appeared to most observers to be a guarantee of victory. Few Westerners realized the extent to which China lacked the cohesive force of nationalism; most Chinese had little knowledge of and less interest in the war. To them the fate of Korea was a meaningless phrase. Chinese troops were poorly trained and their equipment was bad. The navy, estimated as larger than Japan's, lacked both morale and a trained personnel. Naval appropriations had been spent by that remarkable lady, the Empress Dowager, on the Summer Palace near Peking. Against the Chinese giant, Japan could muster relatively small but highly effective forces both on land and sea. Her modernized army and navy were led by capable officers, and quite as important as this was the simple fact that behind these ships and men was a small, compact, literate, proud, and determined people, prepared for any sacrifice in defending the national honor.

During August, Japan and Korea concluded a treaty of alliance, while troops of the former prepared to expel the last of the Chinese. This was done by September 15, and two days later the Chinese fleet was defeated off the mouth of the Yalu River, and four of the ships were destroyed. This gave Japan control of the sea. Japanese armies advanced across the Korean border into Manchuria, while additional forces, landing on the coasts of Liaotung, captured Port Arthur in a single day's engagement. During the winter months of January and February, 1895, the Japanese took Wei-hai-wei, on the northern coast of Shantung. Their Manchurian armies moved slowly, but in early March they had occupied Newchwang and Ying-kow. Peking became their obvious objective, where a frightened and humiliated government was seeking a means of escape.

Western Powers Alarmed

This sense of alarm was not confined to the Chinese government. The presence of Japanese forces in Shantung and the advance of their armies in Manchuria toward the Great Wall were developments that at least some western powers did not view with unqualified approval. Early in the war, Great Britain and Russia offered mediation, and China agreed, for she was now only too ready to admit Korean independence and to pay a war indemnity. The British and the Russian interest at this time was summarized by Charles Denby, American Minister at Peking.

England's advocacy of peace is easily explicable. In the first place her commerce is deranged by the existence of hostilities. The political considerations by which she is influenced are scarcely less forcible. Should rebellion take place in China and should the Manchu power be broken and the Manchus be expelled, the formation of an independent Manchu principality, north of China proper, would be the natural consequence. This principality might easily be converted into a Russian dependency. Such a contingency is not too remote to be regarded with indifference by British statesmen. To this consideration must be added the ever present fear that some turn in the war may justify Russia in interference in Korea.

England hoped in fact for a joint mediation that would include the United States, and when this failed, she approached Japan alone and unsuccessfully. China meanwhile appealed to the United States, Great Britain, France, Germany, and Russia, previous to which the United States had offered its good offices to both China and Japan. To this offer Japan on November 17, 1894, replied significantly (as the years 1931

to 1932 were later to show) that while she did not propose
to push her victories beyond reasonable limits, "those limits can
not, however, be said to have been reached until China finds
herself in a position to approach Japan directly on the subject
of peace."

On the previous day Minister Denby had written in Peking:

History, I think, furnishes no parallel with the condition of
China. There have occurred other examples of nations going to
war while unprepared therefor, but such utter governmental blind-
ness to its own want of preparation and such folly in drifting into
a conflict have never been exhibited elsewhere.

The foundation of the misfortunes of China lies in the over-
weening conceit fostered by seclusion and ignorance among its
governing classes. Proud, haughty, bound up in ceremonial, absolutely ignorant of foreign affairs, the rulers of China are the least
intelligent of her respectable classes.

Chinese councils were in hopeless confusion. On November 18, 1894, Li Hung-chang sent a personal agent to Japan
seeking peace. On November 22, the Chinese Foreign Office
was asking peace on the basis of Korean independence, and
an indemnity. All these efforts failed, Japan replying that
peace would not be discussed until China had dispatched
properly qualified representatives. Late in January, 1895,
China sent a second mission. It consisted of two Chinese
officials of secondary rank, with John W. Foster, former
American Secretary of State, as adviser. Again Japan asserted
that their powers were insufficient, by which she meant that
China was not yet prepared to make peace. This was certainly true, for in February Minister Denby wrote:

It is impossible to say with certainty to-day that China wants
peace. She still has an idea that the foreign powers will intervene
to save her from ruin—an idea to which some force has been given
by the frantic and foolish conduct of people who ought to have
known better. If China knew to-day that the world would stand
aside and let her fight her own battle she would instantly make
peace.

Not until all hope of direct foreign aid had vanished did China appoint Li Hung-chang with full powers to make peace, and by this time Japan had made known that her terms would include the cession of territory. Li spent the weeks prior to his departure for Japan in feverish efforts to prevent any annexation by securing guarantees of European intervention. In vain did Denby seek to impress Li and the foreign office with the imperative need of "a sincere, friendly, *rapprochement* with Japan." Li was determined that Japan would yet be deprived of the fruits of victory, if not by China, then at least by Europe.

The Shimonoseki Negotiations

The peace negotiations were conducted at Shimonoseki. Nine years previously, Ito had met Li Hung-chang at Tientsin, where his views on Korea had received scant attention. At Shimonoseki the tables were turned, for Ito now dictated the terms. He was assisted by Viscount Munemitsu Mutsu. The approach of the conference aroused the greatest interest among the powers. They hoped that Japan would sweep away the remaining restrictions on foreign trade in China to the benefit of all, while at the same time they watched jealously the increasing prestige of Japan in Asia. The United States enjoyed an unusual position, for two of her nationals, John W. Foster and Henry W. Denison, acted as advisers to the Chinese and Japanese missions, respectively.

The negotiations were opened late in March, 1895. Li requested an armistice. When this was refused, except upon onerous terms, he asked for Japan's terms of peace. That day a Japanese fanatic, holding Li responsible for affairs in Korea and the war, made an attempt on his life. Although the wound was not serious, its political effects were great. Stunned by this disgraceful act, Japan granted an immediate armistice. The peace terms were submitted on April 1. They were severe in the extreme, including recognition of Korean independence, cession of a considerable area in south Manchuria, all of Formosa and the Pescadores Islands, a war indemnity of 300,000,000 taels, and commercial concessions. China's counter-proposals were made April 9. They agreed to the independence of Korea, refused any cession of territory save the Pescadores and a small area in Manchuria, and offered an indemnity of 10,000,000 taels without interest. Japan's modified demands were presented on April 10 and were followed by an ultimatum the next day. No further modifications would be allowed, and on April 17, the treaty was signed. Some of its terms, which are here briefly summarized, were to be of the utmost consequence. (1) China recognized the independence of Korea. (2) China ceded to Japan Formosa and the Pescadores, off the coast of Fukien, and the Liaotung peninsula (with Port Arthur), in south Manchuria. (3) China agreed to pay within seven years a war indemnity of 200,000,-000 taels, with interest at five per cent. (4) Four additional treaty ports would be opened to Japanese trade and residence, and under most-favored-nation treatment to all the treaty powers. (5) Japan would be accorded most-favored-nation treatment in China until the conclusion of a new Chino-Japanese commercial treaty.

For Japan, the war had been truly a great victory. She had triumphed both on the battlefield and at the conference table. Her policy of independence and reform in Korea had been vindicated, and the most-favored-nation clause gave her commercial equality with the western states in China. To these phases of her policy, western states had given either informal support or, at worst, no active opposition. When, however, Japan included in her demands cession of Port Arthur and its hinterland, the moment for European action had arrived.

The Triple Intervention

The origins of the triple intervention by which Russia, France, and Germany were to deprive Japan of Port Arthur were complex in the extreme. Before his departure for Japan, Li had visited the Ministers of Russia, Germany, and France, made known the Japanese demands to them, and implored their aid. Russia was the power most intimately concerned with any annexations Japan might make in Manchuria. In March, Mr. Denby wrote:

It is generally thought that she will not permit Japan to annex any portion of Manchuria lying contiguous to her own territory, or so situated as to block her access to the South. In a few years the great trans-Siberian railroad will be completed, and an outlet to the sea accessible at all seasons will become a necessity. . . . Russia will not be in a hurry to develop her plans—unless Japan should take measures of annexation which would tend to hem her in. In that event, it is thought that Russia will forcibly object, and will resort to arms if necessary.

From St. Petersburg in February Minister C. R. Breckinridge had written on Russian policy as follows:

. . . what Russia most needs and wants at this time is outlets upon the Pacific Ocean. Manchuria is thinly populated and too far North to alone fully answer her purposes. Corea and the country about Pekin, one or both, coupled with the other, more nearly meet her requirements. . . .

But if she cannot now get what I am sure she wants, she will at least leave nothing undone to prevent Japan from gaining a foothold upon the continent, and to prevent anything like a protectorate over Corea.

At this time, too, Russia had already considered a route for the Trans-Siberian railroad across northern Manchuria. In these interests Russia could count on the support of her ally, France. It was also at this time that Germany had become ambitious for a place in the Pacific. For many years she had been represented in the Far East by M. von Brandt, a distinguished diplomat who could be counted upon to support China against Japan, and it was probably he who moved the German government to intervene.

The Ministers of these three powers (for England had refused to act with them) presented the views of their respective governments at the Japanese Foreign Office on April 23, 1895, less than a week after the Treaty of Shimonoseki had been signed. In the curious language of diplomacy, these views were tendered as a friendly advice. They asserted that "the possession of the peninsula of Liaotung, claimed by Japan, would be a constant menace to the capital of China, would at the same time render illusory the independence of Korea, and would henceforth be a perpetual obstacle to the peace of the Far East," and to the end that this "peace" might never again be disturbed they advised Japan to return her Manchurian territory to China. There was, to be sure, some humor in the spectacle of Europe's most heavily armed states manifesting such pious concern for the peaceful future of eastern Asia, but there is little wonder that this humor made no appeal to Japan. Confronted by this armed threat, veiled as friendly advice, she offered to renounce all the Manchurian territory save Port Arthur and its immediate vicinity. The three powers refused this concession, and Japan agreed to surrender Port Arthur. She asked that the Treaty of Shimonoseki be ratified and that additional indemnity be granted. This was agreed to, an additional 30,000,000 taels being added to China's bill. From motives which were entirely selfish, Russia, Germany, and France had deprived Japan of what was then regarded as the legitimate spoils of war. Their action was proclaimed in the name of peace. The merits of this claim will receive some attention in later chapters.

SELECTED BIBLIOGRAPHY

R. H. Akagi, *Japan's Foreign Relations* (Tokyo: 1936), ch. 6, "The Sino-Japanese War." Nagao Ariga, *La Guerre Sino-Japonaise*

(Paris: 1896). G. A. Ballard, *The Influence of the Sea on the Political History of Japan* (New York: 1921), chs. 5-6. *History of the Peace Negotiations Between China and Japan* (Tientsin: 1895). Valentine Chirol, *The Far Eastern Question* (London: 1896). Henri Cordier, *Histoire des Relations de la Chine avec les Puissances Occidentales, 1860-1902,* 3 vols. (Paris: 1901-1902). G. N. Curzon, *Problems of the Far East* (Westminster: 1896). Charles Denby, "How Peace Was Made Between China and Japan" in the *Forum,* Mar. and Aug. 1900. Tyler Dennett, "American Good Offices in Asia" in *American Journal of International Law,* vol. 16, no. 1, 1922. E. T. S. Dugdale, *German Diplomatic Documents 1871-1914,* 4 vols. (London: 1930), vol. 3, ch. 1, the Chino-Japanese War and triple intervention. J. W. Foster, *American Diplomacy in the Orient* (Boston: 1904). J. W. Foster, *Diplomatic Memoirs,* 2 vols. (Boston: 1909), vol. 2 on the settlement of the Chino-Japanese War. Edwin A. Falk, *Togo and the Rise of Japanese Sea Power* (New York: 1936), chs. 8-11; excellent for the strategy of the war. A. Gerard, *Ma Mission en Chine 1893-1897* (Paris: 1918). W. E. Griffis, *The Mikado's Empire,* 2 vols. (New York: 1906), vol. 2, bk. 3, chs. 4-5, on the war with China. K. Hara, *An Introduction to the History of Japan* (New York: 1920). A. E. Hindmarsh, *The Basis of Japanese Foreign Policy* (Harvard University: 1936). S. G. Hishida, *The International Position of Japan as a Great Power* (New York: 1905). S. Hsu, *China and Her Political Entity* (New York: 1926), ch. 4, the war and its consequences. H. B. Hulbert, *The History of Korea* (Seoul: 1905). Kikujiro Ishii, *Diplomatic Commentaries* (Baltimore: 1936), ch. 2, Japanese diplomacy, 1853-1900. Philip Joseph, *Foreign Diplomacy in China, 1894-1900* (London: 1928), chs. 3-5. U. Kobayashi, *War and Armament Loans of Japan* (New York: 1922), chs. 1-3. S. A. Korff, *Russia's Foreign Relations During the Last Half Century* (New York: 1922), ch. 3. Alexis S. Krausse, *The Far East* (London: 1900). H. B. Morse, *The International Relations of the Chinese Empire* (London: 1918), vol. 3, ch. 2. G. Ono, *Expenditures of the Sino-Japanese War* (New York: 1922), Pt. 2, economic effects of the war. G. N. Steiger, *China and the Occident* (New Haven: 1927), ch. 3, consequences of the treaty of peace. Tatsuji Takeuchi, *War and Diplomacy in the Japanese Empire* (Garden City: 1935), ch. 10. P. J. Treat, *Diplomatic Relations Between the United States and Japan, 1853-1895,* 2 vols. (Stanford University: 1932), vol. 2, chs. 42-44, the most satisfactory account. J. V. A. MacMurray, ed., *Treaties and Agreements With and Concerning China, 1894-1919,* 2 vols. (New York: 1921). See also United States, *Foreign Relations,* 1894, Appendix I, and 1895, Pt. 1. Vladmir (Zenone Volpicelli) *The China-Japan War* (London: 1896). Vladimir, *Russia on the Pacific and the Siberian Railway* (London: 1899).

CHAPTER XVII

China Pays: The Leaseholds and Spheres

1895-1899

DURING the Chino-Japanese War, Li Hung-chang had been warned by the American Minister in Peking that China would pay dearly for any assistance that Europe might give her. Yet so intent was Li on humiliating Japan that he gave no heed to this advice. On the contrary, he made every effort to gain European support. His labors were given ample reward in the triple intervention when Russia, Germany, and France piously "advised" Japan to surrender south Manchuria in the interests of future peace in the Far East. Japan accepted the advice; it remained for China to pay for it.

France Receives Payment

France was the first to profit. She had been negotiating with China for many months seeking rectification of the Tongking boundary and a commercial treaty. The negotiations lagged. China was not disposed to make concessions until, after the triple intervention, she was given to understand that now was the appropriate time to show her gratitude. Accepting this suggestion, on May 9, 1895, she agreed to the French proposals. Three blocks of territory passed into French hands, and China consented to approach French capitalists if mining properties were to be exploited in Yunnan, Kwangsi, and Kwangtung. In addition, it was agreed that the French railways of Annam might be extended into China proper. This was the first step in the creation of a French "sphere of influence." The terms were formally signed in June, France promptly requesting a railway concession in Kwangsi, which was granted the following year.

Compensation for Russia

Russia's first compensation seemed innocuous enough. Before Port Arthur had been returned to China or the amount of additional indemnity to Japan had been agreed upon, Russia offered China a loan to cover initial indemnity payments. The matter was handled by a Franco-Russian banking syndicate, and the agreement, concluded July 6, 1895, provided for a loan of 100,000,000 gold roubles at four per cent, secured by duties of the Chinese Maritime Customs. This loan was opposed by the British and the German Ministers at Peking, but on March 23, 1896, less than a year later, their two countries arranged for China a joint loan of £16,000,000, which, like the Franco-Russian loan, was charged against the Chinese Customs Service. These two loans were merely the beginnings of a bitter rivalry among European states to provide for China's real or imagined financial needs.

The Trans-Siberian Railway

The Russian gesture of assisting China to pay the indemnity was merely a preliminary move in a much larger and more ambitious policy. Before and during the Chino-Japanese War (as noted in the preceding chapter), Russia was planning to consolidate and expand her interests in eastern Siberia, north China, and Korea. Construction of the Trans-Siberian Railway was begun in 1891. Its completion would link European Russia with Vladivostok, on the Pacific. Two major defects marred this plan: (1) the course of the railroad would lie through the long and difficult country north of the Amur River and thence down the full length of the Maritime

Province; (2) Vladivostok, though possessed of an excellent harbor, was icebound many months of the year. How could these defects be removed?

As one of the chief instruments of the Russian policy, there was created in St. Petersburg on December 22, 1895, with capital derived mainly from French banks, the Russo-Chinese Bank. Its charter was approved by the Russian Minister of Finance, who also retained the right to confirm an elected board of directors. The function of the bank being to develop Russian commercial relations with the Far East, it was endowed with extraordinary powers to collect duties in China and to assist in the construction of railways and telegraphs.

In June, 1896, distinguished statesmen of all the great powers were present in Moscow for the coronation ceremonies of Tsar Nicholas II. Among them was Li Hung-chang, whom the Russian government had designated as the only man who could properly represent China. Insistence upon the appointment of Li was not a matter of chance. He had been in disfavor at Peking when the war with Japan broke out, and the humiliating Treaty of Shimonoseki had not added to his reputation at court. Nevertheless, he hated Japan, and in Russian eyes this was his greatest virtue. Already he had become the leader of the pro-Russian faction at Peking, and on his arrival in St. Petersburg and Moscow, he received particular attention from Lobanov and Witte, who headed the ministries of foreign affairs and finance, respectively. Witte, stressing Russia's financial favors to China, and her leading role in the triple intervention, expressed regret that, owing to lack of railways, she had not been able to come to China's aid during the war. To avoid future repetition of this unhappy fact, he offered Li a secret treaty of alliance against Japan. The two powers would support each other against any move by Japan that threatened Korea, China, or eastern Siberia, and a concession to build the Siberian railway across north Manchuria direct to Vladivostok would be granted to the Russo-

Chinese Bank. The treaty was signed at Moscow on June 3, 1896, though its existence was not admitted by either signatory until 1922.[1] This was a major triumph for Witte. The first defect in Russia's far eastern schemes had been removed, and, incidentally, the future railroad journey to Vladivostok reduced by more than three hundred miles. At the same time, it was this secret treaty of alliance and the Russian ambitions that grew from it that were to lead directly and inevitably to the Russo-Japanese War.

The Chinese Eastern Railway

Three months after signature of the secret alliance, the Russo-Chinese Bank secured a contract with the Chinese government providing for construction of the Chinese Eastern Railway, a section of the Trans-Siberian system, to run directly across north Manchuria toward Vladivostok. The railroad was to be built by the Chinese Eastern Railway Company, a subsidiary of the Russo-Chinese Bank. Although the president of the company would be named by the Chinese government, actual control would rest with a general manager who would be Russian. Perhaps of greatest importance was "the absolute and exclusive right of administration" that the company was to exercise over the "lands actually necessary for the construction, operation, and protection of the line." The company was likewise to exercise "complete and exclusive right to operate the line." China might purchase the road after thirty-six years, or it would revert to her without payment after eighty years. The statutes of the company were to be confirmed by the Russian government; Russian mails were to be carried free of charge, and finally, "the preservation of law and order on the lands assigned to the railway and its appur-

---

[1] At the Washington Conference in January, 1922, the Chinese delegation submitted a telegraphic summary of the treaty. The existence of some secret agreement between China and Russia was rumored as early as 1895 and was usually referred to as the "Cassini Convention."

tenances shall be confided to police agents appointed by the Company," while goods carried on the line would enjoy a one-third reduction from the Chinese import and export duties. In a word, the Chinese Eastern Railway would provide the basis for Russian economic and political control of Manchuria.

South Manchuria Railway Co.

THE SUNGARI RIVER AT HARBIN, MANCHURIA. It was here that the Russians at the close of the nineteenth century built the greatest railway town in the Far East, the most cosmopolitan city in eastern Asia.

Germany's Compensation

But what of Germany? She, too, had joined in the triple intervention, and presumably expected some reward. German interest in the Pacific had been aroused more than a decade before the Chino-Japanese War and had resulted in annexation of numerous islands, including the Marshall group. But these acquisitions were at best scattered and gave Germany no tangible stake in the future of China. A coaling station in — the Far East was thought to be imperative. Plans were formulated in March, 1895, before the close of the Chino-Japanese War, and negotiations with China were opened in December,

1896. In August, 1897, the German Kaiser prepared the way by securing the Tsar's approval to the German plan of occupying Kiaochow, in Shantung province, "the best seaport in Northern China." The choice of this port was made after Germany's far eastern squadron had examined every available harbor on the China coast. China was of course reluctant to surrender territory, even in the form of a lease, for a grant made to one power would immediately bring demands from others. Germany thus appeared to be blocked, unless some pretext for direct action could be found. The exemplary patience of the German Foreign Office was soon rewarded. In the secluded southwest regions of Shantung province, two German Catholic priests were murdered on November 1, 1897. The murder of foreign priests in China was not an unheard-of phenomenon. The striking feature of this case was the application of a new and a vigorous remedy.

A German squadron appeared in Kiaochow Bay on November 14. Its defenses were occupied by the invaders pending the presentation of German demands at Peking, which took place on November 22. These demands called for the erection of a tablet in memory of the priests, an indemnity, dismissal of the governor, expenses to cover the Kiaochow occupation, and preferential treatment for German engineers in railroad construction and the working of mines in the province. China showing no haste in meeting what Germany termed her "just rights," reinforcements in ships and men arrived from Europe in December. It was becoming more obvious to the Chinese Foreign Office that this time there would be no triple intervention. Accordingly, the missionary question was settled. It was agreed that the governor should be dismissed, that indemnity should be paid for the murdered priests, and, as signal proof of China's respect for Christian priests and their doctrines, that the Chinese government should erect three churches, costing 66,000 taels each, provide sites for two of them, and donate additional sums for mission buildings in the district where the missionaries had been murdered. With these preliminaries out of the way, Germany now proceeded to the real business of demanding a lease of Kiaochow, and since no power was prepared to challenge her demand openly, the Chinese yielded, as "a special proof of their grateful appreciation of the friendship shown to them by Germany." The agreements covering this settlement were signed March 6, 1898. The leasehold, granted to Germany for ninety-nine years, covered some two hundred square miles around Kiaochow Bay. Beyond this was provided a neutral zone thirty miles wide. Germany might fortify the place and maintain troops there, but she agreed never to sublet the territory to another power. She also acquired the right to construct two railways in Shantung—one from Kiaochow to Tsinan, and the other from Kiaochow via Ichow to Tsinan. In conclusion, the Chinese government made the following significant commitment:

. . . where foreign assistance, in persons, capital and material, may be needed for any purpose whatever within the Province of Shantung, to offer the said work or supplying of materials in the first instance to German manufacturers and merchants engaged in undertakings of the kind in question.

In this manner Germany established herself in China. A naval base and a coaling station, the right to construct railways, and preferential treatment for German brains and materials —these were the price and presumably the value of two murdered priests.

Russia Leases Port Arthur

German activity in Shantung had aroused the fears of both Russia and France, for neither of these powers looked with favor on an extension of German influence. Particularly in Moscow was there bitterness when the ministry learned that the Tsar had given Berlin a free hand at Kiaochow. While the German-Chinese negotiations were in progress, the Russian Pacific fleet appeared at Port Arthur, merely, as the British were informed, to winter there temporarily. In Russia, the ministers of the Tsar could not agree on policy. Count Witte, father of the secret Russo-Chinese alliance and chief promoter of the Chinese Eastern Railway, hoped to preserve for Russia's Manchurian adventure a predominantly economic character. Mouraviev, the Foreign Minister, frankly labeled the policy as political and advocated seizing Port Arthur and the Liaotung peninsula for the Russian Pacific fleet. His advice was accepted. The "temporary" visit of the Russian squadron became permanent. China was informed that a lease of Port Arthur must be granted, while Witte speeded the negotiations by making available to Li Hung-chang a "gift" of 500,000 roubles. The transaction was embodied in two Russo-Chinese agreements made on March 27 and May 7, 1898. Russia was granted a twenty-five year lease of the southern part of the Liaotung peninsula, including Port Arthur and Talien Bay and adjacent waters, "for the purpose of ensuring that the Russian naval forces shall possess an entirely secure base on the littoral of northern China." Within this leasehold the supreme military and civil administration was to be Russian. Port Arthur itself was created a naval base open only to Russian and Chinese vessels. A commercial open port, later known as Dalny, was to be established on Talien Bay, and the right to connect this port by railway with the main line of the Chinese Eastern was granted. By this provision, Dalny, as well as Vladivostok (and Dalny was an ice-free port), would become the Pacific terminus of the Trans-Siberian system. The second defect in the Russian plan had been eliminated. And if China felt any misgivings at these events, her fears were to be stilled by a Russian guarantee that the building of the railway would "never under any form serve as a pretext for the seizure of Chinese territory or for an encroachment on the sovereign rights of China."

Reactions Within Japan

Whatever effect these words may have had in China, they did not ring true in Japan. Only three years had elapsed since the Chino-Japanese War. Memories were still fresh— memories of a triple intervention in which Russia, France, and Germany had forced Japan to restore Port Arthur, a fortress which she had taken according to the legitimate uses of war, to China. Japan recalled that these military powers of Europe had justified their action on the high plane of safeguarding the future peace of the Far East. Since that intervention, Japan had observed the annexation of Chinese territory by France in the south, and the creation of a naval base and leasehold by Germany in Shantung. She was now called upon to witness the seizure by Russia of Liaotung, the identical territory that Japan herself, after winning it in battle, had been forced to surrender. If in 1895 Japan entertained any doubts as to what Europe meant by "the peace of the Far East," assuredly those doubts were removed in 1898.

The British Policy

Great Britain, opposed at least in principle to the alienation of Chinese territory, saw in the policies of Germany and Russia a threat to her prestige in north China. Fearing Russia in particular, she countered the occupation of Port Arthur by ordering a squadron north from Hong Kong, and by informing China that a leasehold would be sought. Wei-hai-wei, on the northern coast of Shantung directly between Port Arthur and Kiaochow, was the British objective, but it was then occupied by the Japanese, who had captured it during the war and who were to remain in occupation until the indemnity was paid. No obstacle, however, was placed in the British path by the Japanese, for they welcomed and sympathized with Great Britain's fear of Russia. China, too, consented to the lease on the same terms that Russia enjoyed at Port Arthur. German objections from Kiaochow were set at rest by a guarantee that there would be no interference with German commercial interests. In fact the Anglo-German banking syndicate advanced a second loan to China; the Japanese indemnity was paid and her troops withdrawn. On July 1, 1898, the leasehold agreement was signed by China. The territory involved was something less than three hundred square miles, and the agreement was to run "for as long a period as Port Arthur shall remain in the possession of Russia." A second fortress that Japan had taken in war passed into the hands of a European power.

Nor did south China escape the ravages of 1898. In 1860, China had ceded to Great Britain a small area known as Kowloon, opposite the British island of Hong Kong. This cession was extended in 1898 by a lease covering the hinterland of Kowloon, with an area of 376 square miles.

France Leases Kwangchow

France, likewise discovering that the compensation received in 1895 was insufficient, demanded a lease of Kwangchow Bay, on the southern coast southwest of Hong Kong. Its area, including two small islands, was 195 square miles, and the lease was to run for ninety-nine years. This negotiation was also aided by the murder of a priest, for whose life it was agreed that an indemnity of 100,000 francs should be paid, a chapel erected, local officials punished, and a railroad concession granted.

The leaseholds provided the means whereby the powers could force their politico-economic policies upon China. That country was looked upon as a great and undeveloped economic frontier capable of absorbing Europe's surplus capital principally in the building of railroads and the working of mines. Industrial progress along these lines had been advocated at

Peking by ministers of various powers, including the United States, for half a century. Usually their efforts had been fruitless. Chinese conservatism, prejudice, and general opposition to the West and its ways, together with the political instability of the Chinese state, had all conspired to defeat any far-reaching industrial penetration of the Middle Kingdom. To these various obstacles, the leaseholds provided a convenient answer. From these naval strongholds, pressure for concessions could be exerted on the Chinese government, and when railroad and mining rights were secured, they would be under the immediate protection of the foreign troops. Capital might now be invested in large amounts with a reasonable guarantee of profits.

The Spheres of Influence

So keen was the rivalry of the powers in this scramble for economic spoils that each attempted to create in the hinterland of its leasehold a "sphere of influence" or "sphere of interest," defined as "a region pre-empted for further exploitation and possibly for political control." In the first instance, the spheres were created by unilateral action. Their existence was then strengthened by agreements with China whereby the latter pledged herself never to alienate any of the territory in question. Finally, some of the powers agreed in specific conventions to respect the sphere of a rival. France, for example, had in 1895 secured preference for French capital in mining development in Yunnan, Kwangsi, and Kwangtung, three provinces which were soon to be recognized as a French sphere of influence. In 1897, China agreed never to cede the Island of Hainan to any other power, and in 1898 the same promise was made applicable to the three provinces themselves. Great Britain was assured that China would never cede any part of the Yangtze Valley, which the British regarded as their sphere. In Shantung, Germany, as has been noted, was assured preference for German technical advisers and German materials. Britain pledged herself not to interfere with Germany's economic plans in the province, and Germany in turn agreed not to seek railway concessions in the Yangtze Valley. In fact, the German sphere was regarded as covering the entire valley of the Yellow River. Russia strengthened her claim to a sphere including all Manchuria by an exchange of notes on April 28, 1899, with Great Britain. The British were thereby pledged not to seek railway concessions north of the Great Wall, and the Russians would refrain from seeking similar grants in the Yangtze Valley. Shortly after this, China granted Russia a preference in the building of all railways to the north and east of Peking.

Railway Politics in China

This frantic campaign to supply China with railroads may be traced directly to the spineless character of the Peking government and its stupidity in relying on European support during the war with Japan. It is quite true that Europeans had been urging the Chinese to build railways for nearly fifty years, for it was clear that Peking could never control the Empire until communications were improved. But all such suggestions had met with stubborn resistance. The first railroad, from Shanghai to Woosung, a distance of twelve miles, was built by a British firm in 1876, only to be purchased and torn up by the Chinese, so great was popular prejudice against it. By 1888 a line had been built from the Kaiping coal fields to Pehtang and Tientsin. This line was extended north to Shanhaikwan, where the Great Wall meets the sea, in 1894, but opposition to any line connecting this point with Peking remained firm. Before 1893, some construction was undertaken in Formosa, and the Tientsin-Shanhaikwan line was being extended into Manchuria when work was interrupted by the war with Japan. It was the British who had been the primary backers of these northern lines. With the securing of the leaseholds, railway concessions assumed gigantic proportions. For convenience, they may be summarized as follows:

1. Russia: the Chinese Eastern from Manchouli to Pogranichnaya and from Harbin to Port Arthur (approximately 1,500 miles).

2. Germany: from Tsingtao to Tsinan (256 miles).

3. Great Britain: the Peking to Mukden line (525 miles); the Shanghai to Nanking line (195 miles).

4. France: lines to Yünnan extending from the Tongking frontier (300 miles).

5. Belgium: the Peking to Hankow line (750 miles), backed by France and Russia.

6. The United States: the Hankow to Canton line (700 miles).

7. Great Britain and Germany: the Tientsin to Pukow line (630 miles).

The Break-Up of China

One who observed the progress of events in China from 1896 to 1899 could but conclude that the economic and perhaps the political break-up of China was at hand. During the nineteenth century the interests of the foreign powers in China had remained largely commercial. The events of four years under review in this chapter indicated that these commercial interests were soon to be rivaled, if not overshadowed, by the industrial interests of foreign investors. The earlier period had at times witnessed an intense commercial rivalry among the powers to capture the China trade, but an equilibrium, if not an equality, among them had been preserved by means of the most-favored-nation clause. The rights and privileges extended by China to one power were, by reason of this provision, enjoyed by all. Unfortunately, the principle of most-favored-nation treatment had not prevented the creation of spheres of influence, and these spheres proclaimed definitely an era of industrial exploitation. No longer was China to be open to all comers. The several powers—Germany, Russia, France, and Great Britain—had established for themselves in their respective spheres a general preference covering capital, technical advice, and materials for railways and mines. Each power claimed for itself what was in essence an economic preserve in which the special privileges enjoyed would be proportional to the political pressure exerted upon the Chinese government. The day seemed close at hand when the spheres would become protectorates and these in turn would be formally annexed.

Selected Bibliography

K. Adachi, *Manchuria: A Survey* (New York: 1925). M. J. Bau, *The Foreign Relations of China* (New York: 1921), ch. 3 on the struggle for concessions, a pro-Chinese view. M. J. Bau, *The Open Door Doctrine in Relation to China* (New York: 1923), convenient for its presentation of documents, but faulty in interpretation. Clive Bigham, *A Year in China 1899-1900* (London: 1911). Lord Charles Beresford, *The Break-Up of China* (New York: 1899), a book which exerted great influence on American opinion. J. W. Bookwalter, *Siberia and Central Asia* (New York: 1899). For discussions of the leased territories and settlements, see successive issues of *The China Year Book*. *The Cambridge History of British Foreign Policy*, 3 vols. (Cambridge: 1922-23), vol. 3, ch. 3, pt. 4, "Foreign Encroachments in China, 1885-1898." *British Documents on the Origins of the War* (London: 1926 ff.), vol. 1, ch. 1, "Russia and the Far East 1897-99." E. T. S. Dugdale, *German Diplomatic Documents 1871-1914,* 4 vols. (London: 1930), vol. 3, ch. 2, the occupation of Kiaochow. A. L. P. Dennis, *Adventures in American Diplomacy 1896-1906* (New York: 1928) contains many documents previously unpublished but is sometimes weak in interpretation. E. J. Dillon, *The Eclipse of Russia* (London: 1918), ch. 15 on Russia in the Far East to 1905 is an excellent survey by a brilliant journalist. P. H. Clements, *The Boxer Rebellion* (New York: 1915). P. H. Clyde, *International Rivalries in Manchuria* (Columbus: 1928), chs. 3-4. Tyler Dennett, *Americans in Eastern Asia* (New York: 1922), ch. 32. Two works by John W. Foster: *American Diplomacy in the Orient* (Boston: 1904), and *Diplomatic Memoirs,* 2 vols. (Boston: 1909).

A. Gerard, *Ma Mission en Chine 1893-97* (Paris: 1918). W. L. Godshall, *The International Aspects of the Shantung Question* (Philadelphia: 1923), ch. 1, foreign encroachments in China. S. G. Hishida, *The International Position of Japan as a Great Power* (New York: 1905), ch. 8, the struggle for concessions. S. K. Hornbeck, *Contemporary Politics in the Far East* (New York: 1916), chs. 12-13. S. Hsu, *China and Her Political Entity* (New York: 1926), ch. 4. T. Hoshino, *Economic History of Manchuria* (Seoul: 1920). Alexander Hosie, *Manchuria, Its People, Resources and Recent History* (New York: 1904). H. B. Hulbert, *The Passing of Korea* (New York: 1906). Philip Joseph, *Foreign Diplomacy in China 1894-1900* (London: 1928) is the best single volume on the period; see in particular ch. 9 on Germany at Kiaochow, ch. 11, the Russians in Manchuria, and ch. 17, the Anglo-Russian railway agreement of 1899. P. H. Kent, *Railway Enterprise in China* (London: 1907) is a scholarly study. Stephen King-Hall, *Western Civilization and the Far East* (London: 1924), ch. 3. S. A. Korff, *Russia's Foreign Relations During the Last Half Century* (New York: 1922). A. T. Mahan, *The Problem of Asia . . .* (Boston: 1900). H. B. Morse, *The International Relations of the Chinese Empire* (London: 1918), vol. 3, ch. 4, railway development, ch. 5, the break-up of China, and ch. 6, the Hundred Days of reform. S. McCordock, *British Far Eastern Policy 1894-1900* (New York: 1931). T. W. Overlach, *Foreign Financial Control in China* (New York: 1919), an excellent study. Leo Pasvolsky, *Russia in the Far East* (New York: 1922). P. S. Reinsch, *World Politics at the End of the Nineteenth Century* (New York: 1904). Baron Rosen, *Forty Years of Diplomacy,* 2 vols. (New York: 1922), a most revealing discussion. Geo. N. Steiger, *China and the Occident* (New Haven: 1927), chs. 4-5. M. M. Shoemaker, *The Great Siberian Railway* (London: 1904). P. J. Treat, *Japan and the United States 1853-1921* (Stanford University: 1928); and by the same author, *The Far East* (New York: 1928), ch. 29. Alexander Ular, *A Russo-Chinese Empire* (Westminster: 1904). H. M. Vinacke, *A History of the Far East in Modern Times* (New York: 1928). Vladimir, *Russia on the Pacific and the Siberian Railway* (London: 1899). K. S. Weigh, *Russo-Chinese Diplomacy* (Shanghai: 1928). W. W. Willoughby, *Foreign Rights and Interests in China,* 2 vols., rev. ed. (Baltimore: 1927), vol. 1, ch. 6. E. T. Williams, *China Yesterday and To-day* (New York: 1929), ch. 22. *The Memoirs of Count Witte,* trans. and ed. by A. Yarmolinsky (Garden City: 1921).

CHAPTER XVIII

The United States in the Philippines

THE Far East was looked upon with indifference by the
American government and the American people in the
three decades which followed the Civil War. In oriental waters
the American flag lost the prestige enjoyed in the days of the
clipper ships. While it is admitted that William H. Seward, as
Secretary of State, had attempted to play a vigorous role in the
politics of the Pacific, the fact remained that Americans as a
people were simply not interested. The exalted morality of the
Seward-Burlingame Treaty of 1868 in regard to China was soon
repudiated, and the measures taken later to exclude Chinese
from the United States did not elevate American prestige in
Asia. To be sure, Washington was represented in Tokyo and
in Peking by a succession of able, if little known, diplomats,
but in general they functioned as observers of European policy
rather than as exponents of American. In fact, American
policy, such as it was, had not changed since the days when
Kearney, Cushing, and their successors had demanded and received from China the pledge of most-favored-nation treatment.
The even tenor of this settled policy was rudely disturbed by
the Spanish-American War. From this war, so it was said, the
United States emerged as a "World Power," rising above preoccupation with domestic concerns and, like all great powers,
feeling or imagining the need of colonies.

First Lessons in Imperialism

Although the United States had given little heed to the
prophets of imperialism, she was not entirely without experi-

ence in this politico-economic technique. She had secured a
harbor in the Samoan Islands to be used as a naval base in
1878, and, when a decade later her position seemed threatened
by Germany, she employed imperialistic formulas with considerable skill. The Samoan incident was not without
significance.

[It was] the assertion by the United States not merely of a willingness but even of a right to take part in determining the fate of
a remote and semi-barbarous people whose possessions lay far outside the traditional sphere of American political interests.[1]

Embracing the Unknown Philippines

This type of political philosophy, relatively new to Americans, was intensified by the Cuban question. The popular
sympathies of the American people were extended freely to
the oppressed in Cuba, and, although "before the outbreak of
the Spanish-American War not one American in a thousand,
perhaps, had so much as heard of the Philippine Islands,"
these same popular sympathies might with little difficulty be
extended to embrace the oppressed inhabitants of those islands.
Before the Maine was destroyed in Havana harbor, there were
indeed indications that when the appropriate occasion arose,
the United States would not be averse to assuming its share of
the "white man's burden." And yet it is equally clear that
"prior to May 1, 1898, no idea was, perhaps, more remote from
the mind of the American people than the conquest of the
Philippine Islands."[2]

Roosevelt and the Philippines

The origins of a vital and official American interest in the
Philippines may be traced to September, 1897, when Theodore

[1] John Bassett Moore, *The Cambridge Modern History*. The University Press,
Cambridge, 1934. Vol. VII, p. 663.
[2] H. R. Lynn, *The Genesis of America's Philippine Policy*. University of
Kentucky, 1935. A doctoral dissertation in manuscript. p. 8.

Roosevelt, then Assistant Secretary of the Navy, suggested to the President that, in the event of war with Spain, the Asiatic squadron should blockade and, if possible, take Manila. In February, 1898, it was the Assistant Secretary (backed by the moral support of Henry Cabot Lodge) who shortly after the *Maine* disaster instructed Commodore Dewey to hold his squadron in readiness for offensive operations in the Philippines. In the United States, popular indignation against Spain was making itself felt in Congress, which on March 7, 1898, provided $50,000,000 for defense. The tense situation dragged on until April 19, when in a joint resolution, the Congress declared that the people of Cuba were, and of right ought to be, free and independent and that Spain should withdraw from the island, and directed the President to use all military and naval forces to effect these ends. Spain immediately severed diplomatic relations, and in a resolution of April 25, Congress declared that war existed as of April 21.

The United States Violates China's Neutrality

When war broke out, the American Asiatic squadron was lying at Hong Kong, from which, owing to British neutrality, it was forced to depart. It repaired to Mirs Bay, on the southern China coast, for, as Dewey later wrote, "we appreciated that so loosely organized a national entity as the Chinese Empire could not enforce the neutrality laws."

On April 27, Dewey sailed for Manila. His squadron entered Manila Bay on the morning of May 1, crippling or destroying the Spanish ships. A blockade of the city and bay was established, while the administration in Washington was informed that the city could be taken but that 5,000 men would be required to hold it. It was at this point that the momentous decision was made to prosecute the war in the Philippines, but that decision was the result of a conscious policy toward which Roosevelt, Lodge, and their friends had been working for many

PHILIPPINE ISLANDS

Scale of Miles

0   50   100   150   200

Balintang Channel

BATAN IS.

BABUYAN IS

P A C I F I C

S O U T H

C H I N A

S E A

S. Fernando

Baguio

LUZON

Malolos   POLILLO IS

Manila

Cavite

CATANDUANES

MINDORO

MARIN DUQUE

SIBUYAN I.

TABLAS

MASBATE

CALAMIAN IS.

SAMAR

PANAY

Iloilo

LEYTE

CUYO IS.

DUMARAN I.

Puerto Princesa

NEGROS

CEBU   Cebu

BOHOL

CAGAYANES IS.

P A L A W A N

S U L U   S E A

O C E A N

M I N D A N A O

BALABAC I.

Balabac Strait

Zamboanga

BASILAN

SULU

ARCHIPELAGO

B O R N E O

C E L E B E S   S E A

MANHATTAN ENGRAVING CO., N.Y

*From P. J. Treat, "The Far East." New York, 1928. Reproduced by special permission
of the publishers, Harper and Brothers.*

327

months. In fact, it is now evident that long before the termination of the war, "some influence more tangible than Providence was responsible for placing the Americans in the Philippines."

The Prophet of Imperialism

Scarcely had Dewey steamed out of Mirs Bay, on the China coast, on his eventful voyage when the voice of the prophet of imperialism was raised in America. Albert J. Beveridge, speaking before a Boston audience, painted in glowing colors a picture of America's destiny. Visions of an American merchant marine covering the seven seas; of great colonies flying the American flag and buying American products; of American law, order, and civilization making beautiful and bright places hitherto bloody and benighted— these Beveridge conjured up before his delighted audience. Finally, becoming more specific, Beveridge focussed attention upon the Philippines—an island empire of Spain in the Pacific, poorly defended. "The Philippines," he said, "are logically our first target." [3]

Four days after Beveridge made this speech, the American public read of Dewey's victory in Manila Bay.

The country went wild with excitement. "Dewey Days" were celebrated in the principal cities. Streets were renamed for Dewey. Young women wore "Dewey" sailor hats, sipped "Dewey" cocktails, chewed "Dewey Chewies"—a new brand of gum—and wrote letters on "Dewey blue" stationery. Men smoked cigars made of Sampson [Havana] filler and Dewey [Manila] wrappers, while those who were so inclined resorted to the corner saloon and called for Dewey brand whiskey. Meanwhile the President notified Congress that "At this unsurpassed achievement the great heart of our nation throbs, not with boasting or with greed of conquest, but with deep gratitude that this triumph has come in a just cause. . . ." [4]

Those Americans who liked to regard themselves as "patriots" were quick to assume that the Philippines were legitimate prey. Others, more thoughtful, such as Carl Schurz and

---

[3] *Ibid.* p. 17.
[4] *Ibid.* pp. 17-18.

David Starr Jordon, were inclined to pause. They observed that the question was not what the United States would do with Cuba or the Philippines, but rather what these islands would do to the United States.

Nationalism in the Philippines

Thus while Americans discussed and debated their new-found glory, events moved rapidly in the Philippines. Long before the outbreak of the Spanish-American War, the Filipinos had been restive under the rule of Spain. The liberal political leaders who made their appearance in the late nineteenth century directed their attack against the tremendous influence wielded by the Catholic clergy and also against the ruinous commercial restriction inseparable from the Spanish colonial policy. Many of the early revolts were aimed at Spanish officialdom, whose harsh and uncompromising rule was notorious. These outbreaks were local. Filipinos found it difficult to unite. The friars taught them to be submissive to authority, and many were overawed by the military strength of Spain. From time to time the ranks of the liberals were increased by well-to-do and educated Filipinos and by native priests who criticized not only the Spanish administration but also the political influence of the Church. Tenants on large estates held by the friars became increasingly critical of their lot, and when, after 1872, a number of native priests were executed and some Filipinos exiled, many were convinced that both government and Church were prepared to stifle all criticism. As a natural result of this official and pious stupidity, revolutionary leaders and revolutionary societies became more active, and government oppression more severe. José Rizal, one of the most distinguished liberals, a man of broad culture in science and letters, was banished to the southern island of Mindanao, since, as an advocate of education for the people, he was looked upon as a "dangerous" character.

The most serious outbreak of the period preceding the Spanish-American War may be ascribed to a secret revolutionary society called the Katipunan. Among its objectives were the overthrow of Spain's political control, the destruction of the influence of the friars, and the curbing of the power of other great landlords. A rebellion was precipitated in 1896 when a number of the leaders were arrested in Manila. The measures of repression were severe. Many revolutionary leaders were executed, including Rizal, who was accused of fomenting the rising. With the arrival of reinforcements from Spain, the rebellion was finally crushed, the leaders agreeing for a consideration to leave the islands. The Filipinos asserted that this agreement included a promise of reforms. At all events, Aguinaldo and thirty-four of his confederates departed for Hong Kong, where they remained in exile during the months when Dewey was awaiting orders to attack the Spanish fleet in Manila Bay. When, therefore, the Congress of the United States declared war on Spain, asserting that the people of Cuba were, and of right ought to be, free and independent, Filipino rebels were disposed to believe that they, too, would be assisted in the revolt against Spain. This conviction was strengthened when Dewey, after his victory over the Spaniards, made possible the return of Aguinaldo on an American dispatch-boat and supplied him with weapons from the Spanish arsenal at Cavite. The Filipinos were ready for independence, and Aguinaldo was soon at the head of a sizeable force composed of the earlier revolutionists and of trained native forces who had deserted from the Spanish ranks. With this backing, he proclaimed the revolutionary government of the islands on June 23, 1898. Manila was held in a state of siege. By August, sufficient American troops had arrived to render further resistance by the Spaniards futile. It was agreed that the city should surrender after a show of force, but this sham battle developed some realities and five Americans were killed. The surrender was effected on August 13, a few hours after a peace protocol had been signed in Washington between the United States and Spain. To the Filipino revolutionists, the fall of Manila meant that their independence was, as it were, "just around the corner."

Washington Formulates a Policy

In Washington, Dewey's success and the subsequent victory of American and Filipino troops at Manila raised the inescapable problem of expansion. What was the government to do? Was it to be content with the conquest of Manila, or should it proceed to complete subjugation of the islands? What disposition was to be made of them at the close of the war? Speaking before Congress in December, 1897, and again in April, 1898, President McKinley had expressed the view that "forcible annexation" would, by the American code of morality, be nothing short of "criminal aggression." But Dewey's victory was not without its effect on the President's mind, for by June he was expressing the conviction that while war lasted, the United States should take all it could get; after the war, it should keep what it wanted. Dewey's success was no less effective on the popular American mind. To it may be ascribed the fact that forcible expansion could no longer be regarded as "criminal aggression."

The problem which confronted the McKinley administration was complex in the extreme. Filipino revolutionary leaders had received direct assistance from the armed forces of the United States. To these forces and to the administration it was well known that the Filipinos were fighting for independence. Even granting the debatable point that no specific pledges of independence were ever given to Aguinaldo, "strong evidence was at hand to indicate that the latter had been led, or at least had been permitted, to believe that the American authorities were in sympathy with the national aspirations of his people. And, toward the end of July, it had become clear that the insurgents were growing resentful of the manifest disposition of the American authorities to disregard their claims of independence and to reap single-handed the fruits of a joint endeavor—the capture of the city of Manila." [5]

It was in these circumstances that the peace protocol of August 12 was signed, providing among other things that the United States should occupy the city, bay, and harbor of Manila pending the conclusion of a treaty of peace that in turn would determine the final disposition of the islands. The President, it would seem, had already determined that the United States should take the Philippines; but he was not as yet sure that American public opinion would support him.

Public sentiment, so far as it could be judged at the time, was divided. Most of the manufacturing and commercial interests, believing that the islands would provide a gateway to the trade of China, favored their annexation. Agricultural and labor bodies were, as a rule, opposed to annexation. Tobacco, sugar, and allied interests were led to believe that these products from the Philippines would flood the American market duty-free, and therefore at prices ruinously low. Organized labor protested that annexation would place the American workingman at the mercy of the "pauper" labor of the Philippines. Such arguments were good enough, but the average American listened with secret pride to the sonorous pronouncements of Beveridge.

It is God's great purpose [said he] made manifest in the instincts of our race, whose present phase is our personal profit, but whose far-off end is the redemption of the world and the Christianization of mankind.

Here was a philosophy to still the most sensitive conscience. No exponent of European imperialism had ever voiced the creed on a higher plane than this: "Profits" and "religion"— the redemption of mankind.

---

[5] *Ibid.* pp. 56-57.

Peace Negotiations at Paris

While the administration watched the fluctuating trends of public opinion, its representatives met in Paris with those of Spain to conclude a definitive peace. William R. Day, former Secretary of State, Senators C. K. Davis, W. P. Frye, and George Gray, and Whitelaw Reid, formerly Minister to France, were the American commissioners. Their instructions respecting the Philippines required them to secure at least the Island of Luzon, together with commercial privileges in the entire group. Disagreement arose as to what terms to demand. Gray opposed all annexations; Day reluctantly favored the annexation of Luzon and perhaps some additional islands; Davis, Frye, and Reid wanted the entire archipelago. Accordingly, they cabled for instructions, and the President replied that they must demand the entire group. The protests of Spain being unavailing, on December 10, 1898, the treaty was signed. It provided that in receiving the islands, the United States should pay to Spain $20,000,000, not as a purchase but to take care of a bond issue charged against the Philippines. The cession, in fact, was a part of America's indemnity for the war. After a bitter fight, the United States Senate, by a margin of two votes, gave its advice that the treaty should be ratified. Before this ratification was given, the President had already violated the terms of the protocol by ordering the extension of American authority throughout the islands. "Forcible annexation" had ceased to be "criminal aggression." It had become "benevolent assimilation."

These developments came as a shocking revelation to President Aguinaldo and the revolutionary government of the Philippines. They had looked upon the Americans as allies who would assist in delivering them from the hands of Spain, just as in Cuba they had fought for the freedom of an oppressed people. Annexation, therefore, was a rude awakening. The first Filipino Congress had met in September, 1898. It consisted of able men who, despite political inexperience, conducted themselves remarkably well. This Congress adopted a constitution, largely the work of Felipe Calderon, which was proclaimed in January, 1899. Political parties or groups soon made their appearance to wrestle with the new problem created by American annexation. The so-called radicals favored independence at any cost. The conservatives wanted independence if it could be had without war. Supporting Aguinaldo in the radical ranks was Apolinario Mabini, one of the most capable advocates of independence.

President McKinley's instruction to extend American control throughout the islands and the subsequent ratification of the treaty with Spain now precipitated the American-Philippine War. The American forces slowly extended their lines from the city of Manila. Expeditions were dispatched south to occupy the principal islands, in some of which, such as Samar, fighting continued until 1902. In Luzon, after driving the Filipinos from the outskirts of Manila, the Americans advanced to the north. Aguinaldo, defeated at Malolos, retreated further to the north into the mountains, finally taking up his quarters at the little town of Palanan, on the Pacific slope. Guerrilla warfare now ensued. Many captured Filipino leaders were imprisoned, while others were sent into exile to the military prison at Guam. In March, 1901, Aguinaldo was captured, and the next month he took the oath of allegiance to the United States. Fighting still continued in some sections, but the war was virtually at an end. American military rule prevailed, however, until the appointment of William H. Taft as the first civil governor in July, 1901.

Censorship of the Press

While the war was being prosecuted against the Filipinos, the American public had received only the most optimistic reports. A rigid censorship had been established, against which correspondents of the American press protested vigorously in July, 1899. Their pens fell heavily upon the policies of the American military regime. They claimed the American government had not permitted the public to know the real facts in the Filipino fight for freedom. The American volunteers, contrary to official reports, were not willing to prolong their service. In fact, it was charged, and probably with reason, that the entire censorship was designed to protect the Republican administration in Washington from possible political injury. But to these protests and charges the administration paid no heed. A government so recently converted to the imperial point of view could have little sympathy with "petty" interference.

Political Platforms in 1900

With an army of 70,000 men holding the Philippines, the American people plunged into the political campaigns of 1900. The Democratic platform was concise and clear. It condemned the seizure or purchase of distant islands that could be governed only outside the Constitution and whose peoples could never become citizens. The United States, it asserted, could not remain half republic and half empire. It referred to the "inglorious" role of the administration in crushing with military force the efforts of the Filipinos to achieve liberty and self-government.

The Filipinos cannot be citizens without endangering our civilization; they cannot be subjects without imperiling our form of government, and as we are not willing to surrender our civilization nor to convert the Republic into an empire, we favor an immediate declaration of the Nation's purpose to give to the Filipinos: first, a stable form of government; second, independence; and, third, protection from outside interference such as has been given for nearly a century to the republics of Central and South America.

The Republican platform attempted in a few pious phrases to justify the course of the administration. After referring to the necessity of destroying Spanish sovereignty in the islands and to the reponsibility of providing law and order, it observed:

> Our authority could not be less than our responsibility, and wherever sovereign rights were extended it became the high duty of the Government to maintain its authority, to put down insurrection, and to confer the blessings of liberty and civilization upon all the rescued people.
>
> The largest measure of self-government consistent with their welfare and our duties shall be secured to them by law.

How strange this guarantee of "the blessings of liberty" must have sounded in the ears of Filipino patriots who had witnessed the collapse of their own revolutionary government before an army of 70,000 Americans!

The United States and Hawaii

The Philippines, however, were not the sole prize in the victory of American imperialism. A little more than 2,000 miles southwest of San Francisco lay the Hawaiian Islands, known to Americans since 1789. They were a matter of interest to American missionaries as early as 1820, and had become an important point of call in the early Pacific trade. An agent of the United States was appointed at Honolulu in 1821, and a consul in 1824. The first American treaty, which was not ratified, was negotiated in 1826. Daniel Webster, as Secretary of State in 1842, declared that the government of the islands ought to be respected and that no foreign power should take control of them or receive any exclusive privileges in matters of commerce. President Tyler observed that, while virtually all of the trade of the group was in American hands, the United States sought no peculiar advantages or exclusive control. Unauthorized by his government, a British naval officer attempted to seize the islands in 1843, and between 1849 and 1851 the French became somewhat meddlesome and thereby occasioned a reassertion by Webster of American policy. That policy still demanded respect for the independence of Hawaii.

[The United States] can never consent to see those islands taken possession of by either of the great commercial powers of Europe, nor can it consent that demands manifestly unjust and derogatory, and inconsistent with a bona fide independence, shall be enforced against that Government.

Yet at the moment when this policy was affirmed, the conviction was growing that the islands would inevitably be controlled by one of the major powers.

It fell to Secretary of State Marcy in 1854 to propose that arrangements be made for the annexation of Hawaii by the United States. Over protests of the English and the French, a treaty was negotiated, but, because of a provision which contemplated admission of the islands as a state, it was never submitted to the Senate. Matters remained in abeyance during the Civil War. Then interest revived. An American-Hawaiian reciprocity treaty was signed in 1875 after the United States had investigated the strategic value of Pearl Harbor. This treaty was remarkable in two respects. It contained a so-called "non-alienation" clause of the type that, as the reader is aware, European powers forced upon China in 1898, and it conferred upon the United States special privileges which were not to be extended to other powers under most-favored-nation treatment. These striking developments were almost coincident with America's first imperialistic venture in Samoa. By 1881, Secretary Blaine was referring to the "political necessity" of a closer identification of the islands with the United States, and when in 1887 a second reciprocity treaty was concluded, Pearl Harbor was leased as a naval base.

The Annexation of Hawaii

From this time onward, the growing influence of the United States became increasingly apparent. The death of the native

King and the miserable rule of the sister who succeeded him were the occasion for a revolution in 1893 engineered largely by Americans. The successful rebels invited annexation, and President Harrison approved. The approaching change in administrations at Washington threw the question into party politics. President Cleveland withdrew the treaty from the Senate. Later, a second annexation treaty was submitted by President McKinley to the Senate, where, when the Spanish-American War occurred, it had still failed to receive the necessary vote. In Hawaii, the revolutionary republican government, controlled in the main by Americans, opened wide its ports to American ships, and was thus in fact an ally of the United States. Annexation had become inevitable, and since the two-thirds vote of the Senate could not be obtained, annexation was declared by joint Congressional resolution on July 6, 1898.

In addition, at the close of the war, the United States acquired from Spain the Island of Guam, the largest of the Mariana group, which with its excellent harbor became a naval base and an important cable station. Between this island and Honolulu lay two small and uninhabited groups, the Wake and the Midway Islands. The latter had been taken by the United States in 1867, when Seward was asserting a vigorous far eastern policy; the former were occupied by the United States Navy Department in 1899.

By the turn of the century, the United States was possessed of an entirely new geographical relationship with eastern Asia. Hawaii, Midway, Wake, Guam, and finally the Philippines were tangible evidence of an expansion that had not been arrested on the Pacific shores of North America. China and Japan had become the next-door neighbors of the United States. The ultimate consequences of this new relationship, either in their effects upon Asia or upon the United States, were not foreseen clearly in 1898. Yet there was ample evidence on which to conclude that powerful American interests and forces could no longer be excluded from the Far East. In the Philippines, Americans pictured themselves as disinterested crusaders bearing the standards of liberty and civilization to an untutored people. And beyond, so they thought, was China, eager to grasp American ideals and perhaps to buy American products. It was an enticing picture of American power and of an American empire stretching far across the Pacific. Amid the popular acclaim greeting the new imperialism, an imperialism conceived on such a high moral plane, voices of protest could be heard but faintly. It was embarrassing to be told that the United States had broken with the traditions of its past; that self-government, democracy, and equal rights had all been overruled by the mere course of events. It was difficult for Americans to believe that they had forsaken their "established ways to follow the familiar path by which the empires of the past had risen to greatness, and then collapsed as ambition overreached itself, the path along which the modern empires of Europe were struggling in jealous rivalry." [6]

Selected Bibliography

J. B. Bishop, *Theodore Roosevelt and His Time,* 2 vols. (New York: 1920), vol. 1, chs. 9-10, on the war with Spain. J. H. Blount, *The American Occupation of the Philippines* (New York: 1912). C. G. Bowers, *Beveridge and the Progressive Era* (New York: 1932). E. J. Benton, *International Law and Diplomacy of the Spanish American War* (Baltimore: 1908). R. Cortissoz, *The Life of Whitelaw Reid* (New York: 1921). *Autobiography of George Dewey* (New York: 1913). A. L. P. Dennis, *Adventures in American Diplomacy 1896-1906* (New York: 1928), chs. 3-4, on the war in the Philippines and expansion in Hawaii and Samoa. F. R. Dulles, *America in the Pacific* (Boston: 1932), a spirited but not definitive account of American expansion. E. T. S. Dugdale, *German Diplomatic Documents, 1871-1914,* 4 vols. (London: 1929), vol. 2, chs. 31-32. C. B. Elliott, *The Philippines,* 2 vols. (Indianapolis: 1916-17).

---

[6] Foster Rhea Dulles, *America in the Pacific.* Houghton Mifflin Company, Boston, 1932. p. 264.

John W. Foster, *American Diplomacy in the Orient* (Boston: 1903), ch. 13. C. E. Hill, *Leading American Treaties* (New York: 1922), ch. 14. W. F. Johnson, *America's Foreign Relations* (New York: 1916). M. Kalaw, *Self-government in the Philippines* (New York: 1919). M. Kalaw, *The Philippine Revolution* (Manila: 1925). J. H. Latane, *America as a World Power 1897-1907* (New York: c. 1907). F. C. Laubach, *The People of the Philippine Islands* (New York: 1925). B. Laufer, *The Relations of the Chinese to the Philippine Islands* (Washington: 1907). J. A. LeRoy, *The Americans in the Philippines,* 2 vols. (Boston: 1914). Walter Millis, *The Martial Spirit* (Boston: 1931). J. B. Moore, *A Digest of International Law,* 8 vols. (Washington: 1906). H. C. Moncada, *America, the Philippines, and the Orient* (New York: 1932). C. S. Olcott, *The Life of William McKinley* (Boston: 1916). J. S. Reyes, *Legislative History of America's Economic Policy Toward the Philippines* (New York: 1923). Whitelaw Reid, *Problems of Expansion* (New York: 1900). D. R. Williams, *The United States and the Philippines* (Garden City: 1924). D. C. Worcester, *The Philippines Past and Present* (New York: 1914).

There is likewise a tremendous volume of periodical literature on the Philippines and their acquisition by the United States. T. M. Anderson, "Our Rule in the Philippines" in *North American Review,* Feb. 1900. "Aguinaldo's Case Against the United States" in *ibid.,* Sept. 1899. Edward Atkinson, "Eastern Commerce: What is it Worth?" in *ibid.,* Feb. 1900. John Barrett, "The Cuba of the Far East" in *ibid.,* Feb. 1897. John Barrett, "The Paramount Power in the Pacific" in *ibid.,* Aug. 1899. Andrew Carnegie, "The Opportunity of the United States" in *ibid.,* May, 1902. W. W. Cook, "How May the United States Govern the Philippine Islands?" in *Politicial Science Quarterly,* Mar. 1901. C. A. Conant, "The Currency of the Philippine Islands" in *Annals of the American Academy,* Nov. 1902. Charles Denby, "Do We Owe Independence to the Filipinos?" in the *Forum,* June, 1900. J. W. Hillman, "The Inauguration of Civil Government in the Philippines" in *Independent,* Aug. 29, 1901. G. F. Hoar, "Dangers of Colonial Expansion" in *Independent,* July 7, 1898. Harold Martin, "The Manila Censorship" in the *Forum,* June, 1901. L. S. Rowe, "The Establishment of Civil Government in the Philippines" in *Annals of the American Academy,* Sept. 1902. L. B. Shipee, "Germany and the Spanish-American War" in *American Historical Review,* July, 1925. W. H.

Taft, "The People of the Philippine Islands" in *Independent*, May 1 and 8, 1902.

On the constitutional status of the Philippines, see: Carl Becker, "Law and Practice of the United States in the Acquisition and Government of Dependent Territory" in *Annals of the American Academy*, Nov. 1900. Perry Belmont, "Congress, the President and the Philippines" in *North American Review*, Dec. 1899. G. S. Boutwell, "The Supreme Court and the Dependencies" in *North American Review*, Aug. 1901. J. W. Burgess, "How May the United States Govern its Extra-continental Territory?" in *Political Science Quarterly*, Mar. 1899. J. W. Burgess, "The Decisions of the Supreme Court in the Insular Cases" in *ibid.*, Sept. 1901. J. W. Burgess, "The Relations of the Constitution of the United States to Newly Acquired Territory" in *ibid.*, Sept. 1900. Charles Denby, "The Constitution and the Flag" in the *Forum*, May, 1900. G. F. Edmunds, "The Insular Cases" in *North American Review*, Aug. 1901. L. S. Rowe, "The Supreme Court and the Insular Cases" in *Annals of the American Academy*, Sept. 1901.

For the Hawaiian Islands, in addition to many of the references above, see: W. F. Blackman, *The Making of Hawaii* (New York: 1899). G. V. Blue, "The Project For a French Settlement in the Hawaiian Islands, 1824-1842" in *The Pacific Historical Review*, Mar. 1933. D. E. Clark, "Manifest Destiny and the Pacific" in *ibid.*, Mar. 1932. O. W. Freeman, "The Peopling of Hawaii" in the *Journal of Geography*, Apr. 1929. John W. Foster, *American Diplomacy in the Orient* (Boston: 1903), ch. 11, the annexation of Hawaii, and by the same author, *Diplomatic Memoirs*, 2 vols. (London: 1910), vol. 2, ch. 34 on the same subject. T. Harada, "Early Communications Between Hawaii and Japan" in *Mid-Pacific*, Jan. 1931. T'ing-yu Hsieh, "The Chinese in Hawaii" in *The Chinese Social and Political Science Review*, Jan. 1930. Yamato Ichihashi, *Japanese in the United States* (Stanford University: 1932). R. S. Kuykendall, *A History of Hawaii* (New York: 1926), and by the same author, "Early Hawaiian Commercial Development" in *The Pacific Historical Review*, Dec. 1934. Donald Rowland, "The United States and the Contract Labor Question in Hawaii, 1862-1900" in *Pacific Historical Review*, Sept. 1933, and "The Establishment of the Republic of Hawaii" in *ibid.*, Sept. 1935.

CHAPTER XIX

The So-Called "Open Door Policy"

THE conclusion of the Spanish-American War coincided with the revival of an American interest in China. It was affirmed in many quarters that possession of the Philippines would result in a generous expansion of Chino-American commerce and an increase in America's political influence in eastern Asia. During the latter half of 1898, while peace was under negotiation with Spain, these conclusions were given frequent expression in the American press. They were confined, however, to general expressions of opinion, for both the American government and the American people were too immersed in the glories of victory to give attention to specific details of far eastern policy. In fact, most Americans, including John Sherman, the Secretary of State, were, in March, 1898, blissfully ignorant of what was happening in China at that moment. To a nation involved in the Spanish War, the acquisition by European powers of leaseholds and spheres of influence was a circumstance that perhaps might best be described as of academic interest only.

Britain Seeks American Aid

One European power, to be sure, had not viewed the threatened partition of China in this light. Great Britain had long enjoyed the lion's share of China's foreign commerce. Because of her predominant position both commercially and industrially, she had long favored a China market open to all comers on equal terms. She thus viewed with some apprehen-

342

sion the creation of leaseholds and spheres by Germany and
Russia early in 1898. Although she participated in the
concession-hunting, she nevertheless favored in China a policy
of *commercial* equality, and to insure this she sought the aid
of the United States. In March, 1898, she confidentially invited
the United States to co-operate in opposing any action by foreign powers calculated to violate this commercial equality,
which the British termed vaguely but suggestively, "the open
door." This was two days after Germany had concluded her
agreement with China for a lease of Kiaochow and preferential
treatment for German capital in Shantung.

The response of Secretary Sherman to the British overture
observed:

The President is in sympathy with the policy which shall maintain open trade in China, that all his advices up to the present time
indicate no foreign occupation which interferes with that trade or
aims at exclusive privileges, and that he does not see any present
reason for the departure of the United States from our traditional
policy of respecting [sic] foreign alliances and so far as practicable
avoiding interference or connection with European complications.

It is clear from the above that both the President and his
Secretary of State failed to foresee or appreciate the dangers to
free and unrestricted trade that were at least implied by the
leaseholds and spheres then being established by Germany
and Russia. Yet they were not without information as to the
course of events in China. In March, 1898, American Minister
Denby wrote from Peking:

If Germany, France and Russia proposed simply to open new
ports to the trade of the world nobody would object; but they
have not done so. They claim, or will claim, jurisdiction exactly
as if they owned the ceded [leased] territory. They will monopolize the exploitation of the adjacent country. They will construct all
the railroads, and work all the mines. There can be but little
question but that the treaties so far as the [most] favored nation
clause is concerned will fall to the ground.

This warning might well have spurred Washington to some form of joint action with the British, for the most-favored-nation clause had been the basis of America's China policy since 1844. Unhappily, nothing was done, and the British, discovering that it was hopeless to expect aid from America, proceeded, with misgiving, to demand leaseholds and a sphere for themselves.

The ultimate objectives of the European policy of leaseholds and spheres were economic and political. The policy was designed not only to insure investments already made, but also to guarantee by political pressure on China that the way for future investment would remain open. Even as early as 1900, the major European states and their nationals were, financially speaking, heavily entrenched. Some conception of their interests may be gathered from the following:

FOREIGN INVESTMENTS IN CHINA

Great Britain	(1902)	$260,300,000
Russia	(1903)	$246,043,000
Germany	(1902-1904)	$164,282,000
France	(1902)	$ 91,120,000

As against these impressive totals, American holdings in China in 1900 were only $24,700,000, while the total Japanese investments there were not more than $1,000,000. From the standpoint of policy, however, the most striking feature of the American position at the turn of the century was not the small financial stake involved, but rather the fact that general interest was still largely confined to trade, with investments playing but a minor role. In this circumstance may be found at least a partial explanation of the American failure to support the British proposals for an open door. Traders are sometimes less effective than bankers in shaping the course of government.[1]

---

[1] For a detailed analysis of foreign investments and trade with China in these years see C. F. Remer, *Foreign Investments in China.* The Macmillan Company, New York, 1933.

The Policy of John Hay

The change that was due to overtake America's passive policy may be ascribed in large measure to John Hay, who assumed his duties as Secretary of State in September, 1898. To accept this post he had resigned the position of Ambassador to Great Britain, where he had become thoroughly familiar with British views on China. He was thoroughly acquainted, therefore, with that system of free and unrestricted commerce which the British called the open door in China. Although the crisis created by the leaseholds and spheres had reached an acute stage by the summer of 1898, and although Hay assumed direction of the State Department in September, it was not until eleven months later (August 24, 1899) that he called upon W. W. Rockhill, who had been in the diplomatic service both at Peking and Seoul and was excellently informed on the Far East, for specific suggestions on a China policy. Rockhill's response took the form of a memorandum which, for keen and accurate analysis, has rarely been surpassed in American diplomatic documents. Since its proposals became the basis of Hay's so-called "open door policy," a somewhat detailed discussion of its contents is essential.

Rockhill commented first on the unique influence being exerted upon American public opinion by Lord Charles Beresford's book, *The Break-Up of China,* and numerous speeches made by the author during a tour of the United States. Beresford had endeavored to show an identity of interest between England and America in China. Continuing his analysis, Rockhill regretted the lack of a co-operative policy on the part of the diplomatic corps in Peking. He was of the opinion that the cause of stagnation in trade was due to the vacillating policies of the home governments, induced by apathy (a reference perhaps to Secretary Sherman) and lack of knowledge on Chinese affairs. As a result, the Chinese government had been able to evade performance of treaty obligations.

British writers on Chinese questions [he said], and especially Lord Beresford, have advocated in the strongest terms the "open-door policy," or equality of treatment and opportunity for all comers, and denounce in the strongest terms the system of "Spheres of Influence" (or interest) but such spheres have now been recognized by Great Britain as well as by France, Germany and Russia, and *they must be accepted as existing facts.*

The memorandum continued by setting forth that Great Britain had sought to harmonize the open door with the existence of spheres, but had failed to do so since she had recognized special and exclusive investment rights of other powers, particularly those relating to railroads and mines. To Rockhill, it was not clear how extensive these rights might eventually become, and he thus recommended to Hay a policy that would limit them by asking the powers that possessed spheres for assurances respecting future action in their spheres: (1) that they would not interfere with the administration of the treaty ports; (2) that the Chinese treaty tariff should be applied impartially on all merchandise; and (3) that within their spheres the powers would not charge discriminatory railroad rates or harbor dues. Rockhill realized that a policy of a completely open door no longer existed. The spheres had already precluded an open door for investment. In the face of this, the question remained whether or not an open door for trade could be maintained. His three proposals to Hay were designed to accomplish this end, for, as he pointed out, the principle of most-favored-nation treatment had broken down.

We should insist [he said] on absolute equality of treatment in the various zones [spheres], for equality of opportunity with the citizens of the favored powers we cannot hope to have, in view of the well-known method now in vogue for securing privileges and concessions, though we should continually, by every proper means, seek to gain this also.

By means of the three proposals mentioned, then, Rockhill hoped to preserve American commerce with and in China from discriminatory treatment. The proposals were commercial, not political—a consideration of some consequence, in view of the fact that later, and without justification, Americans developed the habit of attaching the principles of Chinese territorial integrity and administrative entity as appendices to Hay's original open door policy.

The Hay Notes of 1899

Acting promptly on the suggestions made by Rockhill, Secretary Hay dispatched his so-called "open door notes" to the principal powers interested in China—to Great Britain, Germany, and Russia on September 6, 1899, to Japan on November 13, to Italy in abridged form on November 17, and to France on November 21. He also communicated on November 11 with Wu Ting Fang, Chinese Minister in Washington, assuring him that the American policy as outlined to the powers in the circular notes was designed to safeguard the interests of China and the legitimate commerce of all nations. This somewhat gratuitous information was followed by a more significant statement:

If we [the United States] should ever in the future, which I do not now anticipate, desire to treat with your Government for any conveniences or accommodations upon the [China] coast, we shall have pleasure in addressing ourselves directly to the Imperial Government of China.

On reading this note the Chinese government may possibly have congratulated itself on the fact that all the strategic harbors on the coast had already been leased.

The preambles of the various notes dispatched by Hay to the powers differed somewhat in wording, but the sense of all was the same. It was stated in each note that the American government was animated by a sincere desire to insure to the United States and all other nations perfect equality of treatment within the limits of the Chinese Empire for trade and navigation, especially within the so-called "spheres of influence or interest" claimed by certain European powers. To this end each of the governments addressed was asked to make the following declarations:

First. [That it] will in no way interfere with any treaty port or any vested interest within any so-called "sphere of interest," or leased territory it may have in China.

Second. That the Chinese treaty tariff of the time being shall apply to all merchandise landed or shipped to all such ports as are within said "sphere of influence" (unless they be "free ports"), no matter to what nationality it may belong, and that duties so leviable shall be collected by the Chinese Government.

Third. That it will levy no higher harbor dues on vessels of another nationality frequenting any port in such "sphere" than shall be levied on vessels of its own nationality, and no higher railroad charges over lines built, controlled, or operated within its "sphere" on merchandise belonging to citizens or subjects of other nationalities transported through such "sphere" than shall be levied on similar merchandise belonging to its own nationals transported over equal distances.

The replies of the powers, while on the whole favorable, were not unconditional acceptances of these American proposals. Great Britain replied informally on September 29 and formally on November 30, accepting the note but excluding Kowloon, opposite Hong Kong. The reply of the German government, delivered by von Bülow on December 4, 1899, although extremely involved, amounted to an acceptance. France concurred December 16, and Japan on December 26. The Russian reply was the least satisfactory, since it made no reference to discriminatory rates. Each reply was conditional upon similar assurances being given by the other powers addressed. Despite all these qualifications, Hay informed the powers on March 20, 1900, that his government regarded their assent to the principles outlined as "final and definitive." Since, however, the replies had varied considerably, the question of what was "final and definitive" was a matter which each might interpret for itself.

Earlier American Policy

In an analysis of the Hay policy thus formulated, one must recall that many commentators on American far eastern policy have asserted that the open door may be traced to the instructions given by Daniel Webster to Caleb Cushing on the eve of the latter's departure in 1843 to negotiate the first American treaty with China, or even to the commercial treaty with the French monarchy in 1778. On both these occasions the American government sought and secured most-favored-nation treatment, but it is at least debatable whether open door may be applied correctly to this principle. The term itself was apparently invented by the British and adopted by the Americans in 1898. In itself, it had no precise meaning, being merely a slogan suggestive of free access—commercial, industrial, and financial—to the markets of China. During the nineteenth century the most-favored-nation principle had accomplished this purpose, for at that time, foreign interests in China were almost exclusively commercial. But by 1899, the creation of leaseholds and spheres had revolutionized the relations of the major powers with China, and to meet this situation, Hay sought a policy that was in some respects new. The spheres were regions where the nationals of the holding power were to enjoy preferential, and in some cases exclusive, privileges. This was a development against which the most-favored-nation principle had proved ineffective, and in view of which it had become a hollow mockery. It had been inserted originally in the China treaties to preserve a status of equality among *trading* nations. It never contemplated the creation of regions of special privilege, and when these regions, in the form of spheres, were established, the principle of most-favored-nation treatment in the broad field of investment collapsed. The spheres destroyed completely any all-inclusive principle of equal opportunity, save such equality as existed between what the Germans enjoyed in Shantung and what the British enjoyed in the Yangtze basin, or what the Russians enjoyed in Manchuria. Rockhill fully realized that equality of opportunity in the spheres was not possible, and, since the spheres "must be accepted as existing facts," one course alone was open to the American government—to limit the special privileges that a sphere-holding power should enjoy.

A Misleading Name

This limited objective was all that Hay asked of the powers in 1899. The term "open door" as applied to it was distinctly misleading. The British had used the phrase in a much broader sense than was specified in the three stipulations of the Hay notes. Lord Beresford and others used it to describe a situation in which spheres of influence could not exist. Rockhill himself stated in his memorandum that the British conception of an open door had been destroyed and that America could hope to secure only a limited application of the principle. But many years were to elapse before this fact was given any recognition in the United States. In the popular mind, the Hay policy, the open door, equality of opportunity, and most-favored-nation treatment were all one and the same. This misconception was not unnatural, but it was most unfortunate. As years passed, it led to serious international friction. Much of this subsequent trouble might have been avoided had there been a better understanding of what Hay asked and what the powers accepted in 1899. Instead, discussions of the Hay open door were, with few exceptions, expressed in vague generalizations, which left the impression on the public mind that Hay in 1899 had asked acceptance of a broad and unqualified principle of equal opportunity. Enough has been said to demonstrate that this was not the case. In fact, Hay's open door notes attempted to preserve only such equality of commercial opportunity as had not been destroyed already by the creation of leaseholds and spheres.

SELECTED BIBLIOGRAPHY

K. Asakawa, *The Russo-Japanese Conflict* (New York: 1904). J. F. Abbott, *Japanese Expansion and American Politics* (New York: 1916). R. H. Akagi, *Japan's Foreign Relations* (Tokyo: 1936), ch. 7, the open door policy. M. J. Bau, *The Open Door Doctrine* (New York: 1923). S. F. Bemis, *The American Secretaries of State and Their Diplomacy,* 10 vols. (New York: 1927-29). Charles Beresford, *The Break-Up of China* (London: 1899). P. H. Clyde, *International Rivalries in Manchuria* (Columbus: 1928). Charles Coates, *China and the Open Door* (Bristol: 1899). A. L. P. Dennis, *Adventures in American Diplomacy* (New York: 1928), particularly valuable for documentary materials. Tyler Dennett, *John Hay* (New York: 1933), ch. 24 on the open door notes. R. K. Douglas, *Europe and the Far East* (London: 1913). R. S. Gundry, "China: Spheres of Interest and the Open Door" in *Fortnightly Review,* vol. 72, p. 37, 1899. F. H. Hitchcock, *Our Trade with Japan, China and Hongkong 1889-1899* (Washington: 1900). H. B. Learned, "Aspects of the Foreign Policy of the United States," Pamphlet 63 of The Historical Association, London, Sept. 1925. F. D. Pavey, "The 'Open Door' Policy in the Philippines" in *North American Review,* Nov. 1899. W. R. Thayer, *The Life and Letters of John Hay,* 2 vols. (Boston: 1915), vol. 2, ch. 26. Shutaro Tomimas, *The Open Door Policy and the Territorial Integrity of China* (New York: 1919). P. J. Treat, *Japan and the United States 1853-1921* (Stanford University: 1928), ch. 9. W. W. Willoughby, *Foreign Rights and Interests in China,* rev. ed., 2 vols. (Baltimore: 1927), vol. 1, ch. 4. For the principal correspondence between Hay and the powers, see United States, *Foreign Relations,* 1899.

CHAPTER XX

Fists of Righteous Harmony: The Boxers

POVERTY, reaching far across the border-line of starvation, had long been a familiar bedfellow of the three hundred or perhaps four hundred millions of hapless souls who made up the bulk of China's population at the turn of the twentieth century. To the masses of China, life had offered rarely, if ever, more than a desperate struggle to survive. A food supply produced by antiquated methods of ancient times failed to fill the stomachs of new generations bred ceaselessly to satisfy the spirits of ancestors. Time was when Europe lived day by day, but China existed hour by hour. There was no reserve, nothing to tide over the crowning misery of famine, plague, and pestilence.

If there were any faint remoteness of truth in the tedious idiocy that hardship brings out men's virtues, we should see in China today a nation of saints.[1]

Long suffering had reconciled the average Chinese to his fate. He had developed the conviction that there wasn't much that could be done about it anyway, and in this he was about right. His vast territory and immense population was a society rather than an organized state. His knowledge reached only to the boundaries of his own village. His struggle to live was circumscribed by the rigid conventions of the Confucian code, and change had no part in that system.

All during the nineteenth century, western states, impelled by commerce, missionary propaganda, and later by prospect of

---

[1] Ralph Townsend, *Ways That Are Dark*. G. P. Putnam's Sons, New York, 1933. p. 81.

industrial exploitation, had been pressing a new world upon China. In the earlier years of the century, their efforts made little imprint on the Chinese mind. Only a fringe of coast towns (the treaty ports) had been touched. Most Chinese had never heard of the so-called "Opium" and *"Arrow"* Wars, and even if they had, they would not have understood the issues involved. It was not until the close of the century, when the creation of spheres of influence brought industrial exploitation to the very heart of the country, that China became aroused. A foreign locomotive roaring its way past the graves of honorable ancestors brought reform and revolution to China.

The reader is already aware that the decline of the Manchu Dynasty preceded by many years the dawn of the twentieth century. To be sure, the dynasty had survived the ravages of the Taiping Rebellion, but its weakness had been revealed, a weakness from which it never fully recovered. Affairs of state remained in the hands of palace cliques that looked upon government solely as a means to personal wealth. Provincialism and an amazing ignorance of the outside world were the common badge of officialdom. To western aggression and the humiliating defeat at the hands of Japan in 1895, China had found no answer. Her plight was well voiced by one of her few honest statesmen, Chang Chih-tung:

Of all countries China has alone for these fifty years proved herself almost irreclaimably stupid. . . . Many of the officials and people are proud and indolent. They contentedly rest in the belief that the old order of things will suffice for these dangerous times. . . . Among our officials there is not one man of discernment: we have no real scholars and no skillful artisans. We are not represented abroad and at home have no schools. . . . With nothing to stimulate the mind, harden the nature, or supply the deficiencies, there seems nothing left for China but to perish miserably in the slough of despondency and despair.[2]

---

[2] From *The Four Hundred Million,* by Mary A. Nourse. Copyright 1935. Used by special permission of the publishers, the Bobbs-Merrill Company. p. 252.

The First Reformers

Happily, however, there were some few Chinese willing to fight for a new and a modern China. These reformers were men of striking courage. It required some bravery in 1898 to imagine that new life could rise from the exhausted soil of Chinese thought. Furthermore, every attempt at reform in the late nineteenth century had met with failure. The first railroads had been torn up because of official and popular prejudice, and it was only by the most gradual degrees that new lines, supplemented by telegraphs and a postal service, had been accepted. In the period before the Chino-Japanese War the few existing ventures in rapid communication "owed their existence to the determination of a few individuals and not to any popular demand. The mass of the Chinese people felt no need for, and little confidence in, such changes. Yet telegraphs, posts, and railways all contributed to the wider spread and interchange of ideas and thus wore down the wall of prejudice and procured an entry for innovations more fundamental." [3]

Between 1860 and 1894, some attempts had been made to reorganize China's military and naval establishments. Li Hung-chang was the leader in this movement. In 1885, a Board of Admiralty was formed. Some ships were purchased, and a body of officers received something like adequate training, but neither army nor navy possessed morale. Local and provincial jealousies dominated their entire spirit; funds that should have been devoted to naval purposes were, at the suggestion of one of the court eunuchs, diverted to build the Summer Palace for the Empress Dowager. In a word, as the war with Japan in 1894 and 1895 showed, the pleasures of the court were of more consequence than defense of the nation.

Some of the early reformers drew their inspiration from knowledge of the West acquired through Christian mission-

---

[3] Meribeth E. Cameron, *The Reform Movement in China, 1898-1912.* Stanford University Press, 1931. p. 14.

aries. Although these views were often distorted by Christian prejudice, this did not lessen their influence on the Chinese mind. After 1860, a little encouragement was given by Prince Kung to western learning, much to the annoyance of reactionaries who ascribed a prolonged drought and famine to this cause. But as late as 1894, there was little evidence to indicate that either the Manchu government or the Chinese people desired or sensed the need of reform.

It is true that in the years after the Taiping Rebellion a portion of the Chinese literati began to take an interest in Western institutions, which formerly they had been inclined to view as the curious ways of a barbarian people, unworthy of imitation by the Middle Kingdom. But to all those who thought that the inauguration of a few railway lines, the formation of one modern army corps and a small navy, and a tentative interest on the part of the government in Western learning constituted an adequate reformation of the Empire the Sino-Japanese War was a rude awakening.[4]

The humiliating defeat by westernized Japan aroused intelligent Chinese to the imperative need for reform. Some of the southern radicals, including Sun Yat-sen, at Canton, memorialized the Throne, requesting constitutional government. Another reformer of great influence in this period was Kang Yu-wei, also from Canton. Trained in the Confucian school, he had early acquired an interest in things western, and his reading, if not deep, had at least been wide. His interpretation of Confucius as a progressive and not a reactionary sage commanded wide attention, and he soon emerged as an advocate of constitutional monarchy, the leader of the right-wing progressives. It was he, acting on behalf of a larger group, who in December, 1895, submitted a grand memorial advocating complete westernization of the Empire. This attempt was abortive, but the foreign aggressions of 1896 to 1898 again stimulated the reformers and added to their ranks a group of unwilling but desperate officials, who saw in reform the Em-

[4] *Ibid.* p. 22.

pire's only hope. In Peking, where Kang Yu-wei had accepted an official position, he appealed to the young Emperor Kuang Hsu to follow the example of Japan. This appeal brought striking results. The young sovereign was the nephew of that august and now elderly lady, Tsu Hsi, the Empress Dowager. She had dominated the young man through all his brief reign, and, although he had outwardly shown her every respect, there were indications that he coveted "the reality and not the mere semblance of power." Unfortunately, the Emperor was physically frail and mentally sensitive. In no struggle could he be counted the equal of this strong-willed and politically experienced woman. These two represented conflicting tendencies at court. The sympathies of the Empress Dowager were with Li Hung-chang and the so-called northern party, conservatives in the main, while the young Emperor leaned toward the more liberal teachings of Weng Tung-ho, his tutor, and the southern reformers such as Kang Yu-wei. In the beginning, the line of cleavage between the two groups was by no means clear, for among the northerners and the Manchus were officials who favored a moderate political house cleaning.

By June, 1898, the Emperor had determined to initiate a radical program of reform. The influence of Kang Yu-wei and the southerners had triumphed. The government was ordered to investigate all branches of western learning with a view to adopting reforms. High officials and members of the Imperial clan were advised to seek western learning. This was the beginning of the now famous "Hundred Days" of reform. Imperial decrees followed each other in rapid succession. The old classical studies were to be replaced by modern and more practical subjects. Schools and colleges modeled on western lines were to be established in every province. The Manchu army was to be modernized and naval colleges founded. Useless posts in government would be abolished; roads would be built, modern bureaus of railways and mines set up, and western works on science translated into Chinese. Overnight, by the simple process of official decree, China was to be remade. Kang Yu-wei and his zealous but impractical reformers dominated the young, well-meaning, but weak sovereign. Among their number there was not one man who realized that the China that had resisted change for centuries could not be reformed in this manner. Prince Kung, who had some appreciation of the nation's needs, was dead, and Li Hung-chang, who would at least have supported moderate reform, had been dismissed from the Foreign Office. In this plight, and lacking practical leadership, the reformers now sought to remove by direct action the chief opponents of their plans.

The Reform Program Collapses

They turned to Yuan Shih-kai, with whose vigorous policy in Korea the reader is already familiar and who at this time was judicial commissioner of Chihli province. To him the Emperor entrusted the program of army reform. Taken into the confidence of the reformers, Yuan was informed that the Empress Dowager and her most trusted adviser, Jung Lu, viceroy of Chihli, must be imprisoned, and to this scheme it appears that the Emperor gave his approval. Yuan, however, refused to be a party to the plot. He warned Jung Lu and through him the Empress Dowager. This lady, in turn, summoned the chief officials of the government, who implored her to resume again the direction of government and thereby end what they regarded as the radical reforms of the Emperor. Accordingly, the person of the Emperor was seized. He was forced to issue an Imperial decree declaring that the Empress Dowager would again direct affairs of state. The reform edicts were declared void, old offices were re-created, and many of the reformers were executed, though Kang Yu-wei escaped. Thus ended an impractical effort to revolutionize China in a day. What would have happened had Yuan Shih-kai remained loyal to the Emperor is mere speculation. Yet it is reasonably certain that the program of Kang and his supporters in 1898 could not have succeeded. The change was too abrupt, and neither the Emperor nor his liberal supporters appear to have possessed the talents necessary for its enforcement.

The Revival of Antiforeignism

Coincident with the reactionary policy that now seized Peking came a renewed wave of antiforeignism in the provinces. A general hostility to foreigners and more particularly to their ways and the institutions they represented was by no means new in China. It had been apparent during all the early years of contact, and the reasons underlying it have been touched upon at some length. Although the Chinese and the foreign traders got along tolerably well, the mass of the Chinese people were suspicious of the foreign "barbarian," an attitude in which they were frequently encouraged by officials. This latter class, drawn exclusively from the conservative literati, was pre-eminently antiforeign. It hated the Westerner with his presumptions of equality. The defeat administered by Japan in 1895 increased the general antiforeign sentiment; this was aggravated further by the subsequent leasehold and railway concessions. The ignorant masses saw the railroads as disturbers of ancestral spirits, and their betters did little to enlighten them. The Christian missionary, too, appeared in a more sinister light. His religion was no less foreign than the railroad. His attempts to control and protect his converts appeared intolerable. After 1897, these conditions resulted in numerous assaults upon foreigners and their property and particularly upon missionaries, whose isolated position exposed them to attack. These attacks were general throughout China, the worst conditions prevailing in the north, where in reality there was less excuse for the government's failure to maintain order. It was there, however, that China had suffered defeat, and there, too, that most of the railroads were being built.

Economic distress added its quota of discontent, for drought and famine prevailed in Shantung, Chihli, and Shansi. Mob action by desperate men was not uncommon; and secret societies, the fear of every Chinese dynasty, flourished.

Next to the family as a social unit, secret societies have been, and probably still are, the most influential factor in Chinese society.

Often they have had an active and influential part in politics. It is estimated that today about half the adult males who can lay claim to any influence are members. Almost everywhere they must be reckoned with by those who would understand the life of a community. Just how ancient are those now in existence is a matter of doubt, although some of them claim to have begun hundreds of years ago. . . . Sometimes . . . they have religious features. Often they have solemn and binding vows of brotherhood, and they may have secret codes.[5]

Among the numerous secret societies of this type which made their appearance in north China in the trying years under review were the Fists of Righteous Harmony, or, as they came to be known by the foreigners, the Boxers. During the later months of 1899, these "patriots" pillaged and looted in north China, their particular victims being native Christians. Since the antiforeign wave was already widespread, these attacks upon native Christians enjoyed popular sympathy. They struck vicariously at the foreigner. The reactionary court at Peking, controlled by the Empress Dowager, took secret delight in these Boxer outrages, officials being instructed to resist all foreign aggressions. In a word, the people, the secret societies, and the court were at one in the hope that the "barbarian" might be expelled.

The Boxers in Control

Here was a situation to which the foreign ministers at Peking could no longer remain indifferent. In Shantung, open

---

[5] K. S. Latourette, *The Chinese: Their History and Culture.* The Macmillan Company, New York, 1934. Vol. II, pp. 199-200.

assistance given to the Boxers by the local governor led to diplomatic protests, the governor's dismissal, and his replacement
early in December, 1899, by Yuan Shih-kai. But the movement
was too far advanced to be arrested by any halfhearted measures of Peking. Attacks were no longer confined to native
converts, for on December 31, a British missionary was murdered in Shantung by members of another secret society, the
Great Swords. Again the enfeebled government made amends
by executing two and imprisoning three of the guilty, but these
acts served to inflame rather than to quiet the populace. Edicts
were issued, on the demand of the legations, to protect the foreigners and the native converts, and in February, 1900, the
Boxers and the Great Swords were ordered suppressed. These
edicts, however, were to no avail. There was no real determination behind the government decrees. Instead, the Boxers
and their allies were moving northward toward Peking. The
position of the court became more difficult, for in the opinion
of many officials, the Boxers now represented a great mass
rising against the foreigner. More missionaries were killed,
and railroad engineers were subjected to attack. So little faith
did the legations now have in the Chinese government that at
the end of May, legation guards were requested from the foreign warships at Taku. On June 3, 450 troops arrived, to be
distributed among the legations of Great Britain, the United
States, Russia, France, Japan, and Italy.

Two days after the arrival of these troops the Boxers cut
the railway connecting Peking with Tientsin, eighty miles to
the southeast, and on June 9, Admiral Seymour, commanding
British ships off Taku, received an urgent appeal for help from
the British Minister in Peking. The British and other foreign
ships mustered a landing force of some 2,000 sailors and marines. Half way to Peking they met determined opposition,
not only from the Boxers but from Imperial troops as well, and
were forced to retire to Tientsin. Casualties had been heavy.

In Tientsin itself, the position of the foreigners was by no means secure. To hold the foreign concessions—British, German, French, and Japanese—in the city was essential if aid were to be carried to Peking, and to the naval commanders it appeared that safety of the concessions was in turn dependent on possession of the Taku forts at the mouth of the river. Their surrender was demanded in an ultimatum of June 16. It was refused, and the forts were taken by storm the following day. The American admiral held aloof from this action on the ground that he had no authority to make war on a friendly state. Tientsin concessions were attacked by the Chinese on the same day, and three days later China declared war on the powers. Meanwhile, the Boxers invaded both Tientsin and Peking. In the former, mission property was destroyed, while in the latter, unguarded foreign buildings were burned and native Christians slaughtered. The chancellor of the Japanese Legation was killed by a Chinese soldier, and a like fate befell Baron von Kettler, the German Minister, at the hands of a Manchu bannerman. The siege of the legations had begun. Imperial troops and Boxers were now combined to destroy the foreigner. For this untimely development, the policy of the Empress Dowager and her conservative cohorts was the immediate cause. As early as November, 1899, she had warned high officials to be prepared for war.

Let no one think of making peace [she had urged], but let each strive to preserve from destruction and spoliation his ancestral home and graves from the ruthless hands of the invaders. Let these our words be known to each and all within our domains.

Yet the government in Washington, like those in Europe, had paid little heed to warnings from the ministers in Peking. They had been advised that Peking either sympathized with the Boxers or was afraid of them, but nothing was done to prepare for the coming storm.

The Siege of the Legations

Within Peking, something less than 1,000 foreigners were now under siege. Most of these were in the legation quarter, while a few remained across the city at the Catholic cathedral, where 2,000 Chinese Christians had taken refuge. By June 11, the foreigners, now completely isolated, made desperate efforts to strengthen their meager defenses. Meanwhile, the Boxers were burning and pillaging in the city, and the American Minister wrote on June 15 that "in no intelligent sense can there be said to be in existence any Chinese Government whatever." The ignorance of the American and other governments at this time is revealed in the fact that on this same day, Secretary of State Hay was trying to communicate with the American Minister, asking: "Do you need more force?" From her palace grounds, the Empress Dowager listened nervously to successive attacks by her own troops and the Boxers on the legation area. At first, thinking only of the complete destruction of the foreigners, she chafed at their heroic resistance. Among her ministers, however, were some who urged caution. Jung Lu, her most trusted supporter, commanded the heavy artillery and refused to permit its use. It was he who saved the foreign community from annihilation. At times, the Empress Dowager weakened. Attacks upon the legations were temporarily stopped. She ordered gifts of fruit and vegetables to the besieged and opened a special market for their convenience. Then the attacks were renewed, and it seemed but a question of time until further resistance would be useless.

In the northern provinces, the Boxer madness had spread, bringing death to 232 missionaries and their families, both Catholic and Protestant. In a few cases these outrages reached as far as the Yangtze, but they were confined largely to the northern provinces and Manchuria. In the south, Li Hung-chang, at Canton, and the Viceroys Chang Chih-tung and Liu Kun-yi, in the Yangtze, maintained order.

The Attitude of Foreign Governments

Diplomatically, a somewhat remarkable situation prevailed. So far as the Peking government was concerned, war prevailed with all the foreign states; but the latter did not choose to proceed on this theory. They maintained that no war existed. On the contrary, the outbreak was to be regarded as a rebellion which Peking was unable to suppress but for which it would be held responsible. The theory was obviously absurd, yet it was adhered to even after Imperial troops had joined the Boxers.

Meanwhile, the foreign departments of the great powers debated what should be done to save the Peking legations. All agreed that something should be done, but as to what it should be and as to who should do it, opinions differed. Organization of an international relief expedition sufficiently powerful to reach Peking was desirable but difficult. The British were engaged in the Boer War. American troops in the Far East were still fighting in the Philippine insurrection. Distance prevented the rapid mobilization of German or French troops. The Russians were guarding their railway in Manchuria. Of all the great powers, Japan alone was in a position to act quickly and effectively. Although she was urged to do so by Great Britain, her plan was blocked by Russia. The ministers of the Tsar had already determined to use the Boxer troubles for their own advantage. Better allow the legations to perish than to permit their rescue by Japan. And so there was unnecessary delay, every hour of which threatened the lives of the foreigners besieged in Peking. The first enthusiasm to save the legations having waned, its place was taken by the petty and jealous rivalries of imperialistic states, each bent on using the Boxer tragedy for its own gain.

The selfish objectives of the powers, however, were not identical. As will be seen in the following chapter, the Russians hoped secretly to make Manchuria a Russian protectorate.

The Germans, stung by the murder of their Minister, were intent on a policy of revenge. The British, the Americans, and the Japanese feared the breakup of China, with resulting restrictions on trade. The United States had long since abandoned the co-operative policy for one of unpredictable independent action. Secretary Hay had observed:

The position of the United States in relation to China makes it expedient that, while circumstances may sometimes require that it act on lines similar to those other powers follow, it should do so singly and without the co-operation of other powers.

To this policy, which has proved most convenient both before and since the Boxer trouble, may be accredited much of the absurd fiction that the government of the United States had ever entertained a very special friendship for China. Acting in accordance with this policy, Hay circularized the powers on July 3, 1900, informing them that, while the United States proposed to hold the Chinese to the "uttermost accountability," it nevertheless sought "a solution which may bring about permanent safety and peace to China, preserve Chinese territorial and administrative entity, protect all rights guaranteed to friendly Powers by treaty and international law, and safeguard for the world the principle of equal and impartial trade with all parts of the Chinese Empire."

The Relief Expedition

While these diplomatic exchanges were taking place and the siege in Peking continued, the foreign concessions in Tientsin had been subjected to intermittent attack. By July 14, sufficient foreign troops having arrived, the city was taken. With Tientsin as a base, plans could be made for an advance on Peking. The troops available were, in the opinion of the military commanders, inadequate; but, as the desperate plight of the besieged became known, desperate methods were adopted. On August 4, the relief expedition left Peking. It included 8,000 Japanese, 4,500 Russians, 3,000 British, 2,500 Americans, and 800 French. It was a truly remarkable force. Troops from America, Asia, and Europe marched through the blistering heat of the Chinese summer to the rescue of their legations. Ten days were consumed in reaching Peking. On August 14, the city was attacked and the legations relieved. The rescue was none too soon, for the imprisoned foreigners had already lost 67 killed and 168 wounded. Fighting continued throughout the city, while the Empress Dowager and her court fled from her capital for a second time before the hated foreigner. And now, the immediate danger gone, the foreign troops and civilians looted the city. The bravery and heroism which had thus far marked the course of events was besmeared by wanton pillage. It is not possible to assess responsibility for this knavery accurately, but it does appear that the Japanese, the British, and the Americans gave the least cause for complaint.

Beyond Peking, expeditions were dispatched to disperse the Boxers in regions where missionaries had been murdered. Because her Minister had been murdered, Germany demanded that Count von Waldersee be placed in command of the allied forces. He reached Peking with reinforcements in October, eager to display the power of German arms. So-called punitive expeditions, most of which were composed of German troops, marauded the countryside far into the spring of 1901. After the first few expeditions had cleared the countryside about Peking, these forays degenerated into useless pillaging. They could be justified neither on grounds of necessity nor on grounds of moral effect.

With the relief of the legations effected, the larger problem of effecting a diplomatic settlement with the Chinese remained. This problem was complicated by a maze of factors. Among the foreigners in China there was a very general demand for revenge. The Chinese court had fled; there was no government in Peking worthy of the name; general confusion prevailed; and the foreign powers were as suspicious of each other as they were of the Chinese. Yet two things were imperative: a common settlement, and the selection of Chinese negotiators on whom some reliance could be placed. Li Hung-chang was the obvious choice, though his selection was not secured without stubborn opposition from Berlin. He was recalled from the south and appointed peace commissioner by the Empress Dowager on August 7, 1900. The approach of peace negotiations brought forth all manner of conflicting proposals. Should guilty Chinese officials be punished prior to the negotiations? Were punishments to be inflicted by China or by the foreign powers? Were there to be annexations of Chinese territory? Were the spheres of influence to be expanded? What safeguards should be erected to forestall similar outbreaks in the future? Not until December 22 had the representatives of the powers and their respective governments agreed upon a joint note which embodied their basic demands and which in turn became the basis of the final settlement, the protocol of September 7, 1901.

Every phase of the complicated diplomatic game as played by the powers during the late summer and the autumn of 1900 was packed with dangerous plays. The Russians, for reasons of their own, had suggested that all the foreign troops be withdrawn. The Germans were determined to expand their influence in north China, were jealous of Russia's influence in Manchuria, and were covetous of England's commercial supremacy in the Yangtze. Between England and Russia, in particular, German diplomacy played with great skill. In October, 1900, while diplomatic chaos in Peking was at its height, an Anglo-German agreement was announced. Both powers agreed to exert their influence to preserve free and open trade at the ports of China, and neither would use the Boxer complications to secure territorial advantages. On the surface, this agreement appeared to be another pledge for a commercial open door. In reality it was not, for Germany had played for Russian favor by excluding Manchuria from the scope of the agreement, while at the same time she guaranteed to her own merchants equality of treatment with the British in the Yangtze. She had likewise played upon Anglo-American commercial rivalry by telling the English that Washington had no permanent intention to maintain the open door, and that the United States was looking to the Pacific as an American lake. To this kind of talk, Lord Salisbury, whose best days were already past, lent an attentive ear. In fact, the Anglo-German agreement was soon to prove of less value than the paper on which it was written. It meant that the Germans regarded Hay's open door policy as quite innocuous.

The Boxer Settlement

By January, 1901, China had accepted the united demands of the powers, and on February 5, the first meeting of the foreign envoys and the Chinese took place. The powers insisted that many of their demands be carried out in advance of the signature of the formal settlement. Among innumerable problems the question of indemnity loomed largest. In this respect, all the powers made extravagant demands, those of Russia, Germany, and France being beyond all reason. When finally all difficulties were overcome, there emerged on September 7, 1901, the famous or perhaps infamous, Boxer Protocol, which set up a new relationship between China and the foreign powers. Although not a treaty, this agreement has been of tremendous consequence. Its provisions merit a somewhat detailed statement:

1. For the murder of Baron von Kettler, German Minister at Peking, China was required to erect a monument and to dispatch a mission of apology.

2. Provision was made for the punishment of guilty Chinese

officials. This included not only executions and exile, but lesser punishments on many provincial and local officials where foreigners had been attacked.

3. For the murder of the Chancellor of the Japanese Legation, reparation and an apology.

4. In desecrated cemeteries monuments were to be erected.

5. The importation of arms and ammunition was to be prohibited for two years, and for a longer time at the discretion of the powers.

6. An indemnity of $332,900,000 (450,000,000 taels), with interest at four per cent, capital to be paid by December, 1940, was demanded. Payments were to be guaranteed by allocation of the unpledged balance of the Chinese maritime customs, the native customs, and the revenue of the salt monopoly. Among the powers the indemnity was divided as follows:

	Taels	Per Cent of Total
Russia	130,371,120	29
Germany	90,070,515	20
France	70,878,240	15.75
Great Britain	50,620,545	11.25
Japan	34,793,100	7.7
United States	32,939,055	7.3
Italy	26,617,005	5.9
Belgium	8,484,345	1.9
Austria-Hungary	4,003,920	.9
Netherlands	782,100	.2
Spain	135,315	
Portugal	92,250	
Sweden	62,820	
Other claims	149,670	

7. A legation quarter was to be set apart in Peking, which might be protected by adequate guards.

8. The Taku forts were to be destroyed, thus insuring an unfortified approach to Peking.

9. Permission for foreign troops to occupy certain posts between Peking and the sea was granted.

10. The Chinese government was required to issue edicts threatening death to members of antiforeign societies, announcing the punishments which had already been inflicted, and requiring provincial officials to be responsible for future acts against foreigners.

11. The commercial treaties were to be revised.

12. The Wai-wu Pu, the Chinese Foreign Office (formerly the Tsungli Yamen), was to rank above other departments of the government.

Here was a settlement that for severity was unrivaled in modern western diplomacy. Wherever possible, China had been forced to carry out its provisions in advance of signing. From 1900 onward, Peking and the road to the sea was never free from foreign troops. In January, 1902, the Chinese Court wended its mournful procession back to Peking. China had had her day, but her humiliation was now greater than ever. Peking, her capital, the Forbidden City, would listen daily to the march of foreign soldiers. Of the Middle Kingdom nothing was left but name. For this unhappy result, two forces were responsible: China herself, and the *western* powers.

Selected Bibliography

E. Backhouse and J. O. P. Bland, *Annals and Memoirs of the Court of Peking* (Boston: 1914). J. B. Bishop, *Theodore Roosevelt and His Time* (New York: 1920). Meribeth E. Cameron, *The Reform Movement in China 1898-1912* (Stanford University: 1931), chs. 1-2, a very scholarly study. Sih-Gung Cheng, *Modern China* (Oxford: 1919), ch. 5. P. H. Clements, *The Boxer Rebellion* (New York: 1915). Tyler Dennett, *John Hay* (New York: 1933), chs. 25, 26, 33. E. T. S. Dugdale, *German Diplomatic Documents, 1871-1914*, 4 vols. (London: 1930), vol. 3, ch. 8. Edwin A. Falk, *Togo and the Rise of Japanese Sea Power* (New York: 1936), ch. 12. C. J. Fox, *The Protocol of 1901* (Tientsin: 1926). S. G. Hishida, *The International Position of Japan as a Great Power* (New York: 1905). Shuhsi Hsu, *China and Her Political Entity* (New York:

1926), ch. 5. Paul King, *In the Chinese Customs Service* (London: 1930). H. B. Morse, *The International Relations of the Chinese Empire* (London: 1918), vol. 3, chs. 7-12. Mary A. Nourse, *The Four Hundred Million* (Indianapolis: 1935), ch. 19. M. J. Pergament, *The Diplomatic Quarter in Peking* (Peking: 1927). P. S. Reinsch, *Intellectual and Political Currents in the Far East* (Boston: 1911). A. H. Smith, *China in Convulsion* (New York: 1901). G. N. Steiger, *China and the Occident* (New Haven: 1927), chs. 6-13. B. L. Simpson, *An Indiscreet Chronicle from the Pacific* (New York: 1922). H. C. Thomson, *China and the Powers* (London: 1902). P. J. Treat, *The Far East* (New York: 1928), chs. 30-31. W. W. Willoughby, *Foreign Rights and Interests in China,* rev. ed., 2 vols. (Baltimore: 1927).

CHAPTER XXI

Origins of the Russo-Japanese War

THE dramatic struggle of forces which occasioned the Russo-Japanese War is a narrative reaching far beyond the bounds of academic interest. In the modern history of the Far East there have been problems peculiar in the main to the nineteenth century and new problems that appeared with the twentieth century; but the root problems from which the Russo-Japanese conflict sprang have been common to both centuries and remain (in modified forms) as contemporary problems today. Western imperialism, the root cause of the war, had, as the reader is well aware, fastened itself upon China in the latter half of the nineteenth century. At the turn of the century, this incubus had all but destroyed the vitality of a hapless China, which, together with Korea, was unable to resist the predatory tactics of western states. The vicious character of these tactics, the fact that their objective was domination of China and her former vassal Korea, had already aroused Japan. The Island Empire of Nippon was called upon to choose between two major policies. She could live quietly within the narrow confines of her island home, trusting in such security as her insular position afforded, while Europe cut and devoured the Chinese melon. Perhaps this would have been the course of wisdom, but history appears to record that it is not the policy which proud, vigorous, and able peoples adopt. Japan's alternative was to beat Europe (and later the United States) at her own game; to adopt imperialism as a policy; to expand as Europe had expanded; and to demand her share of the spoils. Whether wisely or not, it was to this policy that the government turned, supported by the almost unanimous voice of the nation. To the western world, this policy, coinciding with the turn of the century, has appeared as one of *offense* and aggression. To the Japanese it has appeared from the first as the inevitable strategy of *defense*: defense against western domination of the Far East.

Origins of Japanese Imperialism

Adoption by Japan of the imperialistic technique was not, of course, the decision of a few moments. It was influenced by forces which were domestic as well as foreign. Increasing population in the later nineteenth century, the development of urban and the beginnings of industrial life, real or alleged need for colonies, for new markets and new sources of food supply— all these prepared the Japanese mind for the coming struggle. The Chino-Japanese War was a formal announcement of the new policy, when Tokyo, alarmed by the advance of Russia, determined that Korea could no longer be left to the irresponsible guardianship of China. In fact, the war was not unrelated to those ambitious schemes which Mouraviev fifty years previously had initiated on the Pacific slope of Siberia, schemes which could be justified on no reasonable grounds.

Indeed, there was no reason for the Russian advance. There was no need for new areas for colonization, because Siberia was as yet practically untouched. There was no need for an open port, so long as the hinterland was undeveloped. There was no need for a market for Russian goods, for Russia had none to sell. . . . In brief, it may be said that Russia's action was that of a predatory state,—expansion for its own sake under the leadership of a Governor who tried to serve his Tsar too well.[1]

These early conquests led to the desire for others. The Maritime Province remained of questionable value as long as Russia controlled neither Manchuria nor Korea. This fact pre-

---

[1] William L. Langer, *The Origin of the Russo-Japanese War* (from the English original manuscript, published in *Europäische Gespräche,* Hamburg, 1926).

cipitated the Russian advance on Korea in 1880, which was blocked by the British (see p. 265). It was apparent, too, that without adequate means of communication, Russia could hope to do little in the Far East. The result was the plan for the Trans-Siberian Railway, begun in 1891. By 1894, when Japan drove the Chinese out of Korea, the Russian plan for domination of Manchuria, Korea, and perhaps north China was already far advanced. It was directly responsible for the Russian intervention in 1895 to force the return of the Liaotung peninsula, and it was followed quickly by the secret alliance with China in 1896 and the concession to build the Chinese Eastern Railway across north Manchuria. The Russian lease of Port Arthur followed as a natural consequence (1898). The way was thus paved for Moscow to dominate north China.

Russian Influence in Korea

The weakest spot in the Russian scheme, after 1895, was Korea. Japan held the advantage there. But this advantage was sacrificed in the same year, when the Japanese were implicated in a plot which resulted in the murder of the Korean Queen and the flight of the King to the Russian Legation. Of the opportunity thus afforded, the Russians failed to take full advantage. They refused the Japanese offer in May, 1896, to divide Korea into two spheres of influences (Russia to take the northern half), and in its place signed the Lobanov-Yamagata Protocol of June, 1896, an innocuous sort of agreement whereby each would give financial aid to Korea and refrain from interference in her military and police affairs. Two years later, on April 25, 1898, a second agreement was signed, the Nishi-Rosen Convention. Again lip service was paid to the independence of Korea. Neither power would interfere in the internal affairs of the country or lend military or financial advisers without mutual consent. All this was after Russia had leased Port Arthur, and when, in Japan, it was hoped that Russia would be content to confine her activities to Manchuria. This hope was in vain, the Japanese being forced to accept the principle of Russian equality with herself in Korea. That the Russians never intended to take these two agreements seriously is evidenced by the fact that in 1899 and 1900 Moscow was exerting itself to secure land for a naval base at Masampo, not far from Fusan and directly across the straits from Japan.

Had the Russians concentrated on Korea in the period immediately following [1896], they might have gained control of the state. They had the king under their thumb and the Japanese were not a serious obstacle. It seems that the Tsar did assume a rather informal protectorate over Korea, and it is obvious that the naval men were intent on securing a base on the Korean coast, but Witte was still all-powerful in St. Petersburg and insisted that Russia's efforts be confined to peaceful penetration. His policy is reflected in the Russian attempts to get control of the financial and military matters of Korea in the period from 1896 to 1898. The Japanese, of course, protested, arguing that such procedure was contrary at least to the spirit of existing agreements, but their remonstrances were ignored by the Russians. Japan was in no position to fight, at least not without allies. But the Russian policy, not sufficiently vigorous to solve the question in her own sense, was yet sufficiently active to enrage and alarm the Japanese, who from this time onward began serious military and diplomatic preparations for a conflict which they regarded as inevitable.[2]

The trouble was that the Russian policy was not unified. Witte, who dominated foreign affairs from 1896 to 1898, believed in peaceful economic penetration of China, but his policy was dropped in 1898 when Russia leased Port Arthur. From this time on there were divided councils in St. Petersburg— divided between those who favored peaceful penetration and those who were prepared to take by military force whatever was available. Both policies were bound eventually to lead to war, for the lease of Port Arthur by Russia placed Japan in a dangerous and a humiliating position. This was the territory

[2] *Ibid.*

which she had been forced to return to China in the interests of the peace of the Far East. She was for the moment forced to witness Russia supreme in Manchuria and with an equality of interest in Korea. At the time, the government being in no position to fight Russia, most of the Genro favored some compromise.

The Russian advance in Manchuria, coupled with the potential threat to Korea, had the Japanese thoroughly aroused. The British, too, were disturbed. An attempt had been made to replace the English inspector of Korean customs by a Russian; a Russo-Korean bank had been founded; and British and Russian interests were fighting bitterly on the subject of railway construction north and east of Peking. There had been some talk, as early as 1895, of an alliance between England and Japan. This was confined mostly, but not exclusively, to the press. Chamberlain and Ambassador Kato, in London, both favored the idea in 1898, but the Genro were opposed. In Tokyo the government was too weak and finances too uncertain to risk the danger of a war with Russia. There was the possibility (so the Japanese thought) that Germany and France might again support Russia. Accordingly in March, 1898, Japan, as noted, offered the Russians Manchuria as a sphere, on the understanding that Korea should be a Japanese sphere. This proposal was declined, and in its place Japan was given whatever consolation she could find in the Nishi-Rosen Convention.

The Yalu Timber Concession

Meanwhile, beginnings were made in a Russian concession later to be known as the Yalu Timber Company. This remarkable enterprise had its inception in a grant in 1896 by the Korean government to a Russian merchant to cut timber along the Yalu and the Tumen Rivers, which form the northern boundary against Manchuria. Out of this concession three Russian conspirators (including the Minister to Seoul and later the notorious Bezobrazov, a retired officer and councilor to the Tsar) proposed to erect an edifice which would give the Tsar complete control of Korea. All was to be done, under the guidance of the Tsar, through the agency of an East Asiatic Company, which was primarily a political organization. A distinguishing feature of the enterprise, as it was presented to the Tsar in 1898, was that it would give Russia a "fighting vanguard, up to 20,000 men, disguised as lumbermen." Ambitious plans were formed while a preliminary expedition surveyed the territory. The Russian War Department co-operated by sending an officer to make surveys. All north Korea was examined from the standpoint of economic and military development, and surveys were undertaken for a railroad from Port Arthur to Vladivostok. But with divided councils at St. Peterburg, all plans were postponed. There were in fact three factions, each pushing its own policy: (1) Bezobrazov and the Yalu concession group, (2) the Russian navy, which, as noted, had attempted to get a naval base at Masampo, and (3) Witte's policy of peaceful economic penetration in Manchuria and north China, excluding any encroachment in Korea. This was the set-up which prevailed from 1898 to 1900. Then came the Boxer affair and the spread of violence to Manchuria.

The Boxers in Manchuria

The aggressiveness that Russia had displayed in Manchuria since 1898 served to aggravate the Boxers and those sections of the populace that joined with them. Here, too, the movement was directed first against the missionaries and their converts. Five Catholic missionaries were slain in Mukden; others were driven from the field while their converts fell in large numbers before the frenzied rebels. The Russian railroad from Harbin to Port Arthur, then in process of construction, was attacked and sections of the line destroyed. From Aigun, on the Amur, Russian ships were attacked, and the Russian town of Blagovestchensk bombarded. Fearful of their safety, the Russians ordered the Chinese population to cross to the Chinese side, but, since transportation was lacking, about 4,500 were driven into the river to drown or be slaughtered. After these events Russia proceeded to the occupation of numerous strategic points through Manchuria. Her troops moved south along the zone of the railway, taking possession as they went until she had occupied the capital, Mukden, the port of Newchwang, and the railroad southward beyond the Great Wall to Tientsin. In this manner Manchuria passed into the military control of Russia during the very months that the powers sat in judgment on China at Peking.

The Boxer upheaval and the spread of violence to Manchuria presented two possibilities. If the Russian policy were moderate, as Witte had hoped, Russo-Chinese friendship could be renewed. Officially, Russian policy as announced during the Boxer crisis was moderate, but in reality the Tsar had already fallen under the influence of Bezobrazov, who advocated elimination from Manchuria and north China of all but Russian influence. General Kuropatkin, Minister of War, also appeared to favor using the Boxers as an excuse for seizing Manchuria, and even Witte was forced to call for troops to protect his prize hobby, the Chinese Eastern Railway. It is not strange then that in the winter of 1900-1901, while Russians at Peking were making the pretense of a common settlement with the other powers, they were in reality attempting to force upon China separate and secret demands with respect to Manchuria. These included railroad concessions "in the direction of Peking" and an exclusive Russian preference in all railroads, mines, and industrial undertakings in Manchuria, Mongolia, and Chinese Turkestan. Germany would have been content to let the Russians have their way as long as German interests in Shantung and the Yellow Valley were not molested; but England and Japan protested, and in this they were joined by the United States. Temporarily the Russians paused, while

England and Japan began conversations which were to result finally in the Anglo-Japanese Alliance.

The British Policy

Practically, the English had abandoned Manchuria to the Russians in 1899 by the Scott-Mouraviev notes, which relieved the latter of any competition from British railroad men. The Anglo-German agreement of 1900, signed in the midst of the Boxer troubles, was a belated and futile effort to stop the Russians, since the Germans said it did not apply to Manchuria. This in turn strengthened the Russian position. Officially the Russians continued to protest that they would leave Manchuria when the crisis had passed (the view of Lamsdorff and Witte), but in reality the militarists and adventurers who surrounded the Tsar had not the slightest intention of so doing. England, in fact, hoped for an alliance of Germany, Japan, and the United States to stop Russia. But there were too many complications in the way of any such grouping, and while preliminary discussions were under way, Russian negotiations with China were resumed. Witte and Lamsdorff urged withdrawal of Russia's armies to avoid war with Japan. The militarists, while willing to leave south Manchuria, wanted to annex the north. In the settlement finally proposed in the summer of 1901, China was to promise not to give concessions in Manchuria to foreign powers until they had first been offered to the Russo-Chinese Bank. The Chinese delayed. By telling the English and the Japanese what the Russians were doing, they speeded negotiations toward the Anglo-Japanese Alliance. By the spring of 1901, the Russian threat had already paved the way for an understanding between London and Tokyo. Each government needed an ally against Russia. The latter was a growing danger to England in India and north China, and to Japan in Korea. As early as April, the Japanese Minister, Tadasu Hayashi, was instructed to open informal discussions. His

efforts met with a most favorable response in London, while
in Tokyo the Cabinet, headed by Prime Minister Katsura, and
the Genro (Ito, Inouye, and Yamagata) supported the general
idea of a British alliance but differed on questions of principle
and detail. The views of Ito, the nation's most distinguished
leader, were of particular importance. He was not, as has been
said frequently, opposed to an understanding with England,
but he did insist that the proposed alliance should avoid the
Korean question. On this subject he was convinced, though
probably mistakenly, that a direct and satisfactory settlement
could be reached with Russia. To this end he left Japan for
Europe in September, 1901. His mission enjoyed the blessing
of Yamagata and Inouye and the apparent approval of Katsura,
who, however, merely wanted him out of the country in order
to smooth the negotiations with England.

In Russia the proposals presented by Ito were most liberal.
They included:

1. A reciprocal guarantee of the independence of Korea;

2. Reciprocal obligation not to employ any part of Korean
territory for strategic purposes;

3. Reciprocal obligation not to take military measures upon
the coast of Korea which would hamper freedom of passage in
the Gulf of Korea;

4. Russia to recognize Japan's liberty in Korea in political,
industrial, and commercial matters;

5. Russia to recognize Japan's exclusive right to aid Korea
with advice and assistance in the execution of engagements
which devolve upon every well-organized government, and to
dispatch troops when necessary.[3]

If Japan could be set at rest on these points and could be
assured that Russia would not seize a base in Korea, then Russia, said Ito, "might in future do as she liked in China . . .
without meeting with any opposition from Japan." To these

---

[3] *Ibid.*

terms the Russians would not agree. They demanded, in addition to complete freedom on the Russo-Chinese frontier, that the right of Japan to advise Korea be subject to Russian approval in each case. Disappointed, though not convinced that his efforts had failed, Ito left Russia.

The Anglo-Japanese Alliance

The British were meanwhile disturbed by the presence of a leading Japanese statesman in St. Petersburg. If an understanding with Russia were reached, Japan might no longer be interested in London's proposals. The British draft was thus given to Hayashi on November 6. Ito attempted from Russia to postpone its consideration, but Katsura replied that discussions had already proceeded too far to permit delay. On December 8, Katsura reported to the Emperor that Cabinet and Genro favored the alliance. From Europe Ito again wired for delay, but the Genro affirmed their previous action, and the Emperor gave his approval. It appears that Ito alone had any faith in Russia, and this it would seem was misplaced. His colleagues never believed an agreement with Russia possible. As a result they have been accused of rejecting an offer which so distinguished a leader as Ito still believed might form the basis of a settlement. According to Langer, "it is the one questionable point in the Japanese policy, but one should not forget that in point of fact they [the Japanese] were justified in distrusting Russia." [4]

The Anglo-Japanese Alliance was signed on January 30, 1902. The two governments declared that they were "actuated solely by a desire to maintain the *status quo* and general peace in the extreme East . . . [and] specially interested in maintaining the independence and territorial integrity of the Empire of China and the Empire of Corea, and in securing equal op-

---

[4] *Ibid.*

portunities in those countries for the commerce and industry of all nations."

Both powers declared themselves uninfluenced by aggressive tendencies. Great Britain's "special interests" were declared to relate principally to China, while Japan, in addition to interests possessed in China, was declared to be "interested in a peculiar degree politically as well as commercially and industrially in Corea." Under the terms of the alliance, either would be permitted to safeguard these interests if threatened by the aggressive action of any other power or by disturbances arising in China or Korea. If either Great Britain or Japan, in defense of its interests, became involved in war with another power, its ally would remain neutral; but if another power or powers joined hostilities against it, its ally would come to its assistance and conduct the war and make peace by mutual agreement.[5]

Russia Agrees to Evacuate Manchuria

The influence of the first Anglo-Japanese Alliance may scarcely be overestimated. It gave Japan the support necessary to challenge the irresponsible and grandiose plans of Russia in Korea and Manchuria. Its public announcement on February 11, 1902, might well have served as a warning to Russia that her far eastern policies were no longer compatible with peace. Indeed, for a brief period it did appear that the peak of Russian pretensions had passed and that more modest policies would prevail. Although a Franco-Russian declaration, issued in March, was regarded as a reply to the alliance, the fact remained that Russia did modify the demands concerning Manchuria and on April 8, 1902, signed with China a convention agreeing to evacuate Manchuria within eighteen months; that is, by October 8, 1903. Superficially it seemed that the crisis was passed, but this view failed to take account of two

---

[5] For text and documents relating to the Anglo-Japanese Alliance, see *British Documents on the Origins of the War*. London, 1927. Vol. II, pp. 89-120.

circumstances. In the first place, the Russians had signed the agreement only under international pressure. In the second, they had made evacuation conditional on the restoration of order in Manchuria and on the understanding that China would permit no interference by foreign powers. It is fair to conclude that Russia's failure to carry out the evacuation was the immediate cause of the war. Had Russia been content to regard Manchuria merely as a sphere for financial and industrial exploitation, free from military occupation, and open to the trade of other nations, no power would have felt justified in attacking her. Not only Japan, but also England and the United States, had already accepted the obvious fact that Manchuria was a Russian sphere. Japan, however, regarded the Russian military forces in Manchuria as a threat to Korea. She therefore, while watching closely the progress of the evacuation, in August, 1902, again proposed to Russia a peaceful settlement. She suggested:

1. That both powers recognize the independence and integrity of China and Korea.

2. That both agree to refrain from using any part of Korea for military purposes.

3. That Japan's special position in Korea be recognized in return for recognition of Russia's right to take special measures to protect her Manchurian railways and other interests there.

The Reoccupation of Manchuria

To these suggestions the Japanese received only an evasive response. The Russians had gone too far to turn back. Their investments in railroads and the port of Dalny were already heavy. They could ill afford, so they thought, to withdraw their army to please Japan, or to establish an open door policy to please Japan, England, and the United States. During the first six months following signature of the evacuation convention, the Russian troops were withdrawn from some southern areas of Manchuria, but they were concentrated at Port Arthur and the country immediately north. Though late in 1902 and early in 1903 a few troops were taken from Mukden, fresh forces occupied territory near the Korean border. New demands, amounting to a protectorate over Manchuria and Mongolia, were pressed upon China on April 8, 1903, it being made clear that the troops would not be withdrawn until the demands were met. Responsibility for Russia's failure to keep her agreement may be laid to Bezobrazov and similar adventurers who surrounded the Tsar. From the first they characterized the evacuation agreement as "a confession of weakness" unworthy of a great and expanding power. In this they were supported by von Plehve, new Minister of the Interior, who was jealous of Witte and thus identified himself with Bezobrazov and company. Their program entailed threatening Japan by strengthening Russian forces on the Yalu. The timber lands of the region would be exploited with vigor, and other concessions would be sought in Korea. All major undertakings in Manchuria should be brought under Russian control.

In order to satisfy the Americans and other malcontents the doors might be thrown open to foreigners, but the effect of this could be wiped out by an alliance between the Russians and the Manchurian brigands or Hunghuses, who would make the ground so hot for both Chinese and foreigners that the Russians would soon find themselves in complete and undisputed control.[6]

This program received the full support of the Tsar, and in 1903 Bezobrazov returned to the Far East with not only the moral but also the financial backing of His Majesty. The East Asiatic Industrial Corporation again sprang into activity. Agencies were established even in Seoul, the Korean capital. Lumber operations were commenced on both sides of the Yalu, under the protecting hand of reserve officers of the Russian army, while a concession was sought to build a railroad from the Yalu to Seoul. Against these Korean schemes Witte,

---

[6] William L. Langer, *op. cit.*

(Minister of Finance), Lamsdorff (Foreign Minister), and Kuropatkin (Minister for War) protested. On Manchuria opinions were still further divided, for Kuropatkin, like Bezobrazov, demanded military guarantees as a prerequisite of evacuation. And back of all this confusion was the fact that the Tsar was beginning to see himself as the master of half of Asia.

The failure of Russia to carry out her agreement of April, 1902, and the persistent rumors of new Russian demands on China, again aroused the fears of Japan, Great Britain, and the United States. Together they prevailed upon China to refuse the Russians, thus forcing the latter to make concessions. They agreed to open new ports in Manchuria and to respect the treaty rights of other powers. By these acts they satisfied the English and the Americans, who were basically interested only in Manchuria's trade, but not the Japanese, who were equally concerned with strategic matters and who looked with increasing alarm on Russian activities in Korea. Again these concessions seemed to foreshadow hope of a peaceful settlement. The contrary was the case. They were counterbalanced in August, 1903, by an order of the Tsar creating the Viceroyalty of the Far East, by which Bezobrazov and his group were freed completely from the restraining influence of Witte and Lamsdorff. With the "Koreans" (as the Bezobrazov men were known) in power, conflict with Japan was inevitable.

Direct Russo-Japanese Negotiations

With this background of Russian policy in mind, Japan's attitude as she approached direct negotiations with Russia in July, 1903, may now be briefly summarized. The Anglo-Japanese Alliance, negotiated by the Katsura Cabinet, in which Jutaro Komura was Foreign Minister, enabled Japan to formulate a moderate yet a specific policy. Japan's fears were not removed by the Russo-Chinese convention of evacuation of

April, 1902, and in December, a bill for heavy naval expansion was introduced in the Diet. Funds were to be provided by increases in the land tax, but such was the opposition raised in the House of Representatives that it was not until April, 1903, that the government, after various political manipulations with the Seiyukai (majority party), was able to carry its naval program. Coincident with the passage of the naval bill, Minister Uchida at Peking reported the failure of Russia to withdraw her Manchuria troops and pressed for an early determination of policy. Toward the close of April, Katsura, Komura, and Princes Ito and Yamagata decided that Russia might claim priority rights in Manchuria if a similar position were accorded Japan in Korea. Meanwhile, the Cabinet determined to protest vigorously against the Russian policy and to appeal to arms should this protest fail. This decision, when debated before the Throne, was opposed by Ito and Inouye on the ground that the nation was not yet prepared to risk war. The views of the Cabinet were supported by Yamagata, Matsukata, and General Oyama, chief of the general staff, who argued that Japan enjoyed a strategic advantage and that delay would only strengthen the Russians. The Emperor's decision was that Japan should open direct negotiations. Ito's opposition to the government's policy was now removed from the Diet by his resignation as head of the Seiyukai and his appointment as president of the Privy Council.

From the public, too, came a growing demand for a resolute policy against the Russians in Manchuria. Advocates of this course were to be found among the faculties of the Imperial University of Tokyo and the staffs of such metropolitan dailies as the Tokyo and Osaka *Asahi,* the *Jiji,* and the *Osaka Mainichi,* which demanded war with Russia. Some of the papers avoided any direct stand, but as early as June, 1903, seven professors of the law faculty of the Imperial University of Tokyo presented a memorial to the government urging a decisive policy and asserting that war was inevitable. "By November (1903) . . . the public was united in its demand for war." [7] The Cabinet thus found itself between a populace which demanded action and the most distinguished of the Genro, Prince Ito, who counseled peace. Kurino, the Minister in St. Petersburg, was instructed, on July 28, 1903, to open formal negotiations. The Russians delayed their response, but finally, in August, agreed to discuss the situation in Manchuria and Korea. The first Japanese proposals, which were quite moderate, might well have been accepted by Russia. They included:

1. Mutual engagement to respect the independence and territorial integrity of the Chinese and Korean Empires and to maintain the principles of equal opportunity for the commerce and industry of all nations in those countries.

2. Reciprocal recognition of Japan's preponderating interests in Korea and Russia's special interests in railway enterprises in Manchuria, and of the right of Japan to take in Korea and of Russia to take in Manchuria such measures as may be necessary for the protection of their respective interests as above defined, subject, however, to the provisions of Article 1 of this Agreement.

3. Reciprocal undertaking on the part of Russia and Japan not to impede development of those industrial and commercial activities of Japan in Korea and Russia in Manchuria which are not inconsistent with the stipulations of Article 1 of this Agreement.

Additional engagement on the part of Russia not to impede the eventual extension of the Korean Railway into Southern Manchuria so as to connect with the East China and Shanhaikwan-Newchwang lines.

4. Reciprocal engagement that in case it is found necessary to send troops by Japan to Korea or by Russia to Manchuria for the purpose either of protecting the interests mentioned in

[7] Tatsuji Takeuchi, *War and Diplomacy in the Japanese Empire.* Doubleday, Doran & Company, New York, 1935. p. 140.

Article 2 of this Agreement or of suppressing insurrection or disorder calculated to create international complications, the troops so sent in no case to exceed the actual number required and to be forthwith recalled as soon as their missions are accomplished.

5. Recognition on the part of Russia of the exclusive right of Japan to give advice and assistance in the interest of reform and good government in Korea, including necessary military assistance.

6. This Agreement to supplant all previous arrangements between Japan and Russia respecting Korea.

Attempting to evade the issue, Russia sought to have the negotiations transferred to Tokyo and delayed nearly two months before replying to the Japanese note. She consented to discuss Korea only, and she was unwilling to give any assurance on the open door there. She demanded a neutral zone in Korea in the very week that the last of her soldiers should have been withdrawn from Manchuria under the evacuation agreement—an agreement which the Russians had now repudiated completely. Japan's counter proposals showed a willingness to compromise still further by offering a neutral zone in the territory lying on both sides of the Manchurian-Korean frontier. Again the Russians delayed. On December 11, still refusing to discuss Manchuria, they insisted on a neutral zone in Korea but consented to connecting the Korean and Chinese railways. Further exchanges followed, in the last of which Russia omitted the demand for the Korean neutral zone but refused any guarantees concerning Manchuria.

In Japan, by the end of December, 1903, the Foreign Office and the military services were convinced that war was certain. On December 28, an emergency Imperial ordinance was issued, authorizing emergency military expenditures. A supreme war council was established, and two warships were purchased from Argentina. Foreign Minister Komura was prepared, on

January 11, 1904, to break off negotiations with Russia, but was dissuaded by the navy, whose preparations were not yet complete. On January 24, Premier Katsura informed the Emperor that the Cabinet had decided to terminate the negotiations. On February 4, no Russian reply having been received to the final Japanese proposals, the Cabinet made its final decision. That afternoon the Genro (Ito, Yamagata, Matsukata, Oyama, and Inouye) and the Cabinet met before the Emperor. Orders were issued to the army and navy to be ready for operation when diplomatic relations should be severed on February 6.[8] War was at hand.

While Japan and Russia were rapidly approaching a declaration of war, no one of the great European powers or the United States took any steps to prevent the conflict. The British exerted some pressure on Russia in the Persian Gulf and Tibet, but in the main encouraged Japan. France and Germany could ill afford to forsake neutrality, since President Roosevelt had indicated his intention to support Japan if either power should join Russia.

. . . it can at least be said for Japan that her policy was based upon a real need. The argument for self-preservation is in her favor. However great or small her need for Korea was at the time, it is easy to see that she could not afford to allow the peninsula to fall into the hands of some power which would seal it hermetically against Japanese colonization or trade. With the Russians the case was entirely different. If they are honest with themselves they admit, like Kuropatkin, that Russia had no need of expansion in the Far East. . . . The fact was that the predatory tendency of the Russian autocracy had led to expansion, in many cases senseless expansion, in the Far East as in the Middle East.[9]

SELECTED BIBLIOGRAPHY

R. H. Akagi, *Japan's Foreign Relations* (Tokyo: 1936), ch. 8.
K. Asakawa, *The Russo-Japanese Conflict* (Boston: 1904), a re-

---

[8] *Ibid.* pp. 142-144.
[9] See Langer, *op. cit.*, for a full analysis of the Russian materials.

markably scholarly contemporary account of the causes of the war. *British Documents on the Origins of the War,* vol. 2, ch. 9, the Far East 1900-1901; ch. 11, the Anglo-Japanese agreement; ch. 13, Russian policy in the Far East, 1903-1904. *The Cambridge History of British Foreign Policy,* 3 vols. (Cambridge: 1922-1923), vol. 3, ch. 4, pt. 4, the Anglo-Japanese Alliance, 1898-1902. P. H. Clyde, *International Rivalries in Manchuria* (Columbus: 1928), chs. 4-6. Chang Chung-fu, *The Anglo-Japanese Alliance* (Baltimore: 1931). A. L. P. Dennis, *The Anglo-Japanese Alliance* (Berkeley: 1923), to be used with caution. E. J. Dillon, *The Eclipse of Russia* (New York: 1918). E. T. S. Dugdale, *German Diplomatic Documents, 1871-1914,* 4 vols. (London: 1930), vol. 3, ch. 10. Baron von Eckardstein, *Ten Years at the Court of St. James, 1895-1905* (London: 1921). Edwin A. Falk, *Togo and the Rise of Japanese Sea Power* (New York: 1936). Otto Franke, *Die Grossmächte in Ostasien von 1894 bis 1914* (Hamburg: 1923). Kikujiro Ishii, *Diplomatic Commentaries* (Baltimore: 1936), trans. and ed. by W. R. Langdon, ch. 3. Alexander Iswolsky, *Recollections of a Foreign Minister,* L. Seeger, trans. (Garden City: 1921), chs. 2 and 4. Lancelot Lawton, *Empires of the Far East,* 2 vols. (London: 1912). T. J. Lawrence, *War and Neutrality in the Far East* (London: 1904). A. Lobanov-Rostovsky, *Russia and Asia* (New York: 1933), ch. 10. M. J. F. McCarthy, *The Coming Power* (London: 1905). Inazo Nitobe, *The Japanese Nation* (New York: 1912). Leo Pasvolsky, *Russia in the Far East* (New York: 1922), ch. 3, Russian policy, 1895-1905. J. F. Rhodes, *The McKinley and Roosevelt Administrations, 1897-1909* (New York: 1922). R. R. Rosen, *Forty Years of Diplomacy,* 2 vols. (New York: 1922), vol. 1, chs. 16-17, and 22-23. Tatsuji Takeuchi, *War and Diplomacy in the Japanese Empire* (Garden City: 1935). A. Yarmolinsky, trans. and ed., *The Memoirs of Count Witte* (Garden City: 1921). Ken-shen Weigh, *Russo-Chinese Diplomacy* (Shanghai: 1928). H. G. Whigham, *Manchuria and Korea* (London: 1904). V. A. Yakhontoff, *Russia and the Soviet Union in the Far East* (London: 1932), chs. 1-2.

CHAPTER XXII

The Russo-Japanese War and the Peace

A<small>N</small> ancient Chinese authority on war has observed: "The successful fighter plans his victory and then gives battle; the unsuccessful gives battle and then looks for victory." No formula could describe more aptly the attitudes of Japan and Russia on the eve of and during the Russo-Japanese War. Since 1898, when Russia seized Port Arthur, commenced her appropriation of Manchuria, and attempted a strategic and economic invasion of Korea, Japan had been fully conscious of the danger. From 1900 to 1904, while striving for a moderate and a peaceful settlement, she had not neglected to strengthen her international position by allying herself with England or her strategic position by increasing the strength and efficiency of her land and naval services. In man power and in ships she was overshadowed numerically by the Russians, but in morale and equipment she stood supreme. Her naval and her military leaders had profited by experiences of the Chino-Japanese War and the actions incident to the Boxer Rebellion. They had proved their fighting ability and their unsurpassed discipline. The vast majority of her conscript army (probably more than eighty per cent) was composed of literate men who had confidence in their leaders. The leaders in turn were officers who, with few exceptions, could attribute their rank to ability rather than to political preferment. The appointment in December, 1903, of Vice Admiral Togo as commander-in-chief of Japan's fighting squadrons is but one example of the rule which prevailed. Behind these leaders and their men was a factor of equal if not greater importance. The people of Japan, when efforts for a peaceful solution failed, had demanded war. Its purpose being clear to them, they were prepared for any sacrifice. In a very real sense it was a people's war: a war of literate men fighting for an objective they could see and understand.

How different was the position of Russia! She had seized Port Arthur in 1898 to satisfy her undefined ambitions for expansion and jealousy of other European states. Her subsequent exploitation of Manchuria and Korea met no real national need. Her economic, political, and military activities in the valley of the Yalu merely victimized the Russian people for the purpose of enriching a Tsar, a court, and a gang of unscrupulous adventurers. Witte, to be sure, saw the danger, and attempted, when too late, to avoid it. Yet Witte himself was responsible for Russia's economic and political invasion of Manchuria. Russia possessed no statesmanship comparable to that which placed Japan in the Anglo-Japanese Alliance. Until it was too late, she refused to believe that the Japanese would risk war. Her army was illiterate, her navy hopelessly divided and in decay. To her soldiers the war was no more than the commands of officers often wholly unfitted for their task. At home, in contrast with Japan's literate and patriotic populace, the Russian peasants, under the rule of a stupid autocracy, had no understanding of and no heart for a conflict on the remote northeastern slope of Asia.

The Theater of War

In these circumstances, not fully appreciated by the western world at the time, Japan and Russia entered a war that was to be fought on the seas of the Far East and on the Manchurian plains. China, although allied secretly with Russia, proclaimed her neutrality on February 12. Japan's plan of operations was determined in advance by the fact that Russia was already in military occupation of Manchuria, including the zone adjacent to the Korean border. She proposed, therefore, to drive the

Russians from Korea, to destroy Russian naval forces in the Far East and capture their naval base at Port Arthur, and, finally, to break the Russian army proper in south Manchuria. Her immediate problem was to insure uninterrupted communication with Korea and to establish a base of operations there against Manchuria. Until this was done, she would not be in a position to guarantee support for her troops. The distance from western Japan to Korea was not great, but so long as Russian ships operated in the Far East, these sea-lanes would be menaced. For Russia, the immediate problem was one of land (railway) transportation. The Trans-Siberian Railroad was started in 1891. When the war came, it was complete as a single-track line, including the Chinese Eastern, stretching across north Manchuria, with the branch line from Harbin to Port Arthur. However, trains had still to be ferried across Lake Baikal, the roadbed in many places was poor, sidings and rolling stock were inadequate, and, above all, the personnel lacked initiative. On this railroad Russia's ability to prosecute the war would depend.

In February, 1904, as in 1894, Japan fired her first guns before the formal declaration of war. She "was aware of the risks attendant upon the shipment of an expeditionary force to the mainland before the control of the water routes was assured." [1]

Troops were dispatched to Korea simultaneously with the severing of diplomatic relations. The Russians were now alarmed. Never having believed that Japan would make war, they hurriedly, but too late, invoked British mediation. On February 8, a Russian cruiser fired on a Japanese convoy off Jinsen (Chemulpo), the port of Seoul. That night Admiral Togo surprised the Russians at Port Arthur with a destroyer attack which crippled three of the Russian vessels. On the following day, two Russian cruisers, putting to sea at Jinsen,

---

[1] Edwin A. Falk, *Togo and the Rise of Japanese Sea Power.* Longmans, Green & Company, New York, 1936. p. 289.

were destroyed by the Japanese squadron which awaited them. In 1904, Korea lacked the means, even if she had possessed the will, to defend her neutrality.   At the time, Japan's action in Korea and at Port Arthur, taken before any formal declaration of war, was criticized.   The fact was, however, that for her procedure Japan could cite ample precedent.   The formal declarations of war followed on February 10.   The United States declared its neutrality on February 11, and China, as already noted, on the following day.   Great Britain's position was already defined legally by the terms of the Anglo-Japanese Alliance.

China: The Helpless Onlooker

The attitude of China was, of course, quite incompatible with that of a sovereign state.   The Manchus were incapable of doing anything to defend themselves.   For eight years they had been secretly allied with Russia, who was all the while seeking to appropriate their homeland.   They had failed to repudiate the alliance.   They lifted a hand neither to defend themselves nor to assist Japan in driving the Russians from their soil.   Consequently, when the peace was made, China was not considered, and it is questionable whether she deserved consideration.

The military and naval operations of the war, although of great consequence to the student of strategy, can here be no more than mentioned.   A Japanese army was landed at Jinsen on February 8 and 9, and the capital (Seoul) was occupied. Another army landed further north at Gensan.   Its objective was to operate against the Russians in northern Korea and in the valley of the Yalu.   While this movement was under way, another army was landed on May 6 on the eastern shore of the Liaotung peninsula, to the north and east of the Russian leased territory.   Another army followed still farther to the east.   With these forces the Japanese were able to press the

Russians back from the Yalu, either toward Mukden or south to their fortress at Port Arthur.

The Siege of Port Arthur

To capture this stronghold was of great importance. Its position was all but impregnable. The forts lay in the series of hills in which the Liaotung peninsula terminates. Entrenched behind these natural ramparts, protected by heavily constructed subterranean forts, the Russians could well believe themselves safe. Time and again General Nogi sent his forces to the assault across open valleys to certain death. Meanwhile, Japanese forces under Oyama faced, to the south of the Mukden, the Grand Army of the Tsar under General Kuropatkin. To Japan's 125,000 men, Russia had already gathered 158,000. In the Battle of Liaoyang (August 23—September 3), the Russains were driven back but not routed. In October, the Russians

South Manchuria Railway Co.

THE NORTH FORTS AT PORT ARTHUR. In the Japanese leased territory these ruins stand as a memorial to the cost of war—the cost in material, human life, and human bitterness.

attacked at Sho-ho, but the Japanese lines held. Winter now forced the main armies into quarters, while in the south the assaults on Port Arthur continued. The Russian Baltic fleet was already on its way to the Far East. It was therefore essential that Port Arthur and its fleet be destroyed. By repeated attacks, Nogi's men slowly drove the Russians back upon their inner forts. Early in December the fall of the forts on 203 Metre Hill enabled the Japanese to direct their fire on the harbor and fleet. Less than a month later (January 2, 1905), Stoessel surrendered the fortress with 41,000 men, 500 guns, and large stores of munitions and supplies. But the price had been heavy. The siege cost Japan the lives of 20,000 men, and many more were wounded. The sons of her great men were not spared. The elder son of General Nogi had already fallen at the Battle of Nan-shan; the younger fell at Port Arthur.

Japan Tourist Bureau.

GENERAL IWAO OYAMA. Satsuma clansman, Genro, and military strategist, whose tactics defeated General Kuropatkin in the Russo-Japanese War.

The tremendous sacrifice of life and the death of his sons were blows that Nogi never forgot. The power with which he inspired his army was great, but he was not a master of strategy.

In February, 1905, the main armies fought the greatest engagement of the war—the Battle of Mukden. Oyama, with an army of 400,000, attempted to outflank the smaller Russian force of 325,000. The latter retired successfully and reformed their lines seventy-five miles north of the city, where Kuropatkin asked to be relieved of supreme command. General

Linievitch replaced him, though Kuropatkin continued to command the first army.

Destruction of the Russian Fleet

Aided by both the German and the French governments, the Russian Baltic fleet had reached far eastern waters on its

Japan Tourist Bureau.

ADMIRAL COUNT HEIHACHIRO TOGO.
He was "temperamentally incapable of
lifting a finger to gain the slightest
preferment for himself. . . ."

way to Vladivostok. Togo's forces were concentrated off the southern coast of Korea. His scouts sighted the Russians in the early morning darkness of May 27. The fleets converged in the eastern channel of the Korean strait off the islands of Tsushima, where Togo, "crossing the Russian T," virtually destroyed the enemy. One Russian ship reached Vladivostok. The remainder were sunk, captured, or interned in neutral ports. The Japanese lost three torpedo boats. On the sea and at Port Arthur, Japan had been completely victorious. On the plains north of Mukden, the Russian army was still intact. There, Japan's victories had been at best only technical. Each week that passed brought more Russian soldiers into Manchuria. Each advantage won by the Japanese in the field removed them farther from their base. In Russia, there was grave danger of revolt, while both powers had practically exhausted their financial resources. The re-establishment of peace was imperative, yet neither power wished to make the initial move lest it be interpreted by the other as admission of defeat.

Roosevelt as Peacemaker

The need for peace had been recognized by Witte as early as August, 1904. The Tsar would not listen. At the same time, President Roosevelt began to formulate the policy that was finally to make him the go-between for the belligerents. His ideas on a settlement were that Korea should be accepted as a Japanese protectorate, and that the powers should guarantee the neutrality of Manchuria. At the moment, President Roosevelt, through his particularly intimate relations with the German Ambassador, learned that France was reported to be preparing to lead a movement of mediation by neutral powers with a view to territorial compensation in China. John Hay again circularized the powers on January 13, 1905, requesting that the integrity of China and the open door be respected. In February, Japan having sounded both Germany and the United States as to the probability of Russia's discussing terms of peace, President Roosevelt advised her to make the first move. The Germans at this moment seemingly wanted the war to continue, in order to keep Russia occupied in the Far East, though the precise nature of the German policy is by no means clear. The American Minister in Peking, Mr. Conger, was urging the State Department to make some effective move toward peace, observing that:

Had the other Powers [the neutrals] in 1901 and 1902 . . . demanded of Russia the fulfillment of all her promises, made nominally to China, but actually to all the Powers, Manchuria would have been handed back to the Chinese then and, probably, the terrible war averted.[2]

Japan made the first positive move for peace on May 31, three days after the Russian fleet had been sunk. She requested President Roosevelt on his own "initiative to invite the two belligerents to come together for the purpose of direct negotia-

---

[2] Quoted by A. L. P. Dennis, *Adventures in American Diplomacy*. E. P. Dutton & Co., New York, 1928. p. 400.

tions." Accordingly, the President proposed to Russia that he invite the two powers to meet, adding that the invitation to Japan would in no way indicate that Russia had consented. England and Germany also favored peace by this time, yet it was only with the greatest difficulty that the consent of the Tsar to President Roosevelt's invitation was obtained. Washington was selected as the place for the peace conference. Thus far President Roosevelt's diplomacy had been successful. That he was not thinking of Japan or Russia alone may be gathered from his letter to President Wheeler, of the University of California.

You see the significance of the world movement of which we are a part just as I do. I believe that our future history will be more determined by our position on the Pacific facing China than our position on the Atlantic facing Europe.[3]

The Portsmouth Conference

The peace conference was opened August 9 at Portsmouth. Japan was represented by her Foreign Minister, Baron Komura, and her Ambassador at Washington, Baron Takahira; Russia was represented by Count Witte and Baron Rosen. Japan's initial demands, presented at the second session, included:

1. Recognition by Russia of Japan's paramount political, economic, and military interests in Korea.
2. The evacuation of Manchuria by both powers.
3. Transfer to Japan of the Russian leasehold on the Liaotung peninsula, and of the southern branch of the Chinese Eastern Railway from Harbin to Port Arthur.
4. Cession to Japan of the Island of Sakhalin.
5. An indemnity covering the cost of the war.
6. A limitation of Russian naval strength in the Far East.
7. Fishing rights for Japanese in the Pacific territorial waters of Russia.

[3] *Ibid.* p. 406.

Although to the Japanese, regarding themselves as victors, these demands appeared reasonable, they conflicted seriously with the Tsar's command to Witte that he should cede no territory and pay no indemnity. In fact, Russia refused to admit that she was the defeated power. At this point, when the negotiations had reached a deadlock, President Roosevelt again intervened. He warned the Japanese of the dangers of prolonging the war for monetary and territorial considerations. To Russia, he proposed that Japan restore the northern half of Sakhalin, and that an indemnity be paid by Russia for its return and for the expenses of Russian prisoners. The Tsar was moved. On August 28, Witte delivered an ultimatum: Russia would cede southern Sakhalin to Japan, but she would pay no indemnity. On August 29, the Japanese accepted this settlement, and the Treaty of Portsmouth was signed September 5.

The Treaty of Portsmouth was a document of the utmost importance, providing the basic point of departure in the international relations of Manchuria for many years. By Article 2, Russia acknowledged "that Japan possesses in Korea paramount political, military and economical interests, and agreed neither to obstruct nor interfere with the measures of guidance, protection and control which the Imperial Government of Japan may find it necessary to take in Korea." This, the first objective of Japanese policy, was thus fully attained. Article 3 provided for the complete restoration of Manchuria "to the exclusive administration of China," excepting, of course, the Russian leasehold and the railway zone. And Russia declared that in Manchuria she possessed no "territorial advantages or preferential or exclusive concessions in impairment of Chinese sovereignty or inconsistent with the principle of equal opportunity." By Article 4, Japan and Russia agreed to a self-denying ordinance "not to obstruct any general measures common to all countries, which China may take for the development of the commerce and industry of Manchuria." Under this pious and ineffective generalization, Japan was later to be accused of illegally obstructing foreign enterprise in Manchuria. Articles 5 and 6 contained Russia's consent (upon the approval of China) to the transfer to Japan of the Russian leasehold (the southern section of the Liaotung peninsula, Port Arthur, and Dalny), of the southern section of the Chinese Eastern Railway (Changchun to Port Arthur), and also of the coal mines in the area that were owned by or worked by the Russians for the railway. The two powers agreed, in Article 7, "to exploit their respective railways in Manchuria exclusively for commercial and industrial purposes and in no wise for strategic purposes with the exception of the railways in the Liaotung leased territory."

Additional articles ceded to Japan the southern half of the Island of Sakhalin, guaranteed Japan fishing rights in Russian waters, and provided for payment of expenses for Russian prisoners. Supplementary agreements provided for the evacuation of Manchuria by April 15, 1907. The Russian railway was to be turned over to Japan by August 1, 1906. After the troops had been withdrawn, each power might maintain railway guards up to the number of fifteen per kilometer. This was a "right" which the Russians had assumed previously without treaty provisions. It was now to be continued, not by the consent of China but by agreement between Japan and Russia.

The Treaty of Portsmouth provided that the transfer to Japan of the Russian leasehold, railway, and other rights should be conditional upon the consent of China. This provision was a formal recognition of Chinese sovereignty in Manchuria. By it, China was permitted to "save face." Neither Russia nor Japan had requested Chinese permission to fight the war on Manchu soil. It was, therefore, remarkable that they should now seek Chinese approval of the settlement. To Japan, however, the opportunity thus afforded to negotiate with China was of importance, for it enabled the government in Tokyo to adjust by direct negotiation a number of questions arising from the war—specifically, Japan's newly acquired position in south Manchuria. When, therefore, the Treaty of Portsmouth was ratified promptly by both powers in November, Japan sent Baron Komura to Peking to negotiate. These conversations resulted in a formal treaty (December 22, 1905), an additional agreement, and, finally, secret protocols of importance. The Treaty, which was signed by Komura and Yuan Shih-kai, was brief. China agreed to "all the transfers and assignments made by Russia to Japan" in the Treaty of Portsmouth, while Japan agreed "so far as circumstances permit to conform to the original agreements concluded between China and Russia."

In the additional agreements (made the same day as the treaty), Japan secured China's consent to the opening of sixteen cities and towns in Manchuria to international residence and trade. China had previously agreed in commercial treaties with Japan and the United States in 1903 to open a number of Manchurian cities, but she had been blocked by Russia's occupation of the provinces. Japan agreed to withdraw her troops and railway guards "in the event of Russia agreeing to the withdrawal of her railway guards," but this was conditional on the restoration of peace in Manchuria, and was to be only at a time when "China shall have become herself capable of affording full protection to the lives and property of foreigners." Japan was granted the right to improve, so that it might be suitable for commercial use, the military railway line which, during the war, she had constructed from Antung on the Korean border, to Mukden. Maintenance of this railway was to extend over a period of fifteen years. At the end of the period, the line was to be sold to China. Finally, it was agreed by China that a joint stock company of Japanese and Chinese capitalists should be formed to exploit forest wealth on the right bank of the Yalu River, the region in which Russian activity had been so conspicuous on the eve of the war.

The "Secret Protocols"

Lastly, the Chino-Japanese settlement of December, 1905, included the so-called "Secret Protocols." Of these, the most important clause stated:

The Chinese Government engages, for the purpose of protecting the interests of the South Manchuria Railway, not to construct, prior to the recovery by it of the said railway, any main line in the neighborhood of and parallel to that railway, or any branch line which might be prejudicial to the interests of the above-mentioned railway.

For many years this clause was a subject of serious dispute between Japan and China and an occasion for strained relations between Japan and certain western states. Since the Protocols were not published at the time by either China or Japan, their validity was frequently questioned. In reality, the Protocols did not constitute a formal treaty. They were contained in the minutes of the Peking Conference of December 4, 1905. Although it is debatable whether they constituted a binding commitment on the part of China, there is no doubt that they did constitute "a declaration or statement of intention on the part of the Chinese plenipotentiaries."[4] The manner in which these Protocols gave rise to serious international friction will be discussed in subsequent chapters.

Anglo-Japanese Alliance Renewed

Another feature of the far eastern settlement of 1905 was the revision and renewal of the Anglo-Japanese Alliance, effected August 12. The pledge of Korean independence, which had appeared in the first alliance, was discarded. In its place, the paramount political, military, and economic interests of Japan in Korea were recognized. Japan was accorded the right to take such steps of guidance, control, and protection as she might think essential to protect these interests. At the same

[4] League of Nations, *Report of the Commission of Inquiry* (Lytton Report), pp. 44-45.

time, she was to observe the policy of the open door. There was nothing in the agreement to define accurately just what that vague and abused phrase might mean, and, since in the same agreement Great Britain had recognized Japan's "paramount" interest, the open door was not likely to mean much of anything. The position of the United States with respect to Korea was similar to that of England. In July, before the Japanese and the English had renewed their alliance, Secretary Taft visited with Premier Katsura in Tokyo. Their conversations, embodied in a memorandum, contained:

(1) a disclaimer by Japan of any hostile intentions as regards the Philippines, (2) a proposal for an informal understanding with the United States which would make her in certain respects a silent friend to the Anglo-Japanese alliance, and (3) the view expressed by Secretary Taft that Japanese troops might set up Japanese suzerainty in Korea in such fashion that Korean foreign affairs should be under Japanese control.[5]

In conclusion, it may be emphasized again that the group of agreements and treaties which closed the Russo-Japanese War were soon to prove of vital significance. For the time being, Japan was relieved of the Russian menace. Her control over Korea was soon to be complete. In south Manchuria, she had fallen heir to the Russian sphere of influence, with all the preferential privilege which that term implied. In the aggressive development of this sphere she was, however, to encounter the persistent opposition of the Chinese. The problems that arose were intensified by the very nature of the Portsmouth and the Peking Treaties. Although the former treaty was remarkable by reason of the fact that it was based on negotiations and embodied a compromise, its language was frequently general, and the principles that it expressed were often vague. A stipulation, such as Article 4, by which Japan and Russia engaged not to obstruct any general measures, common to all countries, which China might take for the development of the commerce

---

[5] A. L. P. Dennis, *op. cit.* pp. 416-417.

and industry of Manchuria, was a "sonorous nothing"—a masterpiece of verbal trickery.

SELECTED BIBLIOGRAPHY

R. H. Akagi, *Japan's Foreign Relations* (Tokyo: 1936), chs. 9-10. K. Adachi, "Japan's Elder Statesmen and the Peace," in *Review of Reviews,* Oct. 1905. Nagao Ariga, *La Guerre Russo-Japonaise* (Paris: 1908). G. A. Ballard, *The Influence of the Sea on the Political History of Japan* (New York: 1921), chs. 7-9. J. B. Bishop, *Theodore Roosevelt and His Time,* 2 vols. (New York: 1920), vol. 1, chs. 31-32. *British Documents on the Origins of the War,* vol. 4, chs. 23-24, the latter on the Anglo-Japanese agreement of 1905. *The Cambridge Modern History* (New York: 1910), vol. 12, ch. 19. M. R. Coolidge, *Chinese Immigration* (New York: 1909), ch. 23, the anti-American boycott of 1905. A. Cheradame, *Le Monde et la Guerre Russo-Japonaise* (Paris: 1906). Tyler Dennett, *Roosevelt and the Russo-Japanese War* (Garden City: 1925). Tyler Dennett, *John Hay* (New York: 1934). E. T. S. Dugdale, *German Diplomatic Documents, 1871-1914,* 4 vols. (London: 1930), vol. 3, chs. 14 and 16. Edwin A. Falk, *Togo and the Rise of Japanese Sea Power* (New York: 1936), chs. 13-21. Ippei Fukuda, *New Sketches of Men and Life* (Tokyo: 1934), see the chapter on Admiral Togo. Amos S. Hershey, *The International Law and Diplomacy of the Russo-Japanese War* (New York: 1906). A. M. De Wolfe Howe, *George von Lengerke Meyer* (New York: 1920). Shushi Hsu, *China and Her Political Entity* (New York: 1926). U. Kobayashi, *War and Armament Loans of Japan* (New York: 1922), ch. 4. F. McCormick, *The Tragedy of Russia in Pacific Asia* (New York: 1907). G. Ono, *War and Armament Expenditures of Japan* (New York: 1922). G. Ogawa, *Expenditures of the Russo-Japanese War* (New York: 1923), pt. 2, the economic effects of the war. A. Novikoff-Pribov, *Tsushima* (London: 1936). Francis Rey, *La Guerre Russo-Japonaise* (Paris: 1911). R. R. Rosen, *Forty Years of Diplomacy,* 2 vols. (New York: 1922), vol. 1, chs. 23-24. F. E. Smith and N. W. Sibley, *International Law as Interpreted during the Russo-Japanese War* (Boston: 1905). Tatsuji Takeuchi, *War and Diplomacy in the Japanese Empire* (Garden City: 1935), ch. 12. S. Takahashi, *International Law Applied to the Russo-Japanese War* (New York: 1908). H. E. Wildes, *Social Currents in Japan* (Chicago: 1927), ch. 5 on press censorship.

CHAPTER XXIII

Manchuria after the Russo-Japanese War
1905-1910

THE Russo-Japanese War, viewed through conservative Japanese eyes, was a successful venture. By it Japan's undisputed influence in Korea gained recognition, while in Manchuria, Russia surrendered that part of her sphere of influence lying south of Changchun. Yet the war was in no sense a solution of the so-called Manchurian problem. The Manchus had again revealed their inability to defend the Empire. Two great imperialistic powers had fought a war on the choicest provinces of the state. The fame of Manchuria as an economic frontier awaiting exploitation spread not merely to Japan but to imperialists in Europe and America. South Manchuria, where Japan held the former Russian leasehold and railway, commanded particular attention. Its geographical position made it accessible to all the great maritime trading powers. Furthermore, since Japan had fought to preserve the open door and the integrity of China in Manchuria, the assumption was that her newly acquired sphere of influence would be thrown open to all. By this happy prospect British and American merchants and industrialists were especially attracted. Financial imperialists everywhere saw in the defeat of Russia the opening of a great market and the opportunity for greater profits in south Manchuria.

The narrative of Manchuria's international position in the years 1905 to 1910 is extremely complex. So many interrelating factors were involved that simplification results inevitably in generalizations, which at times are inadequate. Some elements

405

of clarity will be gained, however, in treating the subject under
the following arbitrary divisions: (1) the position of Japan, (2)
the position of Russia, (3) Chinese administration in Manchuria, and (4) the policies of western powers, in particular,
Great Britain and the United States.

The Position of Japan

By acquiring the former Russian leasehold in Liaotung, the
railway from Port Arthur to Changchun, and the mining and
other rights pertaining thereto, Japan fell heir in south Manchuria to the special position which previously Russia had enjoyed. Accordingly, she began to develop what was commonly
referred to as a sphere of influence, similar in many respects to
the spheres of European powers in various regions of China
(see chapter 17). From the strategic point of view, her most
valuable asset in Manchuria was the Liaotung leased territory,
containing as it did the naval fortress of Port Arthur (Ryojun)
and the commercial port of Dalny, now to be called Dairen.
To this territory the name of Kwantung province was given,
and an administration, known as the Government General of
Kwantung, was established on August 1, 1906. It was headed
by a governor general, who, in addition to civil administrative
powers, was to protect the newly acquired railway. Since he
was to command the Kwantung garrison, he was to be selected
from among generals or lieutenant generals of the Japanese
army. Appointed by the Emperor, on the advice of the Prime
Minister, he was, nevertheless, responsible to the Minister of
War and the general staff for military administration, mobilization, and tactics. Thus, under a single head were combined
the civil and the military authority in the province, a system
which prevailed until 1919, when a civil administration under
a governor was set up. Under this new administration, the
governor did not control the Kwantung garrison, but he did
control the police in the leased territory and the railway zone.

The management of the railroad lines acquired by Japan from Russia was entrusted by the Japanese government to a company formed for this special purpose and known as the South Manchuria Railway Company. This was a joint stock

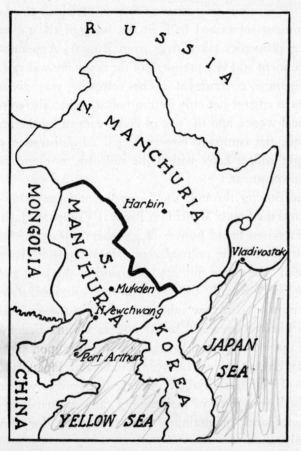

Sketch Map Indicating Approximate Line Dividing South from North Manchuria After the Russo-Japanese War.

company controlled by the Japanese government, which held one half of the shares of capital stock and reserved the right to appoint the principal officers. The railroads over which it assumed control in August, 1906, included the main line from Dairen (the former Russian port of Dalny) to Changchun; the military line from Antung, on the Korean border, to Mukden; and branch lines to Port Arthur, Newchwang, Fushun, and Yentai. Only the governments of Japan and China and the subjects of these countries might become shareholders. Original capitalization was 200,000,000 yen, of which the Japanese government subscribed half, in the form of the railway and mining properties taken over from Russia. Appointment of the president and vice-president of the company was reserved to the Japanese government. The company was given wide powers to engage not only in transportation but also in mining, electrical works, and the sale of goods carried by the lines. In addition, the company possessed civil administrative powers. It might collect taxes within the railroad zone and establish local government.

Functioning through the Government General of Kwantung and the South Manchuria Railway Company, Japan after 1905 exercised broad powers of jurisdiction both in the leased territory and in the railroad zone. In Kwantung, Russia had possessed "the entire military command of the land and naval forces [and] equally the supreme civil administration," and these rights Japan now inherited. Within the railroad zone, Japan likewise exercised broad powers of jurisdiction, which rested upon the original Russian agreements, upon supplementary agreements made between China and Japan, and upon rights of extraterritoriality. Among the powers which Japan exercised were those of maintaining railway guards to protect the lines and maintaining ordinary police for municipal administration.

In addition to these extensive powers which she acquired after 1905, her position in Manchuria was strengthened also by a number of railroad, mining, lumbering, cable, and telegraph agreements with China. In 1907, the military railway from Mukden to Hsinmintun (the northern section of the Peking-Mukden line), which had been built during the war by the Japanese army, was sold to China. The latter undertook to reconstruct the line, borrowing half of the funds from the South Manchuria Railway Company. In the same year, the Chinese government agreed to borrow from the South Manchuria Railway Company half the capital necessary for construction of an eighty-mile railroad from Changchun to Kirin. The line did not prove profitable, and China's failure to meet her payments was a contributing cause to later friction. A third railway agreement concerned the Antung-Mukden line, a narrow-gauge military railway which the Japanese had constructed during the war. In 1905, Japan acquired the right to reconstruct and operate the line. Since reconstruction of the road was not completed by Japan within the time agreed upon, final arrangements for the project were not completed until August 9, 1909, after delivery of an ultimatum at Peking. The line was finished in November, 1911. Further agreements between China and Japan defined more specifically the circumstances under which the latter might work the famous coal mines at

South Manchuria Railway Co.

Open-Cut Coal Mine of the Fushun Colliery, Fushun, Near Mukden, Manchuria. It is one explanation for the interest of China, Japan, and Russia in Manchuria.

Fushun, Yentai, and Penhsihu. The chief lumbering agreement reached between China and Japan in this period provided for a Sino-Japanese joint stock company "for the exploitation of the forests in the regions on the right bank of the River Yalu," which forms a part of the boundary between south Manchuria and Korea. Japan also acquired the right to connect the Kwantung leased territory by submarine cable with the port of Chefoo, in Shantung province. The Russians had previously laid a cable there, which the Japanese had cut during the war. China also agreed to connect her land telegraph offices at such points as Changchun, Mukden, Newchwang, and Antung with Japenese telegraph offices at these places within the railway zones.

From the foregoing brief summary, it is evident that Japan, as a result of the Russo-Japanese War, acquired in south Manchuria specific rights and from them a distinct interest in the region. In railroads and their subsidiary enterprises, she acquired an economic interest; in the former Russian leasehold, she acquired a political interest. The presence of the Kwantung army indicated the need or the desire to protect these enterprises, and thus she acquired the presence of a strategic or military interest.

The Position of Russia

While Japan was a newcomer to Manchuria, with special interests after 1905, Russia had long been established there. Her position dated back to the secret Russo-Chinese Alliance of 1896 and the railroad agreement for the construction of the Chinese Eastern line. These rights were supplemented in 1898 by the lease of Liaotung and the right to join Harbin and Port Arthur by rail. By the Treaty of Portsmouth, it was these latter holdings that Russia lost. In north Manchuria (the area lying north of Changchun), she retained all rights attained by the earlier agreements. She still held the Chinese Eastern main line and its southern branch from Harbin to Changchun.

Within this railroad zone, the Russians exercised virtually complete civil administration, including the powers of taxation and police jurisdiction. After the War, the Russians set up a municipal council for the administration of Harbin (the chief railway center on the line), basing their action on the original railway contract of 1896, by which they were accorded absolute and exclusive administration of the railway lands. Some modifications of this system were made in 1909, when, after protests from China and other powers, the Russians agreed to elected councils, in the choosing of which Chinese and non-Russian foreigners were to enjoy equal rights. In 1907, Russia turned over to China the telegraph lines in north Manchuria outside the railroad zone, which had previously been operated by the railway company. A year later, Russia was granted certain timber concessions in Heilungkiang province.

In brief, although Russia still retained in north Manchuria after 1905 commercial interests of the highest importance, her activities, for the time being at least, lacked the spectacular quality attached to events in the Japanese sphere. This may be explained by a number of considerations. By their defeat, Russians temporarily lost interest in the Far East. The loss of the leasehold and the ice-free port of Dalny, together with the timbering and other concessions in south Manchuria, deprived the Russian sphere of its most valuable assets and, with them, any hope of controlling north China. The policy of Bezobrazov and his following was discredited, while at home, in European Russia, revolution had already threatened the dynasty. Contrasting with this Russian reverse was the vigorous entry of Japan into Manchuria and the consequent rise of Japanese influence in Peking.

Chinese Administration in Manchuria

In Manchuria, the special rights and the influence of Russia after 1898 and of Japan and Russia after 1905 were so great that the position of China, the sovereign power, in name at least, has sometimes been ignored. Yet Manchuria was the homeland of the Manchu Dynasty and, as such, had enjoyed a privileged position since the middle of the seventeenth century. Emigration from China proper to the three Manchurian provinces was usually prohibited and always strictly controlled. The prov-

South Manchuria Railway Co.

PUBLIC SCHOOL FOR CHINESE MAINTAINED BY THE SOUTH MANCHURIA RAILWAY COMPANY AT DAIREN.

inces were governed by a military administration exclusively Manchu in custom and personnel. Three military governors exercised not only military but also civil authority. In China proper, a governor was rarely, if ever, appointed to office in the province of his birth; in Manchuria these positions were held by Manchus. The Russo-Japanese War was responsible for a major revision of this system. In 1907, the military governors were replaced by civil governors under the control of a viceroy or governor general, in the hope that the change would render Manchuria more readily amenable to control from Peking, whose policy at the time was designed to hold both Russia and

Japan to a rigid—and a Chinese—interpretation of their treaty rights. After 1912, when the Manchu Dynasty gave place to the Chinese Republic, both a civil and a military governor were appointed to each of the Manchurian provinces. When in later years the authority of the Republican government failed, the military governors in Manchuria, as in other provinces of China, became the real, and to a large extent the irresponsible, rulers of the land.

The Powers and Manchuria, 1905-1910

Even before the smoke of battle had cleared in Manchuria, the homeland from which the Manchus had imposed their rule upon China in 1644, the forces of international economic politics played with reckless vigor. The six years from 1905 to 1910 witnessed in Manchuria a series of international contests whose political implications were at times of a most serious character. In particular, they were to have far-reaching results upon the policies and the relationships of Japan and the United States.

The Plans of Harriman

During the autumn of 1905, E. H. Harriman, of American railway fame, visited Japan, where he met the Prime Minister, Count Katsura. At the time, Harriman was intent on acquiring a round-the-world railroad and steamship service. To complete this ambition, he was seeking to secure trackage rights over the Trans-Siberian system and to buy from Russia and Japan the Chinese Eastern and the South Manchuria Railway. Katsura was disposed favorably to Harriman's plan and, in October, 1905, concluded with the American magnate a memorandum preliminary to effecting the sale of the line from Port Arthur to Changchun. The plan called for a syndicate which would share equally with the Japanese government in the ownership and operation of the road. It is evident, therefore, that as late

as October, 1905, the Katsura Ministry had no intention of excluding foreign capital from its newly acquired railroad. This
point is significant, for it has been charged frequently that in
1905 Japan was acting on the basis of a long-established policy
to create in south Manchuria an exclusive Japanese sphere.

While Katsura and Harriman were thus paving the way for

South Manchuria Railway Co.

ANSHAN STEEL WORKS OPERATED BY THE SOUTH MANCHURIA RAILWAY COMPANY.

the entry of American capital into Manchuria, the Japanese
public was reviling its government, Baron Komura, its chief
plenipotentiary at Portsmouth, and President Roosevelt, because these had forced upon the victor nation a peace without
indemnity. The rejection of the treaty had been demanded by
mass meetings, offices of newspapers that defended it were
destroyed, and rioting in Tokyo resulted in more than 1,000
casualties and many arrests. Into this atmosphere, charged with
popular indignation, Baron Komura returned on October 16,
entering Tokyo under heavy guard. The government had
already decided to ratify the treaty despite its unpopularity.

Facing public criticism, Komura realized that the Katsura-Harriman plan could not be accepted. He argued that, since China had not yet consented to the transfer of the line to Japan, the government had no power to dispose of its interests. Furthermore, he reminded the cabinet that the railroad was the only tangible financial reward that Japan had gained in the war. Was it necessary or good policy, he asked, to hand over fifty per cent of this asset to American capital? The government made its decision accordingly, and notified Harriman that the plans contemplated in his preliminary memorandum would be carried no further. Although in the United States there were charges that Japan had broken faith, the biographer of Harriman later wrote:

In this thwarting of Mr. Harriman's plans there seems to have been no intentional breach of faith on the part of the Tokyo authorities.[1]

Japan and the Open Door Policy

The year 1906 opened with a change of government in Japan. When the Treaty of Portsmouth and the subsequent Treaty of Peking had been concluded, the Katsura Ministry resigned and was replaced by a government headed by Marquis Saionji. With regard to Manchuria, the new ministry formulated a policy of respecting the sovereignty of China and the principle of equal opportunity. But, concurrently with the adoption of this policy, reports reached London and Washington to the effect that British and American business was virtually excluded from south Manchuria. The chief complaints came from the British-American Tobacco Company, whose agents asserted that the market was closed in areas occupied by the Japanese army, where martial law still prevailed. American tobacco agents reported that they were unable to enter Manchuria at Newchwang, though Japanese agents were allowed

---

[1] George Kennan, *E. H. Harriman, A. Biography,* 2 vols. Houghton Mifflin Company, Boston, 1922. Vol. II, p. 19.

free access. The situation was called to the attention of Japan by Secretary Root in March, 1906:

> We learn [he said] through our agents in China that the action of the Japanese authorities in Manchuria during Japanese occupation is so generally directed towards establishing Japanese commercial interests in the principal towns, and toward acquiring property rights for Japanese in all available quarters as to leave little or no opening for other foreign trade by the time the territory is evacuated.[2]

The Japanese government explained the situation by calling attention to difficulties involved in withdrawing an army of several hundred thousand men. It reaffirmed its purpose to maintain the open door for trade and to remove military restrictions from commercial ports at the earliest possible time. That this had always remained the intent of the Japanese government was supported by the reports of the American Consul General at Newchwang as early as February.

By June, 1906, the situation was clarified somewhat. The civilian wing of the Saionji government having gained ascendency over the military, the American Ambassador wrote from Tokyo that the open door in south Manchuria would prevail. At the same time, he called attention to the harm that had already been done to American-Japanese relations:

> . . . it will occur to any thoughtful person that delay in such matters is very dangerous. Delay means an opportunity for the manufacture and circulation of rumors and the growth of a hostile public opinion in the West, the final issue thus being that when the liberal policy, inevitable from the first, is adopted, the Japanese will be said to have yielded to pressure rather than to the dictates of their own free judgment and volition.[3]

Rumors of Japan's "closed door" policy were, in fact, increasing. In June, a commission of merchants, representing the American commercial interests of Shanghai, visited south Manchuria to investigate and report on Japan's policy. It was

---

[2] United States, *Foreign Relations*, 1906. Pt. I, pp. 171-172.
[3] *Ibid.* pp. 194-195.

assumed that the findings of this body would reveal flagrant violations by Japan of the open door policy. In contrast with these expectations, the commission reported to W. W. Rockhill, the American Minister at Peking, that it could find no evidence of interference by the Japanese with China's customs administration or with the ordinary course of trade. Summarizing all

South Manchuria Railway Co.

DOUBLE TRACKS ON SOUTH MANCHURIA RAILWAY LINES FROM DAIREN TO CHANGCHUN.

the charges that had been made by British and American commercial agents in Manchuria, the commission concluded:

> After a most comprehensive inquiry it is most difficult, if not impossible, to offer any satisfactory evidence to substantiate the theory that the Japanese Government, through the instrumentality of either its military or civil authorities, is at present purposely interfering with or placing any obstacles in the path of other nations for the industrial exploitation of this important part of the Chinese Empire.[4]

Japan was thus absolved of the charge of violating the open door, but, as Ambassador Wright in Japan had observed, the

---

[4] *Ibid.* pp. 209-212.

damage to American-Japanese relations had already been done. The evidence produced by the Shanghai commission never reached the American public; it was tucked away in the archives of the State Department, to be published many years later. In fact, as Minister Rockhill pointed out, China, and not Japan, was responsible for any failure of the open door to operate successfully in Manchuria during the years 1905 to 1907. During 1906 and 1907, the Japanese, the British, and the Americans urged the Chinese government to establish custom houses at the new Manchurian ports, yet it was not until July, 1907, that China took action.

The Anti-Japanese Crusade in California

Concurrent with the open door controversy in Manchuria, there arose in California another crisis in American-Japanese relations. The occasion was the rapid increase in the number of Japanese immigrants reaching San Francisco. The ideas of many Californians respecting oriental immigrants had been shaped two or three decades earlier in the campaigns of heartless violence to which the Chinese immigrants had been subjected. The Chinese, having been excluded effectively (see chapter 13), were no longer a problem, but the same attitude remained to confront their successors, the Japanese. Early in 1905, the anti-Japanese agitation had already grown to alarming proportions. In May, President Roosevelt wrote to Henry Cabot Lodge:

Meanwhile, I am utterly disgusted at the manifestations which have begun to appear on the Pacific slope in favor of excluding the Japanese exactly as the Chinese are excluded. The California State Legislature and various other bodies have acted in the worst possible taste and in the most offensive manner to Japan.[5]

The demand for Japanese exclusion was supported by organized labor and also by a growing section of the public at

---

[5] Thomas A. Bailey, *Theodore Roosevelt and the Japanese-American Crises*. Stanford University Press, Stanford University, California, 1934. p. 3.

large, which, during the negotiations at Portsmouth, had shifted its sympathies from Japan to Russia. Americans who had originally looked upon Japan with curiosity and then admiration were beginning to view her with jealousy and suspicion. These sentiments of hatred were heightened by the arrival in the United States in 1905 of a group of American war correspondents who, not having been permitted to see much of the war in the Far East, now proposed "to get their knives into Japan." [6] In May, 1905, the Japanese and Korean Exclusion League was formed in San Francisco, and in little more than a year it boasted a membership of more than 78,000. Yet despite these manifestations, when, in 1906, San Francisco was devastated by earthquake and fire, the Japanese government and Red Cross contributed to the stricken city $246,000—more than the contribution of all other foreign nations combined. In October of the same year, the San Francisco Board of Education passed a resolution ordering all Chinese, Japanese, and Korean children to be placed in a separate oriental public school. Although many excuses were given for this action, the fact remained that "the Japanese children were set apart because the whites were prejudiced against them, and the root of this prejudice, at least in San Francisco, appears to have been the belief that coolie labor was thwarting the work of the unions and lowering the American standard of living." [7]

Against this discriminatory treatment, the Japanese government protested in the most dignified and restrained tone, and its views were shared in large part by President Roosevelt. Having no intention of permitting San Francisco to plunge the nation into a war with Japan, he characterized the action of the board of education in a message to Congress, as "a wicked absurdity." Yet it was not until the President had used vigorous action that the board's order was rescinded (March 13, 1907). The price of this settlement was a pledge given by

---

[6] *Ibid.*, p. 8, quoting *Japan Weekly Mail*, Oct. 27, 1906. p. 542.
[7] *Ibid.* p. 43.

Japan to co-operate with the United States in controlling immigration. It was this arrangement that later came to be known as "the gentleman's agreement." Under its terms, Japan would no longer issue passports to laborers desiring to emigrate to the United States. With this settlement, a second crisis in American-Japanese relations had passed.

The Hsinmintun-Fakumen Railway

Meanwhile, in Manchuria, other international difficulties appeared. As the reader has seen, the first complaint directed against Japanese policy there concerned the so-called open door in trade. The second was a challenge to Japan's policy respecting railway construction. Late in 1907, a British construction firm undertook to build a railroad some fifty miles in length, for the Chinese government, from Hsinmintun (west of Mukden) northward to the town of Fakumen, provision also being made to extend the line to Tsitsihar, north of the Chinese Eastern. Funds for the Hsinmintun-Fakumen construction were to be provided by a loan from the British and Chinese corporation to the Chinese government. This plan had been under consideration by the Chinese for some years, but in 1907, when the agreement was signed, south Manchuria had become in fact a sphere of Japanese influence over which China no longer exerted unqualified control. It was not surprising, then, that during 1907 the Japanese government protested vigorously against construction of the line, on the ground that it would violate the article in the Peking Protocols of 1905 prohibiting parallel and competing lines. The involved diplomatic correspondence that ensued between China and Japan revolved principally about the question of whether or not the proposed railroad, which would lie within thirty miles of the South Manchuria Railway and parallel to it, was in fact a parallel and competing line, and on this question, the two states naturally disagreed. Japan also based her protest against the line on the

Russo-Chinese agreement of April 8, 1902, by which China was pledged to consult Russia if railroad extensions were contemplated north of Hsinmintun. The Japanese claimed that by the Treaty of Portsmouth they had fallen heir to these Russian rights.

Faced with these Japanese protests, the British financial and construction interests involved appealed to the British govern-

South Manchuria Railway Co.

DAIREN. The wharves and harbor of Japan's great seaport in the Kwantung leased territory, Manchuria.

ment; the Foreign Office, however, refused to support its nationals against Japan. Nor was this surprising. The British had surrendered Manchuria as a field for railroad finance to Russia in 1899, they were allied with Japan under the second Anglo-Japanese Alliance, and they accepted Japan's interpretation of the 1905 protocols. While Japan's interpretation in this case was undoubtedly justified by reason of the geographical location of the proposed line, it is also to be observed that the wording of the 1905 protocol left the Japanese free to place almost any definition they thought fit on the phrase, "parallel and competing lines." As a result, then, of the 1907 negotiations, Japan prevented construction of the Hsinmintun-Fakumen railroad, thereby strengthening her claim to a monopoly in railroad building in south Manchuria.

This Japanese policy was subject to severe criticism both in England and in the United States. It was labeled a violation of the commercial open door enunciated by Hay, with which, as a matter of fact, it had nothing whatsoever to do. It was likewise termed a violation of the Portsmouth Treaty, wherein Japan and Russia had agreed "not to obstruct any general measure common to all countries, which China may take for the development of the commerce and industry of Manchuria." Whatever the framers of this ambiguous article may have meant, it is clear that in 1907 Japan did not regard a loan and a contract bestowed by China on private British interests as a "general measure common to all countries." Perhaps the Japanese were conscious, as early as 1907, that Willard Straight, American Consul General at Mukden, was advocating the introduction of British and American capital "to check the Japanese in Manchuria." The Hsinmintun-Fakumen incident was officially closed in September, 1909, when China agreed that "in the event of its undertaking to construct a railway between Hsinmintun and Fakumen, it shall arrange previously with the Government of Japan."

Russia and Japan

The year 1907 also witnessed a *rapprochement* between the erstwhile enemies, Japan and Russia. During July, the two powers concluded an open convention agreeing to respect the *status quo* in the Far East, and a secret treaty giving a more definite boundary to their respective Manchurian spheres of influence and complete freedom for each in financing railroads and telegraphs. By this means the two powers sought to give a more precise definition to the term "sphere of influence" and mutually to protect their interests therein.[8]

The decision of the Japanese and the Russian governments to forget past differences and to work out amicably the development of their respective spheres was both hastened and intensified after 1905 by the policies of the Chinese government and of American and British financial interests. Harriman's original plan to buy the South Manchuria Railway, the charges that the open door was being violated, and the efforts to put through the Hsinmintun-Fakumen Railway—all these served to convince the Japanese that Chinese and western interests were intent on destroying what the Japanese regarded as their newly won sphere. In China, the so-called spheres of influence rested primarily on the right claimed by the sphere-holding power either to priority or to a monopoly in the financing and constructing of railways. It was on this principle that Japan's sphere was to be challenged repeatedly, though unsuccessfully, in the years 1907 to 1910.

Willard Straight and Manchuria

Since nationals of all the great powers were interested in the prospects for exploitation that Manchuria appeared to offer after 1905, it became the settled policy of China to encourage foreign investment, presumedly in the hope that western finance would effectively destroy Japan's special position. The Hsinmintun-Fakumen Railway concession was China's first step in this direction. Concurrently, the Peking government invited E. H. Harriman to finance a Manchurian loan of $20,000,000. The invitation, even though it could not be accepted because of the financial panic of 1907, served to renew Harriman's interest in buying the Manchurian railways from

---

[8] For text of the Russo-Japanese secret treaty, see E. B. Price, *The Russo-Japanese Treaties of 1907-1916 Concerning Manchuria and Mongolia.* Johns Hopkins Press, Baltimore, 1933. pp. 107-108.

Japan and Russia. In the following year, the proposal to secure
a Manchurian loan from American financiers was revived by
the Viceroy of Manchuria, with the active sympathy, if not the
support, of Willard Straight, the American Consul General at
Mukden. The plan contemplated formation of a Manchurian
bank in which American financiers would enjoy more than a

South Manchuria Railway Co.

A KAOLIANG FIELD IN MANCHURIA. Kaoliang provides food for Manchuria's peasants and refuge for its bandits.

passing interest. When preliminary arrangements had been
completed, Straight returned to the United States at the request
of Harriman, followed closely by Tang Shao-yi as the special
representative of China. Tang's mission was supposedly to
thank the United States for remitting a portion of the Boxer
indemnity. In reality, he was to conclude the Manchurian loan
and to form a triple entente of China, Germany, and the United
States.[9]

---

[9] J. G. Reid, *The Manchu Abdication and the Powers, 1908-1912.* University of
California, Berkeley, 1935. p. 16.

The Root-Takahira Notes

The proposals which Tang placed before Elihu Root called for an enormous loan, to be applied for various purposes, in China proper as well as Manchuria, and to which other banking groups besides the Americans might be admitted. But the troubled state of China's politics made agreement difficult, if not impossible, and the American government was by no means inclined to challenge the Japanese so directly. On November 30, 1908, Secretary Root and Japanese Ambassador Takahira exchanged notes. The policies of the two governments were declared to be maintenance of the *status quo* in the Pacific and defense of the open door in China. Each would respect the territorial possessions of the other and support by pacific means the independence and integrity of China and the principle of equal opportunity. The Root-Takahira exchange was undoubtedly intended as an answer to China's efforts to embroil the United States and Japan in Manchuria. Although Tang Shao-yi was in Washington, he was not informed of it until noon of the day on which the notes were formally signed. For the time being at least, the United States government would not openly challenge Japan's special position in Manchuria. Another crisis in American-Japanese relations had passed. Still another was soon to appear.

The Chinchow-Aigun Railroad

Late in the summer of 1909, Willard Straight returned to China, not as a representative of the State Department but as agent of an American banking group composed of J. P. Morgan and Company, Kuhn, Loeb and Company, the National City Bank of New York, and the First National Bank. Straight's objective was to secure from China a concession for a Manchurian railway to be financed by American capital. If such a concession could be secured, it would not only provide a broad field for American investment but would also smash

Japan's special position in the south. The Chinese readily granted the concession. They had already used Straight for political purposes while he was American Consul General at Mukden, and they now welcomed an opportunity to allow American capital to destroy the Japanese sphere in Manchuria. Accordingly, a preliminary contract was signed October 2, 1909. By it the provincial authorities of Manchuria agreed to the construction of a railroad from Chinchow, in south Manchuria, via Tsitsihar, to Aigun, a Chinese town on the Amur River. Funds necessary for this railroad were to be borrowed from the American banking group, and the railroad itself was to be the security. Construction was to be undertaken by the British firm of Pauling and Company, which had previously secured the contract for the Hsinmintun-Fakumen Railway. Management was to be in the hands of a railway company composed of Chinese, Americans, and British. This plan for the Chinchow-Aigun Railway was a sequel to the original Harriman plan to buy the Manchurian lines from Russia and Japan, the Chino-British project to build the Hsinmintun-Fakumen Railway, and the proposal to establish an American-financed Manchurian bank. The failure of these three projects had not discouraged either Harriman or Straight. The latter, in particular, had convinced himself that American capital was to be the instrument of China's political salvation. However, the Chinchow-Aigun line would cut directly across the Japanese and Russian spheres, and the Japanese would regard it as a serious threat to the earning power of their South Manchuria Railway. For these reasons, the preliminary contract secured by Straight and the Pauling Company, in October, 1909, threatened political complications of the most serious kind.

The Knox Neutralization Proposal

It was at this point that the American State Department, taking notice of the negotiations between the Manchurian authorities and the American bankers, proposed a much broader solution of Manchurian railway affairs. Secretary Knox suggested that those powers which were pledged to that vaguely understood principle called the open door (the United States, Japan, Russia, Great Britain, Germany, and France) should provide China with funds with which to purchase the Manchurian railroads from Japan and Russia. During the period in which China was repaying this great international loan, the Manchurian railroads would be operated by an international board of management. Should this scheme fail of acceptance by the powers, Secretary Knox suggested, as an alternative, that powers wishing to do so unite with the American banking group in financing the Chinchow-Aigun project.

In principle, the Knox so-called "neutralization" proposal had much to recommend it. In practice, it was neither practical nor sincere. Its purpose was not to establish in China as a whole the so-called open door. The idea, as Knox informed the German Ambassador, was to use the alternative proposals of the Chinchow-Aigun Railway and the "neutralization" plan to "smoke Japan out." [10] The fact was that the Russo-Japanese War had given the Japanese an opportunity to develop a sphere of influence in south Manchuria that threatened to overshadow the spheres which Germany, Russia, England, and France had mapped out for themselves at an earlier date. All the powers were intensely jealous of this new and strategic position which Japan held, and the United States, the power which had originally enunciated the open door policy, took the lead in forcing Japan to share the economic advantages she had won in the Russo-Japanese War. Despite this jealousy, the European powers were not prepared to do more than accept the Knox proposal "in principle," which meant, of course, not accepting it at all. Finally, Knox, in broaching his proposal, approached, first, Great Britain rather than Japan and Russia,

[10] Quoted in *ibid.* p. 75.

which obviously were the powers most concerned. The opposition of these two powers was thus a predictable result.

Tokyo and St. Petersburg made what was in reality a joint reply to the Knox scheme. The Japanese asserted that they were not prepared to accept the American neutralization proposal, which involved so radical a departure from the Treaty of Portsmouth and subsequent agreements made with China. They added, most effectively, that they could not see "in the present condition of things in Manchuria anything so exceptional as to make it necessary or desirable to set up there an exceptional system not required in other parts of China." Furthermore, the Japanese were not convinced that international management would add to the efficiency of their already efficient railroad. On the contrary, they were convinced that international control would lead only to political friction. But beyond these stated reasons, Japan was influenced by emotional values arising from the sacrifices made in the Russo-Japanese War. The tangible assets she had acquired as a result of that struggle were by no means large, and she had no intention of surrendering them to satisfy American capitalists or the American Department of State.

The Russian refusal to accept the Knox plan stated plainly that the proposal "would seriously injure Russian interests, both public and private," and was therefore not acceptable. The Chinese Eastern Railway was declared to be a necessary link between Russia and her far eastern possessions and an integral part of the Trans-Siberian system, which Russia had no intention of surrendering.

On the question of the alternative, namely, construction of the Chinchow-Aigun Railway, the Japanese indicated that they were willing to participate in financing and constructing the line, provided it was joined at some point with the South Manchuria Railway. The Russians, while not declining to cooperate, observed that it would "open up a new route giving access from the south not only to the Chinese Eastern Railway, but directly to Russian possessions at Aigun. This [they said] shows adequately the strategic and political importance of the enterprise."

In this manner, the plans of Harriman, Straight, and Knox to finance the railroads of Manchuria came to an end. In their immediate results, they effected a second *rapprochement* between Japan and Russia, at the same time stirring anew Japan's resentment toward the United States. On July 4, 1910 (the date was probably a mere coincidence), Japan and Russia concluded a secret convention. The 1907 line of demarcation between their respective spheres in Manchuria was reaffirmed. They recognized mutually the right of each within its sphere to take all necessary measures for the protection of its special interests, and agreed that neither would seek in the sphere of the other any privilege or concession prejudical to those special interests.[11] In the light of this secret convention, it must be concluded that the efforts of British and of American interests to "smoke Japan out" had not been attended with success. They had, in fact, served only to strengthen the Russian and the Japanese determination to maintain their spheres at all cost.

Selected Bibliography

K. Asakawa, "Japan in Manchuria," in *Yale Review,* Aug. and Nov. 1908. H. F. Bain, *Ores and Industry in the Far East* (New York: 1933). A. J. Barry, "Railway Development in China," in *Journal of the Royal Society of Arts,* London, 1909. J. B. Bishop, *Theodore Roosevelt and His Time,* 2 vols. (New York: 1920), vol. 2, ch. 5. G. H. Blakeslee, *China and the Far East* (New York: 1910). *British Documents on the Origins of the War,* vol. 8, ch. 69. P. H. Clyde, *International Rivalries in Manchuria* (Columbus: 1928). Herbert Croly, *Willard Straight* (New York: 1924). E. T. S. Dugdale, *German Diplomatic Documents, 1871-1914,* 4 vols. (London: 1930), vol. 3, ch. 21 on Germany, the United States, and China, 1907-1908. A. Gerard, *Ma Mission au Japon, 1907-1914* (Paris: 1919). S. L. Gulick, *The American Japanese Problem*

---

[11] E. B. Price, *op. cit.* pp. 113-114.

(New York: 1914), on the immigration problem in California, especially chs. 5-10. Shuhsi Hsu, *China and Her Political Entity* (New York: 1926), ch. 6 on reconstruction in Manchuria. E. J. Harrison, *Peace or War East of Baikal?* (Yokohama: 1910). L. J. Hall, "The Abortive German-American-Chinese Entente of 1907-08," in *The Journal of Modern History,* June 1929. Yamato Ichihashi, *Japanese in the United States* (Stanford University: 1932), chs. 15-16 on anti-Japanese agitation and the Gentlemen's Agreement. T. Iyenaga and K. Sato, *Japan and the California Problem* (New York: 1921), chs. 4-9 on Japanese immigration and California. P. H. Kent, *Railway Enterprise in China* (London: 1907). K. K. Kawakami, *American-Japanese Relations* (New York: 1912), bk. 1, the Manchurian question, 1905-1912, and bk. 3, Japanese immigration and the agreement of 1907. K. K. Kawakami, *Japan in World Politics* (New York: 1917), ch. 4 on land-hunger, the background of the Japanese immigration question; see also ch. 5. K. K. Kawakami, *The Real Japanese Question* (New York: 1921). George Kennan, *E. H. Harriman* (Boston: 1922). Adachi Kinnosuke, *Manchuria: A Survey* (New York: 1925). *The Kwantung Government, Its Functions and Works* (Dairen: 1934). Frederic McCormick, *The Tragedy of Russia in Pacific Asia* (New York: 1907). Inazo Nitobe, *The Japanese Nation* (New York: 1912). S. Okuma, *Fifty Years of New Japan,* 2 vols. (New York: 1909). E. B. Price, *The Russo-Japanese Treaties of 1907-1916 concerning Manchuria and Mongolia* (Baltimore: 1933), a most scholarly study. Yosaburo Takekoshi, *Prince Saionji* (Tokyo: 1933), chs. 51-65 on Japanese politics, 1900-1912. P. J. Treat, *Japan and the United States, 1853-1921* (Stanford University: 1928), chs. 10 and 14. The South Manchuria Railway, *Report on Progress in Manchuria, 1907-1928* (Dairen: 1929).

CHAPTER XXIV

The Annexation of Korea

KOREA in modern times has never enjoyed, politically speaking, a truly independent existence. During the nineteenth century, China, while continuing to claim the peninsula as a vassal or tributary state, failed to assume the responsibilities which suzerainty entailed. In 1876, it will be recalled, Japan, which like China had previously claimed suzerainty over Korea, recognized its independence, being followed shortly in this action by the United States, Great Britain, and other powers. China's refusal to accept this change, her attempts to regain control in Seoul, and her failure to guarantee a stable administration in Korea culminated in the Chino-Japanese War, by which China was finally forced to recognize Korean independence. Having refused to co-operate with Japan in a program for Korean administrative reform, she thereby lost all influence at Seoul. Japan's influence thereafter replaced that of China. But in utilizing the victory, Japan's official agents in Korea were guilty of stupid and inexcusable intrigue. In October, 1895, the Korean Queen was murdered by Korean and Japanese conspirators. At least partial responsibility for this outrage was traced to the Japanese Minister. Its immediate effect was to place the King in the hands of pro-Japanese Koreans. The program of reform continued, only, however, to be interrupted in February, 1896, by the flight of the King to the Russian Legation in Seoul, where, with his ministers, he lived for more than a year. It was the Japanese who were now on the defensive. Having lost the King, their influence was gone. Russians replaced Japanese in advisory posts of influence. Concessions were granted to Russian merchants, grants of timber lands near the Yalu were made to Russians, and to the Japanese it appeared that China had been expelled only to have her place taken by Russia. Japan, to save her position, approached St. Petersburg and concluded the Yamagata-Lobanov (1896) and Nishi-Rosen (1898) agreements. As a result, Japan, though deprived of most of her political influence, was left free to develop her commercial relations with Korea. The rebuilding of this influence became one of Japan's primary objectives in the years preceding the Russo-Japanese War.

To Japan, as the reader is already aware, Korea appeared as a land not only of important but also of essential interest.

. . . [A] glance at the economic situation reveals clearly that Japan was dependent upon Korea as the nearest foreign market, and as a source of raw materials. A disorderly government in Korea would always expose trade and friendly relations to disturbance, while a hostile power in possession of this strategic area would be a menace.[1]

These were the considerations which produced Japan's evolving policy toward Korea in the years 1898 to 1910. The policy itself, which was to control Korea, did not change; the methods used to attain it did. There were three principal stages in this evolution. Japan first sought to control the situation through formal independence supported by Japanese advice. When this failed, a semi- and then a full protectorate was established. Finally, the protectorate was ended with annexation.

As early as 1895, when China was forced to recognize the independence of Korea, some Japanese foresaw the probability of annexation. Successive ministries were questioned by members of the Diet as to their probable policy in case Japan should be called upon to defend the independence of the peninsula;

---

[1] From *Roosevelt and the Russo-Japanese War*, by Tyler Dennett, copyright 1925, by Doubleday, Doran & Company, Inc. p. 97.

all, however, refrained from disclosing this policy. Meanwhile, Japanese commercial interests there having expanded rapidly, in 1900 the Diet was urging the government to complete the construction of a railroad from Fusan, in the south, to Seoul. The contract for this line had been granted in 1896 to a Japanese syndicate. Construction was begun in 1901, and the line opened to traffic early in 1905, when the Russo-Japanese War was in progress. This is but a single example of the many ways in which Japanese enterprises turned to Korea. Japan had been denied a foothold in Manchuria in 1895 by action of the Triple Intervention; but the three intervening powers (Russia, Germany, and France), together with Great Britain, had forthwith secured leaseholds and spheres of influence for the precise purpose of exploiting China.

In what sense was Japan to interpret these manoeuvres? Was it possible for her to see in them anything but a determination on the part of the great European powers to prescribe for and to enforce upon Japan a rule of conduct totally different from that by which they themselves would be bound; and which, if Japan should subscribe to it, would deprive her not only of every advantage attached to her geographical situation off the coast of Asia, but also of every further advantage which she might legitimately (according to the international code of ethics hitherto in force) expect to derive from her rapid development, from her strong and unifying sentiment of nationality, from her tireless industry, and from her heroic military qualities?

Was Japan, in brief, to accept the restrictions of a self-denying ordinance at the very moment when England had reached the climax of her territorial acquisitions in every quarter of the globe, when Russia and Germany were fortifying themselves on Chinese soil almost within sight of the Japanese coast, when France was reforming her administration, strengthening her garrison, and extending her control in Indo-China, when the United States had recently taken possession of the Philippine Islands? [2]

---

[2] Alleyne Ireland, *The New Korea*. E. P. Dutton & Co., New York, 1926. pp. 44-45.

Korea as a Semi-Protectorate

By July, 1903, when Japan opened direct negotiations with Russia on the subject of Korea and Manchuria, she regarded the peninsula as an area in which her interests—political, commercial, and industrial—were paramount and, with respect to her own security, were such as could not be surrendered or shared with any power. This being the case, it was inevitable, when the war with Russia occurred, that in Korea Japan should take steps to strengthen her control and further the prosecution of the war. Accordingly, when her expeditionary forces occupied Chemulpo (Jinsen) and Seoul in February, 1904, she secured consent of the Korean government to the establishment of what might be termed a semi-protectorate. It was agreed that Korea should accept Japanese advice in the improvement of administration and that Japan should guarantee the independence and territorial integrity of Korea and take the steps necessary in case independence were threatened by the action of other powers or by internal disturbance. Neither power would conclude agreements contrary to these provisions except by mutual consent. This preliminary agreement was strengthened in August, when Korea agreed to engage, on the recommendation of the Japanese government, a Japanese financial adviser and a foreign diplomatic adviser.[3] Japan was to be consulted in all cases in which Korea wished to conclude agreements with other powers or to grant concessions to foreigners.

Korea as a Protectorate

Then followed the conclusion of the second Anglo-Japanese Alliance in August, 1905, and the Treaty of Portsmouth in September, by which Japan's special position in Korea was given international recognition. The government thereupon sought

---

[3] For the latter post, an American, Durham White Stevens, was selected.

to implement this recognition by further arrangements at Seoul. The negotiations were conducted by Prince Ito, then president of the Privy Council, who proceeded to Seoul in November. In a personal interview with the Korean sovereign, Ito presented a draft agreement for the establishment of a full Japanese protectorate, which was accepted by the Korean administration on the following day. By this agreement, Japan assumed control of Korea's foreign relations and was granted permission to appoint a resident general at Seoul. Henceforth, Tokyo would do more than "tender advice" in Korean affairs.

Establishment of a Japanese protectorate over Korea met with no opposition from western states. The English, in the second Anglo-Japanese Alliance, had already given their official approval, and no obstacle was raised by the United States, despite the fact that American commercial interests in Korea were rather large. As a matter of fact "the competition between American and Japanese capitalists from 1899 to 1904 was very keen, but in the main the feeling was friendly." [4] Such American opposition as there was came from Protestant missionaries, who in most instances favored a Korea independent in fact, as well as in theory. But the official attitude of the American government was affected both by recent developments in the Pacific and by the personality of President Theodore Roosevelt.

Some Japanese had wanted not only the Philippines but even Hawaii. Having blocked Japanese expansion in the Pacific, seeking the exclusion of the Japanese from the Pacific coast, was the United States also to oppose Japanese expansion in Asia? In fact, there had been for some years a feeling in diplomatic circles, recognized alike by Great Britain, the United States, and Japan, that there must be diplomatic give-and-take, that if the United States might stride across an ocean and seize an archipelago, just as Great Britain, the Netherlands, and France had already done, Japan had at least equal rights to similar liberties. [5]

---

[4] Dennett, *Roosevelt and the Russo-Japanese War*, p. 105.
[5] *Ibid.* pp. 108-109.

Roosevelt himself had no respect for the Koreans, for, as he said, "They could not strike one blow in their own defense." It was but natural, then, that the United States should acquiesce in Japan's "paramount influence."

Ito in Korea

For the supervision of the new protectorate, Japan sent Prince Ito to Korea as resident general. Although he was her ablest and most experienced administrator, this was perhaps the most difficult task of his long and distinguished career. While there were many prominent Japanese who believed that annexation was the only solution of the Korean "problem," Ito was not one of them. Early in 1906, his first act as resident general was to propose to the Korean government a comprehensive program of reform, touching, among other things, on construction of roads and waterworks, the building of hospitals and schools, the reorganization of the court, the police and the judicial system, and the encouragement of industry. Some progress was made, but the program was blocked at many points by the inefficiency of the Korean ministers and their natural resentment toward their Japanese advisers. The resident general could give advice but could not compel its execution. This state of affairs dragged on into 1907, when the Korean King dispatched a secret mission to the Second Hague Conference to seek intervention of the powers to free Korea from Japanese control. When news of these activities reached Japan, it aroused tremendous resentment, causing the hapless Korean Sovereign promptly to declare that he was in no way responsible for the mission. In Tokyo, political factions demanded adoption of a "decisive policy," and the Saionji Ministry determined to give Ito a free hand. Accordingly, in July, the Korean King was forced to abdicate in favor of his son. This was followed by an agreement on July 24 "whereby the Japanese resident general became a virtual regent." [6]   Under its terms all matters of internal administration as well as foreign affairs were placed under Japanese control.

This new formula for Korean affairs produced results which from Japan's point of view were equally disappointing.   There were still many ways in which the advice of the resident general could be nullified.   Although he could veto objectionable laws, it was not by this means that a constructive administration could be built.   By 1909, Ito was still confronted with a stubborn Korean opposition to his plans.   By July of that year, he was finally convinced that neither could an efficient government be formed nor could Japan's interests be preserved by any system short of annexation.   This policy soon had the support of Premier Katsura and his Foreign Minister, Baron Komura. Ito resigned as resident general in June and was succeeded by Viscount Sone.   During July, the government determined on annexation.   In October, while methods to effect the policy were under discussion, Ito went to Harbin to negotiate a better understanding on Manchuria with the Russian Minister of Finance.   There, on October 26, he was assassinated by a Korean fanatic.   His death profoundly affected public sentiment in Japan, and evoked popular demands for immediate annexation.   In Korea, public sentiment was equally aroused.   Viscount Sone resigned on May 30, 1910, and was succeeded by General Terauchi, a powerful militarist who had served as Minister of War since 1902.   On June 17, six hundred gendarmes were sent to Korea, and on the following day, Premier Katsura made public the intended annexation.   By July 1, "the entire kingdom [of Korea] was under strict control of the gendarmerie, in preparation for the final step."   General Terauchi arrived at Seoul on July 23 under heavy guard.   All organs of public opinion were suspended or ruthlessly suppressed. [7]

---

[6] Tatsuji Takeuchi, *War and Diplomacy in the Japanese Empire*.   Doubleday, Doran & Company, New York, 1935.   pp. 162-163.

[7] *Ibid.* p. 165.

His negotiations with the Korean Prime Minister were completed August 20. The treaty of annexation was signed two days later. It conferred all rights of sovereignty in Korea upon the Emperor of Japan. In her announcement to the powers, Japan declared that her own treaties would apply in Korea, that extraterritoriality there was ended, but that the existing tariffs would remain in force for ten years.

In this manner was the international struggle to control Korea brought to a close. In subsequent years, Japan was roundly denounced by sections of western and Chinese public opinion for violating her pledge to maintain Korean independence. The charge, to be sure, was founded in fact, but its greater significance revealed that Japan, like great powers of the West, had been swept into the turmoil of imperialistic rivalry, where, as history has so frequently revealed, pledges have little value. The United States, entering upon an imperialistic crusade in 1898, had likewise listened to the philosophy of imperialism when President McKinley declared that "the march of events rules and overrules human action." For her policy in Korea from 1895 to 1910, Japan offered a like explanation.

In 1910, as in earlier years, Korea had no friends prepared to give more than lip service to her alleged ideals of independence. The bulk of her people were illiterate and bound by poverty. Her royal house and the administration had given ample proof of complete incompetence. A government which had been content to accept the overlordship of China for centuries, and which had failed in every primary domestic duty to its subjects, could claim little respect in the so-called court of world public opinion. It was already clear in 1907, when the Korean King appealed to the Hague conference against Japan, that the sovereign was attempting to preserve his own prerogatives rather than the welfare of his people. Yet there were Koreans, many of whom had been educated in American Protestant missions, who had been inspired by the ideal of a new Korea, literate, prosperous, and free. To these men and women, the annexation of their homeland was a national disgrace.

Korea Under Japanese Administration

The task of governing and developing Korea, which Japan undertook in 1910, was difficult, and for it the Japanese were ill prepared. They had had virtually no experience in colonial administration. Koreans were naturally suspicious of their motives, and the Japanese made the initial mistake of reserving the office of governor general for a high-ranking military officer. This was in keeping with what other powers had frequently done in their colonial dependencies, yet to Koreans it was convincing proof that Japan intended to impose her rule by military force. If in 1910 there remained any possibility that Koreans might be reconciled to Japanese control, it was destroyed by the rule that only a military man could occupy the post of governor general.

Despite this initial mistake, material progress in the peninsula was soon apparent. A new administration was created and was staffed with competent technical experts. The finances of the state were reorganized to provide a system of equitable taxation and adequate revenue. Between 1912 and 1923, nearly five million additional acres of land were placed under cultivation. The value of agricultural products rose from 435,000,000 yen to 1,169,000,000 yen. Reforestation of denuded countrysides was undertaken in 1911, and by 1925, millions of seedlings had been planted. The value of the annual fisheries catch increased from 8,000,000 yen to 45,000,000 yen between 1912 and 1921. During the same years, the annual value of the output of Korean mines was doubled. In 1912, capital investment in Korean railroads was 114,720,385 yen; in 1921, it was 214,906,215 yen. At the time of Korea's annexation, there were scarcely one hundred miles of good road. In 1923, there were 5,000 miles of first- and second-class roads and almost as many miles of third-class. More important than these, however, were the development of irrigation and the undertaking of sanitary projects designed to preserve the denuded lands from floods and their inhabitants from plague. From whatever angle of material progress Korea was viewed, her advancement under Japanese rule was remarkable.

Yet, with all this material advance, the first decade of Japanese rule in Korea was a failure. The program of reform, desirable in itself, was imposed with rigid military severity. Koreans, having little understanding of or appreciation for its purpose, met it with sullen opposition. While many Koreans occupied minor posts in government, they exercised no real influence on its policies, and were completely denied any semblance of representative institutions. The masses of illiterate Koreans were, of course, quite incapable of participating in government at this time, yet encouragement might well have been extended to the small but growing educated class. Many Korean progressives hoped for the restoration of national independence, and their hatred of the Japanese regime increased from year to year. From conditions such as these, the Korean nationalist cause was born.

The Nationalists in Korea

Like other similar movements, Korean nationalism was supported by diverse elements prompted by various motives. There was a nucleus of disinterested idealists to whom national independence alone meant national and cultural honor; disgruntled merchants who were alarmed by the efficiency of Japanese business; would-be politicians who looked to independence as a means of personal advancement; and bewildered farmers and peasants who dreaded reform and especially its personification—the fierce and fearless Japanese gendarme. From the first days of the annexation, the leaders of this national movement worked effectively, for the most part escaping the observation of Japan's secret police. During 1917 and 1918, after the United States had entered the World War, their hopes were renewed by the war-time propaganda that extolled freedom and self-determination for national groups. In 1919, therefore, the Korean "patriots" brought their movement into the open by inaugurating a campaign of protest and passive resistance against Japanese rule. Popular uprisings occurred at widely separated points; crowds refused to disperse when ordered to do so by the Japanese police; troops sent to quell the disturbances acted with extreme severity. Casualties, among both Koreans and Japanese, were numerous. The repressive policy of the government fell heavily upon Korean Christians, many of whom were associated with the nationalist cause—a fact that explains in large part the widespread criticism of Japan that soon appeared in the United States.

In Japan, as elsewhere, public sentiment was shocked by the merciless severity with which the revolt was suppressed. The government was forced to recall the governor general, Count Hasegawa, a militarist, whose regime at Seoul since 1916 must be held responsible in the main for the rebellion. A reorganization of Korean affairs was promptly ordered. The post of governor general was no longer to be reserved for military men. The new appointee, Admiral Saito, though not a civilian, was, nevertheless, recognized as a great administrator and a man of generous and humane character. His appointment symbolized a new and better day for Korea. An ordinary police force was established to replace the hated gendarmerie, and many unpopular regulations were abolished. In some cities and towns, Koreans were to select councils. The results of this changed policy were soon evident.

The general consensus of opinion in Korea in 1922, except in so far as it reflected the feelings of the anti-Japanese extremists, was that Governor-General Saito had been animated by a sincere desire to rule Korea through a just and tolerant administration, that he had accomplished notable reforms, that in the matter of education he had ministered very generously to the cultural ambitions of the

ADMIRAL MAKOTO SAITO. Few statesmen have served Japan better than the late Admiral Saito. As naval commander, as governor general of Korea and Prime Minister of Japan itself, he was the nation's servant until assassinated in 1936 by military fanatics.

people, and that in regard to their political ambitions he had, whilst setting his face sternly against anything which could encourage the vain hope of independence, shown himself eager to foster local self-government, and to infuse into the personal relations of the Japanese and Koreans a spirit of friendliness and co-operation.[8]

This marked improvement in Korean political affairs after 1919 may be traced to a number of excellent reforms and to the

[8] Alleyne Ireland, *op. cit.* p. 72.

spirit and manner of their execution. The stated objectives of these reforms indicated many of the worst abuses which had previously existed. Discrimination between Japanese and Korean officials was to be eliminated; laws and regulations were to be simplified; greater respect was to be shown to native customs and culture; freedom of speech, assembly, and the press were to be recognized; education was to be extended; medical and sanitary services were to be enlarged; and opportunity for advancement was to be given to men of talent. All of these reforms have been applied in varying degrees but with some significant qualifications, such as those on freedom of speech and assembly. These qualifications may be traced not only to the temperament of the Japanese government but also to the attitude of the Koreans themselves. Even under the humane and tolerant administration of Admiral Saito (1919-1927), many Koreans refused to co-operate. Their minds remaining fixed on the ideal of national independence, they withheld both interest and participation in any reform program introduced by any Japanese administration. This passive resistance not only retarded the material and the intellectual growth of the Korean people but also played into the hands of Japanese conservatives and militarists, who feared the liberalism of the Saito policy.

The indictment which Korean nationalists have raised against Japanese rule is a severe one. They have objected to a policy which aims at the absorption and assimiliation of the Korean people. They have objected to what they regard as the autocratic rule of an alien power. They have charged Japan with economic discrimination and with responsibility for the economic ills of the people.

Whether or not Japan's policy of assimilation will result in absorption of the Korean race is a matter in which grave doubt may be entertained, a doubt which is shared by many Japanese. In the early years after annexation, Korean intellectuals believed that Japan was intent upon stamping out both their language and culture. Since 1919, there has been less ground for this charge. Primary-school instruction during the first two years is in the Korean language, after which it is in Japanese, with special classes for instruction in Korean. The use of Chinese characters is taught, with Korean as well as with Japanese pronounciation. Korean history and geography are taught in all schools. Thus, while the system of education is modeled on that of Japan, and conducted, with the exception noted above, in Japanese, it is modified to meet the interests of Korean culture. The greatest contribution made by the system of education which Japan has given Korea has been in the field of agriculture. More than ninety per cent of the population of Korea lives in villages of less than 8,000 inhabitants, and of these, ninety per cent are engaged in agriculture.

Japan Tourist Bureau.

GENERAL TARO KATSURA. Three times Prime Minister between 1901 and 1911, this Choshu clansman was the successor to Yamagata in the politics of the Japanese army and the nation.

Courses in agricultural guidance are given to graduates of common schools in the rural districts, while groups of selected students receive further training at the government experimental stations in the provinces.

The autocratic character of Japan's administration has also been modified. Local autonomy, which has been granted for many years to local bodies, is gradually being extended. The governor general is advised by the Central Council, which is composed of influential Koreans selected from all the provinces.

Its authority, however, is limited to giving advice on questions presented to it by the governor general.

The Agrarian Problem

The final charge, that the Japanese administration in Korea has permitted economic discrimination against Koreans, arises from the fact that in Korea, as in Japan and in many other countries, the farmer has been losing his land. It is perhaps but natural that the Korean nationalists should lay the responsibility for this at the door of Japan's administration. The explanation cannot, of course, be reduced to terms quite so simple. The extent to which Japanese have entered Korean agriculture may, however, be stated briefly.

The total arable land of Korea is 4,500,000 chobu, or about 11,000,000 acres. By terracing, drainage, and reclamation, about 1,000,000 chobu, or 2,500,000 acres, may be added to this arable total in the future. At the close of 1922, the landowners of Korea were classified as follows:

	Chobu	Acres	Per Cent of Total
Koreans	4,129,399	10,117,000	94.14
Japanese	254,753	724,000	5.81
Foreigners	2,372	5,800	.05

At the end of 1931, the figures were:

	Chobu	Per Cent of Total
Koreans	4,119,279	91.5
Japanese	378,895	8.4
Foreigners	3,936	.08

During these nine years, the increase in the cultivation of arable land was 115,686 chobu, almost all of which was the result of reclamation undertaken by Japanese companies. In the above figures, these companies are included under "Japanese owned," though a large number of their shares are held by

Koreans. Population growth in Korea during the same years
was as follows:

	Korean	Japanese	Foreign
1922	17,208,139	386,493	32,129
1931	19,710,168	514,666	38,124

Of the Japanese population at the close of 1932, 49,971 persons, comprising 11,214 households, were engaged in agriculture. Of these, 3,183 households (28.4%) leased their entire
land to others to cultivate; 1,661 (14.8%) leased most of their
land to others to cultivate; 672 (.6%) cultivated half and
leased half to others; 2,683 (23.9%) cultivated their land themselves; 1,703 (15.2%) owned half of the land they cultivated,
renting the remainder from the other owner; and 1,312
(11.7%) rented from others all of the land they cultivated.

To meet the problem of the peasant and his land, the
Government General has since 1912 stressed the necessity of
preventing the formation of large estates through the purchase
of land from owner cultivators. Uncultivated state-owned lands
were leased to farmers on easy terms and later conferred in full
title. Since 1928, the government has made loans to small
landowners through farmer associations in the villages. The
rate of interest is one per cent per month, the loans to be repaid
by the associations within twenty years. Since 1932, further
plans have been effected whereby small farmers obtain loans
to aid them in retaining or purchasing land. The amount of
these loans is limited to 1,000 yen, with interest at three and
one-half per cent.

To protect farmer tenants, as differentiated from owner cultivators, the government completed regulations in 1928 by
which the tenant is protected in his tenancy of land, in maintenance of the land's fertility, in methods of payment of rent
and taxes, and in the settlement of disputes. These regulations
have produced beneficial results at a time when agricultural
distress had been aggravated by the world-wide depression.

It is the general conclusion of students competent to judge

that since 1919, Korea has possessed the best government she has ever known. Assuming that this statement can be proved, the fact remains that it is not an answer to the aspirations of the Korean nationalists. They are demanding free government, even if bad government, by Koreans. Japan has offered them efficient and, in many respects, model government, in which, however, the authority is Japanese. Of their shortcomings in Korea, intelligent Japanese are by no means unconscious. As late as 1931, Count Soyeshima wrote for Japanese readers:

> The greatest defect in the Japanese rule in Korea lies in lack of sympathy and consideration for Koreans on the part of Japanese officials and the Japanese people. [9]

That efforts have and are being made to remove these faults is evident, but Japan has learned since 1910 that the governing of one people by another is, at best, a difficult and a thankless task.

SELECTED BIBLIOGRAPHY

The annual reports (in English) issued by the Government of Korea are indispensable. They have been issued in three series: (1) Korea, H. I. J. M's Residency General, *Annual Report on Reforms and Progress in Korea* (Seoul: 1908-09); (2) Korea, Government General of Chosen, *Annual Report on Reforms and Progress in Korea* (Seoul: 1910-23); (3) Korea, Government General of Chosen, *Annual Report on Administration of Chosen* (Keijo: 1924-34). In these reports, the statistical material is of greatest value.

J. F. Abbott, *Japanese Expansion and American Policies* (New York: 1916). R. H. Akagi, *Japan's Foreign Relations* (Tokyo: 1936), ch. 11 on the annexation of Korea. *British Documents on the Origins of the War,* vol. 8, ch. 69. A. J. Brown, *Report on a Second Visit to China, Japan and Korea, 1909* (New York: 1909). J. O. P. Bland, *China, Japan and Korea* (New York: 1921), ch. 10, the independence movement in Korea. Henry Chung, *The Case of Korea* (New York: 1921), chs. 11-18 on the independence move-

---

[9] See *The Japan Chronicle,* August 13 and 20, 1931.

ment. Henry Chung, *Korean Treaties* (New York: 1919). *Economic Development of Korea and Manchuria* (Tokyo: 1923). W. E. Griffis, "The Statesmanship of Ito," in *North American Review,* Jan. 1910. H. B. Hulbert, *The Passing of Korea* (New York: 1906). T. Iyenaga, "Japan's Annexation of Korea," in *Japan and Japanese-American Relations,* Geo. H. Blakeslee, ed. (New York: 1912). Alleyne Ireland, *The New Korea* (New York: 1926). K. K. Kawakami, *American-Japanese Relations* (New York: 1912), bk. 2, the Korean question, 1905-1912. By the same author, *Japan in World Politics* (New York: 1917), ch. 11 on America and Japan in Korea. E. G. Kemp, *The Face of Manchuria, Korea and Russian Turkestan* (New York: 1911). *Korea, Treaties and Agreements* (Washington: 1921). G. T. Ladd, *In Korea with Marquis Ito* (New York: 1908). Three volumes by F. A. McKenzie: *The Colonial Policy of Japan in Korea* (London: 1906); *The Tragedy of Korea* (New York: 1908); *Korea's Fight for Freedom* (London: 1920). Rentaro Mizuno, "From Korea to Chosen," in *Contemporary Japan,* Sept. 1933. F. H. Smith, *The Other Side of the Korean Question* (Seoul: 1920). Count Soyeshima, "Administration of Korea," in *Japan Chronicle,* Aug. 13, 1931. C. J. D. Taylor, *Koreans at Home* (London: 1904). Tatsuji Takeuchi, *War and Diplomacy in the Japanese Empire* (Garden City: 1935), ch. 13. H. G. Underwood, *The Call of Korea* (New York: 1908). W. H. Wilkinson, *The Corean Government: Constitutional Changes, 1894-96* (Shanghai: 1897).

CHAPTER XXV

China: From Empire to Republic

THE passing of the Manchu Empire, of a dynasty which had ruled China since 1644, and its replacement by the Chinese Republic were events that appealed widely to popular and sentimental opinion in the western world and particularly in the United States. Although the public in western lands was almost totally ignorant of and indifferent to Chinese history, culture, and contemporary affairs, it was pleased to assume that the passing of the dynasty and the rise of the Republic would, as if by magic, alter China from the ancient to the modern, from the oriental to the occidental, from autocracy to democracy, and finally from Confucius to Christ. Americans, in particular, were inclined to pride themselves that in republicanism the Chinese had discovered and adopted a virtue which was essentially American. American popular reactions to the Chinese revolution of 1911-1912 bore, in fact, a marked resemblance to the untutored enthusiasm which greeted Anson Burlingame on his return to the United States in 1868. This philosophy of good will has played an important part in shaping modern American attitudes toward China, attitudes that have determined American interpretations of China's most recent revolutions.

Origins of the Revolution

Contrary to these and other popular assumptions, the passing of the Manchus was caused solely neither by the revolutionary outbursts of 1911 nor by the decade of belated reforms which preceded them. Revolution in almost every aspect of

449

Chinese life had become inevitable at least as early as the middle of the nineteenth century. The Opium and the *Arrow* Wars demonstrated that China would be forced, by the instrument of western imperialistic power, to discard, or at least to modify, her ancient civilization. In the West, the modern age of coal, of iron, of steel, of factories, and of world markets had created a group of highly organized states saturated in doctrines of national imperialism. To combat the invasion of these powers on her soil, China had no effective weapon. At the beginning of the twentieth century, China was a continent, a civilization, a society. She was not a nation, nor yet a state, as the West understood these terms. Her government was social. Its political aspects were negative and ornamental, steeped in corruption and moldering in decay. Such statesmanship as they had ever possessed had long since been forgotten by Manchu leaders; even a revolt so colossal as the Taiping Rebellion had failed to revive their memories. The very idea of reform was repulsive not only to the Manchus but also to Chinese officialdom.

While Japan manoeuvred for time to adopt Western characteristics and catch up with the West, the whole history of Chinese relations with the West implies an underlying instinctive playing for time, in the hope that the West would exhaust itself and China be able to assert once more the superiority of which the Chinese are morally convinced. [1]

Even the Chino-Japanese War (1894-1895) failed to convince the Manchu court of the need of reform. Three years later, the famous "Hundred Days" of reform launched by the young Emperor under the guidance of Kang Yu-wei was brought to a disastrous close, and in 1900, that picturesque old woman, the Empress Dowager, stupidly imagined she could save China and the dynasty by supporting the Boxer terror in 1900-1901.

---

[1] Owen Lattimore, *Manchuria, Cradle of Conflict*. The Macmillan Company, New York, 1932. p. 88.

She had left Peking as the discredited patron of reaction; she was to return as the leader of reform. She had not learned to admire the foreigners; there was little in their conduct in China during the nineteenth century which entitled them to respect or affection. In her eyes they were still worthy of the epithet, "foreign barbarians." But she had come to realize that the foreign powers were strong, stronger by far than the Chinese Empire, despite its more venerable civilization, and that for the sake both of the Chinese people themselves and of the enfeebled Manchu dynasty China must borrow from the West the institutions and ideas which seemed to be the secrets of its power. [2]

From 1902 to 1911 the Manchus struggled desperately with reform, stimulated further by the helpless condition of the Empire during the Russo-Japanese War. But their efforts had been delayed too long. Neither the misgovernment of a century nor the social and economic maladjustments occasioned by the impact of the West could be righted in a decade, least of all by an effete dynasty and by officials lacking in understanding and appreciation of the very reforms they advocated. While young intellectuals trained in the West clamored for a new China, millions of illiterate, wretched peasants continued to submit, without question, to the inevitable—life on the border line of starvation. Between these extremes of intellectual radicalism and peasant conservatism, where would the course of government lie?

Attempts at Reform

The greatest and perhaps the most difficult of all the reforms undertaken by the Chinese government after the Boxer uprising was in the field of education, so long dominated by the Confucian classics and rigid official examinations. When the Empress Dowager and her court returned to Peking from the Boxer exile, announcement was made that stress would be laid on modern and western subjects. Under the direction of

---

[2] Meribeth E. Cameron, *The Reform Movement in China, 1898-1912.* Stanford University Press, Stanford University, California, 1931. p. 57.

Chang Chih-tung, the plan of a complete system of modern education was prepared. The system, modeled largely on the Japanese, was inaugurated in January, 1904. The old system of classical examinations was abolished and was replaced by tests on modern subjects. Chinese students were no longer to draw their inspiration from the past but from the modern, living present. On paper (in Imperial edicts) all this could easily be done; to translate it rapidly into reality was impossible. In a land as vast as China, the building of schools and the training of teachers required enormous expenditures, for which no national revenue was available. The problem was thus passed on to provincial and local authorities, many of whom had no interest in these modern and western innovations. Where a province possessed a viceroy or governor who had ability and was sympathetic to reform, great progress was made, but in most of the provinces, the new schools enjoyed a most precarious existence. Tuition was charged almost everywhere, with the result that children of the poor received no more education than formerly. Competent teachers were rarely obtainable, while officials, in turn, were unwilling to pay for competent instruction. Many Chinese, after studying for a brief period in Japan (at one time there were 15,000), returned to their native land as potential teachers, with little more than a superficial smattering of western and modern learning. Yet, with all these handicaps, education in China made a significant advance in the years just preceding the revolution. The break with the past had received official recognition, and, for good or ill, was soon to have vital effects on the whole fabric of Chinese life.

Attempts to reform the political structure were scarcely less striking. It will be recalled that in China the powers of the central government were largely negative. It was concerned with checking rather than with directing provincial affairs. The provinces having always retained large powers of local autonomy, a highly decentralized state had been the result.

Now all this was to be changed. A committee of ministers was created. The old boards were reorganized or replaced. Chinese and Manchus were to be appointed without racial distinction or discrimination. The autonomy of the provinces was to be severely restricted. All matters of national interest, such as finance, defense, education, police, and justice were to be controlled by Peking. Likewise, in the provinces themselves there was to be a tightening of control over local communities. As in the case of education, these proposals were revolutionary in scope. Since they were the antithesis of government, as the Chinese had previously understood that term, opposition to their enforcement from conservative officials and the masses was inevitable.

Proposals for Representative Government

From the beginning of the reform movement, the liberals and some of the more enlightened conservatives had thought in terms of the establishment of representative government. In 1905, a committee was appointed to investigate. Commissioners, sent to Europe and to the United States to study political organization, recommended on their return the gradual introduction of representative institutions. In September, 1906, an Imperial edict promised the people a constitution when, in the view of the government, their preparation for it was adequate. There was great difference of opinion, however, as to how adequate this preparation should be; but finally, in August, 1907, a constitution was promised for the year 1917. The intervening years were to be employed as a period of training—nine years in which to commence the training of more than 300 million illiterates for representative government.

One of the most characteristic features of Chinese affairs since 1840 has been her inability or her unwillingness to protect either her territory or her peoples from foreign invasion and exploitation. The Opium War, the *Arrow* War, and the troubles in Loochoo, Formosa, Indo-China, and Korea had all revealed the plight of China's armed forces. They lacked equipment, discipline, and leadership. In the Chino-Japanese War, they were no match for Japan's well-trained battalions. They scattered like leaves in the wind before the international forces that relieved Peking in 1900. They were helpless before the armies of Russia and Japan that used Manchurian soil as a battleground in 1904-1905. This unbroken record of defeat and humiliation has frequently been explained erroneously by the statement that the Chinese are a pacific people, as compared with those of other great states, and thus make very poor soldiers. Nothing could be further from the truth than this legend, which has enjoyed wide currency in the United States.

The numerous dynastic changes and the civil wars and rebellions from which the country [China] has suffered from the dawn of history, as well as the growth of China territorially into a vast empire, are sufficient to demonstrate the truth of the assertion that the Chinese are no less human, and no more divine, than other peoples when it comes to fighting and acquiring. [3]

During the Taiping Rebellion, Chinese soldiers, properly equipped and disciplined, and led by able foreign officers, proved themselves excellent soldiers. The plight of China's armies in the first decade of the twentieth century was merely a reflection of the general anarchy and decay which prevailed.

Military Reforms

To this problem the reformers turned their attention. A decree of 1906 contemplated an army to be recruited eventually on a basis of conscription. The new forces were to comprise infantry, cavalry, artillery, engineers, and transports, with a total peace standing of 450,000. A general staff would be created, officers sent for training abroad, and foreign instructors secured.

---

[3] Harley F. MacNair, *China in Revolution.* University of Chicago Press, Chicago, 1931. p. 2.

Arsenals and all the paraphernalia for creating an army machine would be set up. But, like the reforms in education, no army could be built without funds. As a result, the new army depended entirely on the initiative and energy of individual viceroys. Yuan Shih-kai succeeded in building a force of some 80,000 well-trained men, but in most areas of China, the army reforms remained on paper. There were also ambitious plans for building a navy, but by 1911 it had reached a total of only 45,000 tons. Here, too, finance was the main problem. Though contributions were made by many of the provinces, they were small in amount and irregular in payment.

The Campaign Against Opium

More successful than the educational, political, and army reforms was the campaign waged in the last years of Manchu rule against opium. The reader is already aware that the opium trade at Canton was a contributing factor to the first Anglo-Chinese war. In 1858, the importation of opium was legalized.

The imports of Indian opium into China reached their highest point in the years 1871-1880, when over 68,000 piculs were imported, on an average, annually. About that time the Chinese began to grow opium extensively in their own territory, with the double object of making money and displacing the foreign product. The opium was mostly grown in Szechuen and Yünnan. Though less esteemed by connoisseurs than Indian opium, the cheapness of Chinese opium commended it to the poor; and it gradually became a serious rival to Indian opium. No figures are available, but it is not unlikely that in the early years of the present century nearly as much native opium was consumed in China as foreign. [4]

The spread of opium-smoking had thus become a national calamity, destructive of both the physical and the mental well-being of the Chinese people. In the first years of the twentieth

---

[4] L. A. Lyall, *China*. Charles Scribner's Sons, New York, 1934. p. 293.

century, the evils associated with opium had already aroused a certain public consciousness in China, a fact which goes far to explain the success of reforms encouraged by the government. The importance of the question was likewise emphasized in the report of the Philippine opium commission in 1904 and in the resolution of the British House of Commons in 1906, condemning the Indian opium trade. In the same year, Chinese officials, reformers, and many foreign missionaries memorialized the government for opium reform. Accordingly, an edict was issued decreeing abolition of opium-smoking within ten years. Subsequent regulations provided for restriction of the cultivation of the poppy, licenses for addicts (except for persons over sixty years of age, included among whom was the Empress Dowager), and punishment for those who refused to give up the habit. Opium dens and shops would be closed, and negotiations with Great Britain would seek restriction on the Indian trade. These negotiations with the British proved most successful. The Indian government agreed to reduce its exports of opium to China by one tenth annually, over a period of three years, provided that China made similar reductions in domestic production. Later, an Anglo-Chinese agreement was concluded (1911), by which the Indian trade would continue to be reduced until ended in 1917. Indian opium, in the meantime, would not be shipped to any Chinese province where the cultivation of native opium was prohibited effectively. This arrangement brought speedy results. So rapid was the suppression of opium cultivation within China that in 1913 the importation of Indian opium came to an end. This happy result was a product both of the enlightened policy of the British government and the power of Chinese public opinion when thoroughly aroused. That the results were not permanent does not, of course, detract from the historical significance of this truly great reform.

As long as the reform movement was dominated by the vigorous will of the Empress Dowager, ably supported by Yuan

Shih-kai, there was some prospect of tangible results being peacefully attained. But in 1908, the Empress Dowager and the young Emperor, whom she had dominated, died. The throne passed to Pu-yi, an infant two years of age, the son of Prince Chun, who was a younger brother of the late Emperor and who had married a daughter of Jung Lu. Prince Chun became regent, while Yuan Shih-kai, one of the few able officials in Peking, was dismissed from office. Although the regent was not opposed to reform, he was young, weak, and lacking in political ability. As a consequence of this change in administration, the reform program was deprived of a stabilizing and directing force. A step toward representative government was taken, however, in 1909, with the calling of provincial assemblies and, later, of municipal councils. These beginnings were to prepare the way for a national assembly, which met at Peking in October, 1910. Part of its members were appointed, and others were elected by provincial assemblies. It deliberated on questions of reorganizing the national finances and inaugurating an elected parliament. To meet its demands, the government promised to summon a parliament in 1913 and to revise the program of reform with a view to its completion in 1914 instead of 1917. The readiness of the government to submit to the will of the assembly was probably a fatal error, for already the reform program had been too rapid. China was ripe for moderate reform; she was not prepared for revolutionary change.

Attitude of the Powers Toward Reform

While the fate of the Manchu Dynasty in the years 1908 to 1912 depended directly on the attitude of the provinces toward the program of reform, it rested to almost as great a degree on the policies of the great western powers and Japan. These were the years when international financial rivalries played fast and loose with the future of China. While every one of the great powers was solemnly pledging its disinterested support for a reconstructed China, each was seeking merely the enhancement of its own interests therein.

> In their pre-war diplomacy, the six great powers [Great Britain, France, Germany, Japan, Russia, and the United States] . . . neither supported a strong, modernized, centralized, stable government nor the ancient, loosely governed, imperial system . . . instead, they indirectly encouraged internal unrest and rebellion. [5]

British interests exceeded those of all other powers in China, and it was the policy of the British government to maintain this lead. France, to protect her colonies in Indo-China, favored the *status quo*. Germany attempted to use international rivalries in China to break the anti-German entente in Europe. Japan, intent on fortifying what she regarded as her special position in Manchuria, was opposed to political reforms in China and to foreign loans to finance them. The former, she believed, would lead to unrest, and the latter to international friction. Russia consolidated her position in north Manchuria and came to an understanding with Japan.

The policy of the United States was not so consistent in the years 1908 to 1912. Theodore Roosevelt, a realist, was content that Japan should have Korea and that she should divide control of Manchuria with Russia. In return, the Japanese were pledged not to interfere in the Philippines, and by the Gentlemen's Agreement, to prohibit the migration of laborers to the United States. President Taft, supported by Secretary Knox, was not content to leave well enough alone. Washington sought the co-operation of other great powers to "smoke out" Japan. "Dollar diplomacy" was the slogan that described American policy. In the crises, both domestic and foreign, which confronted Peking on the eve of the revolution, the Chinese government "received no concrete assistance from Washington." [6] Under Taft and Knox, the government of the United

---

[5] J. G. Reid, *The Manchu Abdication and the Powers.* University of California Press, Berkeley, 1935. p. 300.

[6] *Ibid.*   pp. 308-311.

States was not interested in "saving" China; it was interested in securing there a broader field for American investment.

China, as she entered the year 1911, was beset with uncertainty in every quarter. The reform program instituted by the dynasty was still largely a paper reform. The provinces remained jealous of any encroachment by Peking. The problem of national revenue had not been solved. Foreign financial assistance had failed because of the ambitions and rivalries of the great powers. The only stabilizing force that remained was the ingrained conservatism of a Confucian society, and even this was threatened by devastating famines, floods, and plagues, which again visited China in 1911. A less patient people would have long since sought relief in revolt. But in China, man was not accustomed to expect much of life; he was born to suffer in silence. Yet even in China, as her history well shows, there was a limit to what man could endure. Along with the Confucian code, his ancestors had bequeathed the right of revolution, a right which the Chinese had frequently used. To the Chinese, it was clear that, when a dynasty could no longer be endured, the mandate of Heaven had been withdrawn, and a new ruler must be found. Here, then, was a philosophy on which the Chinese revolutionists could rely.

Revolutionary Leaders

In 1911, China lacked neither the doctrines nor the agents of revolution. Working against the reformers in Peking were two groups: the one, advocating constitutional monarchy, led by the veteran Kang Yu-wei; the other, demanding republicanism, led by Sun Yat-sen. Kang being an exile in Japan after the Emperor died in 1908, many of his sympathizers turned to republicanism. Since 1895, Sun had been collecting funds (largely abroad) for the organization of his republican rebels. These in turn co-operated with secret societies within China until a vigorous antidynastic movement was well under way.

By the early spring of 1911, only an incident was necessary to precipitate revolt. In April, at Canton, one of the most revolutionary centers, the viceroy was attacked and the Tartar general killed. Other scattered clashes occurred in the valley of the Yangtze.

It was in the upper Yangtze region in particular that public sentiment was aggravated by the attempts of Peking to build a national system of railways. The problem of transportation had long been one of the most serious in China. Commercial development, the relief of famine, and effective control by the central government—all these depended on the construction of railways. Early in 1911, the Peking administration was arranging for a loan from banking groups in the United States, Great Britain, France, and Germany for railway projects in the provinces of Hupeh and Hunan and westward into Szechwan. Portions of these railroads had already been constructed with local capital, but the attempt of Peking to convert the roads into national railways aroused the deep-rooted spirit of provincial and local autonomy. Many of the provinces protested to Peking. In August, at Chengtu (Szechwan province), a mob resisted efforts of the viceroy to arrest a number of local railway stockholders. The uprising spread rapidly throughout the province, drawing its support not only from those interested in the railway question but also from an ever-increasing army of men made desperate by famine. Then came the incident from which the revolution proper arose.

The Revolution Breaks

The explosion of a bomb on October 9 in a factory located in the Russian concession of Hankow led to arrests, the discovery of a revolutionary plot, and the beheading of four prisoners. The revolutionists decided to strike immediately. In Wuchang, across the Yangtze, they were joined in an attack upon the viceroy's yamen by large bodies of mutinous troops, and the city was taken by October 11. Li Yuan-hung, a general who had been second in command of the Imperial troops, was forced to take command of the rebel army. News of the outbreak spread rapidly, particularly in south China, where the Manchus were held responsible for all the ills from which the Empire suffered. In Peking, the government, taking alarm, recalled Yuan Shih-kai to deal with the revolting provinces. The National Assembly, holding its second session in Peking, denounced the viceroys of Szechwan and Wuchang and demanded their punishment. In the name of the five-year-old Emperor, the government issued a penitential decree in which the sovereign took upon himself responsibility for all the calamities that were befalling his people, and again promised further reform. A responsible cabinet was promised. Yuan Shih-kai was appointed Prime Minister, and early in November was elected to

Ewing Galloway.

Li Yuan-hung. He led the republican army in 1911 when the age-old monarchy was overthrown. He was then a Manchu garrison commander and was compelled by the rebels to take over the revolution at the point of a pistol. That is how he turned republican, but his conversion was lasting.

the same office by the Assembly. All this was to no avail; the momentum of revolution was too great to be arrested by words. Cities and provinces throughout the Empire declared their independence. The verdict of the people had already been given.

By early December, China south of the Yangtze was largely under control of the republican rebels, while provinces north of the river remained for the most part nominally loyal to the government in Peking. The rebels were not prepared to challenge Yuan Shih-kai's well-trained battalions, nor could the latter hope to subdue the south except by a prolonged and costly civil war, the outcome of which was beyond prediction. On the assumption, then, that a constitutional monarchy under the Manchus might satisfy the nation at large, Yuan, who was now master in Peking, agreed to a truce and to a peace conference, which met in Shanghai. The regent, Prince Chun, having already resigned, the north was represented in the negotiations by Tang Shao-yi, who had been closely identified with the Harriman-Straight loan negotiations in Manchuria. The south was represented by Wu Ting-fang, formerly Chinese Minister to the United States. The deliberations, prolonged until the last day of December, ended in a deadlock. The south wanted a national convention, so picked that establishment of a republican government would be inevitable, and to this Yuan Shih-kai would not agree.

Sun Yat-sen versus Yuan Shih-kai

Meanwhile, a national council, selected by a variety of procedures, had assembled at Nanking. Presuming to speak for revolutionary China, it straightway elected (December 28) Sun Yat-sen as president of the "republic." Sun had returned to China from Europe, arriving at Shanghai in December, while the peace negotiations were in progress. As a result, by January, 1912, China was in possession of two governments. The southern republican regime under Sun controlled all south of the Yangtze. The Manchus, now dominated by Yuan Shih-kai, held the north. But Yuan's policy had undergone a striking change. He was convinced that the Manchus must abdicate, yet he was determined that the influence of the north should be maintained in whatever government should result. Toward the end of January, an accommodation was made possible. The northern generals had already memorialized the

Throne favoring abdication, thus leaving the Throne without support, while in the south, Sun Yat-sen had offered to resign in favor of Yuan Shih-kai, provided the latter would pledge his undivided support to the cause of republicanism. On February 12, the decrees of abdication of the Manchus were issued, and

Keystone View Co.

DR. SUN YAT-SEN. Intellectually the founder of the Chinese Republic, his influence has been more powerful in death than during his lifetime.

Yuan Shih-kai was instructed to organize a provisional republican government. The former Emperor was to retain his title and was to be accorded the respect due a visiting foreign sovereign. A residence was to be assigned him, his private property was to be respected, and he was to receive an annuity of 4,000,000 taels. The Manchu people were to be assured equality with the Chinese. And so ended the dynasty that had occupied the Dragon Throne since the conquests of the descendants of Nurhachu in 1644.

With the resignation of Sun and his replacement by Yuan as president, the civil war appeared to be ended, with China embarked on her republican career. Nanking was to be the new capital. General Li Yuan-hung, commander of the revolutionary armies, was made vice-president. But China's political problems had not been solved. North and south China had not been reconciled. The followers of Sun Yat-sen were demanding a democratic republic. They expected Yuan Shih-kai to provide what they wanted and then retire. This Yuan had not the slightest intention of doing. He was neither a republican nor a democrat. He needed southern support, and he was pledged to republican government, but he was no friend of democracy, since he knew that China was not prepared for it. Probably from his first assumption of office he planned to restore monarchy and to follow a policy of moderate and gradual reform as the people could be prepared for it. During March, 1912, Yuan took the oath of office, remaining, however, with the backing of his army, in Peking. At the same time, a provisional constitution was promulgated. The work of the republicans, it provided for a government by a president, a vice-president, a national advisory council, and a bicameral legislature, in which most of the power was centered. The first meeting of the council was held in April, when it soon became evident that followers of Sun were in control. As a consequence, parliament was not summoned until the following year. The republic had been launched, but harmony in its counsels was conspicuously absent.

Prospects for the Republic

While the future of the infant republic was not bright, the Chinese could, nevertheless, pride themselves on tangible gains. The Manchu Dynasty, which had burdened the nation with its incompetence for a century, had been overthrown. With it had gone the undisputed control of a scholarly but unintelligent officialdom. The radicals, men trained in western theories of political and social freedom, had won their first victory. It would be their task to transform ancient, autocratic, and conservative China into a modern, liberal, and progressive state. The way for this change had been opened by a remarkably brief and, comparatively speaking, bloodless revolution. There had been little fighting in the engagements on the Yangtze. Many of the Imperial troops went over peaceably to the side of the revolution. There were few disturbances in cities or villages, for the Chinese had long before mastered the art of local self-government; and, finally, there was no foreign military intervention, with all its attendant evils.

And yet, only a beginning had been made. If the new China were to emerge as a democratic and stable republic, there would be many problems to be faced. How would the young radicals meet the problem of educating an illiterate population of more than 300 millions, of providing a real central government in an Empire where local autonomy had long prevailed, of substituting the individual for the family, and of discarding the political wisdom of the sages for the modern political notions of western barbarians? On questions such as these, the future of China's republic was to depend.

Selected Bibliography

The best study of China in the decade prior to the republican revolution is M. E. Cameron, *The Reform Movement in China, 1898-1912* (Stanford University: 1931). G. M. Dutcher, *The Political Awakening of the East* (New York: 1925). Arthur N. Holcombe, *The Chinese Revolution* (Cambridge: 1930), ch. 3, the overthrow of the Manchus. P. W. Kuo, *The Chinese System of Education* (New York: 1915). Paul Linebarger, *Sun Yat-Sen and the Chinese Republic* (New York: 1925). H. B. Morse, *The Trade and Administration of China* (New York: 1920). H. B. Morse, *The Inter-*

national Relations of the Chinese Empire (London: 1918), vol. 3, ch. 15, the downfall of the Empire. F. McCormick, *The Flowery Republic* (New York: 1913). Paul Monroe, *China: A Nation in Evolution* (New York: 1928), ch. 7 on Sun Yat-sen and the nationalistic movement. J. J. Mullowney, ed., *A Revelation of the Chinese Revolution* (New York: 1914). A. M. Pooley, *Japan's Foreign Policies* (London: 1920), chs. 3-4. John Gilbert Reid, *The Manchu Abdication and the Powers, 1908-1912* (Berkeley: 1935). P. S. Reinsch, *Intellectual and Political Currents in the Far East* (Boston: 1911). Jean Rodes, *La Fin Des Mandchous* (Paris: 1919). Sun Yat-sen, *Memoirs of a Chinese Revolutionary* (London: 1918). Stephen King-Hall, *Western Civilization and the Far East* (New York: 1924). Payson J. Treat, *The Far East* (New York: 1928), chs. 36-37. T'ang Leang-li, *The Inner History of the Chinese Revolution* (New York: 1930). H. M. Vinacke, *Modern Constitutional Development in China* (Princeton: 1920), chs. 2-5. W. W. Willoughby, *Constitutional Government in China* (Washington: 1922). E. T. Williams, *China Yesterday and To-Day* (New York: 1929), chs. 23-24, covering the era of reform and the revolution. P. M. A. Linebarger, *The Political Doctrines of Sun Yat-sen* (Baltimore: 1937).

CHAPTER XXVI

The Far East in the World War

THE FIRST PHASE: 1912-1915

IN THE very first years of its existence the young republic of China faced problems of gigantic proportions. The first of these was the problem of government. The second involved financing the new regime through international loans. The third included important developments in Chino-Japanese relations subsequent to Japan's entry into the World War. All of these problems were, of course, closely related. In reality, they were merely various aspects of a single problem—China's failure to preserve her own sovereignty in fact as well as in name. Since 1842, when the British secured the Treaty of Nanking, China had permitted one foreign power after another to impose practical limitations upon her sovereignty. Her tariffs were made by foreigners through their treaties. Her courts had no jurisdiction over the foreign resident on her soil. Strategically choice spots of her territory were occupied as foreign naval bases. The most valuable sections of her most important commercial port—Shanghai—were ruled by foreigners. Foreign concessions existed in many of the treaty ports. Foreign troops, including those of the United States, policed the railroad from the nation's capital, Peking, to the sea. China was not an equal among the great powers. Yet it was the policy of the powers to maintain the fiction of China's statehood, her sovereignty, her independence, her territorial integrity, and her administrative entity. These were the sonorous phrases which fitted so aptly into diplomatic language or into the pious speeches of western politicians.

These limitations upon China's existence as an independent sovereign state have frequently been described during the first two decades of the twentieth century as the cause of all China's woes. It would be more correct to describe them as a result rather than a cause of China's political status. For the republic which was ushered into being in the first months of 1912, China had virtually no preparation. To begin with, only a small minority of her peoples were literate. Even a representative republic presupposes political activity by a fair proportion of the populace. The Chinese, however, were entirely ignorant both of the political theories and of the political forms on which western republicanism was supposed to rest. It is quite true that they had long been conversant with forms of village democracy, and had ruled themselves with remarkable success through the craft, the trade, and the professional guilds. In place of all this, the revolution proposed to "set up an ideal representative democratic system on a territorial [national] basis."

Republican Politics in China

When by March, 1912, the new Chinese republic had acquired a provisional president (Yuan Shih-kai) and a provisional constitution, political parties made their appearance. The first and most important of these was Kuomintang (National People's Party), the successor to the Tung Meng Hui, the secret revolutionary organization of the southern republicans. Opposed to these extreme republicans was the Chin-Pu Tang (Progressive Party), nominally under the leadership of Li Yuan-hung and inclined to support President Yuan. Finally, there were two political factions, the Pei-Yang Military Party and the Chiao Tung, both of which supported Yuan Shih-kai. The Pei-Yang had been founded originally by Li Hung-chang. In 1912, its membership was composed mostly of men who had held office under Yuan in the days when he was building the new northern army under the Empire. It was on this group that Yuan depended primarily for support.[1]

The political issue which confronted China from March, 1912, until April, 1913, centered about Yuan Shih-kai's plan to establish a strong executive government based on the authority of himself and supported by his henchmen, and the plan of the southern republicans to found a parliamentary state. By terms of the provisional constitution, a permanent constitution was to be drafted by a parliamentary committee. Yuan's failure to summon parliament and his known opposition to this plan of constitution-drafting brought forth bitter criticism from the south. Among the southern spokesmen was Sung Chiao-jen, the candidate of the republicans for the office of premier. Outspoken in his denunciation of Yuan, he was assassinated in March, 1913, while in Shanghai on his way to Peking for the opening of parliament. For his act, Yuan was held responsible by the Kuomintang. Such was the tension that when in the following month (April) parliament convened, the president did not attend. Further difficulties arose over the organization of the two houses; before these had been settled the parliamentarians launched an attack on the president's financial policy, which was to involve the young republic in a program of heavy borrowing from western bankers. The real object of the attack was fear of Yuan's increased military power, which would result from a full treasury. The method of attack was to charge that the control measures demanded by the foreign bankers were unbecoming to an independent republic. Nevertheless, Yuan secured his loan, and thereupon proceeded to replace revolutionary provincial governors by his own military appointees. Against this move, Sun Yat-sen and some of his followers rose in an abortive revolt, which resulted in its leader

---

[1] After Yuan's death, the party split into three groups: (1) the Chihli party, under Tsao Kun and Wu Pei-fu (2) the Mukden party, under Chang Tso-lin, and (3) the Anfu Club, under Tuan Chi-jui. In subsequent years, one or another of these so-called parties was to dominate the political life of Peking and for a time the destinies of China.

being forced into exile. What was left of the parliament confirmed Yuan as president. A new constitution was prepared,
but when Yuan discovered that it placed authority in parliament rather than in the president, all remaining members of
the Kuomintang were charged with complicity in Sun's revolt
and were thereupon expelled. Parliament, left without a
quorum, was dissolved in January, 1914. As a concession to
respectability, Yuan prepared his own "constitutional compact," which placed all power in the president's hands. Yuan
was now virtually a dictator. He "was far more powerful
than the emperor he had unseated."[2] The success of Yuan
in creating his own personal government immediately after
the republican revolution was due not only to his own
political capacity and his knowledge of the Chinese people, but
also to the financial backing he received from foreign bankers
and their governments.

China and the Foreign Bankers

Large-scale investment by foreign banks in Chinese undertakings may be said in general to date from the establishment
of the so-called spheres of influence in 1898. After the lapse of
a decade, a number of the sphere-holding powers (Great Britain, France, and Germany) and the United States (which possessed no sphere) were confronted with developments which
had not been clearly foreseen in 1898. In the first place, they
all were alarmed by the rapid development of Japan's paramount influence in south Manchuria. Secondly, the lack
of precise boundaries between the spheres in China proper gave
rise to inter-power disputes concerning rights of preference in
the construction of Chinese railways. For both of these reasons,
British, German, and French bankers thought it desirable to
co-operate in financing construction of the trunk lines which

---

[2] H. F. MacNair, *China in Revolution*. University of Chicago Press, Chicago,
1931. p. 39.

China proposed to build south and west from Hankow, known as the Hukuang railways. In May, 1909, an agreement was reached with the Chinese government. American interests, after demanding a share in the project on the basis of an option which had been granted by China in 1904, were granted permission by China and admitted with the other banking groups in May, 1910. It was understood that the British, German, French, and American bankers should co-operate in undertaking Chinese loans in general, which was a matter of importance, since American bankers had already reached a preliminary agreement to finance currency reform in China and certain industrial projects in Manchuria. This plan for a four-power banking group was practically complete in the spring of 1911. Then followed the revolution and the overthrow of the Manchu Dynasty. The new regime under Yuan Shih-kai needed funds quite as badly as the old, and so negotiation with the foreign banking groups, to which by June, 1912, Japan and Russia had been added, was continued on the subject of a "reorganization loan," which was, so to speak, to set the new republic on its feet. An agreement having been reached between Yuan and the bankers early in 1913, the loan for 25 million pounds sterling was floated in London, Paris, Berlin, St. Petersburg, Brussels, and Tokyo. The American banking group, which had been closely associated with all the preliminary negotiations, did not participate. What is the explanation of its sudden withdrawal?

American Financiers and China

The background which explains the interest manifested by the American government and by private American bankers in financing China is an exceedingly complex story. The reader is already familiar with the ambitions of Harriman to control the Japanese and the Russian railways in Manchuria, of Willard Straight to finance a Manchurian bank with American capital, of Harriman and Straight to promote the Chinchow-Aigun Railway, and of Secretary Knox to "neutralize" the Manchurian lines. These projects, although receiving little, if any, encouragement from President Roosevelt and Secretary Root, represented a policy supported with enthusiasm by President Taft and Secretary Knox. It was a policy commonly referred to as "Dollar Diplomacy" and defined by one of its ablest exponents as:

> . . . logical manifestation of our national growth, and the rightful assumption by the United States of a more important place at the council table of nations. Our export trade is constantly increasing and foreign markets are becoming each year more and more necessary to our manufacturers. The new policy aims not only to protect those Americans already engaged in foreign trade but to promote fresh endeavor and by *diplomatic action* pave the way for those who have not yet been, but who will later be, obliged to sell either capital or goods abroad. [3]

The orthodox version of the relations of the American bankers to the Six-Power Consortium, which had been formed by 1912, is that they participated at the request and on the initiative of the American Department of State. The bankers who formed the American group professed to be interested in Chinese loans not primarily for the profits involved but rather to serve the political purposes of the Taft administration. In his message to Congress in December, 1909, the President referred to the co-operation of the American bankers as the "indispensable instrumentality" which the American government needed to enable it "to carry out a practical and real application of the open door policy." However, it is to be noted that Willard Straight, both as American Consul in Manchuria and as financial agent for Harriman and the bankers, was an enthusiastic advocate of American participation in Chinese finance as a means of blocking the Russians and the Japanese.

---

[3] Willard Straight, *China's Loan Negotiations,* in *Recent Developments in China,* G. H. Blakeslee, ed. G. E. Stechert and Company, New York, 1913, p. 121. Italics are those of the present writer.

It was he who converted the Taft administration to these views. He, in turn, "owed his consular appointment partly to Harriman."

. . . it seems clear that throughout he was acting as an agent of bankers who from the first knew what they wanted, and that his part in the transaction was to win from the State Department the strong diplomatic support which was absolutely essential for the successful prosecution of financial projects in China. [4]

The assumption that the American bankers were not interested primarily in profits appears to be refuted not only by the fact that it was they, and not the State Department, who assumed the initiative, but also by the fact that they showed no reluctance to enter the international syndicate. What is more, American bankers who were not invited to join the American group, "instead of acting as if they welcomed their escape from the performance of an unattractive task, resented their exclusion." [5] Finally, the control measures which the bankers of all groups demanded of China would appear to indicate that the undertaking was not entirely altruistic. These measures, in the case of the reorganization loan, were briefly as follows:

1. The banking groups were to have the right to satisfy themselves as to the purposes for which China required funds.

2. China was to create a system of audit, in which foreigners were to be assigned executive powers, to insure effective expenditure of loan funds for specified purposes.

3. China's salt taxes were to be hypothecated for the service of the loan and administered by the maritime customs or a similar organization under foreign direction in order to safeguard the loan against the recurrence of revolutionary conditions.

4. China was not to borrow through other banking groups until the entire loan had been issued.

---

[4] Jacob Viner, "Political Aspects of International Finance." *The Journal of Business of the University of Chicago,* 1928. Vol. I, pp. 345-346.

[5] *Ibid.* p. 346.

5. For a period of five years, China was to appoint financial agents of the banking groups in the Consortium to "assist" the Chinese government in its work of reorganization.

President Wilson's Policy

Against these control measures the southern republicans in China's first parliament (1913) protested vigorously. These protests constituted the principal point of attack upon Yuan Shih-kai. The existence of this strong republican opposition was well known to all the banking groups. Consequently, when the Wilson administration assumed office in March, 1913, it was asked by the American group whether it, like the previous administration, would request the bankers to participate in the China loan. President Wilson replied that his administration would decline to make any such request because it did not approve the conditions of the loan or the implications of responsibility on its part which it was plainly told would be involved in the request.

The conditions of the loan seem to us to touch very nearly the administrative independence of China itself; and this administration does not feel that it ought, even by implication, to be a party to those conditions. The responsibility on its part which would be implied in requesting the bankers to undertake the loan might conceivably go the length in some unhappy contingence of forcible interference in the financial, and even the political affairs of that great Oriental state, just now awakening to a consciousness of its power and of its obligations to its people. . . .
Our interests are those of the open door—a door of friendship and mutual advantage. This is the only door we care to enter.

Herein, then, lay the explanation of why the American banking group did not participate. To President Taft, the work of the bankers was an "indispensable instrumentality" to preserve the open door and the integrity of China. To President Wilson, in 1913, the bankers appeared as the instrument most likely to destroy them. Curiously enough, before many years had passed, the Wilson administration was to reverse its policy and put the bankers to work in the Four-Power China Consortium of 1920.

In the broadest sense, the Six-Power Consortium of 1912-1913 was the instrumentality that enabled Yuan Shih-kai to consolidate his power, to oust a parliament, and to place his own appointees in strategic posts. The financial negotiations between Yuan and the powers from 1912 to 1914 make it quite clear that, while western peoples bestowed freely their blessing on China's revolutionary republicanism, western bankers, traders, and, with the exception of the first Wilson administration, western governments wanted a China ruled by a strong executive. Since Yuan Shih-kai seemed to meet this need, it was to him that the foreign powers threw their support.

The third major problem which confronted the young republic concerned the relations of China with her small but more vigorous oriental neighbor, Japan. These new relations were occasioned, though not caused, by the outbreak of the World War and Japan's entry as an ally of Great Britain. Between August, 1914, and May, 1915, Japan fell heir to important German properties and interests in the Far East and challenged the position of western imperialists there by affirming her own right to paramount interest in China. These events were of such importance that their consideration in some detail is essential.

Japan Enters the World War

The initial moves which eventually brought Japan into the World War were made apparently by the Japanese government. Late in July, 1914, views were exchanged between Tokyo and London concerning Japan's obligations under the Anglo-Japanese Alliance in the event that Great Britain should become involved in the European War. On August 4, the Japanese Foreign Office informed the press that Japan might be called upon to act under the Alliance. On August 7, the

British Ambassador at Tokyo formally requested Japanese assistance to destroy German ships of war in Chinese waters. Marquis Okuma, the Prime Minister, and Count Kato, the Foreign Minister, favored this British proposal, but were not content that Japanese military and naval operations should be confined to destruction of German warships in Chinese waters. At a cabinet meeting held during the night of August 7, Count Kato asserted that:

. . . though the general conditions were not such as to impose upon Japan the duty to join the war under treaty obligations, it was the proper course to take as a voluntary expression of friendship toward Great Britain under the alliance. He welcomed it as an opportunity to destroy the German influence from eastern Asia and to enhance the international position of Japan.[6]

Early on the morning of August 8, the Cabinet determined to join the war.

This decision of the cabinet to enter the war on the side of the Allies was based upon the general spirit of the Anglo-Japanese Alliance, though not legally obliged, and for revenge upon Germany for her part in the three-power intervention after the Sino-Japanese War of 1894-1895.[7]

Approval of the Genro to the policy of entering the war was

---

[6] Tatsuji Takeuchi, *War and Diplomacy in the Japanese Empire.* Doubleday, Doran & Company, New York, 1935. pp. 169-170.

There were large groups in Japan which favored the nation's entering the war regardless of obligations. Chief among these was the pro-British group, headed by Kato, the Foreign Minister, though it cannot be said that he would have deliberately pushed Japan into the conflict had she not been invited. A large section of the press clamored for war, especially after it became known that the German Pacific squadron was stopping neutral ships. No doubt powerful Japanese shipping interests were behind this, but evidence on the point is not conclusive. It is also possible that a group in the Japanese army which favored Japanese expansion on the mainland welcomed an opportunity to take Kiaochow and hence gave support to the popular demand for revenge for Germany's intervention in 1895.

Supplementary to Takeuchi's account, the best brief treatment of Japan's entry is Charles Nelson Spinks, "Japan's Entrance into the World War," in *The Pacific Historical Review,* December, 1936.

[7] Tatsuji Takeuchi, *op. cit.* p. 170.

given on the evening of the same day. On August 9, it was
decided to give Germany one week in which to reply to an ultimatum. Meanwhile, Count Kato requested the British government to agree to Japanese participation under principles of the
Alliance and not to limit Japan's activities to destruction of
German warships in Chinese
waters. The British requested
delay, observing that a Japanese declaration of war
would be disturbing to the
entire Far East. Kato assured
London that a declaration of
war would not threaten British trade and added that Japan
had no territorial ambitions.
The Foreign Minister asserted
that "popular demand for taking revenge for the three-
power intervention [of 1895]
had been so persistent that
further delay would lead to a
serious political situation in
domestic politics." [8] On August 11, Great Britain asked
Japan to reconsider her decision to make war on Ger-

Japan Tourist Bureau.

SHIGENOBU OKUMA. One of Japan's
most popular party leaders, he fought
untiringly for liberalism under the Constitution. Although favored with the
post of Prime Minister, he never attained the full status of Genro.

many, but when no change was forthcoming, agreed that
Japan might declare war. Britain sought, however, to limit
the Japanese to operations within Chinese waters, her object
being to prevent Japanese occupation of German Pacific
islands, but in this, too, she failed. On August 15, Japan
dispatched her ultimatum to Germany.

[8] *Ibid.* p. 172.

The Ultimatum to Germany

This famous document contained the following "advice," which would seem to indicate that Japan had not forgotten Germany's pious intervention of 1895:

Considering it highly important and necessary, in the present situation, to take measures to remove all causes of disturbance to the peace of the Far East and to safeguard the general interests contemplated by the Agreement of Alliance between Japan and Great Britain, in order to secure a firm and enduring peace in eastern Asia, the establishment of which is the aim of the said Agreement, the Imperial Japanese Government sincerely believe it their duty to give advice to the Imperial German Government to carry out the following two propositions: (1) Withdraw their men-of-war and armed vessels of all kinds from the Japanese and Chinese waters, and disarm at once all that cannot be so withdrawn; (2) Deliver up to the Japanese authorities, by September 15th, without condition or compensation, the entire leased territory of Kiaochow with a view to eventual restoration of the same to China.

Germany was given until August 23 to reply. Since Japan received no response, war was declared. An extraordinary session of the Diet approved, without a dissenting vote, a war budget of 53,000,000 yen, despite the fact that the government did not reveal "the precise causes and procedures" leading to the declaration of war. For this secrecy, the government was criticized severely by members of the House of Representatives, who pointed out that by publication of the diplomatic correspondence on the outbreak of the Russo-Japanese War, the government had won the full confidence and support of the nation. Some representatives questioned whether Japan had any obligations to join the war under the Anglo-Japanese Alliance.

When the Thirty-fifth Diet met in December, 1914, the government was again attacked on the question of the nation's participation in the war and in particular with respect to the future of Kiaochow and the German islands in the Pacific. Count Kato, replying for the government, stated that Japan was not committed to any power on the future status of Kiao-chow. The government was likewise charged, and with some justification, with using the Imperial authority to shield itself from public and parliamentary criticism. So bitter was the conflict between the Cabinet and the lower house that army and navy appropriations were passed only with the greatest difficulty. The Diet was finally dissolved on December 25. As will become apparent later, this tense situation in domestic politics was not without its effects on foreign policy.

The government of the United States was also concerned when it became evident that hostilities might spread to the Far East. The German Ambassador at Tokyo informed his American colleague, on August 10, that "elimination of Germany from the Far East and the transfer of her possessions to Japan would be prejudicial to American interests." [9] China likewise had approached the United States, seeking, in the first instance, American good offices to exclude the area of hostilities from the Far East, an act which the Japanese regarded as distinctly unfriendly. Secretary Bryan suggested to the British that the warring powers consider the Pacific as a neutral area, and Sir Edward Grey replied that he was prepared to entertain a proposal from the United States to England and to Germany that the *status quo* be maintained in China. Meanwhile, the Department of State was disturbed by reports reaching it from the German Minister in Peking to the effect that Japan and Russia had concluded, in 1912, a secret agreement by which Russia, in the event of becoming involved in hostilities in Europe, would lend Japan all practical support in annexing south Manchuria and acquiring Kiaochow, Russia reserving freedom of action in north Manchuria. This supposed agreement was said to have been modified later, by the intervention of Great Britain, to limit Japan's compensation to Kiaochow alone.

---

[9] United States, *Foreign Relations,* 1914 (supplement). p. 165.

Alarmed by these reports, Secretary Bryan expressed his views to the Japanese government in a note of August 19. While refraining from any expression on the merits of the differences between Japan and Germany, he observed:

[The American government] notes with satisfaction that Japan, in demanding the surrender by Germany of the entire leased territory of Kiaochow, does so with the purpose of restoring that territory to China. . . . Should disturbances in the interior of China seem to the Japanese Government to require measures to be taken by Japan or other powers to restore order, the Imperial Japanese Government will no doubt desire to consult with the American Government before deciding upon a course of action. This would be in accordance with the agreement made in the exchange of notes on the 30th of November, 1908 [the Root-Takahira notes]. [10]

China Leans on the United States

On the following day, the Chinese Minister of Communications suggested that German rights at Tsingtao be ceded to the United States for immediate transfer to China, the object being to throw the weight of Japanese resentment against the United States. Secretary Bryan replied promptly to the Chinese that the course proposed would do more to provoke than to avert war. Once again the major problem was China's incapacity to maintain her neutrality and her efforts to place this burden on other powers, in particular the United States. Early in September, the efforts of China to shift her responsibilities upon the United States were revealed to the State Department by the American *chargé* at Peking, John MacMurray. His comments are of sufficient significance to merit extended quotation:

It would seem that, during the first weeks of the war, even the more serious and responsible of the Chinese were deluded by the rumors which were disseminated from Japanese sources to the effect that the American Government was preparing to act in opposition to Japanese interests in China; and upon that delusion

---

[10] *Ibid.* p. 172.

they founded extravagant hopes that the United States would undertake to guarantee China against any territorial aggression or disregard of its sovereignty . . . the suggestion of consultation between the American and Japanese Governments [the Bryan note to Japan, August 19], in pursuance of the Root-Takahira exchange of notes of 1908, seems to have been interpreted in some Chinese quarters as indicating a determination on the part of our Government to insist upon its approval as a condition precedent to any Japanese action in Chinese territory.

On the 27th ultimo Dr. V. K. Wellington Koo, of the Wai Chiao Pu, called upon me informally, professedly at the instance of the President, to inquire as to the precise terms and purport of the American note [to Japan]. . . . In discussing the matter with me, Dr. Koo strongly intimated the view that the Root-Takahira exchange of notes established in favor of the United States a right to be consulted with respect to any action contemplated by Japan in Chinese territories, as though to imply that such rights were held by our Government in trust for the Government of China; and he specified the possible landing of an expeditionary [Japanese] force in Shantung (beyond the limits of the zone of condominium established by the treaty of lease of the Kiaochow territory) as constituting a question in regard to which the Japanese Government would thereby be required to seek the approval of the United States.

Not knowing how peremptorily our Government is disposed to insist upon its suggestion that the Japanese Government would doubtless desire to consult our own in the event that it should judge the situation here to require action, I pointed out to Dr. Koo that that suggestion in terms concerns only the case of internal disorders in China; and I furthermore reminded him that the Root-Takahira exchange of notes, although frequently referred to for convenience as an agreement, was in fact simply a joint declaration of policy rather than a convention establishing a legal status which either party might invoke against the other. [11]

This interpretation of American policy was fully supported by the Acting Secretary of State, Robert Lansing, in his instructions to Paul S. Reinsch, the newly appointed Minister to China. His words described American policy with an exact-

---

[11] *Ibid,* pp. 186-187.

ness which even the Secretary of State perhaps did not fully appreciate.

The United States [said Lansing] desires China to feel that American friendship [for China] is sincere and to be assured that this Government will be glad to exert any influence, which it possesses, to further, by peaceful methods, the welfare of the Chinese people, but the Department realizes that it would be quixotic in the extreme to allow the question of China's territorial integrity to entangle the United States in international difficulties.[12]

While these significant developments in American policy were taking place, the Japanese were proceeding to drive the Germans from Kiaochow. This German naval base in Shantung province, only some 550 miles from the coasts of western Japan, possessed an excellent harbor and was strongly entrenched behind a double line of forts. Like other great European powers, Germany had erected her stronghold on Chinese soil in defiance of any real respect for Chinese sovereignty. Her purpose was to maintain and to promote German trade, German investment, and German prestige in the Far East by political action. Like other European powers, she had claimed with success a vast area in China as a German sphere of influence. This program, it will be recalled, had been carried into effect as early as 1898, only three years after Germany had "advised" Japan to withdraw from the Liaotung peninsula in the interest of preserving "the peace of the Far East." In 1904 and 1905, the Japanese had felt called upon to drive another European power, Russia, from a naval base erected on Chinese soil. The Port Arthur leasehold had been accordingly transferred to Japan, and in 1914 the Japanese had substantial grounds for the belief that what Europe could in China, Japan could likewise do, and that the precedent of 1905 would be followed.

---

[12] *Ibid.* p. 190.

China and her Neutrality

In attacking Kiaochow, Japan proposed to invest the fortress by a land attack, which involved crossing Chinese territory. Again, as in 1904, foreign powers were to fight on Chinese soil. As usual, China's neutrality, which she was not herself willing to defend, was given little consideration, Japan proceeding to land troops at Lungkow to march overland against the fortress. Japan had notified China as early as August 20, and on September 3, China went through the formality of specifying a war zone. In the siege which followed, the Japanese were assisted by a British contingent, whose presence was probably occasioned more by political than by military considerations. The fortress was finally taken on November 7. Meanwhile, the Japanese had occupied the German railway from Kiaochow to Tsinan, a distance of 256 miles, by which they were able to control the hinterland and the industrial properties which Germany had erected in her sphere.

Concurrently with these operations, the Japanese navy had taken possession of German islands in the north Pacific (the Marshalls, the Carolines, and the Marianas). Their ships assisted also in clearing the Pacific and Indian Oceans of German raiders and in convoying Australian and New Zealand forces as far as the Suez Canal. Later, some of Japan's destroyer divisions served in the Mediterranean.

Japan's military and naval activities in the war were, however, of far less significance than her political activities in China. These activities have gained notoriety under the label of the Twenty-one Demands, but are more properly called the Chino-Japanese Treaties and Notes of May, 1915. The Russo-Japanese War was the first major challenge hurled by Japan at western imperialism in China. The Twenty-one Demands, presented to China in 1915, constituted the second.

Chino-Japanese Treaties, May, 1915

The occasion for the policy enunciated by Japan in 1915 was, of course, the preoccupation of the European powers in the World War. Japan was roundly denounced for using this advantage, despite the fact that it is a principle on which national policies have always been advanced. The policy itself, however, was by no means new in 1915. It was merely the natural development of Japanese imperialism, which hoped to supplant western imperialism in China. For some years, increasing numbers of Japanese had been convinced that western imperialism there was a threat to the development and the security of Japan itself. In 1905, to be sure, the advance of Russia in Manchuria and Korea had been effectively stopped, but in subsequent years (1906-1910), successive Japanese ministries felt that their position in south Manchuria was threatened seriously by economic and political schemes of American and British interests. These, in turn, had been defeated with the collapse of the Knox neutralization proposals. Nevertheless, Japan was not satisfied with the attitude of China. She realized that the Chinese would have expelled her gladly from south Manchuria, and that they had consistently encouraged the Americans and the British to break her monopoly in railroad construction. The whole question of the future of Japan's administration in Manchuria was discussed from time to time in the press and as early as 1910 by members of the Diet, who interrogated the government without success. In 1913, Count Komei Kato sought to reach an understanding with the British government on Japan's future policy in China. He informed the British Foreign Secretary that the Japanese people had vital interest in the Kwantung leasehold and were determined to remain in permanent occupation of it.

He stated to the British foreign secretary that if a "psychological moment" should arrive the Japanese government would take up the matter of extending the lease and concessions in Manchuria. [13]

The Katsura Ministry, which approved these views, was soon replaced by a government headed by Admiral Yamamoto. The same views were urged upon this ministry, but it in turn was replaced, on April 16, 1914, by the Okuma government, in which Count Kato became Foreign Minister. One of his first acts was to reorganize the personnel of the diplomatic service, in particular that of the legation and consulates in China. On August 21, Minister Hioki, in Peking, was instructed to inform Yuan Shih-kai that a frank exchange of views between the two governments was imperative. By the end of September, Premier Okuma, together with Yamagata and Oyama, had determined that Japan should seek a firmer position in south Manchuria and Inner Mongolia and that negotiations with China should be initiated after the capture of Kiaochow. When this occurred (November 7), Count Kato's "psychological moment" had arrived. The press began to advocate retention of Kiaochow and a more vigorous assertion of Japanese interests in China. Hioki was recalled from Peking for instructions, which were handed to him on December 3, 1914. The way was paved further when, on January 7, 1915, China revoked her declaration of a war zone and demanded immediate withdrawal of the Japanese troops from Shantung. In Japan "public opinion was raised to a state of high frenzy." On January 18, her demands were presented to President Yuan Shih-kai.

The demands fell into five groups. The first dealt with Shantung, in substance requiring that China assent to all matters previously agreed upon by Japan and Germany relative to German rights and concessions in the province. This was in accord with the precedent established in Manchuria in 1905. The second group dealt with south Manchuria and eastern Inner Mongolia, requiring an extension of the Kwantung lease and the railway concessions to ninety-nine years, in conformity

---

[13] Tatsuji Takeuchi, *op. cit.* p. 184.

with the terms of the French and German leaseholds. Further, Japan demanded that, in both south Manchuria and eastern Inner Mongolia, her nationals should be granted the right to lease or to own land, to conduct business, and to be granted certain mining rights. The building of railroads in these areas was to be subject to Japan's approval. The third group dealt with the valuable coal and iron properties of the Hanyehping Company in the Yangtze Valley; this company was to be made a Chino-Japanese concern, the working of mines in the region to be subject to its approval. The fourth group required a pledge from China not to alienate, by cession or lease, any harbor, bay, or island on her coast. The fifth group, which contained the most objectionable clauses, the acceptance of which would have reduced China almost to a Japanese protectorate, was labeled "requests." China was asked: (1) to engage Japanese political, financial, and military advisers; (2) to grant to Japanese schools, temples, and hospitals the right to own land in the interior; (3) to place the Chinese police under Chino-Japanese control, or to engage Japanese as supervisory officials, in certain localities; (4) to purchase her munitions from Japan, or to establish an arsenal under Chino-Japanese management; (5) to grant Japan the right to construct certain railway lines; (6) to consult Japan first should she desire capital for railways, mines, and harbor works in Fukien province; and (7) to grant Japan freedom for religious propaganda.

For many years after 1915, this Japanese program provoked a storm of criticism in western states. This was somewhat remarkable, since the Japanese program involved little which western imperialists had not themselves practiced in China. In the main, the criticism may be attributed not so much to what Japan was attempting to do but rather to the fact that Japan, an oriental state, was doing it, and at a time when western imperialists were not in a position to defend themselves. The most valid criticisms of Japan's policy have been made by Japanese themselves. One Japanese scholar of distinction said:

. . . the actual demands were far in excess of the purposes . . . sought. One can easily understand Japan's anxiety to obtain security for her vast economic interests in South Manchuria and the Liaotung Peninsula. Her desire for extension of the lease of Port Arthur and Dairen and the term of her railways and other related rights and interests was quite natural. But what justification was there for Japan to demand the right of owning land, of residing and carrying on business outside of the regions specified by treaty, in a country where extraterritoriality operates? Japan should have known better because of her own experience with consular jurisdiction until very recent years. Her demand that Japanese should be employed in the service of China was nothing short of being preposterous. If Japanese experts should prove superior or more suitable to China's needs, they would be so employed by China of her own accord. The demand for a veto on economic development of South Manchuria and Eastern Inner Mongolia and the demand for mining operations in the Yangtse region were clearly at variance with the spirit of the open door which, until this time, Japan had so honorably upheld. To demand a share in police work of a sovereign nation was in direct violation of the sovereignty of that country. So also was the demand that China should buy arms from Japan. Military matters are considered secret by every nation. Japan had no right to make such a demand. Even the attempt to impose alien religions has always met with the "none-of-your-business attitude." Of course the demand for the right of preaching only provokes a smile. What do the Japanese think of the customary demand of Christian nations for such a right in making treaties with non-Christian nations? [14]

After Japan had presented her demands, the negotiations were conducted by a conference beginning February 2. By April 17, after twenty-four conferences, the Chinese had agreed in detail or in principle to fifteen of the demands. At this point their resistance stiffened, and Minister Hioki informed his government that an ultimatum was necessary. Tokyo, however, sought acceptance of a revised list, which postponed consideration of group 5, with the exception of the article on loans in Fukien. If China accepted, Japan would agree to return

---

[14] Yamato Ichihashi, *The Washington Conference and After.* Stanford University Press, Stanford University, California, 1928. pp. 291-292.

Kiaochow, on certain conditions, to China, at the close of the war. On May 1, the Chinese refused these proposals, and on May 7, Japan delivered an ultimatum which was accepted by China on May 9. On May 25, a series of treaties was signed, and notes were exchanged by the two governments. Among the principal provisions of these treaties and notes, the following may be mentioned:

Manchuria:

1. The lease of Port Arthur and the South Manchuria and Antung-Mukden Railways was extended to ninety-nine years.

2. Japanese subjects might lease land in south Manchuria for erecting commercial and industrial buildings or for farming.

3. Japanese subjects might reside and travel there and engage in business.

4. Joint Chino-Japanese agricultural enterprises were to be allowed in eastern Inner Mongolia.

5. Japanese residents referred to above were to be subject to the police, law, and taxation of China. Detailed provisions were made covering extraterritorial provisions, Japan promising to waive extraterritoriality when the judicial system of Manchuria was reformed adequately.

6. China was to open suitable places in eastern Inner Mongolia for trade and residence of foreigners.

Shantung:

1. China agreed to accept all engagements made by Japan and Germany respecting German rights and interests in Shantung.

2. Under certain conditions, Japanese capitalists were to finance a railroad from Chefoo or Lungkow to the Kiaochow-Tsinan line.

3. China agreed to open cities in Shantung to residence and trade of foreigners.

4. China agreed not to alienate any territory in Shantung.

Yangtze region:

1. China would give her approval to any future agreement between Japanese capitalists and the Hanyehping iron interests. The company was not to be nationalized nor was it to contract foreign loans without the consent of Japanese capitalists.

Non-alienation of territory:

1. This demand was modified to permit China to make a voluntary declaration that she would not alienate any of her territory.

Fukien province:

1. China declared that she had not granted and did not intend to grant to foreign nations concessions to build on the coast of Fukien province any dockyards, coaling stations, or naval bases.

By these, the principal provisions of the treaties and notes, Japan, while strengthening greatly her legal rights and interests in China, did immense damage to the cause of Chino-Japanese relations. The Chinese had long resented the pretensions of western imperialists, but in 1915 they were still more inclined to resent the pretensions of Japanese imperialism. Western opinion, both official and unofficial, leaped to the defense of China, but in view of the record which the West had already established there, it may be questioned whether this "sympathy" for China was anything more than a weapon with which to strike vicariously at Japan.

The United States and the Chino-Japanese Treaties

On May 11, 1915, after the United States had learned of the Japanese ultimatum, the Secretary of State dispatched notes to Japan and China stating:

[The American government] cannot recognize any agreement or understanding which had been entered into or which may be entered into between the Governments of Japan and China, impairing the treaty rights of the United States and its citizens in China, the political or territorial integrity of the Republic of China, or the international policy relative to China commonly known as the open door policy.

This note, coupled with the popular resentment aroused against Japan, led to the assumption that the United States was protesting officially against Japan's policy. This was not the case. On the contrary, during the course of the Chino-Japanese negotiations, the Department of State raised no objection to sixteen of the twenty-one demands. The demands that were not questioned included those respecting Shantung, south Manchuria, and eastern Inner Mongolia. These were the very points on which such pronounced anti-Japanese sentiment was raised in the United States in subsequent years. Of the five demands which did appear objectionable to the American government, two were considered to be violations of the principle of the open door, and three were regarded as violations of China's sovereignty and administrative entity. Japan conceded to the American objections in each case. She dropped four of the demands. The fifth was embodied in an exchange of notes whereby China asserted that she would not permit any power "to construct a dockyard, a coaling station for military use, or a naval base or to set up any other military establishment on the coast of Fukien Province, nor shall they allow any like establishment to be set up with any foreign capital on the said coast."

So ended the negotiations of 1915. In Japan, the policy of the Okuma Ministry was soon subjected to a series of bitter parliamentary attacks on the character of its Chinese policy. The government was accused of having approached China at an inopportune moment, of using military pressure, of creating an anti-Japanese movement in China, and, conversely, of sacrificing the interests and prestige of Japan in having offered to restore Kiaochow to China. A resolution of censure, however, failed, the vote being 232 to 133. While it is true that these attacks on the Okuma government were inspired largely by partisan politics, it is equally true that many Japanese disapproved the nation's policy.

SELECTED BIBLIOGRAPHY

J. O. P. Bland, *China, Japan and Korea* (New York: 1921), ch. 2, Yuan Shih-kai, 1912-1916. By the same author, *Recent Events and Present Policies in China* (Philadelphia: 1912). *British Documents on the Origins of the War.* Meredith E. Cameron, "American Recognition Policy Toward the Republic of China, 1912-1913," in *The Pacific Historical Review,* June, 1933. P. H. Clyde, "The Open Door," in relation to the Twenty-one Demands, in *Pacific Affairs,* Sept. 1930. Henry Chung, *The Oriental Policy of the United States* (New York: 1919). A. C. Coolidge, *The United States as a World Power* (New York: 1908). Sih-Gung Cheng, *Modern China* (Oxford: 1919), especially ch. 8 on economic concessions and foreign investments. C. Collum, "Prince Katsura," in *Contemporary Review,* Nov. 1913. E. T. S. Dugdale, *German Diplomatic Documents, 1871-1914,* 4 vols. (London: 1931), vol. 4, ch. 2, the United States and the Far East, 1909-1913. John S. Ewart, *The Roots and Causes of the War, 1914-1918,* 2 vols. (New York: 1925), vol. 1, ch. 11 on Japan's entry into the war. R. Fujisawa, *The Recent Aims and Political Development of Japan* (New Haven: 1923), especially ch. 1. A. Gerard, *Ma Mission au Japon, 1907-1914* (Paris: 1919). H. H. Gowen, *An Outline History of Japan* (New York: 1930), ch. 28. W. L. Godshall, *The International Aspects of the Shantung Question* (Philadelphia: 1923), chs. 2-3. H. A. Gibbons, *The New Map of Asia* (New York: 1916). Stanley K. Hornbeck, *Contemporary Politics in the Far East* (New York: 1926). M. C. Hsu, *Railway Problems in China* (New York: 1915). N. D. Harris, *Europe and the East* (Boston: 1926). Alexander Iswolsky, *Recollections of a Foreign Minister* (Garden City: 1921). Kikujiro Ishii, *Diplomatic Commentaries,* trans. and ed. by W. R. Langdon (Baltimore: 1936), ch. 5, the diplomacy of Japan during the World War. K. K. Kawakami, *Asia at the Door* (New York: 1914). L. Lawton, *Empires of the Far East,* 2 vols. (London: 1912). A. Lobanov-Rostovsky, *Russia and Asia* (New York: 1933), ch. 11, Russia in the Far East, 1905-1914. T. F. Millard, *Our Eastern Question* (New York: 1916), chs. 2-4 on the revolution and reconstruction in China. Gotaro Ogawa, *Conscription System in Japan* (New York: 1921). G. Ono, *War and Armament Expenditures of Japan* (New York: 1922). R. P. Porter, *Japan, the New World Power* (Oxford: 1915). Paul S. Reinsch, *An American Diplomat in China* (Garden City: 1922), chs. 1-5 on Yuan Shih-kai. Michel Ribaud, *Le Japon pendant la Guerre Européenne* (Paris: 1919). Charles N. Spinks, "Japan's Entrance into the World War," in *The Pacific Historical Review,* Dec. 1936. Willard Straight, "China's Loan Negotiations," in G. H. Blakeslee, ed., *Recent Developments in China* (New York: 1913). B. De Siebert, *Entente Diplomacy and the World, 1909-1914* (New York: 1921), bk. 1, ch. 1 on Russia, Japan, and the United States in China, 1909-1914. P. J. Treat, *Japan and the United States, 1853-1921,* rev. ed. (Stanford University: 1928), ch. 11, Japan and the war. Tatsuji Takeuchi, *War and Diplomacy in the Japanese Empire* (Garden City: 1935), ch. 15 on the Sino-Japanese negotiations of 1915. W. R. Wheeler, *China and the World War* (New York: 1919), ch. 1. W. W. Willoughby, *Foreign Rights and Interests in China,* rev. ed., 2 vol. (Baltimore: 1927), vol. 2, ch. 42, railway loans and foreign control.

CHAPTER XXVII

The Far East in the World War
(Continuea)

CHINA ENTERS THE WAR

CHINA'S republican revolution appears to have entered a new phase as the year 1914 drew to a close. Theorists, doctrinaires, and other "dangerous" characters had been weeded from posts of authority. Sun Yat-sen and many of his so-called radical following were in exile in Japan, while, at Peking, President Yuan Shih-kai was well on the road to dictatorship, whither he had proceeded by the most approved and time honored methods. His most dangerous opponents had been removed by either assassination or exile. The parliament had been purged of the revolutionary (Kuomintang) members. A new constitution, the Constitutional Compact (May, 1914), had been conveniently devised whereby virtually all power reposed in the person of the President, whose term of office was extended in such manner as to make his retirement extremely improbable. Many of the old forms, such as veneration of the memory of Confucius and state worship at the Temple of Heaven, were restored. Throughout the provinces, Yuan's military agents assumed control. All this was made possible because a select group of bankers (English, French, German, Russian, and Japanese), supported by their respective governments, through the famous reorganization loan early in 1913, had provided Yuan with funds. And, it should be added, only the temporary concern of President Wilson to safeguard China's administrative entity deprived American bankers of their share in this project of international finance, the object of which was forcible suppression of revolution against Yuan's arbitrary government.

Government Under Yuan Shih-kai

Between 1911 and 1914, China had passed from the feeble absolutism of the Manchus to the republican despotism of Yuan Shih-kai. Parliamentary democracy as advocated by the southern revolutionists was discredited. Opposed and throttled by Yuan, its application in China was feared by most of the foreign powers. Philosophically, it was said that China was ill suited to democracy or republicanism, by which it was to be inferred that the nation's only hope lay in a return to monarchy. In the spring of 1915, a "peace preservation" society made its appearance as an advocate of the monarchical system. One of its leading personalities, Yang Tu, published a pamphlet extolling the merits of constitutional monarchy. His arguments assumed new force when Dr. Frank J. Goodnow, later President of Johns Hopkins University but at the time adviser to Yuan Shih-kai, observed that historical development and contemporary conditions, rather than the mere ephemeral desires of the people, determine the ideal form of government. It was Dr. Goodnow's opinion that monarchy was better suited to China than republicanism.

At first, Yuan did little to encourage, and nothing to stop, the growth of this movement toward monarchy, though for publicity purposes he declared himself opposed to the change. Nevertheless, as the movement grew both at Peking and in the provinces, Yuan was preparing to accept the throne. From all sides, he was begged to save the nation by restoring monarchy with himself as sovereign. During the autumn of 1915, "elections" were held in the provinces, the results revealing Yuan and monarchy as the choice of the nation. In fact, the victory seemed too decided. Such unanimity is not frequently found in China. Yuan, with appropriate modesty, at first declined even this "people's mandate"; on second thought he consented, and the enthronement was announced to take place early in 1916.

The Opposition to Yuan

Meanwhile, Sun Yat-sen had not been idle. From his exile in Japan, he sent agents to rebuild the revolutionary cause and to strike at Yuan's government. Among the enemies of Yuan's regime was one Taso Ao, a young and brilliant official who had encouraged the uprisings in 1911, and who had since held office in Peking. It was he who now instigated revolt in Yunnan, which soon spread to other provinces. Popular feeling was so strong that some of Yuan's trusted lieutenants appeared ready to desert him. Faced with this widespread opposition, Yuan delayed his enthronement, announcing in March, 1916, that monarchy would not be restored. Many of the southern provinces had by this time declared their independence, despite the fact that Yuan made the concession of establishing a responsible cabinet under Tuan Chi-jui. To this, the southern provinces that had revolted replied by choosing Vice-President Li Yuan-hung their chief executive. From this division, the country was saved on June 6 by the death of Yuan. But Yuan's passing did not mean a return of stable government in any form—monarchical or republican.

An apparent unity was, for the moment, attained under the presidency of Li Yuan-hung. Li had commanded the rebel troops against the Manchus in 1911, had been elected Vice-President of the new republic, and now as late as 1916 had been chosen chief of the provinces that revolted against Yuan's scheme of monarchy. If not a profound believer in republicanism, he was willing at least to try new theories in old China. His Vice-President was General Feng Kuo-chang, who had failed to support Yuan when the 1915 revolts occurred. Tuan Chi-jui again became Premier, and parliament reassembled. All the machinery for parliamentary government was thus at hand, but there were lacking both experience and a united desire on the part of its agents. The confusion that followed was not due solely to the petty jealousies of the rival politicians who now began their struggles for control. These were bad enough in themselves. Beyond them were still larger questions, with the general character of which the reader is familiar. There was the traditional jealousy between the northern and the southern provinces, and also the ingrained opposition of all provinces to any centralization of power in Peking. In the government itself, there was strife between the President and the Premier. The latter was no less a militarist and a dictator by nature than Yuan Shih-kai, and he had the advantage of the support of the military governors who controlled the provinces. These factors go far to explain how China's revolution degenerated once more into a struggle between rival personalities and groups, each seeking power at the expense of the nation.

While these domestic squabbles were in progress, China remained, as always, subject to the international rivalries of the great powers. Germany, France, England, and Russia were preoccupied with the World War, yet this fact, instead of lessening pressure upon China, served rather to expose that country to the rival policies of Japan and the United States. This conflict, as it appeared in 1916-1917, was merely a new phase of the struggle between Japanese and American interests in Manchuria following the Russo-Japanese War. In Manchuria, the Japanese had sought successfully to consolidate their sphere of influence. Americans, sometimes supported by their government, had sought unsuccessfully to destroy it. In 1915, Japan, by the treaties and notes which followed the Twenty-one Demands, had extended her influence still further, and again the challenge to Japan's policy came from the United States. This time, however, it was to take the form of a comprehensive attack upon the spheres of all the powers. The principal agent in this renewed American attack was Paul

S. Reinsch, whom President Wilson had sent to Peking as American Minister. To understand the nature of this episode in international exploitation, it will be necessary to present in some detail a number of railway proposals which were before the Chinese government during 1916 and 1917.

Railway Politics Again

In May, 1916, the Chinese government concluded a preliminary contract with the Siems-Carey (American) Company to finance and construct 1,500 miles of railways in widely separated regions of China. The primary purpose of the roads was to give Yuan Shih-kai military control of the country. The first line, connecting the provinces of Shansi and Kansu, was to cross Inner Mongolia, thus encroaching upon what was usually regarded as Russia's sphere of influence. The second was to run southwest from Hunan into Kwangsi, the French sphere. The third line, in Chekiang province, invaded what the British regarded as their sphere. The Russians protested the right of China to make such a concession to other than Russian capitalists, their protest being based on an exchange of notes between Peking and St. Petersburg in June, 1899. Dr. Reinsch urged the State Department to challenge the Russian protest; but the American International Corporation, which was associated with the Siems-Carey Railway and Canal Company, being prepared to accept from China an alternate concession that would not invade the Russian sphere, informed the Department of State that it did "not wish to become involved in political controversies between the Chinese and Russian Governments." Dr. Reinsch, characterizing this attitude as one endangering the rights of Americans to do business in China, from this time on adopted a policy designed to force, if possible, the fulfillment of the original contract, regardless of the wishes of the American investors. The American Minister became, in other words, the champion of what he regarded as the "rights" of American investors in China.

Following these developments, a supplementary contract was concluded between China and Siems-Carey, with a preliminary advance of $500,000 in gold being made by the American International Corporation and accepted by the Minister of Communications in the Cabinet of President Li Yuan-hung. At this point, the Cabinet raised the question as to whether the Siems-Carey contracts would require approval by the Chinese Parliament. Curiously enough, Minister Reinsch, who frequently appeared in the role of champion of the Chinese people, held that these contracts did not require parliamentary approval. He was likewise convinced that the purposes of Siems-Carey were basically altruistic and were not designed "purely for construction profits." But, despite the Minister's efforts, the American International Corporation refused to proceed until the question of the validity of the Russian claims had been settled by St. Petersburg and Peking. Nevertheless, Dr. Reinsch had the support of Secretary Lansing, who instructed him on November 2, 1916, to inform the Chinese that the United States could not recognize the Russian claim to an exclusive sphere in the region of the projected railway.

Having raised the question of American rights in Inner Mongolia, Dr. Reinsch next challenged the Russians in north Manchuria and the Japanese in south Manchuria, where railway concessions had been granted recently by China to these powers. The proposal for the Japanese lines rested on the Chino-Japanese railway agreement of October 5, 1913, while that for the Russian lines was said to rest on an agreement between China and the Russo-Asiatic Bank (March 27, 1916). The American Minister based his action on the Chino-American preliminary contract (October 2, 1909; see p. 426) for construction of the Chinchow-Aigun Railway, and, without authorization from the Department of State, he raised with the Japanese Minister the question of American-Japanese co-operation in railroad construction in Manchuria. Dr. Reinsch felt that Japan should be made to see that her "special position" in Manchuria did not go beyond the special grants and concessions she had received from China, and in this view he was again supported by Secretary Lansing. Yet, in 1915, Secretary Bryan had informed Japan that the United States frankly recognized that "territorial contiguity" (quite apart from specific international agreements) created "special relations" between Japan and Manchuria. The lines which Japan proposed to finance were based on specific agreements, yet Dr. Reinsch continued to oppose the Japanese on the theory that he was safeguarding American rights and in particular those of American bankers. These latter, however, appeared to have no more desire to enter the Japanese sphere than they had previously shown in the case of the Russian sphere. The real problem was whether there existed in China an open door for investment and industry.

The Spheres of Influence

Historically, this problem was not new. It was traceable to the fact that in 1898-1899 spheres of special preference were recognized generally in China by the European powers. The existence of these spheres was quite compatible with the Hay open door stipulations of 1899, but not with the general principle of equal opportunity in industry and finance. Although this fact must have been obvious from the first, it was not accorded frank and official recognition by the powers until 1917. The occasion was provided when France and England, in addition to Russia, protested the validity of the Siems-Carey concessions.

In April, 1917, the French Minister at Peking protested the right of China to grant railway concessions to Americans in Kwangsi province, on the basis of a Franco-Chinese agreement (September 24, 1914). Minister Reinsch felt that the preoccupation of Europe with the War was the opportune moment that the United States might use to force the European powers to abandon their spheres. The French government, however, made its position quite clear by stating that it possessed in Kwangsi province preferential rights which resulted from valid engagements with the Chinese government.

Meanwhile, the British government protested against the proposed American railways in Hupeh and Hunan on the basis of a Chino-British agreement (September 9, 1905) granting a preference to British capital. The American government was thus faced with the fact that railroad enterprises of its citizens were blocked north of the Great Wall by Russia, in the province of Kwangsi by France, in Hupeh and Hunan by England, and in south Manchuria by Japan. It was obvious, then, that previous attempts of the American government to create equality of industrial opportunity had failed. Accordingly, Secretary Lansing addressed the British government on August 24, 1917, stating:

> The reservation of whole provinces and larger areas in China for railway construction, for mining or for other industrial enterprise by any one Power, appears to the American Government to be decidedly at variance with the policy of the "open door" and equality of commercial opportunity to which the British Government has subscribed.

To this the British government replied:

> . . . it is a cause for regret that a régime whereunder specific areas are earmarked for the enterprise of specific countries has gradually taken the place of a régime of free railway construction. They [the British government] are of opinion, however, that it would be a mistake not to recognize that such a transition has actually taken place. [1]

Nevertheless, because of the special conditions created by the War, Great Britain was prepared to welcome the co-operation

---

[1] United States, *Foreign Relations*, 1917. pp. 191-195.

of American capital in constructing railroads within the British sphere; the sphere itself, however, was not to be surrendered.

The United States and the Spheres

The significance of this episode in international railroad finance was indeed great. At no time since 1899 had the question of the so-called open door been so clarified. In principle, the policy for which the United States stood in 1917 was highly desirable. Its object was establishment of a market in China open freely and on equal terms to the commerce and industry of all nations. Its realization would have destroyed all claims to spheres of influence. The policy, too, was one by which the United States, which possessed no spheres, had everything to gain. On the other hand, the sphere-holding powers believed they had much to lose by adoption of the American view. Their spheres rested on special privileges granted by China, antedating even the Chino-Japanese War. These privileges (such as preference in railroad construction) were in many cases not recognized by the United States, but that fact in no way served to invalidate them. Russia, for instance, had never held herself accountable to the United States in matters concerning Manchuria. France, Germany, Japan, and Great Britain adopted a similar view in their respective spheres. It is not necessary to enumerate all the engagements granting special preferences which China had signed between 1896 and 1917. The fact remains that they were concluded; and, undesirable as these agreements were, they were accepted by the powers concerned. They created areas of special privileges which Mr. Rockhill recognized when he advised Secretary Hay on Chinese policy in 1899. When, therefore, Secretary Lansing refused in 1917 to admit that an era of special privilege had been created in China, it would seem that he either was ignorant of or was disregarding facts which had been common knowledge in the State Department for eighteen years.

The United States, China, and the War

The positive efforts of the United States to exert a wider influence in China by destroying the spheres of influence were affected also by military events of the World War. On February 3, 1917, the American government severed diplomatic relations with Germany and, in a communication to all the neutral powers (including China), requested them to do likewise. China, after protesting against Germany's submarine warfare, on March 14 severed diplomatic relations. The American invitation to the neutral powers had been urged upon the Chinese government with the utmost vigor by Minister Reinsch. The Chinese, according to Reinsch, feared that, if relations with Germany were severed, the Allies would confer upon Japan a mandate to reorganize the Chinese military. The Minister thereupon assured the Chinese that his government would be disposed to assist China in undertaking "the requisite [military] measures independently with American financial assistance and guidance." [2] On being advised of these developments, the Department of State enjoined upon Minister Reinsch the utmost caution and secrecy. Here, then, was the explanation of China's action: assurance, by the American Minister, of financial assistance and guidance. By this means, China hoped once again to use the United States as a buffer against Japan.

China's severance of diplomatic relations with Germany was in many respects a disturbing event. So far as the Chinese people at large were concerned, there was in 1917 probably less hatred of Germany than of some of the Allies. Yuan Shih-kai appears to have offered to join the Entente Powers in 1914 and again in 1915, but the offers were declined. After Yuan's death in June, 1916, China had again lapsed into a period of domestic strife, during which the possibility of entering the War was not considered. Then came the American

---

[2] *Ibid.* (supplement 1). p. 403.

overture to sever relations, and immediately China's politicians weighed the advantages not only of breaking diplomatic relations with Germany but also of declaring war. These ideas were encouraged further when, on April 6, 1917, the United States herself declared war on Germany. Many Chinese officials believed that if China entered the War, the Allies would be willing to compensate her by remitting some of the Boxer indemnity payments, by increases in the tariff, and by removal of foreign troops from the Peking-Tientsin area. Negotiations to this end were actually opened with the Allies as soon as relations with Germany were severed. China's military leaders saw in the War an opportunity to secure foreign loans and thus consolidate their power. The so-called patriots clamored for war in order that China might have a seat at the peace conference, where, backed by the moral support of the United States, she could more effectively strike at Japan's newly acquired position in Shantung.

All of these questions were debated feverishly as early as March, but nothing was, or could be, settled. The reasons were not far to seek. Official corruption at Peking and in the provinces was unprecedented. The government lacked a policy and the authority to carry one into effect. Revolutionary leaders and some of the southern provinces were again threatening revolt. In Peking, President Li Yuan-hung and the Parliament, acting in the name of constitutionalism, were immersed in a political battle against the Premier, General Tuan Chi-jui, who was closely associated with the military governors. The Parliament, fearing that war funds would be used to strengthen the military clique and the governors, opposed war. Finally, late in May, the President dismissed Tuan, much to the annoyance of the militarists who wanted the Parliament dissolved.

At this juncture in China's domestic turmoil, the United States informed Peking that:

The Government of the United States learns with the most profound regret of the dissension in China, and desires to express

the most sincere desire that tranquillity and political coordination
may be forthwith reestablished.

The entry of China into war with Germany, or the continuance
of the *status quo* of her relations with that Government, are matters of secondary consideration. The principal necessity for China
is to resume and continue her political entity and to proceed along
the road of national development on which she has made such
marked progress. [3]

On the surface, this advice appeared as merely the pious
wish of a friendly power. Coming, however, as it did, contemporaneously with American efforts to destroy the spheres
of influence, and with the attempts of the American Minister
at Peking to dominate the course of Chinese policy, the American note was interpreted in Japan as a conscious American
attempt to interfere in China's domestic politics. Officially, the
Japanese Foreign Office took the view that:

. . . while the United States may not have intended by the
communication to take one side as against the other [namely, the
side of the President and Parliament against Premier Tuan and
the militarists], the action in effect did so and was used by certain
political elements in Peking to strengthen the position of the
President. [4]

As a result, the American advice, whether disinterested or not,
served only to increase tension by arousing further Japanese
suspicions of American policy.

How China Entered the War

With affairs in Peking at an impasse, President Li appealed
to General Chang Hsun, then in military control of Anhwei
province, to attempt mediation between Parliament and the
militarists. As might have been expected, the general advised
dissolution of Parliament. This, carried out on June 13,
resulted promptly in a revolt of the three southernmost

---

[3] *Ibid.* pp. 48-49.
[4] *Ibid.* pp. 60-61.

provinces of Kwangtung, Kwangsi, and Yunnan. Undaunted by this resistance, General Chang moved many of his troops into Peking and announced restoration of the Manchu Emperor. In this extraordinary move, General Chang had not consulted other powerful northern militarists. Led by Tuan Chi-jui, the former Premier, the disgruntled generals advanced upon Peking and with equal promptness restored the Republic. By this time, President Li, having experienced enough of politics, retired in favor of Vice-President Feng Kuo-cheng. For good or ill, the way was now clear for some form of positive policy. The militarists were in full control; there was no parliament to obstruct action either by debate or by raising embarrassing constitutional questions. So, by presidential proclamation, China on August 14 declared war on Germany. This act was in direct violation of the provisional constitution which theoretically was still supposed to prevail. As recompense for entering the War, the treaty powers who were arrayed against Germany postponed for five years the Boxer indemnity payments (though Russia postponed only one third of the sums due her) and increased the tariff duties to an effective five per cent.

Naturally, China, a nation torn by domestic strife, could take no effective part in the prosecution of the War. Her military leaders, in fact, never entertained the slightest intention of doing so. Concerned only with the problem of consolidating their own authority, they were soon able to do so through war loans negotiated with foreign powers.

American-Japanese Tension

The developments outlined in the preceding pages made it quite clear to the governments of Japan and the United States that their respective policies toward China were viewed with mutual and growing suspicion. This was the more regrettable, since both were waging a common war against Germany, who, incidentally, was attempting to aggravate the discord which it knew to exist between Washington and Tokyo. In the Japanese Diet, the government was subjected to repeated questions that revealed a desire for a better understanding with the United States on the subject of China. As a result, on June 14, 1917, the Terauchi Ministry announced the appointment of Viscount Kikujiro Ishii as Ambassador Extraordinary and Minister Plenipotentiary, whose mission would congratulate the United States upon its entry into the War. On the following day, Aimaro Sato, Japanese Ambassador in Washington, in the course of conversations with Secretary Lansing, made the following important statement:

That Japan has special and close relations, political as well as economic, with China, is well and has long been understood by the American Government. In a note dated March 13, 1915, addressed to Viscount Chinda, my predecessor, by Mr. Bryan, the then Secretary of State, he recognized this state of affairs and declared that the activity of Americans in China had never been political. Reposing confidence in this statement, the Japanese Government has attached no importance to the recent rumor repeatedly finding its way to the press despatches from China to the effect that the American Minister [Dr. Reinsch] at Peking was more or less involved in the present political crisis in China. Again, with regard to the recent important representations made by the American Government to the Chinese Government relative to the political situation in China [see p. 503] without previously consulting Japan, the Japanese Government does not entertain the slightest doubt as to the fair and unselfish motives of the United States Government. However, it is constrained, much to its regret, to recognize as a fact that, since the Japanese public is specially sensitive toward Chinese problems, this action of the American Government, in conjunction with the rumor aforementioned, has generated in the minds of a certain part of the people a feeling of uneasiness. [5]

In view of these circumstances it was the hope of the Japanese government that the United States would find an opportunity for "confirming the statement made by Mr. Bryan."

_____

[5] _Ibid._ p. 259.

In his reply on July 6, 1917, Secretary Lansing observed that the American government was pleased to reaffirm the statements of Secretary Bryan. He called attention to the fact that:

. . . while Mr. Bryan's note thus expressed the views of the United States in regard to international relations in the Far East, I do not find that it anywhere went to the extent of stating or recognizing that Japan has special and close relations, political as well as economic, with China as a whole, as your excellency stated at our interview on June 15 last. Mr. Bryan merely said that the United States recognized that territorial contiguity created special relations between Japan and the districts of Shantung, Southern Manchuria and East Mongolia, but he did not admit that the United States might not in the future be justified in expressing its views in regard to Chino-Japanese relations involving even these districts. . . . I ought to make it clear to your excellency that I had no intention in our conversation of June 15 to convey the impression that this Government recognized that Japan possessed in China a paramount interest. It was my intention to vary in no way the formal declaration of Mr. Bryan, and, as I recall my language, I did not employ the word "paramount" but spoke of "special" interest in the same sense in which the term was used in the note of March 13, 1915. [6]

Mr. Lansing then reminded the Japanese Ambassador that, though the United States did not consult Japan *before* giving advice to China, it did bring the note to Japan's attention immediately following its presentation, "notwithstanding the fact that the Japanese proposals of 1915 [the Twenty-one Demands] were made to China several weeks before Japan acquainted the United States with them in accordance with the exchange of notes in 1908 [the Root-Takahira Notes]." [7]

The Lansing-Ishii Notes

On reaching Washington, Viscount Ishii first sought an agreement with the United States on the basis of accepting the

---

[6] *Ibid.* p. 261.
[7] *Ibid.* pp. 260-262.

American policy of abolishing spheres of influence in return for recognition of Japan's special position in China. His proposal was not approved by Tokyo, for no Japanese government would have dared to surrender the sphere in south Manchuria. Secretary Lansing then proposed a joint declaration pledging the two governments to respect the territorial integrity of China and the principle of the open door and equal opportunity. Viscount Ishii felt that a public reassertion of these principles would create in the public mind the impression that Japan had violated them; he wished rather a statement of Japan's special position in China which, he said, was similar to that of the United States in the Central American republics. The problem was to find a phrase to describe this position—a phrase to which both countries could agree. Secretary Lansing was opposed to the term "paramount interest," despite Viscount Ishii's reference to its use by Secretary Seward in the case of Mexico. The term "special interest and influences" was also suggested, and this in turn was reduced to "special interest." [8]

Finally, on November 2, 1917, the famous Lansing-Ishii exchange of notes was made. Following the precedent which had been set by Mr. Bryan, the notes declared:

The Governments of the United States and Japan recognize that territorial propinquity creates special relations between countries, and, consequently, the Government of the United States recognizes that Japan has special interests in China, particularly in the part to which her possessions are contiguous.

The territorial sovereignty of China, nevertheless, remains unimpaired and the Government of the United States has every confidence in the repeated assurances of the Imperial Japanese Government that while geographical position gives Japan such special interests they have no desire to discriminate against the trade of other nations or to disregard the commercial rights heretofore granted by China in treaties with other powers.

The Governments of the United States and Japan deny that they have any purpose to infringe in any way the independence or

---

[8] Tatsuji Takeuchi, *War and Diplomacy in the Japanese Empire*. Doubleday, Doran & Company, New York, 1935. pp. 202-203.

territorial integrity of China and they declare, furthermore, that they always adhere to the principle of the so-called "open door" or equal opportunity for commerce and industry in China.

Moreover, they mutually declare that they are opposed to the acquisition by any Government of any special rights or privileges that would affect the independence or territorial integrity of China or that would deny to the subjects or citizens of any country the full enjoyment of equal opportunity in the commerce and industry of China. [9]

In explanation of the negotiations, the State Department issued a press statement on November 6, when the notes were made public. The statement complimented Viscount Ishii on having "performed a service to the United States as well as to Japan."

There had unquestionably been growing up [it continued] between the peoples of the two countries a feeling of suspicion as to the motives inducing the activities of the other in the Far East, a feeling which, if unchecked, promised to develop a serious situation.

To remove this distrust, then, was the objective of the Lansing-Ishii exchange—an objective which was hardly realized. The correspondence reveals that the two countries were by no means in agreement with respect to Japan's relationship to China. It is obvious that the Japanese government regarded itself as possessing "special and close relations, political as well as economic, with China." It attempted to secure from Secretary Lansing an admission that this was what Secretary Bryan had meant in his note of March, 1915. In this it failed, as it did likewise to secure formal recognition of "paramount interest." However, it did secure from the United States a declaration that "special relations" create "special interests." This was a delightful compromise in the matter of language. It admitted the existence of a unique relation between Japan and contiguous parts of China without attempting to define

[9] United States, *Foreign Relations*, 1917. pp. 264-265.

what the real character of that relationship was. The Japanese government was satisfied that the phrase "special interests" meant a *political* interest; the American government was likewise convinced that it did not.

SELECTED BIBLIOGRAPHY

In addition to many references given with the preceding chapter, the following may be noted.

N. Ariga, *La Chine et la grande guerre européene* (Paris: 1920). G. H. Blakeslee, ed., *Recent Developments in China* (New York: 1913). C. B. Fletcher, *The New Pacific* (London: 1917), ch. 16. B. G. Hendrich, *The Life and Letters of Walter H. Page* (Garden City: 1924). K. K. Kawakami, *Japan in World Politics* (New York: 1917).

CHAPTER XXVIII

The Far East in the World War
(Continued)

THE SIBERIAN ADVENTURE AND THE
VERSAILLES CONFERENCE

AFTER four years of devastating conflict, when, on November 11, 1918, the armistice was signed, statesmen and diplomats of Europe turned their attention to the problem of rebuilding what war had destroyed. The War, it was said, had closed a dark chapter in human history. A new and brighter era was promised, in which democracy would be safeguarded; the rights of free peoples restored and preserved; diplomacy conducted on the high plane of self-determination, with open covenants openly reached; and old jealousies, suspicions, and national rivalries submerged in an elevated practical idealism. In most of the lands affected by the conflict, war-weary people grasped at the thought of a new era. Little did they suspect, nor were they permitted to learn, that four months before the armistice was signed, a new world conflict had begun, a conflict the full significance of which may not even yet be apparent. This new struggle was precipitated by the revolutionary outbreaks that rocked Russia during 1917-1918 and led to her complete withdrawal from the World War.

First Moves to "Assist" Russia

In March, 1917, after the United States had severed diplomatic relations with Germany but before the American declaration of war (April 6), the strategic importance of the

Trans-Siberian Railway had been impressed upon the American government. The March Revolution in Russia, which overthrew the regime of the Tsars, had just occurred, and on April 2, four days before the American declaration of war on Germany, the new liberal Russian government was asked by the United States whether it would welcome an inspection of the railroad with the prospect of increasing its efficiency with equipment and expert assistance from America. The British government, likewise disturbed by the inability of Russia to maintain herself in the War, had suggested through Ambassador Page that American management of the Trans-Siberian line would aid the Russians in a military sense. Mr. Page informed Secretary Lansing that:

This seems so important a suggestion looking *towards future American-Russian trade* that I send it for your investigation if you think wise. [1]

Although they resented "outside advice," the Russians accepted the American offer on April 9, and, as a result, the American Advisory Commission of Railway Experts, headed by a distinguished railroad engineer, John F. Stevens, reached Petrograd in June. Its official purpose was to discover methods whereby the United States might render immediate assistance to Russia in the prosecution of the war against Germany. Its proposals, which were accepted by the Russian government in August, provided for the establishment of railway assembly plants at Vladivostok and the supplying of railway engineers, equipment, and technical operators to be used both in Siberia and European Russia. Stevens was cautioned by Secretary Lansing that he must in no way create the impression that the railway commission either represented or spoke for the American government. Meanwhile, in the United States, the Railway Service Corps, a group of technical experts under Colonel George Emerson, was preparing to proceed to Russia to direct

---

[1] United States, *Foreign Relations*, 1918 (Russia). Vol. III, p. 184. Italics are those of the present writer.

operation of Russian railroads in accordance with the recommendations of the Stevens Commission. Its work was to be financed by a Russian loan floated in the United States.

The Bolsheviks in Power

These carefully laid plans were progressing toward a practical stage when, in the autumn and early winter, the Bolshevist revolutions occurred. The Allied and Associated Powers were confronted immediately with the problem of how they could maintain Russia in the War without giving aid to a Marxian government, with which they had not the slightest sympathy. The Russian revolutions themselves had thrown the country (including Siberia) into the utmost confusion. The American Railway Service Corps was unable to land at Vladivostok in December, a circumstance that so disgusted Mr. Stevens that he suggested that the United States dispatch a man-of-war and five thousand troops to Siberia. "Time is coming," he said, "to put [the fear] of God into these people [the Russians]." Before the end of December, 1917, the American and the Japanese governments, having exchanged views on Siberian policy, found themselves in agreement that the dispatch of troops to Siberia by either power would be unwise. This, it was feared, would have the effect of unifying the Russians under the Bolshevik power, a result which no capitalistic state desired. There was an added complication in Russia's ownership and operation of the Chinese Eastern Railway, which stretched across the Russian sphere of influence in north Manchuria. There, General Horvat, an official of the former Tsarist and Kerensky regimes, remained in control of Russian interests, though threatened by Bolshevik agitators.

By January, 1918, an American, a British, and a Japanese cruiser were dispatched to Vladivostok, presumably to maintain order. Concurrently, the French government, acting on reports of the killing of French nationals, informed Washington that it proposed to send troops to Siberia for the purpose of preserving that territory from the Marxian "contagion." The Russian Ambassadors at Tokyo, London, Paris, and Washington (who, incidentally, represented a Russian government which no longer existed) informed Secretary Lansing that Japan intended to invade Siberia. Ambassador Morris, in Tokyo, while denying that the Japanese government had any such policy at the time, significantly observed:

. . . the [Japanese] army is powerful and the General Staff, I believe, would welcome and probably exaggerate any occurrence which might afford an excuse.

At the same time, American and Allied Ambassadors in Europe were advocating joint military intervention in Siberia by Japan and the United States, on the dual theory that Japan must not be permitted to act alone and that it would not require many troops to ruin utterly the authority of the Bolsheviks. There was an ever-present possibility that Japan would act alone, this view being impressed upon the State Department by the American Consuls at Vladivostok and Harbin, who reported frequent assaults upon Japanese and predicted that if the United States did not take over the railroads, Japan would be forced to do so.

Fear and Hatred of Bolshevism

Among the Allied and Associated Powers, there was agreement respecting Siberia on only one point—a common hatred and fear of the Bolsheviks. The British War Office was willing to let Japan alone occupy the Siberian Railroad to check the "Reds." It was suggested that the Japanese were willing to act alone if the reluctance of the United States could be overcome. The "orderly elements" in Russia would welcome the Japanese, since the danger of German domination of Russia was imminent. A still greater danger, in the view of the British

War Office, would be a German-Japanese domination of the world, but this happily could be avoided by bringing Japan directly into opposition to Germany in Siberia.[2] Furthermore, there were plenty of "respectable" White Russian leaders, such as Horvat and Ataman Semenov, a thoroughly unscrupulous and bloodthirsty Cossack, who were willing to accept foreign financial support to attack the rising power of Red Russia. In April, when one Japanese was killed and several were wounded by armed Russians in Vladivostok, some troops were landed to police the city. In Harbin, Mr. Stevens was trying to discover what, if anything, could be done to restore traffic on the Chinese Eastern Railway, which was functioning in a half-hearted way under the remnants of General Horvat's regime. Colonel Emerson had meanwhile been authorized by Washington to confer on railroad matters with the Bolsheviks. This brought forth the comment from Stevens that:

> The new administration of the Chinese Eastern are bitterly anti-Soviet. My opinion is that the principal object . . . is to provide stronger means for fighting the Soviet, even by force of arms. We are thus placed in impossible situations of trying to help two bitterly opposing [Russian factions] with the usual result facing us [of] antagonizing both.

Nevertheless, Mr. Stevens wished to remain at Harbin to prevent Japan from "controlling [the] entire transportation system of Manchuria."

The Czechs Reach Vladivostok

During May, the situation became more complex. The first contingents of Czechoslovakian troops, seeking to make their way from European Russia to the western front to continue fighting with the Allies, reached Vladivostok. These

---

[2] British militarists recognized that Japanese intervention would be at the expense of American, French, and British prestige in Siberia, but they took consolation in the view that the Japanese people were not "psychologically constituted to dominate or administer foreign populations. . . ." At the time when these views were conveyed by the British War Office to France, Great Britain and Japan were allied in arms.

troops had been serving with the Russian armies prior to the revolutions of 1917. Their object was to continue the war against Austria in the interest of an independent Czech state under President Masaryk. They had already reached an agreement with the Bolsheviks whereby the latter consented to their retirement from Russia via the Trans-Siberian Railway. Difficulties arose, however, when the Czechs (numbering some 50,000) refused to surrender their arms. Meanwhile, being encouraged by the Allies to oppose the Bolsheviks, the Czechs, toward the end of May, clashed with Soviets in western Siberia. The fighting soon spread to central Siberia, breaking out wherever Czech contingents were scattered along the Siberian Railway. This development led to reports that the Soviet power was about to collapse and that a unified Allied intervention would meet with little opposition. Dr. Reinsch, the American Minister in Peking, wanted intervention in order to prevent alleged German or Japanese control of Siberia. Stevens and Horvat, in Harbin, favored it to destroy the Bolsheviks. The General Staff in Tokyo wanted intervention in order that Japan, rather than some other power, might control eastern Siberia against the Bolsheviks and dominate the Chinese Eastern Railway in Manchuria. To this end, it was prepared (along with some of the British military) to support Ataman Semenov as a leader of White Russian factions. All the while, the conflict between the Czechs and the Bolsheviks along the western and central line of the Siberian Railway continued, and on June 25 those Czechs who had already reached Vladivostok decided to return westward to assist their brethren. They requested support in munitions and troops from the Allies. Here was a critical turning point in the whole Siberian affair. For, when the Allies and Associated Powers responded, they inevitably (all official protestations to the contrary notwithstanding) took sides with the Russian reactionaries, who everywhere established themselves in the wake of Czech victories over the Reds. Preparatory to their return westward, the Czechs overthrew the Vladivostok Soviet in order to use the city as a base, and small forces of American, British, French, and Japanese troops were landed.

The United States Proposes Intervention

Events now moved rapidly. The American government decided on July 6 to propose that Japan and the United States each dispatch 7,000 troops to guard the line of communications of the *westward*-moving Czechs. Two days later, the British, French, and Italian governments were expressing annoyance caused by rumors that Japan and the United States were planning to act alone. There was activity, too, among White Russians. General Horvat was attempting to launch one government from Harbin, while a Russian grand duke was en route to Vladivostok to establish another. In western Siberia, "White" governments appeared as fast as the Czechs defeated the Reds. In Tokyo, the Cabinet of Premier Terauchi, backed by the General Staff, was prepared not only to accept the American invitation but also to dispatch an independent expedition on its own initiative. On July 17, 1918, came the American motion to the Allied Powers, proposing military action in Siberia. The purposes set forth by the American government were threefold: (1) "To help the Czechoslovaks consolidate their forces and to get into successful co-operation with their Slavic kinsmen," (2) "to steady any efforts at self-government or self-defense in which the Russians themselves may be willing to accept assistance," and (3) "to guard military stores which may subsequently be needed by Russian forces." Japan informed the United States on August 2 that in response to its proposal, troops would be sent to Siberia, reserving the question of the dispatch of additional troops if these should be needed. On the following day, the United States made a public announcement of the joint intervention.

Railroad Jealousies

The decision of the Allied and Associated Powers to dispatch troops to Siberia precipitated anew the question of control and operation of the Trans-Siberian and the Chinese Eastern Railways. In order to block the plan of the Japanese General Staff to control the Chinese Eastern and thereby extend the Japanese sphere into north Manchuria, Stevens proposed that the railways be placed under the military control of the Allies and that their operation be assigned to himself with his advisory commission and the Emerson Railway Service Corps. The ambitions of the Japanese military were to Stevens an unqualified annoyance, blocking, as they did, his desire to monopolize for Americans the work of reorganizing the Russian lines. The plan was placed before the Japanese government on August 20, buttressed by the argument that the American railway men in Manchuria and Siberia were not representatives of the United States but agents of the Russian people, paid by Russian funds.[3] The response of Tokyo was not favorable, and the lines continued to pass gradually under Japanese military control, the position of Japan having already been greatly strengthened by a Chino-Japanese agreement (March, 1918) for joint defense of the Siberian border. This was supplemented by further agreements with Peking (May, 1918) whereby Japan had been granted the right to station "guards" on the northwestern sections of the Chinese Eastern.

As the weeks passed, bitterness between the American railway men and the Japanese military increased. The latter could see in the activities of the Stevens group only a repetition of economic politics as played by Americans in Manchuria following the Russo-Japanese War. The Americans, in turn, regarded Japanese policy with suspicion. Even Ambassador

---

[3] These funds were provided by American loans to the Kerensky "liberal" government, which no longer existed.

Morris, whose statements were rarely based on rumor, was of the opinion that:

Recent events seem to support the statement constantly repeated that the General Staff [Japanese] has a definite policy in Siberia and that it proposes to pursue this policy leaving to the Foreign Office and Viscount Ishii the task of explaining after the event.

Although the Japanese government was prepared to accept some form of joint American-Japanese plan for running the railroads, it was not prepared to consent to exclusive American control. There was opposition, too, from other sources. The British agreed to the plan only in "principle," withholding official approval. The "White" Russian Ambassadors in Peking and Washington complained that Russian rights in the Chinese Eastern were not sufficiently protected by the American plan. As Ambassador Morris, in Japan, pointed out:

The advent of Allied forces [in Siberia] has led to the hope among former [Russian] officials, civil and military, that they will now regain the power and influence they had before the revolution. The attitude of these officials indicates that they will be relentless in their endeavor to suppress all liberal or moderate movements. Possibly nothing but their inevitable failure will bring them to reason.

This was quite true, for the Allied forces had no sooner reached Siberia than "White" Russian factions resumed their attacks upon the revolutionary elements. To add to the confusion, the Japanese press was now publishing stories to the effect that the American Railway Service Corps was in fact a selected group of agricultural experts and industrial promoters who would use their connection with the Russian railways as a cloak to establish American interests and control.

The Railroad Agreement of 1919

Nevertheless, by January, 1919, the United States and Japan had agreed upon a plan of railroad management. The roads

were to be supervised by an inter-Allied committee, while
their administration was to be in the hands of Stevens and a
technical board in which various nationals would be represented. On paper, the problem of transportation in north
Manchuria and Siberia was settled, but in fact, this agreement
led only to further trouble. The Minister of Communications
in Kolchak's "White" and collapsing government was made
chairman of the inter-Allied railway committee. A Kolchak
supporter was placed at the head of each railway, and the lines
were operated, not in the interest of the Russian people, but in
the interest of Kolchak and those elements that called themselves "White." As General Graves, commander of the American troops, observed, "The majority of the people of Siberia
enjoyed about the same value from the operation of these railways as did the people of Liberia."

The Kolchak Regime

While the allies in arms were thus struggling for control of
the Siberian and north Manchurian railway systems, a "White"
Russian government had been declared at Omsk by Admiral
Kolchak, a former officer in the Tsar's navy. From Omsk,
Kolchak, who had the support of British and French imperialists, declared himself the supreme ruler of Russia, and proceeded to pose as the champion of the so-called law-abiding
and respectable elements of Russian society against the terrors
and destruction of the Red revolution. At the same time,
Kolchak surrounded himself with former Tsarist officials,
whose primary thought was to regain the power they had lost.
The Siberian peasants who refused to take up arms in support
of these aristocratic and formerly privileged groups "were
kicked, beaten with knouts and murdered in cold blood by the
thousands, and then the world called them 'Bolsheviks.' In
Siberia, the word Bolshevik meant a human being who did not,
by act and word, give encouragement to the restoration to

power of representatives of Autocracy in Russia." [4] Nevertheless, this Kolchak government was supported not only by the British, the French, and at times by the Japanese, but also by some of the American consular representatives in Siberia and the Russian division of the Department of State.

In addition to the armies of Kolchak's government, other bands of so-called White Russians under Cossack leaders such as Semenov operated in eastern Siberia. Semenov and his followers, who at times received direct support from both the British and the Japanese and from the American Red Cross, were guilty at the time of the most indescribable excesses against their fellow Russians. The fact was that "the Allies in Siberia had become so enmeshed in Siberian affairs [contrary to the stated purposes of the intervention], in their determination to destroy Bolshevism, that they could protest only feebly against Czarist Russian excesses, if they protested at all." [5] Despite the fact that the United States, in proposing the Siberian intervention, made it quite clear that there was to be no interference with the internal affairs of Russia, the commander of the American troops testified that "all Allied representatives and the United States State Department representatives were solidly behind Admiral Kolchak and the more hopeless the cause of Kolchak became the more bitter his supporters became towards everyone who did not assist him." [6]

That Kolchak's cause was hopeless became evident in the late summer of 1919, when the White armies were defeated in the Ural region. The anti-Bolshevik front soon collapsed, the Whites retreating eastward. In November, Omsk was abandoned to the advancing Soviet armies. The regions to the east, where Kolchak authority was supposed to prevail, became chaotic, and Kolchak's administrators were soon replaced by mushroom governments of a mixed liberal and

---

[4] William S. Graves, *America's Siberian Adventure*. Peter Smith, New York, 1931. p. 101.

[5] *Ibid.* p. 147.

[6] *Ibid.* p. 244.

radical complexion—the Political Center. Such a government existed at Irkutsk, and to this government, Kolchak, who had placed himself under the protection of the retreating Czechs, was surrendered.[7] The futile attempt of the Allied and Associated Powers to save Siberia from Bolshevism had failed. Furthermore, the jealousies that marked the origins of the intervention and the struggle to control the railroads appeared to indicate that the powers never had any intention of refraining from interference in Russian affairs. On the contrary, they hoped, by turning back the course of the Russian revolution, to profit both politically and economically as a result of the venture.

The Western Allies Withdraw

The downfall of Kolchak convinced the United States, Great Britain, and France that the attempt to establish a White Siberia had failed. In January, 1920, Washington announced that the American troops and railway experts would be withdrawn, this being accomplished by March. The British and the French did the same. A contingent of Canadian troops had withdrawn earlier. These Canadian soldiers had apparently found it impossible to serve under the stupid command of General Knox, whom the British had sent to support Kolchak. Thus the United States, the Canadians, and the European Allies washed their hands of the whole Siberian affair. The Czechoslovaks had been "helped"; the military stores which were to be guarded had been saved for Kolchak and Semenov. To this degree, the announced purposes of the intervention had been carried out. The third objective—to steady any efforts at self-government in which the Russians themselves would be willing to accept assistance—had been interpreted by all the Allies in a somewhat curious way. Each

---

[7] Elena Varneck and H. H. Fisher, editors, *The Testimony of Kolchak and Other Siberian Materials,* translated by Elena Varneck. Stanford University Press, Stanford University, California, 1935. pp. 215-216.

nation engaged in the intervention assumed that by the term "Russians" was meant only White Russians. These had been aided, and when the efforts failed, the whole fiasco was abandoned—abandoned by all save Japan.

Japan Remains in Siberia

Japanese policy in the Siberian affair was complicated by a number of considerations. Geographically, the Japanese were much more concerned with the political fortunes of Siberia and the spread of Bolshevism than were the western powers. Her powerful military leaders regarded the Russians as their traditional enemy. Her politicians and the military were afraid of any political disturbances in north Manchuria and along the Chinese Eastern that might affect the stability of Japan's sphere in south Manchuria. For these reasons, Japan had, from the beginning of the intervention, reserved the right to determine and to augment the strength of her expeditionary force. The result was that at one time her troops in Siberia and along the Chinese Eastern reached the total of some 75,000 men. This policy, which had been initiated by the Terauchi and was carried forward by the Hara Ministry, was attacked in the Diet. The government was charged with maintaining an army in Siberia for the specific purpose of interfering in the internal affairs of a foreign state. When the United States announced the withdrawal of its troops, the Japanese Ministry, while expressing regret that it had not been consulted prior to the decision, was pleased to note that there was no official American objection to the continued maintenance of Japanese troops in Siberia. These exchanges led to further Diet attacks on the government, which was accused of sending the troops to Siberia without parliamentary sanction. Further, the military authorities were accused of working at cross purposes with the Foreign Office, as Ambassador Morris had hinted previously. Despite these attacks, the government refused to state what its future policy in Siberia would be. Finally, in March, the ministry issued a public statement which attempted to justify the continued occupation of eastern Siberia on the ground that chaotic political conditions endangered the lives and property of Japanese residents. The government added that it had no territorial designs and would withdraw its troops as conditions improved.

Intervention Opposed in Japan

Throughout the early months of 1920, it was quite clear that Japan's military occupation of eastern Siberia was contrary to the wishes of informed Japanese opinion. Then, in June, came news of an "incident" which enabled the government to prolong its military policy. At Nikolaevsk, a "massacre" of Japanese soldiers and civilians, including the consul, had occurred. Immediately, the government determined upon the occupation of strategic points in Russian Sakhalin until a responsible Siberian government, with which negotiations could be opened, had been established. This incident, coupled with the political turmoil which had accompanied revolution, was all that was needed to enable the Japanese military to prolong their occupation of Siberian soil, an occupation which was not terminated until 1922.

The Versailles Conference

While the long and futile Siberian intervention was in process, the Allied and Associated Powers had assembled their delegates in Paris to decide on terms of peace that should be offered to Germany. Two major far eastern powers, Japan and China, were represented at this conference. Neither of these powers was concerned primarily with the European settlement. And, although they had been associated in the war against Germany, they came to the conference as enemies rather than as allies. Japan had been a party to the War since

1914. The objectives she sought were defined rather clearly from an early date. China, on the contrary, had not entered the War until 1917. Her purposes were by no means well defined, and during 1918, her energies had been wasted in continuous civil war which left neither time nor resources for prosecution of the war against Germany. When the armistice was signed in November, 1918, the Chinese government proceeded, however, to draft the program it proposed to demand in Paris. In this respect, as will be seen, it was able to present a united front in its international program, even while at home the civil strife continued unabated.

Japan, which was represented at Paris by Prince Saionji and Baron Makino, wanted two things: cession to herself of former German islands in the northern Pacific (the Carolines, the Marianas and the Marshalls) and the transfer to herself of the German leasehold and other concessions in Shantung province. As early as 1915, the European Allies by secret conventions had agreed upon the distribution of the spoils they hoped to win from Germany. Following this example, Japan, in 1917, made agreements with Great Britain, France, Russia, and Italy whereby these powers would support Japan's claims as stated above. Furthermore, in 1915, China consented in advance to whatever decision the peace conference might reach with respect to Shantung. Again, in 1918, after China had entered the War, she made further agreements with Japan, confirming the latter's position with respect to the German holdings. Finally, the Japanese hoped that the peace conference would recognize their claim to "racial equality."

Chinese Demands

China was represented at the conference by her Minister for Foreign Affairs, Lu Cheng-hsiang, with whom were associated Wellington Koo, Minister to Washington, and Alfred Sze, Minister to London. The peace program submitted by these delegates concerned only incidentally the issues involved in the War. It was, in the main, a demand that China be relieved from what she termed the "unequal treaties," such as those which included the conventional tariff, extraterritoriality, the Boxer indemnity, foreign concessions, and the right to maintain foreign troops on Chinese soil. It was China's purpose to use Japan's occupation of Kiaochow as the occasion to challenge all the exceptional rights that foreigners had acquired.

China was promptly informed that this general program could receive no consideration at a peace conference whose specific purpose was to make peace with Germany. In fact, before the peace conference assembled, China had been informed by the Allied ministers in Peking that she had fallen far short of the duties of a co-belligerent and that many of her officials had shown a positive bias in favor of the Central Powers. This was taken "as a frank warning that China's official inaction during the war would react to her disadvantage at the peace conference." [8]   Accordingly, China altered her program and sought first to prevent the transfer of the German rights in Shantung to Japan.

The Japanese Case

Japan's claims were presented to the peace conference late in January, 1919. Against the Kiaochow claim, Koo argued that all agreements with Germany had been canceled when China entered the War and that direct restoration of the German rights to China was in accord with the principles which the conference had adopted. To this the Japanese replied that Japan had taken the Kiaochow leasehold from Germany and was in actual occupation of it. They revealed further that in September, 1918, the Chinese had for the second time confirmed the Japanese contention.

---

[8] Robert T. Pollard, *China's Foreign Relations, 1917-1931.* The Macmillan Company, New York, 1933. p. 48.

The Chinese delegates were fully aware that the legal force of their arguments was weakened considerably by the existence of the Sino-Japanese agreements of May, 1915. Consequently, shortly after filing their first brief, they submitted a second asking for the abrogation of all of the treaties and notes signed following the presentation of the Twenty-One Demands.[9]

The Japanese were not slow to attack the legal weakness of the Chinese case. The result was that during February and March no action was taken by the conference. Meanwhile, the Chinese returned to a presentation of their broader claim for relief from the "unequal treaties." To this the conference merely replied that China's desires might receive consideration at some more appropriate time.

Reasons for China's Failure

By the middle of April, the question of the disposal of the German rights in Shantung still remained unsolved. Secretary Lansing had urged as a compromise that these rights be ceded to the Great Powers with a view to their restoration to China. It was also suggested that Shantung be assigned as a mandate under the League of Nations. To these proposals the Japanese replied that unless their wishes were met, they would not sign the treaty. The Japanese were insistent that the Chino-Japanese agreements of 1915 and 1918 were valid, and even President Wilson conceded unwillingly that in this respect the Japanese were on solid ground. Accordingly, the conference decided that Germany's rights in Shantung should pass to Japan. The Japanese, on their part, asserted that:

The policy of Japan is to hand back the Shantung peninsula in full sovereignty to China, retaining only the economic privileges granted to Germany and the right to establish a settlement under the usual conditions at Tsingtao.

China immediately protested this settlement. In Peking there were mass demonstrations of students, and in Versailles

9 *Ibid.* pp. 62-63.

the Chinese delegation refused to sign the treaty. Nevertheless, the treaty affected China to an important degree. By it, her former agreements with Germany, including the Boxer Protocol and indemnities, were abrogated. These advantages China could weigh against reverses at Versailles. She failed to secure the direct restitution of Kiaochow. She was defeated in her attempt to have the Japanese agreements of 1915 and 1918 declared invalid. She did not secure consideration of the "unequal treaties," though the powers did intimate that these matters would be considered later. Intelligent Chinese were not surprised at this result. They realized that China's complete failure to stabilize her own government and her equal failure to assume any responsibility after she had declared war on Germany had alienated well-informed western opinion.

The Japanese Failure

Japan was likewise disappointed with the Versailles settlement. The peace conference had determined in January that the German colonies, instead of being annexed directly by victorious powers, were to be ceded to the principal Allied and Associated Powers and later entrusted to various of these powers as mandates. This meant that Japan, instead of acquiring full sovereignty over German islands in the north Pacific, would merely administer the islands as a mandatary on behalf of the League of Nations. In addition, the Japanese wished to insert in the League covenant the principle of racial equality. This principle they stated as follows:

The equality of nations being a basic principle of the League of Nations, the High Contracting Parties agree to accord, as soon as possible, to all aliens, nationals of states, members of the League equal and just treatment in every respect, making no distinction, either in law or in fact, on account of their race or nationality.

When this eminently just principle was rejected by the framers of the covenant, the Japanese found themselves defeated on a second point. It is not surprising, therefore, that they refused to make concessions regarding German rights in Shantung. In Japan itself, the peace settlement was not popular. However, the government was attacked on its method of conducting the negotiations rather than on the peace program itself. Members of the Diet pointed out that in western states members of parliament were well informed on the progress of the negotiations at Versailles, while in Japan the government had never taken the legislature into its confidence. To some extent these attacks were inspired by party politics, yet they fell with telling force on the ministry of Premier Hara, the first commoner to head any government in modern Japan.

SELECTED BIBLIOGRAPHY

R. S. Baker, *Woodrow Wilson and World Settlement* (New York: 1922). J. O. P. Bland, *China, Japan and Korea* (New York: 1921), ch. 8 on Japan's policy in China. M. J. Bau, *The Foreign Relations of China* (New York: 1921), ch. 9. P. H. Clyde, "Manchuria and Siberia: 1918," in *Contemporary Japan*, June, 1934. Sih-Gung Cheng, *Modern China* (Oxford: 1919), ch. 9 on Shantung. W. P. Coates and Z. K. Coates, *Armed Intervention in Russia 1918-1922* (London: 1935), especially chs. 8 and 14. C. K. Cumming, *Russian-American Relations, 1917-1920* (New York: 1920). A. L. P. Dennis, *The Foreign Policies of Soviet Russia* (New York: 1924). D. R. Francis, *Russia from the American Embassy* (New York: 1921), especially ch. 19. Louis Fischer, *The Soviets in World Affairs*, 2 vols. (London: 1930), vol. 1, chs. 2, 4, 5, 8. Patrick Gallagher, *America's Aims and Asia's Aspirations* (New York: 1920). W. L. Godshall, *The International Aspects of the Shantung Question* (Philadelphia: 1923), ch. 4. W. S. Graves, *America's Siberian Adventure, 1918-1920* (New York: 1931), a most illuminating account by the commander of the American military forces in Siberia. Ching-Lin Hsia, *Studies in Chinese Diplomatic History* (Shanghai: 1925). Kikujiro Ishii, *Diplomatic Commentaries* (Baltimore: 1936), ch. 7 on the League of Nations. K. K. Kawakami, *Japan and World Peace* (New York: 1919). By the same author, *Japan's Pacific Policy* (New York: 1922), pt. 6, on the Siberian intervention. K. Adachi, *Manchuria, A Survey* (New York: 1925). V. K. W. Koo, *China and the League of Nations* (London: 1919). Robert Lansing, *The Peace Negotiations* (Boston: 1921). Henry Cabot Lodge, *The Senate and the League of Nations* (New York: 1925). A. Lobanov-Rostovsky, *Russia and Asia* (New York: 1933), ch. 13 on Soviet policy in Asia. P. N. Miliukov, *Russia To-Day and To-morrow* (New York: 1922), ch. 10. H. K. Norton, *The Far Eastern Republic of Siberia* (London: 1923), chs. 4-10 on the Siberian intervention, and 11-15 on the Far Eastern Republic. Leo Pasvolsky, *Russia in the Far East* (New York: 1922), chs. 5 and 7. H. S. Quigley, "Far Eastern Republic: Product of Intervention," in *American Journal of International Law*, Jan. 1924. H. S. Quigley, "Rise and Fall of the Far Eastern Republic," in *The Chinese Social and Political Science Review*, Jan. 1924. P. S. Reinsch, *An American Diplomat in China* (Garden City: 1922), chs. 19-21 on China and the Peace Conference. Charles Seymour, *The Intimate Papers of Colonel House*, 4 vols. (Boston: 1928), vol. 3, ch. 13 on Wilson's policy in Siberia. G. H. Scholefield, *The Pacific: Its Past and Future* (New York: 1919), ch. 6 on Germany and Pacific islands, and ch. 17 on British dominions in the Far East. F. L. Schuman, *American Policy Toward Russia Since 1917* (New York: 1928). George Stewart, *The White Armies of Russia* (New York: 1933). Tatsuji Takeuchi, *War and Diplomacy in the Japanese Empire* (Garden City: 1935), ch. 18 on the Siberian intervention, and ch. 19 on Japan at the Paris Conference. Y. Takekoshi, *Prince Saionji* (Kyoto: 1933), ch. 70 on Saionji at the Peace Conference. A. J. Toynbee, *Survey of International Affairs, 1920-23* (Oxford: 1925), pt. 6, ch. 2 on foreign intervention in Siberia. Elena Varneck and H. H. Fisher, editors, *The Testimony of Kolchak and Other Siberian Materials* (Stanford University: 1935). W. W. Willoughby, *Foreign Rights and Interests in China*, 2 vols., rev. ed. (Baltimore: 1927), vol. 1, ch. 9 on Shantung and the Paris Conference.

CHAPTER XXIX
The Legacy of the World War

THE interest of western peoples in the Far East during 1918 to 1920 was centered largely upon the events related in the preceding chapter. The Siberian intervention was understood, though mistakenly, to be an effort to assist the Russian people. It had something of the appeal of a moral crusade. Likewise, at Versailles, the Chinese delegates took full advantage of President Wilson's peace program and presented with great popular effect the picture of an abused and helpless China victimized by the imperialists of Europe and, in particular, of Japan. To China, which had long since lost many of the attributes of a sovereign state, the Wilsonian program, resting on the high moral plane of respect for the independence and sovereignty of all peoples, appeared most applicable. Why should China not enjoy the new equality that, following the World War, was to govern the relationship of states? Why should China not be relieved from the burden and the stigma of the "unequal treaties"? These Chinese aspirations were supported almost unanimously by western public opinion. In the so-called court of world opinion, China's victory could not be questioned. Yet, despite this moral triumph, not a single great power represented at Versailles was prepared to surrender the privileges resting on the "unequal treaties" that it enjoyed in China. Why was it that the world that listened so sympathetically to the recital of China's "wrongs" was prepared to do nothing about them? The answer to this question involves a consideration of China's domestic politics (1918-1920) and also of the attempts of international finance to control her destinies.

Chinese Politics, 1918-1920

As the reader is already aware, establishment of the Chinese Republic had served to increase rather than to diminish domestic political strife. Yuan Shih-kai had been accused of seeking to destroy the revolution in order to advance his own political fortunes. Yet it is questionable whether his political shortcomings exceeded in any degree the political hypocrisy of many southern republican revolutionists, who themselves were seeking office rather than the welfare of the Chinese people. From the time of Yuan's death, in June, 1916, China continued to advance toward complete political chaos. In March, 1917, Dr. Reinsch, the American Minister, who was notable for his tendency to present China's case in the most favorable light, was forced to admit the prevalence "of unprecedented official corruption." The military governors of the northern provinces were virtually in open revolt against Peking. The parliament had been dissolved. An abortive attempt to re-establish the monarchy had resulted in an open breach with the southern provinces and an attempt to establish an opposition government at Canton.

By the early months of 1918, this conflict between north and south China had developed to alarming proportions. The northern elements were led by a group of military men closely associated with General Tuan Chi-jui and Acting President Feng Kuo-chang. Among these northern leaders the most outstanding characteristic was the existence of "personal rivalries and discordant aims." But this predominance of personal aims was even more marked among southern leaders, headed by Sun Yat-sen, whose influence had declined rapidly. Dr. Reinsch reported that in south China, the home of republican idealism, "There is the same desire of the military to control as is found in the North." While the old Parliament, which had been expelled from Peking, continued to hold sessions at Canton, without a quorum, elections were being held for a new Parliament to meet at Peking. The cost of getting a member elected to either house was estimated by the American Minister at between $20,000 and $30,000.

The sporadic civil war continued on into 1919. At the beginning of the year, the southern forces were in possession of half of Fukien and Hunan, practically all of Szechuan, and a portion of Shensi, in addition to the four provinces of Kwangtung, Kwangsi, Kweichow, and Yunnan. An armistice had been concluded late in 1918, but this did not mean that fighting ceased. Hsu Shih-chang, who replaced Feng as President, exerted himself to re-establish internal peace, but these efforts were handicapped by recurring monthly deficits of $5,000,000. These were met in part by loans from Japanese banks, the proceeds of which were squandered largely on the military establishment. The President himself lacked military support, most of the northern armies being con-

Ewing Galloway.

PRESIDENT HSU SHIH-CHANG. He was the puppet of the militarists. When President of republican China, he acted as guardian of the boy Emperor, a condition of affairs that could obtain only in China. He was an old scholar and monarchist and the bosom friend of the great Yuan Shih-kai, the first President of China.

trolled by provincial military governors who were guarding their own political fortunes rather than those of the nation. A peace conference which assembled at Shanghai during January, 1919, accomplished nothing, neither the civilian nor the military elements being willing to make concessions in the interest of the general welfare. The northern militarists were from the beginning opposed to the conference. The President was irresolute, and the southern representatives, supposedly representing China's republican and democratic elements, devoted themselves entirely to political intrigue designed to strengthen their position in doubtful provinces. At the time, the opposing military forces of north and south China in the field numbered between 800,000 and 1,000,000 men, a considerable portion of whom maintained themselves by preying upon the country they happened to occupy. In many of the provinces, local authorities turned to cultivation of the poppy to produce opium and thus revenue, while brigandage and piracy continued unabated.

A second meeting of the Shanghai peace conference, held during April and May, 1919, was also abortive. The irresolute President Hsu again failed to achieve peace, and his influence in Peking was soon overshadowed by a military faction known as the Anfu Club. The southern government at Canton had likewise failed to show any real desire to make peace.

This complete failure of China's leaders to display any statesmanship at home was coincident, it will be recalled, with the passionate appeal made by the Chinese delegation before the Versailles Conference. This ability of the Chinese to present a united program before the Conference, while at home the nation was torn by civil war, is one of the most striking features of China's recent history. Its explanation is to be found, in part at least, in the personal character of Chinese politics. The forces which controlled Chinese politics in 1919 were not new. The northern military or Peiyang Party had originated some twenty years earlier in the modern army created by Yuan Shih-kai when he was Viceroy of Chihli. It assumed no political significance, however, until after the revolution of 1911, when control of the state passed from the civilian mandarinate to the military. During the presidency of Yuan Shih-kai, the Peiyang Party consisted of two groups, the Anhui clique and the Chihli clique. The Anfu Club, which was formed in 1918, drew its military membership largely from the Anhui clique supplemented by members of the Cabinet and by parliamentarians whose election was owing to a liberal use of funds by General Hsu Shu Cheng, second in command of the Mukden troops in south Manchuria. Among the military governors closely associated with the Anfu Club was Chang Tsolin, of Mukden, together with the governors of Anhui, Shensi, Kansu, Hunan, Honan, and Chekiang. In opposition to this dominant Anfu Club, the Chihli faction controlled the central Yangtze Valley, including the military governors at Nanking, in Kiangsi, and at Hankow. In Chihli province itself, Tsao Kun, the military governor, was attempting to play with both cliques. Commenting on conditions in December, 1919, the American Minister stated:

To the unbiased observer it would appear that neither the Anfu party nor the radical extremists of the south had any ardent desire to find a practical solution of the difficulties in the way of peace. The constitutional questions which were the nominal cause of the civil war, while still invoked in moments of stress by the southern party, actually have largely drifted into the background and the disagreement has rendered itself into a struggle between two groups of professional politicians and military leaders.[1]

To this stupid conflict between north and south China there was added in 1920 a renewed outburst between the dominant Anfu Club and the Chihli party. The northern leaders who inspired this movement against the Anfu regime were General Tsao Kun, of Chihli, and his able supporter, General Wu Pei-fu. In 1918, General Wu had been sent by the Peking government with an army to hold Hunan province against south China. His expedition was a marked success; but, after a brief period, Peking diverted to other channels funds that should have been used for the support of Wu's armies. Accordingly, in May, 1920, General Wu, with the approval of his chief, Tsao Kun, withdrew his armies northward, placing them along the Peking-Hankow railroad with the ultimate objective of attack-

---

[1] United States, *Foreign Relations*, 1919. Vol. I, p. 397.

ing and driving the Anfu Club from the capital. At this point, General Chang Tso-lin, of Mukden, joining Tsao Kun and Wu, presented at Peking their demands for re-organization of the government and expulsion of the principal Anfu leaders. The issue was now clearly drawn between Tsao Kun and Wu

on the one hand, and Tuan Chi-jui and General Hsu Shu-cheng, known as Little Hsu (see chapter 34), the Anfu leaders, on the other. Chang Tso-lin retired to Manchuria, massing his troops at the Great Wall in a position to support whichever side offered the better bargain. Fighting began in and about Peking during July, and at the critical stage, Chang Tso-lin threw his forces against the Anfu armies. Their complete defeat was a matter of only a few days. The Anfu party was destroyed. It remained to be seen what substitute the vic-

Ewing Galloway.

GENERAL WU PEI-FU. Great commander of Chinese armies, and the sword arm of his patron, Tsao Kun.

torious Chihli generals would provide.

A new cabinet was organized. Its personnel was far abler than that of the Anfu days, but its members were dependent entirely upon the support of Tsao Kun and Chang Tso-lin. Furthermore, although a people's convention had been advocated by Wu Pei-fu during his march on Peking, the idea did not appear to recommend itself to the new masters of government, Chang and Tsao. In fact, it was already becoming apparent that a new rivalry was developing between Tsao Kun and his Chihli forces and the intruder, Chang Tso-lin, from Manchuria. The settlement became, therefore, a contest between these two military chiefs to strengthen their own personal power, rather than an effort to establish a stable central government. By the autumn of 1920, there was small reason to believe that government by the Chihli clique would be any improvement over the previous Anfu regime. In south China, conditions were no better. The withdrawal of General Wu's troops from Hunan province opened the way for an advance by southern armies, but, far from taking advantage of this, the south was now involved in its own personal and factional strife.

Ewing Galloway.

MARSHAL TSAO KUN. Another of China's military presidents and head of the famous Chihli military party.

These, then, were the political conditions which prevailed in China during the years 1918 to 1920. So long as such conditions did prevail, it was hardly probable that even the eloquence of China's delegates at Versailles would be accorded serious consideration. Yet, in 1919, the principal powers represented at Versailles were vitally interested in China's future. Something of the character of this interest now remains to be set forth.

Politics and Finances

It will be recalled that in June, 1912, a Six-Power Consortium had been formed to undertake a so-called reorganization loan to the new Chinese Republic. The total loan was to be for £60,000,000. In May, 1913, a £25,000,000 series of the reorganization loan was issued by five of the six banking groups, the Americans not participating since it was President Wilson's view that the control measures demanded by the consortium infringed China's administrative independence. The World War, following in 1914, destroyed temporarily development of the consortium idea. German bankers could no longer participate with those of the Allies. Furthermore, British and French bankers no longer had funds available for investment in China. In Russia, the communist revolution ended financial co-operation with Russia's former allies. Thus, for all practical purposes, the consortium ceased to exist. Of its original members, Japan, alone being in a position to invest freely in the Chinese market, made haste to gain a position of primacy. Her aggressive politico-economic policy, as revealed in the Twenty-one Demands of 1915, was, however, of doubtful value, inasmuch as it alienated Chinese opinion and created in the West a pronounced suspicion of Japan's motives. In the following years (1916-1918), Japan adopted a policy of financial assistance to China. Loans were made to the Peking government and many of the provincial governments by Japanese bankers, with the support, and sometimes at the request, of Tokyo. In explanation of this, it should be observed that China needed funds, and the British, French, and German bankers who had financed her in the past were, because of the War, no longer in a position to do so. Japan took the business, and with it her influence and interest in China increased. Since most of the Japanese loans were made to north China, they aroused tremendous opposition in the south, while in western capitals, fear was expressed that Japanese money was being used for political purposes and that Japan would soon enjoy a financial monopoly. These fears were responsible for a movement initiated by the British early in 1917 to revive the international consortium.

The British government suggested to Japan that the United States be invited to re-enter the consortium, and in January, 1917, Japan, in turn, informed the United States that she fa-

vored the idea, provided the consortium confined its activities
to political loans for administrative purposes. In March, 1917,
the group of American banks which had been associated with
the first (or Six-Power) consortium of 1912 was invited by
the British, French, Russian, and Japanese groups to participate
in a supplementary re-organization loan to China of from
£10,000,000 to £20,000,000, half of the loan to be issued in
Japan and half in the United States. The American bankers
welcomed this invitation as "an exceptional opportunity again
to promote the legitimate commercial aspirations of our country in the Far East. . . . They fear, if this opportunity be not
availed of, that it will be more than could be hoped for that
such favorable circumstances for the promotion of American
commercial prestige in the Orient will again present themselves."[2] However, the State Department, "in view of the
political conditions and disturbances now existing in China,"
was not prepared to define its policy. But, as China wanted
money, the British informed Washington that "the only member of the Allied Governments which at present is in a position
to furnish them with the money they desire is Japan, which
would consequently acquire a predominant position in Chinese
financial matters."[3] Accordingly, the British and the American Ministers in Peking were instructed to advise China that
the time was "inopportune"—that is, that it was undesirable-
that China should borrow from Japan. In fact, Secretary Lansing informed Dr. Reinsch that if a consortium loan should be
made, "Japan would be the lender and would have the backing
of the Allied Group. This is undesirable." This fear of Japanese competition in China's financial affairs inspired the
United States by November, 1917, to give serious consideration
to re-entry of the American group.

No tangible progress was made, however, until June, 1918,
when Secretary Lansing addressed a communication to Presi-

[2] *Ibid.*, 1917. p. 127.
[3] *Ibid.*, 1917.

dent Wilson advocating that an American banking group re-enter the consortium. The Secretary stated that there were three matters in prospect in which "it will be very advisable to have American financiers interested." First, Japanese interests were seeking to control China's tobacco and wine industries, which had already been pledged by China to secure the loans of a Chicago bank. Second, if America should loan China funds for completion of the Canton-Hankow railway, which had previously been under British control, it would enable American interests "to control a very important railroad" and might possibly induce both Britain and France to abandon their claims to spheres of influence in that region. Third, a currency loan, continued from the old consortium, would probably be advanced to China. Japan had invited American participation, but would proceed alone if the Americans declined. President Wilson approved Lansing's proposal, on the understanding that the control measures of the loans would not infringe upon China's sovereignty. Furthermore, it was the American idea that "industrial" as well as "administrative" loans should be made by the new consortium, a proposal to which the Japanese and the British, each claiming a sphere of interest, were obviously opposed. The American plan was presented to the interested governments as a comprehensive international scheme for financing China. The old consortium was to be dissolved. A new consortium, including the United States, Great Britain, Japan, and France, would take its place.

The Japanese Exemptions

Negotiations among the various governments and among their respective banking groups continued with some success until June, 1919, when the Japanese bankers informed the Americans that "all the rights and options held by Japan in the regions of Manchuria and Mongolia, where Japan has special interests, should be excluded from the arrangements for pooling provided for in the proposed [consortium] agreement." [4] This Japanese claim was based on the special relations that Japan was said to have with these regions, and which "have been recognized by Great Britain, the United States, France and Russia on many occasions." Reference was made by the Japanese bankers to their previous statement, made in 1912 when the first consortium was being formed, that it should not operate to the prejudice of Japan's special rights and interests, and to the Lansing-Ishii notes.

The American bankers, supported by the British and French, replied that exclusion of Manchuria and Mongolia from the activities of the proposed consortium "must be inadmissible." It was their view that the "special interests" to which the Japanese bankers referred "never had to do with economic matters." Accordingly, the three groups referred the question back again to their governments. Secretary Lansing informed Tokyo on July 30, 1919, that the Japanese reservation could not be accepted, and in August, the British government addressed the Japanese on the essential point involved.

One of the fundamental objects of the American proposals [said the British memorandum] as accepted by the British, Japanese and French Governments, is to eliminate special claims in particular spheres of interest and to throw open the whole of China without reserve to the combined activities of an International Consortium. This object can not be achieved unless all the parties to the scheme agree to sacrifice all claim to enjoy any industrial preference within the boundaries of any political sphere of influence. [5]

The response of the American government to Japan's claim to special treatment in Manchuria and Mongolia was, if anything, more pointed than the British. Japan's reservation was

---

[4] Carnegie Endowment for International Peace, *The Consortium*. Washington, 1921. p. 19.

[5] *Ibid.* p. 30. It will be noted that Great Britain was, at this time, disposed to surrender her sphere of influence. In explanation, it may be suggested that the British would prefer making such a sacrifice to seeing the Japanese become more firmly entrenched in Manchuria.

regarded as an "intermixture of exclusive political pretensions in a project which all the other interested Governments and groups have treated in a liberal and self-denying spirit and with the purpose of eliminating so far as possible such disturbing and complicating political motives; and it [the American government] considers that from the viewpoint, either of the legitimate national feeling of China or of the interests of the Powers in China it would be a calamity if the adoption of the Consortium were to carry with it the recognition of a doctrine of spheres of interest more advanced and far-reaching than was ever applied to Chinese territory even in the period when the break-up of the Empire appeared imminent." [6]   Secretary Lansing went on to state that such Japanese enterprises in these regions as were already well developed and could thus be regarded as vested proprietary interests would naturally be excluded from the consortium, but the United States was not prepared to accept a geographical reservation.

A Question of "Special" Relations

To these objections, raised by Great Britain and the United States, the Japanese replied in March, 1920, by stating that south Manchuria and eastern Inner Mongolia were contiguous to Korea and stood in close and special relation to Japan's national defense and economic existence.   In addition, it was Japan's view that the Bolshevik revolution in Russia had exercised an unwholesome influence on the Far East. Since Manchuria and Mongolia were the gateways through which these revolutionary influences might reach Japan itself, the government was not prepared to surrender its claim to special interest and treatment there.   Accordingly, although Japan was prepared to enter the consortium, she proposed to reserve the right to take such steps as were demanded by her security in all loans affecting south Manchuria and eastern Inner Mongolia,

[6] *Ibid.* pp. 31-32.

and she set forth in detail the various undertakings existing or proposed which she was not prepared to share with the other powers. In reply, the British and the American governments characterized the Japanese position as "ambiguous and general in character." The American government felt that Japan should be prepared to rely on the good faith of the other consortium powers not to countenance undertakings inimical to Japan's vital interests. In fact, the British were prepared to give Japan a written assurance to this effect. Finally, in May, 1920, a representative of the American bankers visited Tokyo, and after extended discussions the Japanese group withdrew its more objectionable reservations. As a result, an agreement was reached whereby the South Manchuria Railway system and feeder lines were to be excluded from the joint activity of the consortium, while in the territory west of this system, Japanese railway plans were to be undertaken in common with the consortium powers. In September, 1920, China was informed of the agreement and later was invited to participate through a Chinese banking group.

Significance of the Consortium

In 1920, therefore, the way had been opened for an era of international co-operation in financing China. Four great powers, Great Britain, the United States, France, and Japan, had agreed to undertake in common the burden of China's financial needs. With the exception of the reservations permitted to Japan, all China was to be the field for the new consortium. The old system of spheres of influence was all but destroyed, the spheres having rested in main on the financial and industrial preference claimed by a given power in a particular region. All this was done, of course, in the name of preserving China. In reality, China's "salvation" was not a primary concern either of the bankers or of the consortium powers. Of all the powers interested in China in these years, the United States alone was opposed to the system of spheres of influence, and this in large part because the Americans had never succeeded in acquiring a sphere. As late as 1918, the British, the French, and the Japanese were all supporting strongly the sphere idea. The British and the French both protested to the United States when the American Siems-Carey Corporation threatened to invade the British and French spheres. It was not until the British, exhausted by the European War, realized that their financial primacy in China was threatened by Japan that they saw in the consortium a means by which Japan might be stopped. To stop Japan, the British were at last prepared to surrender their sphere of influence, and France followed suit.

The policy of the American government was more consistent than that of either Britain or France. Holding no sphere herself, the United States had been opposed to the entire system. She had, in fact, never recognized the spheres as such, though she had in 1915 and again in 1917 recognized Japan's "special interests" in Manchuria. Prior to this, however, American financiers and the Department of State had repeatedly challenged Japan's paramount position in south Manchuria. During the Wilson administrations, the United States was represented in Peking by Minister Reinsch, a vigorous champion of China's "rights" and of American "rights" in China. The views of Reinsch, to whom Japan appeared as a constant threat to these rights, were not without their effect upon the State Department and the President. As a consequence, the same administration which withdrew its support from the consortium bankers in 1913 urged the same bankers to return to the consortium in 1918. By following this policy, the American government accomplished a number of things. It appeared in the role of a savior of China; it opened new fields to American investment by destroying, in part, the spheres of influence; and, finally, it took an active part in attempting to obstruct Japan's rapid march toward financial primacy in the Chinese Republic.

China and the Consortium

The altruistic view of the new consortium of 1920, as voiced in America, did not escape challenge from the Chinese. To them, the main object of the consortium was to harvest exorbitant profits from loans forced upon an unwilling China. China, they observed, had neither been invited to participate in the negotiations leading to the formation of the consortium nor been so much as informed of its existence until it had been formed. It is not surprising that China viewed the scheme with undisguised suspicion, seeing in it only a financial monopoly, the purpose of which was to deprive her of a competitive market in which to borrow. In an effort to allay such fears, the council of the consortium, in May, 1923, issued a statement. In it, the bankers contended that, by their refusal to lend to China, they had encouraged the use of native savings and had arrested the profligate expenditures which were leading the country into bankruptcy. The consortium, in the opinion of the bankers, was an agency for the preservation, not for the destruction, of China. But still the Chinese remained unconvinced.

To Chinese who desired a place of respect for their country in the community of nations, the events recorded in this chapter brought increased disillusionment. Thoughtful Chinese knew that Great Britain, France, and the United States had supported the consortium idea not primarily to save China, but rather to arrest the growing influence of Japan. They knew that these powers were serving their own interests first, and those of China only incidentally. Slowly they were beginning to realize that China could not depend on foreign powers for her political salvation. As long as her own house remained chaotic and without leadership, China would continue to be a prey to international intrigue.

In effect, the results of the new consortium in the decade following 1920 were negative.

[It] was expected to increase the American holding of Chinese government securities [but it] has had no such effect. The Consortium has done no more than to prevent certain loans. It has maintained some solidarity among possible lenders to China. It is the answer of the foreign financial and political leaders to the difficult problem presented by Chinese government borrowing in the past. The American government, after rejecting it in 1913, returned to the principle of the Consortium in 1918. The reason for the Consortium lies in the actual situation in China and in the experience of the foreign financial groups with China, with each other, and with the international political situation in the Far East.[7]

SELECTED BIBLIOGRAPHY

Julean Arnold, "Changes in the Economic Life of the Chinese People," in *The Chinese Social and Political Science Review,* Feb. 1922. Henry C. Adams, "International Supervision over Foreign Investments," in *American Economic Review,* Mar. 1920. Joseph Barnes, ed., *Empire in the East* (New York: 1934), ch. 5, "Battle of the Bankers." A. J. Brown, *The Mastery of the Far East* (New York: 1919). J. O. P. Bland, *China, Japan and Korea* (New York: 1921), ch. 4, "The Republic of Today," and ch. 5, "Civil War as a Profession." M. J. Bau, *The Foreign Relations of China* (New York: 1921), chs. 24-25 on the consortium. Sih-Gung Cheng, *Modern China* (Oxford: 1919), chs. 2-4 on Chinese politics and government, 1911-1918. Carnegie Endowment for International Peace, *The Consortium* (Washington: 1921). F. V. Field, *American Participation in the China Consortiums* (Chicago: 1931). P. Gallagher, *America's Aims and Asia's Aspirations* (New York: 1920.) Feng-hua Huang, *Public Debts in China* (New York: 1919). K. K. Kawakami, *Japan and World Peace* (New York: 1919), ch. 10 on "The Japanese Advance in China." C. F. Remer, *Readings in Economics for China* (Shanghai: 1922). C. F. Remer, *Foreign Investments in China* (New York: 1933). C. S. See, *The Foreign Trade of China* (New York: 1919). A. J. Toynbee, *Survey of International Affairs, 1920-1923* (Oxford: 1925), pt. 6, ch. 3 on

---

[7] C. F. Remer, *Foreign Investments in China.* The Macmillan Company, New York, 1933. pp. 331-332.

the Four-Power Consortium. United States, *Foreign Relations,* 1917-1920, are rich in diplomatic correspondence on the consortium. H. M. Vinacke, *Modern Constitutional Development in China* (Princeton: 1920), chs. 9-10.

CHAPTER XXX

The Legacy of the World War
(Continued)

THE WASHINGTON CONFERENCE

WHEN the World War, with its wanton and futile destruction of life and property, came to a close, public opinion in practically all lands demanded some tangible guarantees of permanent peace. The Covenant of the League of Nations was the immediate answer to this popular demand. Among its various provisions was one that stated:

> The Members of the League recognize that the maintenance of peace requires the reduction of national armaments to the lowest point consistent with national safety and the enforcement by common action of international obligations.

Here was a tangible principle by which, it was hoped, peace might be preserved and the horrors of another World War avoided. But, though the statesmen and politicians of Europe, Asia, and America paid eloquent tribute to the principle of disarmament while peace was being made at Versailles, their actions were in direct opposition to it. By 1920, the victorious Allied and Associated Powers (in particular the United States, Great Britain, and Japan) had embarked upon a naval race so appalling as to frighten even the naval experts. In the United States, the Naval Service Appropriation Act (August 29, 1916) increased naval expenditures of $155,029,000 for 1915-1916 to $1,268,000,000 for 1917-1918. This was followed in 1919 by a famous three-year program of construction designed to give the United States the most powerful navy afloat. To this program, the Japanese replied the same year with a plan for constructing fourteen powerful ships. In Great Britain, the first of the "Hood" class battleships was under construction in 1917, and by 1921, work had commenced on three similar vessels. There could be no doubt that by June, 1921, a naval race between England, Japan, and the United States was in progress. The World War, instead of reducing armaments, had led to their increase.[1]

This threatening naval race was an indication of a disturbing political change which had resulted from the War. Prior to the War, Germany and Russia had offered the greatest threat to the British Empire. The Allied victory had temporarily removed this danger, but in its place British imperialists were forced to recognize in the Americas the tremendous power of the United States and in Asia the rising power of Japan. During the war years, Japan's advance in China had been at the expense of both Great Britain and the United States. Both powers were jealous of an oriental state that had already challenged their positions in the Far East. Furthermore, the British had emerged from the War convinced that a policy of Anglo-American friendship must be followed at all cost. Yet, in Asia, England was linked with Japan by the historic Anglo-Japanese Alliance. In the days of the Russo-Japanese War, the Anglo-Japanese Alliance had enjoyed a wide popularity in the United States. But by 1920, Americans had been taught to believe that Japan was the natural enemy of the American territorial and commercial empire in the Far East. From this they concluded, though mistakenly, that the third Anglo-Japanese Alliance of 1911 would involve Great Britain in what was referred to as "the inevitable American-Japanese war." These American fears were shared to a large degree by Canadians. Consequently, the British, at the time of the Imperial Conference of 1921, were confronted with the task of restrain-

---

[1] For the most adequate discussion of the Washington Conference, see Yamato Ichihashi, *The Washington Conference and After.* Stanford University Press, Stanford University, California, 1928.

ing Japan and with the risky business of terminating an alliance with her in order to placate the feelings of Americans and Canadians. Quite apart, too, from considerations involving Japan, Great Britain wanted a general understanding with the United States, which had failed to accept the Versailles settlement, was not a member of the League of Nations, and whose future course in foreign policy was beyond prediction.

Canada and the Anglo-Japanese Alliance

British imperial policy reached a crisis on June 29, 1921, when Premier Meighan of Canada informed the British Imperial Conference meeting in London that:

Canada opposed renewal of the [Anglo-Japanese] Alliance in any form because the reason for its existence was past, such entanglements were incompatible with the League of Nations idea and both the United States and China would regard any such treaty with mistrust, as implying benevolent neutrality towards Japanese aggression. He reminded the Conference that good Anglo-American relations were the touchstone of British policy and the hope of the world.[2]

He had proposed to Lloyd George, as early as February, a conference of Japan, the United States, China, and the British Empire to deal with Pacific problems. This opposition to renewal of the alliance was bitterly resented by Australia and New Zealand, who felt that such action would wound Japan, that the United States could not be depended upon, and that the British Empire needed an ally in the Far East. It was in the midst of this crisis that the American government approached Great Britain, France, Italy, and Japan, suggesting the advisability of a conference on the limitation of armament and problems of the Pacific and the Far East. Formal invitations were addressed to these powers and to China on

---

[2] J. Bartlet Brebner, "Canada, The Anglo-Japanese Alliance and the Washington Conference," in *Political Science Quarterly*, March, 1935.

August 11, 1921, and on October 4 Belgium, the Netherlands, and Portugal were invited to participate.

Invitations to Washington Accepted

In the United States, Great Britain, Canada, and China, the American invitation was received with enthusiasm. On the Continent, the response was less dramatic. A number of conferences held since the War had produced few tangible results. Europe likewise was at a loss to understand why the United States, which had refused to associate itself with the League, should now propose a conference to deal with subjects that might properly be dealt with by the League. The Japanese, too, were suspicious. Although they were quite prepared to discuss limitation of armament, they were surprised when informed that political problems of the Far East were to be linked with the general question of naval limitation. Why was the Far East selected rather than Europe, where "problems" were quite as numerous? The government in Tokyo was as embarrassed as the United States would have been had Japan proposed that a conference be convened at Tokyo to discuss limitation of armament and problems of Central America and the Caribbean. Nevertheless, Japan, like the other powers addressed, accepted the American invitation, even though her acceptance did not dispel the impression that Japan was being called before a court of justice. It was well known that the United States disapproved of Japan's policy in China and in Siberia, that American interests had supported China in the Shantung dispute, and that the government of the United States had attempted to prevent Japan from falling heir to the former German submarine cables in the western Pacific.

Organization of the Conference

The Washington Conference, both by the nature of its origins and by the problems to be dealt with, consisted of two conferences, the one dealing with naval limitation, the other with political problems of the Far East, by which was meant China. Proceedings were opened on November 12, 1921, when President Harding declared to the assembled delegates and guests that the American people wanted "less of armament and none of war." He was followed immediately by Secretary of State Charles Evans Hughes, who electrified his international audience by calling upon Great Britain, Japan, and the United States to scrap sixty-six battleships, existing or in course of construction and aggregating a total of 1,876,000 tons. The plan also called for a ten-year holiday in naval construction. Despite the amazing character of the American proposal, it was accepted "in principle" by all the powers as a basis for discussion, and the conference thereupon proceeded to the difficult task of agreeing on its detailed application. After prolonged and secret negotiations between Hughes, Balfour (of England), and Admiral Kato (of Japan), known as the "Big Three," these three powers accepted a capital-ship ratio for their respective navies of 5-5-3, as provided by the American proposal, and agreed to maintain the *status quo* in their Pacific fortifications and naval bases, excluding Hawaii, Australia, New Zealand, the islands along the coast of the United States and Canada, and the islands composing Japan proper. France was assigned by the American proposal a capital-ship strength of 1.75 in the above ratio. With this she was far from satisfied. She was piqued further by the attitude of the Italians, who seemed prepared to accept any limitation, as long as they were granted parity with France. On the question of submarines and auxiliary craft, the views of the powers were so divergent that no agreement could be reached.

Pacific Fortifications

Meanwhile, a troublesome disagreement had arisen with respect to fortifications in the Pacific Ocean. The Japanese

government interpreted the expression, "the islands composing Japan proper," to include Amami-Oshima and the Bonin
Islands, on the ground that they were within the administrative
jurisdiction of the home government. On the other hand,
Hughes, Balfour, and even Kato regarded these islands as
within the zone where the *status quo* in the matter of fortifications was to be maintained. The Japanese government felt that
its right to increase the fortifications of these islands was most
reasonable. If the United States were permitted to increase the
strength of Pearl Harbor, 2,100 miles from San Francisco, it
was argued that Japan was surely entitled to the same privilege
in islands only 600 miles from the coast of Japan. In the end,
a verbal understanding was reached by the "Big Three," applying the *status quo* in matters of fortifications to the Philippines,
Guam, Hongkong, Amami-Oshima, the Bonins, Formosa, and
the Pescadores. As far as the Far East was concerned, the
naval agreements reached at Washington were significant in
two respects: (1) the *status quo* would be maintained in the
principal insular naval bases of the Pacific, with the exception
of Hawaii, and (2) the United States was accorded superiority
to Japan in capital ships as represented by a ratio of 5 to 3.

Scrapping the Anglo-Japanese Alliance

Before this important naval agreement had been reached,
the Conference had announced its solution to the political
problems centering about the Anglo-Japanese Alliance. This
solution took the form of the Four-Power Pacific Treaty, signed
by the United States, the British Empire, France, and Japan.
These powers agreed to "respect their rights in relation to
their insular possessions and insular dominions in the region
of the Pacific Ocean" and to confer together in case these
rights appeared threatened in any controversy. The ratification
of this treaty, which was to remain in force for ten years, was
to terminate the Anglo-Japanese Alliance of 1911. The main

significance of this treaty lay in the fact that it provided a convenient means of disposing of the Anglo-Japanese Alliance. The policies of the United States and Canada had prevailed, the Alliance being superseded by a rather innocuous agreement by which the signatory powers were pledged not to attack each other for at least ten years.

China's "Bill of Rights"

During the negotiations leading to the limitation of naval armament, the Conference was also dealing with problems of the Pacific and Far East, which proved to be primarily the problem of China and of Japan's relationship thereto. Early in November, the Chinese delegation presented what came to be known as China's "Bill of Rights." This included:

1. The Powers were to respect China's political and administrative independence, and China and the powers were to apply the open door policy.

2. The powers were asked to agree not to conclude any treaty affecting China without previously notifying China and giving her an opportunity to participate.

3. All agreements claimed by the powers respecting China were to be declared, and any not so declared were to be deemed null and void.

4. All limitations upon China's political, jurisdictional, and administrative freedom were to be removed.

5. Definite terms of duration were to be applied to China's commitments, which were without time limit.

6. China's rights as a neutral were to be respected in future wars to which she was not a party.

In response to these Chinese demands, the far eastern committee of the Conference adopted the following resolution:

It is the firm intention of the powers attending this conference hereinafter mentioned, to wit, the United States of America, Belgium, the British Empire, France, Italy, Japan, the Netherlands, and Portugal:

1. To respect the sovereignty, the independence, and the territorial and administrative integrity of China;

2. To provide the fullest and most unembarrassed opportunity to China to develop and maintain for herself an effective and stable government;

3. To use their influence for the purpose of effectually establishing and maintaining the principle of equal opportunity for the commerce and industry of all nations throughout the territory of China;

4. To refrain from taking advantage of the present conditions in order to seek special rights or privileges which would abridge the rights of the subjects or citizens of friendly States and from countenancing action inimical to the security of such States.[3]

American opinion was divided as to the value of this resolution. By some it was described as a solution to the problem of the Pacific, while others, less superficial in judgment, saw it in terms of "general principles." It was described as a set of "glowing but somewhat vague rules . . . so general that they could be printed in a wreath and used as Christmas cards." Actually, the force of the resolution would depend largely on China herself, and, unfortunately, China's condition in 1921-1922 was not at all what the Chinese delegation pictured it to be. What were the conditions?

Who Represented China?

The Chinese press had accepted President Harding's invitation to the Conference with enthusiasm, yet it was difficult to see how China, involved in domestic chaos, could take full advantage of it. The Peking government was living on borrowed money. Financial panic threatened during the later months of 1921. In November, the Department of Finance failed to meet payments on a loan made by an American bank.

---

[3] United States Senate, document 126, 67th Congress, 2nd Session. pp. 459-460.

The personnel of the Cabinet was changed frequently. Salaries of civil employees of the government were many months in arrears. At Canton, a rival government had been formed, with Dr. Sun Yat-sen as "President of the Republic of China." This administration, refusing to recognize Peking, declared that it would maintain a separate delegation at the Washington Conference; when this was refused by Secretary Hughes, the Canton authorities announced they would not recognize the validity of any decisions reached by the Conference.

Despite the conditions prevailing in China, the Conference did attempt to give the Chinese some relief from limitations upon their sovereignty. Among these limitations was the conventional or treaty tariff, which dated back to the Treaty of Nanking (1842), and which had prevented China from raising adequate revenues from customs duties. In a new treaty that the Conference finally adopted, China was to be allowed an effective five per cent rate. Steps were to be taken to apply certain additional surtaxes, while the Chinese themselves were to abolish likin (internal transit duties, which were exceedingly burdensome on trade).

The Nine-Power Open Door Treaty

One of the most widely publicized acts of the Conference was its acceptance of the so-called Nine-Power Treaty, dealing primarily with the historic open door policy. The first article of this treaty restated the resolution which the Conference had already adopted concerning China (see p. 554). The powers (Article 2) agreed to make no treaties infringing these principles, and pledged themselves (Articles 3 and 4) not to establish spheres of influence, though existing spheres were not to be interfered with. China promised (Article 5) not to permit discrimination in the administration of her railways. Respect for China's neutrality was guaranteed (Article 6). Article 3, referred to above, was of special significance, since it sought, for the first time by treaty, to define more clearly the open door policy, about which there had been so much confusion. It reads:

With a view to applying more effectively the principles of the Open Door or equality of opportunity in China for the trade and industry of all nations, the Contracting Powers, other than China, agree that they will not seek, nor support their respective nationals in seeking:

(a) Any arrangement which might purport to establish in favor of their interests any general superiority of rights with respect to commercial or economic development in any designated region of China;

(b) Any such monopoly or preference as would deprive the nationals of any other Power of the right of undertaking any legitimate trade or industry in China, or of participating with the Chinese Government or with any local authority, in any category of public enterprise, or which by reason of its scope, duration, or geographical extent is calculated to frustrate the practical application of the principle of equal opportunity.

It is understood that the foregoing stipulations of this Article are not to be construed as to prohibit the acquisition of such properties or rights as may be necessary to the conduct of a particular commercial, industrial, or financial undertaking or to the encouragement of invention and research.

China undertakes to be guided by the principles stated in the foregoing stipulations of this Article in dealing with applications for economic rights and privileges from Governments and nationals of all foreign countries, whether parties to the present Treaty or not.

These provisions, taken together with Article 4, prohibited any power from acquiring a sphere of influence by future action. It will be observed at once, therefore, that the open door, as defined by the Nine-Power Treaty, was a policy quite different from that set forth by John Hay in 1899. The latter was designed to create equality of treatment for trade and commerce within a sphere of influence. The former was designed to make impossible the creation of spheres of influence in the future.

Extraterritoriality

On the subject of extraterritoriality, to which China had objected on numerous occasions, the Conference agreed to the appointment of a commission to inquire into the practice of extraterritorial jurisdiction and into the laws and judicial administration of China. Members of the commission were to report to their respective governments such changes in China's judicial administration as might lead to relinquishment by the powers of their extraterritorial rights.

China had also raised objection to the maintenance on her soil of foreign troops and foreign post offices without treaty authorization. On these subjects, the Conference passed resolutions. The first provided that China might request the foreign ministers in Peking, together with Chinese officials, to discuss the question of whether or not these troops were required to protect life and property of foreigners. The second provided that foreign post offices, except those operating in leased territories, were to be abolished.

Another Chinese demand called for the surrender of all electrical telegraph stations maintained in China without the expressed consent of the Chinese government. The powers maintaining stations included Japan, France, Great Britain, and the United States. The Conference agreed that the powers were not to use their stations for other than official business, and that all other stations operating without Chinese authorization were to be sold to China. Stations existing in the zone of the South Manchuria Railway, in leased territories, and in the French concession at Shanghai were to be dealt with by China and the power operating the station.

In order to prevent secret agreements with China, the powers at the Washington Conference agreed to make public all their treaties and private contracts made with the Chinese government.

The Chinese Eastern Railway

Although Russia was not represented at the Conference, the subject of the Chinese Eastern Railway was considered at length. China was informed that the powers were not satisfied with such protection as she had afforded the line during the troubled years of the Russian Revolution and the Allied intervention. The Chinese delegation was further advised that:

> The Powers . . . reserve the right to insist hereafter upon the responsibility of China for performance or non-performance of the obligations toward the foreign stockholders, bondholders, and creditors of the Chinese Eastern Railway Company. . . .

On the subject of her railways in general, the Conference expressed the hope, somewhat piously, that the Chinese government would effect the unification of her railway systems, using such foreign financial and technical assistance as might be necessary.

At Washington, China also sought cancellation of the various leaseholds held by foreign powers and of numerous treaties, conventions, and notes, which were described as "restrictive stipulations." These included not only the Treaties and Notes of May, 1915, but also the Anglo-Japanese Alliance, a number of Russo-Japanese conventions regarding Manchuria, the Root-Takahira and the Lansing-Ishii Notes, and various non-alienation agreements whereby China was pledged not to cede portions of her territory. As far as the Anglo-Japanese Alliance was concerned, China's wishes were met. This was done, however, to satisfy Canada and the United States, rather than to meet the Chinese demand. The validity of other agreements to which China objected was not challenged successfully.

The Shantung Question

Of all the questions China hoped to settle at the Conference, the return of Shantung was stressed most frequently by

the Chinese delegates and press. The decision of the Versailles
Conference, transferring the German rights to Japan, had provided Chinese politicians with an effective weapon for stirring
resentment against Japan. The Chinese delegates desired the
powers to force a revision of the Versailles settlement. This
the Japanese resisted. They continued to insist that the question of the return of Shantung be settled by direct negotiations
beween themselves and China. In this view, they were supported by Hughes and Balfour, and it was announced during
the Conference that the Chinese and Japanese delegates had
agreed to "conversations" on the subject of Shantung. The
resulting treaty provided that Kiaochow would be restored to
China within six months after the treaty became effective.
Japan would receive compensation for public properties purchased or constructed by the Japanese. The Japanese garrison
at Kiaochow would be withdrawn within thirty days, and the
troops and guards along the Tsingtao-Tsinan Railway within
six months. The railway and its properties would be transferred to China at a cost of some 53,000,000 gold marks, plus
the sums expended by Japan for permanent improvements and
additions. These sums were to be paid in Chinese treasury
notes secured by the properties and revenues of the road, and
pending their redemption China would retain a Japanese
traffic manager and chief accountant. Kiaochow was to be
opened by China to foreign trade and residence. On December
10, 1922, the Kiaochow leasehold was transferred to China.
An official ceremony was announced to mark this historic
occasion, but "hardly one prominent Chinese, other than the
members of the Rendition Commission, was present to witness
the consummation of what had been represented at Versailles
and Washington as the passionate desire of the whole Chinese
nation." [4]

When the time came for the Japanese to withdraw their garrison the bandits of the outlying region prepared to descend upon

[4] H. G. W. Woodhead, in *North China Herald*, December 23, 1922.

the city. The Chinese were forced to ask the Japanese to supply them with arms for their newly organized police, and these had to be sent from Japan.[5]

Yap and the Cables

One of the most troublesome problems that confronted the Washington Conference was the American-Japanese controversy over a tiny island in the western Pacific known as Yap. During the Versailles Peace Conference in 1919, the victorious powers had conferred upon Japan a mandate over the islands of Micronesia (the Marianas, the Carolines, and the Marshalls), which the Japanese navy had occupied during the War. More than a year later (November 12, 1920), the American government informed Japan that the Supreme Council of the Peace Conference, when conferring the mandate on Japan, had, at the request of President Wilson, reserved for future consideration the final disposition of Yap (one of the Carolines), with a view to reaching a later agreement to place the island under international control as a cable station. For this reason, the American government assumed that Yap had not been included in the Japanese mandate. The Japanese insisted that it had been included. This Japanese claim was strengthened on December 17, 1920, by action of the Council of the League of Nations, which confirmed the Japanese mandate as "all the former German islands situated in the Pacific Ocean and lying north of the equator." Accordingly, the United States addressed itself to the Council, setting forth the alleged American reservation. The Council replied that it had no thought of challenging rights acquired by the United States through the part it had played in the War and in making the peace, but that the situation had been complicated by the failure of America to ratify the peace treaty and to join the League. Furthermore, it pointed out that any complaint that the United States entertained should be addressed not to the League but to the Prin-

---

[5] P. J. Treat, *The Far East*. Harper & Brothers, New York, 1935. p. 474.

cipal Allied and Associated Powers, to which the German colonies had been ceded. Japan, meanwhile, wanted to know why the American government had delayed more than a year before presenting its protest concerning the disposition of Yap, an island which Tokyo regarded as of great importance. What, then, were the actual reasons underlying this dispute?

During the World War, a telegraph company, formed in Germany but supported largely by Dutch capital and subsidized by the German and Dutch governments, owned cables running from the island of Guam to Yap, and there diverging, one line going south to the Dutch Celebes, the other going north to Shanghai. An American company owned cables running from San Francisco to Guam, from Guam to the Bonin Islands, from Guam to Manila, and from Manila to Shanghai. During interruptions of the Guam-Manila cable, American messages were diverted to Yap and Shanghai over the German-Dutch system. This alternate route was regarded by Americans as of importance in maintaining uninterrupted communication with China and the Philippines. The seizure of Yap by the Japanese in 1914 and the diversion of the Shanghai cable into one of the Japanese islands (Nawa, of the Loochoo group) placed this alternate route under the control of Tokyo. To prevent this situation from becoming permanent, President Wilson had been advised by his communications expert at Versailles, in 1919, to seek international control of the former German cable system. If the United States could prevent Japan from holding the cable, the Americans would then be in possession of two lines of cable communication with China and the Philippines. In addition, Wilson's advisers objected to Japanese possession of Yap and other Micronesian islands on the ground that it would weaken American naval control in the Philippines, that Guam would be exposed to a possible Japanese attack, and that American influence in the western Pacific would suffer generally. Thus the United States was opposed to Japanese occupation of the mandated islands, but, since this occupation could not be avoided, it became the policy to insist on a reservation concerning Yap and control of its cables. This was the situation which prevailed when the Washington Conference met late in 1921.

Secretary Hughes announced on December 12 that the American and Japanese delegations had reached a settlement concerning the troublesome island. Two months later, this settlement was embodied in a treaty. It set forth that Germany had renounced, in favor of the Principal Allied and Associated Powers, all her rights over her overseas possessions. Great Britain, France, Italy, and Japan had conferred a mandate upon Japan; but the United States, not having ratified the Treaty of Versailles, did not participate in the final confirmation of the mandate. For this reason, the United States and Japan were now concluding a special treaty defining the rights of the two governments and their nationals in the Japanese mandate, particularly with respect to Yap. Among its provisions were the following: (1) The United States gave its consent to the Japanese mandate; (2) all rights and privileges granted to members of the League by terms of the mandate were to be accorded to the United States; (3) American citizens were guaranteed free access to the island of Yap, on an equal footing with Japanese, "in all that relates to the landing and operation of the existing Yap-Guam cable"; (4) citizens of the United States were to enjoy unrestricted rights of entry and of residence in Yap. In this way, an international dispute, which was bitter and at times extremely dangerous, was brought to a close. Just why the United States went out of its way to oppose Japanese control of Yap has never been made quite clear. The American government has never exercised any of the cable privileges which it secured under the treaty,[6]

---

[6] The development of wireless communication may account for the failure of the United States to exercise its privilege under this treaty.

and, ten years after the treaty had been signed, not a single American was resident in Yap.

Summary of the Conference

The Washington Conference concluded its work on February 6, 1922. When account is taken of the international politics to which the Conference owed its origins, it is perhaps surprising that it was able to accomplish many tangible and harmonious results. On naval limitation, it succeeded in scrapping an immense amount of tonnage and establishing a capital-ship ratio for Great Britain, the United States, and Japan of 5-5-3, thus conceding American parity with the British fleet and holding the Japanese navy to a secondary position. Beyond this, it could not go. Although the delegates breathed the language of peace and good will, each power was concerned with disarming its rivals rather than itself. The British accepted parity with the United States in capital ships from necessity, not from desire. They realized that the United States could outbuild them. Japan accepted the ratio of 5 to 3 because it was all the United States would concede and because the Japanese were well aware that Washington could stand a naval race better than Tokyo. The treaty maintaining the *status quo* in fortifications and naval bases in certain insular possessions in the Pacific was of appreciable value, though it must be conceded that the United States, by excluding Hawaii from the *status quo* zone, enjoyed a naval advantage not accorded to Japan. To this extent, the force of the agreement was weakened; it lessened Japanese faith in the peaceful intentions of the United States.

Toward China, the Conference was generous, not to say lavish, in its use of words. Delegates from every power voiced their good will to the great oriental republic. The old phrases pledging China's sovereignty, territorial integrity, and administrative entity were employed with an eloquence never before surpassed. As far as words were concerned, China was surrounded with friends at Washington. This friendship was conditioned, as far as western powers were concerned, by two things. In the first place, the western powers were opposed to the idea of surrendering their special privileges in China as long as these could be retained with safety. At the same time, it was profitable for them to pose as the friends of China in order to restrain Japanese influence at Peking. Thus, while western peoples looked upon themselves as the saviors of China against Japanese aggression, Japan was the only power in 1922 to return a leasehold to China. It is true that the Conference did outline a carefully qualified program by which China might at some time in the future be relieved of some of her international disabilities. Yet it should not be forgotten that the Conference powers that pledged their unswerving adherence to the principle of China's sovereignty and independence were at the very moment the chief violators of that principle. To those powers that enjoyed the conventional tariff, extraterritoriality, settlements, concessions, and the right to maintain their troops on Chinese soil, the principle of China's sovereignty had become little more than a polite and convenient expression.

Granting, however, that the Conference powers were seeking their own, rather than China's, interests, the fact remained that China herself was in large part responsible. Many of her leaders who spoke passionately of the ideals of the Chinese people were at best merely professional politicians seeking political advantage. At Versailles in 1919, and at Washington in 1921, they demanded respect for the Chinese people, yet at home they had done nothing for the very people whose interests they claimed to champion. For China, the obvious lesson of the Conference was the fact that she could expect little of the powers until she had faced her own domestic problems. The powers had promised "to provide the fullest and most unembarrassed opportunity to China to develop and maintain for herself an effective and stable government." It remained to be seen whether or not China was prepared to exert herself to this end.

SELECTED BIBLIOGRAPHY

G. A. Ballard gives a very suggestive treatment of *The Influence of the Sea on the Political History of Japan* (London: 1921). George H. Blakeslee devotes ch. 4 to the Washington Conference in his *Recent Foreign Policy of the United States* (New York: 1925). The influence of Canadian politics on the conference was first developed by J. B. Brebner, "Canada, the Anglo-Japanese Alliance and the Washington Conference," in *Political Science Quarterly,* Mar. 1935. R. L. Buell, *The Washington Conference* (New York: 1922), while of value, was too contemporary to be definitive. A. Bullard, *The A. B. C.'s of Disarmament and the Pacific Problems* (New York: 1921). Hector C. Bywater, *Sea-Power in the Pacific* (Boston: 1921), the analysis of a British naval expert; see in particular chs. 3, 4, 5, 6, 7, 8, and 10. C. Chao, "The Shantung Negotiations," in *The Chinese Social and Political Science Review,* Apr. 1923. Valentine Chirol, *The Occident and the Orient* (Chicago: 1924). Henry Chung, *The Case of Korea* (New York: 1921). A. L. P. Dennis, *The Foreign Policies of Soviet Russia* (New York: 1924). A. L. P. Dennis, *The Anglo-Japanese Alliance* (Berkeley: 1923), special pleading against the alliance. G. M. Dutcher, *The Political Awakening of the East* (New York: 1925). Louis Fischer, *The Soviets in World Affairs,* 2 vols. (London: 1930), vol. 1, ch. 8 on Siberia and the Washington Conference. W. L. Godshall, *The International Aspects of the Shantung Question* (Philadelphia: 1923), ch. 5. Sydney Greenbie, *The Pacific Triangle* (New York: 1921), ch. 18 on Australasia, ch. 19 on Japan and Asia, and ch. 22 on Australia and the Anglo-Japanese Alliance. Yamato Ichihashi, *The Washington Conference and After* (Stanford University: 1928), the most scholarly work on the subject. K. K. Kawakami, *Japan's Pacific Policy* (New York: 1922). Ushisaburo Kobayashi, *Military Industries of Japan* (New York: 1922). P. T. Moon, *Imperialism and World Politics* (New York: 1926). H. K. Norton, *China and the Powers* (New York: 1927). H. S. Quigley, "The Shantung Question in International Law," in *The Chinese Social and Political Science Review,* Feb. 1922 Charles Seymour, *The Intimate Papers of Colonel House,* 4 vols.

(Boston: 1928), vol. 4, ch. 12 on the Shantung question. Henry W. Taft, *Japan and America* (New York: 1932), pt. 2, ch. 2 on the Washington Conference. A. J. Toynbee, *Survey of International Affairs, 1920-23* (Oxford: 1925), pt. 6, ch. 4 on the Washington Conference, and appendix 5, for texts of the treaties. Tatsuji Takeuchi, *War and Diplomacy in the Japanese Empire* (Garden City: 1935), ch. 20. W. S. Thompson, *Danger Spots in World Population* (New York: 1929). W. W. Willoughby, *China at the Conference* (Baltimore: 1922), the contemporary account of an adviser to the Chinese government. By the same author, *Foreign Rights and Interests in China*, 2 vols., rev. ed. (Baltimore: 1927), vol. 1, ch. 10. For the Conference minutes and documents, see *Conference on the Limitation of Armament* (Washington: 1922). P. H. Clyde, *Japan's Pacific Mandate* (New York, 1935).

CHAPTER XXXI

Japanese Immigration and Exclusion

LESS than two years after the Washington Conference had reinforced official harmony between the United States and Japan, the friendly relations of these states were again seriously threatened by a problem in human migration, the presence in California and other states on the Pacific Coast of what was regarded there as a large and growing Japanese population. To many Americans, the coming of these Orientals was cause for alarm—something destructive of indefinable American standards and ideals. From this attitude of alarm, created by the presence of a people alien in race and in color, was born the specter of the "Japanese menace," this in turn leading in 1924 to a national policy excluding the Japanese. Since that date the exclusion policy has remained one of the numerous stumbling blocks in the path toward American-Japanese amity.

Acting on Precedent

In surveying the events that led both directly and indirectly to Japanese exclusion, the student of American history will observe that the policy, not to mention the method of its enforcement, was in no sense new. Historically, the United States, to be sure, had been a country which immigrants entered with the utmost freedom. This policy had been applied not only to Europe but also to Asia. As late as the decade preceding the World War, gross immigration, most of which was from Europe averaged nearly one million annually. It will be recalled, too, that as late as 1868 the United States, in the Seward-Burlingame Treaty respecting China, had pledged itself to the principle that man possessed an inalienable right to change his home and his allegiance. By the turn of the century, however, the government of the United States, under constant pressure from the states of the Pacific Coast, had come to the conclusion that these inalienable rights could no longer be enjoyed by the Chinese, whose exclusion created a somewhat unsavory chapter in American history (see chapter 13). When, therefore, the "Chinese menace" of the late nineteenth century was followed by the "Japanese menace" of the early twentieth century, both a policy and a method of procedure were already at hand. But, whereas a policy of exclusion could be applied with impunity to a weak and ineffective state like China, its application to Japan involved dealing with an established nation which had long since been recognized as one of the so-called great powers.

Nature of Japanese Migration

Contrary to popular notions, the history of Japanese emigration in general is confined to very recent years, and, compared with the migrations of European peoples, has been numerically insignificant. It was not, in fact, until 1884 that the Japanese government sanctioned emigration of laborers. In that year, Japanese laborers began to enter Hawaii at the instance of sugar-plantation owners. Between 1868 and 1924, the Japanese government issued only 1,186,605 passports to all types of emigrants, indicating the very limited character of Japanese migration. Of these emigrants, 238,291 were destined for Hawaii, and 198,070 for continental United States. By 1927, Japanese residing in foreign countries, including children born there of Japanese parents, numbered only 676,262, or far less than the total number of passports issued from 1869 to 1927, which was 1,250,000. Of these Japanese living abroad, 140,709 were in continental United States and 129,387 in the Hawaiian Islands. Of the former, about fifty per cent were American-born, and thus presumably American citizens, while, of the latter, about sixty per cent were Hawaiian-born. From these facts, it becomes evident that Japanese emigration had been conspicuously small.[1]

Numbers of Japanese immigrants reached the Hawaiian Islands before the close of the nineteenth century. By 1890, 12,360 had entered the islands; in 1900 the Japanese population was 61,111. By 1910, the figure had risen only to 79,675; but this is explained perhaps by the fact that during the decade some 40,000 Japanese left the islands for continental United States and Canada. By 1920, the Japanese in Hawaii numbered 109,274, of whom 48,658 were native-born, and in 1930, 139,631, of whom 91,185 were native-born. From 1910 to 1920, the alien Japanese population of the islands remained almost stationary, while after 1920 it decreased. The Hawaiian Islands, it will be recalled, were annexed by the United States in 1898, though prior to that date the American government had maintained a naval base at Pearl Harbor. These facts made the racial composition of the islands' inhabitants a matter of some concern to Washington. It was frequently assumed, though never proved, that the native-born Japanese could not become loyal Americans. When it was pointed out that alien and citizen Japanese formed 16 per cent of the total population of Hawaii in 1900, 41 per cent in 1910, 40 per cent in 1920, and 37 per cent in 1930, alarmists were convinced that the Japanese had already created a political problem of the utmost consequence.

Japanese in the United States

Japanese immigration to continental United States did not assume sizeable proportions until after 1900. The Japanese

---

[1] For much of the following summary the author is indebted to Yamato Ichihashi, *Japanese in the United States*. Stanford University Press, Stanford University, California, 1932.

population of the United States in 1870 was 55; in 1880, 148; in 1890, 2,039; but in 1900, it had jumped to 24,326; in 1910, to 72,157; in 1920, to 111,010; and in 1930, to 138,834. This steady and rapid growth of the Japanese population was by no means due entirely to immigration. The figure of 1910 includes 4,502 native-born Americans; that for 1920, 29,672 native-born Americans, and that for 1930, a still larger proportion. Of the Japanese immigrants who reached the United States between 1886 and 1908, 39.3 per cent were classified as laborers (farmers, fishermen, artisans, and laborers); 21.5 per cent were merchants; 21.4 per cent were students; and 18.1 per cent were officials, tourists, and so forth. Women constituted but a small proportion of these immigrants. As compared with other immigrant groups, the Japanese represented a satisfactory average with respect to material possessions or money, to literacy, to general intelligence, and to peaceful behavior. The causes of this immigration were varied, but in the main it was impelled by a desire on the part of the immigrants to improve their economic status, though some came in order to escape Japan's military conscription. The movement of Japanese from Hawaii, Canada, and Mexico to the United States was also caused in the main by the greater economic opportunities offered. Once in the United States, the Japanese tended to remain on the Pacific Coast. In 1930, of the 138,834 Japanese residents, 120,251 lived in the Pacific Coast states. Obviously, therefore, it was in that area that the so-called "Japanese problem" made itself felt.

The reception accorded the Japanese immigrant was, from the first, by no means cordial. He inherited the attitude that many Americans had already assumed toward the Chinese. Like the Chinese, he was "a yellow man" from a strange and allegedly mysterious part of the world. Again, the discovery was soon made that the Japanese wore peculiar clothing, ate fish without cooking it and, worst of all, worshiped weird un-Christian gods. As early as 1887, only shortly after the

Chinese had been excluded, the cry was raised in California that the "Japs must go." It had little effect, for at the time there were only 400 Japanese in the entire state. In 1890, Japanese cobblers in San Francisco were attacked by members of the shoemakers' union, and two years later a Japanese restaurant was attacked by members of another union. At the same time, there was agitation for exclusion of Japanese children from public schools attended by children of the white race. The year 1900 marked a revival of the campaign in California to exclude Japanese laborers along with the Chinese.

. . . not only was a resolution adopted urging Congress to re-enact the Chinese exclusion law, but it was further resolved [by a mass meeting] to urge the adoption of an Act of Congress or such other measures as might be necessary for the total exclusion of all classes of Japanese other than members of the diplomatic staff. It added, "such a law has become a necessity not only on the grounds set forth in the policy of Chinese exclusion but because of additional reasons resting in the fact that the assumed virtue of the Japanese—i.e., their partial adoption of American customs—makes them the more dangerous as competitors." [2]

During 1901, in a message to the state legislature, the Governor of California called attention to the "danger in the unrestricted immigration of Japanese laborers." He declared that the cheapness of Japanese labor was a menace to American labor. The result was a joint resolution of the state legislature (to be followed by a similar resolution in Nevada), asking the United States Congress to restrict Japanese immigration. The growing fear of the Japanese immigrant had already been stated in great detail by the United States Industrial Commission (1900), which had affirmed that the Japanese were even less desirable than the Chinese, that they had most of the vices of the Chinese and none of their virtues, and that, as a class, the Japanese laborer was "tricky, unreliable, and dishonest." To this point, the agitation against the Japanese had

---

[2] *Ibid.* p. 231.

been in large part the work of labor leaders and politicians seeking the labor vote, but in 1905, newspapers joined the campaign, and the legislature again demanded that Congress restrict immigration. Japanese were assaulted in San Francisco, and their business establishments were wrecked.

The California School Incident

It was while this state of affairs prevailed that the San Francisco Board of Education passed a resolution (October 11, 1906) directing the principals of public schools to send all Chinese, Japanese, and Korean children to the city's oriental school (see chapter 23). This action, which was given wide publicity in the press, brought protests to the Board from both Japanese and American groups. In Japan, the resolution was described as "unfair" and "discriminatory." Opinion in the American press was divided. When the resolution was actually enforced, Japanese in San Francisco appealed to Tokyo, which in turn protested to the American government, resting its claims on the Japanese-American treaty of 1894. The subsequent investigation conducted by the federal government of the United States revealed that, at the time, there were exactly ninety-three Japanese students attending the public schools of San Francisco, and that prominent leaders in the State of California wished Japanese children in the United States to have the same school privileges as children of other nations. In contrast with this sane procedure, a California member of the House of Representatives, presumably speaking for his constituents, had declared from the floor of the House (March 13, 1906):

A close acquaintance shows me that unblushing lying is so universal among the Japanese as to be one of the leading national traits; that commercial honor, even among her commercial classes, is so rare as to be only the exception that proves the reverse rule, and that the vast majority of the Japanese people do not understand the meaning of the word "morality," but are given up to practice of licentiousness more generally than any nation in the world justly making any pretenses to civilization.

Absurd distortion and falsehood of this type was typical of the methods which the California agitators thought necessary to adopt in their efforts to whip up a pronounced racial and political prejudice against the Japanese.

The Gentlemen's Agreement

As a result of intervention by the federal government, the San Francisco Board of Education was prevailed upon to rescind the objectionable resolution (March 13, 1907), while the immigration act of the previous month forbade the entry of Japanese laborers from Hawaii, Mexico, and Canada. In addition, President Roosevelt concluded with the Japanese government the famous Gentlemen's Agreement (1907-1908), according to which "the Japanese government agreed to issue passports for America only to non-laborers, laborers returning from a visit in Japan, and the parents, wives, and children of domiciled laborers, as well as to laborers who had an already possessed interest in a farming enterprise in the country." The immigration act excluding entry from Hawaii, Canada, and Mexico was enforced by the United States; the executive agreement, known as the Gentlemen's Agreement, was enforced by Japan, which, to make it more effective, applied it voluntarily to the Hawaiian Islands and in a measure also to Mexico. That the agreement worked most effectively may be observed from the fact that from 1909 to 1913 the number of Japanese, both immigrants and non-immigrants, to enter the United States annually was only 4,288. It was the understanding, too, of the Japanese government that as long as it enforced the agreement, the United States would not adopt a policy of exclusion.

Any menace which may have existed in a system of unrestricted Japanese immigration was removed effectively by

1908, but the agitation against the Japanese did not cease. In 1908, the Asiatic Exclusion League, meeting in Seattle, condemned the Gentlemen's Agreement on the ground that it permitted the ruler of a foreign state to determine what class and what numbers of persons might come to the United States. During 1909, the California legislature considered many anti-Japanese bills and passed a resolution favoring Japanese exclusion. Similar activities were also in evidence in the States of Oregon, Nevada, and Montana. In 1910, the California state party platforms (Republican, Democratic, and Socialist) all contained demands for oriental exclusion, meaning in particular the Japanese. In the midst of this popular agitation, the California State Commissioner of Labor completed a report on the Japanese in the state. To the chagrin of the anti-Japanese groups, it was discovered that the report regarded oriental labor as essential to much of the agricultural industry of the state. The result was that its contents were promptly "buried." The following year (1911) a new American-Japanese Treaty was concluded. Although it contained no specific provision enabling the United States to exclude Japanese, the Japanese government agreed to maintain the limitations provided for by the Gentlemen's Agreement. For these reasons, the California legislature protested against the treaty. Once it was ratified, however, many legislators expressed themselves as satisfied; it appeared that the anti-Japanese crusade was ended, but not for long. California in 1913 passed its notorious alien land law, the stated purpose of which was to prevent any alien not eligible to citizenship from owning land. This law was directed primarily against the Japanese. The law itself, though legally correct, was not, as is sometimes affirmed, in violation of the Japanese-American Treaty of 1911; it was, nevertheless, discriminatory, for it was based on the federal law withholding naturalization from peoples who are neither white nor black. Economic conditions in California may have had some bearing on the enactment of the law, but it was, in the main, clearly an expression of racial prejudice.

After the passage of the alien land law, and during the period of the World War, there was little anti-Japanese agitation in California. Then, in 1919, the movement was revived for political purposes, looking toward the general election of 1920. A new alien land law, which strengthened the previous law, was passed in this year. Under it, aliens ineligible to citizenship could acquire real property only as provided in the treaty. They could no longer lease land for agricultural purposes. Three years later, the law was amended to prohibit cropping contracts with the result, in the case of the Japanese, that those who had not owned land prior to the passage of the law could now work it legally only as hired labor.

The Picture Brides

Another phase of the anti-Japanese movement concerned what were commonly referred to as "picture brides." The Gentlemen's Agreement permitted the coming to the United States of the "parents, wives, and children of domiciled [Japanese] laborers." It has already been noted that of the early Japanese immigrants, the vast majority were young men. To be more specific, in 1900, there were only 410 married women in a Japanese population of 24,326; in 1910, there were 5,581 in a population of 72,157; and in 1920, there were 22,193 in a population of 111,010. These figures indicate that after the enforcement of the Gentlemen's Agreement, a larger proportion of Japanese women were admitted to the United States. Some of these women were the so-called "picture brides." This name arose from a long-established custom in Japan whereby an exchange of photographs might constitute the beginning of the preliminary arrangements looking toward marriage. Marriage between a Japanese immigrant in the United States and a woman in Japan was effected in this way by the heads of the two households and was regarded as perfectly valid. The legality of the marriage was not questioned by the United States after 1917, but, since it was not recognized as valid by any of the states of the American Union, a second ceremony had been required by the American immigration authorities at the port where the bride entered. Nevertheless, the pious advocates of Japanese exclusion, attacking the admission of the picture brides as immoral, broadened their campaign to oppose the entry of all Japanese women, whether picture brides or not, as contrary to the spirit of the Gentlemen's Agreement. To meet this irresponsible clamor of the exclusionists, the Japanese government in 1921 announced that it would no longer issue passports to picture brides. This ruling meant, of course, enforced celibacy to most Japanese immigrants in the United States and the creation of all the problems associated with celibacy.

Ineligibility for Citizenship

The preceding chapter has revealed how, in the face of all this anti-Japanese movement, official amity between Japan and the United States had been reinforced by the Washington Conference. Yet the Conference had no more than adjourned when new bitterness was added to the Japanese view of America. There had always been some uncertainty as to whether Japanese might become American citizens by naturalization. Some few had been admitted to citizenship, but, in the main, such petitions had been denied by the lower federal courts. Then, in November, 1922, the Supreme Court, in the Ozawa Case, decided against naturalization of Japanese. It was thus clear that the existing American naturalization law discriminated on a racial basis, and that Japanese were ineligible to citizenship. In Japan, this decision outweighed all the verbal protestations of friendship for Japan that had issued from American throats during the Washington Conference.

Post-War Immigration Restrictions

This ruling of the Supreme Court, declaring Japanese ineligible to citizenship under the existing naturalization law, coincided with a new emergency in the development of general immigration to the United States. Immediately after the World War, the United States appeared to be threatened by an unprecedented volume of immigrants from the devastated states of Europe. There was a wide and popular demand that this movement be stopped, or at least drastically curbed. The sentiment was intensified by a revived nationalism, a product of the War itself. This particular nationalism manifested itself in a form of antiforeignism directed against aliens in general, who it was assumed were, at worst, radicals and pacifists and, at best, un-American. As early as October, 1918, an act of Congress had excluded anarchists and similar classes. This legislation was strengthened in June, 1920, resulting in sensational deportations of so-called "reds." The presence of these allegedly undesirable groups was of less real consequence, however, than the situation created by industrial demobilization following the War. At a time when American industry was readjusting itself to a peacetime level, a constant flood of new immigrant labor might have entailed serious results. At all events, some sort of effective restriction having been demanded, the Emergency Quota Act was approved in May, 1921. It based immigrant quotas on three per cent of the number of persons born in any given country and residing in the United States in 1910. In May, 1922, the act was extended for a period of two years, while investigations looking to the adoption of some permanent immigration policy were continued.

Japanese immigrants were not included within the Emergency Quota Acts. This was due to a provision making the acts inapplicable to aliens from countries whose immigration

was regulated in accordance with treaties or agreements dealing solely with immigration, such, for instance, as the Gentlemen's Agreement. To this exception, the anti-Japanese groups
in California and elsewhere on the Pacific Coast were vigorously opposed, and they continued to urge, not a quota for
Japan, but complete exclusion. To this end, the California
State Board of Control prepared a report on "California and
the Oriental." It was submitted by the Governor to the Secretary of State with the statement that:

> ... the people of California ... are determined to exhaust every
> power in their keeping to maintain this state for its own people.
> [By this, the Governor presumably meant anyone so long as he was
> not an Oriental.] This determination is based fundamentally upon
> the ethnological impossibility of assimilating the Japanese
> people. ...

Such was the official attitude of California when in 1924
Congress undertook the drafting of legislation to replace the
Emergency Quota Act. The general immigration act that resulted does not concern this discussion; but it should be noted
that it adopted the system of quotas, which were fixed at two
per cent of the 1890 census. When the subject of the oriental
immigrant was introduced, Representative Albert Johnson of
the State of Washington, the chairman of the House Committee on Immigration and Naturalization, presented the official views of the Pacific Coast, which favored exclusion of
aliens ineligible to citizenship. The bill as drafted by the
House committee exempted, in the main, the same classes as
were exempted under the Gentlemen's Agreement. Thus the
change proposed was largely in method of enforcement. The
committee supported its plan by stating that it was undesirable to admit aliens ineligible to citizenship and that Japan
should logically be placed on the same basis as other oriental
states. Furthermore, it had already become clear that Congress, ever jealous of its prerogative to control immigration,
disapproved of the Gentlemen's Agreement, a purely execu-

tive arrangement. The exclusion clause was adopted by the House by a vote of 323 to 71 (37 not voting).

In the Senate, opinion had been somewhat more liberal. Secretary of State Hughes had suggested that aliens entitled to enter the United States under provisions of a treaty or an agreement relating solely to immigration be excepted from any requirement excluding aliens ineligible to citizenship. Under this plan, Japan would have been exempted under terms of the Gentlemen's Agreement and, like European countries, would have been placed on a quota, which in her case would allow 146 immigrants annually. The Senate committee supported this proposal of the Secretary of State.

The Hanihara Letter

Meanwhile, the Japanese Ambassador in Washington had (with the approval of the State Department) addressed a note to the Secretary of State explaining the character of the Gentlemen's Agreement, to which so much opposition had already arisen in Congress. In the course of this note, Ambassador Hanihara stated:

It [the Gentlemen's Agreement] is in no way intended as a restriction on the sovereign rights of the United States to regulate its immigration. This is shown by the fact that the existing immigration Act of 1917, for instance, is applied to Japanese as to other aliens.

It was because of the fact that discriminatory immigration legislation on the part of the United States would naturally wound the national susceptibilities of the Japanese people, that after thorough but most friendly and frank discussions between the two Governments, the Gentlemen's Agreement was made for the purpose of relieving the United States from the possible unfortunate necessity of offending the national pride of a friendly nation.

The Japanese Government have most scrupulously and faithfully carried out the terms of the agreement as a self-imposed restriction, and are fully prepared to continue to do so as officially announced at the time of the conclusion of the present treaty of commerce and navigation between Japan and the United States. In return the Japanese Government confidently trust that the United States Government will recommend, if necessary, to the Congress to refrain from resorting to a measure that would seriously wound the proper susceptibilities of the Japanese nation.

The note called attention to the fact that during the years that the Gentlemen's Agreement had been in operation (1908 to 1923) the excess of Japanese admitted to the United States over those departing had been only 8,681, or an annual average of 578. The note then concluded:

Relying upon the confidence you have been good enough to show me at all times, I have stated or rather repeated all this to you candidly and in a most friendly spirit, for I realize, as I believe you do, the grave consequences which the enactment of the measure retaining that particular provision would inevitably bring upon the otherwise happy and eventually advantageous relations between our two countries.

The State Department expressed itself as in accord with Japan's view of the Gentlemen's Agreement, and Secretary Hughes forwarded copies of the correspondence to the chairmen of the House and the Senate committees on immigration. However, in the House, the immigration bill containing the Japanese exclusion clause was adopted. In the Senate on April 14, Senator Lodge declared that the note of the Japanese Ambassador contained a "veiled threat." He was supported by Senator Reed, who added that the words of the Japanese Ambassador forced him to vote for Japanese exclusion rather than continuance of the Gentlemen's Agreement. As against the "veiled threat" theory, Senator Sterling observed that Japanese exclusion should be adopted only on the ground of sound policy and not on the pretext of an alleged threat. This statesmanlike suggestion appeared to receive little consideration, for the Senate voted 71 to 4 to exclude aliens ineligible to citizenship.

It was thus clear that both Houses of Congress were as one

in their determination to exclude Japanese. With this policy, the American executive was in complete agreement, but it was opposed to the method employed. Therefore, in signing the general immigration bill, which included the exclusion clause, the President stated:

In signing this bill which in its main features I heartily approve, I regret the impossibility of severing from it the exclusion provision which in the light of existing law affects especially the Japanese. . . . We have had for many years an understanding with Japan, by which the Japanese Government has voluntarily undertaken to prevent the emigration of laborers to the United States; and in view of this historic relation and of the feeling which it inspired, it would have been much better in my judgment and more effective in the actual control of immigration, if we had continued to invite the cooperation which Japan was ready to give and had thus avoided creating any ground for misapprehension by an unnecessary statutory enactment. That course would not have derogated from the authority of the Congress to deal with the question in any exigency requiring its action. There is scarcely any ground for disagreement as to the result we want, but this method of securing it is unnecessary and deplorable at this time. If the exclusion provision stood alone, I should disapprove it without hesitation if sought in this way at this time.

In this manner, then, the organized opposition to Japanese immigration that had commenced in San Francisco in 1905 was finally enacted into a national policy—a policy resting, in the main, on racial discrimination. Following the passage of the exclusion law, the American Ambassador at Tokyo resigned his post, voicing, as he did so, his disapproval of the method employed by Congress. At the same time, the Japanese government lodged its official protest at Washington, in the course of which it asserted:

It is not denied that, fundamentally speaking, it lies within the inherent sovereign power of each state to limit and control immigration to its own domains, but when in the exercise of such right, an evident injustice is done to a foreign nation in disregard of its proper self-respect, of international understandings or of ordinary rules of comity, the question necessarily assumes an aspect which justifies diplomatic discussion and adjustment. . . .

In Japan, indignation at the passage of the law was expressed in every quarter.. In the United States, opinion was divided. Most newspapers published in the East were critical of the act, describing it as "an unnecessary affront to Japan." In the West, and on the Pacific Coast, press opinion was for the most part favorable.

Since 1924, there has been no "problem" of Japanese immigration. There has remained, however, a decided problem in American-Japanese relations. Japanese resentment against the exclusion policy has continued. Organized protests against the law have been voiced in the United States by the National Foreign Trade Convention, and Chairman Johnson, of the House committee that had written the bill containing the exclusion clause, has been reported as favoring placing Japan on a quota basis, a policy which is supported by many newspapers on the Pacific Coast. To any such change, however, the California Joint Immigration Committee, representing state organizations such as the American Legion, the State Federation of Labor, and the Native Sons of the Golden West, remained unqualifiedly opposed.

SELECTED BIBLIOGRAPHY

J. F. Abbott, *Japanese Expansion and American Policies* (New York: 1916). R. C. Adams, *A Statistical Study of the Races in Hawaii* (Honolulu: 1925). R. C. Adams, *The Peoples of Hawaii* (Honolulu: 1925). R. H. Akagi, *The Second Generation Japanese Problem* (New York: 1926). Thomas A. Bailey, "California, Japan, and the Alien Land Legislation of 1913," in *The Pacific Historical Review*, Mar. 1932. R. L. Buell, *Japanese Immigration* (Boston: 1924), a brief but valuable account. George H. Blakeslee, *The Recent Foreign Policy of the United States* (New York: 1925), ch. 5 on Japanese exclusion. W. R. Crocker, *The Japanese Population Problem* (New York: 1931), an excellent study. A. H. Charteris, "Australian Immigration Laws and their Working," in *Problems of the Pacific,* J. B. Condliffe, ed. (Chicago: 1928). S. L. Gulick, *American Democracy and Asiatic Citizenship* (New York: 1919), and by the same author, "Japanese in California," in *Annals of the American Academy of Political and Social Science,* Jan. 1921. T. Harada, *The Social Status of the Japanese in Hawaii* (Honolulu: 1927). K. S. Inui, "California's Japanese Situation," in *Annals of the American Academy of Political and Social Science,* Jan. 1921. T. Iyenaga and K. Sato, *Japan and the California Problem* (New York: 1921). Yamato Ichihashi, *Japanese in the United States* (Stanford University: 1932), the most comprehensive and the most scholarly treatment of the whole subject. K. S. Inui, "Oriental Immigration in British Colonies and Dominions," in *The Far Eastern Review,* Nov. 1933. United States, *Japanese Immigration,* hearings before the Committee on Immigration and Naturalization of the House of Representatives, 66th Congress, 2nd Session, July, 1920 (Washington: 1921). Two books by K. K. Kawakami, *American-Japanese Relations* (New York: 1912); and *The Real Japanese Question* (New York: 1921). An article by the same author, "Japan's Policy Toward Alien Immigration," in *Current History,* June, 1924. G. Kennan, "The Japanese in the San Francisco Schools," in *The Outlook,* June 1, 1907. E. G. Mears, *Resident Orientals on the American Pacific Coast* (Chicago: 1928). R. D. McKenzie, *Oriental Exclusion* (Chicago: 1927). H. F. MacNair, "The Chinese in the British Empire and the New World," in *The Chinese Social and Political Science Review,* July, 1922. J. F. Normano, "Japanese Emigration to Brazil," in *Pacific Affairs,* Mar. 1934. Rodman W. Paul, *The Abrogation of the Gentlemen's Agreement* (Cambridge: 1936). Chester Rowell, "The Japanese in California," in *World's Work,* June, 1913. R. N. Lynch, "The Development of the Anti-Japanese Movement," in *Annals of the American Academy of Political and Social Science,* Jan. 1921. P. J. Treat, "California and the Japanese," in *Atlantic Monthly,* Apr. 1921. P. Scharrenberg, "The Attitude of Organized Labor towards the Japanese," in *Annals of the American Academy of Political and Social Science,* Jan. 1921. P. J. Treat, *Japan and the United States* (Stanford University: 1928). Henry W. Taft, *Japan and America* (New York: 1932), pt. 2, chs. 3-8. A. J. Toynbee, *Survey of International Affairs 1924* (London: 1926), pt. I, sec. 2, on U. S. immigration restriction, 1921-1924.

CHAPTER XXXII

Constitutional Government in Japan

THE STRUGGLE BETWEEN BUREAUCRACY AND LIBERALISM

THE history of constitutional government in Great Britain, France, and the United States is measured by centuries. In Japan, it is still measured by decades. Less than fifty years have elapsed since the Emperor Mutsuhito bestowed, as a voluntary gift upon this people, the Constitution of February 11, 1889. Representative government in the national sense dates only from the meeting of the first Imperial Diet, in 1890. Subsequent years have focused western attention in large part upon Japan's dramatic position in international affairs, yet this position should not exclude some consideration of the nation's domestic political thought and its application. The subject would seem to derive added importance from the fact that the Japanese Constitution is "a document embodying Japanese [not western] political principles under the cloak of [western] representative institutions."

Nature of the Constitution

The government that the makers of modern Japan designed under the Constitution (see chapter 15) was neither parliamentary nor democratic. On the contrary, its strongly centralized forces were to be controlled by a powerful bureaucracy. The Constitution itself, although given in recognition of a popular demand, was not submitted to the people or passed upon by them. The rights of sovereignty remained in the

Emperor, not the people, and were to be exercised by him according to the provisions of the Constitution. In all this there was no suggestion of a monarchy controlled by the will of a sovereign parliament. Yet the Constitution owed its existence in some measure to words of the Imperial Oath (1868), which had declared that: "An assembly widely convoked shall be established, and thus great stress shall be laid upon public opinion." Between the conception of popular government as suggested by the Imperial Oath, and the conservative regime established by the Constitution, there was obviously a wide gulf. From it have emerged the forces of Japanese liberalism, seeking the overthrow of bureaucracy; while, in turn, bureaucracy and special privilege have sought to entrench themselves still further by conservative interpretation of the Constitution.

The Political Parties

It will be recalled (see chapter 15) that, prior to the promulgation of the Constitution, political parties had appeared under such names as the Jiyuto (Liberal Party) and the Kaishinto (Reform or Progressive Party). The former had advocated bestowal of popular sovereignty, while the latter, less radical in its tendencies, had sought rather to control the monarchy to some degree by constitutional limitations that would confer real powers upon the Diet. From as early as 1875, the government showed a pronounced dislike of the parties. The constitutional implication that the Ministers of State (the Cabinet) were responsible to the Emperor rather than to the Diet was meant to relegate them to a position of little consequence. Nevertheless, some nine political parties, indicative of the confusion of political thought, and including the Jiyuto and the Kaishinto, were represented when the first session of the Diet met, in 1890. Of the 300 seats in the House of Representatives, 170 were occupied by members of the liberal parties. From the outset, they were able not only to force the passage of popular legislation but also to block budget proposals of the government. This attitude of the parties was a challenge to the central theory of the Constitution, which was opposed to popular control of policy. The vigor of the parties was indeed disturbing in a state where the Emperor was, in theory at least, an absolute monarch. However, in practice, the Emperor does not determine policy or administer it. These functions have been performed by various and powerful elements of the bureaucracy, who, in so doing, have themselves departed from the letter of the Constitution. Thus in their long struggle to control policy, the political parties have, in ignoring the letter of the Constitution, merely imitated the practice of their alleged superiors—the bureaucrats.

The Cabinet had been functioning for five years when the first session of the Diet was called, at which time Aritomo Yamagata of Choshu, one of the most distinguished Genro, a decided militarist, and the organizer of the modern Japanese army, was Minister President, or Premier. His successor, Masayoshi Matsukata, of Satsuma, who assumed office in 1891, was, if anything, less inclined than Yamagata to humor the politicians. The second session of the Diet was convoked in November, 1891, but the threatening attitude of the parties led to its dissolution in December, while the elections of the following February revealed all the worst features of bureaucratic corruption. The Cabinet entered its own official candidates, and the prefectural governors were ordered to insure their election. The government employed bribery and police interference to an alarming degree in its effort to defeat party candidates. Riots characterized the election. A number of persons were killed, and several hundred were wounded, yet all to little purpose, for the Matsukata Ministry succeeded in electing only ninety-five of its candidates. From this time, it was evident that even bureaucratic cabinets could ill afford to ignore the influence of the despised politicians. It thus became the policy of the clan statesmen, who were to head successive ministeries, to find some compromise scheme whereby the parties might be permitted to participate in government, yet without giving them ultimate control.

. The parties themselves remained united in their opposition to the government during the first four sessions of the Diet, until 1894, when this unity was shattered. Prince Ito, who succeeded Matsukata as Premier, had won in part the support of Itagaki and his Liberal Party. Its support, however, was not sufficient to prevail against Okuma and the Kaishinto, and both the fifth and sixth sessions were ended by dissolution. At this point, the war with China (1894-1895) played into the hands of the clan statesmen. Party interests were subordinated to the national policy. The Liberal Party and other groups continued to support Ito, while Itagaki entered the Cabinet (1896), after resigning, formally at least, his presidency of the party. Here, indeed, was a curious political compact. The most radical of Japan's early political parties, the champion of popular sovereignty, had made a qualified alliance in government with the powerful clan bureaucracy of the Choshu, represented by Ito, the Premier.[1]

Faced with this alliance between the Liberals and the Choshu, Count Okuma reorganized and strengthened his Reform Party (Kaishinto) to form the Shimpoto (Progressive Party) in 1896. On the surface, the new party demanded a government responsible to the Diet. Its principles evidently were not strongly rooted, for later (in 1896), Okuma, like Itagaki, resigned formally his leadership to become Minister of Foreign Affairs in the new Cabinet headed by Matsukata, the Genro and clan statesman of Satsuma. This *modus vivendi* was short-lived, being terminated in 1897, when the Shimpoto discovered that actually its voice carried no weight in matters of policy.

The unhappy results of these brief flirtations of the parties

[1] See Harold S. Quigley, *Japanese Government and Politics*. D. Appleton-Century Company, New York, 1932. p. 209.

with the bureaucrats led in June, 1898, to a union of the Jiyuto and Shimpoto to form the Kenseito (Constitutional Party). In reality, though not formally, Okuma and Itagaki were its leaders. Its declared purpose was to force recognition of Cabinet responsibility to the House of Representatives. Since the new union party was destined to control the House, the Genro were forced to advise that Okuma and Itagaki be summoned to form a Cabinet. This was done in the very month that the party was formed. Okuma became Premier and Minister of Foreign Affairs, while Itagaki was given the post of Home Minister. All members of the Cabinet were party men, save the Minister of War and the Minister of Marine (Navy). It appeared that the goal of responsible government had been achieved within eight years of the Diet's history. And now this phenomenal achievement was sacrificed on the altar of factional strife. After only four months in office, and before it had faced the Diet, the Cabinet resigned (October, 1898). As a union party, the Kenseito had already ceased to exist. Jiyuto members retained the party name of Kenseito, while the Shimpoto adopted the term *Kenseihonto* (Original Constitutional Party). The programs of the two remained essentially alike, but the bitter party strife between them nullified their efforts against the clan bureaucrats. In fact, the party members, like the bureaucrats, were interested primarily in gaining office and power. The cry for responsible government was merely a means to this end. To this fact, the failure of responsible government in 1898 must be attributed. The parties had been given their opportunity and had failed. Twenty years were to elapse before they would again have a cabinet of their own making.

The Bureaucrats Control

To replace the discredited party leaders, the Genro turned to one of their own members, the arch militarist Yamagata.

The restored system was that which had evolved by 1896—bureaucracy seasoned with party influence so far as required to secure the passage of necessary legislation. The parties were compensated with offices and with legislation of a liberal, but not a radical, character. Thus the experience and astuteness of the genro and their political descendants, the oligarchs who stood on the top rung of the bureaucratic ladder, continued to be utilized, while a very gradual liberalizing process operated concurrently. Too facile condemnation of party opportunism may mean overlooking the important fact that Japan's progress toward democratic politics had been accomplished in circumstances of peace and order that have promoted economic and social progress.[2]

From 1898 to 1900, the Kenseito supported the Yamagata Cabinet, but in the latter year the fourth Ito Cabinet was formed. On the eve of this event Ito and a brother Genro, Count Inouye, had engineered the organization, out of the Kenseito, of a new party, the Seiyukai, designed to give practical effect to the new working arrangement between bureaucracy and party politics. Although the immediate result was an increase in party prestige, Ito made it quite clear that bureaucracy had surrendered none of its essential control. The Emperor's prerogatives, which included that of selecting his ministers in complete disregard of party, were unaffected. In a word, the Seiyukai surrendered to Ito, in return for such concessions as the latter might be willing to make. Yet it should not be forgotten that Ito himself was responsible for the organization of a political party whose influence was to grow with succeeding years. From 1900 to 1915, the Seiyukai remained the largest party in the House of Representatives, at times holding an absolute majority. Its chief party rival was the Kenseihonto, now known again as the Shimpoto, of which Okuma had become president. It was logical, therefore, for the Seiyukai to enjoy a virtual monopoly of such favors as the government found it convenient to extend.

After Ito resigned the Premiership, in 1901, this post was

_____
[2] *Ibid.* p. 211.

held alternately until 1913 by General Taro Katsura, of
Choshu, the clan's successor to Yamagata's military bureaucracy, and Marquis (later Prince) Saionji, a civilian and liberal
bureaucrat who had succeeded Ito as president of the Seiyukai

PRINCE KIMMOCHI SAIONJI. In 1937 he was the only surviving member of Japan's
illustrious Genro (Elder Statesmen), and as always, he was the most human of
them all.

in 1903. The Katsura Ministries covered the years 1901 to
1906, 1908 to 1911, and 1912 to 1913. Although Katsura included no party men in his Cabinets, and was at first opposed
by the Seiyukai, he succeeded in retaining, in the main, the
support of the party. The Saionji Ministries held office during
the years 1906 to 1908 and 1911 to 1912. Saionji, in contrast
to Katsura, did appoint some party men to the Ministry.

Power of the Army

The circumstances which brought about the fall of the second Saionji Ministry, in December, 1912, illustrate a factor which has been and which still is of the greatest significance in Japan's constitutional development. The nation, it will be recalled, had recently annexed Korea, and the General Staff was demanding the creation of two new army divisions for its protection. This demand was the culmination of ever-increasing military expenditures, which had followed Japan's success in the Russo-Japanese War.

... [Saionji] disliked the vicious circle in which military ideas move, he was not to be impressed by alarmist tactics, and, above all, he objected to the cost of thus expanding the standing army. Most of his Cabinet were with him; but General Uehara, the Minister for War, insisted, and when the proposal was definitely rejected by a majority of the Cabinet, he resigned. The constitution required that the Minister for War and the Minister of Marine should be respectively a general and an admiral on the active list, so the last word was always with the defence forces, for no officer would be bold enough to accept a portfolio in defiance of the General Staff and the Admiralty Board. There was no other course, therefore, but for the whole Cabinet to resign. Uehara's resignation was handed in on December 2, 1912, and that of the whole Cabinet immediately followed.[3]

The incident was proof of the tremendous constitutional power of the military and naval services to control and to fashion national policy.

A new premier and ministry had to be found, and the choice of the Genro fell again on Katsura—a fair indication that the wishes of the army would not be opposed. From the outset, the Katsura Cabinet was unpopular both within and outside the Diet. When the House of Representatives met in January, 1913, Seiyukai leaders accused the Premier of using

[3] A. Morgan Young, *Japan Under Taisho Tenno, 1912-1926*. George Allen & Unwin, Ltd., London, 1928. p. 21.

the Throne to bolster his personal interests and those that the Cabinet represented. Against such an attack Katsura had sought to protect himself by organizing his own political party, the Rikken Doshikai (Constitutional Fellow-Thinkers' Society). Its membership was drawn largely from the Kokuminto (Nationalist Party), which had appeared two years earlier, replacing the Shimpoto. In the Diet, however, the Rikken Doshikai occupied only ninety-three seats.

Another effort on Katsura's part to put a better face on affairs was the creation of a Council of National Defence, by which he apparently hoped to camouflage the army and navy with an array of highly respectable gentleman behind whom they could maintain their position without its being subject to continual attack.[4]

Meanwhile, the Diet had been twice prorogued within a week; disorders broke out in Tokyo; representatives known to be supporters of the government were beaten in the streets; newspaper offices were attacked and police boxes overturned; and the military were called before peace was restored. Riots also occurred in Kobe, Osaka, and Kyoto. It was plain that the nation did not want Katsura, and that in his selection a fundamental constitutional question was involved. Who had advised the Emperor to summon Katsura to the Premiership? Obviously these unnamed advisers of the Throne had erred, for the Throne itself could do no wrong. From the floor of the House of Representatives came a challenge that sounded harshly in bureaucratic ears. Representative Yukio Ozaki affirmed that there were advisers and ministers among the bureaucrats "who always mouth 'loyalty' and 'patriotism,' and who advertise themselves as the sole repositories of these qualities, but what they actually do is to hide themselves behind the Throne and shoot at their political enemies from this secure ambush. The Throne is their rampart. Rescripts are their missiles." To this challenge, the bureaucrats of the Katsura Ministry replied feebly by attempting to cast the

---

[4] *Ibid.* p. 26.

shadow of treason upon Ozaki. "Our Constitution," they declared, "definitely states that the Emperor is divine and super-human, and the fact of his sanctity cannot in its nature depend on the responsibility of Ministers of States." This, of course, was the purest quibbling, as the ministers well knew. The Katsura Cabinet was doomed. Resignation of the ministers was accepted in February, 1913.

The Naval Scandals

The choice of the Genro now fell on Admiral Count Yamamoto, whose ministry prevailed until March, 1914. Although not a party cabinet, it had the support of the Seiyukai. Its downfall was occasioned by the popular protest which followed disclosure of naval scandals, of which the ministry itself was quite innocent. The House of Representatives cut 30,000,000 yen from the naval estimates, while the Peers followed with a cut of 70,000,000 yen. To this the Lower House, which was seeking to establish its sole right to control money matters, refused to agree. All attempts at compromise failing, the Cabinet resigned.

A difficult task now beset the Genro in finding a successor to Admiral Yamamoto. A number of distinguished men, such as Prince Tokugawa and Viscount Kiyoura, were considered; but the choice finally fell on Marquis Okuma, aged, but still vigorous, whose ministry was to survive during two and a half stormy years in Japanese history (April, 1914 to October, 1916). Okuma, who was in no sense popular with the Elder States-men, appears to have consented, before taking office, to the army demands for two new divisions, thus making himself acceptable to Yamagata and the General Staff. For political support in the Diet, Okuma turned naturally to the Doshikai, which, in a manner, could trace its descent from the old Kaishinto. The general election of 1915 gave this party a majority, and its former relation with the now deceased Katsura was severed with the adoption of a new name, Kenseikai (Constitutional Party). This election was significant in that it was the first in which a government, after defeat in the Diet, appealed to the electorate. Although the Cabinet was not composed exclusively of party men, it did appeal to the principle of popular responsibility. But this precedent did not go unchallenged. When Okuma resigned, in October, 1916, his logical successor, Viscount Kato, president of the Kenseikai majority party, was not chosen to head a responsible cabinet. Instead, the Genro, now dominated by Yamagata, turned to a Choshu clansman and militarist, Marshal Seiki Terauchi.

The Terauchi Cabinet, though not a party government, sought and received the support of the Seiyukai, much to the chagrin of the Kenseikai, which likewise sought the Premier's favors. The elections of 1917 gave the government a majority, composed of the Seiyukai and a group of independents. Here again was a compromise by which a bureaucratic and irresponsible cabinet might function by means of such favors as it saw fit to bestow on its temporary political allies in the Lower House. This convenient arrangement was rudely interrupted in August, 1918, by events which were the product of the World War. Japan's wartime prosperity, with its unprecedented increase of wealth among certain classes, ushered in an era of lavish and ill-advised extravagance. Prosperity was no longer just around the corner; it was a reality. Employment increased, and wages rose, but not so rapidly as prices of the staple foodstuffs—rice and fish. The trouble first broke out in some remote fishing villages, where angry wives raided the rice shops (August 4, 1918). These "rice riots" spread with great rapidity to the great cities such as Kyoto, Osaka, and Kobe. Premises of firms that the mobs thought responsible for the increased prices were burned. Troops soon suppressed the rioters. There were many casualties and more arrests, followed, in some cases, by the death penalty. Order promptly being restored, the government attempted by

emergency measures to meet the popular protest. Nevertheless, it seemed that the Terauchi Ministry had outlived its
usefulness. It resigned in September, 1918.

The First Commoner

Again the Genro were summoned to find a premier. The
ranks of the Elder Statesmen had now been reduced to
Yamagata, Matsukata, and Saionji. On the advice of the first
two, the Emperor ordered Saionji to form a cabinet, but this
the liberal Saionji declined, insisting that the time had arrived
to recognize democratic development by calling a commoner,
the president of the Seiyukai, Takashi Hara. To this suggestion, Yamagata and Matsukata finally agreed, though reluctantly, and Hara's party government took office in September,
1918. The new Premier, the first untitled leader to hold
this office, had through his entire career been identified with
the party. A man of great personal force, he was inclined to
be unscrupulous, was in no sense a reformer, and owed his
power in large part to the personal loyalty that he inspired
among his political followers. He will be remembered not
as a great statesman but as the man whose privilege it was to
head Japan's first responsible government. His years in office
(September, 1918 to November, 1921) were filled with stirring
events: the Versailles Peace Conference, the inter-Allied Siberian intervention, the formation of the Four-Power Consortium,
and the calling of the Washington Conference. Furthermore,
the Hara party ministry symbolized the rapid wartime expansion of Japan's capitalistic enterprise and with it the spread
of liberal and democratic philosophies, though Hara himself
was by no means a democrat. It appeared to indicate that
the power of the clan bureaucrats had been crippled, if not
completely destroyed. In the general election of May, 1920,
Hara was given an overwhelming Seiyukai majority, and was
pushing his policies vigorously when on November 4, 1921,

he was assassinated at Tokyo station by a youth who asserted
that his act was in protest against the corruption of politics.
That politics was corrupt under Hara there is no doubt.
Hara's Minister of War was General Baron Giichi Tanaka

KOREKIYO TAKAHASHI. From 1904 when during the Russo-Japanese conflict he
negotiated Japan's first great war loans, he remained until his death by assassination
in 1936 the indispensable personality in the world of Japanese public finance, banking, and politics.

(one of Yamagata's lieutenants), who became the agent of
reckless expenditure on the military services. It was thus clear
that, although the Hara government represented belated recognition of a constitutional principle, it did not bequeath a higher
code of political conduct.

Hara was succeeded both in the Premiership and in the presidency of the Seiyukai by his Minister of Finance, Korekiyo Takahashi. Takahashi, a man of liberal principles, finding himself unable to control either his Cabinet or the party, resigned the Premiership after a brief seven months in office (June, 1922). The Seiyukai had fallen a prey to internal factional strife, with the result that the Genro turned from the party politicians and summoned Admiral Tomosaburo Kato, who had represented Japan at the Washington Conference, to form a government. Japan now witnessed a succession of aristocratic and non-party cabinets. Admiral Kato was succeeded in September, 1923, by Admiral Gombei Yamamoto, and he, in January, 1924, by Viscount Keigo Kiyoura, president of the Privy Council. The parties in these years wasted their energies in factional revolts and new group alignments. For example, the Seiyukai was weakened when a group led by Takejiro Tokonami formed the Seiyuhonto in January, 1924. The principal result was to make the Kenseikai the most powerful single group in the Lower House, and, when Kiyoura resigned, Prince Saionji, now the only surviving Genro, recommended Viscount Taka-akira Kato, the party's chief, for Premier. Since the Kenseikai held only 155 seats, a coalition Cabinet was formed, including ministers from the Kenseikai, Seiyukai, Kakushin Club, and the Peers. The army and navy Ministers, as always, were selected from the services, while the Foreign Minister was a non-party man. It was during Kato's tenure that the manhood suffrage bill was passed (March, 1925).

Manhood Suffrage

The suffrage in Japan had been determined previously by the electoral laws of 1889, 1900, and 1919. All included as a voting qualification the payment of a stated sum in direct national tax. In 1890, the electorate numbered some 450,000. In 1900, it was increased to approximately 1,000,000; in 1919, to 2,800,000 and in 1925, to 12,500,000. This was a male suffrage, the voting age being 25 years. Under the first electoral law, many of the poorer former samurai and persons of education were disqualified because of inability to meet a property qualification. The first manhood suffrage bill was introduced in 1903. A similar bill passed the Lower House in 1911, only to be defeated by the Peers. The proposal was agitated widely again in 1919, and in 1920, the Diet was dissolved because the government feared the result of a vote. In 1925, the manhood suffrage bill, in recognition of a popular demand that could no longer be ignored, was proposed by Viscount Kato's coalition ministry. Since 1925, a movement to enfranchise women has received increasing popular support.

The political shuffling that followed passage of the manhood suffrage law brought new strength to the Seiyukai. General Baron Giichi Tanaka, who since the passing of Yamagata had become the most influential of the Choshu leaders, accepted the presidency of the party, which was also joined by Ki Inukai, a liberal politician of great ability. In fact, the Seiyukai was revived by an apparent union of militarism and liberalism. Nevertheless, the Kato Ministry survived until the death of the Premier (January, 1926), who was succeeded both as Premier and head of the party by Reijiro Wakatsuki. To balance the increased power of the Seiyukai, the Kenseikai and Seiyuhonto united (March, 1927), forming the Minseito (Democratic Party), which now controlled the Lower House. In April, Wakatsuki's Cabinet resigned when challenged by the Privy Council in connection with relief measures concerning the Bank of Taiwan. The Genro recommended General Tanaka, who formed a Seiyukai Cabinet, excepting, of course, the portfolios of war and marine. Since the Seiyukai was in the minority, the government dissolved the Diet (January, 1928), but failed to secure a majority in the subsequent general election, despite a lavish use of campaign funds. The government was able to survive the meeting of the Diet only because some of the small party groups, in a no-confidence vote, failed to support the Minseito.

"In the Name of the People"

During 1928 Japan, among other states, had signed at Paris the Treaty for the Renunciation of War, commonly referred to as the Kellogg Pact or the Pact of Paris. According to the wording of the treaty, the sovereigns or presidents of the various states signed "in the names of their respective peoples." No exception to this phraseology was taken by Tanaka or his Seiyukai Cabinet, but in the ratification, the Privy Council insisted on a statement that the phrase was inapplicable to Japan. The incident was a convenient occasion for the Minseito to attack the Seiyukai, even though the alignment did not strictly follow party lines. Some of Japan's foremost liberals were opposed to the phrase "in the names of their respective peoples." Their argument was that in this form the treaty violated Japan's Constitution. More specifically, they asserted that the Japanese people, not the Emperor, were the subject of the treaty. This might be well enough in countries where the sovereign reigned but did not rule; but in Japan, where the Emperor, according to the Constitution, both controlled and exercised the supreme sovereign authority and concluded treaties, the people could not become the subject of a treaty. The controversy was interesting in that it revealed the efforts of the older conservatives and liberals alike to maintain what was no longer tenable, namely, that Japan was an absolute monarchy. The effort to separate the Japanese people from the policy accepted by the Emperor in the terms of the Kellogg Pact might find justification in a literal reading of the Constitution, but it was no longer tenable in the light of Japan's political development during three decades of constitutional rule.

Tanaka's Cabinet, resigning in July, 1929, was succeeded by that of Yuko Hamaguchi, president of the Minseito. In the

Lower House, the opposition parties far outnumbering the Minseito, the House was dissolved. The general elections gave the government its needed majority, though there was little to choose between in the election platforms of the two major parties. Both were pious and vague summaries of general principles to which anyone might subscribe without committing himself to detailed action. The parties, in fact, were pledged to no higher principle than the maintenance of party government, which in turn was the avenue to power.

The London Naval Treaty

The most significant constitutional test that confronted the Hamaguchi Cabinet arose in connection with the signature and ratification of the London Naval Treaty of 1930 (see chapter 38). The treaty embodied a compromise with the original Japanese proposals. This compromise was acceptable to the Premier and the Foreign Office but not to the navy. Despite this opposition, the treaty was signed by the Japanese delegates. Then came the question of ratification. The Supreme War Council held that the government should not have signed without approval of the Naval Staff. Before the Privy Council, the Premier stated that the chief of the Naval Staff had been fully informed on government action and had withdrawn his opposition. If such had been the case, the constitutional position of the military services as advisers of the Emperor was not affected. Actually, the reverse was the case, for the government had given orders to sign the treaty against emphatic opposition from the navy. In other words, the navy, acting within its constitutional right to advise the Throne directly, had been defeated by the Cabinet, the civilian and responsible wing of the government. There can be no doubt that at the time public opinion favored the treaty, this fact presumably having been made clear to the Emperor by the Genro and officials of the Imperial Household. The precedent established in this case is likely to be of significance in Japan's future constitutional development.

While the struggle over the London treaty still filled the public mind, Premier Hamaguchi was shot and wounded seri-

BARON K. SHIDEHARA. He was Minister for Foreign Affairs in Japan at the time of the outbreak in Manchuria in 1931. He headed the civilian liberals as opposed to the military.

ously at Tokyo station. Although he lived for another year, he could no longer participate actively in politics. Baron K. Shidehara, Minister for Foreign Affairs, became Acting Premier. In April, 1931, the Cabinet resigned. Reijiro Wakatsuki, who succeeded to the headship of the party, was chosen

Premier, and reappointed most of the Hamaguchi ministers. The new government advocated retrenchment, a policy which had gone far to alienate the army when the Manchurian outbreak occurred in September. The Cabinet was subject immediately to attack by the Seiyukai on its foreign policy. Within its own councils, there was dissension, and from various sources came suggestions for a coalition government to meet the Manchurian emergency. In December, the ministry was forced to resign. The Genro, still holding, however, to the idea of a party cabinet, called Tsuyoshi Inukai, president of the Seiyukai, to head a new ministry. A general election, held in January, 1932, gave the Seiyukai a handsome majority.

The End of Party Cabinets

This unbroken succession of party cabinets, which Japan had enjoyed since Viscount Kato took office in July, 1924, was ended by the dramatic "May 15th Case" of 1932. More than forty young officers and cadets of the army and navy, with whom were associated a number of civilians, had planned the assassination of important government officials and other forms of direct action. This, they hoped, would precipitate a national emergency and force the creation of a "strong" government to undertake the reconstruction of the state. Their motivation lay in what was described as the stagnation and decline of capitalistic economy, the failure of the parliamentary system, and the growth of communistic thought. They hoped for the establishment of national socialism. Late in the afternoon on May 15, a number of these "patriots" assassinated Premier Inukai at his official residence. Simultaneously, abortive attempts were made to destroy the main offices of the Bank of Japan, the Mitsubishi Bank, the Metropolitan Police Building, and the headquarters of the Seiyukai Party. Order was promptly restored by the police and the military. The Seiyukai immediately chose Dr. Kisaburo Suzuki, a leading member of

the House of Representatives, as head of the party. Suzuki
was passed over, however, by the Genro and other counselors
of the Throne, who believed the emergency demanded a national cabinet. The task of forming this government fell to

GENERAL SADAO ARAKI. In appearance he is the least soldierly of Japan's war
lords. His expression is ascetic and kindly, yet emotionally he is the personification
of Bushido, "The Way of the Warrior."

Admiral Viscount Makoto Saito, former Governor General of
Korea. His ministry was drawn from both the major parties,
the House of Peers, the army and navy, and unaffiliated leaders.
The most significant appointments were those of Korekiyo
Takahashi, Minister of Finance, and Lieutenant General Sadao
Araki, Minister for War.

The Saito Cabinet was designed with the hope of creating

national confidence at a time when Japan's international position was threatened by the policies of the League of Nations and the United States toward the Manchurian affair. It was likewise expected to act as a stabilizing force in the confused state of domestic politics. Under the impetus of an intensified nationalism, the established political parties had lost most of the prestige gained during the previous decade. The political stage was filled with the declamations of extremists and reactionaries of all types. Party politicians, sensing their own weakness, were not averse to profiting through the new vogue of super-patriotism. A group of Minseito members under the leadership of Kenzo Adachi formed, in August, 1932, the Kokumin Domei (National Union), the aims of which were of distinctly fascist flavor. As the international tension relative to Manchuria intensified, the demands for strong government increased. Neither the political parties nor the super-nationalists were satisfied with the Saito Cabinet. Its policies were not extreme, and in this lay its greatest virtue. It survived during the troubled months of 1933, resigned in July, 1934, and was followed by the Ministry of Admiral Keisuke Okada, who, like Admiral Saito, was selected because of his moderate views and his aloofness from party and factional groups. A number of the ministers who had served during the closing months of the Saito regime continued in office. These included Foreign Minister Koki Hirota, War Minister General Hayashi, and Navy Minister Admiral Osumi.

The Minobe Affair

During the regime of the Okada Cabinet, a delicate constitutional question that threatened the very existence of the government arose unexpectedly. A conservative member of the House of Peers, with the object of embarrassing the government, interpellated the Minister of Education on the general subject of "delinquency" in national education and public thought. Was the government, through the Department of Education, exercising proper control over the public mind in what was described as a time of "crisis"? To these charges, the Minister of Education replied in a tactless and provocative manner, whereupon the interpellator, Baron Kikuchi, of the House of Peers, in order to substantiate his charge that "dangerous thought" was prevalent in the educational world, singled out for attack the liberal constitutional theories of one of Japan's greatest scholars, Dr. T. Minobe. The particular point to which exception was taken was Minobe's theory of sovereignty. Minobe held that the Constitution distinguished between the Emperor and the state, and that, despite Article IV, sovereignty did not reside in the Emperor alone. In other words, the state was to be regarded "as a legal personality, the Emperor as an organ of the state, and sovereignty as vested in the state although exercised in the name of the Emperor." This constitutional view had been raised as early as 1913 against the more conservative and absolute views of those who held that the Emperor and the state were inseparable. There was thus nothing new in the theory. It had likewise enjoyed extensive discussion in authoritative works on constitutional law that had long been used in the government universities. How was it, then, that in 1935, all the elements of the extreme "right"—nationalists and super-patriots, both military and civilian—denounced it as treason, and that the life of Dr. Minobe himself was in grave danger? The answer is that these extreme elements (most of which favored a dictatorship in some form) discovered in the Minobe theory a weapon by which, under the cloak of patriotism, they could strike at the moderate and passive Okada government. They could raise the cry of "dangerous thought," because the Minobe theory conceived of the Emperor as:

> . . . an organ of state possessed of an extensive prerogative that is to be exercised, not on the advice of elder statesmen, nor army

and navy chiefs, nor bureaucrats, but rather on the advice of a ministry dependent on the House of Representatives.[5]

Despite the furore that the extremists kept alive for months, the Okada Cabinet did not fall.

Conclusion

The preceding discussion has shown some of the striking features of Japan's political development through four and a half decades of constitutional government. Despite the confusion of recent years, Japanese governments have found it impossible to function independently of the Diet. Nevertheless, the principle of party government has not been adopted, though there have been many party cabinets. The low esteem in which the principal parties have been held in recent years is both a natural product of the times and also a product of the character of the parties themselves. For the most part, they have been groups giving their allegiance to personal leaders rather than to major issues of policy. Their programs have lacked both character and distinctiveness. Like parties in the western world, they have needed funds, and this has led to their alignment with powerful financial interests. In fact, many pages might be filled with the criticisms that in recent years have been hurled at the major parties in Japan. Many of them are justified. Yet in passing judgment upon the parties, it should be recalled that their experience covers little more than half a century, and that they have been the most effective single force in liberalizing the processes of Japan's government.

SELECTED BIBLIOGRAPHY

In addition to the titles listed at the end of chapter 15, see also the following:

G. C. Allen, *Modern Japan and Its Problems* (New York: 1927).

---

[5] K. W. Colegrove, "The Treaty-Making Power in Japan." *American Journal of International Law*, 1931. Vol. 25, p. 274.

T. A. Bisson, "Democracy in Japan," in Foreign Policy Association, *Information Service,* June 25, 1930. E. W. Clement, *Constitutional Imperialism in Japan* (New York: 1916). George M. Dutcher, *The Political Awakening of the East* (New York: 1925), ch. 4. Galen M. Fisher, *Creative Forces in Japan* (New York: 1923), ch. 2. Rikitaro Fujisawa, *The Recent Aims and Political Development of Japan* (New Haven: 1923), in particular, chs. 2-5. Ippei Fukuda, *Sketches of Men and Life* (Tokyo: 1933), includes essays on some of Japan's modern statesmen. Stephen King-Hall, *Western Civilization and the Far East* (New York: 1924). Tamon Maeda, "Political Difficulties of the Japan Diet," in *Pacific Affairs,* June 1931. H. Vere Redman, "How the Cabinet Is Controlled," in *Contemporary Japan,* Dec. 1932. Tai Sekiguchi, "Political Conditions in Japan after the Application of Manhood Suffrage," in *Pacific Affairs,* Oct. 1930. Tatsuji Takeuchi, *War and Diplomacy in the Japanese Empire* (Garden City: 1935), ch. 23 on Japan and the Pact of Paris from the standpoint of domestic politics. A. Morgan Young, *Japan in Recent Times* (New York: 1929). Sakuzo Yoshino, "In the Name of the People," in *Pacific Affairs,* Mar. 1931, a discussion of the constitutional issue in Japan.

CHAPTER XXXIII

Chinese Nationalism and the Powers

1922-1928

THE delegations that professed to speak for China at the Versailles and the Washington Conferences, and so eloquently ascribed the woes of their native land to the vicious imperialism of foreign powers (in particular Japan), did not represent, in any real sense, the geographical area commonly referred to as China. No single government existed that could, properly speaking, claim to represent an authority covering this area. In fact, there had been no such authority since the collapse of Yuan Shih-kai's regime in 1916. The military governors whom Yuan had appointed soon became a law unto themselves in their respective provinces. In and about Peking, the more ambitious of these war lords fought for control of the so-called republican government. For a time, the political spoils were enjoyed by the Anfu party, which, as will be recalled, was displaced in 1920 by its chief rival, the Chihli faction, associated with Chang Tso-lin of Manchuria. In such an atmosphere, there was little place for the Parliament that President Li Yuan-hung had dissolved in 1917. Most of its members retired to Canton, where, at a safe distance, a rival government was set up, under the leadership again of Sun Yat-sen, with the announced purpose of maintaining constitutionalism. But here, too, there was no more freedom from internal strife than in the north. Sun's leadership was soon submerged in a directory that claimed, though it did not exercise, authority over most of China south of the Yangtze. The real power in the south, as elsewhere, remained with the militarists. In the spring of 1918, Sun and his immediate associates found it expedient to retire to the settlement of the despised foreign imperialists in Shanghai.

Student Revolutionaries

These reverses suffered by Sun and his Kuomintang following were countered in some degree during 1919-1920 by public campaigns conducted by student unions. The protests of the students were aimed at the general political anarchy of the nation, and, although it was not at first connected with the Kuomintang, which was essentially a Canton faction, the two groups became more closely associated after 1920. From student enthusiasm the Kuomintang was soon to profit. Meanwhile, General Chen Chiung-ming, one of Sun's revolutionary associates since 1911, captured Canton. Returning from Shanghai with his followers, in 1921 Sun was elected President of the "Chinese Republic" by the remnants of the 1913 Parliament. The fact that these representatives did not constitute a quorum appears to have been regarded as of no importance. It was at this point, with the Chihli group in power at Peking, while Sun and his "Parliament" ruled at Canton, that China presented her case at the Washington Conference.

In the spring of 1922, civil war broke out between the armies of Chang Tso-lin, of Manchuria, and Wu Pei-fu, the most powerful militarist of the Chihli faction, then controlling Peking. To the aid of Wu came the armies of the "Christian" General Feng Yu-hsiang, then military governor of Shensi province. Chang was forced to retire north of the Great Wall, where he declared himself independent of Peking, which, in fact, like many other war lords, he actually was. President Hsu, who was completely powerless in the hands of General Wu, resigned in June, 1922. For the ensuing year, the Presidency was occupied again by Li Yuan-hung, whose influence, it was thought, might win the submission of the southern prov-

Underwood & Underwood.

MARSHAL CHANG TSO-LIN. The brilliant ex-bandit who made of the homeland of the Manchus his own private domain.

inces. Parliament was again summoned, but its policy was little better than that of the militarists. For some time, too, General Tsao Kun, of Chihli, had looked with envious eyes on the Presidency. Accordingly, President Li was driven out and the Parliament bribed into electing Tsao to his place (October, 1923). The policy of the new President was to unite China by force. In this, his armies were enjoying some success, when new warfare broke out in the north between Tsao's chief lieutenant, Wu Pei-fu, and Chang Tso-lin, the master of Manchuria. While this conflict was at its height, Peking was seized suddenly, in October, 1924, by the armies of Feng Yu-hsiang, former ally of Wu. Feng imprisoned President Tsao Kun and arrested such members of Parliament as could be seized. With Chang Tso-lin threatening him from the north and Feng from Peking, Wu Pei-fu fled with a small body of troops to the Yangtze. Feng, now controlling the capital, announced himself commander of the Kuominchun, or National People's Army, and appointed a new Cabinet. Tsao Kun was forced to resign. Under the dictation of Feng and his troops, the new Cabinet demanded that the former Manchu Emperor, who still resided in Peking and retained his Imperial rank according to the abdication agreement of 1912, resign the title. This the former sovereign, who was now known as Pu-Yi, refused to do. He took refuge in the Japanese Legation.

With Wu Pei-fu and the Manchu Emperor out of the way, Generals Feng and Chang now bestowed the title of Chief Executive on the former Anfu leader, Tuan Chi-jui (November, 1924). The two "king-makers" then retired from the capital—Feng to Kalgan, where his armies controlled an indefinite area northwest of Peking, and Chang to his private realm, Manchuria. Through 1925, a series of private wars was fought between these rival brigand-generals and their allied war lords south of the Wall. The principal result of these indecisive campaigns that ravaged the country was a new alliance against Feng between the erstwhile enemies, Wu Pei-fu and Chang

Tso-lin. This combination being, for the time, too strong for General Feng, he retired for rest and study to Moscow. This was soon followed by the retirement of Chief Executive Tuan Chi-jui. As there was some difference between Generals Chang

Ewing Galloway.

GENERAL FENG YU-HSIANG. The so-called "Christian General" was among the ablest of China's war lords in the early days of the Republic.

and Wu as to what kind of government should be established, for a time it is doubtful that any existed. Finally, in December, 1926, Chang Tso-lin assumed command of what was called the northern armies and in June, of the following year, proclaimed himself dictator of the northern military government.

While the foregoing period of private wars, brigandage, and

unqualified treachery prevailed among the war lords of Peking and the north, what had been the fortunes of Dr. Sun's republican and allegedly constitutional government at Canton? Sun owed his restoration to power at Canton in 1921 not to any popular or constitutional demands but rather to the military power of his ally, General Chen Chiung-ming. The latter was no friend of popular government. He was opposed to Sun's election as President and to Sun's whole theory of government.

. . . Ch'en had opposed Dr. Sun's plan of establishing a National Government independently of the Peking Government. He wanted the support of the Tuchüns [military governors] of Yunnan, Kweichow, Szechuan and Hunan for his own ambitions, and in return supported and encouraged them in their schemes of a Federated Government of autonomous provinces. For they disliked Sun's plans of a Centralised Government, which would mean a surrender of their semi-independent position in the provinces. They had to pay a nominal allegiance to Sun Yat-sen as President of the Southern Republic, as they were themselves at war with the Peking militarists. But they had no intention of accepting Sun Yat-sen's authority, although they could not afford to repudiate it publicly.[1]

This conflict in policy between Dr. Sun and General Chen soon resulted in an open breach. The occasion was General Wu Pei-fu's victory at Peking, the elevation of Li Yuan-hung again to the Presidency, and the summoning of the original Parliament of 1913. This Parliament included the greater part of the members of Sun's legislature at Canton. They obeyed the summons to Peking, it would seem, largely because of the prospect "of receiving a salary from the Customs Surplus." A group in the re-convened Peking Parliament wired Sun to resign the southern Presidency now that Parliament had been re-established in the north. This Sun refused to do, despite the fact that for the moment his authority was gone. Taking advantage of this situation, General Chen

---

[1] Tang Leang-li, *The Inner History of the Chinese Revolution.* George Routledge & Sons, Ltd., London, 1930. p. 141.

proceeded to drive Sun from Canton and to set up an autonomous government of his own. From the refuge of some warships that had remained loyal to him, Sun attempted unsuccessfully to recapture Canton. He did manage, however, to destroy a good part of the city and to kill a large number of his own countrymen, noncombatants, to whom he gave no warning of the attacks. All these efforts proving futile, Sun again took refuge in Shanghai. By the close of 1922, it appeared that he and his Kuomintang following were definitely in eclipse. The revolution of 1911-1912 seemed lost, unless new life could be infused into the revolutionary party.

Russia and the Kuomintang

The inspiration for a reorganized Kuomintang came from Soviet Russia. In part, this was a natural result of the Russian Revolution, which had overthrown the autocracy of the Tsars and their oppressive aristocracy. In part, too, it resulted from what the revolutionary Chinese were pleased to term the failure of the Versailles and the Washington Conferences to deal justly with China. From as early as 1918, Sun Yat-sen had sympathized with the aspirations of the Russian Revolution. This sympathy was strengthened in 1920, when Moscow declared void all the "unequal" treaties which had been forced upon China by the Tsarist government. The following year, Russian agents formed the nucleus of the Chinese Communist Party, which in 1923 was instructed to work in co-operation with Sun. From this time, the Kuomintang adopted the general policy of admitting communists to its membership. At the same time Adolf Joffe, special envoy of the Soviet government, assured Sun of Russian support in his efforts to achieve Chinese unification and complete independence from imperialistic control. Russia was prepared to support Sun in achieving his political program of the Three People's Principles: nationality, popular sovereignty, and the people's livelihood, commonly interpreted as socialism. No efforts, it was agreed, would be made by Russia to establish a communist state, which, it was acknowledged, was impractical for China.

Meanwhile, General Chen and his autonomous government had been expelled from Canton, to which Dr. Sun was able to return early in 1923. The new government that he set up was, like that of the war lords, arbitrary and oppressive in the extreme. Sun was soon joined by Michael Borodin, who arrived as Russia's unofficial representative to further the cause of China's national revolution. He was promptly appointed by Sun as adviser to the Kuomintang, with the special task of assisting in its reorganization. Although many of the veterans of the Kuomintang, such as Wang Ching-wei, were opposed to the new policy of association with Russia, Sun was able to dominate the first national congress of the party, held in January, 1924. The manifesto issued by the congress declared that:

> . . . the aim of the Revolution was not merely the overthrow of the Manchu Dynasty, but the establishment of a strong and efficient Government, which would liberate the Chinese people from the dominating influence of the Imperialist Powers, and restore China as an independent nation, by lifting her from the semicolonial status to which she had been reduced.[2]

The result, then, of the congress was the appearance of a reborn Kuomintang, highly organized, strongly influenced by Russian advisers, and pointedly anti-imperialistic in its policies. Its more efficient organization and its increased numbers drawn from communist ranks greatly enhanced its immediate power. At the same time, doubts were expressed as to whether or not constitutional democrats and communists could maintain a workable and permanent union. That these doubts were well founded was soon evident. Within the ranks of the Kuomintang (non-communist) members, a Left and a Right faction appeared. Sun associated himself with the former and, to-

---

[2] *Ibid.* p. 166.

gether with his more able lieutenants, Wang Ching-wei, Hu Han-min, and others, established a political council which soon became the political dictator of the party, ignoring the Right faction completely.

Death of Sun Yat-sen

These developments were complicated further by conditions that prevailed within the city of Canton itself. There a regime of extortion finally drove the merchant class, its chief victim, to organize a private militia called the Merchants' Volunteer Corps. Originally, the purpose of the Corps appears to have been purely protective and local, but the dictatorial policy of Sun's government and the growing influence of the Left wing of the Kuomintang and of the communists soon led it to plan for the overthrow of Sun's republic and the restoration of a government under General Chen Chiung-ming. Early in the autumn of 1924, this middle-class revolt against Sun had spread widely throughout Kwangtung province. In October, Sun succeeded in crushing the Merchants' Volunteer Corps. Some of the richest sections of Canton were destroyed, amid much looting and loss of life. It was at this point, while Sun's prestige in the south was threatened seriously, that he was invited to visit Peking to discuss with Feng Yu-hsiang, Chang Tso-lin, and Tuan Chi-jui the reorganization of the northern government on a basis satisfactory to the Kuomintang. He accordingly left Canton and proceeded north by way of Shanghai and Japan. His trip was punctuated with speeches directed against the foreign imperialists in China, their "unequal" treaties, and their concessions and settlements. Yet at the very moment, Sun was proceeding to the refuge of his residence within the French concession at Shanghai, which on previous occasions had afforded him a safe retreat. From Japan, Sun learned that the situation in Peking was no longer favorable to his plans. Nevertheless, he proceeded to Tientsin where, a sick man confined to his bed, he devoted himself to the organization of the workers and to the establishment of branch parties of the Kuomintang. On December 31, 1924, he set out for Peking, where on March 12, 1925, he died leaving a political will, the importance of which may scarcely be overestimated, though its authenticity has been called into question. Its appeal was directed to his followers.

The work of the Revolution is not yet done. Let all our comrades follow my "Plans for National Reconstruction," "Fundamentals of the National Reconstruction," "Three Principles of the People," and the "Manifesto" issued by the First National Convention of our Party, and strive on earnestly for their consummation. Above all, our recent declarations in favor of the convocation of a National Convention and the abolition of the unequal treaties should be carried into effect with the least possible delay.[3]

The death of Sun Yat-sen was not an unwelcome event to China's militarists. It meant that the revolutionary elements had been deprived, so it seemed, of their moral leadership. Few dreamed in the spring of 1925 that Sun Yat-sen would wield a far greater influence when dead than when alive. The immediate effect within the Kuomintang was dissension and personal rivalry. The Right favored co-operation with the northern militarists and the unification of China on that basis. Another faction favored expulsion of the communists and dismissal of the Russian advisers. Other forces within the party included a group led by Hu Han-min, who had been placed in charge at Canton when Sun left for Peking; a military faction, led by Tang Chi-yao, supported by troops from Yunnan; and still another group led by Sun Fo, the only son of Sun Yat-sen.

Within a few weeks of Sun's death, civil war was again raging about Canton. The Yunnan military faction was defeated, and many who opposed the communists were expelled from the party. Announcement was likewise made that the Kuomintang would no longer co-operate with Peking. Canton

---

[3] For a brief discussion of the writings of Sun Yat-sen mentioned in this will, see H. F. MacNair, *China in Revolution*. University of Chicago Press, Chicago, 1931. Chapter 6.

itself set up a soviet government, which promptly served to alienate the Right-wing elements of the party. To meet this emergency, a committee dictatorship (probably suggested by Borodin) was declared, in which the principal leaders were

Underwood & Underwood.

GENERAL CHIANG KAI-SHEK. Since 1927 he has been China's "strong man." He is a soldier, a dictator, a politician, and a professed Christian. He repudiated the communists after rising on their shoulders to leadership in nationalist China.

Wang Ching-wei and General Chiang Kai-shek. Although at the time General Chiang was practically unknown, he was soon, with Borodin's assistance, made commander-in-chief of the Kuomintang armies. As a youth he had studied for the army in Japan, had become a follower of Sun Yat-sen, and had studied in Moscow in 1923, when Sun turned to the Russians for aid. Returning to China with the Russian advisers, he was made director of the military academy at Whampoa, near Canton.

The committee dictatorship maintained its power into 1926, when the Second Kuomintang Congress, meeting at Canton, again declared for co-operation with Russia. Only a minority, however, seems to have favored the powerful influence of Borodin, a fact which in many cases may be attributed to jealousy. This seeming party unity was, however, not fundamental. A break was already forecast between Borodin and General Chiang. When, in February, 1926, the former was absent from Canton, Chiang arrested a group of Russian and Chinese communists, thus breaking the Russian control and at the same time freeing himself by military power from the civilian influence of his colleague dictator, Wang Ching-wei. Two months later, Chiang, to prove his impartiality, ousted a number of Right-wing members of the Kuomintang. Meanwhile, he resumed friendly, if somewhat strained, relations with Borodin, at the same time making preparations for a military campaign into central and north China.

The first moves of the Kuomintang armies were made in the spring of 1926. Kwangtung and Kwangsi provinces already being controlled by General Chiang, his troops first entered Hunan. The armies were officered by men trained at the Whampoa Military Academy. They were assisted, too, by a number of Russian military advisers and by Chinese propagandists, who preceded the troops, announcing their coming in the name of Sun Yat-sen and the Three People's Principles. Although the Nationalists, as they now called themselves, met with stubborn resistance at many points, their march to the Yangtze was in the main an uninterrupted succession of victories. Propaganda and treachery in the ranks of the northern militarists hastened the victory of the southerners. By April, 1927, the greater part of China proper had submitted, or was prepared to submit, to the Kuomintang. In the northeast, the provinces of Shantung and Chihli still remained under the sway of Chang Tso-lin.

Hankow versus Nanking

With the unification of China by force within reach of the Kuomintang, its power was again broken from within. The new weakness centered in the opposing policies of Borodin and General Chiang. The former was seeking a government based on organization of the Chinese masses—the peasants and the laborers; the latter was visualizing a middle-class regime based on the money-power of the merchants, bankers, and capitalists. The conflict led to an open break. The Left wing of the Kuomintang established itself at Hankow. General Chiang, now clearly identified with the Right, ruled at Nanchang, the capital of Kiangsi. The Hankow group, hoping thereby to discredit Chiang, endeavored unsuccessfully to instigate attacks on the foreign interests in Shanghai. In March, troops, allegedly communists from Hunan, attacked the foreign residents of Nanking. These acts, however, served only to give General Chiang the full backing of the Shanghai capitalists. By the middle of April, he had set up his own government in Nanking, which now disputed with Hankow for leadership of the Kuomintang. The outcome in this conflict was determined in large part by the decision of one of the northern militarists, Feng Yu-hsiang. Among the militarists and propertied classes there was general fear of the so-called radical character of the Hankow pro-Russian group, with its plans for an agrarian revolution. Accordingly, Feng united with Chiang, demanding that the agrarian and social revolution be abandoned, that the Chinese communists be suppressed, and that their Russian advisers be sent home. This was followed by the seizure of Hankow by a Nationalist general and the banishment of Borodin and his immediate followers. Yet, even with this "house cleaning," the Kuomintang was by no means free from internal and personal strife. Among General Chiang, Hu Han-min, and Wang Ching-wei, the outstanding leaders of the party, there was mutual and petty distrust. In August, 1927, Chiang retired from office. Presumably, he hoped by this move to bring about the union of the Nanking and Hankow factions. Instead, there ensued a period of unqualified confusion in which personal jealousies overshadowed completely the patriotism of China's leaders. By December, 1927, Chiang returned to Shanghai from Japan, proceeding in January to Nanking, where he was not only restored as commander-in-chief of the Kuomintang armies but was also made chairman of the party's Executive Committee and of the Military Council. The revolution had returned definitely to control by middle-class policies.

The Nanking government, dominated by Chiang, now dispatched its armies against the northeastern war lords, Chang Tso-lin and Chang Tsung-chang. Chiang himself did not enter Peking. This honor he delegated to his ally, General Yen Hsi-shan. It was a peaceful occupation. A few days previously, Chang Tso-lin, the Manchurian war lord, had left Peking on his last journey to Mukden.

The objective of the Nationalist armies was now theoretically attained. In theory, all of China proper had submitted to Nanking, which was promptly named the new capital of the Republic, while Peking, the old "Northern Capital," became Peiping, or "Northern Peace." Despite internal conflicts on policy and bitter personal feuds, the Kuomintang armies had achieved a sensational victory in their march from Canton to Peking. Yet the victory was more apparent than real, as succeeding years were to show.

In main, then, China's domestic political history from 1922 to 1928 centered about the efforts of the Kuomintang to overthrow the succession of militarists who ruled in these years at Peking. During the period, however, it was the Peking government which, in international affairs, was recognized by the foreign powers as the legitimate government of China. To Peking fell the responsibility of conducting China's foreign relations and of carrying into effect such obligations as China assumed at the Washington Conference. If these were troubled years in China's domestic history, they were equally so in her contacts with the outside world, for, as a matter of practical policy, the powers were forced to deal with various of the so-called governments that claimed to speak for China.

It will be recalled that the Washington Conference had passed a number of resolutions concerning China. One of the more important of these dealt with the Chinese conventional tariff, which was to be revised so as to yield an effective five per cent. The new schedule of rates was determined by a commission of Chinese and foreign representatives, which met in March, 1922. With some difficulty, this work was completed, and the new rates became effective in January, 1923.[4]

The Washington Conference had also agreed to abolish foreign post offices maintained on Chinese soil without treaty authorization. The principal governments involved were Great Britain, France, and Japan. By the end of 1922, these three governments had closed some ninety post offices. In addition, the Japanese government withdrew the troops it had maintained at Hankow since 1911.

Early in 1923, the government in Peking again raised the question of abrogation of the 1915 Treaties and Notes. Taking advantage of the fact that the original Russian lease of Kwantung (twenty-five years) would expire in March, 1923, but for the extension to ninety-nine years that Japan had secured in 1915, the Peking authorities informed the Japanese Minister that relations between the two countries should now be improved by abrogation of all the 1915 agreements. The government was well aware that Japan would not consent. Its action

---

[4] For a detailed account of China's foreign relations in the years 1922 to 1928, see Robert T. Pollard, *China's Foreign Relations*. The Macmillan Company, New York, 1933. Chapters 8-9.

could be interpreted only as a play to popular support among the more vocal elements of Chinese society. The Japanese reply merely reaffirmed what had already been said at the Washington Conference, namely, that the treaties had been signed and ratified by the two governments and that as far as Japan was concerned, they were valid. In this view, the Japanese government had already received tacit, if not verbal, confirmation from the other great powers.

At the same time, the Chinese were negotiating with the British for the return of the British leasehold of Wei-hai-wei, which had been promised conditionally at Washington. A draft agreement, concluded in May, 1923, contained the following stipulations: The territory was to remain a separate administration area; its municipality was to remain open to trade and residence; the foreign taxpayers were to assist in the government; and for ten years, subject to renewal, China was to provide the British government a station, without charge, for use of the British Asiatic fleet during summer months. To this agreement, the Chinese objected, negotiations thereupon (1924) being suspended indefinitely. Restoration of Wei-hai-wei to Chinese control was not finally effected until October, 1930. [5]

Question of Extraterritoriality

The Washington Conference had also provided that before May, 1922, a commission should be constituted to inquire into the operation of extraterritoriality. This was in answer to China's demand for the abolition of consular jurisdiction. But such was the confusion resulting from China's annual civil wars that it was not until May, 1923, that Peking announced itself ready to receive the commission in November of that year. Even this invitation proved to be premature, and the meeting of the commission was obstructed further by the attitude of the French government. France was demanding that

---

[5] See The China Year Book, 1931. p. 483.

China, in resuming payments of the Boxer indemnity, do so in gold francs at the pre-war rate of exchange. Upon China's refusal, France announced that she would withhold her ratification of the Washington treaties. This deadlock continued until February, 1925, when the gold franc issue was settled by compromise, and France consented to ratify the treaties. These formalities were completed by August, when the two Nine-Power Treaties concerning China, which had been signed at Washington in 1922, for the first time became legally effective. The powers were now in a position to co-operate in carrying them into effect.

These technicalities had no sooner been removed than problems of more serious import appeared. By 1925, many Chinese in the seaport towns were clamoring for an antiforeign policy far more radical than the program that China had submitted at the Washington Conference. Student agitators, in particular, were unrestrained in their public verbal attacks upon the foreign imperialists. They found it a convenient and a popular practice to attribute all of China's troubles to the privileged position enjoyed by the foreigners under protection of the "unequal" treaties. A group of these student agitators collected a mob in the International Settlement of Shanghai (May 30, 1925) to protest against the treatment of Chinese laborers in Japanese factories. The fact that working conditions in Chinese-owned mills were far worse than in the Japanese-owned mills appears to have been ignored by the students and their following. Frightened by this public and mob demonstration, a police inspector of British nationality gave the order to fire. Nine Chinese were killed. But this was not all. Within a few days, Shanghai found itself within the grip not only of a general strike but also of a boycott on all foreign goods. Riots directed against foreigners occurred in many cities along the Yangtze. At Canton, fighting broke out between troops in the British and the French concessions and a mob of Chinese students, workmen, and soldiers. The result was a boycott of British goods in Canton, and at Hong Kong, a strike which crippled the trade of that important British port for many months. The foreigners in China were unanimous in the belief that their use of force was justified in terms of self-defense. On the other hand, Chinese students, agitators, and "patriots" were more determined than ever to destroy whatever special privileges the hated foreigner enjoyed. Even Chinese conservatives found it expedient to give public lip-service to this more radical program. The reactionary government at Peking played for popular support by protesting promptly to the powers the Shanghai incident of May 30. The note implied that China would be content with nothing less than complete equality with other states. The powers replied that, as a preface to any revision of China's foreign relations, the Chinese would be required to show "their willingness and ability to fulfill their obligations." The powers added that they were prepared to continue with the program outlined at the Washington Conference.

Accordingly, in October, 1926, China and the powers convoked a tariff conference at Peking, which resulted in a resolution adopted by the powers granting China tariff autonomy in 1929. China agreed that, simultaneously with the granting of tariff autonomy, she would abolish effectively likin, a form of internal taxation on goods in transit. The conference then considered measures to be taken in the intervening years. These discussions were interrupted in December by the civil wars that raged about Peking. The foreign representatives indicated their willingness to proceed with negotiations whenever a government recognizable as such appeared, but by the summer of 1926, the Peking war lords were too much concerned with the Nationalist advance from Canton to give further consideration to the tariff.

Concurrently with the tariff discussion, China was negotiating with the powers for relinquishment of extraterritoriality. The foreign representatives on this commission commenced their work in January, 1926. Silas Strawn, the representative of the United States, acted as chairman. The commission's report, completed in September, did not favor the abolition of consular jurisdiction. While admitting that China had made some progress in the modernization of her laws and the administration of justice, the report condemned the fusion of administrative and judicial functions, the procedure of the military, and its interference with the courts. The commission was of the opinion that China had not as yet entrusted the administration of justice to a judiciary free from unwarranted interference by the government. Furthermore, modern codes had not been completed or enforced effectively. The commission recommended that China establish a more regular system of law enactment, that more modern courts and prisons be provided, and that adequate funds be set aside for their maintenance. When China had made material progress with this program, the powers might consider abolition of extraterritoriality by some gradual means. In other words, China was told that on the basis of the then existing conditions, abolition of consular jurisdiction was unthinkable. It was now quite clear that the extravagant claims to the effect that China had put her house in order—claims which were presented with great eloquence by the Chinese delegation at the Washington Conference—were not founded in fact.

The Antiforeign Campaign

To China's politicians, however, this was a matter of small consequence. They had discovered that their own political fortunes could thrive more speedily on a campaign of antiforeignism than on any other basis. By 1925, it was quite evident that antiforeignism would play a major role in the program of the Nationalists. It assumed two aspects. The first was a well-concerted propaganda against Christianity, a vulnerable target because of its close association with the foreign imperialists. The second took the shape of popular demand, not for gradual revision of the "unequal" treaties, but for their immediate abrogation. The process by which this more vigorous program took effect is illustrated by affairs at Canton in 1926. It will be recalled that in 1925 Canton had by means of a boycott virtually closed the port of Hong Kong. When this boycott was finally terminated, the Canton government, of which Eugene Chen was Foreign Minister, informed the powers that certain special and temporary taxes would be imposed on foreign trade. The ministers of the powers represented at Peking protested this action as a direct violation of the treaties, whereupon Chen informed the powers that the real authority in China was at Canton, not Peking. There was, in fact, some point to this remark, since at the moment the Nationalist armies were engaged in their triumphant march northward to the Yangtze, where their capital, as will be recalled, was soon established at Hankow. The boycotts that the Chinese had directed so successfully against the British at Shanghai, Canton, and Hong Kong had already convinced the British government that a change in the policy of the powers toward China was desirable. This view was stated in a memorandum from Great Britain to the Washington Conference powers on December 18, 1926. The memorandum reviewed China's changing political fortunes since 1922, recommended that regional governments in China be permitted to collect surtaxes authorized by the Washington Conference, and suggested that the powers again indicate their willingness to negotiate a revision of the treaties, at the same time reminding China that she was under obligation to observe existing treaties.

While these proposals were being considered by the powers, the British concession at Hankow and at Kiu-kiang were invaded by Chinese mobs, and the foreigners were forced to withdraw. Had such events occurred prior to the World War, Great Britain would have promptly employed the old gunboat policy; but in 1927, she accepted the events and surrendered the two concessions, both of which had been established in

1861. This was indeed a marked reversal of British policy—a policy that had since 1840 led and dominated that of other foreign powers in China. Had the British government decided that the time had come for the foreigners to surrender their special and privileged position?

The negotiations between the British and the Hankow (Nationalist) government for the rendition of the two British concessions were concluded early in March, 1927. Toward the end of the month, the Nationalist armies captured Nanking. This triumph of the southerners was followed by what appeared to be a well-organized attack upon all foreigners in the city. Among the victims of these murderous attacks were nationals of Great Britain, the United States, Japan, France, and Italy. Foreign buildings, including consulates, were pillaged and burned. To prevent further attacks upon the surviving foreigners, American and British warships in the river shelled portions of the city. The Nanking outrage occurred within a few days of the solemn declaration by the Hankow government that its foreign policy would not countenance the use of force. Despite this fact, the demands of the powers for reparation were exceedingly moderate. They included punishment of the commanders of the responsible troops, a written apology from the commander-in-chief of the Nationalist army, and reparation for personal injuries and material damage. Most of the powers hoped to settle the Nanking affair by joint action. In contrast, the Hankow Nationalists sought to make individual settlements, by which means they hoped to drive a better bargain. They attempted further to lay responsibility for the affair on defeated northern soldiers and on the general conditions created by the "unequal" treaties. Meanwhile, the break between the Hankow radicals and conservative factions of the Kuomintang (see p. 621) was coming to a head. The new Right-wing government that was soon established at Nanking wanted temporarily the support of the foreigners, but later was looked upon with favor by the foreign powers themselves. It was not until the following year (1928), however, that the affair was finally settled by an exchange of notes between the powers concerned and the Nanking government.[6]

While the Nationalists were, in the manner described, forcing the foreign powers to deal with them as a *de facto* government in south and central China, the government in Peking was likewise seeking treaty revision. Treaties were negotiated on a basis of equality with Austria in October, 1925, and with Finland in October, 1926. To meet the pressing need for funds to finance the campaign against the Nationalists, Chang Tso-lin announced that the Washington Conference surtaxes would be applied. Collection of the tax, since it had not been authorized by treaty, was refused by Sir Francis Aglen, the British Inspector General of Customs. Chang accordingly dismissed him and appointed another British subject to the post. Although the powers protested this action, the new Inspector General, A. H. F. Edwards, assumed office.

Treaty Revision

On the problem of treaty revision, the Peking government adopted the policy of approaching the powers individually. In April, 1926, it informed Belgium, a country whose opposition would probably be ineffective, that it desired to revise the Chino-Belgian Treaty of 1865. The new treaty, it was added, would be based on equality and reciprocity. Negotiations to this end were in progress when Chang Tso-lin was forced from Peking in 1928. The powers then extended *de jure* recognition to the Nanking government, and a new Chino-Belgian treaty was concluded on November 22, 1928. This treaty recognized Chinese tariff autonomy but accorded the Belgians most-favored-nation treatment. Belgium surrendered the principle of extraterritoriality. This, however, was not to take effect until January, 1930, by which time China was to have made de-

---

[6] For the texts of these notes, see *The China Year Book*, 1929-1930. pp. 893-901.

tailed arrangements with the Belgian government for the assumption by China of jurisdiction over Belgian subjects. These negotiations with Belgium constituted a kind of test case by which the Chinese sought to prove their ability to end the "unequal" treaties by unilateral action.

In 1926, the Peking government challenged France by declaring null and void a number of commercial agreements, but showed a ready willingness to negotiate in the face of French opposition to unilateral action. A revision of China's commercial treaties with Japan was also demanded, with the implied threat that if satisfactory revision were refused, the treaties would be abrogated. With the establishment of the Nationalist government at Nanking in 1927, and the expulsion of the northern militarists from Peking in 1928, China was in a better position to proceed as a unit to treaty revision. The Nanking government announced that its purpose was to continue the fight against the "unequal" treaties. It declared its treaties with Spain (1864) and Portugal (1887) terminated. The Italian and Danish treaties meanwhile having expired, China declared that they were thereby abrogated. Other "unequal" treaties were also soon to be abrogated and replaced by new ones based on equality. In the meantime, foreigners would be subject to interim regulations. Japan was notified that, pending the signing of a new Chino-Japanese treaty, these regulations would be applied to Japanese. Japan replied that the Sino-Japanese treaties in question were still in force and that she reserved the right to take whatever action she deemed necessary, if the Chinese carried their threat into effect. While tension between Japan and China was increasing, the United States and China concluded a treaty (July, 1928) by which Washington conceded the Chinese complete tariff autonomy, carefully guarded, however, by most-favored-nation treatment. By the close of 1928, the Nationalist government had, in addition, negotiated new treaties with Germany, Belgium, Italy, Denmark, Portugal, Spain, Norway, Sweden, Great Britain, and France, all of which provided for tariff autonomy. It remained only for a similar agreement to be concluded between Nanking and Tokyo. Because of the general tension in Sino-Japanese relations and China's threat of unilateral action, this remained a particularly difficult task. It was not until May, 1930, that a tariff agreement between the two countries could be effected. With its conclusion, China may be said to have regained the tariff autonomy that she had surrendered nearly a century earlier at the close of the First European War.

China's success in regaining tariff autonomy in 1930 was due to many factors, but principal among them was the unity that for the moment at least had been achieved under the national government. Revolutionary China, under the banner of the Kuomintang, had since 1926 won a striking victory over localism. The northern war lords had been driven from Peking. Nanking emerged without a serious rival. At the Versailles Conference and at the Washington Conference, the Chinese had talked. A decade later, at Nanking, they were in a position to act.

SELECTED BIBLIOGRAPHY

American Relations with China (Baltimore: 1925), for post Washington Conference Relations. Leon Archimbaud, "French Interests in the Far East," in the *Asiatic Review,* Jan. 1929. Hallet Abend, *Tortured China* (New York: 1930), a graphic descriptive account of conditions in China by a correspondent of *The New York Times.* P. S. Buck, "Missionaries of Empire," ch. 8 in *Empire in the East,* Joseph Barnes, ed. (New York: 1934). George H. Blakeslee, "Outstanding Facts in the Present Situation in China," in *Annals of the American Academy of Political and Social Science,* July, 1928. J. S. Burgess, *The Guilds of Peking* (New York: 1928). J. O. P. Bland, *China: The Pity of It* (London: 1932). For an account of the history of the Kuomintang, see *The China Year Book,* 1928. J. B. Condliffe, ed., *Problems of the Pacific* (Chicago: 1928). A. G. Coons, *The Foreign Public Debt of China* (Philadelphia: 1930). H. O. Chapman, *The Chinese Revolution, 1926-1927* (London: 1928). "American Policy in China," in Foreign Policy

Association, *Information Service,* May 11, 1927. In *ibid.,* "The Rise of the Kuomintang," June 22, 1928. S. D. Gamble, *Peking: A Social Survey* (New York: 1921). F. Goodnow, *China: An Analysis* (Baltimore: 1926). Rodney Gilbert, *What's Wrong With China* (New York: 1932). Arthur N. Holcombe, *The Chinese Revolution* (Cambridge: 1930), see in particular ch. 8 on the dictatorship of the Kuomintang. S. K. Hornbeck, *China To-Day: Political* (Boston: 1927). G. W. Keeton, *The Development of Extraterritoriality in China,* 2 vols. (London: 1928). A. M. Kotenev, *Shanghai: Its Mixed Court and Council* (Shanghai: 1925). A. M. Kotenev, *Shanghai: Its Municipality and the Chinese* (Shanghai: 1927). H. B. Morse, "Concessions and Settlements in China," in *The Nineteenth Century and After,* July, 1928. W. H. Mallory, "China's New Tariff Autonomy," in *Foreign Affairs,* Apr. 1929. W. H. Mallory, "The Passing of Extraterritoriality in China," in *Foreign Affairs,* Jan. 1931. C. A. Macartney, *Survey of International Affairs, 1925* (Oxford: 1928), vol. 2, pt. 3, ch. 8 on the tariff conference; ch. 7 on the Boxer indemnity and the gold franc dispute; ch. 9 on the rendition of Wei-hai-wei; and ch. 11 on the Shanghai incident, May 30, 1925. Sobei Mogi and H. Vere Redman, *The Problem of the Far East* (London: 1935), the section on China. H. F. MacNair, *Modern Chinese History: Selected Readings* (Shanghai: 1927). By the same author, *China's New Nationalism and Other Essays* (Shanghai: 1926). Paul Monroe, *China: A Nation in Evolution* (New York: 1928), ch. 12, Yen Hsi Shan the model governor. Mary A. Nourse, *The Four Hundred Million* (Indianapolis: 1935), ch. 23, "The Nationalists Come into Power." C. K. Peake, *Nationalism and Education in Modern China* (New York: 1932). R. T. Pollard, *China's Foreign Relations, 1917-1931* (New York: 1933), a well-documented survey. H. S. Quigley, "The United States in the Pacific" (Aug. 1927-June, 1929), in *Pacific Affairs,* Aug. 1929. R. T. Rich, *Extraterritoriality and Tariff Autonomy in China* (Shanghai: 1925). C. F. Remer, *The Foreign Trade of China* (Shanghai: 1926). *Report of the Commission on Extraterritoriality in China* (Washington: 1926). Frank H. Simonds, *American Foreign Policy in the Post-War Years* (Baltimore: 1935). G. E. Sokolsky, "The Kuomintang," in *The China Year Book,* 1929-1930, ch. 26. Sun Yat-sen, *San Min Chu I: The Three Principles of the People* (Shanghai: 1928). Sun Yat-sen, *Memoirs of A Chinese Revolutionary* (London: 1918). Sun Yat-sen, *The International Development of China* (New York: 1929). M. T. Z. Tyau, *Two*

Years of Nationalist China (Shanghai: 1930), propaganda issued by the bureau of information of the Nanking government but valuable for some of its statistical material. A. J. Toynbee, *Survey of International Affairs, 1926* (Oxford: 1928), pt. 3, ch. 1, on Chinese civil wars in 1926; chs. 7-9 on conflicts at Canton; and chs. 10-12 on troubles in the Yangtze Valley. A. J. Toynbee, *Survey of International Affairs, 1928* (Oxford: 1929), pt. 4, ch. 1, the victory of the Kuomintang; ch. 2, relations between China and the foreign powers. A. J. Toynbee, *Survey of International Affairs, 1927* (Oxford: 1929), pt. 3, the Chinese civil war, dissensions in the Kuomintang, and decline of Russian communist influence in China. A. J. Toynbee, *Survey of International Affairs, 1931* (Oxford: 1932), pt. 4, ch. 3 on extraterritoriality; ch. 2 on internal conditions in China. A. J. Toynbee, *Survey of International Affairs, 1930* (Oxford: 1931), pt. 4, ch. 1 on the survival of the Kuomintang at Nanking, and ch. 2 on relations between the Nanking government and the foreign powers. Sakutaro Tachi, "Legal Aspects of the Leased Territories," in *Contemporary Japan,* June, 1932. Ralph Townsend, *Ways That Are Dark* (New York: 1933). Kyoson Tsuchida, *Contemporary Thought of Japan and China* (London: 1927). H. G. W. Woodhead, *The Truth About the Chinese Republic* (London: 1926). T. C. Woo, *The Kuomintang and the Future of the Chinese Revolution* (London: 1928), chs. 1-4 on the history and organization of the Kuomintang. Chao-Kwang Wu, *The International Aspect of the Missionary Movement in China* (Baltimore: 1930), a study of the legal position of the missionaries under the treaties. Edith E. Ware, *Business and Politics in the Far East* (New Haven: 1932). T. C. Wang, *The Youth Movement in China* (New York: 1927). J. W. Wheeler-Bennett, *Documents on International Affairs* (London: 1929-31), vol. for 1928 contains texts of treaties negotiated by China with the United States and Belgium; vol. for 1929 contains correspondence regarding proposed abolition of extraterritoriality; vol. for 1930 gives text of the Sino-British convention for the rendition of Wei-hai-wei, and the Sino-British agreement with reference to Boxer indemnity funds.

CHAPTER XXXIV

Russia and China, 1905-1929

THE victory won by the Chinese revolutionary and Nationalist groups in the years 1927 and 1928 was made possible in some considerable degree by direct aid given by communist Russia. This aid was a natural product of the policy of friendship announced by the Soviet as early as 1919, a policy designed to throw into bold relief the selfish and aggressive interests of the so-called imperialistic states. Yet, within two years of the establishment of Nationalist China, Nanking and Moscow were engaged in hostilities, if not in a formally declared war. Sudden shifts of this type in Russo-Chinese affairs arose from the dual character of Russian policy in China. From as early as 1860, the Russian government had sought to pose as the friend and protector of China. It played this role with striking success in 1860, when it professed to exert influence to save the Manchu court from the wrath of British and French armies then marching to Peking. In 1895, it took the initiative with Germany and France to save China from the territorial demands of victorious Japan. In 1896, it concluded with Peking a secret alliance, designed, so it appeared, to preserve China from further Japanese aggression. But these practical demonstrations of Russian esteem were at best feeble attempts to disguise what was clearly a policy of imperialism. The Russian efforts to control Manchuria and Korea down to 1904 have already been dealt with (chapter 21). The Russo-Japanese War checked, but did not end, Russia's imperial ambitions in the Far East. She lost her interests in Korea and south Manchuria, but retained her hold on north Manchuria. She was now faced with an imperialistic competitor, Japan, with whom she divided Manchuria as a sphere of influence. The two powers, once the war was over, adopted a policy of guaranteeing mutually the special interests they claimed in Manchuria. They sought, furthermore, to extend and to define their "special" positions in Mongolia. To Russia, the control of Mongolia might compensate for the loss of south Manchuria and, by keeping open a Russian road to Peking, nullify in large measure Japan's victory in Manchuria.

Russia's position in north Manchuria was not affected directly by the Treaty of Portsmouth. Having retained the main line of the Chinese Eastern Railway and the branch line from Harbin to Changchun, within the zone of these railroads she continued to exercise jurisdiction as she had done before the war. Her rights south of Changchun had, of course, passed by the Treaty to Japan. Japan, in turn, soon recognized a fundamental weakness in the Treaty of Portsmouth. It failed to provide an adequate and common Russo-Japanese policy for the protection of their respective spheres of influence. In both countries, influential leaders (Yamagata, Ito, and Isvolsky) favored a *rapprochement* to this end. Its fulfillment was made easier when France, Russia's ally, concluded a treaty with Japan (June 10, 1907) in which the two powers assumed guardianship of the peace in somewhat indefinite areas of Chinese territory. Thus encouraged, Russia accepted a series of agreements with Japan, the first concerning the junction of their railways at Changchun (June 13, 1907), the second concerning commerce and navigation (July 28), the third concerning fisheries (signed the same day), and the fourth concerning two political agreements, one public and one secret (July 30). The full significance of these two political agreements was not revealed for many years. By them, Japan and Russia gave more specific definition to their spheres of interest in Manchuria and Mongolia and retained for themselves freedom of action within these spheres. More specifically, a line of demarcation was drawn between north and south Manchuria. Each of the powers pledged itself not to obtain, in the sphere of the other, railway and telegraph concessions, or to obstruct the granting of such concessions to the sphere-holding power. Russia pledged herself not to obstruct the further development of political relationships between Japan and Korea. In return, Japan recognized Russia's special interests in Outer Mongolia and pledged herself to refrain from interference prejudicial to these interests.[1]

Her interest in north Manchuria strengthened by the agreements of 1907, Russia proceeded in 1908 to consolidate her position by forming at Harbin, the center of her railway administration, a municipal council. This action was based on the Russo-Chinese railway agreement of 1896, which gave to the Chinese Eastern absolute and exclusive administration of its lands. The action was promptly protested by China, on the ground that the same agreement reserved to China the task of protecting the line. A settlement was finally reached on the understanding that municipal administrations in the railway towns were not to be under exclusive Russian control. They were to be in the hands of a committee chosen by delegates who in turn were elected by the inhabitants under a property qualification. Against this arrangement, various foreign powers, including the United States, protested that a Russian-controlled railway company was requiring foreign residents in Harbin to comply with local regulations, contrary to the general treaty provisions establishing extraterritorial rights for foreigners in China. Later (in 1914), some of the powers did

---

[1] E. B. Price, *The Russo-Japanese Treaties of 1907-1916 Concerning Manchuria and Mongolia*. Baltimore, 1933, chapter 3. The line of demarcation between north and south Manchuria was as follows: "Starting from the northwestern point of the Russo-Korean frontier, and forming a succession of straight lines, the line runs, by way of Hunchun and the northern extremity of Lake Pirteng, to Hsiushuichan; thence it follows the Sungari to the mouth of the Nunkiang, thereupon ascending the course of that river to the confluence of the Tola River. From that point, the line follows the course of that river to its intersection with Meridian 122° East of Greenwich." Used by special permission of the publishers, The Johns Hopkins Press.

agree conditionally that their nationals might pay the same taxes as were collected from Russians.

It was while these Russian efforts were under way at Harbin that Willard Straight was proposing and futhering establishment of a Manchurian bank, financed with American capital, to undertake industrial development in Manchuria. This was followed by the American proposal to construct a railroad from Chinchow to Aigun, which in turn gave rise to the Knox proposal to "neutralize" the Russian and Japanese Manchurian railways. The general implications of these various schemes have already been discussed (chapter 23). It may now be noted that they led directly to the conclusion, on July 4, 1910, of two additional Russo-Japanese conventions, only one of which was then made public. In contrast to the agreements of 1907, those of 1910 made no mention of the independence and territorial integrity of China or of the principle of equal opportunity. In 1907, these powers had agreed to defend the *status quo* by all peaceful means, but in 1910 they agreed to defend it by whatever measures they might judge necessary. In the new secret convention, they agreed to ,recognize the right of each, within its own sphere, to take freely all measures necessary for the defense of its interests. Neither power would hinder the "consolidation and further development" of the special interests of the other. Each was to refrain from political activity within the other's sphere. In a word, Japan and Russia were bound to a mutual defense of the special interests that each claimed in Manchuria.

By 1910, it was quite clear that Japan and Russia professed to possess a monopoly in the financing and construction of railways in Manchuria. This was the principal feature of the special interests which they claimed there. In an attempt to forestall extension of this monopoly to enterprises other than railroads, China, in September, 1910, invited American bankers to offer a loan to be used both in China proper and in Manchuria for currency reform and industrial development. The offer was accepted, and three European banking groups (British, French, and German) asked to be admitted. The Russians and Japanese had also been invited by the American bankers to participate. Their governments, however, were alarmed by this new venture of foreign capital in Manchuria. In Russia, annexation of north Manchuria was considered, but these extreme views were set aside in favor of maintaining Russia's full privileges there looking to annexation at some future date. In the meantime, pressure would be exerted upon China even to the extent of military demonstrations on the frontier. Pressure, indeed, was exerted by Russia, but it failed to prevent China from agreeing (February, 1911) to a four-power loan for currency reform and industrial development in Manchuria, in which American, British, French, and German banking groups were to participate. This loan agreement was protested by both Japan and Russia. Their governments held that it granted to the participating banking groups a preference in the matter of industrial loans for Manchuria. This would endanger their special interests, which, it was now revealed, were not to be confined to railway enterprises.

Mongolian Independence

Adding to these complications, the Mongols threw off the suzerainty of China in 1911, proclaimed an independent Mongolia, and sought Russian recognition. Russia, while refraining from granting immediate recognition, did give immediate and direct aid. Following close upon these events came the republican revolution in China proper. The time seemed ripe for Russia to carry out her plans both in north Manchuria and in Mongolia. She informed the American government that she held in north Manchuria, Mongolia, and western China special interests and rights founded on her treaties and conventions with China, and that in these areas she would reserve the right to take such protective measures as circumstances might force upon her. This led Japan to make a similar reservation on eastern Inner Mongolia, which bordered south Manchuria, the Japanese sphere. To this, the American government agreed, on the understanding that the rights and interests to be protected were covered by treaty or convention.[2]

The Chinese revolution and the overthrow of the Manchus had blocked, for the moment, the currency reform and industrial loan. The Japanese, however, were prepared to participate in it only on condition that the loan would not affect adversely their special interests in south Manchuria. The Russians, while inclined to block the entire consortium scheme, also consented to participate, under a reservation similar to Japan's. On this condition, the Russian and Japanese banking groups entered the consortium; the loan agreement was concluded, but its proceeds were not used in Manchuria, Mongolia, or western China. Furthermore, the Americans, at President Wilson's suggestion, had already withdrawn. Finally, Japan and Russia concluded a new secret treaty (July 12, 1912), by which they defined the boundary between their expanded spheres of interest. Russia recognized Japan's special interests in eastern Inner Mongolia. Japan recognized Russia's in western Inner Mongolia.

Meanwhile, on March 10, 1912, China's republican government promulgated the first of its numerous provisional constitutions, in which Outer Mongolia was declared to be a part of the Chinese Republic. This declaration was wholly contrary to existing facts, for, at the time, the Mongols were completely independent of Peking, were still receiving direct aid from Russia, and were recognized as independent by St. Petersburg later in the same year. Moreover, it was quite evident in 1912 that the Mongols had no desire to be a part of China. Nevertheless, Russia was disposed to compromise on this important question and thus avoid an open break with Peking. In November, 1913, notes were exchanged between the Russian

[2] *Ibid.* p. 72.

and Chinese governments by which Russia recognized that Outer Mongolia was under the "suzerainty" of China, while China recognized the right of Outer Mongolians to provide their own internal administration. Political and territorial questions affecting international relations were to be settled by future negotiation. As a result, a tripartite convention between China, Outer Mongolia, and Russia was signed June 7, 1915. This convention provided a beautiful example of diplomatic quibbling. It was agreed that Outer Mongolia could not conclude treaties with foreign powers on "political and territorial questions," but that she could conclude treaties of a "commercial and industrial nature." For the moment, this was all that Russia desired. Political control would follow naturally, once her commercial and industrial interests in Mongolia were developed.

Fearing that the inroads of Russia into Outer Mongolia would soon penetrate Inner Mongolia also, China took steps in 1914 to consolidate her grip on this area. Here, too, as in Outer Mongolia, she claimed sovereignty over a people who were not Chinese and who had no desire to be incorporated into China proper. Accordingly, Peking encouraged the emigration of Chinese settlers to eastern and southern Inner Mongolia, dividing the area into three administrative districts: Jehol, Chahar, and Suiyuan. In 1928, after the Nationalists had established themselves in Nanking, these districts became provinces, in which, as a result of immigration, Chinese settlers outnumbered the Mongols and in many cases appropriated their lands.

Japan's Position

It is evident that the revolt in Outer Mongolia and the results of the Chinese revolution worked distinctly to the advantage of Russia. They enabled her to exert a special interest in the new autonomous Mongolian state. In contrast, Japan's position in south Manchuria and eastern Inner Mongolia had not been so favored. The opportunity to rectify this situation came in 1915. The World War had broken out; Russia, England, and France were fully occupied with the European struggle. At this opportune moment, Japan presented China with the so-called Twenty-one Demands, group two of which dealt with her special interests in south Manchuria and eastern Inner Mongolia. Japan secured the extension of the Kwantung leasehold and of her ownership of the south Manchurian and other railroads to ninety-nine years; the right of Japanese to lease land and to enter, reside, and travel in the Japanese sphere; the privilege of exploiting certain mining properties; the preference of Japanese nationals when China employed political, financial, or military advisers in these areas; and the immediate control of the Kirin-Changchun Railway.

On the whole, the treaty and exchanges of notes of May 25, 1915, might reasonably be said to confirm Japan, in principle, in most of the claims which, bit by bit, that country had built up since 1906. And it might of course be added that by implication, they conferred on Russia a similar recognition of her parallel claims.[3]

Japan's next step was to secure, in 1916, Russia's consent to her strengthened position in south Manchuria and eastern Inner Mongolia. This was obtained through a group of agreements, public and private, at a time when Russia, hard pressed in the European war, was in no position to bargain. Each power pledged itself not to be a party to any arrangement or political combination directed against the other. The secret convention set up a defensive alliance. Russia and Japan recognized that their "vital interests" required that China should not fall under the political domination of any third power hostile to Russia or Japan. If such a threat should appear, the two powers would consult together and take such measures as might be mutually agreed upon. If a war in defense of these "vital interests" should occur, either ally might

---

[3] *Ibid.* p. 82.

call upon the other for aid. By this means, Japan was compensated for the relative advantage Russia had won earlier in Outer Mongolia.

This important series of public and secret agreements (1907, 1910, 1912, and 1916) concluded by Japan and Russia, concerning the border lands of northeastern China, by which they had sought to cement their "special," and finally their "vital," interests, were affected materially by the Russian revolutions of 1917. The Provisional (Russian) government under Kerensky accepted the previous commitments of the Tsarist regime, but when the Bolsheviks assumed power, they made it clear that Russia was starting anew and that treaties of the former government deemed contrary to communist philosophy would not be recognized. In 1918, it will be recalled (see chapter 28), certain of the Allied and Associated Powers intervened in Siberia and north Manchuria, the Russian sphere. The purpose of this interevention was two-fold: its was designed (1) to check the spread of communism and to re-establish a capitalistic regime in Russia, and (2) to prevent Japan (one of the intervening Allies) from extending her influence in the affected regions of northeastern Asia. North Manchuria was for a time under the control of Russian anti-communist factions, working in more or less close co-operation with the intervening Allies, while the Chinese Eastern Railway was policed by Chinese and Japanese troops. During 1920, all the Allied troops were withdrawn from Manchuria and Siberia, with the exception of the Japanese, who remained until the close of the Washington Conference. Meanwhile, the Chinese government had in 1920 concluded an agreement with the Russo-Asiatic Bank (successor to the Russo-Chinese Bank; see p. 311) by which China was to take over management of the Chinese Eastern Railway. This agreement, while supported by France, was never recognized by Bolshevik Russia. The latter was, in fact, already seeking to resume diplomatic relations with China and to regain control of the former Tsarist railroad.

The first step toward this end was taken by Soviet Russia in 1919, in the form of a declaration transmitted indirectly to the Chinese government. Denouncing the former imperialistic policy of Russia, it renounced all the acquisitions made by the Tsar's government that deprived China of Manchuria and other regions. A somewhat similar declaration was made by Soviet Russia in 1920, in which the significant point was made that, though the policy of the Tsars could never be continued by the Soviet, this government did retain certain rights and interests in the Chinese Eastern Railway. The Soviet government, in other words, had no intention of surrendering all that had been won from China by the previous regimes. Indeed, there would appear to be little doubt that the Soviet authorities were drawing a clear distinction in their own minds between those special rights which they were prepared to surrender to China and others which would be retained at all cost. This is illustrated by events in Outer Mongolia during the years of the Russian revolutions and the Allied intervention.

"Saviors" of Mongolia

The political chaos which infested Siberia and north Manchuria during the years of the Allied intervention spread also to Outer Mongolia. This condition enabled China to annul the three-power agreement of 1915, thus canceling the autonomy of Outer Mongolia and reasserting the direct sovereignty of Peking. Three personalities—Semenov, Hsu Shu-cheng, and Baron Ugern-Sternberg—as adventuresome and unscrupulous as modern history provides, were instruments in this attempted reassertion of Chinese sovereignty. The first was that disreputable "White" Russian, Ataman Semenov, who in fighting Bolshevism pictured himself as the creator of a Pan-Mongolian state including Outer and Inner Mongolia, portions of Siberia, and even part of Tibet. Not only the Japanese General Staff, but also British and certain American interests provided this ruthless cut-throat with funds which enabled him to murder in cold blood any Mongolian or Siberian suspected of being "red" on whom he could lay his hands.

For sheer infamy, Semenov enjoyed the close rivalry of the Chinese General, Hsu Shu-cheng.

[Hsu Shu-cheng was] known as "Little" Hsu, an amazing personality, quick, efficient, unscrupulous, treacherous, a delightful conversationalist, producing ideas with the rapidity of a trip-hammer, capable of murdering his best friend in the courtyard of his house after a feast of friendship, and in the end being himself murdered by the soldiers of the "Christian General" Feng.[4]

"Little" Hsu also wanted to set up a state in Mongolia. What was more, he had an army that Japan had financed to assist China's efforts in the World War. When the War was over, "Little" Hsu managed to hold on to most of this army and a good deal of the money and to set himself up as a commander of the Northwestern Frontier Defense Force.

He got himself a fleet of motorcars and rushed between Peking and Kalgan and across the Gobi Desert from Kalgan to Urga, the capital of Mongolia. Back and forth he rode, working great plans for his Mongolian kingdom.[5]

It was he who canceled the autonomy of Outer Mongolia, attempted to colonize it with Chinese, and ruled those who came under his sway by methods "so outrageous and with an arrogance so unbearable" that few Mongols could possibly desire any further connection with China. It has been observed, indeed, that the method by which China regained Mongolia was quite as imperialistic and brutal as anything used by foreign imperialism, against which China had so frequently protested.

When "Little" Hsu's party collapsed, his place on the Mongolian stage was taken by Baron Ungern-Sternberg, "half Magyar, half Russian, married to a Manchurian princess and

---

[4] From *The Tinder Box of Asia,* by George E. Sokolsky, copyright 1933, reprinted by permission from Doubleday, Doran & Company, Inc. p. 178.

[5] *Ibid.* p. 178.

deeply versed in Buddhistic mysticism, apparently quite mad." [6] The Baron appeared at Urga in October, 1920, accompanied by a mob which could hardly be described as an army. His object was to set up a theocratic Buddhist state to include Mongolia and, if possible, Manchuria and Tibet. But by this time most of the Allies were getting out of Siberia. The effort to crush Bolshevism under the guise of "aiding the Russian people" had failed. The "Red" armies already controlled a substantial part of central Siberia. In November, 1920, Soviet troops moved against Sternberg. Moscow, informing China that she would no longer tolerate the presence of "White" counter-revolutionary bands that used Outer Mongolia as a base, offered to assist China in suppressing them. Upon China's refusal, Soviet troops, accompanied by political agents, entered Mongolia. Taking advantage of this assistance, the Mongols revolted and set up the People's Revolutionary Government of Mongolia, which asked immediately for continued aid from Russia. A Russian army remained at Urga to protect the new state, whose independent position was soon confirmed by a secret Russo-Mongolian treaty. In time, the Russian connection became still closer when the revolutionary government became the Socialist Soviet Republic of Mongolia.

Russo-Chinese Agreements, 1924

During 1923, negotiations took place between the Chinese government and a Soviet mission at Peking, looking to a settlement of outstanding questions in north Manchuria and Mongolia and to the resumption of diplomatic relations, but it was not until May, 1924, that a series of agreements was concluded. The first agreement re-established diplomatic relations between China and Russia and prohibited propaganda by either state directed against the political and social system of the other. It was declared that all treaties of the Tsarist government made

---

[6] *Ibid.* p. 179.

either directly with China or with third powers, affecting the sovereign rights of China were canceled. Russia surrendered her share of the Boxer indemnity and also her extraterritorial privileges. All this appeared to indicate a policy of respect for China. (What was more, Russia recognized that Outer Mongolia was an integral part of the Republic of China and agreed to respect China's sovereignty therein.) Practically, this seeming reversal in Russia's Mongolian policy meant nothing save that Moscow was playing a shrewd game of diplomacy. She would save China's "face" by recognizing her sovereignty over Mongolia, at the same time continuing to assist the independent Mongolian state which she had done so much to establish.

As to Russian interests in north Manchuria, the agreement of 1924 affirmed China's right to recover at some future time the Chinese Eastern Railway and provided that all outstanding questions between the two powers should be settled by a conference to be called later in the year. Until such time as this conference had completed its work, the Chinese Eastern Railway would be managed under the terms of a provisional agreement. This agreement set up the principle of equal representation (Chinese and Russian) in the management of the road, though the post of manager, the key position, was to be held by a Russian, and all non-Soviet Russians in the employ of the railroad were to be dismissed. The Russo-Asiatic Bank, representing the French bondholders of the railway, ineffectively protested this agreement. In this manner, a provisional settlement between Russia and China was reached. However, these agreements were of questionable value, for Manchuria, at the time being under the control of Chang Tso-lin, enjoyed a practical independence of Peking. As a result, Russia concluded in September a separate and similar though not identical agreement with Chang in Mukden. As will be seen later, a final settlement of the Chinese Eastern problem was never concluded by Russia and China. The agreements of

1924, although granting China greater participation in the management of the line than she had previously enjoyed, also enabled Soviet Russia to regain a position of influence in north Manchuria, the historic Russian sphere. They failed, nevertheless, to work smoothly, and the years following were filled with exceedingly dangerous "incidents" between the Manchurian authorities and the Soviet manager of the Chinese Eastern.

THIS MAP SUGGESTS THE COMPARATIVE LAND AREAS OF RUSSIA, MANCHOUKUO, AND JAPAN.

In one respect, even after these agreements of 1924 had been made, Russia's far eastern program was far from complete. Her special interests in Manchuria had not been recognized by Tokyo. This defect was remedied by the Russo-Japanese Convention of January, 1925. By this convention diplomatic relations between the two powers were resumed, and, perhaps of greater significance, the Treaty of Portsmouth was declared to be in full force. Other treaties concluded prior to 1917 were to be re-examined. It remained to be seen whether Japan and Soviet Russia would seek mutual protection of their "special" Manchurian and Mongolian interests, as Japan and Tsarist Russia had done.

Before this question could be answered, the fate of Manchuria was involved with the rise of the Nationalists at Nanking in 1927, and the extension of their power to Peking in the following year. Marshal Chang Tso-lin was forced to surrender Peking to the Nationalists. He died in June, 1928, from injuries received when his train was bombed near Mukden. This event was of great national consequence. Chang Tso-lin had been an unqualified enemy of the Kuomintang and the Nationalists, but his eldest son, Chang Hsueh-liang, who succeeded him as Manchurian dictator, threw in his lot with the Nationalists, raising the flag of the Kuomintang at Mukden in December, 1928. Manchuria, with its Russian and Japanese spheres of influence, was immediately thrown open to the antiforeign, anti-imperialistic propaganda of the Kuomintang. Two weeks later, young Marshal Chang celebrated his advent to power by the summary execution at Mukden of General Yang Yuting, who for many years had been his father's chief of staff. The way was thus opened for the spread of Nationalist agitation to all parts of Manchuria. Its attacks were directed against Japanese imperialism and special interests in south Manchuria and Russian in north Manchuria. For the moment, however, the Japanese were too strong. Nationalist China was not yet prepared to cross swords with Tokyo. Russia seemed less dangerous. She had already surrendered some of her interests in China, and this the Nationalists interpreted as an indication of weakness. If Russia were now challenged by China, she might forego what still remained of her interests in the Chinese Eastern Railway. Then, with Russia forced from north Manchuria, the Nationalists would direct their attack against Japanese interests more strongly entrenched in south Manchuria.

The Russo-Chinese "War"

The first blow was struck in May, 1929, when Chinese police at Harbin raided the Soviet Consulate, arresting Soviet consular officials and private citizens who were attending what was alleged to be a communist meeting. Thirty-seven of those arrested were later sentenced to terms of from two to nine years at hard labor, the charge being that they were engaged in communist propaganda and conspiracy against the Chinese state, in violation of the Russo-Chinese agreements of 1924. Two months later (July 10, 1929), Chinese authorities seized the telegraph system of the Chinese Eastern Railway, dissolved all Soviet unions in the railway zone, and closed the offices of the principal Soviet mercantile concerns. The Soviet general manager of the railway was dismissed, and wholesale dismissals, arrests, deportations, and internment of Soviet railway employees followed. Having gained control of the central administration of the railway at Harbin, the Chinese sought to extend this control to the entire system. To aid them in this, they employed a considerable number of "White" Russians in technical positions. The Soviet government protested promptly in an ultimatum giving China three days to release all Soviet citizens and to restore the management of the railway to its status prior to July 10. It likewise proposed a Russo-Chinese conference to settle all railway problems. In her reply, China attempted to justify her arbitrary action on the ground that Russia had used Chinese soil to carry on communist propaganda contrary to the 1924 agreements, and that she had imprisoned Chinese without cause on Russian soil. No indication was given that China was prepared to restore the joint management. Accordingly, Russia severed diplomatic relations, ordered the return of all her diplomatic and consular agents, and severed communications between the Trans-Siberian and the Chinese Eastern Railways. China also severed diplomatic relations and issued a public manifesto, designed for western rather than Chinese consumption. Russia was accused of violating her declarations of 1919 and 1920 and her agreements of 1924. In particular, she was accused of communistic propaganda dangerous to all capitalistic states. The manifesto concluded by taking advantage of an historical myth commonly accepted in the West that the Chinese have been and are an extraordinarily pacific people.

China only knows [said the manifesto] to devote her entire energy to the preservation of peace, and world peace is always the aspiration of the Chinese people. China will do her best to uphold the spirit of the Kellogg Anti-War Pact as compatible with her right of self-defence.[7]

While these charges and counter-charges filled the world press, troops of both powers were concentrated at border points, principally near Manchouli, in the west, and Suifenho, in the east, where the Chinese Eastern Railway enters Siberia. Outside powers, too, were becoming interested. Russia and China had both signed the Kellogg Anti-War Pact, even though ratifications had not yet been exchanged, and the United States reminded China of her obligations under the Pact. A suggestion, assumed to be similar, was conveyed verbally to Russia through France. China replied that she would observe the Pact and resort to force in self-defense only, and the Russians took a like stand. The only question not answered by this exchange was what constituted self-defense.

In August, these protestations of peace gave place to military activities on the Siberian-Manchurian frontier, where both the Chinese and the Russians had assembled large forces. In the border engagements that followed, each side accused the other of aggression. The Chinese were assisted by considerable numbers of "White" Russians, but neither in morale nor in equipment were they any match for the Russian forces,

---

[7] *The China Year Book*, 1929-1930. p. 1225.

which were supported by bombing planes. Late in November, the Soviet troops forced the Chinese from the Hingan Mountains and cut their communications with Harbin. "The demoralized Chinese soldiery burnt, looted and murdered in their wild flight from the front," and hostilities in the undeclared Russo-Chinese War were ended. A preliminary settlement, the Habarovsk Protocol, was signed on December 22. It provided for a conference to settle all outstanding questions. Meanwhile, the Chinese Eastern Railroad was to be restored to the joint management which had preceded China's seizure of the line. In May, 1930, China sent Mo Teh-hui, President of the Chinese Eastern, to Moscow for the proposed conference. There he waited six months for the conference to open. The Soviets insisted on discussing questions of trade and diplomatic relations. The Chinese would discuss nothing but the railroad. A compromise was finally agreed upon, but the conference made little progress. Conditions in China were far from stable. Russia could afford to delay, in the hope that she might again profit through China's internal troubles. In a word, the Moscow conference was still engaged in its dreary and unproductive course when, in September, 1931, hostilities broke out in south Manchuria between the Chinese and the Japanese. China's attempt to oust the Russians from their north Manchurian sphere had failed.

SELECTED BIBLIOGRAPHY

Joseph Barnes, ed., *Empire in the East* (New York: 1934), ch. 3 on Soviet Siberia. *North Manchuria and the Chinese Eastern Railway* (Harbin: 1924). F. Deane, "The Chinese Eastern Railway," in *Foreign Affairs*, Sept. 1924. Walter Duranty, "Russia Watches East As Well As West," in *Asia*, Feb. 1936. Louis Fischer, *The Soviets in World Affairs*, 2 vols. (London: 1930). Stanley K. Hornbeck, "American Policy on the Chinese Eastern Railway Dispute," in *The Chinese Social and Political Science Review*, Jan. 1930. Tao-fu Kuo, "Modern Mongolia," in *Pacific Affairs*, Aug.

1930. E. Kann, "Mongolia and Its Currency System," in the *Chinese Economic Journal,* Dec. 1928. W. Karamisheff, *Mongolia and Western China* (Tientsin: 1925). H. L. Kingman, *Effects of Chinese Nationalism upon Manchurian Railway Developments, 1925-1931* (Berkeley: 1932). Chia-pin Liang, "History of the Chinese Eastern Railway," in *Pacific Affairs,* Feb. 1930. Vera A. Micheles, "Russia and China in Manchuria," in Foreign Policy Association, *Information Service,* Aug. 7, 1929. C. A. Macartney, *Survey of International Affairs, 1925* (Oxford: 1928), vol. 2, pt. 3, ch. 4, the Soviet-Japanese Treaty of 1925, and ch. 2, treaties between China and the U. S. S. R. *Outer Mongolia: Treaties and Agreements* (Washington: 1921). H. D. Robinson, "Mongolia, Its Trade Routes and Trends," in U. S. *Commerce Reports* (Washington: 1930). A. J. Toynbee, *Survey of International Affairs, 1920-1923* (Oxford: 1925), pt. 6, ch. 1 on Russia, China, and Outer Mongolia. A. J. Toynbee, *Survey of International Affairs, 1926* (Oxford: 1928), pt. 3, ch. 6 on the Chinese Eastern Railway. A. J. Toynbee, *Survey of International Affairs, 1929* (Oxford: 1930), pt. 4a, ch. 4 on the Chinese Eastern Railway; and pt. 4b on the Japan-U. S. S. R. fisheries treaty, 1928. S. M. Wolfe "The People's Republic of Mongolia," in *Contemporary Review,* Mar. 1929. Victor A. Yakhontoff, *Russia and the Soviet Union in the Far East* (London: 1932), chs. 6-7.

These titles should be supplemented with reference to successive issues of *The China Year Book.*

CHAPTER XXXV
China and Japan, 1922-1931

MANY bonds of interest—cultural, economic, and even political—have served to create particularly intimate relationships between the Chinese and the Japanese. These, partaking little of the spectacular, have escaped notice in the West, where, consequently, a distorted view of Chino-Japanese relations prevails. Unfortunately, suspicion and even open distrust have all too frequently intruded themselves, leading to hostilities, with or without a declaration of war, between these neighboring peoples. The causes contributing to this unhappy state of affairs require explanation. They are exceedingly complex. Essentially, they all belong to two dominant movements in the modern history of eastern Asia: (1) the rise of Japan as a great nationalistic and imperialistic power, and (2) the emergence of a revolutionary and nationalistic movement in China. Both of these movements were in turn conditioned to some considerable degree by western imperialism, which, by the beginning of the twentieth century, was firmly rooted upon Chinese soil. In the Russo-Japanese War (1904-1905), Japan struck the first decisive blow against the power of western imperialism in China. She saved China from Russia but not from imperialism, for Japanese exploitation was more efficient than Russia's had ever been. What Japan failed to do in 1905, the World War did by 1919—it all but destroyed Europe's imperialistic stake in China, leaving Japan the dominant imperialistic power. Her increased influence was gained at the expense of both Europe and the United States. It was this changed condition that led in large measure to the calling of the Washington Conference. At this Conference, the western powers were confronted with a dilemma. Desiring to block Japan wherever possible, they paid lip service to China's aspirations for sovereignty and equality among the nations, yet at the same time they sought to preserve such of their pre-war imperial interests as might be salvaged.

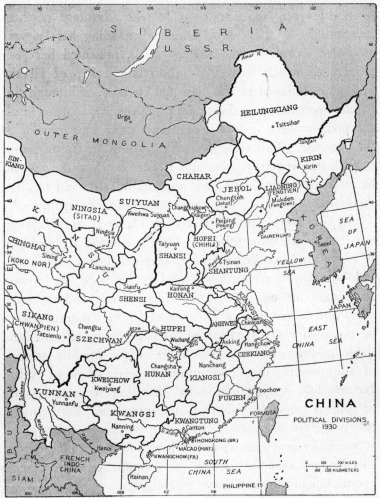

Courtesy of George B. Cressey and of the "Geographical Review," published by the American Geographical Society of New York.

Accordingly, when the Washington Conference assembled, most of the delegates, influenced by these practical considerations and also by the general and popular liberalism inspired by the Wilsonian program of world settlement, spoke in glowing but somewhat vague terms of the new and sovereign China, which, it was assumed, would emerge in the new world order. In turn, the Chinese delegates, who had failed miserably with their program presented at the Versailles Conference in 1919, were not slow to take advantage of these protestations of friendship. China, demanding her "rights" as a free sovereign state among equals, presented her "bill of rights," which was designed to relieve her of all the indignities imposed by the "unequal" treaties. Although this Chinese program was directed against the imperialism of all the great powers, it was designed to strike in particular at the Japanese. This was good strategy. By it, China hoped to push the western powers into a position where they would be forced to forego their own imperial interests and to align themselves openly against the imperialism of Japan.

In part, the aspirations voiced by China at the Washington Conference were fulfilled. On the surface, a philosophy of liberalism prevailed at the Conference tables. This attitude was expressed in treaty pledges given by the powers "to respect the sovereignty, the independence, and the territorial and administrative integrity of China." China was to be accorded every opportunity to develop an effective and stable government. As expressions of the friendly attitude of the powers, these commitments were of some value. Nevertheless, it should be noted that they were expressions of general principles subject to interpretation. Furthermore, they were not retroactive. By them, no power was required to surrender anything which it already held in China. They merely provided a general prohibition against further encroachments upon China's sovereignty.

To this general program, Japan gave her full support.

She adhered likewise to those other Conference settlements by which it was proposed to accord China greater freedom in the matter of the tariff, and to review the status of extra-territoriality. In addition, Japan agreed to surrender many of the post offices that she, like other powers, maintained on Chinese soil. Finally, the Japanese reached a special agreement with Peking by which the former German lease-hold at Kiaochow was returned to China. When, however, the Chinese demanded cancellation of the Treaties and Notes of May, 1915, and challenged in particular Japan's "special interests" in south Manchuria, the Japanese made it perfectly clear that such proposals would not be considered. Japan took the position that her interests in Manchuria rested upon a legal treaty basis which she would not permit to be called into question. Nor was her attitude challenged by any of the powers other than China. In fact, it was quite clear before the Washington Conference adjourned that China had not been wholly successful in her attempt to play the western powers against Japan.

Cordial Relations

From 1922 until 1927, Chino-Japanese relations were more cordial than at any period in the previous decade. To be sure, Chinese Nationalists never ceased their demand that the special privileges of foreigners and of the foreign powers be destroyed. During 1925, their wrath was directed mainly against the British, following the outbreaks at Shanghai and Shameen (see p. 625), and in 1927, against the British and Americans at Nanking. Although the interests of all foreigners were involved in these incidents, the Japanese government took no active steps to intervene. Its policy was still dictated by the liberalism of the Washington Conference and perhaps also by expediency. For the moment, Tokyo was content that British and American, rather than Japanese, gunboats should drop their shells on Nanking (see p. 629).

But Japan's moderation in these years, when British and American ships were firing upon the Chinese, was more than mere expediency. It resulted from a conscious liberal policy that derived its inspiration from the Washington Conference and was fostered by a number of Japanese governments, in particular the Kato Cabinet, which took office in 1924. This government included such outstanding liberals as Wakatsuki, Hamaguchi, and Baron Shidehara, the Foreign Minister. It was at this time, too, that Sun Yat-sen visited Japan again on his way to Peking (see p. 617), and it was understood that he came to some sort of understanding with leading Japanese statesmen regarding Japan's position in Manchuria. Whether Sun embraced the Japanese view is not clear, but it is certain that his relations with individual Japanese leaders at this time were most cordial. This friendly Japanese policy, of which Baron Shidehara was the principal author, continued without serious break until 1927, by which time the Chinese Nationalists had established themselves in the Yangtze Valley. The confusion that attended the advance of the Nationalists and their pronounced campaign of antiforeign propaganda forced the powers, including Japan, to define their relation to the civil conflict. Speaking before the Japanese Diet in January, 1927, Baron Shidehara declared that Japan proposed:

To respect China's sovereignty and territorial integrity and scrupulously to avoid interference in her domestic strife.

To promote solidarity and economic rapprochement between the two nations.

To assist the Chinese to attain the realization of their just aspirations.

To exercise patience and toleration with regard to the existing situation and simultaneously *to use all reasonable means of protecting Japan's legitimate rights and interests*.[1]

---

[1] Italics are those of the writer.

In a word, Japan would exercise forbearance, but she would not be unmindful of the important interests that she held in China. Although the policy of Shidehara was moderate, it never contemplated the surrender of Japan's treaty rights. As early as June, 1927, troops from Japan's Manchurian garrison at Port Arthur were sent to Shantung with the announced purpose of protecting the lives and property of Japanese residents, which were said to be imperiled by the advance of the Nationalists. This action foreshadowed a decided shift in Tokyo's policy.

The Wakatsuki Cabinet (Minseito), which resigned in the spring of 1927, was succeeded by the more militaristic and conservative Seiyukai Ministry, with General Baron Tanaka as Premier. Tanaka, previously Minister of War, was now the leader of the Choshu military clique. As Premier, he retained also the post of Foreign Minister, much to the regret of Japanese liberals, who foresaw that a more vigorous Chinese policy would result. The instructions issued subsequently to Japan's representatives in China, both diplomatic and military, were soon spoken of in Japan as "the positive policy." Tanaka emphasized the distinction to be drawn between Japan's interests in China proper and her interests in south Manchuria and eastern Inner Mongolia. In the latter areas, because of Japan's "special interests," it was her duty to maintain peace and order.

√ The announcement of the "positive policy" passed without crisis. By April, 1928, the Chinese Nationalists were advancing north to drive Chang Tso-lin from Peking. Chang's position was weak, and it soon became apparent that unless he received aid, the Nationalists would reach not only Peking but also Manchuria, where their antiforeign policy would be directed to the destruction of Japanese interests. On April 18, General Tanaka, Premier and Foreign Minister, General Shirakawa, Minister of War, and Admiral Okada, Minister of the Navy, decided upon the dispatch of Japanese troops to Tsinan, in Shantung province, for the purpose "of protecting the Japanese residents." This decision, which was made without the presence of any civilian representative of the Foreign Office, was bitterly attacked by the liberal Tokyo press as unwarranted. The government attempted to protect itself by announcing that there would be no interference in China's domestic affairs and that the troops would be withdrawn as soon as the danger to Japanese residents was removed. Despite these assurances, Tanaka's first venture into "the positive policy" was far from popular. It was denounced by liberals in Japan, by the Nationalists in China, and generally by the press of western countries. The situation was aggravated in May, when the Nationalists and the Japanese exchanged shots at Tsinan, which resulted in deaths and injuries to soldiers and civilians, both Japanese and Chinese. In the Diet, it was charged that Tanaka sent the troops for political purposes and failed to protect the lives of the Japanese residents of Tsinan, since the presence of foreign troops had served only to inflame the Chinese. Meanwhile, the Japanese commander had ordered Chiang Kai-shek to withdraw his troops some miles from Tsinan, whereupon the Tokyo militarists decided that reinforcements must be sent to Tsinan. Feeling was still running high when, on June 4, Chang Tso-lin met his death as his train was bombed entering Mukden. At the time, Chang had given up Peking and was hurrying to his Manchurian capital. The responsibility for Chang's death remains a matter of dispute, but it seems quite certain that both Japanese and Chinese were involved.

The death of Chang Tso-lin raised his son, Chang Hsueh-liang, to the post of Manchurian dictator. Young Chang soon showed a pronounced friendship for the Nationalists. In July, he was "advised" by the Japanese Consul General in Mukden, acting "in his individual capacity" but also on instructions from General Tanaka, to delay the reported union of Manchuria with the Nationalist cause. At the same time, Tanaka demanded from the Nationalists at Nanking an apology for the Tsinan affair, with indemnity and guarantees of future security. Concurrently, he decided to pursue a more moderate policy and gradually to withdraw the troops from Shantung. This decision was the result of general criticism in Japan of Tanaka's methods. It forced him to adopt a more liberal policy and in January, 1929, to concede tariff autonomy to China. Two months later, Japan and China were happy to reach a settlement and to be rid of the Tsinan affair. Both governments expressed their regret. The Chinese promised to secure the safety of Japanese residents, and Japan agreed to withdraw her troops.

Meanwhile, the death of Chang Tso-lin was not without its political effect in Japan. Chang's train had been bombed as it entered Mukden through an underpass of the Japanese-owned South Manchurian Railway. In Japan, the press was not permitted to discuss what was referred to as "a grave Manchurian incident." In the Diet, the Minseito opposition demanded publication of a full report. This demand was voiced by members of the House of Peers also. There was opposition to publication of the report by high military authorities, since it would involve disciplinary measures on the commander of the Kwantung garrison and thus reflect upon the honor of the army. Caught between the demand for publicity and the desire for secrecy, the Tanaka Ministry resigned in July, 1929. It was succeeded by a Minseito government led by Premier Hamaguchi, but, though the Minseito had been loud in its demands for publication of a report, these demands ceased the moment it took office. "The grave Manchurian incident" was to be regarded as closed. Yet this could not disguise the fact that Chino-Japanese relations were passing through a critical period. With Manchuria opening her doors to the advancing Nationalists and subjecting Japanese interests to a virulent propaganda of antiforeignism, further trouble was assured.

The cause of "the positive policy," of which Tanaka happened to be the official spokesman, lay in a multitude of problems which beset internal affairs in Japan itself and also in

China. The former will be discussed in a subsequent chapter
(see chapter 37). The latter involved the whole cycle of disorders that had preyed upon the Chinese people since the collapse of Yuan Shih-kai's government in 1916. These years had
witnessed the rule of numerous Chinese military governors,
two attempts to restore the monarchy, the rise and fall of various so-called parliaments, the declared independence of several
provinces, and, finally, the rivalry between Peking and Canton
for control of the nation. They were years in which all foreign
interests in China were subject to constant danger and, at times,
to open attack. All the western powers were apprehensive, yet,
because of her increasing investments and her geographical
position, none was so much concerned as Japan.

It was difficult at times for any government to know where
the actual authority in China rested. Even the Nanking Nationalist government, established in 1927, never succeeded in
securing complete unity. It was attacked by powerful war
lords, who repeatedly threatened its existence. Within its own
ranks, there was schism resulting in the retirement of many of
its leaders to Canton, where they acted independently of Nanking whenever it served their purpose to do so. There was, in
fact, save in moments of national crisis with foreign powers, no
real nationalism in China. The bulk of the Chinese people,
accustomed to think primarily in terms of the local community
and the family, had no interest in national or foreign affairs.
It is hardly surprising, then, that in Japan, and to a lesser degree elsewhere, more aggressive nationalists and imperialists
held the view that China had forfeited her right to further consideration at the hands of the powers. The Washington Conference had promised China an unembarrassed opportunity to
work out a stable and unified government, but, they argued,
she had failed to do so, having wasted her effort in civil strife.
They could point to China's failure to equip herself with a
proper budgetary system, and to the increase in her domestic
indebtedness to meet the costs of civil war. Not a few Japanese

were alarmed by the growth of the Kuomintang, which had "introduced into the nationalism of China an additional and abnormal tinge of bitterness against all foreign influences, and has expanded its aims so as to include the liberation of all Asiatic people still subject to 'imperialistic oppression.'"[2]

Encouraged by gains made at the Washington Conference, China's Nationalists, despite internal feuds, had presented a strong front to the foreign powers. The economic boycott had proved itself a weapon of great power, especially when accompanied by political propaganda. This propaganda was used most effectively in the schools, whose textbooks showed that their authors had sought "to kindle patriotism with the flame of hatred." Students were induced to engage in political activities and to threaten the ministers of their government when the latter failed to take strong action against the foreigners. As a consequence, the foreign powers became alarmed. Seeing little effective improvement in China's internal affairs, they became reluctant to surrender their remaining special privileges.

Communism in China

There was always hope, of course, that Nanking would be able to effect a truly national regime; but against this hope stood three major obstacles. Many of China's so-called armies owed their allegiance to a particular leader rather than to the nation. In the second place, banditry existed in all parts of the country. This, largely an economic question, could be dealt with only by a major economic readjustment. No such thing was contemplated in the middle-class program of the Nanking government. Neither could banditry be suppressed by force so long as the nation lacked adequate means of communication. Finally, there was the threat of communism. The communist movement in China had its beginnings in the period 1919 to

---

[2] League of Nations, *Report of the Commission of Enquiry* (The Lytton Report), p. 18.

1924, communists, after 1922, being admitted to the Kuomintang (see p. 615). For a time in 1927, when the Nationalists
had reached Hankow, the party influence of the communists
was so strong that the Nationalist movement became almost a
communist revolution. Then came the purging of the Kuomintang, the expulsion of Russian advisers, and the saving of
the Nationalist revolution for the middle classes. This, of
course, did not mean that communism had disappeared. Some
units of the Nationalist army, already having turned communist, were responsible for uprisings in Kiangsi and Kwangtung.
Between 1928 and 1931, the movement spread to Fukien and
Hunan. At the same time, Nanking was confronted by a non-
communist revolt, led by northern militarists and supported by
Canton troops in Hunan. This enabled the Red armies to
assume the offensive; by 1931, a large part of the provinces of
Fukien, Kiangsi, and Kwangtung were under communist control. In addition, there were communist areas in all parts of
south China and, in the north, in the provinces of Hupeh,
Anhwei, and Kiangsu. Wherever the communists established
themselves, they made their appeal on a program of debt cancellation, distribution of land seized from large private owners
and religious institutions, simplification of taxation, and development of irrigation projects, credit systems, and co-operatives,
together with public schools and hospitals. Consequently, by
1931, communism had "become an actual rival of the National
Government."

Japan, as China's nearest neighbor and largest customer,
suffered more than any other power from the "lawless conditions" touched upon in preceding pages.[3] More than two
thirds of the foreigners in China were Japanese. These could
not but suffer if they were subject to Chinese law, justice, and
taxation as it was administered in the years between 1927 and
1931.

[3] *Ibid.* p. 23.

Japan felt it impossible to satisfy Chinese aspirations so long as satisfactory safeguards to take the place of her Treaty rights could not be hoped for. Her interests in China, and more especially in Manchuria, began to be more prominently asserted as those of the other major Powers receded into the background. Japan's anxiety to safeguard the life and property of her subjects in China caused her to intervene repeatedly in times of civil war or of local disturbances. Such action was bitterly resented by China, especially when it resulted in an armed clash such as occurred in 1928 at Tsinan.[4]

Thus it was that the claims of Japan were regarded by China as a more serious challenge to her national aspirations than the claims of all other powers together. Despite all this, Japan's policy might not have developed on lines widely different from those of other powers had it not been for the special position she occupied in south Manchuria. It is necessary, then, to review in some detail some of the factors which occasioned Chino-Japanese friction in that area.

The reader is already familiar with the fact that after 1922 Chang Tso-lin, the Manchurian dictator, pursued a policy of complete independence at Mukden and later established himself in control of Peking. In 1925, Chang's position in Manchuria was seriously threatened by the revolt of one of his generals. He was saved largely through the action of Japan in not permitting the troops of the rebels to cross the South Manchuria Railway. Nevertheless, Chang was so opposed to the presence of the Japanese that he would gladly have destroyed their sphere of interest had he possessed the power to do so. During 1928, Chang showed increasing impatience with Japanese influence in Manchuria, particularly resenting Japan's "advice" that he should hold himself aloof from the civil strife in China. Where Chang Tso-lin resented Japanese advice, his son and successor at Mukden, Chang Hsueh-liang, openly defied the Japanese by declaring his allegiance to the Nanking government (1928). The area of Japan's sphere was thereby

---

[4] *Ibid.* p. 23.

thrown open to the organized propaganda of the Kuomintang, which insisted on the recovery of all sovereign rights and the abolition of the unequal treaties. Associations were formed to conduct a series of anti-Japanese campaigns. All this was done in the name of a Manchuria reunited with China. In reality, the administrative union was superficial, for the old officials continued to rule in Manchuria, their power depending not upon Nanking but upon their own Manchurian armies. These armies numbered a quarter of a million men, their maintenance absorbing eighty per cent of the Manchurian budget. In addition, there was "nepotism, corruption and maladministration." It was this condition of affairs that contributed to the failure of the Manchurian authorities when they seized the Chinese Eastern Railway from Russia in 1929 (see p. 650).

Japan's Special Position

Having failed to drive out the Russians, the Manchurian authorities and their Nationalist supporters turned the full force of their antiforeignism against Japan. Japan's sphere of influence at the time rested on a multitude of treaty rights and alleged rights based first on the Treaty of Portsmouth (1905) and subsequent supplementary agreements. These rights included the Kwantung leased territory, containing Dairen and Port Arthur, and the former Russian railway reaching northward to Changchun. In addition, Japan held the railroad from Mukden to Antung, on the Korean border. Out of these beginnings had grown the powerful South Manchuria Railway Company, controlled by the Japanese government and including among its properties the coal mines at Fushun and Yentai. The company not only engaged in many branches of business, but also administered the railway zone, where it levied taxes. After 1910, Japan exercised extraterritorial rights over the large number of Koreans who resided in Manchuria, thus again increasing her interest in the area. The year 1915 brought the

Treaty and Notes of May, concerning south Manchuria and
eastern Inner Mongolia. The territorial leasehold and the railway concessions were extended to ninety-nine years. Japanese

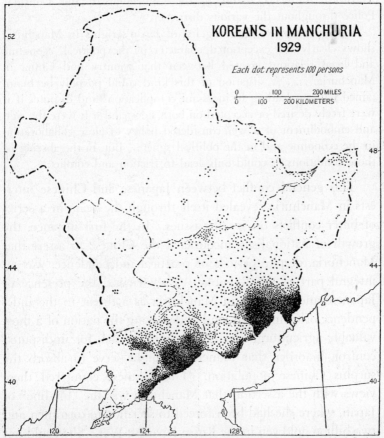

KOREANS IN MANCHURIA
1929

Each dot represents 100 persons

Courtesy of the "Geographical Review," published by the American Geographical Society
of New York.

subjects secured the right to engage in business and to lease
land.

These treaties and other agreements gave to Japan an important
and unusual position in Manchuria. She governed the leased territory with practically full rights of sovereignty. Through the South
Manchuria Railway, she administered the railway areas, including

several towns and large sections of such populous cities as Mukden and Changchun; and in these areas she controlled the police, taxation, education and public utilities. She maintained armed forces in many parts of the country: the Kwantung Army in the Leased Territory, Railway Guards in the railway areas, and Consular Police throughout the various districts.

This summary of the long list of Japan's rights in Manchuria shows clearly the exceptional character of the political, economic and legal relations created between that country and China in Manchuria. . . . A situation of this kind could possibly be maintained without leading to incessant complications and disputes if it were freely desired or accepted on both sides, and if it were the sign and embodiment of a well-considered policy of close collaboration in the economic and in the political sphere. But, in the absence of those conditions, it could only lead to friction and conflict.[5]

This general conflict between Japanese and Chinese interests in Manchuria revealed itself through the years in a series of bitter conflicts on specific issues. In the first instance, the growth of nationalism encouraged the Chinese to assert that Manchuria, despite periods of practical independence, was an integral part of the Republic. They viewed the presence of Japanese and Russians in Manchuria as a threat to the independence of China itself, and as depriving the nation of a most valuable agricultural area. They wished, too, for undisputed control, in order that Manchuria might serve to absorb the surplus Chinese population. The Japanese countered these views with the assertion that Manchuria was the "life-line" of Japan, where she had been forced to sacrifice 100,000 men and two billion gold yen in the Russo-Japanese War. She could not contemplate a reassertion of the Russian menace or the rise in Manchuria of a powerful and aggressive China. Japan's "special position" was not merely a matter of legal treaty rights, but also one of patriotic sentiments not subject to clear definition. Thus, Japan's claim to a special position in Manchuria and China's aspirations to regain full sovereignty were, by their nature, irreconcilable.

[5] *Ibid.* p. 38.

As already noted, Japan had, in maintaining her position in Manchuria, followed two policies since 1922: (1) the so-called friendly policy of Baron Shidehara (1922 to 1927 and 1929 to 1931), and (2) the so-called positive policy of Baron Tanaka (1927 to 1929). The former depended on diplomatic action; the latter depended on the threat of military pressure. Each of these policies was used, on occasion, to meet specific issues as they arose.

Railway Problems

From as early as 1905, a principal difficulty in Chino-Japanese relations in Manchuria was the question of railroads. In the building of Manchurian railroads, political considerations always overshadowed the economic. This was true when Russia built the Chinese Eastern in 1896, when Japan fell heir to the southern branch in 1905, and also in later years when the Chinese themselves began railroad construction. In 1906, when the South Manchuria Railway Company was formed, the principle of its political as well as its economic function was an accepted fact. The company from the beginning looked with favor on the construction of only such Chinese lines as would act as feeders to it. A number of these lines it financed. Its policy and the question of its rights and privileges led to numerous disputes with the Chinese, these being aggravated after 1924 when the Manchurians began to build their own lines with Chinese capital and without regard to their effects on the Japanese railway system. The Japanese resented this, terming it a violation of the so-called secret protocols of December, 1905 (see p. 420). These protocols had provided that China would not permit the building of "any main line in the neighborhood of and parallel to that railway [the South Manchuria], or any branch line which might be prejudicial to the interests of the above-mentioned railway." After 1924, Japan protested, on the basis of this clause, China's construction of the Tahushan-Tungliao and the Kirin-Hailungcheng Railways, but the Chinese proceeded to open and operate the lines despite the protest. Instances of this type incited considerable bitterness between the two powers. There appeared to be little chance of an amicable settlement, since neither power would agree with the other on what constituted a "parallel," a "competing," or a "prejudicial" line.

Another serious issue concerned Chinese government railroads in Manchuria constructed with Japanese money. Among these were the Kirin-Changchun, the Kirin-Tunhua, the Ssupingkai-Taonan, and the Taonan-Anganchi Railways. The Japanese capital invested in these, including interest and arrears, by 1931 amounted to 150,000,000 yen. The Chinese refused to meet payments on these loans or to make provision for them. They offered the excuse that the railroads were strategic and political, that they had been built largely as feeders to the South Manchuria Railway, that they were overcapitalized and unable to earn the necessary returns, and that an impartial investigation would justify the Chinese stand in each case. To add to these disputes, there was the question of the proposed Tunhua-Kwainei Railway, which, when built, would complete the line from Changchun to the northern Korean border. The Japanese insisted that this line should be built and that they should participate in financing it. The Chinese refused because they feared its strategic value to Japan. The legal merits of this dispute, which dated back to 1909, were highly involved, and after 1928 were a major issue between the two states. Furthermore, there were disputes over through-traffic agreements between the Japanese and Chinese lines, charges of unfair rate cutting, and, lastly, the attempt of the Chinese to develop at Hulutao a new seaport, the prime purpose of which was to draw traffic away from Dairen and the South Manchuria Railway.

Closely related to these disputes were those arising out of the Manchurian Treaty and Notes of May, 1915. The Chinese continued to claim that this treaty was the result of coercion and was therefore lacking in fundamental validity. Consequently, they refused to carry the treaty into effect except when it was convenient to do so. Although many Japanese did not approve the policy that had resulted in the treaty, they asserted, and in this they appear to have been legally quite correct, that it was valid and therefore binding upon China. The western powers tacitly supported the Japanese in this view, while the Chinese, unable to make a legal case, continued to demand return of the leased territory and full recovery of the South Manchuria Railway as their "national rights," or, failing this, the deprivation of the line of its political functions, leaving it a purely economic enterprise. They objected to the Japanese railway towns, which were based on the original Russo-Chinese Agreement of 1896, by which the railroad company had "absolute and exclusive administration of its lands." They objected to many of the contracts by which the railway acquired land. These rights also rested on the original agreement, which permitted the company to acquire land "actually necessary for the construction, operation and protection of the line." They also objected to the practice whereby the company levied taxes in the railroad zone. Though this followed from the right of the company to administer its lands, the Chinese claimed it violated their sovereignty. They objected, too, to the maintenance of Japanese railway guards. The Japanese based this right on their treaty of December, 1905, and on the ground that conditions in Manchuria made it inevitable. The Chinese denied this, declaring that their administrative integrity was violated. They objected to Japan's consular police, maintained as a part of Japan's extraterritorial administration. They objected to, and they imposed restrictions on, the right of Japanese and other foreigners to reside, travel, and conduct business in the interior of south Manchuria and eastern Inner Mongolia. This objection was based on the Chinese claim that the treaty was invalid and that the privileges could not be extended until extraterritoriality was withdrawn. On most of these points, the Japanese case appears to have been legally sound, but legalities made small appeal to those Chinese who were talking the language of nationalism.

Koreans in Manchuria

Adding to all these points of friction was the presence in Manchuria of some 800,000 Koreans, who were Japanese subjects. Japan claimed that Koreans, as Japanese subjects, were entitled, like Japanese, to acquire land, and this the Chinese denied. Japan, on her part, refused to recognize the naturalization of Koreans as Chinese subjects. Japanese consular police were employed to protect the Koreans; this the Chinese resented. Finally, after 1927, the Chinese authorities in Manchuria adopted a policy of discrimination against Koreans who were not naturalized, with the result that the wretched Koreans found themselves in an impossible situation between the demands of their home government and the government of their adopted land.

These various issues between Japan and China were of long standing. They represented the cumulative effect of the western imperialism that Great Britain had imposed upon China, and other western powers, including the United States, had readily accepted after 1842. The Japanese position in Manchuria was different in degree rather than in kind from the position held by the great western powers in China. The distinction to be noted is that Japan's imperialism coincided with the rise of China's nationalism; that of the western powers (England, France, and the United States) preceded this development. The West was no longer prepared to fight for the spoils of China; but this attitude Japan, influenced by her geographical position with respect to Chinese nationalism and Russian communism, was not prepared to adopt. Since Chinese aspirations would not be silenced, and Japan would not forego her special position, a conflict of some kind appeared inevitable. History would seem to indicate that in such cases pretexts in abundance are soon found. In the case of Manchuria, there were three: The Wanpaoshan affair, the anti-Chinese riots in Korea, and the strange case of Captain Nakamura.

The first of these incidents took its name from a small village, Wanpaoshan, a few miles north of Changchun. Here a Chinese leased a tract of land from its Chinese owners (April, 1931), the lease agreement providing that it would be null and void if its terms were not approved by the Chinese district magistrate. Shortly thereafter, the lessee subleased the land to a group of Korean farmers. In this contract there was no requirement for official approval, but the sublease was made by the lessee without having secured official approval of his own lease. The Koreans commenced construction of a dam in a nearby river and of a canal to carry water to their fields. This canal passed through the lands of Chinese farmers near the river. When the work was well advanced, the Chinese farmers protested to their authorities, police arrived on the scene, and the Koreans were ordered to stop construction and to leave the land. At the same time, Japanese consular police arrived from Changchun to protect the Koreans. A joint investigation followed, the police meanwhile having been withdrawn, but no conclusion was reached. The Chinese maintained that the rights of the Chinese farmers were violated by the canal. The Japanese maintained that it was unfair to hold the Koreans responsible for an error in lease procedure of which they had no knowledge. Thus matters stood early in July, when the Chinese farmers drove the Koreans away and filled in much of their ditch. Again the Japanese consular police appeared. This time the Chinese were driven away, and, under Japanese police protection, the Koreans resumed their work.

News of these events appeared promptly in the Korean press, amplified by all the best devices of sensational yellow journalism. There followed a series of anti-Chinese riots throughout Korea, in which it appears that more than one hundred Chinese were killed and nearly four hundred were wounded. The Chinese claimed that the Japanese authorities encouraged the rioting. The Japanese replied that the riots were spontaneous and a natural result of China's discriminatory policy against Koreans in Manchuria. To China's official protest, Japan replied expressing regret and offering compensation to the families of the dead. Diplomatic efforts to settle the Wanpaoshan affair continued through the summer, but without complete success.

The Nakamura Affair

In western Manchuria, simultaneously with these events in the summer of 1931, Captain Shintaro Nakamura, of the Japanese army, was murdered by Chinese soldiers. Captain Nakamura, at the time, was on active duty. While traveling to western Manchuria, his passport was examined by Chinese authorities in Harbin, where he represented himself as an agricultural expert. When he reached the vicinity of Taonan, he was arrested by Chinese soldiers, shot, and his body cremated in order to destroy evidence of the deed. Reports of Nakamura's death aroused the Japanese, in particular the authorities of the Kwantung army. Under pressure of Japanese resentment, the Chinese, who had first sought to evade responsibility, agreed to investigate the case. This investigation proving abortive, the Chinese instituted a second. These delays occasioned further Japanese resentment. Meanwhile, there were diplomatic exchanges between Peking and Tokyo. On the afternoon of September 18, the Japanese Consul at Mukden was informed that the Chinese commander held responsible for the shooting of Nakamura had been brought to Mukden and would be tried by court-martial. It appeared, therefore, that the case was approaching a peaceful settlement.

The Chinese Boycott

Unfortunately, although the Wanpaoshan affair and the Nakamura case might have been subject to diplomatic settlement, the anti-Chinese riots in Korea again released forces that were by no means so susceptible to amicable adjustment. In the hands of the Chinese, the economic boycott was not a new or an untried weapon. Its origins may be traced back to that passive resistance by which the Chinese peasant had frequently protested against flagrant misuse of government authority. Its practical use in international affairs dated back to 1905, when the Chinese instituted, against the United States, their first boycott on a large scale. The causes of this boycott were varied, but in the main they centered about the harsh methods by which the United States enforced the provisions of its exclusion policy against the Chinese. This was followed in 1908 by the first boycott against Japanese goods, occasioned by the seizure of a Japanese ship and the subsequent acceptance by the Chinese government of Japanese demands delivered in the form of an ultimatum. Another anti-Japanese boycott followed in 1915, brought on by the Japanese expedition to Shantung and the presentation of the Twenty-one Demands. The next anti-Japanese boycott came in the years 1919 to 1921. It was designed to bring pressure on Japan in connection with the Shantung question. Student organizations took a more active part than in previous boycotts, and, as a result of their propaganda, there was more effective co-operation from Chinese consumers. In 1923, another boycott accompanied China's demand for the return of the leased territory in Manchuria. Two years later, boycotts were instituted against Great Britain and Japan after the so-called Nanking Road affair at Shanghai. The movements subsided in 1926 but were renewed again in 1927, the year in which the Nationalists established their capital in Nanking. Early in 1928, a local boycott of Japanese goods was started at Amoy, and, after the Tsinan affair, this boycott became nationwide. It continued on into 1929, with most serious effects on Japanese trade. Finally, in 1931, the anti-Chinese riots in Korea provided the excuse for another boycott against Japan, which was most effective at Shanghai, Tientsin, and in the middle Yangtze region.[6]

The effects of these various Chinese boycotts on Chino-Japanese relations in the years just preceding 1931 were very considerable. The material loss in trade was heavy. The Japanese were inclined to overestimate and the Chinese to underestimate this feature. The Chinese argument was that the boycott was a moral protest on the part of a weak nation against the aggression of a strong one. The Japanese held that the boycott, since it was actively fostered by the Kuomintang Party and the national government, was an aggressive political weapon by which China was attempting to deprive Japan of her legitimate treaty rights. In a word, they regarded the boycott as practiced by China as an instrument of warfare incompatible with peace-time relations. In conclusion, it must be observed that when to the accumulation of Manchurian disputes there were added popular hatreds engendered by the boycott propaganda, the stage had been set for an open clash between Tokyo and Nanking.

SELECTED BIBLIOGRAPHY

T. A. Bisson, "Basic Treaty Issues in Manchuria between China and Japan," in Foreign Policy Association *Reports,* Dec. 23, 1931. P. H. Clyde, "Manchuria, No Man's Land of Asia," in *Survey Graphic,* July, 1928. W. R. Crocker, *The Japanese Population Problem* (London: 1931). Shuhsi Hsu, "The Manchurian Question," in *Problems of the Pacific, 1929,* J. B. Condliffe, ed. (Chicago: 1930). A. E. Hindmarsh, *The Basis of Japanese Foreign Policy* (Cambridge: 1936). Zenichi Itani, *The Export of Japanese Capital to China* (Tokyo: 1931). South Manchuria Railway Co., *Japanese Investments and Expenditures in Manchuria, 1907-1926* (New York: 1929). *The Kwantung Government, its Functions and*

---

[6] For a full discussion of Chinese boycotts, see C. F. Remer and W. B. Palmer, *A Study of Chinese Boycotts.* Johns Hopkins Press, Baltimore, 1933.

Works (Dairen; 1929). K. K. Kawakami, "Manchuria, the Crux of Chino-Japanese Relations," in *Foreign Affairs,* Apr. 1928. K. K. Kawakami, "Manchurian Backgrounds," in *Pacific Affairs,* Feb. 1932. Yosuke Matsuoka, "Manchuria, Its Past and Present," in *Problems of the Pacific, 1929,* J. B. Condliffe, ed. (Chicago: 1930). Shiroshi Nasu, "The Problem of Population and Food Supply in Japan," in *Problems of the Pacific,* J. B. Condliffe, ed. (New York: 1928). E. F. Penrose, *Population Theories and Their Application with Special Reference to Japan* (Stanford Univ.: 1934). M. Royama, "The South Manchuria Railway Zone and the Nature of its Administration," in *Pacific Affairs,* Nov. 1930. C. F. Remer, *A Study of Chinese Boycotts* (Baltimore: 1933). B. P. Torgasheff, "Manchuria from the Metallurgical and Fuel Standpoints," in *Chinese Economic Journal,* Apr. 1929. A. J. Toynbee, *Survey of International Affairs, 1929* (Oxford: 1930), pt. 4a, ch. 1 on civil war in China, ch. 2 on treaty revision, and ch. 3 on status of foreign concessions and settlements. Tatsuji Takeuchi, *War and Diplomacy in the Japanese Empire* (Garden City: 1935), ch. 22 on the Tsinan incident of 1928, and ch. 24 on the death of Chang Tso-lin. Teijiro Uyeda, "The Future of the Japanese Population," in *Pacific Affairs,* June-July, 1933. C. W. Young, *The International Relations of Manchuria* (Chicago: 1929). By the same author, *Japan's Special Position in Manchuria* (Baltimore: 1931); *The International Legal Status of the Kwantung Leased Territory* (Baltimore: 1931); and *Japanese Jurisdiction in the South Manchuria Railway Areas* (Baltimore: 1931).

CHAPTER XXXVI

The Conflict in Manchuria and Shanghai

A FEELING of intense bitterness had pervaded Chino-Japanese relations by 1931. In those parts of China where large Japanese groups were to be found—Shanghai, portions of Shantung, and more especially south Manchuria—this feeling was particularly in evidence. Even though both governments presumably hoped for a peaceful settlement of their mutual problems, irresponsible individuals and groups on both sides were ever likely, through overzealous and ill-advised actions, to precipitate a crisis. In China, both within and outside the ranks of the Kuomintang Party, such groups were numerous. In Japan, the most restive element was to be found among the junior officers of the army and within various reservist organizations. The feeling was perhaps even stronger among the younger Japanese officers attached to the Kwantung army. All of these groups, Chinese and Japanese, were prepared either to create or to take advantage of minor incidents and thus to produce an open clash. In Manchuria, such incidents frequently took the form of attempts (often by bandits) to tamper with the roadbed of the South Manchuria Railway, the most obvious embodiment of Japan's imperialism. These cases had occurred with alarming frequency after 1926. They added to the cumulative tension that existed in the late summer of 1931.

On the night of September 18, an explosion occurred on or near the South Manchuria Railroad, a few miles north of the city of Mukden, and just south of the Peitaying, or North Barracks, where between 8,000 and 10,000 Chinese troops were quartered. The explosion brought to the scene a Japanese military patrol of one officer and six men who were engaged in practicing defence maneuvers along the line. While examining the extent of the damage, which was slight, the Japanese allege that they were fired upon, at first by a small party in ambush, and, when it was driven away toward the North Barracks, by a larger body of Chinese troops. The Japanese summoned reinforcements from Mukden, which, when they arrived (500 strong), drove the Chinese from the ground between the railway and the barracks, a distance of some 250 yards, and attacked the barracks. By morning, it was in the hands of the Japanese, its 10,000 occupants having retired to the north. All this was denied by the Chinese. They asserted that no explosion occurred, or if it did, the Japanese were responsible, that no Chinese troops fired upon the railroad, and that the subsequent attack upon the barracks was entirely unprovoked. Whatever the truth behind these conflicting stories may be, the fact remains that the high command of the Kwantung army believed, or said it believed, that the Chinese were precipitating an attack. In Manchuria, at the time, there were some 220,000 Chinese troops. The Japanese had 14,000, which were brought into action on the night of September 18 in defense of Japan's Manchurian interests. The Chinese, denying the validity of this motive of self-defense, asserted that their troops, far from provoking an attack or offering resistance, retired from the North Barracks as rapidly as possible. It is alleged that at the time they were under strict orders to avoid provoking the Japanese military in any way.[1]

While the North Barracks were being occupied, Japanese

---

[1] A great variety of interpretations and conclusions have appeared on the subject of this so-called Manchurian incident of September 18. For the present, it must be asserted that the evidence is contradictory and unsatisfactory. That some sort of explosion occurred there appears to be no doubt. This is attested both by the Japanese and by the Lytton Report. But there is no agreement as to who caused it. To the suggestion frequently made that the Japanese themselves were responsible, they have replied with some force that, assuming that Japan wanted an "incident" in order to bring an open clash, she had only to wait for one of the frequent provo-

troops from the Mukden station of the railway attacked and captured the walled city, occupied Chang Hsueh-liang's great arsenal, and drove the Chinese troops from the East Barracks. These events were reported during the night to the headquarters of the Kwantung army at Port Arthur. Troops from Liaoyang, Yingkow, and Fenghuangsheng were ordered to Mukden. The Port Arthur fleet was sent to Yingkow (Newchwang), and reinforcements were asked from the army in Korea. The operations of the Japanese troops were extended immediately to many strategic points on the South Manchuria Railway, where large bodies of Chinese troops were concentrated. At Changchun, the northern terminus of the railway, the Japanese met stout resistance from the Chinese garrisons, numbering about 10,000 men, but succeeded, on September 19, in capturing the barracks. Kirin was then occupied (September 21). Many of the Chinese troops thus routed, assembling on the Peking-Mukden Railway, became concentrated on the southern border of Manchuria.

---

cative acts of irresponsible Chinese civilians or soldiers. It has been suggested also that the incident of September 18 partakes of the nature of a myth (see Ben Dorfman, "The Manchurian Incident," *Harpers Magazine,* September, 1934).

The Japanese military in Manchuria attempted to justify their action on the night of September 18, not on the alleged explosion, but rather on the claim that they were attacked by troops from the North Barracks. In this connection, the findings of the Lytton Commission are of some interest. They imply that because the Japanese "had a carefully prepared plan to meet the case of possible hostilities," and because "this plan was put into operation," and because the Chinese "had no plan of attacking the Japanese troops, or of endangering the lives or property of Japanese nationals at this particular time or place," the aggression came from the Japanese side—that is, that the Japanese precipitated the attack. The Report adds that the Chinese "were surprised by the Japanese attack," but offers no evidence in support of this assertion. It concludes with the statement: "The military operations of the Japanese troops during this night . . . cannot be regarded as measures of legitimate self-defence. In saying this, the Commission does not exclude the hypothesis that the officers on the spot may have thought they were acting in self-defence." If, indeed, the Japanese did precipitate the attack, they most assuredly could have entertained no such hypothesis. Finally, it should be observed that, though the Chinese had no plan of attack "at this particular time or place," they did have a most comprehensive plan of attack upon all Japanese interests in Manchuria, which plan was presumably to be put into operation at a favorable moment (see K. K. Kawakami, *Manchoukuo, Child of Conflict.* The Macmillan Company, New York, 1933. p. 59).

The Conflict in Tokyo

First news of the Manchurian clash reached the War Department in Tokyo early on the morning of September 19. At

GENERAL JIRO MINAMI. Minister of War in Japan in 1931 and a vigorous exponent of the military tradition.

a special Cabinet meeting summoned during the morning, Baron Shidehara, the Foreign Minister, insisted that military operations be confined to the narrowest possible limits. Premier Wakatsuki announced that a policy of non-aggression would be followed. The force of this action was, however, promptly destroyed when the Minister of War, General Minami, after consultation with the Chief of the General Staff and the Inspector General of Military Education, stated that "the army need not consult the cabinet as to the measures to be taken to meet the exigencies of the future, but would leave it to the commander-in-chief of the Kwantung army to exercise his discretion." [2] At this stage, the War Department's policy contemplated the dispatch of additional troops if the Chinese attempted counter-attacks, and the movement of troops from Korea, without authorization of the Cabinet, in case of emergency. The Cabinet was to be permitted to decide whether the crisis was to be the occasion for settling all oustanding disputes concerning Manchuria and Mongolia. Finally, the War Department decided that a policy of non-aggression did not necessarily mean that Japanese troops should be confined to the stations they then occupied in Manchuria. On September 21, the War Minister sought, *as a matter of form,* Cabinet approval of an army decision to dispatch additional troops from Korea. This was opposed by Baron Shidehara and Finance Minister Junnosuke Inouye, on the ground that it was not in keeping with the Cabinet's policy of non-aggression. Scarcely had the Cabinet adjourned, without reaching a decision, when news was received that the garrison commander in Korea had, without specific instructions from the General Staff, dispatched 4,000 troops to Manchuria. Premier Wakatsuki and Baron Shidehara were in the position of having to accept the troop movement as an accomplished fact before the government had given its decision. To the open clash in Manchuria was thereby added a new crisis between the civilian and military wings of the government in Tokyo.

This conflict (see p. 592) was not new. On the contrary, it was deeply rooted in Japan's constitutional system, which conferred upon the Ministers of War and Marine extraordinary privileges enjoyed by no other member of the

Cabinet save the Premier. The problem created by this political setup had for the most part been kept in the background, because of the army's reluctance to appear publicly as an active force in politics. Nevertheless, the army had taken an increasing interest in political affairs since 1925 and was actively involved in them as a result of the critical relations that developed between Tokyo and Nanking during the summer of 1931. During 1930, the navy had voiced vigorously its protest against the London Naval Treaty, but its claims were defeated by the government. As a result, the army was determined that its independence in matters of policy should not be treated in like manner. The army made it known that its appropriations could not be curtailed. In August, 1931, General Minami, in an address to division commanders, denounced Shidehara's conciliatory policy in Manchuria and declared that liberal propaganda was attempting to discredit the army's legitimate needs for national defense. The extraordinary procedure of allowing this address to be made public indicated that the Minister of War intended his remarks for general rather than private consumption. The Japanese press interpreted the move as an attempt to discredit armament reduction, as a bid by the army for public political support, and as a notice that unless the government solved the Manchurian problem, the army would be forced to do so. This was the background, then, that served to explain the dispatch of further Japanese troops to Korea in the face of strong civilian opposition in the Cabinet.

China Appeals to the League

On the same day that the additional Japanese troops moved into Manchuria (September 21), the Chinese government invoked Article 11 of the Covenant of the League of Nations, requesting the Council to prevent further aggravation of the unhappy condition in Manchuria. The Council responded by requesting the governments in Nanking and Tokyo "to refrain from any action which might aggravate the situation or prejudice the peaceful settlement of the problem." Means were also to be sought to enable both powers to withdraw their troops. At the same time, the United States (not a member of the League) was to be informed of these developments.

Prompt action by the League was made possible because the Council was in session when the incident occurred. But, far from being in a position to cope adequately with the forces at work in Manchuria, the League was utterly unprepared for the crisis. Students and observers in close association with the League described the atmosphere of Geneva as one in which "no shadow of crisis had been cast . . . no warning or indication that the peace of the East was in danger. . . . The Far East, when thought of at all, was thought of only as a vast territory. . . ." [3] The explanation of this shocking ignorance and this pious faith in the peace of the Far East lay not in the fact that there had been "no warning or indication," for these had appeared in rapid succession during the summer of 1931, but rather in the fact that the League was essentially a European-controlled organization concerned primarily with European affairs, and that during 1931 these affairs had all but excluded any others from its attention. In a word, the League, which had just failed to meet successfully the economic crisis in Europe, was now appealed to by China to solve the riddle of imperialism in northeastern Asia.

The fact that China appealed to the League was promptly interpreted as showing her unswerving loyalty to the Covenant, to the Pact of Paris, and to the abstract principle of international peace. It could not, of course, be denied that China boasted many pacifists of high principle, but these were not the men who dictated China's policy in appealing to the League. That policy was based on long experience in contacts with foreign states. The idea was that a weak China's greatest weapon of defense lay in her power to play one foreign state against

[3] "The League and Manchuria," *Geneva Special Studies*. Vol. II, no. 10, pp. 3-4.

another. These tactics had been used repeatedly and with varying success against the foreign powers in the late nineteenth and early twentieth centuries. In 1931, China sought to use the same weapon by playing the League against Japan. By so doing, she won an immediate and striking moral victory. Her diplomats were able to picture Nanking as the unselfish champion of the world's peace machinery, a machinery constructed with much labor since the close of the World War. As a natural consequence of this able strategy, China enjoyed, during subsequent developments in the Manchurian affair, the overwhelming support of popular, though often ill-informed, world opinion.

Action at Chinchow

Japan's reply to the League was prefaced by a number of significant decisions in Tokyo. The first was the temporary victory of the Foreign Office, which proposed to deal with the League, over the War Department, which at first opposed any interference by or correspondence with the League on the subject of Manchuria. The second was the Cabinet's decision to insist on direct negotiations with China. The government then clarified its position by stating that military action in Manchuria had been taken to forestall imminent disaster to Japan's vested interests, that the government had no territorial designs, that direct negotiations were the best means of meeting the situation, and that the troops would be withdrawn to the railroad zone as the danger to Japanese life and property was removed. China having already responded to the League resolution, the Council expressed its satisfaction with the replies on September 30. But in Tokyo, by the beginning of October, the War Department was "in firm control of the government, directing the nation's policy towards the League as well as the Manchurian developments." [4] This displacing of civilian by military control was not without effect in Manchuria, where on

---

[4] Tatsuji Takeuchi, *op. cit.* p. 357.

October 8, the Japanese bombed the city of Chinchow, in southwestern Manchuria. Here, Chang Hsueh-liang had established temporary quarters for the government of Liaoning province, formerly located at Mukden. The real purpose of this move was to warn Chang that he would be met by force if he attempted to re-establish his former control over Manchuria. Late in the day, the War Department in Tokyo formulated the general lines of its policy. These included acceptance by China of full responsibility for the incident of September 18, immediate settlement of all important Manchurian questions *with the local authorities* rather than with Nanking, maintenance of the *status quo* in Manchuria until a new government appeared, and resistance to any interference by the League. Against this program, the opposition, led by Baron Shidehara, was powerless. Already, on October 4, General Honjo, commanding the Kwantung army, had expressed the hope that a new regime would appear in Manchuria.

The bombing of Chinchow, followed by new Chinese protests, brought the Council of the League into action again on October 13. Following China's recital of events at Chinchow, Japan circularized the Council with a dispatch which had been presented to Nanking, on October 9, charging China with violating her pledge to the League not to aggravate the situation. Nanking was accused of making no effort to restrain the activities of anti-Japanese societies, which were jeopardizing the lives and property, as well as the liberty of trade, of Japanese subjects in China.[5] Matters were complicated further on October 15, when the Council, in opposition to Japan, decided to invite the United States to be represented at its further meetings as an observer. The reason given was that the Pact of Paris, of which the United States was a signatory, was involved; but the motive behind this action was the desire of the League to increase its strength and thus bring pressure to bear on Japan. This action served to alienate the Japanese Foreign

---

[5] "The League and Manchuria" in *Geneva Special Studies*. Vol. II, no. 11, p. 11.

Office, which objected on legal grounds, and brought from the Japanese War Minister a statement that no good could be expected from intervention by the League or other third parties. Nevertheless, the Council, again in opposition to Japan, voted, on October 24, that Japan should withdraw her troops to the railroad zone by November 16 and that China should assume responsibility for the lives and property of Japanese in Manchuria. Japan countered by announcing five principles, which she proposed as the basis of direct negotiations with China. These included:

1. Mutual repudiation of aggressive policies and conduct.
2. Respect for China's territorial integrity.
3. Complete suppression of all organized movements interfering with freedom of trade.
4. Effective protection throughout Manchuria of all peaceful pursuits undertaken by Japanese subjects.
5. Respect for the treaty rights of Japan in Manchuria.

The Nonni River Battle

But, while resolutions were being discussed in Geneva and principles were being enunciated in Tokyo, the march of conflict continued in Manchuria. Civil war, which the Chinese claim was instigated by the Japanese, broke out in northwestern Manchuria between two Chinese generals, Ma Chanshan, governor of Heilungkiang province, and Chang Hai-peng, the garrison commander at Taonan. To stop the northern advance of the latter, General Ma destroyed the Nonni River railway bridge of the Taonan-Anganchi Railroad, a Chinese road built with capital supplied by the South Manchuria Railway. The Japanese demanded its immediate repair. General Ma delayed, and his troops, contrary to orders, fired on unarmed railway employees at the bridge. Ma was then ordered to complete repairs by November 3, failing which, Japanese engineers protected by troops would undertake the work.

Nothing was done by November 2, when a Japanese ultimatum ordered the Chinese to withdraw their troops from the river. Fighting soon followed. The Japanese repaired the bridge and, advancing northward, drove General Ma's troops north of the Chinese Eastern Railroad and occupied Tsitsihar on November 19. Meanwhile, Chinese armies had reorganized and entrenched themselves in southwestern Manchuria, on the Taling River. These forces, outnumbering the Japanese troops in Manchuria two to one, were supplemented by much larger numbers of disbanded Chinese troops and bandits operating both east and west of the Liao River and in Chientao, in southeastern Manchuria. The situation was further complicated during November by two outbreaks at Tientsin, threatening the lives and property of Japanese in that city. To relieve the small Japanese force in Tientsin, the Kwantung army sent a relief expedition by way of Chinchow, where large Chinese forces were concentrating. By November 29, conditions at Tientsin having improved, the relief expedition withdrew without taking Chinchow. The Chinese reoccupied the district, and irregulars invaded and raided the country around Mukden. This condition led the Japanese military to seek reinforcements and to drive the Chinese from Chinchow. On January 3, 1932, the Japanese occupied Chinchow.

The Lytton Commission

In Geneva, concurrently with these events, the Japanese proposed (November 21) that the League dispatch a commission of inquiry, on the ground that a solution would require a real knowledge of conditions *both in Manchuria and also in China proper.* The Chinese, not welcoming this suggestion, continued to insist that withdrawal of the Japanese troops from Chinese soil was the essential prerequisite of a solution. Then, on December 10, the Council adopted a resolution to appoint a commission to study and report on any circumstances threatening to disturb the peace between China and Japan. Japan and China both accepted this action with reservations. Japan declared that she was not precluded from taking such steps as might be necessary to protect Japanese interests from bandits and lawless elements rampant in various parts of Manchuria, while China observed that she would not condone further action by Japan under the pretext of meeting existing lawlessness in Manchuria.[6]

American Policy

The progress of events in Manchuria had by this time seriously affected relations between Japan and the United States. As early as September 22, Henry L. Stimson, American Secretary of State, had told the Japanese Ambassador in Washington of the American government's concern lest the Manchurian affair should involve the Nine-Power Treaty of 1922 and the Pact of Paris (the Kellogg-Briand Treaty of 1928). A few days later (September 25), Secretary Stimson addressed identic notes to China and Japan, expressing the hope that further conflict would be avoided. The United States had already been informed by the League Council of its procedure, and on September 24 had notified the Council that it was "in whole-hearted sympathy" with its procedure. This was followed by advice from the Secretary of State to the Council "that the League in no way relax its vigilance." At the same time, the United States, acting independently, would "try to reinforce League action." This was of great advantage to the League, but the fact remained that the United States was still unrepresented in its councils. Geneva was already aware that the American government was willing to permit Prentiss B. Gilbert, American Consul at Geneva, to sit with the Council to discuss the bearing of the Kellogg Pact on

---

[6] The membership of the Commission included: The Earl of Lytton (British), General Henri Claudel (French), Count Aldrovandi (Italian), Major General Frank R. McCoy (American), and Dr. Heinrich Schnee (German).

Manchuria. An invitation to this effect was accordingly extended on October 16, and was accepted by the State Department within a few hours, and on the same day Prentiss Gilbert took his seat at the Council table.

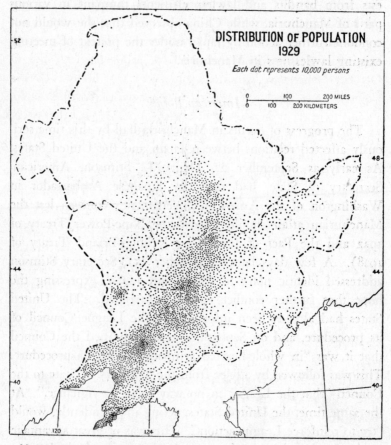

DISTRIBUTION OF POPULATION
1929

Each dot represents 10,000 persons

MANCHURIA. *Courtesy of the "Geographical Review," published by the American Geographical Society of New York.*

This action of the Council inviting the United States to send a representative to sit with the Council had been opposed vigorously on legal grounds by the Japanese government. It held that the matter was fundamental and not a mere question of procedure. If this were so, it would require a unanimous vote. The Council, however, held that only procedure was involved, and the invitation was extended against Japan's single vote. This aroused the resentment not only of the Foreign Office and the War Department in Tokyo but also of the general public. A few weeks earlier, when first news of the Mukden incident reached Tokyo, public opinion in Japan was highly critical of the army authorities. This was particularly true of the liberal press and the labor parties. But in October, when an American observer was invited to the Council over Japan's protest, first suggestions that Japan should withdraw from the League appeared in the press. However, the more liberal opinion, which favored co-operation with the League, was still supported by the general public. By November, this popular support was shifting toward a more vigorous and independent policy. The Minseito Party, identified with Shidehara's moderate views, was attacked by the Seiyukai opposition, which in previous years had been associated with Tanaka's strong policy. Ki Inukaï, the party's president, assailed Shidehara for his alleged failure to appraise world opinion of the threat to Japanese interests in Manchuria that had existed prior to the outbreak at Mukden. There was division, too, within the ranks of the Minseito Cabinet. The result was that, on the day following the Council's creation of a commission of inquiry (December 10), the Minseito Cabinet resigned and was replaced by the Seiyukai, with Inukai as Premier and Lieutenant General Sadao Araki as Minister of War.

Japan's opposition and the hesitancy of any American administration to be too intimately identified with the political activities of the League resulted in instructions to Prentiss Gilbert to refrain from discussion unless the invocation of the Kellogg Pact were considered. On October 17, Great Britain, France, Italy, Germany, and Spain reminded China and Japan of their obligations under Article II of the Pact, the United States following suit on October 20. It appeared, then, that Mr. Gilbert's presence at the Council meetings was not without effect. A month later, however, when on November 16 the Council reassembled in Paris to review the situation since its last meeting at Geneva, on October 24, the striking thing was that no American observer sat with the Council members. To be sure, General Charles G. Dawes, American Ambassador at London, went to Paris to confer with members of the Council in the event that the Kellogg Pact or the Nine-Power Treaty were discussed, but he was not instructed to sit with the Council. As one commentator has said:

If attending meetings was sound policy for Mr. Prentiss Gilbert, why not for General Dawes? If it was legally correct in the first instance, why not in the second?

The inference appeared to be that the American administration had come to regard its representation at the Council as something involving more than a mere matter of procedure. Did it feel that the United States was being drawn too deeply into the machinery of the League? Whatever the answer to this question may be, it was quite clear that the Japanese government and public was becoming more and more sensitive to what it regarded as American "meddling." By the end of 1931, the Japanese public had been converted to the almost unanimous view that the actions of the army in Manchuria were justified measures of self-defense. At this very moment, the United States announced a policy which could result only in bitter Japanese opposition.

The Stimson Doctrine

The immediate occasion explaining the appearance of the so-called Stimson Doctrine was the southern drive of the Kwantung army, which resulted, on January 3, 1932, in the occupation of Chinchow and the retirement of Chang Hsueh-liang's army south of the Great Wall. On January 7, 1932, after consultation with the British, French, and Italian Ambassadors, Secretary Stimson addressed identic notes to Japan and China. The notes asserted that Japan's military operations had destroyed the last remaining administrative authority of the Chinese Republic in south Manchuria and that the United States would not admit the legality of any such *de facto* situation. Furthermore, the United States would not recognize any treaty or agreement concluded by China and Japan impairing the treaty rights of the United States in China, including those which related to the sovereignty, the independence, or the territorial and administrative integrity of China; and, moreover, that it would not recognize any situation, treaty, or agreement brought about by means contrary to the covenants and obligations of the Pact of Paris.[7]

Japan replied on January 16, that in her China policy she had no intention of adopting "improper means," that the Manchurian government had collapsed because the Chinese authorities had either resigned or fled, and that the people of Manchuria would determine their own political future. It added that there could be no question as to the binding power of the Nine-Power Treaty and the Pact of Paris, but that the unsettled condition of China might in material respects modify the application of these treaties. It reminded the American government that Japan was deeply concerned with the welfare of Manchuria, that the very existence of Japan was at stake, and that it hoped the United States would soon

[7] Henry L. Stimson, *The Far Eastern Crisis*. Harper & Brothers, New York, 1936. pp. 87 ff. Stimson observes (p. 88) that American policy to the close of 1931 was predicated on the hope of moderate action from within Japan. As a matter of fact, American policy prior to January, 1932, served to stimulate Japan's supernationalism. The close co-operation between Washington and Geneva, the moral encouragement extended to the League, and the acceptance, in opposition to Japan, of the invitation which brought an American observer to the Council table, had all served to destroy any American policy of conciliation several weeks before the appearance of the Stimson Doctrine.

The non-recognition doctrine was predicated on three specific considerations. Unless Japan's military actions were checked, the United States would suffer: (1) Material damage to her far eastern trade, (2) the ill effects of a crippled peace machinery, and (3) incalculable harm "to American prestige in China." *Ibid.* p. 90.

reach a "correct appreciation of the situation." These views were fully endorsed by the Japanese press. The Stimson Doctrine, far from modifying Japan's policy, served to unite the public behind the new Inukai Cabinet.

Developments at Shanghai

Concurrently with these events, China's anti-Japanese boycott, which followed close upon the Wanpaoshan affair and the Korean riots, had grown to alarming proportions. Japan's trade with her great continental neighbor was in imminent danger of collapse. In Shanghai, anti-Japanese sentiment, being particularly strong, resulted in giant demonstrations by unions, guilds, student organizations, and representatives of the Kuomintang Party. Millions of dollars worth of Japanese goods were seized throughout China by anti-Japanese associations. It was the most effective boycott that China had ever undertaken. Then, on January 9, 1932, two days after announcement of the Stimson Doctrine, the official daily organ of the Kuomintang Party expressed regret that an attempt by a Korean on the life of the Japanese Emperor had failed. The Japanese colony of Shanghai was aroused to fury. Before the matter was settled by a Chinese apology, a Chinese mob attacked five Japanese Buddhists, two of whom were priests, in Chapei, a suburb adjoining the International Settlement. This attack resulted in the death of one of the priests. Japan demanded dissolution of all anti-Japanese associations. Clashes between Chinese and Japanese in Shanghai continued, resulting in an ultimatum to the Chinese mayor on January 27. This was accepted the following day, but in the evening, hostilities broke out between Chinese troops and Japanese sailors in Chapei. At the time, the Japanese were preparing to defend their sector of the International Settlement under a state of emergency, which had been declared by the foreign municipal council.

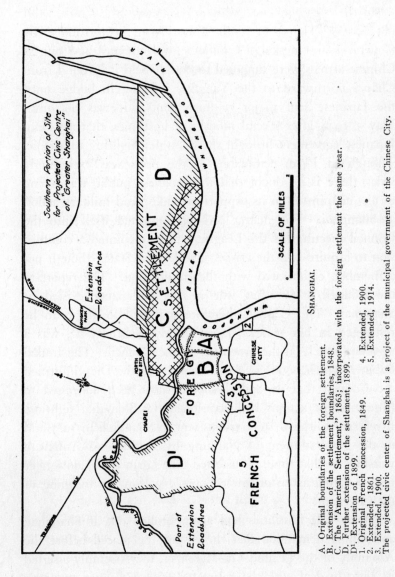

SHANGHAI.

A. Original boundaries of the foreign settlement.
B. Extension of the settlement boundaries, 1848.
C. The "American Settlement," 1863; incorporated with the foreign settlement the same year.
D. Further extension of the settlement, 1899.
D¹. Extension of 1899.
1. Original French concession, 1849.   4. Extended, 1900.
2. Extended, 1861.   5. Extended, 1914.
3. Extended, 1900.
The projected civic center of Shanghai is a project of the municipal government of the Chinese City.

In the Shanghai area, unlike Manchuria, the Chinese did not retire. The Nineteenth Route Army, commanded by General Tsai Ting-kai, a Cantonese, did not turn and run, as Chinese armies were supposed to do. It held its ground from Chapei northward to the Yangtze, refusing to budge until the Japanese sent major reinforcements. It was not until May 5, 1932, after several months of hostilities, that a Chino-Japanese agreement brought the Shanghai fighting to a close. Though in Japan censorship of the press was exceedingly strict, there is no doubt that the Japanese public was by no means unanimous in its support of widespread military action at Shanghai. The matter promptly injected itself into the Council meetings of the League, which appointed a commission to inquire into the crisis. The United States, though not a member, co-operated with the commission. The report to the Council stated that war in all but name existed at Shanghai. The Council therefore appealed to Japan to be restrained in her policy. Japan's reply, February 23, was a vigorous attack on the procedure of the Council. The Inukai Cabinet, which now had a safe majority in the Diet, informed the Council that its appeal should have been addressed to China, whose actions had occasioned the Shanghai fighting. It referred to the western troops sent to Shanghai in 1927 and to the bombardment of Nanking by British and American warships at that time. It asserted that Japan could no longer regard China as an organized people within the meaning of the Covenant.

Meanwhile hostilities had again broken out at Shanghai, and China demanded that the dispute be placed before the Assembly of the League. On March 11, the Assembly asserted its right to deal with the entire far eastern dispute and gave its full adherence to the Stimson Doctrine of non-recognition. These resolutions aroused further resentment in Japan, where the view was held that the League was refusing stubbornly to take account of realities and was thus obstructing, rather than forwarding, a permanent settlement. In addition, the Japanese were alarmed by a restatement of the Stimson Doctrine made on February 23 in a letter from the Secretary of State to the chairman of the Foreign Relations Committee of the Senate.[8] It affirmed that the Nine-Power Treaty and the others made at the Washington Conference were all "interrelated and interdependent." Among these was the Washington Naval Treaty. The letter then continued by stating that:

The willingness of the American government to surrender its then commanding lead in battleship construction and to leave its positions at Guam and in the Philippines without further fortification was predicated upon, among other things, the self-denying covenants contained in the Nine-Power Treaty, which assured the nations of the world not only of equal opportunity for their eastern trade but also against the military aggrandizement of any other power at the expense of China.

This vigorous official threat directed at Japan was supported by a body of unofficial opinions expressed by prominent Americans, advocating the economic boycott as a means of enforcing respect for treaties.

Appearance of Manchoukuo

The prolonged hostilities at Shanghai, the stubborn resistance of the Nineteenth Route Army, and the international complications resulting from the character of the International Settlement, all served during the first three months of 1932 to center world attention on events at this unique city.

---

[8] *Ibid.* pp. 165-178. The purposes of this letter were: (1) To encourage China, (2) to inform the American public on policy, (3) to suggest a common course of action to the League, (4) to remind the British government that it was a joint author with the United States of the open door policy and the Nine-Power Treaty, and finally (5) to remind Japan "that if she chose to break down one of the group of treaties arrived at at the Washington Conference, other nations might feel themselves released from some of those treaties which were as important to her as the Nine Power Treaty was to us." Used by special permission of the publishers, Harper & Brothers.

In the popular mind, Manchuria was all but forgotten. Events there had moved no less rapidly, though indeed they were less spectacular, until, on March 1, by which time Japanese military action had been extended to the country about Harbin, a Manchurian convention meeting in Mukden announced the founding of the new independent state of Manchoukuo, with Pu-yi, former Manchu Emperor of China, as regent. The government of Manchoukuo immediately notified the powers of its establishment and asked recognition. This request was ignored by all states save Japan. On March 18, Tokyo intimated that if the new state proved to be stable, recognition would be accorded. In the meantime, its policy would be one of watchful waiting. The decision on recognition rested, in fact, not so much on events in Manchuria as on those in Japan itself.

Before the close of 1931, as already noted, the War Department in Tokyo had taken the lead in formulating the nation's policy toward Manchuria and China. Public support gravitated to this new leadership, and the Foreign Office, under Shidehara, was largely discredited. The elections of February, 1932, while putting the more aggressive Seiyukai into power, did not arrest the growing popular distrust of parliamentary and party government. Advocates of "strong" government and "positive" policies looked with as much suspicion upon the Diet as they had already shown toward the Foreign Office. Growth of these views in a time of national crisis resulted in a series of political assassinations. The victims included Junnosuke Inouye, former Minister of Finance and a leader of the Minseito (February 9), Baron Takuma Dan, financier (March 5), and finally the Premier, Ki Inukai, who was shot on May 15 at his official residence by a band of men in military and naval uniforms. This alarming crisis in the nation's history was met by the appointment of a nonparty cabinet headed by Admiral Viscount Saito, who had served so ably as Governor General of Korea.

With the installation of this cabinet, demands for the recognition of Manchoukuo became more pronounced. In June, Premier Saito stated that the new state could no longer be ignored. Concurrently, Manchoukuo's Foreign Minister urged upon the commander of the Kwantung army and the president of the South Manchuria Railway Company the ne-

Department of Foreign Affairs, Hsinking, Manchuria.

PREMIER CHENG HSIAO-HSU OF MANCHOUKUO, GENERAL NOBUYOSHI MUTO, AND SECRETARY HAYASHIDE AT A MEETING IN THE PRIME MINISTER'S OFFICE ON SEPTEMBER 16, 1932.

cessity of immediate recognition. In July, General Muto was appointed commander of the Kwantung army, governor of the leased territory, and special ambassador to Manchoukuo. In August, Tokyo announced that recognition would be accorded Manchoukuo, this promise being carried into effect by a protocol signed by Japan and Manchoukuo on September 15.

Concurrently with these events, the commission of inquiry for which the Council of the League had made provision by resolution on December 10, 1931, proceeded to the Far East and conducted an extensive investigation. Its itinerary included parts of Japan, central and north China, and Manchuria. Its findings, known generally as the Lytton Report,[9] were made public from Geneva on October 2, 1932, three weeks after Japan had recognized the independence of Man-

Department of Foreign Affairs, Hsinking, Manchuria.

CHENG HSIAO-HSU, FIRST PREMIER OF MANCHOUKUO. He is typical of the old-school classical scholar and poet, representative in many ways of the finest traditions in oriental life.

choukuo. This report consisted of ten chapters. The first three dealt with the background of Chinese-Japanese relations. From this point, the report discussed the hostilities in Manchuria and at Shanghai, the creation of Manchoukuo, the effects of the Chinese boycott on Japan's economic interests, and the position of Manchuria in the economic life of the

[9] League of Nations, *Appeal by the Chinese Government, Report of the Commission of Enquiry.* Geneva, October 1, 1932.

Far East. The concluding chapters set forth the principles and conditions of a proposed settlement.

That the commission discarded the Japanese claim that her actions in Manchuria were legitimate measures of self-defense has already been indicated. On the subject of Manchoukuo, the commission concluded that the new state was not the product of any spontaneous movement by the people of Manchuria, but owed its existence to the presence of Japanese troops and to the efforts of Japanese civil and military officials. It regarded the creation of Manchoukuo as in no sense a solution of the Manchurian problem. In dealing with the Chinese boycott, which had precipitated the serious clash at Shanghai, the commission found that the movement had the official support and frequently the direction of the Kuomintang Party, that the methods of the boycott were often illegal, and that they were not suppressed by the authorities or the courts. But on the question of whether or not the organized application of the boycott to the trade of one particular country (Japan) was consistent with friendly relations or in conformity with treaty obligations, the commission failed to express an opinion. This was the more striking since the commission had not failed to pass judgment on the events of September 18.

In proposing its principles and conditions of settlement, the commission observed that, while the issues between China and Japan were not in themselves incapable of solution by arbitral procedure, the handling of them by their respective governments had so embittered their relations as "to make a conflict inevitable." It observed further that the issues involved were not so simple as they were frequently represented to be. On the contrary, they were, in the view of the commission, exceedingly complicated and without parallel, and "only an intimate knowledge of all the facts, as well as their historical background, should entitle anyone to express a definite opinion upon them." As a solution, the commission discarded either a return to the *status quo ante* or an acceptance of Manchoukuo. As conditions of a satisfactory solution it suggested:

1. A settlement conforming to the interests of both Japan and China.
2. Consideration of the interests of Soviet Russia.
3. Conformity with existing multilateral treaties.
4. Recognition of Japan's interests in Manchuria.
5. Establishment of new treaty relations between Japan and China.
6. Effective provision for settlement of future disputes.
7. Establishment of Manchurian autonomy.
8. Establishment of internal order in Manchuria and security against external aggression.
9. Encouragement of an economic *rapprochement* between Japan and China.
10. International co-operation in Chinese reconstruction.

The commission then outlined a procedure by which it hoped that a settlement, conforming to the above principles, might be made a reality. This included:

1. An invitation from the Council to Japan and China to discuss a solution.
2. The summoning of an advisory conference to recommend a constitution for a special autonomous regime in Manchuria.
3. A meeting at the same time between Japan and China, if necessary with neutral observers, to settle specific issues in Manchuria.
4. The embodiment of the results of these discussions in four separate instruments:
   a. A declaration by China establishing an autonomous Manchuria.
   b. A Sino-Japanese treaty dealing with Japanese interests.

c. A Sino-Japanese treaty of conciliation, arbitration, non-aggression, and mutual assistance.

d. A Sino-Japanese commercial treaty.

The public reception accorded the findings and suggestions of the Lytton Report was far from uniform. In the western world, approval was general. In China, opinion was divided, for the idea of an autonomous Manchuria made no appeal to the Nationalists of the Kuomintang. In Japan, condemnation of the report was virtually unanimous. The press attacked the report on many grounds: Its denial that Japan had acted in self-defense, its failure to adjudge China guilty of illegal use of the boycott, and its verdict that Manchoukuo was no solution. Finally, it characterized the suggested principles of solution as "utterly unworkable." On November 18, the Japanese government submitted its observations on the Lytton Report to the League. These observations insisted that Japan's actions on September 18, 1931, were legitimate measures of self-defense, that the maintenance of Manchoukuo was the only solution, and that the proposals of the commission must therefore be refused. The Council of the League commenced its consideration of the report on November 21. Heated debates between the Japanese and Chinese representatives followed, and on November 28, the Report, against Japan's wishes, was referred without action to the Assembly of the League. Here, again, Japan's views on Manchuria and the Lytton Report were presented by her chief delegate, Matsuoka. For China, Dr. Yen demanded that the Assembly accept the findings of the Lytton Commission and declare that Japan had violated the Covenant, the Pact of Paris, and the Nine-Power Treaty. Representatives of many of the smaller powers called for censure upon Japan, while the great powers continued to advocate conciliation. Finally the Assembly again referred the Manchurian affair to its special Committeee of Nineteen. Under this procedure, the recommendations of the Lytton Report were adopted as a basis of settlement. Further efforts at conciliation were to be made through the Committee of Nineteen and representatives of Soviet Russia and the United States. Japan, objecting to American and Soviet representation on any conciliatory committee, insisted that its work be confined to aiding the matter of direct negotiations between Japan and China.

The year 1933 opened with further military operations by which the territory of Manchoukuo was extended to include the province of Jehol. Toward the end of January, the Committee of Nineteen announced that efforts at conciliation had failed. It recommended to the Assembly, on February 17, 1933, a solution in harmony with the findings of the commission. On February 20, the Saito Cabinet decided to withdraw from the League should the Assembly adopt a draft resolution that the committee had prepared. Four days later, the report of the Committee of Nineteen was adopted. Among its recommendations was the statement: "They [the members of the League] will continue not to recognize this regime [Manchoukuo] either *de jure* or *de facto*." Mr. Matsuoka, after declaring that Japan had "now reached the limit of endeavors to co-operate with the League," withdrew from the Assembly. On March 27, Japan gave notice at Geneva of her intention to withdraw from the League. In making this decision, the government observed:

The conclusion must be that in seeking a solution of the question the majority of the League have attached greater importance to upholding inapplicable formulae than to the real task of assuring peace, and higher value to the vindication of academic theses than to the eradication of the sources of future conflict.

SELECTED BIBLIOGRAPHY

Joseph Barnes and F. V. Field, *Behind the Far Eastern Conflict* (New York: 1933). *The British Year Book of International Law, 1933* (Oxford: n.d.), "The Stimson Doctrine of Non-Recognition," by A. D. McNair. Edward Bing-Shuey Lee, *Two Years of the Japan-China Undeclared War* (Shanghai: 1933). Thomas Baty, "A Daniel Come to Judgment," in *Contemporary Japan*, Dec. 1933. R. L. Buell, "American Policy Toward the Sino-Japanese Dispute," in Foreign Policy Association *Reports*, Feb. 1, 1933. T. A. Bisson, "Japan and Manchoukuo," in Foreign Policy Association *Reports*, June 22, 1932. T. A. Bisson, "The United States in the Pacific: A Survey of the Relations of the United States with Pacific Countries from September 1, 1931, to September 1, 1932," in *Pacific Affairs*, Dec. 1932. Paul H. Clyde, "Manchuria and American Opinion," in *Contemporary Japan*, Sept. 1933. Vera M. Dean, "The Soviet Union and Japan in the Far East," in Foreign Policy Association *Reports*, Aug. 17, 1932. Ben Dorfman, "The Manchurian Incident," in *Harpers Magazine*, Sept. 1934. F. R. Eldridge, *Dangerous Thoughts on the Orient* (New York: 1933). Ippei Fukuda, "A Revaluation of Count Uchida," in *Contemporary Japan*, Sept. 1932. O. M. Green, "China and the Feetham Report," in *Nineteenth Century and After*, Aug. 1931. S. L. Gulick, *Toward Understanding Japan* (New York: 1935); the author, having long been a resident of Japan, has a sympathetic understanding of the Japanese character. Shuhsi Hsu, "Japan's Rights and Position in Manchuria," in *The Chinese Social and Political Science Review*, July, 1932. Shuhsi Hsu, "Manchurian Backgrounds," in *Pacific Affairs*, Feb. 1932. C. C. Hyde and L. B. Wehle, "The Boycott in Foreign Affairs," in *American Journal of International Law*, Jan. 1933. Kikujiro Ishii, *Diplomatic Commentaries*, trans. and ed. by W. R. Langdon (Baltimore: 1936). K. K. Kawakami, *Manchoukuo Child of Conflict* (New York: 1933). Two volumes prepared for the Council on Foreign Relations by Walter Lippmann, *The United States in World Affairs, 1931* (New York: 1932), and *The United States in World Affairs, 1932* (New York: 1933). Owen Lattimore, *Manchuria, Cradle of Conflict* (New York: 1932), one of the most penetrating books on Manchuria. L. A. Lyall, *China* (New York: 1934), ch. 12 on Manchuria; the treatment is superficial. J. B. Moore, "An Appeal to Reason," in *Foreign Affairs*, July, 1933. Chih Meng, *China Speaks* (New York: 1932), a Chinese view of the *Manchurian incident. Manchurian Year Book, 1931* (Tokyo: 1931). C. F. Remer, *A Study of Chinese Boycotts* (Baltimore: 1933). Of the greatest value for their statistical and economic material is the series of five *Report* [s] *on Progress in Manchuria*, published at Dairen by the Research Office of the South Manchuria Railway

Company; they cover the following periods: 1st report, 1907-1928; 2nd report, to 1930; 3rd report, to 1932; 4th report, to 1934; and 5th report, to 1936. Edgar Snow, *Far Eastern Front* (New York: 1933). J. A. B. Scherer, *Japan, Wither?* (Tokyo: 1933). J. Shinobu, *International Law in the Shanghai Conflict* (Tokyo: 1933). Henry L. Stimson, *The Far Eastern Crisis* (New York: 1936). Yasaka Takaki, "World Peace Machinery and the Asia Monroe Doctrine," in *Pacific Affairs,* Nov. 1932. A. J. Toynbee, *Survey of International Affairs, 1931* (Oxford: 1932), pt. 4, ch. 3 on the Manchurian incident. A. J. Toynbee, *Survey of International Affairs, 1932* (Oxford: 1933), pt. 5, chs. 1-2 on Manchuria, and chs. 3-4 on Shanghai. Tatsuji Takeuchi, *War and Diplomacy in the Japanese Empire* (New York: 1936). Henry W. Taft, *Japan and America* (New York: 1932), chs. 9-14 on Manchuria and Shanghai. Kenzo Takayanagi, "On the Legality of the Chinese Boycott," in *Pacific Affairs,* Oct. 1932. Quincy Wright, "The Manchurian Crisis," in *American Political Science Review,* Feb. 1932. H. G. W. Woodhead, "Thoughts on the Manchurian Crisis," in *Contemporary Japan,* June, 1933. W. W. Willoughby, *The Sino-Japanese Controversy and The League of Nations* (Baltimore: 1935), rich in documentary material but of questionable value in matters of interpretation.

Among official publications are:

League of Nations, *Report of the Commission of Enquiry,* (Lytton Report; Geneva: 1932), and the *Supplementary Documents* (Geneva: 1932). China's official case as presented to the League Commission is published in V. K. W. Koo, *Memoranda Presented to the Lytton Commission,* 3 vols. (New York: 1932-1933). Japan's case is printed in two volumes: *The Present Condition of China,* and *Relations of Japan with Manchuria and Mongolia,* rev. ed. (Tokyo: 1932). See also *Documents on International Affairs, 1932,* J. W. Wheeler-Bennett, ed. (London: 1933).

CHAPTER XXXVII

Revolution in Modern Japan

ALTHOUGH the clash of arms that rocked Manchuria and Shanghai in the years 1931 and 1932 was occasioned by prevalent chaos in China, it was likewise a product of revolutionary forces within Japan. The late nineteenth century had witnessed Japan's first modern revolution in the Restoration of 1868, in the abolition of feudalism in 1871, and in the establishment of bureaucratic constitutionalism in 1889. This laid the foundation for the political struggle during the first three decades of the twentieth century between bureaucracy and liberalism (see chapter 32). The conflict was signalized by the rise of political parties and by their struggle to achieve responsible party government. By 1920, the principle of party government was all but established, and by 1925, with the granting of manhood suffrage, Japan appeared to be advancing rapidly toward the goal of democratic liberalism. This political development was a natural product of a profound change in the economic and social structure. This economic and social revolution traced its origins to the rise of a middle class in the late Tokugawa period. It was stimulated by the abolition of feudalism and by the Chino-Japanese Wars, and reached its peak in the wave of industrialization which swept the country during the World War. A nation that had been pre-eminently agricultural was transformed in little more than one quarter of a century to one controlled by industry.

Effects of Industrial Revolution

The effects of this industrial revolution penetrated every phase of the national life. It created a powerful capitalistic and wealthy class which sought to control government through the medium of political parties. It created an industrial proletariat cut adrift from the manners and traditions of rural and essentially feudal life. It brought a new demand for raw materials to feed machines, materials which had to be purchased abroad, and for foreign markets in which to sell the products of a machine age. It broke the ancient unit of society, the family, with its paternalistic control, and for it substituted the individual as employer or employee. It caused the growth of crowded cities. It created a labor movement steeped in the doctrines of socialistic control. It brought great wealth to the few, a bare existence to the laborer, and debt and poverty to the farmer. From the West, it imported new luxuries and a new extravagance that challenged the feudal tradition of Bushido (see pp. 69-70) and, by so doing, threatened the prestige of groups that sought to maintain their power by perpetuation of that tradition. It was accompanied by a remarkable increase in population, by pressure to expand beyond narrow boundaries, and by the doubtful honor of becoming one of the world's so-called great and "troublesome" powers.

Japan's movement toward industrialization followed immediately upon the opening of the country to foreign intercourse and the abolition of feudalism. The first advance was in the field of commerce and foreign trade based upon home industries of the previous feudal regime. The foreign demand for Japanese raw silk gave the first impetus to an industry that was financed by the wholesale dealers of Yokohama. Foreign demand likewise stimulated the production of potteries and a host of miscellaneous artistic works of handicraft for which the Japanese were famous. By the time of the Chino-Japanese War, a wide variety of industries had appeared: iron and steel, shipbuilding, machinery, cotton, wool, ceramics, glassware, and paper. Because of lack of capital and lack of experience, many of these industries received direct guidance and assistance from the government. They were, moreover, able to adopt from the outset the most modern machinery and techniques that the West had to offer, and their progress was stimulated further by the industrial booms of 1895, 1905, and 1914.

Perhaps the most striking of the early Japanese industries was that of shipbuilding. In 1853, when Commodore Perry reached Uraga Bay, Japan had no vessels that could venture beyond the coasting trade. By 1893, the great Nippon Yusen Kaisha was entering successfully the competitive field of ocean transportation. In 1896, Japanese shipyards produced a tonnage of slightly less than 8,000; in 1919, they produced a tonnage of 611,000, and soon after made Japan the third-ranking maritime power. To cite another example, it was at the time of the Chino-Japanese War that the Japanese cotton industry made its first great advance. With the Russo-Japanese War came the development of weaving. Between 1893 and 1913, the value of exports of yarn increased from 1,109,000 yen to 33,605,000 yen, and of cotton cloth from 59,000 yen to 70,997,000 yen.[1] During the World War, England was no longer able to supply her former cotton markets in India and China. Japan sought to meet their needs, and the result was an unprecedented expansion of her industry. The increase in the exports of Japanese cotton manufactures continued to the peak year of 1925, when they were valued at 571,500,000 yen, and by 1933, Japan had surpassed Great Britain as an exporter of cotton textiles.[2] A further example of Japan's modern industrial expansion was provided by the steel industry, which grew with remarkable speed during the World War.

In this rapid march toward industrialization, Japan faced a complex of factors, some favorable, others adverse. She was handicapped by lack of capital and by her limited national wealth. Her natural resources in the form of iron, coal, and

[1] For the rise of Japan's cotton textile industry, see Freda Utley, *Lancashire and the Far East*. George Allen & Unwin, Ltd., London, 1931. Chapters 4-8.

[2] American Council (Institute of Pacific Relations), *Memorandum on the American Cotton Textile Trade with the Far East*, March 23, 1934.

oil were so limited as to make industrialization on a large scale impossible without heavy importations. Her labor, however, was cheap and abundant, the workers being docile, industrious, and willing to work long hours for little pay. Furthermore, as already noted, the most modern machinery and techniques could be installed and applied with no loss occasioned by the scrapping of old plants. But of even greater advantage than these was the "low," or rather the simple, standard of living, which permitted a real wage beyond competition of western states. Again, although the Japanese laborer, so recently released from feudalism, was ambitious and enterprising, he still retained much of the blind patriotism of retainer to overlord, and in the new industrial state this attitude was reflected in loyalty to employer. He was likewise literate and intelligent and thus able to grasp the technique of his task in the machine age with relative ease. In a word, the forces which favored the rise of Japanese industry were human, while those which hampered it were material.[3]

Problems of Population

The process of urban industrialization was, however, only one of the many phases of Japan's economic and social revolution. To it were added problems of population and of agriculture. Population in modern Japan has increased with alarming rapidity. During the seventh and eighth centuries, Japan's population ranged between 5 and 9 millions. During the late Tokugawa period (1750-1867), it remained stationary at about 26 million.[4] By 1872, it had increased to nearly 35 million, by 1889 to 40 million, and by 1909 to 50 million. By 1925, the

---

[3] For a fuller discussion of these forces, see Sobei Mogi and H. Vere Redman, *The Problem of the Far East*. J. B. Lippincott Company, Philadelphia, 1935. Chapter 3.

[4] Japan's population during more than two hundred years of the Tokugawa period varied only slightly. Exclusive of the samurai and their families, who numbered between two and three millions, population in various years of the late Tokugawa period was:

1750	25,900,000	1828	27,200,000
1780	26,000,000	1848	30,000,000

population of Japan proper (exclusive of the colonies) was 59½ million, by which time the annual increase was close to one million. The census of 1930 gave a total for Japan proper

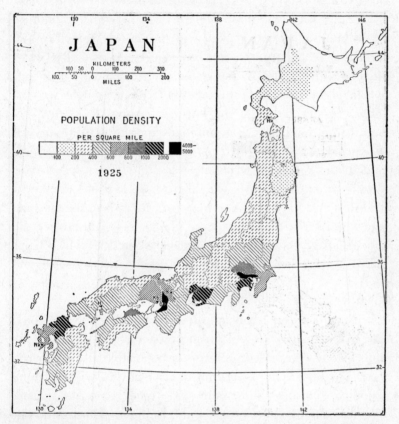

POPULATION DENSITY OF JAPAN BY PREFECTURES, 1925. The largest cities are indicated by initials: O, Osaka; N, Nagoya; T, Tokyo; K, Kyoto; Kb, Kobe; Y, Yokohama; H, Hiroshima; Nk, Nagasaki; Hk, Hakodate. *Courtesy of John E. Orchard and of the "Geographical Review," published by the American Geographical Society of New York.*

of 64½ million. This was increased further to 69 million in 1935.

As late as 1935, despite industrialization, nearly half of Japan's population was employed in agriculture, primarily, of course, in the cultivation of rice, which, with fish, is the nation's staple food. The problem of providing food for a rapidly increasing population was accentuated by geographical factors. The area of Japan proper was only 147,000 square miles, less

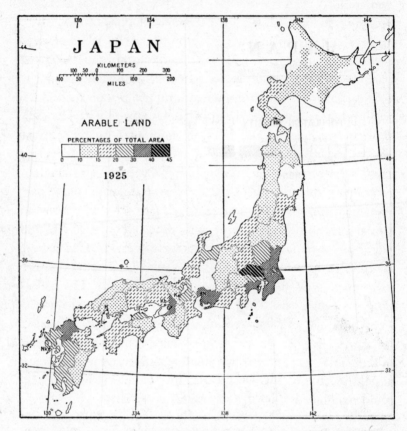

PERCENTAGE OF ARABLE LAND IN RELATION TO TOTAL AREA BY PREFECTURES, 1925. *Courtesy of John E. Orchard and of the "Geographical Review," published by the American Geographical Society of New York.*

than the area of the State of California, and, of this total, only one sixth was arable. In 1932, the average farm holding was about 2½ acres per household. At the same time, 34 per cent of the farm households had holdings averaging less than 1¼ acres, and 69 per cent had less than 2½ acres. Thus, even at the peak of her industrialization, Japan was properly described as "essentially a nation of farmers," with agriculture remaining basic in the national economy. But, a high land tax produced an increasingly heavy burden upon the farmer, while trading and industry were favored at the expense of the agricultural economy. In the main, Japanese farmers belonged to one of three classes: (1) Large landowners employing farm labor or renting land to tenants, (2) average landholders who cultivated part of their land, renting the remainder to tenants, and (3) tenant farmers. After 1900, when industrialization made such rapid progress, tenant holdings increased far more rapidly than those of freeholders, and by 1930 more than 50 per cent of all rice land in Japan proper was worked by tenants.[5] While Japan's industrialists were adopting progressive and modern techniques, the attitude of the farmers and small landowners remained conventional and conservative—a heritage of the feudal age, and the profits of agriculture went largely to the wholesale merchants and speculators on the rice exchange. As in other parts of the world, the farmer was in no position to compete with the power of organized capital. His education was elementary and conservative, and was supplemented by compulsory military training in "blind obedience." Socially, to be sure, the farmer was held in high esteem, another relic of the feudal age, but this was small recompense for an average annual income of 281 yen for a family of four, which at best could maintain life on the subsistence level only.

Problem of Food Production

With her strikingly limited acreage and the rapid increase in population, Japanese agriculture was hard pressed to meet the growing demand for food. Despite the lack of natural fertility in much of the soil, intensive cultivation (of a kind unknown in the West) produced an extraordinarily high yield

---

[5] D. R. Bergsmark, *Economic Geography of Asia.* Prentice-Hall, Inc., New York, 1935. Chapter 20.

of rice, sufficient, in fact, to feed the nation. Yet these results were attained at the price of diminishing returns. By 1930, it was taking more labor and more fertilizer to produce a bushel of rice in Japan than it took twenty years earlier. While some farmers remained prosperous, the majority were working under diminishing returns.[6] Naturally, this fact occasioned serious concern to successive Japanese governments, for it was estimated that within the next generation Japan's population would increase by more than 20 millions. The question was obvious. If a population of 60 millions had forced Japanese agriculture into the sphere of diminishing returns, how would the nation survive when population reached 90 million? Since the area of arable land could not be increased, and since rice cultivation was already proving too costly, it appeared that the nation would be forced, as the only alternative to limitation of families, to adopt a changed diet involving greater imports of wheat, a reduction in the amount of rice grown at home, and a reduction in the number of farmers. This conclusion raised the question, "How would Japan pay for her increasing importations of food?"[7]

Industrialization, advancing through the first decades of the twentieth century, appeared to be the answer to this question. Between 1914 and 1918, when Japan waxed rich on war profits, the soundness of the answer was not questioned. But in subsequent years, its efficacy was challenged. It was soon apparent that industrialization could be built and maintained only against the greatest difficulties. Foreign markets for her manufactured goods were difficult to find. In the relative sense, foreign trade shrank in the post-war years. Countries that formerly imported on a large scale set up their own industries. Furthermore, Japanese industry was in danger of increasing production costs. The nation could not rely on her

---

[6] W. R. Crocker, *The Japanese Population Problem*. George Allen & Unwin, Ltd., London, 1931. p. 67.

[7] See *ibid.*, chapter 6, for a discussion of industrialization as a solution of Japan's problem.

own industrial resources. Her iron ore was scarce; her coal
was expensive and of poor quality. Her dependence on the
mineral wealth of China exposed her industry to political factors—the instability of the Chinese state and the rise of Chinese

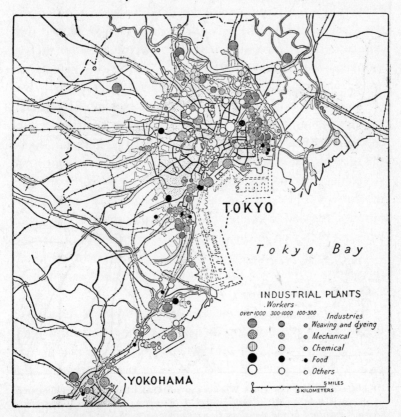

INDUSTRIAL PLANTS AND THEIR WORKERS IN THE TOKYO BAY CITIES. Built-up areas
are shown in light stipple. *Courtesy of G. T. Trewartha and of the "Geographical
Review," published by the American Geographical Society of New York.*

nationalism. Furthermore, in the decade following the World
War, nearly 50 per cent of Japan's exports consisted of silk,
while 25 per cent consisted of cotton, and of these two, making
up the bulk of the trade, two countries, the United States and
China, consumed 65 per cent of this export total. Here was a
vital weakness in Japan's industrial scheme: "A dependence on

two commodities and on two countries."[8] These various considerations made industrialization difficult but not hopeless.

INDUSTRIAL PLANTS AND THEIR WORKERS IN THE OSAKA BAY CITIES. Built-up areas are shown in light stipple. *Courtesy of G. T. Trewartha and of the "Geographical Review," published by the American Geographical Society of New York.*

Relief from Emigration

As a supplementary solution of her problem of food and population appeared the possibility of emigration. The idea was indeed sound, for Japan, with her dense population, possessed a falling birth rate and a rising conception of the standard of living. Here, then, was a possibility of relief, and by

[8] *Ibid.* p. 185.

1930 there were probably one million Japanese living abroad, despite the general tendency to regard the race as a people unwilling to migrate. But the significant facts were that Japan's colonies, such as Korea, were already heavily populated and marked by a low standard of economy, and that migration to countries of the western hemisphere was either prohibited or strictly controlled. In China and Manchuria, Japan's immigrant farmer could nowhere compete successfully with native labor. By 1925, there appeared to be only four areas that might absorb some of Japan's surplus population: (1) Eastern Siberia, (2) Borneo and New Guinea of the East Indies, (3) some of the south Pacific Islands, and (4) some of the states of South America, particularly Brazil. But in each of these areas, there were practical, not to mention increasing political, difficulties to be overcome. As late as 1931, the prediction was made that an outlet for 50,000 Japanese emigrants annually was perhaps essential to save the country from social collapse.[9]

The Farm Riots

The tendencies in agriculture and industry that have been briefly sketched in preceding pages created profound discontent among Japan's farming population and a labor movement among her industrial workers. Tenant disputes occurred with alarming, though quite natural, rapidity; farmers attacked the homes of their landlords; and force was used, when necessary, to impose membership in peasant associations. These outbreaks were disturbing to government, but in the main were productive of little practical improvement in the farmer's lot. His natural conservatism, reinforced by feudal traditions of loyalty and docility, his relative ignorance, and his lack of capacity for organized effort rendered him all but helpless in the struggle to attain economic and social justice. In this re-

[9] *Ibid.* p. 202.

spect, his fellow workers in the cities enjoyed at least a more favorable prospect.

Socialism

Labor and socialistic movements made their appearance in Japan shortly after the abolition of feudalism in 1871. Following the Chino-Japanese War, the Japan Labor Association encouraged workers to organize unions looking to eventual socialistic control. A Social Democratic Party soon followed, which numbered among its members Sen Katayama and Iso Abe. Its program included abolition of armaments, socialization of land and capital, equal distribution of wealth, and equal political rights for all the people. The party was promptly dissolved by government order. In the liberal revival of 1906, following the Russo-Japanese War, the Japanese Socialist Party was formed, but this party, too, suffered the fate of its predecessor, and repressive measures, including prison terms, were provided for participation in socialistic demonstrations. In 1912, a trade-union movement under the guise of a friendly association of workers was begun by Bunji Suzuki. Its membership grew rapidly to 27,000, including intellectuals and liberals as well as wage earners. With the World War came vast profits to Japanese industry, but wages were slow to rise, and with the rice riots of 1918 (see p. 595), demands were made by labor for increased pay. In the labor disputes that followed, 7,800 workers were jailed [10] on the blanket charge of disturbing the peace.

Immediately following the World War, there was renewed activity among Japan's labor and socialistic leaders made possible by the growth of liberal-bourgeoisie democracy. The number of trade unions increased rapidly, and labor leaders were confronted with the alternative programs of slow parliamentary reform and revolutionary reconstruction. Strikes were frequent, particularly in the dockyards, where the work-

[10] Sobei Mogi and H. Vere Redman, *op. cit.* p. 179.

ers demanded the right of collective bargaining. In 1920, the
Japan Federation of Labor was formed from the friendly association of 1912, but this move, far from unifying the workers,
revealed a split between the followers of socialism and the
followers of communism. Despite this, the advance of liberalism was again emphasized in 1923, when the government
permitted the trade unions to nominate workers' delegates to
the International Labor Conference, thus giving to Japanese
labor the opportunity to observe labor conditions and organization in the West. Again, the results did not serve to unify
Japan's workers. Conservatives within the Japan Federation
of Labor sought to confine its efforts to trade unionism. This,
in turn, alienated the left-wing elements, who leaned toward
communism, causing them to form in 1924 the Japanese Labor
Union Council, which was dissolved by the government in
1928. Meanwhile, with the granting of manhood suffrage, an
attempt was made to form a united proletarian party, but this
was likewise dissolved by government order in 1926. The
workers had by 1928 failed to unite effectively for either political action or for collective bargaining. The only exception
to this general rule was the case of the Japanese Seamen's
Union. Lack of funds to sustain long strikes was one cause of
the failure. Aid to Japanese labor was promised by the liberal
Hamaguchi government in 1930, but the trade-union bill that
it introduced was defeated through the combined efforts of the
large employers of labor and the House of Peers. As late as
1933, it was estimated that less than ten per cent of Japan's
industrial workers were organized in any form.[11]

Proletarian Parties

In the realm of politics, as in the sphere of unionism, the
failure of Japanese labor to assert itself effectively was equally
marked. As noted, the Farmer-Labor Party, the first national

---

[11] *Ibid.* p. 189.

proletarian party, organized in 1925 on the occasion of the introduction of manhood suffrage, was suppressed immediately by the government. As a result, the right-wing elements, represented by the Japan Federation of Labor, after expelling the left-wing communists, formed in March, 1926, the Labor-Farmer Party. This party soon became a nest of quarreling in cliques. The question of the readmission of communists led to the secession of the Japan Federation of Labor, together with such right-wing leaders as Iso Abe and Toyohiko Kagawa. These in turn formed the Social Democratic Party, which rejected communism and supported parliamentary reform. Contemporaneously, the left wing of the Federation of Labor and the right wing of the Japan Farmers' Union reorganized the Japan Labor-Farmer Party, which became the real center of communist activity. It was suppressed, as noted, in 1928, by the Tanaka government, when alleged communists were arrested throughout Japan in wholesale fashion. From this time on, shifts and counter shifts among the proletarian groups followed with baffling rapidity.

Prior to the Manchurian incident, Japan, like all large modern states, had failed to solve the problem of the production and distribution of wealth. The confusion that existed in her domestic and foreign policy was a direct product of the struggle of group interests within Japan to share in the national wealth. The tenseness of the domestic struggle was increased by the post-war growth of economic nationalism abroad and the consequent depression on Japan's economic machinery. It will be convenient, then, to summarize these contending forces within Japan as they existed prior to 1931 and as they contributed to Japan's subsequent policy in Manchuria.

Summary of Conditions

First: Japan suffered from a poverty of land and a density of population. There were nearly 450 people to each square mile of land, and nearly 3,000 people to every square mile of arable land, or twice the ratio of population to arable land in China. Mineral resources were likewise scarce. Her iron ore was less than sufficient to supply the blast furnaces of the United States for two years, and much of this was of low quality. Her coal was of better quality and somewhat more plentiful, but it was far from meeting the needs of an industrialized state. Her oil resources were almost nonexistent, the annual production being less than daily production in the United States. Her population was increasing at the rate of more than three fourths of a million per year. Entrance of Japanese immigrants had been prohibited by the United States, while other countries imposed heavy restrictions.

Second: Japan was called upon to choose between maintenance of a low standard of living in a predominantly agricultural society and the introduction of a new economy based on industry. The actual course that the nation pursued was a compromise between the two. Great industries and an efficient merchant marine were indeed built, but the change from an agricultural to an industrial economy was not complete. Nevertheless, it did increase tremendously Japan's dependence on the outside world for food, raw materials, and markets. Furthermore, the change placed enormous power in the hands of a few industrialists and bankers. At the close of the World War, Japan was a creditor nation, but in the succeeding decade she encountered an unfavorable balance, until in 1933 her foreign debt was nearly 1½ billion yen. To meet this situation, government and industrialists sought to increase exports, to decrease imports, and to extend national boundaries. The method used was the fostering of a nationally controlled economy to eliminate waste and to minimize, as far as possible, dependence on foreign sources. But since Japan did not produce cotton, wool, oil, iron, and coal in sufficient quantities to feed her growing machines, foreign dependence continued. When the United States raised its tariff walls still higher in

1930, Japan increased her tariffs. When the Chinese instituted their greatest Japanese boycott, in 1931 and 1932, Japan attacked Shanghai.[12]

Third: Of no less significance, too, was the fact that Japan's new industrial machinery was owned to a remarkable degree by a small group of families, of which the best known were the Mitsui and Mitsubishi. According to an estimate made in 1931, eight families controlled 37.6 per cent of bank deposits, 72.9 per cent of trust properties, and 25.9 per cent of liability reserves of insurance companies. Obviously, with this centralized control of finance, there was no room for the growth of a large middle class. The control of industry slipped more and more into the hands of a few great interests. These, in turn, by their control of the banks, were able to direct the policy of government.

Fourth: By 1930, Japan's non-propertied classes (owning property of less than $500 or having an income of less than $400) composed nearly 85 per cent of the population, yet indirect taxes and excises paid by all consumers contributed 57 per cent of the national budget, while only 43 per cent was met by taxes on income and property.[13] This maldistribution was most striking in the rural communities. In 1930, only 30 per cent of farming families owned all their land, 30 per cent owned no land at all, and 40 per cent owned a portion of their land. The rent paid by tenants was excessive, amounting in some cases to two thirds of their gross income. In 1931, there were 5,000 disputes between tenants and landlords over rents. To aggravate the situation, the tendency was for the farmer to slip further and further into debt. In 1930, farmers' debts were estimated at 4,000,000,000 yen, and this had increased to the staggering estimated sum of 6,000,000,000

---

[12] For a fuller discussion of Japanese conditions as affecting foreign policy, see Joseph Barnes and Frederick V. Field, *Behind the Far Eastern Conflict*. Institute of Pacific Relations, New York, 1933.

[13] *Ibid.* p. 15.

yen in 1936. In a word, by 1930 the problem of the distribution of wealth in Japan remained wholly unsolved.[14]

Fifth: The existence of these cumulative problems was impressed more and more upon the Japanese national mind during the decade that followed the World War by a series of disturbing events, both national and international. The Siberian intervention proved costly. Chinese policy at Versailles and Washington was irritating, and it was disturbing to trade. The Tokyo earthquake of 1923 imposed another burden on the nation. The American immigration law of 1924 was a direct thrust at Japan. The hopeful future predicted for China at the Washington Conference did not appear to be borne out by events, and, as a result, Japan, of all foreign powers, suffered most. The year 1927 witnessed a domestic banking crisis in Japan, followed two years later by the general world economic collapse. Economic nationalism and rising tariffs threatened to exclude Japanese goods from world markets. Many of Japan's factories were closed. Unemployment increased. Prices fell. Discontent which had previously found expression through the feeble trade unions and the schismatic proletarian parties sought a new outlet.

Japanese Fascism

This was the occasion, then, for the rise of what may be called, for want of a better term, Japanese fascism.

Because of purely Japanese conditions and traditions, one of the centers of this discontent was the army. Its young officers were recruited largely from country districts. Trained in a discipline which reveres the Emperor and the interests of his empire above everything else, they provided a fertile field for agitation and propaganda against the capitalist factions and the parties which were considered their political puppets. Corrupt elections, political scandals, government subsidies to powerful industrial interests became

---

[14] This statement of fact does not imply that the problem had been solved in western countries.

the focus of attack. The structure of parliamentary government, not indigenous to Japan, was itself challenged. The movement was inchoate, unofficial, and partly underground, but even before September 18, 1931, it had resorted to one of its most frequent weapons, political assassination.[15]

Fascism has been defined as implying the rule of the disciplined and resolute few over the undisciplined and irresolute many, as something undemocratic and antiparliamentarian, as national rather than international, as tending to dignify the state rather than the individual, or any group of individuals, except, of course, the resolute group in whose hands power is concentrated. [16] These were indeed the ideas which animated various groups in Japan on the eve of the Manchurian incident. Furthermore, there existed in Japan all the conditions necessary for a fascist movement: (1) proletarian support against unrestricted capitalism, (2) military support to carry the program into effect, (3) a general popular dissatisfaction with existing conditions, and (4) a sort of crisis in national affairs to justify fascism's ruthless methods.

The proletarian backing for Japanese fascism took definite shape in the summer of 1931, when Katsumaro Akamatsu, chief secretary of the Social Democratic Party, representing the extreme right of the proletarian movement, announced that he would henceforth adhere to national socialism, defined as anticapitalistic, antiparliamentarian, and national. He drew with him a large following both from the Social Democrats and from the Farmer-Labor Party, which was distinctly more radical, and in 1932 he formed the Nationalist Socialist Party. It was fairly easy for Social Democrats to accept belief in the new faith. They had no strong international obligations; they feared communism, and they had failed to gain their objectives through parliamentary action. This last was very effective in turning democratic proletarians into undemocratic

---

[15] Joseph Barnes and Frederick V. Field, *op. cit.* p. 16.

[16] Sakuzo Yoshino, "Fascism in Japan." *Contemporary Japan,* September, 1932. p. 185.

fascists. The proletarian parties had secured representation in the Diet for the first time in 1928, but they received very little popular support in the general election of 1930. Their failure was due partly to themselves.

But the main reason was that the chief political leaders, in consort with financial magnates, had made strenuous efforts to curb the activities of the proletarian parties by all sorts of devious methods, including ingenious application of the laws and recourse to police force.[17]

Thus Social Democrats despaired of gaining their objectives by constitutional means and turned to the short-cut methods promised by national socialism.

The conversion of the left-wing proletarians (including communists) to national socialism was made easier by its promise of direct action. The creed was not what they wanted, but they argued that it was at least better than constitutional reform. They observed likewise a recurring world-wide nationalism, which at the time was affecting the policies even of Soviet Russia. As opportunists, then, they found in national socialism a medium for immediate action.

Support of national socialism by the Japanese army also became pronounced on the eve of the Manchurian incident. In Japan, the army, from the time of the Meiji Restoration, was supposed to hold itself aloof from politics and to devote its energies entirely to the military side of national defense. But like most human ideals, this one was rarely honored. In fact, the Constitution of 1889 thrust the army and navy into politics by giving the Ministers of War and of Marine, always high-ranking officers of the service, direct access to the Throne, a privilege enjoyed by no other member of the Cabinet save the Premier. Even the post of Premier was more frequently occupied than not by an admiral or a general. The life of every cabinet depended on the good will of the army and navy, for, without this, no officer would accept a post in the

17 *Ibid.* p. 189.

government. No government, therefore, was free to pursue a policy that threatened to interfere with the constitutional prerogatives of the two services. The reader has already observed the fate which befell the second Saionji Cabinet, wrecked in 1912 by the army's demand for additional forces in Korea. However, it was true that the army and navy were content with this substance of power; their political influence was not flaunted openly; their objectives were sought quietly by powerful army leaders working behind the political scene. With the growing national discontent after 1925, however, dissatisfaction spread within the army and in particular among the younger officers, who, as noted, were drawn mainly from rural areas where they were well acquainted with the plight of the farmers. High-ranking officers were soon forced to take note of growing discontent among their juniors, and decided in the summer of 1931 to enter publicly the political arena. General Minami, Minister of War in the Wakatsuki Cabinet, addressing the divisional commanders (see p. 683), emphasized the dangers in Manchuria, indicated that Japan might be compelled to use force there, and suggested that the army must put a stop to propaganda derogatory to the military. This speech was, contrary to custom, made public. This was the more noteworthy, since the views expressed in it were supposed to be at variance with those of the civil wing of the government. [18] At the same time, army officers, in addressing reservist organizations throughout the country, demanded political reform and denounced the corruption of capitalists and political parties.

Additional specific reasons explaining the swing of the army toward national socialism and fascism were evident. The negotiation of the London Naval Treaty in 1930 (see p. 601) indicated that the civilian branch of the government was gaining control of national defense. If such a treaty could be accepted despite bitter naval opposition, the army, it was

---

[18] *Ibid.* p. 191.

argued, was due to suffer a similar fate. This seemed to be borne out by the vigorous proposals of Finance Minister Inouye in the Wakatsuki Cabinet to reduce military expenditure. With tension increasing in Manchuria, the army saw its control of national defense slipping into the hands of party politicians.

When, therefore, in September, 1931, Japan's interests in Manchuria were subject to threat, real or imagined, most elements and groups in the nation were already psychologically prepared for vigorous action. For a quarter of a century, Japan had invested in Manchuria not only her wealth but also her sentiment. These interests on foreign soil had become an integral part of the national mind, as essential, so it was thought, as the homeland itself. Viewed through the eyes of a Japan in social and economic crisis, Manchurian interests in 1931 were to be preserved regardless of cost.

Japanese Politics Since 1931

The course of Japanese politics since 1931, as expressed in the failures of responsible party government, the rise and fall of ministries, the recurrence of political assassination, and, finally, the active participation of the army in politics, is at once a dramatic and perplexing narrative. In December, 1931, the Wakatsuki (Minseito) Cabinet was replaced by the Inukai (Seiyukai) Ministry. The assassination of Premier Inukai on May 15, 1932, led to the appointment of Admiral Makoto Saito as head of a super-party national government. In July, 1934, the Saito Cabinet resigned and was replaced by a similar national government under the Premiership of Admiral Okada. This government survived until the disastrous army mutiny of February 26, 1936, when it was succeeded by yet another national government under Premier Hirota. The Hirota Ministry lasted less than a year, resigning on January 23, 1937, and being followed by the government of General Senjuro Hayashi.

But no mere recital of cabinet changes can suggest the fundamental conflict that has been raging within Japan's political life. The character of this conflict cannot be stated in simple terms, but it is possible to suggest some of its more

KOKI HIROTA. Ambassador, Foreign Minister and Prime Minister (March, 1936, to January, 1937). He returned to the Foreign Ministry again in the Cabinet of Prince Konoye in June, 1937.

striking features. Among these should be mentioned: (1) The active participation of the army in politics with the dual objective of (a) promoting some form of national socialism, perhaps fascism, at home, and (b) developing Japanese imperialistic expansion on the Asiatic continent; (2) the struggle of the so-called liberal factions (the capitalists, industrialists, party politicians, and the intellectual liberals) to revive the lost prestige of party and responsible government and the general ideals of a so-called liberal and democratic society. During the past six years, neither of these schools has been able to command a sufficient following to crush the other. The result has been a succession of what might be termed middle-course governments, which have sought to pick their way carefully between political extremes.

The Murder of Premier Inukai

The fall of the Minseito Cabinet in December, 1931, was occasioned by the Manchurian policy of the army and by growing discord within both the Cabinet and the party. The following February, the Seiyukai won an unprecedented majority in the general election. This majority, however, did not signify a real victory for the Seiyukai or for parliamentary government. At best, it indicated little more than a general desire for a new administration to deal with the Manchurian crisis. The political tension of succeeding months culminated in the notorious "May 15th (1932) Case," in which a group of reactionaries, principally young naval officers and military cadets, attempted to force establishment of a military dictatorship by terroristic methods. They succeeded in murdering Premier Inukai at his official residence, but their efforts to destroy with bombs the main offices of the Bank of Japan, the Mitsubishi Bank, the Metropolitan Police Building and the headquarters of the Seiyukai Party proved abortive.

The Saito Cabinet

To quiet the popular unrest, of which this reactionary outburst was but one manifestation, the Emperor called upon Viscount Admiral Makoto Saito, one of the most tried and respected of Japan's administrators, to head a national government. The Saito Cabinet included members of both political parties, of the House of Peers, and representatives of non-party interests. The War Ministry continued to be headed by Japan's most philosophical militarist, Lieutenant-General Sadao Araki, who had occupied the post since the fall of the Wakatsuki Cabinet in December, 1931. Despite the fiery political pronouncements with which Araki startled and annoyed western governments, it was, in the main, his prestige that held the reactionary terrorists in check after the "May 15th Case." For more than two years, the Saito Cabinet maintained a balance, a precarious equilibrium, in the face of growing discontent. To agrarian distress at home were added growing tension with China and Russia, trade disputes with Japan's foreign markets, and uncertainty on the naval setup in the Pacific. These, combined with financial scandal within the administration, forced the Ministry's resignation in July, 1934.

The Okada Cabinet

Although the Saito Cabinet was not a party ministry, both the Seiyukai and the Minseito were pledged to support it. This pledge, however, the former on occasion disregarded. When the Cabinet finally resigned (July 3, 1934), Prince Saionji, the surviving Genro, recommended Admiral Keisuke Okada to the Emperor. To the public, this choice came as a complete surprise. Like the choice of Admiral Saito two years earlier, it was designed to meet the naval conversations that were approaching and to check the reactionary tendencies of the national socialists and so-called fascists. But Okada lacked the prestige of Saito, and, partly because of this and partly because of political inexperience, he failed to get a pledge of support from the Seiyukai. The Cabinet's position was thus weakened from the outset, despite the continuance in office of three ministers who had served under Admiral Saito: Koki Hirota as Foreign Minister, General Senjuro

Hayashi as Minister of War, and Admiral Mineo Osumi as Minister of the Navy. The political parties were offended further when Admiral Okada gave the remaining key ministerial posts of Home Minister and Finance Minister, respectively, to Fumio Goto and Masanobu Fujii, both non-party men. Faced with a hostile Seiyukai majority in the House of Representatives and a somewhat skeptical attitude on the part of the public, the Okada Cabinet was constantly on the defensive.

The Liberal Revival

In the Diet, Premier Okada's major support, therefore, came from the minority party, the Minseito, whose political tenets were alleged to be somewhat more liberal than those of the Seiyukai. The general election of February 20, 1936, altered the composition of the Diet materially. The Minseito was returned with a majority. Still more noteworthy was the increased vote cast for the proletarian parties, whose candidates in some of the large cities, such as Tokyo, were supported by the intellectuals and salaried groups. The Shakai Taishuto (Social Democratic Party) candidates received more than half a million votes. In contrast, most of the various reactionary right-wing candidates were defeated. As far as the results of this important election may be judged at close range, they indicated a reviving faith in liberal representative government. It is also to be noted that they were probably the cleanest elections ever held under the Constitution.

The February Assassinations

Within one week of this apparent liberal victory, Tokyo was the scene of an appalling political crime. Early on the morning of February 26, amid darkness and falling snow, a group of conspiring army officers led some 1,400 troops from their barracks to the heart of the capital. Designated officers appeared at the homes of five of the nation's most able and respected statesmen. In the dawning light, they murdered Admiral Viscount Makoto Saito, Lord Keeper of the Privy Seal, who in his long career had served the nation with honor and distinction; Korekiyo Takahashi, Minister of Finance, whose genial personality, political integrity, and fearlessness had won international recognition; and General Jotaro Watanabe, Inspector General of Military Education. The assassins intended to dispatch Premier Okada also, but by mistake killed Colonel Denzo Matsuo, his brother-in-law. Admiral Kantaro Suzuki, Grand Chamberlain of the Imperial Household, escaped with serious wounds. For three and one-half days, the rebel troops occupied many of the official buildings of the capital, crowning their treason by disregarding a direct command from the Emperor to surrender. When the enlisted men finally did yield, their officers were seized and imprisoned, and many of them were later condemned to death.

The February rebellion was the most serious upheaval in the history of twentieth-century Japan. The rebel leaders, their minds warped by a philosophy of super-patriotism, regarded their methods as Japan's only salvation from what they called the greed and corruption of capitalists and politicians. Their solution was to remove by force those statesmen who symbolized the liberal regime. The nation as a whole remained calm in the face of this national crisis. It was stunned by the army's failure to maintain discipline among its young officers, a failure which many attributed to its political ambitions and its alleged desire to found a military fascist state.

The Hirota Cabinet

The Okada Cabinet, which promptly resigned, was succeeded by a ministry headed by Koki Hirota, who had been Foreign Minister in the previous administration. Hirota was able to form his government (March 9) only after prolonged conversations with the military. Acceptance by General Juichi Terauchi of the post of War Minister was understood

GENERAL SENJURO HAYASHI. Minister of War in two of Japan's cabinets, he became Prime Minister in February, 1937. A moderate militarist himself, his problem was to reconcile the army and the parliamentarians. Political sentiment was solidly against him in the May, 1937, election and his ministry resigned.

to be on the understanding that the government would proceed to "renovate" and "reform" the administration. Although the army's program was not too clearly defined, it leaned heavily toward national socialism. Like its two predecessors, the Hirota government was a compromise. It failed to please the army pro-fascist groups, on the one hand, and the political parties and parliamentarians, on the other. The Premier adopted a moderate course designed to improve Japan's relations with both China and Russia. When, however, the Diet met in January, 1937, the latent conflict between army and civilian political forces broke out in a bitter attack by members of the House on War Minister Terauchi and the policies of the military. Lacking any effective reply to these charges, the army resorted to its customary tactics of demanding dissolution of the Diet. Premier Hirota refused to stoop to this level and, instead, resigned with his Cabinet on January 23. The Emperor then called upon General Kazushige Ugaki, recently retired Governor General of Korea, to form a cabinet. General Terauchi, however, announced that the army would not co-operate with Ugaki, which meant that no officer would accept the post of war minister under him.[19] The Emperor accordingly called upon General Senjuro Hayashi, who had been Minister of War in two recent cabinets, to form a government. When this new government took office, during the first week of February, it was predicted that its life would be a short one. Its personnel, with the exception of Toyotaro Yuki, Minister of Finance, commanded less popular confidence than did that of its predecessor, the Hirota Ministry. The best that could be said of the new government by contemporaries was that the Premier was moderate among military men and without political experience. Public criticism of Hayashi was so strong in the general election of the early summer of 1937 that he resigned. He was succeeded as Premier by Prince Fumimaro Konoye.

---

[19] The army's refusal to co-operate with General Ugaki in forming a cabinet was interpreted as a serious infringement of the imperial prerogative which the army is sworn to defend. It has, in fact, become increasingly difficult, if not impossible, for the army to justify on constitutional grounds its political action in recent years. The army's opposition to Ugaki was based largely on personal and political feuds within the army itself. Cf. article by Hugh Byas in The New York Times, January 31, 1937.

SELECTED BIBLIOGRAPHY

A General Survey of Education in Japan (Tokyo: 1933). M. Anesaki, *Art Life and Nature in Japan* (Boston: 1933). M. Anesaki, *Religious and Social Problems of the Orient* (Boston: 1923). William Axling, *Kagawa* (London: 1932). G. C. Allen, *Modern Japan and Its Problems* (New York: 1927). T. A. Bisson, "The Rise of Fascism in Japan" in Foreign Policy Association *Reports,* Oct. 26, 1932. T. A. Bisson, "Japan's Trade Expansion" in Foreign Policy Association *Reports,* Oct. 10, 1934. A series of articles by Tsunego Baba in *Contemporary Japan:* "Trade Unions and the Labour Movement," June, 1932; "Making Parliament Popular," Mar. 1933; "Our Liberals Look Ahead," Sept. 1933; "Towards Parliamentary Revival," June, 1934; "Our Parliamentarism and World Politics," Mar. 1935; "The Political Outlook," Mar. 1936. J. E. De Becker, *Principles and Practice of the Civil Code of Japan* (Yokohama: 1921). J. I. Bryan, *Japanese All* (London: 1928). J. I. Bryan, *Civilization of Japan* (New York: 1928). George H. Blakeslee, "The Japanese Monroe Doctrine" in *Foreign Affairs,* July, 1933. Edward C. Carter, "American Foreign Policy and the Peasant and Soldier in Japan" in *Annals of the American Academy of Political and Social Science,* July, 1933. J. B. Condliffe, "Industrial Development in the Far East" in *The Chinese Social and Political Science Review,* July, 1928. Kenneth W. Colegrove, *Militarism in Japan* (Boston: 1936). F. R. Eldridge, "Japan's Drive For World Trade" in *Current History,* Aug. 1934. *Financial and Economic Annual of Japan* (Tokyo). Ippei Fukuda, *New Sketches of Men and Life* (Tokyo: 1934); see sketches of Koki Hirota, Senjuro Hayashi, Baron Seinosuke Go, and Ruyuhei Murayama. Ippei Fukuda, "Korekiyo Takahashi—Japan's Sage of Finance" in *Contemporary Japan,* Mar. 1933. Ippei Fukuda, "Araki—The Man of the Crisis" in *Contemporary Japan,* Dec. 1932. F. V. Field, *Economic Handbook of the Pacific Area* (New York: 1934). G. E. Hubbard, *Eastern Industrialization and Its Effect on the West* (London: 1935). W. L. Holland, ed., *Commodity Control in the Pacific Area* (Stanford University: 1935). Ushisaburo Kobayashi, *Basic Industries and Social History of Japan.* Shigeharu Matsumoto, "Party Battles in Japan" in *Pacific Affairs,* Apr. 1932. J. E. Orchard, *Japan's Economic Position* (New York: 1930). H. Vere Redman, "Sen Katayama" in *Contemporary Japan,* Mar. 1934. M. D. Kennedy, *The Changing Fabric of Japan* (London: 1930). K.

K. Kawakami, "Japan's Political Murderers" in *International Conciliation,* Apr. 1936. Emil Lederer, "Fascist Tendencies in Japan" in *Pacific Affairs,* Dec. 1934. H. G. Moulton, *Japan: An Economic and Financial Appraisal* (Washington: 1931). Inazo Nitobe, *Japan* (London: 1931). Inazo Nitobe, *Japanese Traits and Foreign Influences* (London: 1927). J. A. B. Scherer, *Japan's Advance* (Tokyo: 1934). O. Tanin and E. Yohan, *Militarism and Fascism in Japan* (New York: 1935). S. Uyehara, *The Industry and Trade of Japan* (London: 1926). Freda Utley, *Lancashire and the Far East* (London: 1931). H. E. Wildes, *Social Currents in Japan* (Chicago: 1927). A second volume by the same author, *Japan in Crisis* (New York: 1934), is of much less value.

CHAPTER XXXVIII

Naval Politics in the Pacific

THE subject of naval armaments is merely one aspect, though a major one, of the larger subject of international politics. Until the time of the World War, the Pacific Ocean claimed only secondary consideration in the planning of naval strategists. This was not surprising, since the North Atlantic and the Mediterranean were still the centers of the world's greatest naval strength. But a material change in this setup was occasioned by the War. Both the United States and Japan emerged as great naval powers. The consequences were far-reaching. Great Britain's command of the seas was no longer a reality. The ability of the United States to control the eastern Pacific and to exert greater influence in the western Pacific could no longer be overlooked. In the Far East, Japan, too, had "profited" by the War. The resulting increase in her military and naval power placed her in a position to challenge the interests in China and the western Pacific that had been created by European and American imperialism, and possibly to take them over for herself. If, indeed, the World War was negative in that it failed to settle Europe's difficulties, it was at least positive in creating new difficulties in the Pacific and the Far East.

The Washington Conference

The Washington Conference of 1921 and 1922 (see chapter 30), called to consider the question of armament limitation and political problems of the Far East, was expected to solve the difficulties of this new alignment of powers in the Pacific.

Unhappily, the Washington Conference, like the Versailles Conference, was not unaffected by the principle that the solution of one problem is the creation of another. The solution of the naval question which was proposed by the United States and finally adopted by the Conference powers at Washington involved acceptance of a capital-ship ratio. This ratio, in turn, was based in main on the then-existing naval strength of the powers in capital ships. From this emerged the capital-ship tonnage ratio of 5-5-3 for Great Britain, the United States, and Japan, respectively. The United States also proposed that this ratio of capital-ship tonnage should be extended to measure total naval strength, that is, that proportionate allotments of auxiliary craft be made to each power. Fundamentally, the American ratio proposal rested on nothing more substantial than an attempt to perpetuate naval strength as it then existed among the great powers. The proposal was most advantageous to the United States. By its adoption in the matter of capital ships, the United States won parity with the British navy, achieved a 5 to 3 superiority over Japan, and relegated the capital-ship tonnage of France and Italy to the figure 1.67 in the above ratio. On grounds of logic and policy, the American proposal was attacked by both France and Japan. The latter insisted on a ratio of 10-10-7, and accepted 5-5-3 reluctantly and only in view of the agreement to maintain the *status quo* in certain fortifications in the Pacific. Submarines and auxiliary craft were not limited. On the positive side, the Conference could claim a ten-year naval holiday in capital-ship construction for the three great naval powers. On the negative side was the obvious weakness of a ratio system based on existing tonnage.

The conference at Washington in 1921, like the Paris Peace Conference, did not attempt to uproot the matted growths of tradition, established ideas and vested interests which were forcing the world to a new outburst of navalism. Instead, it sought only to imprison them within the fragile limits of the *status quo*.[1]

The Rome Conference

In 1924, a second naval conference assembled at Rome. The League of Nations desired to extend the principles established by the Washington Naval Treaties to other powers, both members and non-members of the League. The United States refused to attend this conference, but Great Britain, Japan, and Soviet Russia did participate. Russia demanded a capital-ship tonnage of 400,000, greater than that possessed by Japan and second only to that of Great Britain and the United States. She likewise demanded demilitarization of the Korean Straits. These demands were sufficient to wreck the conference. Its collapse was not caused by the Russian demands alone, but rather by the fact that most of the participating powers were not prepared to accept existing naval strength as the basis for limitation. The argument advanced by many of the powers was this:

Supposing that the Washington Conference, instead of taking place in 1921-1922 had been held in 1881, the year in which the United States fleet reached the lowest tonnage recorded in its history, the application of the criterion referred to, based on the *status quo*, would have resulted in the ratio figure of the Chilean fleet being higher than that of the United States fleet. Why, then, should Chile, at the Rome Conference, have been expected to accept existing naval forces as the standard of measurement of future naval armaments? [2]

The Preparatory Commission

During 1925, the League of Nations, which had been wrestling with the joint problems of security and disarmament,

---

[1] Walter Millis, *The Future of Sea Power in the Pacific*. World Peace Foundation, New York and Boston, 1935. p. 21.

[2] Giovanni Engely, *The Politics of Naval Disarmament*, trans. by H. V. Rhodes. Williams & Norgate, Ltd., London, 1932. p. 13.

decided to pave the way for a disarmament conference by setting up a preparatory commission to study technical questions involved in arms limitation and reduction. On the subject of naval armament, the principal task of the commission was to find an acceptable standard for measuring fleet strength. Here, two principal schools of thought developed, the one proposing to measure fleet strength in terms of total or global tonnage, the other in terms of tonnage in different categories of ships.

The Geneva Conference

While the Preparatory Commission was engaged in technical studies, the United States invited the British, the French, the Italians, and the Japanese to agree to further naval limitation, supplementary to the Washington agreements and covering auxiliary craft. It appeared that the object of this move was to avoid a naval race in auxiliary-craft construction, which had not been covered by the Washington Treaty. Specifically, the United States proposed to extend the 5-5-3 ratio to auxiliary craft in the case of herself, Great Britain, and Japan, and to discuss what allotments should be made to France and Italy. France and Italy declined the invitation, but Japan and Great Britain accepted. The conference opened at Geneva in June, 1927. Whereas at Washington, in 1921, Great Britain and the United States were in the main aligned against Japan, at Geneva the Anglo-Saxon powers were in opposition. At Washington, the British had agreed in principle to parity with the United States. At Geneva, the Americans interpreted this as an exact mathematical parity to be extended to all categories of ships. In addition, the United States maintained that cruisers constituted a single class, while the British said they should be divided into two classes: light and heavy cruisers. The British, aware of the fact that the

United States contemplated the building of several of the heavier cruisers, were willing to extend the 5-5-3 ratio only to this type of vessel. For these and other causes, the conference could reach no agreement. Perhaps the major obstacle was the unwillingness of the Conservative Party to accept exact tonnage equality with the American fleet. The argument was expressed by Winston Churchill in August, 1927, when he said:

> We hold . . . that the principle of naval equality must be based, not on mere numbers or tonnage, but must take into consideration the quite different conditions of the two communities. We feel that our island Empire is dependent for its inherent and integral existence, and, indeed, for its daily bread, upon our power to keep open the paths across the ocean.[3]

The failure of the Geneva Conference and the announcement of Great Britain that seventy cruisers were essential to maintain her security would have precipitated an Anglo-American naval race had it not been for the tactful policy of the Cabinet in cutting by 66 per cent its cruiser-building program during the following year. Thus, although there was no agreement between the United States and Great Britain as to the meaning of "parity," it became the settled policy of the latter to avoid naval competition with the United States. To this end, the British naval program for 1928-1929 was reduced considerably. Meanwhile, in 1928, the Pact of Paris had been signed, and President Hoover indicated that the time had arrived to translate its idealism into practical naval agreements. He indicated that the United States proposed to retain the ratio principle, but, in applying it to auxiliary craft, existing strength was not to form the basis, as it had at Washington. The obvious reason for this change in American policy was that the United States was far weaker than Great

---

[3] *Ibid.* p. 41.

Britain in existing cruiser strength. The proposal was unpopular with the British, but, since they were in no position financially to risk a naval race with Washington, the United States could afford to insist on its view. From the practical standpoint of capacity to build, the United States was in a position to enforce a mathematical parity. The principle was indeed accepted in main by Ramsay MacDonald and the Labor Cabinet in 1929. There followed a part suspension of the building programs of the two powers in the autumn of that year.

The naval policies of Great Britain, the United States, and Japan were clarified somewhat toward the close of 1929. The British favored reduction in the size of capital ships and of gun caliber and an increase in the replacement age of vessels. Their cruiser demands were reduced to fifty, of which fifteen were to be 10,000-ton vessels. In contrast, the United States was opposed to reducing the displacement of capital ships and wanted twenty-one 10,000-ton cruisers. In all, British cruiser strength was provisionally fixed at 339,000 tons, as against 315,000 for the United States. Each power was prepared to accept less than 200,000 tons in destroyers, and both were prepared to abolish submarines if other powers would do the same. The Japanese, though willing in principle to reduce the size of capital ships, clung to the submarine and demanded a ratio of 10-10-7 for cruisers. And so with Great Britain and the United States at least closer to an understanding than they had previously been, London invited the powers, including France and Italy, to a naval conference to meet in January, 1930. Despite official denials, there was a general impression that the United States and Great Britain would present something approaching a united front at the Conference—an impression not favorably received by the other large naval powers. The primary purpose of the Conference was to deal with those categories of ships not limited by the Washington Treaties.

The London Conference

The London Naval Conference opened in an atmosphere of crisis. This was occasioned by Franco-Italian naval rivalry, the evident desire of France to construct a large navy, and the inability of the British to abide by their pre-conference understandings with the Americans if France and Italy materially increased their fleets. In fact, the London Naval Treaty was made possible only by introduction of the "escalator" clause, which would permit Great Britain increased naval strength if France and Italy should embark on a program of naval expansion. Japan's demands presented another difficulty for the Conference. The Japanese had never been thoroughly satisfied with the 5-5-3 capital-ship ratio established at Washington, and they went to the London Conference determined to secure a 10-10-7 ratio covering all auxiliary combat ships. To this demand, the United States and the British Dominions would not agree. Compromise provided the way out of this dilemma, for, though the Japanese accepted a 10-6 ratio for large cruisers, they received a higher ratio in lighter auxiliary craft and parity in submarines.

Of first importance in the positive accomplishments of the London Treaty was the clause which extended for five years (1931 to 1936) the naval holiday in capital-ship construction. This meant that the five powers agreed to postpone the construction of thirty-two capital ships in all, each one of which would have cost at least $40,000,000. It meant, further, that by 1936 the effective capital-ship strength would have been so reduced by age as to challenge the very existence of this type of ship in future navies. The London Treaty also provided for the scrapping of three British capital ships, three American, and one Japanese. After the Treaty, therefore, the United States and Great Britain retained fifteen capital ships each, and Japan retained nine. The Treaty thus gave the United States its mathematical parity with Britain in capital ships. It defined more specifically aircraft carriers, which had been limited by the Washington Conference, and stipulated the caliber of guns they might carry. It provided also, under certain restrictions, for the installation of aircraft landing and flight platforms on capital ships and cruisers.

The limitations on cruiser strength embodied in the Treaty applied to Great Britain, the United States, and Japan only. Here the problem of reaching agreement was difficult, because the Americans wanted large cruisers with heavier guns; the British wanted smaller cruisers with lighter guns; and the Japanese wanted, as noted, a larger cruiser ratio than the capital-ship ratio they had been granted at Washington. The final limits granted to each power by the Treaty were these:

Cruiser Sub-Categories	United States	Great Britain	Japan
Cruisers with guns of more than 6.1 inches	180,000	146,000	108,400
Cruisers with guns of 6.1 inches or less	143,500	192,200	100,450
Total	323,500	338,200	208,850

This gave the Japanese a 10-6 ratio in heavy cruisers, which was less than they had demanded, but a higher ratio in light cruisers. In destroyers, the three powers accepted a tonnage ratio of 10-10-7.03. On the question of submarines, though the British policy of complete abolition was not favored, somewhat stricter rules were laid down to cover the use of these vessels. Each of the three powers reduced its submarine tonnage to 52,700. [4]

The London Treaty, however, produced a vital change in Japan's naval program, a change of vital import in later naval developments. The Japanese press had welcomed the invitation to the Conference, and the government had announced its policy to be: (1) a navy menacing no other power, (2) a general reduction of armaments, and (3) acceptance of an

---

[4] See B. H. Williams, *The United States and Disarmament.* Whittlesey House, New York, 1931. Chapter 12.

inferior ratio, provided that it gave Japan adequate defense in any contingency. For its chief delegate to the Conference, Premier Hamaguchi and Foreign Minister Shidehara selected former Prime Minister Reijiro Wakatsuki, of the Minseito Party. Specific instructions to the Japanese delegation included: (1) a 70 per cent ratio relative to the United States in 10,000-ton (8-inch gun) cruisers; (2) a 70 per cent gross tonnage ratio relative to the United States for all auxiliary craft; and (3) opposition to radical reduction or abolition of submarines. The personnel of Japan's delegation, which included the Minister of the Navy, Admiral Takarabe, had a distinct bearing on Japan's later naval policy. Takarabe was a son-in-law of Admiral Count Gombei Yamamoto, who had twice been Premier, and who was still regarded as the ultimate power in the Satsuma naval clique. However, this leadership was no longer unchallenged in naval circles, which affected materially the position of Admiral Takarabe.

When the Conference opened, the Japanese government, acting on the advice of the navy, declined the American proposal for a 10-6 ratio in heavy cruisers. Later, a compromise was reached between the Japanese Ambassador, Matsudaira, in London, and Senator Reed, of the United States (see p. 601). This compromise was opposed by the naval members of the Japanese delegation, but the dispatch reporting it to Tokyo was signed by Admiral Takarabe, since, had he failed to attach his seal, he would have been responsible for the breakup of the Conference. In Japan, a sharp division arose between the Foreign Office, which was inclined to favor the compromise rather than wreck the Conference, and the Naval General Staff, which was irrevocably opposed to concession on any of the three fundamental demands. Responsibility for making a decision thus fell to Premier Hamaguchi. In deciding in favor of the compromise plan, Hamaguchi explained to naval leaders in Tokyo that his action was taken in an effort to save the Conference, to promote international

peace, and to guarantee Japan's future by reserving full freedom of action after 1936. Japan's acceptance of the Reed-
Matsudaira compromise was thus given in the face of the

ADMIRAL KANJI KATO. The most vigorous member of the Japanese Naval Staff.
He was uncompromising in his demands for naval parity with Great Britain and the
United States.

hostile opposition of Admiral Kanji Kato, Chief of the Naval
Staff, and his many supporters. In London, the Japanese
delegation made clear the fact that acceptance was in no
way to prejudice Japan's complete freedom to reassert her
position in 1936.

What, then, were the effects in Japan of this diplomatic victory won by the civilian Foreign Office over the Naval Staff? During the negotiations in London, the Japanese public had been "educated" by naval leaders to a belief in the essential soundness of the original demands. There was no countervailing propaganda from peace societies. When the Treaty, with the compromise plan, was accepted, the press in general received it with approval. Baron Shidehara defended the Treaty with eloquence in the Diet. He denied that it had been forced upon Japan by other powers. The Seiyukai (minority) Party, conservative members of the House of Peers, military and naval leaders, and some members of the Privy Council (to which the Treaty would be submitted for approval) immediately joined hands to attack the Minseito government. Both the content and the method of concluding the Treaty were subjected to bitter criticism. The Seiyukai reminded the government that the Chief of the Naval Staff had asserted publicly that under the Treaty the nation was not properly safeguarded, to which Premier Hamaguchi made the significant reply that it was the government and not the Naval Staff that was responsible to the Diet on the question of security. Here, indeed, was the crux of the issue. The London Naval Treaty was merely incidental to a larger constitutional question. Was the civil government supreme over the naval and military staffs even in the matter of policy affecting national defense? Specifically, it was charged that the government was guilty of exceeding its constitutional powers in signing the Treaty without giving regard to the views of the Naval Staff. This the government denied, saying that the views of the naval authorities had been given consideration. In the Upper House, critics of the government argued that matters of national defense could be decided properly only by the staffs of the military services. The Premier replied that the question was one of concluding a treaty and that this function belonged constitutionally to the Cabinet.

In this view, the government was supported by leading constitutional jurists and the press.

There followed an intense struggle between the government and the naval authorities, resulting in the forced resignation of a number of high naval authorities from the General Staff. Then, before the Privy Council, the Naval Treaty was subjected to searching criticism. The Council finally recommended unconditional ratification—an action which was approved by popular opinion. The Hamaguchi government had won a specific victory. Nevertheless, it had not solved the larger constitutional issue, the conflict between the Cabinet and the supreme command. [5]

The Naval Conversations of 1934

From the foregoing remarks, it must be clear that the evolution of Japanese naval policy had by 1930 an intimate connection with questions that were domestic, political, and constitutional in character. During the London negotiations, the Japanese had indeed suggested the adoption of "naval equality" as a principle among the powers. Nothing came of it at the time. The London agreement had provided for another conference, which was to meet in 1935. Preliminary discussions were commenced by the United States and Great Britain as early as June, 1934. In October, they were resumed, this time with Japan included. The British, reviving their earlier demands for greater cruiser strength, appeared ready to make concessions to their Japanese colleagues. The Japanese proposed that an end be put to all ratios, and that all navies be limited by a common upper total tonnage without regard to the types of ships to be built. They likewise

---

[5] For a full discussion of the constitutional features of the issue, see Tatsuji Takeuchi, *War and Diplomacy in the Japanese Empire*. Doubleday, Doran & Company, New York, 1935. Chapter 25.

proposed the substantial reduction of all tonnage and the abolition of heavy battle craft, which they described as "offensive."

Along with Japan, the United States was favorable to reduction, but she wished any reduction to result in the same relative or ratio strength established by the London Treaty. The United States maintained that relative naval strength could not be altered without affecting the "political" treaties regarding the Far East that had been concluded at Washington. The Japanese replied that they were not dealing with political questions, but with a question that was purely naval. Into this American-Japanese dispute, the British entered as go-betweens. The Japanese had intimated that, if granted parity, they would not build to the full limit. The British, therefore, worked out a suggested compromise to give Japan equality in theory, limited by a definite understanding that would keep her actual strength below that of England and the United States. This the Japanese rejected. From this time onward, British opinion become more favorable to the American case.

The United States had advanced the argument that the existing ratios had already established "equality of security," which was far more desirable and equitable than mere parity. Basically, the argument was sound, though it should be remembered that in view of this, the United States would have difficulty, on grounds of equity, in justifying her previous demands for parity with Great Britain. Replying to the American "equality of security" argument, the Japanese asserted that the ratio did not give this security, since the character of naval warfare had changed. To this they added that Japan was prompted by considerations of prestige. The ratio of 5-5-3 sounded too much, they thought, like the ratio "Rolls-Royce—Rolls-Royce—Ford." In December, 1934, these preliminary conversations were terminated.

The End of the Washington Treaty

On the very day of adjournment of these naval discussions in London (December 19), the Japanese Privy Council in Tokyo decided to notify the powers that Japan's obligations under the Washington Naval Treaty would terminate, with the agreement itself, at the end of 1936. This signified Japan's purpose to insist on a new approach to the whole subject of naval limitation. News of Japan's intention to denounce the Treaty was conveyed to the American State Department on December 29. At the same time, the American Navy Department announced a program of naval maneuvers in the central Pacific. In Japan, it appeared that Washington was resorting to a policy of intimidation. Protests of peace organizations in the United States were of no avail. The American maneuvers were held during 1935, followed by similar exercises on the part of the Japanese fleet.

More significant to Japan than these maneuvers was the new naval policy of the Roosevelt administration, which was designed to build the American navy to the full strength permitted by treaty. This policy was fixed by the Vinson Bill, which became law in March, 1934. During the previous ten years, annual naval expenditure in the United States for all purposes had been in the neighborhood of $330,000,000. The new policy was to require more than $500,000,000 annually, and this policy was well advanced when, in 1934, the preliminary naval talks were conducted in London. The American building program did not dissuade the Japanese from denouncing the Washington Naval Treaty. Furthermore, France and Italy announced their opposition to further limitation by ratio, being joined in this view, in July, 1935, by the British. In its place the British proposed that each naval power should announce its program, stipulating the number and kind of vessels it would build in a given period.[6]

The failure of the three great naval powers to reach an agreement in 1934-1935 resulted in the complete breakdown of the naval treaties concluded since the Washington Conference in 1922. On January 1, 1937, naval limitation in the area of the Pacific Ocean was merely a matter of history. There remained, if not the probability, at least the possibility of renewed naval competition among the powers, and principally between Japan and the United States, for mastery of the Pacific. There was a tendency in Great Britain and the Dominions, and in the United States to hold Japan wholly responsible for the collapse of the whole framework of naval limitation. Japan, to be sure, was responsible, but she shared that responsibility with the other great naval powers.

The Naval Theory

Naval competition, as it had developed in the Pacific area during the twentieth century, was a direct product of the Industrial Revolution and imperialistic expansion. The theory on which it was based found its ablest exponent in the person of Captain Alfred Thayer Mahan, of the American navy, whose theory of sea power in history had been expanded and elaborated by naval propagandists throughout the world. The theory stressed the idea that command of the sea in peace, as well as in war, was essential to a nation's greatness. It was pre-eminently the theory of the imperialist. Prior to the World War, Great Britain was the sole successful exponent of the Mahan idea. From the War, two new champions of the theory emerged: the United States and Japan.

The sudden conversion of the United States to the sea-power theory was never explained on logical grounds. Osten-

---

[6] W. H. Shepardson, *The United States in World Affairs.* Harper & Brothers, New York, 1936. Chapter 10.

sibly, the large navy was to defend the United States from attack in case Germany emerged victorious from the War, but this possibility was given little consideration. Much more important was the fact that the American public mind, not unaffected by war psychology, was receptive to the idea that a big navy was a good thing. The navy men themselves, for obvious reasons, wanted as large a fleet as possible. The wartime program that resulted bore no practical relationship to the European conflict. The destruction of the German navy destroyed the ostensible reason for the building program, but the program itself remained.

During the same war years, Japan had embarked on a building program almost as large as that of the United States. She had been encouraged in this by Great Britain, her ally. The Japanese public probably had no more precise idea as to what would be done with a great navy than did the Americans, except for the rather vague notion that it would ultimately give Japan control of the western Pacific.

Consequently, when the World War ended, three great naval powers were contending for command of the seas. In this circumstance, it was logical that Mahan's theory of sea power should be subjected to searching criticism. The Washington Conference and the others that followed it were attempts, albeit somewhat feeble, to avoid the clash that was inevitable if the Mahan theory were carried to its absurd and logical conclusion by all three powers. The naval conferences failed, not because limitation or reduction was in itself impossible or impractical, but because *general* reduction and limitation was never sought by the powers. On the contrary, each power sought to disarm its potential enemy. Each strove to emerge from the conference room with its own position strengthened and that of its imagined adversary weakened. In a word, the old imperialistic technique was not abandoned. It was preserved at the conference tables and in the "educational" campaigns to which the peoples were subjected.

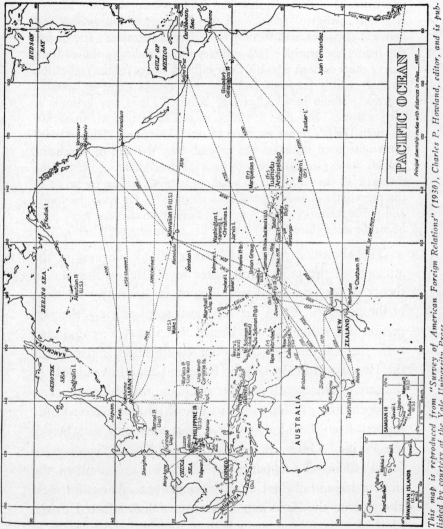

PACIFIC OCEAN

Principal steamship routes with distances in miles. 4500.......

This map is reproduced from "Survey of American Foreign Relations" (1930), Charles P. Howland, editor, and is published by courtesy of the Yale University Press.

A recent Japanese War Office pamphlet, to take a random example, supports its arguments for vast additional military preparation with the observation that "the military strength of the Empire
is a sane, powerful force, with which to crush evil actions and
heretical doctrines, and thereby to declare the Empire's law of justice before the world. This military force radically differs from
that of other nations who use their military forces for the realization
of their selfish purposes and who are always eager to attain a
superior position in all spheres of activity." It is easy to smile at
such naiveté. But does it differ so much, at bottom, from Mr.
Norman Davis's recent assertion of our [American] claim to naval
superiority over Japan on the ground that "the aim to which the
United States is dedicated is to be a good neighbor, respecting the
rights of all the nations both weak and strong and to cooperate in
the promotion of world peace and progress"? Or with the frank,
and public, assumption of American naval men that our navy must
be strong enough to fight Japan in her home waters? [7]

The absurdities that had become all too obvious in the
attempts of the great naval states to realize on the Mahan
theory of sea power renewed interest in alternative solutions
of the problem. From the American point of view, the suggestion was made that the United States navy be constituted
with the sole idea of defending continental United States,
the Hawaiian Islands, and the Panama Canal, surrendering to
the care of others such outposts as Guam, the Philippines, and
the open door in China. This form of solution received little
support from British Dominions and territories that border
the Pacific. Others suggested that the United States grant
Japan's demand for parity, as Great Britain admitted the
similar demand of the United States in 1922. As against these
alternatives, the American naval imperialists adhered to the
ideal of a navy large enough to challenge the supremacy of
Japan in her own waters.

Fewer alternatives confronted Japan's naval men. Their
primary function was to provide a navy that could control

---

[7] Walter Millis, *op. cit.* p. 30.

the western Pacific and thus keep open lines of communication with the Asiatic continent. Their power supported Japan's territorial advance in northeastern Asia and extended the Japanese sphere of commercial interests on the mainland and to islands of southeastern Asia. These functions had, by 1937, strained the nation's resources to a dangerous degree. Faced with the complexities of her policy in China, and threatened by the increasing military power of Russia in Siberia, there appeared to be little chance that Japan would embark on a naval race with the United States.

Perhaps the most regrettable feature of American-Japanese naval relations in the early months of 1937 was the persistence of a condition voiced in the preceding year by one of the ablest exponents of friendship between the two states. "Surprising," he said, "as it may seem to many Americans, Japan entertains a genuine fear of the American Navy." [8] This fear may be explained both by the superior strength of the American navy and by the open secret that it is geared to the Pacific and the Far East, Japan being the potential enemy. Furthermore, the end of the Washington Naval Treaty has, in the view of the American government, brought an end likewise to the agreement to maintain the *status quo* in Pacific fortifications. The Japanese would like to see this agreement prolonged, since it would exclude further American fortifications in Guam, among other places. In October, 1936, the British also suggested that the agreement be maintained. The United States, in contrast, held to the view that the Washington agreements, by their interrelated character, must stand or fall together.

Transpacific Airways

The naval position of the United States in the Pacific was strengthened immeasurably in 1936 by the opening of the transpacific airline operated by Pan American Airways, the

---

[8] K. K. Kawakami in *The Washington Post,* January 19, 1936.

ships of which fly from Oakland to Hawaii, Wake, Midway, Guam, and Manila. Wake Island was placed under the jurisdiction of the Navy Department in December, 1934, and in the following year, the Department granted permits to Pan American Airways to construct landing facilities at Wake, Midway, and Guam. Passenger service over this route began in October, 1936. At the same time, it was announced that Hong Kong would be the terminus of the transpacific line where connections might be made with the Chinese National line. The Japanese, meanwhile, have developed an airline from Japan to the Japanese Mandated Islands. Both lines are commercial. Both can readily be turned to military purposes. Thus, while the United States appears to be withdrawing from the Philippines, her transpacific airlines link her more closely than ever with eastern Asia, and with the potentialities of conflict in an arena that lies more than 4,000 miles across the Pacific.[9]

SELECTED BIBLIOGRAPHY

R. H. Akagi, *Japan's Foreign Relations* (Tokyo: 1936). A series of three articles in *Contemporary Japan* by Seiho Arima: "Security and Naval Limitation," Mar. 1933; "Japan and the Naval Conference," Sept. 1934; and "The London Naval Conversations," Mar. 1935. Admiral Kanji Kato, "Fundamentals of Disarmament" in *Contemporary Japan,* Mar. 1936. H. F. Bain, "Singapore's Control of Key Mineral Resources" in *Foreign Affairs,* July, 1929. Tristan Buesst, "The Naval Base at Singapore" in *Pacific Affairs,* Apr. 1932. Yun-yo Chang, "American Imperialism" in *Pacific Affairs,* Mar. 1930. Great Britain, *Documents of the London Naval Conference, 1930* (London: 1930). Kikujiro Ishii, *Diplomatic Commentaries,* trans. and ed. by W. R. Langdon (Baltimore: 1936). Tatsuo Iwabuchi, "Admiral Kato and the Japanese Navy" in *Contemporary Japan,* Dec. 1934. K. K. Kawakami, "The Unsolved Naval Problems of the Pacific" in *Pacific Affairs,* Oct. 1931. Ippei Fukuda, *New Sketches of Men and Life* (Tokyo: 1934), sketch on "Ad-

---

[9] For a discussion of recent American policy, see T. A. Bisson, "American Policy in the Far East." Foreign Policy Association *Reports,* February 1, 1937.

miral Kanji Kato and Naval Disarmament." Walter Lippmann, *The United States in World Affairs* (New York: 1933), ch. 12 on reduction and limitation of armaments. E. G. Mears, *Maritime Trade of Western United States* (Stanford University: 1935), especially chs. 13, 19, and 20. Walter Millis, *The Future of Sea Power in the Pacific* (New York: 1935). Walter H. Mallory, "Security in the Pacific" in *Foreign Affairs,* Oct. 1934. Vernon Nash, "The Japanese-American War Myth" in *International Conciliation,* Apr. 1936. Kichisaburo Nomura, "Japan's Demand for Naval Equality" in *Foreign Affairs,* Jan. 1935. Gumpei Sekine, "Japan's Naval Claims" in *Contemporary Japan,* Dec. 1933. W. H. Shepardson, *The United States in World Affairs* (New York: 1935), especially chs. 10-12. W. T. Stone, "The London Naval Conference" in Foreign Policy Association *Information Service,* May 28, 1930. Tatsuji Takeuchi, *War and Diplomacy in the Japanese Empire* (Garden City: 1935), ch. 25 on the London Naval Treaty. J. W. Wheeler-Bennett, *Documents on International Affairs, 1930* (London: 1931), documents on the London Naval Conference. By the same compiler, *Documents on International Affairs, 1934* (London: 1935), for Japan's naval relations with the United States, the subject of naval armament, and the denunciation of the Washington Naval Treaty. J. W. Wheeler-Bennett, *The Disarmament Deadlock* (London: 1934). Kisaburo Yokota, "A Security Pact for the Pacific Area" in *Contemporary Japan,* Dec. 1933. Keichi Yamasaki, "The Japanese Press on the London Naval Treaty" in *Pacific Affairs,* July, 1930.

CHAPTER XXXIX
Manchoukuo

THE new State of Manchoukuo made its appearance on the world's political stage on March 1, 1932, in circumstances complex in the extreme. Japan and China were engaged in what could be described only as an undeclared war. The conflict at Shanghai was at its height. The Commission of Enquiry (Lytton Commission), sent to the Far East by the League of Nations, was conducting its investigations. Day-to-day developments in eastern Asia were being watched jealously and apprehensively by every major power possessing interests in China. The situation recalled tense days in 1895, when Russia, France, and Germany, hoping to block any increase in Japanese influence in China, intervened, and forced the return of the Liaotung peninsula in the name of the "peace" of eastern Asia. With the birth of Manchoukuo, the specter of western intervention again appeared, clothed as usual in such phrases as "the preservation of China's integrity" or "the safeguarding of the world's peace machinery." Among those elements in the western world that favored intervention, economic sanctions proved most popular. Yet these were not applied. Though western public opinion had been whipped into a frenzy of denunciation against Japan's policy, it was not prepared to support its allegedly moral pronouncements by more than words. Finally, on the eve of the establishment of Manchoukuo, two significant developments had occurred to tighten the diplomatic tension: (1) The effective fighting strength of the American navy was concentrated in the Pacific; (2) on February 24, 1932, Secretary Stimson, in a letter to Senator Borah, informed the world that if the Nine-Power Treaty respecting China were disregarded, then all the treaty structure of the Washington Conference would, in the opinion of the American government, collapse with it. Despite these gloomy forebodings, the makers of Manchoukuo proceeded with their task.

Origins of Manchoukuo

It is common practice to credit Japan with full responsibility for the appearance of the new state. The future historian will probably offer origins far more complex than this superficial interpretation would imply. In general, it may be said that Manchoukuo was a result of many forces. First, Manchuria, historically speaking, was not a part of China proper. Geographically, it lay beyond the Great Wall. Culturally, it produced a regionalism of its own. While Manchus in China became Chinese, Chinese, when they moved northward, became Manchurian, at least in politics.[1] Western political forms present no parallel to the historic relationship that has existed between Manchuria and China. In the last years of the Manchu rule and throughout the period of the Republic, official China sought by mandate and decree to make Manchuria an integral part of China proper. Officially, indeed, it was so regarded by the foreign powers. In reality, its peculiar regionalism remained. Politically, its fortunes were usually quite distinct from those of China south of the Wall. Nevertheless, this regionalism did not result in the concept of a legal political separation from China. Manchuria was content to remain nominally a part of China as long as her regional cultural heritage was not molested. After 1928, the corrupt rule of Chang Hsueh-liang, coupled with his declared policy of making Manchuria an integral part of nationalist China, tended to increase this spirit of regionalism.

[1] For the development of this subject, see Owen Lattimore, *Manchuria: Cradle of Conflict*. The Macmillan Company, New York, 1932. Chapter 3.

Of itself, this regionalism would not have created an independent Manchuria had it not been for the September incident, the collapse of Chang Hsueh-liang's regime and the necessity of forming some new government to take its place. Accordingly, Chinese and Manchus who were not members of Chang's collapsing regime, or who were hostile to it, organized local independent governments in the three Manchurian provinces of Fengtien, Kirin, and Heilungkiang. In these efforts, they had the active encouragement of Japanese agents, in particular of the Kwantung army. A movement toward uniting these separate provincial governments was well advanced by January 1, 1932, resulting in a proclamation on January 7 favoring an independent Manchurian and Mongolian state. These plans were carried forward rapidly. On March 1, the provisional government of Manchuria, which meanwhile had been formed from the provincial administrations, announced the independence of a new state, Manchoukuo. The former Manchu Emperor of China, Hsuan Tung, known by his personal name, Pu-yi, was inaugurated as Regent on March 9.

The Regency

For two years, Manchoukuo functioned under a sort of provisional constitution, with Pu-Yi acting as Chief Executive. Legally, his powers were extensive, embracing the executive, legislative, and judicial functions. He possessed the power to declare war, to make peace, and to conclude treaties. He was advised in all important matters by a Privy Council. His administrative functions were exercised through a State Council, or Cabinet, presided over by a Prime Minister. The legislative power was exercised with the consent of a Legislative Council; the judicial function was exercised through courts established according to the organic law. A Supervisory Council possessed full and independent authority to audit state accounts. The rights of the people of the new state included many of the usual guarantees found in modern constitutions, such as personal liberty, property rights, the protection of the state irrespective of race or faith, appointment to public office, trial by legally constituted courts, and freedom from unlawful taxation.

Creation of Empire

During 1933, preparations were made for drafting a permanent constitution, it being evident from the first that the government would be monarchical in form. Accordingly, on March 1, 1934, Regent Pu-yi was enthroned as Emperor Kangte, and Manchoukuo became officially Manchoutikuo (Empire of Manchuria). Under the new organic law, with the Manchu Throne restored to its ancestral home, the state is centralized completely in the Throne. The Emperor represents the state, exercises the sovereign rights in accordance with the organic law, issues ordinances for the execution of laws and the maintenance of order, declares war, makes peace, concludes treaties, and commands the military and naval forces. As under the original law, the central administration is in the hands of the State Council, over which presides the Prime Minister, who enjoys extensive powers. All branches of the new government were staffed from the beginning with Japanese advisers, in such capacities as vice-ministers and legal and technical experts. It would appear that much of the development that has taken place since 1932 has been due to the organizing skill and energy of these men.

The principle of centralization of power was carried likewise into the reorganization of the former provinces of Manchuria. The early administration of Manchoukuo covered five provinces: The original Three Eastern Provinces (Fengtien, Kirin, and Heilungkiang), Jehol, and the Mongol territory of Hsingan, in western Manchuria. In 1934, however, the local administrative system was revised completely, making provision for ten provinces, two special municipal districts (Harbin and Hsinking, the capital), a special district in north Manchuria, and four subdivisions of Hsingan province. In 1936, the total population was estimated as slightly less than 33,000,000.

The Japanese leased territory of Kwantung and the South Manchuria Railway zone were not incorporated in the new state. They remained under Japanese jurisdiction. Until the end of 1931, Japanese jurisdiction in Manchuria had been exercised through four services: (1) The Kwantung government in the leased territory, (2) the South Manchuria Railway Company in the railroad zone, (3) consuls in various consular districts, and (4) the Kwantung army or garrison. After 1931, the Japanese army, which was the most aggressive single force in Japan's Manchurian policy, unified these services in the person of Marshal Nobuyoshi Muto, who became commander of the Kwantung army, governor of the leased territory, and Ambassador to Manchoukuo. Later, in 1934, the South Manchuria Railway was placed under the direct supervision of the same official. In Tokyo, unification of control in Manchurian affairs was effected by establishment of the Manchurian Affairs Bureau, its president being the Minister of War. In this way, the Japanese army dominates not only the execution of Japanese policy but also the formulation of policy in Tokyo. The post of Japanese Ambassador to Manchoukuo, which combines the important functions already mentioned, has always been held by a high-ranking officer of the army. The successors to the late Marshal Muto have included General Takashi Hishikari, General Jiro Minami, and General Kenkichi Uyeda. The result has been to make Japan's Manchurian policy since 1932 distinctly the policy of the Japanese army.

Japanese Immigration

Apart from its views on the strategic importance of Manchuria, the Japanese army has given active support to two movements designed to cement the relations of the new state with Japan. A concerted attempt has been and is being made to settle Japanese on Manchurian lands—an experiment that has proved costly and thus far has not been attended with unqualified success, because most Japanese peasants have not the remotest desire to live in Manchoukuo. In the second place, the army has sought to encourage the formation of a so-called Japan-Manchoukuo economic bloc. While some progress has been made in the creation of economic interdependence, it is not entirely clear that the program can proceed indefinitely without encountering well-nigh insurmountable obstacles within Japan, some of which have already appeared.

Japanese Investments

Despite obstacles in the path of Japanese immigration and the creation of an economic bloc, the industrial development of Manchoukuo, through an influx of Japanese capital, has been phenomenal. Much of this investment has been consumed in the construction of cities, such as Hsinking, the capital, railroads, new harbors, such as Rashin and Hulutao, and highways. In the period from 1932 to 1935, inclusive, it is estimated that Japan's Manchurian investments totaled 788,-000,000 yen.

In the economic development of the new state, there is a considerable measure of state control of industry through official management of specially created companies that control enterprises that are closely related to national defense or that may be regarded as public utilities. The policy has been applied most extensively in the fields of mining, oil, distilling, and so forth. In the oil industry, for instance, the government of Manchoukuo exercises a monopoly through the Manchuria Petroleum Company. This industry provides an outstanding example of the influence of the Kwantung (Japanese) army upon the policies of the new state. The object of the army

from the first has been to insure state control over capital in all
key industries. This is obviously designed to create an efficient
economic state machine capable of functioning effectively in
the event of war.

One of the most important changes effected under the new
regime was the unification of all Manchurian railroads under
the management of the South Manchuria Railway Company.
For this purpose, the company established the General Direction of Manchoukuo State Railways, beginning operation of
the lines in March, 1933. By 1936, the South Manchuria Railway Company was operating, in addition to its own original
lines, state railroads with a total mileage of more than 4,000.
A considerable proportion of this mileage represents railroads
constructed or extended since 1932. Some of these are primarily commercial, while others are designed for military and
strategic purposes. Among the important lines completed
since 1932, the following should be noted: (1) the Koshan and
Hailun to Heiho line, which connects Tsitsihar and Harbin
with the Amur River, thus penetrating the heart of north
Manchuria and giving direct access to the Russian town of
Blagoveshchensk; (2) the Hsinking-Paichengtzu and Wang-
yehmiao-Halunarshan lines, which give direct access to western
Manchuria close to the borders of Outer Mongolia; (3) the
Harbin-Lafa and Tunhua-Tumen lines, which open central
Manchuria to the north Korean ports of Seishin, Rashin, and
Yuki; (4) the Tumen-Hulin line in eastern Manchuria, which
connects the Korean border with the Ussuri River region and
the Maritime province of Siberia; and, finally, (5) the Chin-
lingssu-Jehol line, which penetrates westward into the mountainous province of Jehol.

The Chinese Eastern Railroad

Both the political and the economic development of Manchoukuo were conditioned from the first by the presence of

the Chinese Eastern Railway with its important southern
branch reaching southward from Harbin to Hsinking. It will
be recalled that, prior to the Manchurian incident of 1931, this
railroad had been operated under joint Sino-Russian management. After 1931, Chinese interests were appropriated by
Manchoukuo. The new state, like China in 1929, was opposed
to Soviet Russia's fifty-per-cent control and management of the
line. If joint Russo-Chinese management had failed, it was
obvious that Manchoukuo, closely allied with Japan, would
find such an arrangement even less palatable, for it was alleged
that the Chinese Eastern Railway zone was one of the gateways through which communist propaganda entered China.
From the Russian point of view, the emergence of Manchoukuo, dominated as it was by Japanese policy, rendered further
Russian participation in the management of the line a matter
of questionable value. If Russia refused to sell her interests to
the new state, the latter could, with little difficulty, by construction of other lines, render negligible their economic value.
Both politically and economically, the sale of Russian interests
in the line to Manchoukuo appeared as the natural solution.

Accordingly, in May, 1933, the Russians informed the Japanese that they were prepared to sell. Japan replied that
Manchoukuo would be the proper purchaser but that Tokyo
would be pleased to render good offices. Month after month
the negotiations at Tokyo dragged on with seemingly little
progress. The Russians offered to sell for 250,000,000 gold
rubles (approximately equivalent to 600,000,000 yen); Manchoukuo offered only 50,000,000 yen. The Soviet soon reduced
its figure to 500,000,000 yen, but no agreement could be
reached, and the negotiations were broken off for six months.
When the negotiations were resumed, the Soviet price was
200,000,000 yen, plus 30,000,000 yen for retirement allowances
to Soviet employees. Manchoukuo offered 100,000,000 yen.
This difference was gradually bridged, until in March, 1935,
agreement was reached at 140,000,000 yen, plus 30,000,000 for

retirement allowances. Accordingly, the Chinese Eastern Railway (now known as the North Manchuria Railway) passed into the possession of Manchoukuo. One third of the purchase price was paid in cash, and the remainder was to be taken in goods supplied over a period of years. In an exchange of notes between Japan and Russia, the former guaranteed the fulfillment by Manchoukuo of its obligations under the transfer.

As soon as the important North Manchuria Railway was acquired by Manchoukuo, it was placed under the management of General Direction. Its position among other state-owned lines was complicated, however, by the broad five-foot Russian gauge, which made it impossible to interchange rolling stock. This difficulty was overcome in part on August 31, 1935, when, in the course of a single day, the Hsinking-Harbin line was reduced to standard gauge, making possible through train service from Dairen to Harbin. It is possible that a similar alteration in gauge will later be applied to the main line.

Manchoukuo and Siberia

The sale of the North Manchuria Railway materially improved relations between Russia and the allied states of Manchoukuo and Japan. Nevertheless, other dangerous causes of friction remained. This friction is a direct result of the contemporaneous development of Japanese interests in Korea and Manchoukuo, and of Soviet interests in the Amur region and the hinterland of Vladivostok. In main, the present friction between Japan and Soviet Russia in eastern Siberia is a resumption of the older conflict with Tsarist Russia, though the objectives of both states have undergone considerable change. The reader will recall that Russia's aggressive policy in the Far East was ended temporarily by her defeat in the Russo-Japanese War. From that time until the consolidation of Soviet power after 1920, Russia's role in northeastern Asia was passive. More recently, Soviet policy has contemplated a reassertion of Russian influence on the Pacific. Until 1937, the policy had remained basically defensive, its object being to insure eastern Siberia from military attack. To this end, the Soviet authorities have encouraged with great energy the political, economic, and social development of the region eastward from Lake Baikal. This program included the settlement of immigrants from European Russia, rapid double-tracking of the Trans-Siberian Railway and the construction of additional lines, preparations for exploiting mineral and timber wealth, the development of more scientific agriculture, large reinforcements to Russia's far eastern army, and the erection of powerful fortifications on the Amur River and at Vladivostok. Thus, while Russia has surrendered a strategic railroad in Manchoukuo, the strength of her position in eastern Siberia has steadily increased. Once this internal development has reached a greater stage of maturity, the question will again arise whether or not Russia will attempt to resume the imperialistic policy that Mouraviev and Witte followed in the nineteenth century. Meanwhile, the military strength of eastern Siberia remains a matter of concern to Manchoukuo and her Japanese protectors.

Manchoukuo and Mongolia

While border "incidents" continued to keep alive friction on the Amur during 1935 and 1936, a more dangerous situation arose on the Manchoukuo-Mongolian border, where boundary lines are as yet indefinitely drawn. Border clashes in 1935 resulted in a Manchoukuo-Mongolian conference. Manchoukuo asked an exchange of diplomatic representatives, which Outer Mongolia, controlled by Soviet Russia, refused. The result was the failure of the conference to provide any machinery for the settlement of border disputes. In the disputes that continue to harass this region, Manchoukuo and Japan are seeking to unite the Mongols of Outer Mongolia with those of Manchoukuo, while Soviet Russia wants Outer Mongolia to continue nominally as an independent people's republic but under Russian control. The precise extent to which Russia dominated the affairs of Outer Mongolia in 1937 was not ascertainable. Nevertheless, it was apparent that this control differed in extent rather than in kind from similar Japanese control in Manchoukuo. Soviet authorities have denied the existence of any "special relations" between Russia and Outer Mongolia, yet the fact remains that the Red Army and Mongolian forces have acted together on Mongolian soil, that Westerners wishing to enter Outer Mongolia must have their passports visaed in Moscow, that trade between China and Outer Mongolia is rigidly restricted and under the supervision of Russians, that the bulk of Mongolia's commerce is with the Soviet Union, and that Russia and Outer Mongolia have been joined in a mutually protective alliance. Russia's official spokesmen deny the charge that their Mongolian policy savors of the older imperialism of the Tsars. As against these statements, the facts of Russian policy in Outer Mongolia since 1921 indicate marked similarities between the objectives of Tsarist Russia and Communist Russia in the Far East.

Manchoukuo and China

The relations of Manchoukuo with China proper and Inner Mongolia have likewise been far from peaceful. From the founding of the new state, China, in company with the members of the League of Nations and the United States, has refused to recognize it. Fighting between the forces of Chang Hsueh-liang and the Japanese, which had subsided late in 1932, was renewed in January of the following year. The city of Shanhaikwan (where the Great Wall meets the sea) was captured by the Japanese, thus throwing open the road to Peking. With this strategic city in their possession, the Kwantung army moved westward in Jehol province, the capital of which, Chengteh, opened its gates to the invaders, while its Chinese defenders retreated south of the Great Wall. By these events, the power of Chang Hsueh-liang in Manchuria was completely broken. With his forces concentrated in the Peiping area, he was regarded by the Japanese army as a threat to the southern border of Manchoukuo. Accordingly, Japanese forces advanced south of the Wall toward Peiping. On May 31, 1933, a truce was signed at Tangku by the representatives of Tokyo and Nanking. Among the terms of this agreement was a clause providing for establishment of a demilitarized zone stretching along the Great Wall from the Manchurian border. All Chinese troops were withdrawn from this area and replaced by a Chinese police force. By this means, any threat of military action against Manchoukuo from the south was removed. China refused, of course, to recognize Manchoukuo, but at the same time practical business and some official relationships were renewed. After the beginning of 1935, China resumed postal relationships with the new state, as other members of the League had previously done. At the same time, Manchoukuo has suffered heavily from the loss of her export market in China. This loss is attributable to several factors: the Chinese boycott, tariff barriers, and China's loss of buying power.

Extraterritoriality

Despite Manchoukuo's troubled role as Japan's buffer state facing Communist Russia and chaotic China, internal development under Japanese guidance has been remarkable. In view of this, Japan now contemplates the early surrender of the extraterritorial rights that she, together with other foreign powers, enjoyed in Manchuria prior to 1931. The abolition of extraterritorial jurisdiction will follow the execution of an extensive program of reforms now in progress. Among these may be mentioned: (1) Industrial laws designed to safeguard the activities of Japanese subjects in Manchoukuo, such as the trade mark, the patent and invention laws, and laws relating to

mining, marketing, stock-farming, banking, currency, foreign
exchange, and rural credit; (2) complete reform of the system
of taxation; (3) establishment of a system of national police;
(4) erection of a judicial system based on modern codes; and
(5) formation of an efficient postal administration. When this
program was already well under way, Japan, in February, 1935,
appointed a preparatory committee to consider relinquishment
of its extraterritorial rights. Subsequently, Japan announced
that these rights would be surrendered gradually and that her
administrative rights in the South Manchuria Railway zone
would likewise be transferred to Manchoukuo. Finally, in
June, 1936, a Japan-Manchoukuo extraterritoriality treaty was
signed. In return for Japan's promise of gradual abolition,
Japanese subjects in Manchoukuo are granted freedom "to
reside and travel and engage in agriculture, commerce and
industry, and to pursue callings and professions, whether public
or private." They are likewise accorded all rights relating to
land.

Manchoukuo and the West

Although Manchoukuo has not been formally recognized
by any states save Japan and San Salvador, various national
groups have displayed considerable interest in the new state
and have sought to promote their commercial intercourse with
it. Beginning with 1934, a number of trade missions visited
Hsinking. The first of these was the British Industrial Mission, representing the British Federation of Industries. This
was followed in 1935 by a German economic mission
and in 1936 by a Belgian trade mission. An American
economic mission, which visited Japan and China in 1935,
did not go to Manchuria. In April, 1936, a Manchoukuo-
German trade agreement was concluded through the good
offices of the Japanese government. In Japan and Manchoukuo,
this agreement and the previous agreement for the sale of the
North Manchuria (Chinese Eastern) Railway have been inter-

preted as implying recognition of Manchoukuo by both Russia and Germany.

SELECTED BIBLIOGRAPHY

Material on the State of Manchoukuo is fragmentary and of uneven value. Among the most reliable information on the economic development of the state is that contained in the 4th and 5th *Report* [s] *On Progress in Manchuria,* published by the South Manchuria Railway Company (Dairen: 1934 and 1936). There are a number of publications issued by various departments of the Manchoukuo government. Department of Foreign Affairs, *A General Outline of Manchoukuo* (Hsinking: 1932 and 1934). Department of Finance, *Annual Returns of the Foreign Trade of Manchoukuo.* Department of Finance, *Monthly Returns of the Foreign Trade of Manchoukuo.* Department of Foreign Affairs, *Information Bulletins.* The Central Bank of Manchou, *Manchoukuo's Business and Finance.*

Daniel R. Bergsmark, *Economic Geography of Asia* (New York: 1935), discusses economic resources in ch. 26. Tsuenta Yano and Kyoichi Shirasaki, *Nippon: A Chartered Survey of Japan, 1936* (Tokyo: 1936), trans. by Z. Tamotsu Iwado, contains a useful supplement on Manchoukuo. George B. Rea, *The Case for Manchoukuo* (New York: 1935), is poorly organized special pleading. A useful volume giving an official Japanese view of Manchoukuo is Hirosi Saito, *Japan's Policies and Purposes* (Boston: 1935). For Manchoukuo's position in international affairs, see various publications of the League of Nations, and also the Manchurian series of *Geneva Special Studies,* issued by the Geneva Research Information Committee. Various issues of the *Manchoukuo Year Book* (Tokyo) are also of value.

CHAPTER XL
Revolution in Contemporary China

THE political history of China since 1927, when the Nationalist Government[1] of the Republic was established at Nanking, presents an involved and confusing narrative. The constant wranglings of politicians, the phenomenon of almost continuous civil war, the temporary secession of entire provinces, and the existence of a widespread communist movement —these and numerous other disturbing forces have composed the factual political history of China during the past ten years. Although there are contemporary indications that Japan's policy in Manchoukuo, north China, and Inner Mongolia, together with Soviet Russia's "peaceful conquest" of Outer Mongolia, has aroused the Chinese to a new national consciousness, it still remains for history to determine whether or not they will erect a unified political structure. At the beginning of 1937, a truly national government, as that term is understood in the western world, could not as yet be said to exist. Not only were there areas within China proper that repudiated completely the authority of Nanking, but there were also others that, at best, paid to it merely a nominal and doubtful allegiance.

Failures of Nationalism

The historical and fundamental explanation of China's failure to provide herself with a unified political system is that the idea is new to her. In China, political systems have usually

---

[1] Since October, 1928, the Nationalist Government has been known as the National Government.

been incidental and therefore weak. They have ever been subordinate to Chinese culture, Chinese civilization, and Chinese society. Unhappily for themselves, the Chinese now live in a world that surrounds them with highly organized political units. They are thus forced to choose between providing themselves with the same effective political system and submitting to some form of foreign control. Neither course is welcomed by the average Chinese. To him, government, with its modern implications, both in theory and practice, is repugnant. Herein lies the explanation of why China has not enjoyed greater success in creating a national political structure.

Contrary to what is so frequently assumed, China's attempts to erect a national government did not originate as a result of Japan's continental imperialism. They preceded it by many years, and, illogically enough, were essentially a protest against Manchu efforts to repel the foreigner by creating centralization in government. It is only since Europe, crippled by the World War, could no longer pursue her old imperialism, that the full force of Chinese resentment has been turned against Japan. Upon this antiforeign resentment, the major power of Chinese nationalism, such as it is, has rested. The evidence appears to indicate that without the pressure of foreign imperialism there would have been no nationalist movement in China. Even this sentiment, which seeks to save the soil of China from foreign control, has failed as yet, in a political sense, to unify the Chinese. It has failed to destroy the dominant local character of their government and to weld them into a cohesive political unit.

Divisions in the Kuomintang

Suspicion of all centralized authority has been by no means the only obstacle retarding the growth of a national political structure. It will be recalled that at the time the Nationalists made their triumphant march from Canton to the upper Yangtze (1927), the Kuomintang Party included within its membership the Communists and was under the overpowering influence of Comrade Borodin and the Communist program. The economic program that these Communist Russians proposed to apply was such as could not be acceptable to the conservative, capitalistic, and middle-class elements in the Kuomintang. Although there were other factors involved, it

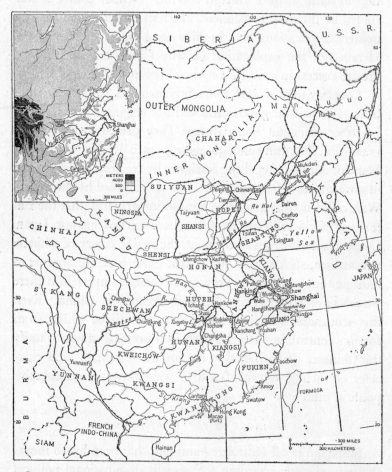

CHINA AND NORTHEASTERN ASIA, 1936. Illustrating the complicated politico-geographical relations of China, Soviet Russia, and Japan (Manchoukuo). The inset emphasizes the high mountain and plateau barriers that focus the Yangtze Valley on Shanghai. *Courtesy of John E. Orchard and of the "Geographical Review," published by the American Geographical Society of New York.*

was mainly this conflict that occasioned the split in the Kuomintang, with the resulting establishment of two governments, the one, the left wing, at Hankow, and the other, the right wing, at Nanking, under the leadership of the man who has, more than any other, dominated Chinese political life during the past ten years, General Chiang Kai-shek. From the first, the Nanking government, with which Hankow later joined forces, after the expulsion of Borodin, was anti-Communist. Its financial backing was supplied by the principal Chinese bankers of Shanghai. The Kuomintang that thus emerged with the establishment of the Nanking regime was restored to its "pure" basis. It accepted Sun Yat-sen's Three Principles (nationalism, democracy, and livelihood, the last implying economic equality); it denounced communism, imperialism, and the rule of the war lords (tuchuns); it accepted the adherence of new bourgeois elements, while peasant and labor unions were disarmed and reorganized on a more conservative basis. This is merely to say that the reorganized Kuomintang of 1928 was controlled by men who adopted a political philosophy that was conservative, capitalistic, bourgeois, and anti-Communist. Since 1928 this Kuomintang Party has been the principal government of China, exercising authority over such areas as it could control. The administration has been conducted, of course, by the National Government at Nanking, which, however, is the creation of, and therefore is subordinate to, the Kuomintang.

The National Government

The National Government derives its authority from two committees elected by the National Congress of the Kuomintang: the Central Executive Committee and the Central Supervisory Committee. Political policy and administration are controlled by the Central Political Council, which is composed of the two committees mentioned above. This body formulates the policies which are to be executed by the National Government. The organic law under which the National Government operated, until the end of 1931, gave to its President very extensive powers, which more recent revisions have restricted. Since 1931, the government has operated under a Provisional Constitution, which is to apply for what is termed the period of political tutelage. According to this document, the sovereignty of the Republic of China is vested in the people as a whole, but governing powers are to be exercised by the Kuomintang. Many of the articles are expressed in very general terms, susceptible to varied interpretation. For example:

Art. 40.—Both capital and labor shall develop productive enterprises in accordance with the principle of cooperation and mutual benefit.

On other questions, the Provisional Constitution is quite specific.

Art. 85.—The power of interpreting this Provisional Constitution shall be exercised by the Central Executive Committee of the Kuomintang of China.

The final draft of a permanent constitution was promulgated on May 5, 1936.[2] It is proposed that this constitution shall be submitted to a national people's congress for adoption, after which the Provisional Constitution will cease to have effect.

The National Government, as it has existed under the Provisional Constitution, consists of five *Yuan* (representing a division of powers): the executive, the legislative, the judicial, the examination, and the control. Each is responsible to the Central Executive Committee of the Kuomintang. In practice, the President of the Executive Yuan is the head of the government, corresponding in a rather loose way to the position held by a prime minister. The functions of the various Yuan are briefly as follows:

---

[2] For the text of the Provisional Constitution, see *The China Year Book*, 1933, pp. 396-398. For text of proposed permanent constitution, see *ibid.*, 1936, pp. 150-155.

1. The Executive Yuan, as the highest executive organ, prepares bills on legislative matters, budgets, amnesties, declarations of war, and so forth, for submission to the Legislative Yuan.

2. The Legislative Yuan decides all matters of legislation, budgets, amnesties, declarations of war and negotiations for peace, and so forth.

3. The Judicial Yuan is composed of the Supreme Court, the Administrative Court, and the Commission for the Disciplinary Punishment of Public Functionaries.

4. The Examination Yuan is composed of an examination commission and a ministry of personnel.[3]

5. The Control Yuan is entrusted with the functions of impeachment and auditing.

Directly subordinate to the National Government is an impressive military machinery consisting of:

1. The National Military Council, created in 1932, which functions as a supreme military directory;

2. the Board of the General Staff, headed by a chief of the General Staff;

3. the Directorate-General of Military Training;

4. a military Advisory Council; and, finally,

5. the Metropolitan Garrison Headquarters.

Provincial Administration

In the sphere of provincial administration, the National Government increased the number of provinces. After 1907, there were twenty-one provinces, including eighteen in China proper and three in Manchuria. To these, the National Government added: Jehol (now a part of Manchoukuo), Suiyuan

---

[3] The organic law of December, 1931, contained a provision that all public functionaries should be appointed to office only after passing examinations set by the Examination Yuan. This provision was found to be inconvenient and was accordingly struck from the law.

and Chahar (formerly special administrative districts in Inner Mongolia), Chinghai, Ninghsia (formerly a portion of Kansu), and Hsikang (formerly western Szechwan). In theory, the provincial governments are headed by boards of administrative members appointed by the National Government. In practice, many of the provinces are still controlled by the military bureaucrats of the old regime.[4]

While the Kuomintang and its agent, the National Government, have devoted much time to the elaboration of impressive constitutional documents and organic laws, their chief concern has been to maintain themselves in power. Though China was declared after 1928 to be united under the new government, the fact was that this unity existed in name only. In the first years of its existence, the actual authority of Nanking extended only to the provinces on the lower Yangtze. Provinces in the northwest and in the south were ruled by their own military tuchuns who from time to time were allied temporarily with Nanking for the sake of political expediency. Much of the nation's territory, too, was controlled by the Communists, while the Kuomintang itself had not fully recovered from the factionalism of 1927. The most serious threat to the life of the Nanking regime came, as always, from south China, where left-wing elements of the Kuomintang took the position that Chiang Kai-shek had merely replaced the former northern war lords with his own military rule. The result was a Canton revolt which set up a rival government for Kwangtung and Kwangsi. This government, after declaring itself the true heir to the Chinese revolution, launched a military attack on Nanking, which was halted only when the Manchurian outbreak of 1931 occurred. Temporarily, all factions of the Kuomintang gave their support to Nanking, where practical authority was divided between Chiang Kai-shek, Wang Ching-

---

[4] In 1932, it was proposed to replace the committee system of provincial administration with the pre-Nationalist practice of having provincial governors. This was reaffirmed with slight modifications in 1934.

wei, and Hu Han-min. This alliance of right and left wings was short lived, and by 1933 Chiang Kai-shek was confronted with the extension of Japanese influence in north China and a renewal of the left-wing revolt at Canton.

Chinese Fascism

Nevertheless, the Kuomintang survived, despite internal attacks on its authority. By the close of 1936, Chiang Kai-shek was heading what was frequently described as a dictatorship, by which he controlled the party, the government, and the army. Supporting this Kuomintang dictatorship are a number of Fascist-like organizations, such as the C. C. Corps, which takes its name from the Chen brothers, who have been the most powerful manipulators in the administrative end of the Kuomintang. Side by side with the C. C. Corps are the Blue Shirts. Warned by the opposition that ousted him temporarily from the government in 1931, Chiang Kai-shek took steps to strengthen his personal position. The result was organization of the Blue Shirts, a military corps inspired by Chiang's most trusted lieutenants from the Whampoa Military Academy. A reported function of the Blue Shirts is that of "removing" persons whom General Chiang finds objectionable. Other groups within the "dictatorship" included in 1935: (1) the followers of Wang Ching-wei, who at the time was President of the Executive Yuan; (2) the so-called returned student group, who number among their leaders Sun Fo, T. V. Soong, and H. H. Kung; (3) the remnants of the so-called "Political Science Party," a mixture of militarists and politicians who date their influence from the early days of the Republic. These various groups stand for a confusing complex of policies, which has resulted in division and dissension within the Kuomintang. This, in turn, has provided the pretext for Chiang Kai-shek's dictatorial methods.

The Chinese Communists

Little of a definite nature is known of the origins of the contemporary Communist movement in China or of its present stability and influence. There can be no question, however,

Ewing Galloway.

T. V. Soong (Sung Tze-wen). One of the chief political lieutenants of Chiang Kai-shek., With C. T. Wang he negotiated China's new tariff treaties of 1928.

that it has enjoyed a rapid development, has threatened the very existence of the National Government, and has exerted a profound influence upon the political, economic, and social thinking of the Chinese. Concerning its origins, the Lytton Report observed:

The Communist movement in China, during the first years of its existence, remained restricted within intellectual and labour circles, where the doctrine gained considerable influence in the period 1919-1924. Rural China was, at that time, scarcely touched by the movement. The manifesto of the Soviet Government of July 25th, 1919 declaring its willingness to renounce all privileges "extorted" from China by the former Tsarist Government, created a favourable impression throughout China, especially amongst the intelligentsia. In May 1921, the "Chinese Communist Party" was formally constituted. Propaganda was especially conducted in labour circles at Shanghai, where red syndicates were organized. In June 1922, at its second congress, the Communist Party, which did not then number more than three hundred members, decided to ally itself with the Kuomintang. Dr. Sun Yat-sen, although opposed to the Communist doctrine, was prepared to admit individual Chinese Communists into the party. In the autumn of 1922, the Soviet Government sent a mission to China, headed by Mr. Joffe. Important interviews, which took place between him and Dr. Sun resulted in the joint declaration of January 26th, 1923, by which assurance was given of Soviet sympathy and support to the cause of the national unification and independence of China.

After these beginnings, Soviet advisers were sent from Moscow to reorganize the Kuomintang and its army. In 1924, the Kuomintang Congress approved the admittance of Communists to membership, on the understanding that they were not to foster a proletarian revolution. By 1924, membership in the Communist Party was 2,000, while membership in the red syndicates that it organized was about 60,000. With this growing influence, the Communists were able to propose to the Kuomintang, in 1926, a program of land nationalization, elimination of military leaders opposed to communism, and the creation of an army of Communists, workmen, and peasants. Although the proposal was defeated, it indicated the increased influence of the Communist element. Its eventual victory seemed assured, for the Nationalist Government, which was established at Hankow in 1927, was under Communist control. As the Lytton Report observed: "The

Nationalist Revolution was almost on the point of being transformed into a Communist Revolution." There followed the
appearance of the bourgeois government at Nanking and,
ultimately, the expulsion by Kuomintang members of the
Communists from Hankow. The outcome was the creation
of a "purified" Kuomintang, drawing its principal support
from the propertied classes and resting on a conservative right-
wing philosophy.

The fact that the Chinese Communists were expelled from
the Kuomintang did not eliminate them as a factor in China's
political turmoil. Communist revolts occurred in Kiangsi and
at Canton in 1927. Their activities were encouraged, too, by
dissension within the Kuomintang and by the civil conflicts
in which the Nanking government soon became involved.
From 1928 to 1931, the principal strongholds of the Communist groups were in Kiangsi, Fukien, and Hunan. By 1931, the
National Government, which had sent three expeditions
against the Reds, had failed to suppress them. In part, this
failure was due to attacks upon its authority by northern
militarists and by armies from Canton. The failure was due
also to the popularity that the Communists enjoyed in many
areas that they occupied—a popularity which could be traced
to their program of social and economic reform.

The Communist Program

In China, the Communist program thus far has struck
directly at the privileged position of the landlords and the
propertied classes. When an area was occupied, the Communists first attempted to sovietize it, suppressing by terror
all opposition by the propertied classes.[5] The resulting govern-

---

[5] Terroristic methods in China are in no sense a monopoly of the Communists.
They have been used perhaps quite as extensively by the National Government. Even
before the Nanking Government was officially established, the groups which supported Chiang Kai-shek used the weapon of terror at Shanghai. "To avoid Com-

ment is exercised by committees elected by a congress of workers and peasants. These committees are usually controlled by special agents of the Chinese Communist Party. Administration is conducted through departments of finance,

Ewing Galloway.

Dr. C. T. (Cheng-ting) Wang. In 1937 he arrived in Washington as China's Ambassador. Educated in American universities, he is one of the ablest of China's diplomats and statesmen.

rural economy, education, hygiene, posts and telegraph, communications, military affairs, and so forth.

In bringing their program to bear upon a given community, the Communists usually began with a mandate canceling all

munistic complications, a 'white massacre' took place in Chapei in the course of which numerous alleged Communists were killed, not by troops, but by so-called 'white' labourers, in reality a body of hired thugs." *China Year Book*, 1929-1930. p. 1157.

debts. Large landed estates were then seized either from landowners or from religious institutions and distributed among the small farmers and the landless proletarians. Taxation was simplified by reducing it to a percentage of the crop. Rural communities were aided by irrigation projects, the establishment of co-operative societies of various kinds, and the development of rural credit systems. Thus far, the Communist movement in China has been rural rather than urban. Its appeal has thus been directed to the small farmers, tenants, and landless peasants. To these groups, it has given land and relief from the financial oppression of previous regimes, which by their system of taxation sought to pauperize those who were already impoverished. In the cities where communism has appeared, it has demanded, and in some cases won, shorter hours of labor and increased pay. The measure of success which the Chinese Communists have won may be attributed to their direct assault upon the worst features of landlordism and industrialization. In the struggle for control of the Chinese masses, the Communists have presented to the peasants and workers a more appealing program than can be offered by the present Kuomintang, whose primary concern has been the protection of propertied classes.

Extent of Communist Control

The Chinese soviets by 1932 controlled an area of more than 300,000 square miles and about 90,000,000 of the population, a position which they held until the close of 1933. For a time, they were allied in Fukien with the famous Nineteenth Route Army, which, after its striking defense of Shanghai against the Japanese in 1932, deserted the cause of the National Government.[6] During 1934, National Government armies

---

[6] General Tsai Ting-kai, commander of the Nineteenth Route Army, was sent to Fukien in 1932 to fight the Communists. As noted, he made an alliance with them and, when defeated, fled to Hong Kong. Later, he appeared in the United States, where he was entertained naïvely as China's foremost patriot. He listened to

under the command of Chiang Kai-shek broke much of the Communist power in Kiangsi and Fukien but never completely destroyed it, for the main Communist armies moved westward into Hunan and western Szechwan. In all, the Nationalists have waged, since 1927, six campaigns to dislodge the main Communist armies from south of the Yangtze. Their success by 1935 was tempered by the fact that the Communist armies had not been annihilated, and that in northwestern China, whither the Reds retreated, they occupied a more fertile country and one less easy to attack.

Educating the Conservatives

The National Government campaigns of 1934 and 1935 against the Communists gave evidence of the fascist tendencies in the Nanking regime that have already been noted. Chiang's Blue Shirts acted as a terrorist society aiming at the suppression of all radical opposition to his government. Government armies were subjected to courses in "political education." The Nationalists sought closer union with the landlords of affected areas, while at the same time they promised a broad but indefinite program of social and economic reform. Supplementing these was the "New Life Movement," designed to strengthen the moral temper of the people and to renew their faith in China's ancient cultural heritage.[7] During 1935 and 1936, the anti-Communist campaigns were strengthened materially by this program, yet the National Government was unable to rout the Communist armies in western China and in Kansu. Some of the semi-independent provincial armies, in fact, showed an increasing reluctance to fight their own

addresses of welcome at American luncheon clubs intended as tributes to Tsai as a patriot and to the cause of the National Government. At the time, Tsai was a political exile from National China. *Cf.* Ralph Townsend, *Asia Answers.* G. P. Putnam's Sons, New York, 1936. pp. 4-5.

[7] See Frederick V. Field, "The Recent Anti-Communist Campaign in China." *Far Eastern Survey,* New York, August 14, 1935.

countrymen in the Red armies. This sentiment was said to be particularly strong among the troops of the Tungpei, or Northeastern, army under the command of Chang Hsueh-liang, former dictator of Manchuria, whom the Japanese had ousted in 1931. When, therefore, Manchoukuo troops entered Suiyuan in Inner Mongolia in 1936, Chang called upon the National Government to resist them and to support the "National Salvation" movement by fighting Japanese imperialism, instead of Chinese Communism.

Kidnaping a Dictator

These proposals came at a time (November, 1936) when some of Chiang Kai-shek's best troops had been captured by the Red armies in the northwest. The Reds, in turn, made overtures to the semi-independent armies of the northeast (nominally forces of the Nanking government) to form a united front against Japan. Faced with the proposal of a union between the northern armies and the Communists, Chiang Kai-shek met Chang Hsueh-liang and the northern commanders at Sianfu, in Shensi, during December. Chiang is declared to have opposed a popular front and to have demanded suppression of the Reds. On the morning of December 12, Chiang Kai-shek was seized by commanders of the northern armies acting for Chang Hsueh-liang. After being held for ten days, the head of the Nanking government was liberated, returning to Nanking with his captor, Chang, who submitted himself to trial on the charge of treason. The farcical "trial" and subsequent pardon of Chang Hsueh-liang was regarded as a part of the bargain by which Chiang Kai-shek agreed to assist in a united front against Japan. At the beginning of 1937, it was still uncertain what effect the Gilbertian "kidnaping" of Chiang Kai-shek would have upon Chinese politics.

Industry in Modern China

China's contemporary revolution has been conditioned by economic as well as political factors. The birth of modern Chinese industry dates only from about the beginning of the present century. It began at a time when the Chinese had already acquired a broad demand for foreign manufactured goods. When these sources were either shut off or at least restricted by the World War, factory industry in China enjoyed a remarkable growth. These new industries were in some cases financed by Chinese, in others by foreign capital. Increase in the number of cotton mills was particularly marked. After the war, the cotton industry continued to grow until it had replaced a large proportion of the imports and was becoming a noticeable element in the foreign market. Smaller industries that have also expanded include the glass, cigarette, and rubber goods. Naturally, most of this industrial development has been without government aid. Another feature has been the conflict between Chinese-owned industry and the foreign-owned mills located in the treaty ports and the foreign settlements and concessions. In addition, there has remained, side by side with factory industry, rural manufacturing among the peasants, which in some cases has not only survived but also expanded in recent years.[8]

The policy of the National Government toward industry has been conditioned by the government's lack of political stability. Political chaos has prevented application of any consistent industrial policy and in many cases has tended to drive industry into the foreign-controlled areas of the treaty ports. On paper, the National Government formulated elaborate plans for industrialization on the basis of a capitalistic society. Whether these will be carried out or modified toward social-

[8] For a concise but satisfactory discussion of industry in modern China, see G. E. Hubbard, *Eastern Industrialization and Its Effect on the West*. Oxford University Press, London, 1935. Chapter 3.

istic or communistic philosophy will depend on future politics. Practically, the interest of the Nanking government in industry has been "that of a tax-collector." [9] The conditions of labor have been, and remain, deplorable. Low wages, lack of supervision, the prevalence of the subsistence standard, the difficulty of securing co-operative action between Chinese and foreign-owned factories—these and many other considerations are involved in the present status of Chinese labor.

The National Economic Council

Recognizing that its own life would probably depend on the financial and economic reconstruction of the country, the National Government created, in 1933, the National Economic Council. At that time, the leading members of the Council included: Wang Ching-wei, President of the Executive Yuan; Sun Fo, President of the Legislative Yuan; T. V. Soong, former Minister of Finance; Chiang Kai-shek, then Chairman of the Military Affairs Commission; and H. H. Kung, Vice-President of the Executive Yuan and Minister of Finance. Seven administrative departments were created within the Council and were charged with work in the following fields: roads, hydraulic engineering, agriculture, health, the cotton industry, sericulture, and co-operative affairs. The powers and functions of the Council were defined as follows:

To plan, examine and approve projects for economic reconstruction or development; to examine and approve the necessary expenditure required for these projects; to supervise and direct them, and to execute directly special projects.

Assistance from the League of Nations

Since 1931, the National Government and the Council have had the technical collaboration of the League of Nations in this

[9] *Ibid.* p. 205.

work of reconstruction. The League has sent twenty-seven experts in various fields as advisers to the Council, but progress has been hampered by lack of funds. The most notable progress has been made in the fields of highway construction, water conservancy, public health, and agricultural rehabilitation. Within a period of three years, 20,000 kilometers of roads were constructed, nearly fifty per cent of which were macadamized. The Chingho irrigation project in northwest China, completed in 1935, is, to date, the most successful project of the Council. Many other projects were well advanced by the end of 1936. Much of the Council's success, it would appear, has been due to the technical advice and supervision of League experts.

Japan and the League in China

The striking success of the League's technical collaboration with the Council aroused much resentment among official and business groups in Japan. This led on April 17, 1934, to a press statement by the spokesman of the Japanese Foreign Office, which was interpreted as a warning to western states (including the United States) that Japan could not remain indifferent to activities in China that she regarded as prejudicial to her interests. Since Japan, said the spokesman, had incurred "special responsibilities in East Asia," which arose from her geographical position and mission, she might be called upon to act alone and on her own responsibility. Therefore, Japan was opposed in principle to any joint operations in respect to China, "undertaken by foreign powers, even in the name of technical or financial assistance." It was Japan's belief that such undertakings would inevitably acquire "political significance"—a point of view for which, it may be added, there was much historical basis in the conduct of many nations, including Japan.

Although this Japanese declaration was made informally by the spokesman of the Foreign Office to press representatives, it was nevertheless expressive of Japan's disapproval not only of some forms of technical advice which Europe was giving China, but also of certain western loans made and contemplated. In June, 1933, the Chinese government had concluded with the United States Reconstruction Finance Corporation and the Grain Stabilization Board a $50,000,000 loan in American cotton, wheat, and flour. The Chinese government was also considering a reconstruction loan under the auspices of the League of Nations. At the time that China contracted for these American credits in kind, her need for them was questionable, for her own market was already depressed. The Japanese Ambassador in Washington asserted that most of the cotton and wheat was resold and the proceeds used by the Chinese government for the purchase of arms, which presumably would be used against Japan. The diplomatic correspondence between various western capitals and Tokyo that followed the Japanese statement of April 17 has not been made public. It appeared that both Japan and the great powers of the West hoped, for the time being at least, to avoid the issue raised by Japan's so-called Asiatic Monroe Doctrine.

The Leith-Ross Mission

During 1935 and 1936, the United States and Great Britain gave renewed evidence of their desire to cement commercial relations with the National Government. An American economic mission, headed by Cameron Forbes, former American Ambassador to Japan, visited China to investigate industrial conditions. Upon its return to the United States, it reported favorably upon the progress made under the Nanking regime. Sir Frederick Leith-Ross, chief economic adviser to the British government, arrived in China on a similar mission in September, 1935. On the eve of his departure nine months later, he predicted, in a lengthy statement to the press, a profitable future for British trade with China and emphasized China's need for capital goods, her tendency to kill legitimate trade by prohibitive tariffs, her need for greater political stability, and her need for an amicable settlement with Japan.

Political Status of "North China"

The political status of north China has been a serious problem since the conclusion of the Tangku Truce in May, 1933 (see p. 769). In the winter of 1934-1935, clashes occurred between Chinese and Manchoukuo-Japanese forces in eastern Chahar (Inner Mongolia). A settlement was reached at the Tatan Conference in February, 1935. Since that time, the Kwantung (Japanese) army has exerted pressure upon the northern Chinese authorities in the hope of creating an "autonomous" state comprising the provinces of Hopei, where Peiping is located, Shantung, Shansi, Suiyuan, and Chahar. The exact political status that this "autonomous" state would occupy was never made quite clear. It was evident, however, that it would be free from Nanking's control and that under Japanese influence it would act as a buffer against anti-Japanese movements in China, and, in the case of Chahar, against the penetration of communist influence from Outer Mongolia and Soviet Russia.

The background of this scheme may be traced in the briefest outline. In 1933, a demilitarized zone was created in Hopei province, south of the Great Wall. The purpose was, as far as the Japanese were concerned, to remove the remnants of Chang Hsueh-liang's army from the southern border of Manchuria. Chang, however, continued to be the central figure in the continued anti-Japanese movements in the northern provinces. It was this situation that provided the Kwantung army with a pretext for ousting Chang from the northern provinces and replacing his influence with that of an "autonomous" state controlled by pro-Japanese factions. By 1936, Chang's armies had retired from Chahar and Hopei, and the distinctly anti-Japanese organs of government, such as the

Peiping Political Council and the Peiping branch of the National Military Council, had been dissolved, their functions being taken over by men who were alleged to be more friendly to Japan. But the new northern leaders, late in 1936 and early in 1937, were resisting Japanese pressure for an autonomous state quite as effectively as their predecessors. The only north-

The New York Times.

IN 1935, IMPERIALISTIC GROUPS IN JAPAN FAVORED CREATION OF AN AUTONOMOUS NORTH CHINA, FREE FROM THE POLITICAL CONTROL OF NANKING AND UNDER THE TUTELAGE OF MANCHOUKUO.

ern area that by 1936 was openly supporting the new state idea was the "East Hopei Autonomous Anti-Communist Council." This government, under Yin Ju-keng, controlled the demilitarized zone in eastern Hopei, where it enjoyed the practical protection of the Kwantung army. By February, 1937, the larger autonomous state had not materialized. For reasons that are not yet clear, the Chinese refused to co-operate. Its leading architect and principal agent of the Kwantung army, Major General Kenji Doihara, sometimes called the Japanese Lawrence, was recalled to Japan.

One significant effect of this political confusion in the north China area was an extraordinary influx of foreign goods (mostly Japanese) through the demilitarized zone. It was alleged that some of these goods paid a small duty (but lower than the Chinese tariff) to the East Hopei Autonomous Council, while others, landed at remote points on the coast, paid no duty at all. By this means, Japan, it was charged, was attempting to demoralize the entire customs administration in north China. The Maritime Customs made the following report in 1936:

> The Customs staff remain at their posts but all their prerogatives and means of enforcing the laws enacted by constitutional authority have been wrenched from them. Quoting the so-called Tangku Truce Agreement as their authority the Japanese authorities have reduced the Customs to a state of impotence; our preventive patrols are no longer allowed on the Great Wall at Shanhaikwan; our officers within the so-called demilitarized zone have to go without protection against the rough Japanese and Korean elements engaged in illegal activities.[10]

At the beginning of 1937, however, it appeared that the basis of these charges had been removed and that the Maritime Customs was again functioning.

---

[10] *The China Year Book,* 1936. p. 140. The Chinese government protested to Tokyo against the wholesale smuggling, while representations were also made at Tokyo by the American and British governments.

China and Mongolia

Coincident with these developments in the regions about Peiping, the National Government met further embarrassment in its relations with the Mongols. It will be recalled that, after 1928, Nanking organized Inner Mongolia on a provincial basis, in the hope of perpetuating Chinese dominance over the Mongol peoples of this area. After the creation of Manchoukuo, the Japanese set aside all the uncolonized Mongol districts in Manchuria as a quasi-autonomous Mongol province called Hsingan, wherein the Mongols enjoy self-government, are permitted to raise their own troops, and are protected against Chinese colonization. Some Japanese have hoped that this might be the beginning of a Pan-Mongol state under Japanese protection. Such a state would obviously have to include the provinces of Inner Mongolia, where Chinese control is still something of a fact, and also Outer Mongolia, now under the protection of Soviet Russia (see chapter 34).

Status of Outer Mongolia

Although the Soviet authorities have repeatedly denied the existence of special political relationships between Moscow and Outer Mongolia, they nevertheless concluded, on March 12, 1936, with the Mongolian People's Republic a protocol of great significance. This protocol is described as a gentlemen's agreement giving tangible expression to a relationship that has existed since 1934. It provides:

1. "In the event of the menace of attack," the signatories will "consider jointly the situation" and take all necessary measures for their mutual protection.

2. In the event of attack upon the territory of one of the signatories, the other will render all necessary aid, including military assistance.[11]

---

[11] For the text of this protocol, see *The China Year Book*, 1936. p. 21.

The Chinese government, on April 7, 1936, protested against the conclusion of this protocol on the ground that "Outer Mongolia being an integral part of the Republic of China, no foreign state has the right to conclude with it any treaty or agreement." To this, the Soviet government replied:

1. That it did not regard the signing of the protocol as an infringement of Chinese sovereignty;

2. that the protocol did not admit or contain any territorial claim; and, finally,

3. that the signing of the protocol did not introduce any changes in the juridical or factual relations between Moscow and China or between Moscow and Mongolia.

The only conclusion that could be drawn from these exchanges was the destruction of the fiction of Chinese sovereignty in Outer Mongolia. Viewed impartially, it appeared at the beginning of 1937 that Soviet Russia had won a significant diplomatic victory. Almost unnoticed by the outside world, and without protest from either the League of Nations or the United States, Russia had detached Outer Mongolia from the sphere of Chinese influence and sovereignty.[12]

German-Japanese Anti-Communist Pact

China's political fortunes were also involved in the conclusion on November 25, 1936, of a so-called anti-communist pact between Japan and Germany. Setting forth that its object is to guard against "communistic disintegration," the agreement binds the signatories to confer upon necessary measures of defense and to "carry out such measures in close co-operation." A supplementary protocol provides that the two states will "take stringent measures against those who at home or abroad work on direct or indirect duty of the Communistic Interna-

---

[12] For a discussion of Japanese efforts to influence Outer Mongolia, see T. A. Bisson, "Outer Mongolia." Foreign Policy Association *Reports,* November 20, 1935.

tional or assist its disintegrating activities." [13] The Japanese Foreign Minister explained the adherence of his government on the ground of communistic activities in China, Mongolia, and Manchoukuo. In reality, the agreement was not merely the result of the alleged communist menace but also of the desire of military and fascist groups in Japan to link their state with the fascist nations of Europe against Russia. It was likewise hoped that the agreement would encourage the fascist groups in China to resist any compromise with the Chinese Reds. In 1937, it was as yet too early to pass judgment on this question. The year opened with the complex of Chinese politics still unsolved.

Selected Bibliography

Julean Arnold, "Agriculture in the Economic Life of the New China," in *The Chinese Social and Political Science Review,* July, 1922. Julean Arnold, *China: A Commercial and Industrial Handbook* (Washington: 1926). Julean Arnold, "The Commercial Problems of China," in *Annals of the American Academy of Political and Social Science,* Nov. 1930. Joseph Barnes, ed., *Empire in the East* (New York: 1934), chs. 4 and 6. O. E. Baker, "Land Utilization in China," in *Problems of the Pacific,* J. B. Condliffe, ed. (Chicago: 1928). J. W. Bennett, "China's Perennially Unemployed," in *Asia,* Apr. 1931. Pearl S. Buck, "Chinese Women," in *Pacific Affairs,* Oct. 1931. J. L. Buck, *Chinese Farm Economy* (Chicago: 1930). On education in modern China, see various issues of *The China Year Book.* "Communism in China," in *Foreign Affairs,* Jan. 1931. Grover Clark, *The Great Wall Crumbles* (New York: 1935). J. B. Condliffe, "Industrial Development in the Far East," in *The Chinese Social and Political Science Review,* vol. 12, 1928. J. B. Condliffe, *China Today: Economic* (Boston: 1932). Han-seng Chen, "Economic Disintegration in China," in *Pacific Affairs,* April and May, 1933. *Report of the Hon. Mr. Justice Feetham to the Shanghai Municipal Council,* 4 vols. (Shanghai: 1931-32). On economic conditions and foreign trade in China, most valuable surveys are published by the Dept. of Over-

---

[13] Text of the agreement and supplementary protocol is in *Contemporary Japan,* December, 1936. pp. 514-515.

seas Trade of the British Government. Lady Hosie, *Portrait of A Chinese Lady* (New York: 1930). G. E. Hubbard, *Eastern Industrialization and Its Effect on the West* (London: 1935), ch. 3. Eduard Kann, *The Currencies of China* (Shanghai: 1927). D. K. Lieu, *China's Industries and Finance* (Shanghai: 1928). Sobei Mogi and H. Vere Redman, *The Problem of the Far East* (London: 1935). W. H. Mallory, *China: Land of Famine* (New York: 1926). H. B. Morse, *The Gilds of China* (Shanghai: 1932). C. F. Remer, *A Study of Chinese Boycotts* (Baltimore: 1933). Two articles by George E. Sokolsky in *The New York Times Magazine:* "China and America: A Study in Tempos," Aug. 2, 1931; and "When War Strikes the Chinese Village," Aug. 16, 1931. S. T. Ting and D. K. Lieu, "China's Cotton Industry," in *Problems of the Pacific,* 1929, J. B. Condliffe, ed. (Chicago: 1930). J. B. Taylor, *Farm and Factory in China* (London: 1928). R. H. Tawney, *Land and Labour in China* (London: 1932). A. J. Toynbee, *Survey of International Affairs,* 1935, 2 vols. (New York: 1936); see vol. 1, pt. 2. Ralph Townsend, *Asia Answers* (New York: 1936).

CHAPTER XLI

The United States and Philippine Independence

WHEN the United States took over the Philippine Islands from the incompetent hands of Spain in 1898-1899, the American government had little practical experience in the management of colonial affairs. Imperialism in eastern Asia was for the United States a new and untried venture. Prior to the Spanish-American War, most Americans had no more than heard of the islands. Annexation of territory remote from American shores and peopled by inhabitants alien in race, language, and tradition was a phenomenon that to Americans was both novel and perplexing. The decision to keep the islands had not been prefaced by any general schooling of Americans in the ways of colonial administration. Few Americans had any intelligent idea as to what should be done with them. To be sure, American imperialists saw in the Philippines an opportunity to amass wealth, but the average American was conscious only of a somewhat vague responsibility to civilize the Filipinos and to prevent their falling a prey to any other power. The general idea was expressed with almost poetic fervor by Henry Watterson, to whom the annexation of the Philippines meant that the United States had come of age.

From a provincial huddle of sovereignties held together by a rope of sand we rise to the dignity and prowess of an imperial republic incomparably greater than Rome.[1]

---

[1] Quoted in *Literary Digest*, July 2, 1898.

The Philippine Censorship

But if the American people were ignorant of the real state of affairs in the Philippines in 1898-1899, the fault was not entirely theirs. A rigid press censorship was maintained in the islands, and no correspondent was permitted to write anything that might "hurt the Administration" in Washington. As a consequence, the public was treated to only the most optimistic view of the American military occupation, while news of the Filipino insurrection against the United States was controlled even more strictly. On the subject of future policy in the Philippines, the Republican platform of 1900 was delightfully vague and noncommittal. It observed that it was the duty of the American government "to maintain its authority, to put down insurrection, and to confer the blessings of liberty and civilization upon all the rescued people," and promised that "the largest measure of self-government consistent with their welfare and our duties shall be secured to them by law."

This was the paternalistic philosophy of those who were determined that the United States should keep the Philippines and thus become an Asiatic power. But there was a question as to the competence of the Federal government to acquire, to hold, and to govern territories as colonial dependencies. In turn, this question involved the problem of whether the Constitution followed the flag. If so, then the Philippines would be brought within the American tariff wall, the coastwise shipping laws and internal revenue laws would be extended to them, and finally, no immigration restrictions could be raised against Filipinos. If, however, the Constitution did not follow the flag, then Congress might legislate arbitrarily and exploit the islands for the benefit of the people of the United States.

The Constitution and the Flag

The Republicans, holding that the Constitution did not follow the flag, assumed that the United States might govern the islands as a colony. The Democrats took a different view. They wished the Philippines to have their independence, and by supporting the argument that the United States could not under the Constitution administer colonies, they hoped to force the Republicans to choose between the evils of incorporating the islands with the American Union and granting them independence. It was in the midst of such political and constitutional arguments that the United States set about to provide a government for the Philippines.

The first step was the appointment by President McKinley, in January, 1899, of a commission headed by President Jacob G. Schurman of Cornell University to conduct investigations in the islands and to report recommendations. Other members of the commission included Charles Denby, Dean C. Worcester, Major General E. S. Otis, and Rear Admiral George Dewey. Its investigations were conducted during 1899, a preliminary report being completed in November and a final report in January, 1900. The striking features of the Schurman commission report were: (1) Strong prejudices in favor of American ideals of self-government and of American methods of government, and (2) a recommendation for a modified form of territorial government for the Philippines. After not merely assuming, but also affirming, the superiority of the American system of separation of powers, the commission expressed regret that the Filipinos appeared never to have recognized the unrivaled qualities of this American plan. In a word, it was assumed from the beginning that what the Filipinos needed was American ideals and American political practices.

The Taft Commission

Acting upon this debatable assumption, as expressed in the Schurman report, the President appointed the Taft commission, which reached the Philippines in June, 1900. It was composed of William H. Taft, Dean C. Worcester, Luke E.

Wright, Henry C. Ide, and Bernard Moses. The functions of this commission were stated by Elihu Root, the Secretary of War. It was to provide, first, for the establishment of municipal government, permitting the populace to participate to the full extent of their ability, of which, however, the commission would be the judge. Later, the commission was to consider provincial administration and report when the central government, in its opinion, might be entrusted to the civil authorities. Finally, the military governor was to remain as chief executive, subject to the legislative power of the commission. In main, the commission was to be guided by the "bill of rights" of the American Constitution, not including the right of trial by jury. The less civilized tribes of the islands were to retain their tribal organization, while education, particularly primary, was to be fostered and the use of the English language encouraged.

In July, 1901, Taft was inaugurated as civil governor, the military power being restricted to those districts where the insurrection against American rule still continued. This was followed by the Congressional Act of 1902, by which provision was made for a Philippine legislative assembly, which, in turn, might select two resident commissioners to the United States House of Representatives. In addition, it stipulated that all laws passed by the Philippine government were to be reported to Congress, which retained the power to annul them. After this, the office of military governor was abolished, and the civil governor became governor general in February, 1905. The first Philippine legislative assembly was elected on a limited franchise in 1907. It exercised the legislative power with the commission, which at this time was composed of five Americans and four Filipinos. This form of administration, while giving the Filipinos some participation in political affairs, was essentially colonial and reserved all ultimate power to the Americans.

The Democrats and Independence

The Democratic victory in the United States in 1912 held great significance for the Filipinos. It is true that some Republican leaders had given lip service to the idea of eventual independence for the Philippines. Their statements, however, were vague, and their policies were so little designed to encourage independence that the Filipinos welcomed the advent of the Democrats to power. Republican members of the Philippine commission were recalled, and their places were taken by Democrats, who were now outnumbered by Filipinos. Francis B. Harrison was appointed Governor General. The policy of the Wilson administration was announced to be ultimate independence for the Philippines. Every act of the administration would be designed to prepare for this event. In 1916, the Jones Act provided for: (1) a Philippine Senate to replace the commission as the upper house of the legislature; (2) broadening the suffrage qualifications; and (3) appointment of all officers, save a specifically excepted few, by the Governor General, with the advice of the Philippine Senate. From 1916 to 1921, the Filipinos thus enjoyed an extraordinarily large measure of self-government. It is true that this newly found power was not always exercised wisely, but at least the Democrats gave the Filipinos the chance to learn in the school of practical politics.

The American Contribution

The contribution that the United States made to the political, social, and economic life of the Philippine Islands during more than three decades of American rule there cannot as yet be appraised with accuracy. If it was the purpose of the American government from the first to accord the Filipinos their independence, the character of American rule will be judged by the degree to which it has fitted the inhabitants of the islands to rule themselves. Many of the factors that enter into such a problem are intangible. Others more material in nature are susceptible of some degree of measurement.

The first difficult problem with which the United States had to deal was the suppression of the Philippine insurrection and the restoration of order. Since the Philippine nationalists had some justification for the belief that the United States had betrayed them in denying independence as soon as the Spaniards were ousted from the islands, it was natural that bitterness should linger on for many years. The moderate policy that was followed once the revolt was suppressed did much to allay this feeling. Civil courts were soon re-established, and, functioning under new codes of criminal and civil procedure, they soon gained the confidence of the people. Law enforcement was entrusted to municipal police, who were assisted by the Philippine Constabulary, a native police body that was at first under American officers. As years passed, the problem of policing the islands was simplified as an ambitious program of road construction was carried out. This program, however, in 1937 still left many districts without adequate communication of this kind. Some railroad building, supplementing a single line that existed under the Spanish regime, was also encouraged under private enterprise, with, on the whole, disappointing results to investors.

Educational Reforms

Public education and public health were, of course, stressed in the beginning by the American administration. Even before the termination of military rule, more than a thousand elementary schools had been opened. An education law of 1901 that made English the medium of instruction was designed to further the course of American administration rather than the interests of the native peoples. Although secondary and technical schools and finally a university were founded, the growth of the educational system was hampered by inadequate revenues. Greater advancement was made in the realm of public health. Smallpox, cholera, and the plague had all flourished in the days of Spanish rule. They could be overcome only by eradication of unsanitary living conditions, which were common throughout the islands. To this task, the public health service applied itself with most encouraging results. The primary problem was in the cities, which, in the space of a few years, became clean and healthy centers.

The Imperialists Return

When the Republicans returned to power in 1921, they professed themselves to be mightily shocked by the Democratic experiment in Filipino self-government. Governor General Harrison was replaced by Major General Leonard Wood, an able administrator but essentially a bureaucrat. Under the administrations of Presidents Harding, Coolidge, and Hoover, the Filipinos were given no reason to believe that they might expect independence in the near future. Although President Wilson, in 1919, had informed Congress that it was now the liberty and the duty of the United States to grant independence, no action was taken, and it was soon apparent that the succeeding Republican administrations did not regard the Filipinos as capable of looking after themselves, or at least this was the reason given for delaying independence indefinitely. When the Philippine legislature passed a bill in 1927 providing for a plebiscite on the question of independence, President Coolidge vetoed it on the extraordinary ground that the Filipinos did not yet comprehend the virtues of the American principle of the separation of powers.

Depression and Freedom

The cause of Philippine independence was, however, revived in the United States, not on the basis of political theorizing, but rather as a result of the world economic depression of 1929 and subsequent years. In the stress of the depression, the argument was advanced that American business was injured by the competition of Philippine products, principally sugar. American labor, likewise, wished to bar Filipino immigrants. For twenty years, Philippine products had entered the United States duty-free, while American products had free entry to the islands. Since 1920, sixty per cent of Philippine imports had been American goods, and more than seventy per cent of Philippine exports went to the United States. As early as 1929, when the Smoot-Hawley Tariff Bill was before Congress, an amendment providing for Philippine independence failed of passage by only five votes. This encouraged such organizations as the National Grange and the American Federation of Labor to continue the independence crusade. While motivated by selfish interests, they were able to base their action on the declared purpose of the American government, as expressed in the preamble of the Jones Act of 1916.

During 1931 and 1932, Congress was flooded with bills proposing Philippine independence. In January, 1933, Congress passed, over President Hoover's veto, the Hawes-Cutting Bill, granting independence to the Philippines after a transition period of ten years. Since this act was not acceptable to the Filipino legislature, it was amended, at the suggestion of President Roosevelt, and accepted as the Tydings-McDuffie Bill in 1934. In its amended form, the act provided for the surrender of American military bases in the islands and left the question of naval bases for ultimate settlement on terms satisfactory to both the United States and the Philippines. This act was promptly accepted by the Philippine legislature.

By February, 1935, a Philippine constitutional convention had provided a new constitution, which was approved by President Roosevelt. In November, the new Philippine Commonwealth government was inaugurated with Manuel L. Quezon as President.

The Transition Period

During the ten-year period that must elapse before full independence may be achieved, if then, the structure of the government of the Philippine Commonwealth is changed but slightly from what had previously prevailed. The major modification is in political ideology rather than in fact. Sovereignty and ultimate responsibility still remain, during the transition period, with the United States. Under the new Constitution, the Philippine legislature has been changed from a bicameral to a unicameral body. An elected Filipino President takes the place, as chief executive, of an American-appointed Governor General. Briefly described, the Constitution of the Philippine Commonwealth is democratic in principle and republican in form. The franchise is limited to literate male citizens twenty-one or more years of age. Guarantees of personal liberty are contained in a bill of rights, while the principle of separation of powers is likewise adopted. The powers of the Philippine President are extensive. He is chosen by direct popular vote for a six-year term and is not eligible for immediate re-election. The system of government being unitary, the President heads the entire administration. He has power of supervision over local government, commands the armed forces of the state, and may suspend the writ of *habeas corpus*. His power of appointment covers all departments, including the courts, subject only to the approval of a commission on appointments.

The Philippine legislature is a unicameral body known as the National Assembly, the members of which are apportioned according to provinces on a basis of population. They are elected for three-year terms.

The Constitution also provides limitations upon the use and disposal of natural resources belonging to the state. It makes provision, too, for the growth of state socialism.

The state may, in the interest of national welfare and defense, establish and operate industries and means of transportation and communication and, upon payment of just compensation, transfer to public ownership utilities and other private enterprises to be operated by the government.

There is also a provision giving the National Assembly power to regulate the relations of capital and labor. During the ten-year transition period, the limitations upon Philippine independence contained in the Independence Act are appended as part of the Constitution. In other words, they will pertain until July, 1946, when complete independence will presumably be achieved.

When the Commonwealth was established, American officials in the Philippine service were replaced by Filipinos. However, President Quezon secured the services of General Douglas MacArthur of the United States Army as his chief military adviser. For the maintenance of internal order and for national defense, the government plans a standing army of about 20,000, which, as a result of compulsory military training, will be supported in the course of some ten years by a reserve of half a million.

Philippine Finances

The biggest single problem that faced the young Commonwealth was the question of revenue. This, in turn, was intimately connected with the new economic status of the islands, resulting from the independence policy. During 1934, three acts of the American Congress precipitated the process of divorcing the Philippine Islands from American economic life, of which they had previously been an integral part. The first of these was the Jones-Costigan Bill (May 9, 1934), which, among other things, limited American importations of Philippine sugar on a quota basis. The Philippine Independence Act of the same year limited the quantity of the principal Philippine exports entitled to free American entry during the first five years of the Commonwealth government. At the end of the fifth year, the Commonwealth government will be required to levy an export tax amounting to five per cent of the American duty, which will be increased to twenty-five per cent in the tenth year, when the full American duty will be imposed. Finally, the Revenue Act of 1934 provided for a processing tax on a number of vegetable oils.

The importance of these provisions and restrictions on the importation of Philippine sugar into the United States may be realized when it is recalled that, since 1913, Philippine sugar had entered the American market duty-free. By 1920, the Philippine sugar industry had become the most important in the islands. In 1934, half a million Filipino farmers, laborers, and their families were engaged in the cultivation of sugar cane, and the industry's investment was estimated at $250,000,000. The value of the annual sugar crop was about $75,000,000, or about 40 per cent of the total value of all agricultural products. Philippine sugar exports in 1932 were valued at $60,000,000, or 63 per cent of the total value of all exports. Whereas, prior to passage of the Jones-Costigan Act, the Philippines had exported 88 per cent of their total crop to the United States, after the act, because of increased production and the quota, they could dispose of only about 63 per cent in the United States.

The excise tax on coconut oil imported into the United States from the Philippines, authorized by the Revenue Act of 1934, was equally serious in threatening the economic life of the islands. The coconut-oil industry was the second largest in the islands, involving several millions of the farming population. As a result of these taxes, it was predicted commonly in 1935 and 1936 that Philippine sugar and oil would be forced from the American market, with serious results to both industries and thus to the economic stability of the Commonwealth.

Another factor affecting the stability of the Commonwealth government was the position occupied by American investments in the Philippines. These, while not heavy in agriculture, have provided the major impetus to Philippine industry. The future of these investments will, of course, bear a direct relation to the prosperity of the Commonwealth. By 1935 there was a marked tendency for Filipino political leaders and American investors to seek modifications of the Independence Act, modifications designed to make it bear less heavily on the economic life of the islands. These and other economic problems involved caused some Filipinos to question the desirability of full independence. On the other hand, American agriculture and labor continued to demand independence in full, in order to free the American farmer and the American laborer from Philippine competition. It may be granted that both the Filipino nationalists and a long-accepted policy on the part of the American government have played their part in bringing about the present Philippine Commonwealth with its promise of future independence. Yet it is doubtful whether the promise of independence would have been so readily given had it not been for the selfish considerations that motivated American agriculture and labor. A specific policy of independence was adopted only after the Philippines had, in the opinion of many Americans, become a liability. Not all American opinion, however, subscribed to this view. The fact that the future of the American naval establishment in the Philippines has not yet been determined indicates that the United States may not be prepared as yet to withdraw completely from the islands. The decision on this question will doubtless be affected by American relationships not only to the Philippines but also to the Far East as a whole.

American Interests in Asia

The contemporary aspects of American interests in the Far East can be treated here only in the briefest outline. As background to such a discussion, it will be recalled that the principle of most-favored-nation treatment was the foundation of America's far eastern policy. It was on the basis of this principle that the United States, like the imperialistic powers of Europe, insisted upon the enjoyment, both in China and Japan, of such privileges as extraterritoriality and the conventional tariff, of which the former is still exercised in China. After acquisition of the Philippines, the United States, seeking to protect her commercial interests in China, enunciated the open door policy, and later, the policy of China's territorial integrity, while at the same time she sought unsuccessfully for a coaling station on the central China coast. Subsequently, the United States exerted diplomatic pressure to break the spheres of influence held by European powers and Japan, in the hope of providing wider investment opportunities for American capital in China.

Trade and Investments

These various phases of American diplomatic policy in the Far East were designed primarily, though not exclusively, to promote: (1) American commercial interests in China, and (2) after the dawn of the twentieth century, American investments. Popularly, the commercial interests of the United States in the Far East, including Siam, British Malaya, and the Dutch East Indies, are usually thought of as large. As a matter of fact, between 1900 and 1914, only about five per cent of American exports and eleven per cent of imports were

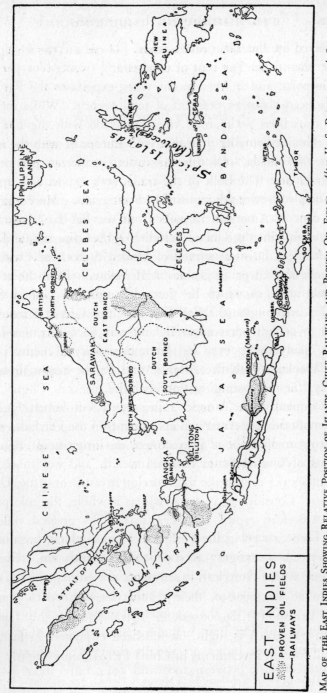
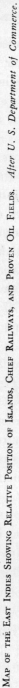

MAP OF THE EAST INDIES SHOWING RELATIVE POSITION OF ISLANDS, CHIEF RAILWAYS, AND PROVEN OIL FIELDS. *After U. S. Department of Commerce.*

involved in the far eastern trade. These increased in post-war years to ten per cent of exports and twenty-four per cent of imports, and in very recent years, exports to the Far East have been about 15 per cent of total exports. While increase has thus been noticeable, American trade with the Far East has remained smaller than that with Europe or with the single state of Canada. Of this far eastern trade, 42 per cent is with Japan. The bulk of the trade, both export and import, consists of raw and semifinished materials. More than 85 per cent of American imports from the Far East have been non-competitive products, including rubber, tin, silk, and furs. A detailed statistical survey of United States trade with the Far East is given in Tables I-III below.[2] From these, the conclusion appears to be that although the United States is dependent upon the Far East for important raw materials, their availability has never in any way been threatened, nor is it likely to be, even in wartime, unless an enemy power can blockade both the Atlantic and Pacific approach to the United States, a seeming improbability.

Coupled with America's important but relatively small oriental trade are American investments in the Far East, which in 1935 totaled about $750,000,000, an insignificant figure in terms of United States national wealth and not more than about six per cent of the total foreign investment of the United States. Considering eastern Asia as a whole, the role played by American capital has been small. Its greatest influence has been exerted in the Philippines, from which, presumably, American sovereignty is soon to be withdrawn. Even in China, where American investments are estimated as a maximum at $200,000,000, their relative importance to those of the British ($1,189,000,000 in 1931) and of the Japanese ($1,137,000,000) is slight. It has been estimated, in fact, that of all foreign investments in China in 1931, only slightly more

---

[2] These tables are reproduced from Miriam S. Farley, "America's Stake in the Far East—I: Trade," *Far Eastern Survey*, New York, July 29, 1936.

TABLE I

UNITED STATES TRADE WITH THE FAR EAST

(Five-year averages; in millions of dollars, and as per cent of total Imports and Exports)

	Japan				China[a]				Philippines				British Malaya				Netherlands India			
	Value		Per cent		Value		Per cent		Value		Per cent		Value		Per cent		Value		Per cent	
	Imports	Exports	Imports	Exports	Imports	Exports	Imports	Exports	Imports	Exports	Imports	Exports	Imports	Exports	Imports	Exports	Imports	Exports	Imports	Exports
1910-14	85.0	45.3	5.0	2.1	38.5	31.4	2.3	1.4	19.4	22.6	1.1	1.0	24.6	2.9	1.5	0.1	9.2	3.1	0.5	0.1
1921-25	335.4	241.9	9.7	5.5	160.7	128.7	4.7	2.9	80.1	51.9	2.3	1.2	153.2	8.0	4.4	0.2	55.0	17.2	1.6	0.4
1926-30	379.6	246.0	9.4	5.1	155.9	134.6	3.9	2.8	114.1	73.7	2.8	1.5	249.8	12.6	6.2	0.3	87.5	33.8	2.2	0.7
1931-35	148.2	169.6	8.6	8.4	55.5	75.6	3.2	3.7	89.1	47.7	5.2	2.3	82.5	3.7	4.8	0.2	38.0	10.2	2.2	0.5

	French Indo-China				Siam				Asiatic Russia				"Other Asia"				Total Far East			
	Value		Per cent		Value		Per cent		Value		Per cent		Value		Per cent		Value		Per cent	
	Imports	Exports	Imports	Exports	Imports	Exports	Imports	Exports	Imports	Exports	Imports	Exports	Imports	Exports	Imports	Exports	Imports	Exports	Imports	Exports
1910-14	0.001	0.2	(b)	(b)	0.1	0.5	(b)	(b)	1.7	1.1	0.1	1.1	0.07	0.001	(b)	(b)	178.6	107.1	10.6	4.9
1921-25	0.2	1.1	(b)	(b)	0.3	1.2	(b)	(b)	0.5	1.1	(b)	(b)	0.09	0.02	(b)	(b)	785.5	451.2	22.8	10.3
1926-30	0.1	1.9	(b)	(b)	0.5	2.4	(b)	(b)	1.0	2.1	(b)	(b)	0.12	0.07	(b)	(b)	988.7	507.2	24.5	10.6
1931-35	0.8	1.2	(b)	(b)	0.2	1.2	(b)	(b)	0.6[c]	0.2[c]	(b)	(b)	0.03	0.53	(b)	(b)	414.7	309.8	24.2	15.3

[a] Including Hong Kong and Kwantung. [b] Less than 0.1. [c] 1931-34.

TABLE II

PRINCIPAL UNITED STATES EXPORTS TO FAR EAST, 1929 TO 1934

	Value of total exports to Far East (000 $)		Per cent of total exports of commodity to										Approximate percentage of exports to total production of commodity	
			Japan		China[a]		Philippines		Other		Total Far East			
	1929	1934	1929	1934	1929	1934	1929	1934	1929	1934	1929	1934	1929	1934
Agricultural products and manufactures														
Raw cotton	133,561	131,299	14.3	30.5	3.0	5.0	(c)	(c)	0.1	0.2	17.4	35.7	55	58
Cotton cloth, duck, and tire fabric	13,139	5,712	0.1	(c)	0.5	0.3	13.2	21.3	2.7	1.4	16.5	23.3	7	4
Tobacco, bright flue-cured	21,663	11,962	4.2	1.7	11.6	8.6	(c)	(c)	2.8	0.5	18.6	10.9	55	55
Cigarettes	11,311	2,903	0.4	0.2	50.6	4.3	13.7	41.6	2.9	1.0	67.6	47.2	7	3
Wheat, grain[b]	9,831	6,679	7.6	23.0	1.2	42.2	(c)	(c)	(c)	(c)	8.8	65.2 }	18	5
Wheat, flour[b]	22,085	3,534	2.1	(c)	19.1	10.3	5.6	10.5	0.4	(c)	27.3	21.0		
Milk, condensed, etc.	6,724	2,361	8.8	0.7	10.7	3.9	21.8	48.3	4.4	5.6	45.8	58.6	4	2
Fish, canned	4,649	891	(c)	0.1	1.8	0.8	10.0	7.5	12.0	0.8	24.8	9.2		
Leather	4,607	1,462	3.5	1.5	3.1	1.8	2.6	4.8	1.4	1.0	10.7	9.2	9	6
Forest products														
Western cedar, logs and timber	3,734	696	94.7	92.2	(c)	0.1	(c)	(c)	(c)	(c)	94.7	92.3		
Douglas fir, logs, timber, sawmill products	13,384	4,894	22.7	20.0	18.0	26.5	0.4	0.4	0.1	0.2	41.3	47.1		
Wood pulp	566	5,450	20.3	74.5	0.5	3.7	(c)	(c)	(c)	0.2	20.8	78.4		
Paper and manufactures	6,544	4,352	2.0	1.5	8.5	11.1	4.8	7.6	2.2	2.7	17.6	23.1		
Petroleum products														
Crude petroleum	2,911	8,048	7.7	16.0	(c)	0.2	(c)	(c)	(c)	(c)	7.7	16.2	3	4
Gasoline, naphtha, etc.	11,955	5,820	1.9	5.2	1.2	2.3	1.1	3.8	0.1	(c)	4.5	11.3	14	5
Kerosene	29,527	5,491	6.5	3.9	22.6	17.2	3.0	4.3	3.2	1.0	35.2	26.4	35	18

814

Gas oil and fuel oil	6,151	8,800	11.8	25.7	2.6	2.3	2.2	3.0	(c)	(c)	16.6	31.0	8	8
Lubricating oil	9,690	4,916	3.2	3.4	3.1	2.7	0.9	1.0	2.3	1.3	9.5	8.4	31	29
Paraffin wax	2,231	523	3.5	0.1	10.7	5.6	0.5	0.8	0.5	0.1	15.8	6.7	51	42
Iron and steel manufactures														
Scrap iron (including tin plate scrap)	3,449	13,129	39.9	64.7	4.5	3.6	0.2	(c)	(c)	(c)	44.6	68.4		
Tin plate and terneplate	13,429	8,249	24.5	21.5	15.8	18.8	3.2	4.6	3.4	3.9	47.0	48.9		
Other semi-manufactures	11,242	3,994	7.0	6.2	1.3	1.3	5.0	8.1	3.3	1.6	16.6	19.2		
Pipes, tubes, etc.	6,339	1,688	5.5	2.8	0.6	3.2	3.4	3.1	7.8	3.6	17.3	12.8	6	6
Other steel mill products	6,687	1,989	2.9	0.8	1.9	2.9	4.0	5.7	2.3	1.3	11.2	10.7		
Advanced manufactures	8,732	3,134	4.0	2.2	2.1	4.0	2.4	3.7	1.5	1.3	10.0	11.3		
Automobiles, parts, etc.	41,792	22,548	3.5	7.0	0.9	1.9	1.1	1.8	2.3	0.7	7.8	11.3	12	11
Industrial machinery	27,368	12,267	3.0	5.2	1.6	2.8	2.0	2.5	3.3	1.9	9.9	12.5	13	10
Electrical machinery and apparatus	12,648	5,431	3.5	1.0	3.2	2.8	1.7	1.9	1.9	2.5	10.4	8.2	5	6
Aircraft, parts, etc.	1,423	4,804	4.9	1.8	8.5	22.0	1.3	0.3	0.8	3.1	15.6	27.2	13	37
Miscellaneous														
Tires and tubes	6,260	1,591	4.3	0.3	1.4	1.8	4.3	8.9	5.9	2.2	16.0	13.3	4	2
Other rubber and manufactures	3,429	719	1.7	1.5	1.2	2.2	4.3	3.4	1.8	1.0	9.1	8.1		
Fertilizers and materials	10,645	2,878	29.6	15.9	1.1	0.3	9.9	5.8	11.5	0.8	52.1	22.9		
Copper and manufactures	4,560	9,417	1.3	17.3	0.7	1.1	0.3	0.4	0.1	0.1	2.5	18.9		
Coal tar dyes, etc.	4,471	2,270	14.7	7.0	46.9	32.3	0.5	0.3	0.2	0.6	62.2	40.3	13	9
Industrial chemicals	3,706	2,268	9.2	4.9	1.5	2.2	1.6	2.3	0.7	0.8	13.2	10.5	6	5
Photographic goods	3,891	2,459	5.7	6.6	2.6	5.6	2.7	1.3	1.3	1.7	12.3	15.9		

a Including Hong Kong and Kwantung. b Exports to Far East abnormally large on account of U. S. loan and subsidy. c Less than 0.1.

TABLE III

PRINCIPAL UNITED STATES IMPORTS FROM FAR EAST, 1934

	Value of imports from Far East (000 $)	Per cent of total imports of commodity from						Domestic production
		Japan	China[a]	Philippines	Netherlands India	British Malaya	Total Far East	
Crude rubber	89,427	....	....	0.1	16.2	74.1	91.4	None; reclaimed rubber supplies about 20% of consumption.
Raw silk	71,440	97.2	2.2	....	....	....	99.4	None.
Sugar	61,459	....	....	52.3	....	....	52.3	Including Hawaii, etc., supplies about 55% of consumption.
Tin	33,099	....	6.9	....	4.4	62.6	73.9	Slight; reclaimed tin supplies about 30% of consumption.
Coconut oil	7,372	....	....	100.0	....	....	100.0	Supplies about half of consumption.
Copra	4,713	....	....	84.6	11.6	1.7	98.0	None.
Dessicated coconut	2,212	....	....	97.6	....	....	97.6	None.
Furs	10,631	4.6	21.5	7.1	....	....	26.1	Little or none.
Cotton manufactures	7,094	10.7	4.4	....	....	....	22.2	Of varieties imported, small.
Tung oil	6,852	....	100.0	....	....	....	100.0	Supplies great bulk of consumption.
Tea	5,909	14.1	6.4	....	15.5	0.3	36.3	Insignificant.
Hides and skins	4,247	....	8.0	0.1	3.8	....	12.0	None.
Potteries, etc.	4,242	57.9	1.1	....	....	....	59.0	Of some varieties, none; of others, insufficient because they are by-products.
Spices	4,132	0.7	4.2	....	30.6	2.8	38.6	Supplies about two thirds of consumption.
Carpet wool	3,888	....	34.8	....	....	....	34.8	Of some varieties, none; of others, small.
Bristles	3,729	19.3	59.2	....	....	....	78.5	None.
Cigars and cheroots	3,080	....	....	90.4	....	....	90.4	Insufficient because they are by-products.
Manila hemp	2,790	....	....	98.5	1.5	....	100.0	Supplies about 95% of consumption.
Crabmeat, etc.	2,228	78.0	....	....	....	....	99.4	None.
Palm oil	2,156	....	....	....	54.6	0.6	55.2	Supplies part of consumption.
Sisal and henequen	1,898	....	....	0.1	34.1	0.1	34.3	None.

a Including Hong Kong and Kwantung.

Table IV

PRIVATE LONG-TERM INVESTMENTS OF THE UNITED STATES ABROAD

(U. S. Department of Commerce estimates; in millons of dollars)

	1900	1909	1912	1930 Direct	1930 Portfolio	1930 Total	1935 (1) Direct	1935 (1) Portfolio	1935 (1) Total
Europe	10	350	200	1,469	3,461	4,929	1,460	2,083	3,543
Canada	150	500	400	2,049	1,893	3,942	2,130	1,634	3,764
Mexico and Central America	195	750	840	931	38	969	855	42	897
West Indies	60 (2)	145 (2)	228	1,072	161	1,233	975	132	1,107
South America	35	100	175	1,631	1,411	3,042	1,570	1,367	2,937
Africa				115	3	118	130	2	132
Australia and New Zealand				155	265	419	155	250	405
Far East (3)	5	175	{ 50	366	603 (4)	969 (4)	373	385 (4)	758 (4)
Other Asia			10	53	...	53	62	...	62
Total	500 (5)	2,020 (5)	1,903 (6)	7,841	7,834	15,675	7,710	5,895	13,665
Add: Bank capital				125	...	125	125	...	125
Deduct: Net repurchase of securities by foreigners				...	630	630	...	1,100	1,100
Net total	500 (5)	2,020	1,903 (6)	7,966	7,204	15,170	7,835	4,795	12,630

(1) Estimates of direct investments for 1935 can be considered as only approximate until such time as a new and detailed study is made, according to the Department of Commerce. The estimates of portfolio investments are subject throughout to the deduction for net repurchases by foreigners. Although based upon rather extensive data, this deduction still cannot be considered as exact.

(2) Including Porto Rico.

(3) Japan, China, Philippine Islands, Netherlands India, British Malaya, French Indo-China, and Siam. For corrections of these figures see footnotes, Table V.

(4) Holdings of certain Chinese securities excluded because of doubtful value. See Table V, note 6.

(5) Includes life insurance guarantee investments of $45 millions not separated by areas.

(6) This figure should be raised by $200 millions according to Paul D. Dickens of the Department of Commerce. The estimates for 1909 and 1912 are the work of private investigators, and are only roughly comparable.

SOURCE: Estimates for 1935 from information supplied by the Department; estimates for earlier years adapted from *A New Estimate of American Investments Abroad*, Washington, 1931, pp. 8, 24.

TABLE V

PRIVATE LONG-TERM INVESTMENTS OF THE UNITED STATES IN THE FAR EAST

(U. S. Department of Commerce estimates; in millions of dollars)

	1930			1935		
	Direct	Portfolio	Total	Direct	Portfolio	Total
Total all countries [1]	7,841	7,834	15,675 [2] [3]	7,710 [2]	5,895	13,605
Total Far East	366 [2]	603 [3]	969 [2] [3]	373 [2]	385 [4]	758 [2] [4]
Japan	61	383	445	60	327 [5]	387 [5]
China	130	... [8]	130 [8]	125	7 [6]	132 [6]
Philippine Islands	81	85	166	100	51 [7]	151 [7]
Netherlands India	66	135	201	68 [8]	...	68 [8]
"British Malaya" [9]	27	...	27	20	...	20

(1) Subject to the correction for bank capital and repurchase of foreign securities (noted in Table IV) making total investments $15,170 millions in 1930 and $12,630 millions in 1935.

(2) Plus an undetermined share of the $125 millions of American bank capital invested abroad. See also note 8 regarding the understatement of investments in Netherlands India in 1935.

(3) Subject to a deduction of $50 millions, according to the Department of Commerce, for estimated repurchase abroad of outstanding foreign securities issued in the United States. Repurchase of securities is not given for individual countries separately.

(4) Subject to a deduction of some $190 millions for repurchase of Japanese and Philippine securities. See notes 5 and 7.

(5) Probably at least 50% of this sum, or $164 millions, has been repurchased from American investors. In 1931 alone $100 millions were repurchased in Japan, according to the U. S. Department of Commerce (*The Balance of International Payments of the United States in 1931*, p. 50). In 1933 the New York Office of the Yokohama Specie Bank estimated for the American Council that 80% of Japan's outstanding foreign issues had been repatriated (*Memorandum on United States Investments in Japan*, July 6, 1933). But the Mitsubishi Economic Research Bureau has recently given a figure of only 33% (*Japanese Trade and Industry*, p. 84). We have adopted as a conservative estimate for American issues the figure of 50%, which corresponds approximately with the repatriation figure for total Japanese foreign issues as reported by the U. S. Department of Commerce for the end of 1935 (quoted in *Moody's Governments*, Vol. 8, No. 59, p. 1089).

(6) Holdings of certain Chinese government obligations are not included because of their doubtful value. For 1930, the total value of Chinese security holdings was estimated at $42 millions by C. F. Remer in *Foreign Investments in China* (p. 301).

(7) Philippine bond issues have been repatriated in part, according to information supplied by the New York agency of the Philippine National Bank. Out of $57,730,000 of Philippine government and municipal bonds outstanding on June 30, 1936, the Philippine government held $19,475,500 and the Philippine National Bank $6,400,000, leaving $31,854,000 in outside hands. There are no adequate data concerning repurchase of private issues. In addition, there are American rubber investments, valued at $23 millions in 1929, and smaller miscellaneous properties.

(8) This figure is obviously too small, for the investment of one American oil concern, The Standard Vacuum Oil Co., is now $70 millions.

(9) Includes Siam and French Indo-China.

SOURCE: Figures in the table itself are from U. S. Department of Commerce; for 1930, from *A New Estimate of American Investments Abroad*, Washington, 1931, pp. 8, 20; for 1935, from information supplied by the Department.

than six per cent were American. A statement of these foreign
investments is given in Tables IV-VII.[3] At the beginning
of the twentieth century, it was predicted optimistically that
American investments in the Far East were about to witness
an unprecedented expansion. In more recent years, there has
been a marked waning of this optimism, a point of view which
has increased since the establishment of the Commonwealth
government in the Philippines.

TABLE VI

AMERICAN PRIVATE LONG-TERM INVESTMENTS IN CHINA, 1930 (¹)

(In millions of dollars)

Business investments	155.1
Transportation	10.8
Public utilities	35.2
Mining	.1
Manufacturing	20.5
Banking and finance	8.5
Real estate	8.5
Import and export	47.7
Miscellaneous	2.1
Not analyzed	4.9
Securities and obligations of the Chinese government	41.7
Total	196.8

(1) Unlike Tables IV and V, this includes the property of Americans
domiciled in China.

SOURCE: C. F. Remer, *Foreign Investments in China*. New York,
1933. pp. 274-308.

The Cost of a Policy

Recently, American students have attempted to estimate
the cost of the far eastern policy of the United States. Briefly
summarized, their tentative findings follow:

---

[3] These tables are reproduced from William W. Lockwood, Jr., "America's Stake
in the Far East—II: Investments." *Far Eastern Survey,* New York, August 12,
1936.

The National Cost

Approximate annual cost of the Foreign Service in China, Japan, and Siam	$905,745
Approximate annual cost of the Far Eastern Division of the Department of State	71,451
Approximate annual cost of the Far Eastern Division of the Bureau of Foreign and Domestic Commerce	12,000
Approximate annual cost of Commercial Attachés' offices in the Far East	139,100
Approximate annual cost of Agricultural Attachés' offices in the Far East	34,860
Approximate annual expenditures for army equipment and maintenance of personnel in the Far East	11,000,000

In addition to the above sum, some considerable proportion (what proportion it is impossible to say) of the annual army appropriations would be chargeable to the conduct of far eastern policy. U. S. army appropriations in recent fiscal years have been:

      1934...... $350,000,000
      1935......   568,000,000
      1936......   402,000,000
      1937......   383,000,000

| Since U. S. naval policy is directed perhaps 90 per cent toward the maintenance of far eastern policy, at least this amount may be charged to the cost of that policy. For the year 1935, this proportion amounted to .... | 589,276,636 |
| Total cost of far eastern policy (1935), exclusive of the general army appropriation...... | $601,439,792 |

In contrast to the above cost, the credits that the United States derives from her interests in the Far East are drawn from two major sources, trade and investments. United States trade with the Far East in 1935 totaled $837,020,000. Of this $510,171,000 represented imports and $326,849,000 exports. Of this total, trade with Japan accounted for 43 per cent—30 per cent of imports, and 62 per cent of exports; trade with Kwantung accounted for 1 per cent; with the Dutch East Indies, British Malaya, French Indo-China, and Siam, 24 per cent; with the Philippines, 18 per cent; with China and Hong Kong, 14 per cent. What portions of this return are a result of American expenditures under the costs of American policy shown above? The naval appropriations do not apply, for the navy, which accounts for 96 per cent of the cost of far eastern policy, is not an asset in the American-Japan trade, nor in the American trade with southeastern Asia. Even in the case of the remainder of the trade (18 per cent with the Philippines and 14 per cent with China and Hong Kong), although the navy has promoted it to some degree, it would probably continue even were there no American navy.

The conclusion to be reached then is that at most 20 per cent to 30 per cent of American trade with the Far East, or between $167,000,000 and $251,000,000 for 1935, has any dependence on the

TABLE VII

AMERICAN PRIVATE LONG-TERM INVESTMENTS
IN THE PHILIPPINES, 1932 ([1])

(In millions of dollars)

Mines	2.6
Real estate ([2])	12.1
Bank capital	0.8
Bonds ([3])	114.0
Manufacturing	35.5
Merchandising	30.5
Agriculture ([4])	10.6
Forest and lumbering	6.5
All other	45.2
Total	257.8

(1) Unlike Tables IV and V this includes the property of Americans domiciled in the Islands.
(2) Exclusive of agricultural land.
(3) Predominantly insular government bonds, but also includes provincial, municipal, railway, and utility bonds.
(4) Only land devoted to agriculture.
SOURCE: Estimates of the Bureau of Insular Affairs of the War Department, quoted in U. S. Department of Commerce, *Economic Notes on the Philippine Islands* (Division of Regional Information, Special Circular No. 303, July 1, 1934).

item of $589,000,000 devoted to the navy. It should be noted, moreover, that the naval expenditure exceeds the total of either imports or exports with all of the Far Eastern countries.[4]

Returns to American capital resulting from the total far eastern trade in 1935, estimated most liberally, may have been as high as $83,000,000, but on the basis of the 20 per cent to 30 per cent of the trade that may have been promoted by national expenditure, the return was only between $17,000,000 and $25,000,000.

The return on American investments in the Far East, which in 1935 totaled about $750,000,000 at 6 per cent, was about $45,000,000. Of this sum, the return from China and the Philippines was between $25,000,000 and $30,000,000.

While the interests of the United States in the Far East cannot be estimated accurately on the simple basis of the incomplete and approximate figures here presented, these figures nevertheless suggest the heavy deficit that is involved.

It should be noted (a) that the trade and investment figures quoted above—43 per cent and 23 per cent respectively—are with Japan, and (b) that it is no international secret that the American navy is maintained in the Pacific vis-a-vis Japan alone. In other words, the primary use of the navy, if it be considered an active force in the Pacific, is directed against the country with which existing American commercial relations are overwhelmingly greatest. It is therefore conceivable that the largest item in the cost sheet of maintaining the Far Eastern policy [of the United States] is an instrument directed against the country bringing in much the largest financial return.[5]

Striking though the above conclusion may be, it does not represent a new tendency in American far eastern policy, nor may it be said that the policy has ever been motivated exclu-

---

[4] These tentative conclusions are presented by Frederick V. Field, "America's Stake in the Far East—III: The Cost." *Far Eastern Survey*, New York, August 26, 1936.

[5] *Ibid.*

sively with a view to furthering American commerce and investments. For the past century, the American stake in the Far East has included, as well, sentimental, religious, and humanitarian values. These, like the ever-present issue of political prestige, defy exact measurement. Nevertheless, their influence has been considerable. During the twentieth century, in particular, the American public, whose knowledge of the Far East has always been fragmentary, tended to assume an attitude of moral and sentimental guardianship toward China, while at the same time it developed somewhat fantastic fears of Japan. These attitudes were in part a result of propaganda, and in part a natural sympathy for China's allegedly helpless condition and a human protest against the rise of new Japan, whose increasing influence overshadowed American prestige in the Orient. Since the World War, these attitudes have been shared in some measure by the peoples of Europe. They made possible the verbal opposition by the League of Nations and the United States to Japan's Manchurian policy. They were largely responsible, too, for the non-recognition doctrine thus far maintained against Manchoukuo. In the popular mind, the non-recognition doctrine signified the moral indignation with which western public opinion viewed Japan's alleged breach of international engagements. In the view of western governments, however, the moral issue, if one existed, was subordinate to practical politics. To them, the creation of Manchoukuo was indicative of Japan's paramount influence in the Far East. It was this claim to paramount influence, rather than the new state of Manchoukuo, which Europe and the United States refused to recognize. As long as Japan asserts that claim and the United States refuses recognition, danger spots will continue to darken the face of American policy in the Far East.[6]

[6] For a discussion of the most recent developments in United States policy, see T. A. Bisson, "American Policy in the Far East." Foreign Policy Association *Reports*, February 1, 1937.

SELECTED BIBLIOGRAPHY

George H. Blakeslee, *Conflicts of Policy in the Far East* (New York: 1934). D. P. Barrows, *A History of the Philippines* (Indianapolis: 1924). R. L. Buell, Foreign Policy Association *Information Service,* Apr. 30, 1930. Grover Clark, *The Balance Sheet of Imperialism* (New York: 1936). F. R. Dulles, *America in the Pacific* (New York: 1932). George M. Dutcher, *The Political Awakening of the East* (New York: 1925), ch. 5 on the Philippines. Frederick V. Field, *Economic Handbook of the Pacific Area* (New York: 1934). F. C. Fisher, "The Status of the Philippine Islands Under Independence," in *The American Bar Association Journal,* Aug. 1933. W. C. Forbes, *The Philippine Islands* (Boston: 1928). J. W. Garner, *American Foreign Policies* (New York: 1928), ch. 3 on imperialism and the Philippines. Hermann Hagedorn, *Leonard Wood,* 2 vols. (New York: 1931). G. L. Kirk, *Philippine Independence* (New York: 1936). M. M. Kalaw, "International Aspects of Philippine Independence," in *Pacific Affairs,* Jan. 1933. Bruno Lasker, *Filipino Immigration* (Chicago: 1931). C. K. Leith, *World Minerals and World Politics* (New York: 1931). H. C. Moncado, *America, the Philippines and the Orient* (New York: 1932). G. M. Malcolm, *The Commonwealth of the Philippines* (New York: 1936). Nathaniel Peffer, *Must We Fight in Asia?* (New York: 1935). *Problems of the Pacific, 1936* (Chicago: 1937). J. S. Reyes, *Legislative History of America's Economic Policy Toward the Philippines* (New York: 1923). W. H. Shepardson, *The United States in World Affairs* (New York: 1935), ch. 8 on the independence of the Philippines. A. J. Toynbee, *Survey of International Affairs, 1933* (Oxford: 1934), pt. 4, ch. 7. A. J. Toynbee, *Survey of International Affairs, 1935,* 2 vols. (New York: 1936), vol. 1, pt. 2. P. G. Wright, *The American Tariff and Oriental Trade* (Chicago: 1931). P. G. Wright, *Trade and Trade Barriers in the Pacific* (Stanford University: 1935).

CHAPTER XLII

The Changing Scene—Japan

THE narrative told in the foregoing pages is, as the reader is perhaps all too well aware, a story of *contacts*—commercial, military, and diplomatic—between the West and the Far East. At intervals, some attempt has been made to introduce the political and institutional life of both Japan and China, where these appeared to form an indispensable background. In the century that has elapsed since the English East India Company lost its commercial monopoly at Canton, or in the briefer interval since Commodore Perry first anchored his ships in Uraga Bay, the western impact upon China and Japan has wrought profound changes in the daily life, the habits, and the thought of these eastern peoples—changes the nature of which can be but briefly suggested in these concluding pages.

It is not surprising that the western world has pictured the Far East in terms of fixed ideas. To Americans, the name "Japan" has often conjured visions of matchless cherry blossoms, of dainty ladies in silk kimonos sipping ceremonial tea, of innumerable temples and shrines, of paper houses, and of exquisite dolls; and, side by side with these, of saber-rattling soldiers sworn to ideals of world conquest, aided and abetted by inscrutable diplomats whose mysterious cunning no western mind may hope to fathom. This is the Japan of the tourist and of the imagination. Against it must be seen another Japan of paddy fields where millions of peasant feet tramp knee-deep in slime to produce the nation's food; of cotton factories where daughters of Nippon toil with machine precision; of cities where white-collared clerks compute the profits of their betters. This is the Japan of reality, where the struggle of the individual to survive must take precedence over cherry blossoms, moon-viewing, and naval ratios.

Modern and contemporary Japan, seen through western newspapers, magazines, and books, has been all too frequently a land of quaint beauty, unhappily, however, inhabited only by the Arakis of war and the Mitsuis of industry. These are the men who create what commonly passes for news: the invasion of alien territory or the capture of a new foreign market. Little space remains in modern journalism for their humbler countrymen, the teachers, the painters, the writers, the poets, the farmers, the petty tradesmen, and the laborers. And yet, if a nation may be said to possess that intangible attribute known as the soul, it is, in Japan, given its truest expression through these commoner folk and through those who with pen or brush interpret their thought and life. The beauty of Japan's pictorial art, the depth and richness of its literature, the suggestiveness of the *tanka* (the thirty-one syllable poem), the uproarious merriment in which the plebeian classes delight, and the happy behavior which makes this land "a paradise for children"— these form a truer approach to the spirit of Japanese life than the sonorous pronouncements of a minister of war.

It is not alone in the spheres of politics, war, and industry that modern Japan has been and remains subject to revolutionary tendencies. Like its predecessor of feudal days, the new political and industrial aristocracy, which created modern Japan with its bureaucracy of militarism and big business, has hoped to discipline the masses by the old techniques. The bureaucrats of the Tokugawa regime used and expanded the stern philosophy of Bushido (The Way of the Warrior), exalting it as a code of virtuous conduct applicable to all, in their vain endeavor to perpetuate an effete feudal society. Likewise, the modern military bureaucrat, his control jeopardized by the growth of popular and responsible government, has sought to preserve his prerogatives by an appeal to the old virtues—to Bushido, to Shintoism with its reverence for the Emperor, to Japan's divine and civilizing mission. With equal determination, he has sought by censorship to arrest the new social forces, for the most part western in origin, which threatened the stability of the family as the unit of society or which encouraged the physical or intellectual freedom of the individual. Despite their efforts, Japan has changed and continues to change; she is westernized, and yet retains much of her oriental culture; she has become a hybrid civilization, half eastern, half western—a complex defying accurate analysis. When General Araki declared that Japanese peasants would fight even with spears to preserve the spiritual culture of the Orient against the fads and *isms* of the West, he wore a uniform designed by a Prussian tailor, rode in a motor car made in an American factory, sat in a war office filled with occidental furniture, and wrote with a fountain pen—not the brush of the calligrapher.

In the heart of modern Tokyo, the traveler may see the temple-like roofs of the Imperial Palace surrounded by massive walls of stone and sheltered by stately pines—a monument to feudal days. Around it lies a city modern in appearance and tempo, with wide paved streets crowded with the traffic of electric trams, busses, and taxicabs, flanked by steel and concrete office buildings, department stores, and theaters, and thronged with men and women who have put on western clothes, who enter western-style cafés to eat with knives and forks instead of chopsticks, who sit through American and European movies, who are proud of their symphony orchestras, their Takarazuka girl revues, their Sapporo and Kirin beer, who dance to American jazz, and who ride home in the subway. This is the Tokyo where golf and baseball are taken for granted, where the accomplished geisha girl gives place to the taxi-dancer and the movie star, and where radio speeches commemorate the divine origins of the Japanese state. These are but suggestive of the external, material changes in Japanese life, which, in turn, are indicative of a still more significant westernization, both intellectual and emotional.

The fundamental basis of this conglomerate picture of change is Japan's modern system of education. Prior to the Tokugawa period, beginning in 1603, most education was controlled by the Buddhist priesthood. The schools were the temples; the textbooks were the Buddhist sutras. After 1603, the educated classes turned more to Confucianism, honoring the sage with no less enthusiasm than his own countrymen. There was some instruction in the native history and literature, and, on the part of the intellectual radicals, some knowledge gleaned secretly from Dutch books at Nagasaki—secretly, because the government frowned on all foreign ideas save Chinese philosophy. In the years that followed the Restoration of 1868, all this was changed. Western education was adopted, largely, at first, on the American model. This attempt to assimilate western methods of thought was a staggering task, because China (not Greece or Rome) provided the cultural background of the Japanese. Is it surprising, then, that twentieth-century Japan is a confused mixture of East and West, which, contrary to the poetic mandate, *have* met?

No less striking has been the transition in what the Japanese write and read. The modern Japanese newspaper with its enormous circulation, picture supplements, advertising stunts, and the whole paraphernalia of commercial journalism (yellow press included) is distinctly a product of twentieth-century westernization. Beside it, the periodical press and the commercial publishers cater to the persistent hunger of Japanese readers.

The material changes in Japanese civilization are mirrored perhaps most effectively in modern fiction, supplemented by the writings of scholars and scientists immersed in western learning. These writings have challenged the old and intolerably dry historical annals, though it may be questioned whether they surpass in artistic value the classical romances of the early Japanese court or the universal humor of the *Hiza Kurige* (Shanks' Mare), that early nineteenth-century novel relating the extraordinary adventures of those Rabelaisian heroes, Yaji and Kita. After the Restoration of 1868, Japanese writers followed the prevalent impulse of their age. Shakespeare, Scott, Lytton, and Beaconsfield were translated. Theirs was the original inspiration to Japan's modern men of letters. Then came the works of Turgenev and Dostoevski. Novelists of the Meiji era (1868 to 1912), influenced by foreign techniques, at first fared ill in the general conservatism of the older generations, who at best were engrossed in economic modernization to the exclusion of letters. Their neglect, however, has not dimmed the fame of such writers as Futabate Hasegawa, Ichiyo Higuchi, and Koyo Ozaki.

The Russo-Japanese War (1904-1905) brought in its train Japan's school of literary realists and the doctrine of naturalism. Katai Tayama, ignoring all tradition, laid bare universal problems of sex to an astonished Japanese public in his novel, *The Bed*. Most prominent among those who resisted the school of naturalism should be mentioned Soseki Natsume, whose masterpiece, *I Am a Cat,* has been translated into many languages; Kafu Nagai, who revived the characters of the past and the romances of the geisha; and Junichiro Tanizaki, with his studies of modern women.

The prosperity that came to Japan with the World War created a comfortable group of writers living in bourgeois ease and yet moving slowly toward socialistic philosophy and providing the background for the Marxian advocates who appeared in the wake of the Russian revolutions. All of which is simply to suggest that significant change and a spirit of restless uncertainty pervades modern Japanese literature. It is a whirl of opposing influences, where even the immediate goal cannot be foreseen.[1]

The world of the theater also reveals the contemporary and more complex life of Japan. Before the appearance of the present generation, the Japanese centered their theatrical arts in the classical *Noh,* or lyrical drama, and the *Kabuki,* or melodrama. The Noh was an outgrowth of early religious dances combined with popular tales from history and legend and poetry from various sources. In the performance, it presented something akin to ancient Greek drama: the chorus, the stately demeanor of the actors, often masked, and a prevalent religious theme. There was no scenery, but the costumes were elaborate. The audience, composed of the cultured and privileged classes, came not to be amused but to be instructed. It followed, book in hand, the chanting of an ancient and difficult language.

In contrast, the Kabuki was the theater of the common people, revealing not an ancient world of gods but rather the drama of history, of life, and of manners. Here there was no scarcity of scenery or costuming, and the performance took place on a large revolving stage. All the actors were men, since immorality, it was feared, would result from the joint appearance of both sexes. Although the plays of the Kabuki had reached artistic triumph by the eighteenth century in the writings of Chikamatsu and Takeda, the privileged classes, while honoring the actors of the Noh, despised the Kabuki and numbered its actors among the outcasts of society—an attitude which did not disappear until after the Restoration of 1868. Then came the modern western theater, in which the purely contemporary, industrialized Japan is revealed and side by side with this the movie palaces showing both foreign and domestic films. Within the space of a few decades, the leading stars of the Kabuki have lost in mass popularity to the rising stars of the films. The American and European tourist is still

---

[1] See Hakucho Masamune, "Modern Fiction." *Contemporary Japan,* June, 1932.

taken to the Noh and the Kabuki, but in neither of them will he see or hear the modern Japan.

It may be affirmed that prior to the modern period of westernization, there was no field of human expression in which the Occident and the Orient were further apart than in the realm of music. As eminent and sympathetic a student of the Japanese as the late Basil Hall Chamberlain referred to this art as "the strummings and squealings" of Orientals. After vain endeavors to find from authorities, both native and foreign, the true nature of the Japanese scale, he was forced to the conclusion that: "Be the scale what it may, the effect of Japanese music is, not to soothe, but to exasperate beyond all endurance the European breast." Indeed, few experiences can be more disappointing to the western ear, accustomed to the full harmonic richness of the symphony orchestra, than the sad wailings, strummings, and rhythms of the Japanese flute, the *koto,* a sort of lyre, the *samisen,* a kind of three-stringed guitar, and numerous drums. Not unnaturally, therefore, first impressions of Japanese music are that it is largely a primitive method of producing disagreeable noises, simple in composition and entirely lacking in beauty of harmony and tone.

More serious students of Japanese music are, however, by no means in accord with such hasty and superficial judgments. Much of Japan's music must be heard and appreciated in its proper setting; that is, as an accompaniment to the singing or chanting of poetical songs. The listener who is unacquainted with the tradition and symbolism of the song fails necessarily to find in the accompaniment an appropriate background.

Much has been done in recent years to bridge the gap between eastern and western music in Japan. Tokyo has acquired its symphony and jazz orchestras, and its brass bands. A new music, both classical and popular, is appearing, in which western techniques have given a new fullness to the atmosphere of Japanese music. Modern popular songs blare from loudspeakers on the *Ginza,* the Broadway of Tokyo, where the

Japanese youth, no less than the American, sways to the tempo of modern rhythm. It is all very modern. Yet still from the quiet countryside and from the seclusion of the Japanese home come plaintive notes of the bamboo flute, and from the tea-houses where geisha songs relax the tired businessman, the discordant twangings of the samisen.

In many forms of artistic expression, Japan has long been the envy of Westerners. The proportions of a room, the arrangement of flowers, the placing of a picture, the designing of a garden have all been subjects of admiration, and deservedly so. They gave to Japan the suggestive qualities of a picture—an ideal unspoiled by the details of reality. Especially was this true of the Japan seen through the works of her painters and block-print artists. From the time of her earliest contacts with China, Japan absorbed the artistic genius that accompanied the spread of Buddhism. To these classical forms was added in the Tokugawa period the products of *Ukiyoe,* which developed hand in hand with popular drama and popular literature. Ukiyoe art, both hand-painting and color prints, was essentially the art of the people. Its subjects were drawn from the common scenes of daily life: a landscape, a bird resting at sunset, a fisherman arranging his nets, the night watchman making his rounds in a rainstorm, a bridge over a mountain stream, a courtesan accompanied by her attendants. To the classical devotees, it was a vulgar art, but it was none the less the real life of the people. Unfortunately, the Japan found in the prints of Hiroshige is fast disappearing. After the Restoration, western influence played no less upon Japanese art than on other phases of the nation's life. In his effort to adopt western subjects and western techniques, the Japanese artist produced extraordinary creations, which may or may not be art. The traveler may still marvel at the atrocious anatomical proportions of female nudes which disfigure many a Japanese exhibit. Nevertheless, the old native art has not been lost.

Its school still flourishes, along with many of the moderns who are creating in art the life of a hybrid civilization.

Japan, which during the past seventy-five years has witnessed these wholesale transformations—political, economic, social, and cultural—and which continues to change from day to day, must necessarily at times appear baffling to American students. Even where there is the will to understand, the barrier of language remains. Few Westerners can discuss Japanese culture in its own tongue. This is a matter of no little significance, for Japanese thought, as expressed in the language, flows in channels widely divergent from those of European expression. Translations from the Japanese are, to be sure, increasing, but they must ever remain a secondary and not a primary source. Culturally, the Japanese enjoy an advantage over the Anglo-Saxon world, for their knowledge of English, imperfect though it may be, has opened to them the entire field of western learning. If any generalization upon the modern Far East be true, it is that Japan knows the West far better than the West knows Japan.

CHAPTER XLIII

The Changing Scene—China

IF it be hazardous to attempt even an approximate appraisal of the changes which have overtaken Japan during the past century, it is more hazardous to attempt it in the case of China. Yet so much has been said and written on the westernization of that land that the subject cannot be dismissed without some comment. In seeking historical perspective, perhaps it will be appropriate to recall the glowing word picture voiced by Anson Burlingame in 1868, when as China's plenipotentiary he sketched before a delighted American audience a China pleading for the blessings of western civilization and eager for modernization, both material and cultural. What Burlingame affirmed, the subsequent history of China has called in question. This is not meant to imply that the western impact has been without effect upon the Chinese pattern. It does imply that westernization in things external, so prevalent in the treaty ports where foreigners reside, does not necessarily mean the creation in China of a new and essentially western civilization. Establishment of the Chinese Republic in 1912 was greeted very generally in the United States as a significant victory for democracy and for a popular national state. Actually, it may be questioned whether or not China has enjoyed as much of democracy or of nationalism as she did in the days of the Manchus. To be sure, the China of the twentieth century has had her revolutionary democrats, her republican and constitutional parties, her parliaments and cabinets, and her numerous constitutions. Unhappily, these manifestations of the western political technique have not as yet resulted in

834

the reality of popular sovereignty. On the contrary, they produced the era of war-lord rule (1916 to 1927), with its perpetual civil wars and its serene disregard of life and property; the dictatorship of the Kuomintang, with its philosophy of middle-class control; the more recent and more personal dictatorship of Chiang Kai-shek, with its fascist implications; and, finally, the communist revolution, with its arbitrary and wholesale confiscations.

Government was one of China's notable achievements in the long era which preceded western contacts. There was, under the ablest rulers from the time of the Han Dynasty (206 B.C.), a prosperity and contentment rarely surpassed in the history of any great people. The essential feature was that:

The state was regarded as an enlarged family and the attitudes of a patriarchal society permeated the whole. The people were to be reasoned with and educated quite as much as commanded.[1]

With its monarchy and bureaucracy, it was at the same time largely a government of checks and balances. Actual power remained in the local units: the family, the clan, the village, and the guild. Although the character of these groups might vary from one locality to another, they were all permeated with the common principle of group responsibility, perhaps the greatest stabilizing force in Chinese life.

With the modern political revolution resulting from the influence of the West, China attempted to introduce novel and foreign institutions and yet to preserve the essential qualities of the old. Then came the revolution of 1911, the abolition of monarchy, and the destruction of the old official hierarchy, the old examination system, and much of the Confucian philosophy. Their place was taken by a sort of mad enthusiasm for western forms of capitalistic republicanism, mingled later with communist doctrines. The direction that these new institutions of government will take is as yet by no means

---

[1] K. S. Latourette, *The Chinese: Their History and Culture*, 2nd ed. rev., 2 vols. in one. The Macmillan Company, New York, 1934. Vol. II, p. 26.

clear. It may well be that the Chinese have only entered upon the beginnings of their political revolution. There can be no question that in recent decades the Chinese have acquired an appreciation of western political nationalism to which they were previously strangers. Nevertheless, they appear loath to carry it to an extreme that would sacrifice that local autonomy which for centuries was the basis of Chinese democracy.

In economics, as well as politics, the force of western civilization is reshaping the life of China. These changes are no less striking, though they are less complete, than those in Japan. China's foreign commerce has developed from the little group of foreign factories huddled together on the river bank outside the walls of Canton into a trade that has made Shanghai one of the great seaports of the world. Historically, the economic life of the Chinese was subject to minute regulation at the hands of local agencies—families, partnerships, guilds, and secret societies. There was no theory of *laissez faire*. At least eighty per cent of China's population (and probably more) derives its livelihood from agriculture and from occupations connected directly with it. Furthermore, in China, it is the labor of man, not of horses or oxen or machinery, that sows and reaps the nation's food. It may be that something like half of China's farmers cultivate their own lands, but be the percentage what it may, it is to this group that China has owed much of her social stability.

Today, in contrast, social stability is conspicuously absent. The collapse of the old empire, the advent of western political techniques among the politically minded, and the growth in the seaport towns of a *laissez-faire,* capitalistic industry—all these have created a confusion in Chinese thought which for the present defies accurate analysis. Beside the centuries-old household and guild industries, there has appeared in China the modern factory, accompanied by mass production and sweated labor on starvation wages; labor unions have begun to replace the guilds. In westernized cities of the seacoast, the "successful" Chinese businessman dines and dances in western-style hotels and clubs, while his less fortunate compatriot sleeps on the ground in some foul-smelling alley or gathers his evening meal from the refuse cast from some foreign ship along Shanghai's waterfront. As yet, this western industrialization of China is in its infancy. Beyond the coast and the river-towns, changes are less apparent. There the bulk of China's millions "are simply following with little if any understanding methods inherited from the past." Often superstition or religion rather than intelligence dictates the methods employed.

Religion, too, in China has changed under western influence. This is not to say that China has adopted Christianity or that she appears likely to do so. While there may be as many as three million professed Christians in China, this total is less than one per cent of the population. In the theological aspects of Christianity, the Chinese have displayed comparatively little interest. Their response to Christian philosophy has been far more pronounced in matters of education, philanthropy, public health, and medicine. In fact, it may be affirmed that the revolutionary movement in China has been directed away from rather than toward religion in any of its conventional forms. The state religion was destroyed with the Manchu Dynasty; Confucianism thereby lost much but by no means all of its hold on the people; Buddhism was forced more directly into the social rather than the spiritual sphere, while the beliefs of Taoism were denounced by radical reformers. In all of this, the leaders of young China followed a well-established technique. They honored a more material and rationalistic view of life than was offered by Buddhism, Taoism, or Christianity. Since religion in China, as in other countries, had frequently been used by those in power to perpetuate their influence, it was but natural that it should be attacked by the revolution. In the case of Christianity, there was the added incentive that it had been associated with what was regarded as the unscrupulous imperialism of the foreign powers. Finally, it may be that these antireligious attitudes, while symptomatic of modern skepticism, are in reality expressive of an idea fundamental to Confucianism, namely, that man knows little about the gods and therefore should have little to do with them. One thing, at least, is quite clear. The present gives little indication of what the future for religion in China will be.

The most interesting and probably the most significant changes wrought in China as a result of western influence concern social customs and organization. The real power of Confucian philosophy was its emphasis upon a code of social relationships and behavior. Through its principles, an orderly society was achieved, resting upon rigid organization of the family, the inferior status of women, the mutual protection that was offered by almost innumerable and powerful secret societies, and the economic relationship maintained by the guilds. The well-established conventions that controlled Chinese social life insisted above all else on "proper form." In fact, correct performance of an ancestral ceremony was regarded quite as important as the principle or motive underlying the act. Closely associated with this was what the Chinese call "face." "Face" is not susceptible to simple definition. It is a principle designed mainly to safeguard the individual from public humiliation in a highly conventionalized society. The contemporary Nanking government, in dealing with foreign governments, insists on the fiction that its control is national and that it is able to afford ample protection to foreigners in the interior. It knows perfectly well that this is not so, but public insistence upon this fiction "saves face."

In contrast to the stable, conservative, conventional China of the old days, the revolution has produced a young China that is decidedly unstable, liberal in one spot and radical in another, and completely unconventional according to Confucian standards. Where western ideas have penetrated deeply, the head of a family no longer rules as an absolute monarch in his household. Sons and daughters are apt to disregard the mandate of the elders in matters of marriage. As in Japan, marriages take place at a more mature age; there are fewer children, and there is no longer the same insatiable desire to propagate male heirs. Divorce has increased, and the individual man and woman is no longer sacrificed to the conventions of the group, as was the case in old China. The mingling of the sexes in public and the craze for social dancing and western movies could never exist in a China which had not undergone profound change. The beginnings of a feminist movement and a self-assertiveness on the part of women that, in educational and economic affairs, they are on a par with men is at least indicative of the gap between the old and the new.

As early as the Tang Dynasty (618 A.D.), perhaps earlier, the Chinese had developed the art of printing, not from movable type but from carved wood blocks. This was a circumstance of the utmost importance in the early development of Chinese civilization. It meant not only the printing of books, but also the preservation of their contents for later generations. Not forgetting that Emperor Shih Huang-ti of the Ch'in Dynasty, as remote as the third century B.C., ordered and effected the burning of the classics, it is to be noted that the Chinese have prized books highly. Many libraries, both official and private, were collected. Nevertheless, the succession of dynastic struggles, foreign invasions, and civil wars that has punctuated Chinese history has left but few of their treasures. Far too much of China's classical literature has been preserved only in fragmentary form. It is to be noted also that since all but a small fraction of China's millions have always been illiterate, literature affected the masses only indirectly, through the teachings and behavior of the officials and scholars. The difficulties of mastering the complex written language of characters was another obstacle to the spread of literacy.

During the past thirty years, it has been proposed that an alphabet of phonetic signs be substituted for the written characters. This would undoubtedly simplify matters for future generations of Chinese school children, but there is no present indication that it will be done. Peoples do not readily cut themselves adrift from their literary heritage. Under a phonetic system, China's ancient literature would become to her peoples a closed book. In the more popular movements for mass education, undertaken since the establishment of the National Government, the Chinese have clung to their ancient method of writing. Some progress has been made, however, toward the spread of the *mandarin* dialect as the common language of speech.

The impact of western thought on Chinese literary and scholastic circles has indeed been impressive. Traditional interpretations of Chinese history have been questioned, and with this has come, as in the writings of Hu Shih, a new approach to Chinese philosophy. It is noteworthy that the great majority of the younger Chinese who have studied in western lands during the twentieth century have devoted themselves to the political and social sciences. They assumed too frequently that a political institution or technique that suited Chicago would work equally well in Canton. More recently, there has been an increasing interest in the natural and mathematical sciences, in which the Chinese have been decidedly backward. More and more thoughtful Chinese are coming to realize that political oratory is no substitute for plague prevention, municipal sanitation, healthy citizens, or intelligent schooling. Knowing their countrymen well, they do not underestimate the difficulties in presenting a philosophy of action rather than one of words. The Taoist doctrine of inaction has left a bold imprint on the Chinese mind. This is illustrated in many ways. Since the first foreign contacts, it has been the Chinese policy to play one foreign power against another, hoping that in the enusing struggle the original problem, whatever it might be, would disappear. It was this attitude that dictated Chinese action in the Manchurian outbreak of 1931. Rarely did it occur to the Chinese that their own house was in chaos and that they alone could put it in order. Nevertheless, in the thinking of contemporary Chinese writers, there is evidence of a more realistic approach.

Popular literature—fiction, novels, drama, and even philosophy—has broadened its scope as a result of the revolution. The significant thing is that even many of the conservative scholars have come to accept the vernacular, or *pai hua* (plain speech), as a suitable medium for literary expression. The publication of books, magazines, and newspapers has increased from year to year. It is quite impossible to estimate, as yet, the value or the influence of the periodical press, for the great majority of its organs have been bitterly partisan, devoting much of their space to questionable political propaganda. However, it must be observed that the modern press and popular literature in general have brought to the literate classes in China a new and broader world of ideas. If China's modernization compares unfavorably with the progress made by Japan, it should not be forgotten that China's problem was immeasurably greater. The extent of her territory, the countless numbers of her peoples, the localization of their society, the grip of the Confucian system, the conviction of superiority arising from centuries of a highly developed culture, and the almost complete lack of any national political consciousness—these and other features of Chinese life have made difficult the process of change. In view of the personal character of Chinese politics, the remarkable thing is not that the revolution has been marked by chaos, but rather that this chaos has not been greater.

The fine arts in China have long constituted one of the great triumphs of the race. Not only in their painting but also in calligraphy, in the creation of jade objects, in ceramics, and in bronzes, their artistic expression has merited the highest praise. But like the fate which befell many of China's libraries, most of her finest paintings have been lost. In part, this was due to their age and the perishable materials used; in main, it was due to wars and a spirit of wanton plunder. Finally, the collapse of Chinese civilization during the past century of western intercourse served to destroy, rather than to create, artistic expression. Western influence is, to be sure, seen in most of the contemporary art of China. Its value is as yet questionable, since much modern art is created in haste to meet the demands of an occidental market.

Of music in China, there has been no lack, if indeed one may apply this term to the tootings and squeakings of what is commonly called a Chinese orchestra. To most western ears, Japanese music is difficult to bear; to the same ears, the strains of a Chinese orchestra are intolerable. Yet music has not been without its cultural value in the folk songs and religious ceremonies dating from the earliest historic times. Esthetic values frequently defy appraisal. It may be that no revolutionary change is involved in the progress from China's indigenous music to the howlings of an American jazz band in one of Shanghai's night clubs.

Of contemporary China there is little that the historian may say, unless it be that contemporary China is revolution. The Industrial Revolution in the West, with its political and social consequences, is more than a century old. In Japan, its development through less than half a century has been rapid and its effects profound. In China, it has just begun. Future historians will tell of its struggles to remake more than 400 millions of people.

Index

A

Abaca, 25
Adams, John Quincy, 125-126
Adams, Will, 92
Agrarian problem, Korea's, 445-447
Agriculture:
  Chinese, 20, 32
  Japanese, 20-21
  Korean, 22, 24
  Manchurian, 12
  of Formosa, 24-25
  of Indo-China, 17
  Philippine, 25
  Siberian, 18
Aigun, 425-426, 638
Airways, Transpacific, 755-756
Albazin, 86
Alcock, Sir Rutherford, 202
Allied and Associated Powers, 643
Allies, withdrawal of western, 522-523
Amazon River, 9
Amban, 15
Ambassadors, 91
American:
  Congress, 139-140
  consular courts, 137
  exports, 814-815
  financiers, 471-474, 638-640
  flag, 799-800
  foreign policy, 122-128, 183-188, 190-195, 331-332, 345-351, 480-482, 501-504, 689-694, 798-824
  Geographical Society of New York, 12
  imports, 816
  interests in Far East, 122-128, 183-188, 190-195, 331-332, 344, 349-351, 480-482, 501-504, 689-694, 798-824
  Japanese tension, 505-510
  Korean Treaty, 261-262
  press, 334-335
  private investments, 344, 817-819, 821
  Revolution, 182
  State Department, 397
  tariff policy, 799
  trade, 99, 108-111, 116, 133-134, 182-188, 342, 810-824
  treaties, 141-143, 240, 246, 349
Amherst, Lord, 100-101, 105

Amoy, 10, 78-79, 85, 119-120, 131, 135
Amur, 19, 86, 177-178, 183
Analects, 40
Ancestor worship, 38
Angell mission, 238-240
Anglo-Chinese War, 124-128, 130, 135-136, 141
Anglo-French Wars, 181-182
Anglo-Japanese Alliance, 380-381, 391, 402-404, 550-551, 553-554
Anhwei Province, 6
Anjiro, 88
Annam, 17, 241-242, 244-245, 247, 294
Anshan Steel Works, 414
Anti-Communist Pact, 795-796
Antiforeignism, revival of, 358-359, 627-630
Anti-Japanese crusade, 418-420
Antung, 401
Arab trade, 46, 75, 123
Araki, General Sadao, 604, 827
Architecture, Japanese, 59
Army, power of Japanese, 60-61, 65-70, 592-594
Arrow War, 131, 146-148, 155
Art, 69, 826, 832, 841
Arthur, President, 239
Artisans, 67
Artists, Japanese, 832-833
Asan, 297, 299
Ashikaga Takauji, 63-64
Asia:
  American interests in, 122-128, 183-188, 190-195, 331-332, 344, 349-351, 480-482, 501-504, 689-694, 798-824
  political and physical map of, 5
Assassinations, February, 731-732
Astronomy, 43, 81
Atlases, 26
Augustinians, 81
Aulick, Commodore, 184
Austrian traders, 99

B

Baku-fu military camp, 61-62
Balfour, Captain, 132
Banks, Manchurian, 638-640

843

Determinative
Bacteriology

Relations.
1842 on →

Date

APR 15 60
MAR 24 61
APR 14 '61

PRINTED IN U.S.A.